OXFORD STUDIES IN
MEDIEVAL EUROPEAN HISTORY

General Editors

JOHN H. ARNOLD   PATRICK J. GEARY
and
JOHN WATTS

Medieval Rome

Stability and Crisis of a City, 900–1150

CHRIS WICKHAM

OXFORD
UNIVERSITY PRESS

OXFORD
UNIVERSITY PRESS

Great Clarendon Street, Oxford, OX2 6DP,
United Kingdom

Oxford University Press is a department of the University of Oxford.
It furthers the University's objective of excellence in research, scholarship,
and education by publishing worldwide. Oxford is a registered trade mark of
Oxford University Press in the UK and in certain other countries

First Edition published in 2015

Impression: 1

Published in the United States of America by Oxford University Press
198 Madison Avenue, New York, NY 10016, United States of America

British Library Cataloguing in Publication Data
Data available

Library of Congress Control Number: 2014934069

ISBN 978–0–19–968496–0

Printed and bound by
CPI Group (UK) Ltd, Croydon, CR0 4YY

For Leslie, again

Acknowledgements

I am, as usual, very grateful for the help of friends while writing this book. Sandro Carocci and Marco Vendittelli, the real experts, gave me advice from the start, and read the whole book for me; I could not have finished it without their detailed critiques. Alessandra Molinari read and critiqued Chapter 3 and Leslie Brubaker Chapter 6; for critiques of parts of chapters I am also indebted to Caroline Goodson, Alessia Rovelli, Emanuela Montelli, Lila Yawn, and Emanuele Conte; the discussions I had with all these framed my understanding of the city. I had further help, in the form of advice and information, offprints, bibliography, or all three, from Frances Andrews, Ermanno Arslan, Giulia Barone, Antonio Berardozzi, Federico Cantini, Cristina Carbonetti Vendittelli, Michael Clanchy, Robert Coates-Stephens, Marios Costambeys, Paolo Delogu, Tommaso di Carpegna Falconieri, John Doran, Lisa and James Fentress, Sergio Fontana, Patrick Healy, Hagen Keller, Mauro Lenzi, Conrad Leyser, Isa Lori Sanfilippo, Jean-Claude Maire Vigueur, Federico Marazzi, Maria Laura Marchiori, Oren Margolis, Jean-Marie Martin, Roberto Meneghini, Giuliano Milani, Emanuela Montelli, Laura Moscati, Cecilia Palombelli, Susanna Passigli (who opened up for me the Jean Coste archive at a critical moment), Anna Rapetti, Serena Romano, Riccardo Santangeli, Julia Smith, Lucrezia Spera, and Laura Vendittelli. I am indebted also to Sue Bowen and Philippa Byrne for the typing, Emily Winkler for the index, and to Harry Buglass for the maps. In Rome, I was helped constructively by the guardians of all the archives I visited, not excluding those several, not cited here, which turned out to have nothing unpublished in them; and by the librarians of a dozen libraries. I am particularly grateful here to the library of the École Française de Rome, which was my primary research library from start to finish and which is a wonderful place to work in. It must finally be noted here that the text of the book is essentially the same as that of *Roma medievale. Crisi e stabilità di una città, 900–1150*, published in 2013 by Viella editrice of Rome; only a few small changes and additions have been made to it for the English version.

I wrote this book while being Chair of the History Faculty Board (Head of Department) in Oxford, in 2009–12. It was fascinating to be doing two such very different, but equally stimulating, things at once. I do not think it was that experience which explains the rather greater stress on political action in this book than in most of my prior writing, as that was part of my project from the start; but I do think it at least partly explains the favourable write-up in the book of Innocent II, one of the most hard-nosed, cynical, and devious popes of my entire period of study.

Birmingham
July 2014

Contents

List of Maps

List of Illustrations

Picture credits: 3.1–2: Roberto Meneghini and Riccardo Santangeli Valenzani, I fori imperiali *(Roma, 2007), reproduced with permission; 3.3, 4.1–2, 6.5–7: Leslie Brubaker; 6.1–4: Monastero di S. Clemente.*

List of Popes, 872–1216

(only those popes of the crisis century who had
very little recognition in Rome have original
names and offices added)

John VIII (872–82)

Marinus I (882–4)

Hadrian III (884–5)

Stephen V (885–91)

Formosus (891–6)

Boniface VI (896)

Stephen VI (896–7)

Romanus (897)

Theodore II (897)

John IX (898–900)

Benedict IV (900–3)

Leo V (903)

Christopher (903–4)

Sergius III (904–11)

Anastasius III (911–13)

Lando (913–14)

John X (914–28)

Leo VI (928)

Stephen VII (929–31)

John XI (931–6)

Leo VII (936–9)

Stephen VIII (939–42)

Marinus II (942–6)

Agapitus II (946–55)

John XII (955–64)

Leo VIII (963–5)

Benedict V (964)

John XIII (965–72)

Benedict VI (972–4)

Boniface VII (974, 984–5)

Benedict VII (974–83)

John XIV (983–4)

John XV (985–96)

Gregory V (996–9)

John XVI (997–8)

Silvester II (999–1003)

John XVII (1003)

John XVIII (1003–9)

Sergius IV (1009–12)

Benedict VIII (1012–24)

John XIX (1024–32)

Benedict IX (1032–45, 1045–6, 1047–8)

Silvester III (1045)

Gregory VI (1045–6)

Clement II (1046–7)

Damasus II (1048)

Leo IX (1049–54)

Victor II (1055–7)

Stephen IX (1057–8)

Benedict X (1058–60)

Nicholas II (1059–61)

Alexander II (1061–73)

Honorius II, Cadalo bishop of Parma (1061–72)

Gregory VII (1073–85)

Clement III (1081–1100)

Victor III, Desiderio abbot of Montecassino (1086–7)

Urban II (1088–99)

Paschal II (1099–1118)

Theodoric bishop of Silva Candida (1100)

Albert bishop of the Sabina (1102)

Silvester IV, Maginulfo archpriest of S. Angelo in Pescheria (1105–11)

Gelasius II (1118–19)

Gregory VIII, Mauricio bishop of Braga (1118–20)

Calixtus II (1119–24)

Honorius II (1124–30)

Anacletus II (1130–8)

Innocent II (1130–43)

Celestine II (1143–4)

Lucius II (1144–5)

Eugenius III (1145–53)

Anastasius IV (1153–4)

Hadrian IV (1154–9)

Alexander III (1159–81)

Victor IV (1159–64)

Lucius III (1181–5)

Urban III (1185–7)

Gregory VIII (1187)

Clement III (1187–91)

Celestine III (1191–8)

Innocent III (1198–1216)

Abbreviations for Primary Sources and Journals

AASS	*Acta sanctorum*
AM	*Archeologia medievale*
ASF	Archivio di Stato di Firenze, fondo documentario
ASF	Rocchettini di Fiesole Archivio di Stato di Firenze, fondo documentario, Fiesole, S. Bartolomeo della badia dei Rocchettini
ASR	Archivio di Stato di Roma
ASR, SCD	ASR, fondo Benedettini e Clarisse in SS. Cosma e Damiano
ASRSP	*Archivio della Società romana di storia patria*
ASV	Archivio Segreto Vaticano
ASV, A. A. Arm. I–XVIII	Archivio Storico Vaticano, Archivum Arcis, Armari I–XVIII [the basic repository of early single-sheet documents and private cartularies in the Vatican Archive]
BAV	Biblioteca Apostolica Vaticana
BISIME	*Bullettino dell'Istituto storico italiano per il medioevo*
Bullaire Cal. II	*Bullaire du pape Calixte II 1119–1124. Essai de restitution*, ed. U. Robert, 2 vols (Paris, 1891), vol. 2
CDC	*Codex diplomaticus Cajetanus*, I–II = *Tabularium Casinense*, I–II (Montecassino, 1887–91), vol. 2
CF	*Il Chronicon Farfense di Gregorio di Catino*, ed. U. Balzani, 2 vols (Rome, 1903)
ChLA, LV	*Chartae latinae antiquiores*, LV, ed. R. Cosma (Zurich, 1999)
CJ	*Codex Iustinianus*, in *Corpus iuris civilis*, II, ed. P. Krueger (Berlin, 1929)
CVL	BAV, Codices Vaticani Latini [the fondo Galletti is CVL 7854–8066]
DBI	*Dizionario biografico degli Italiani*
'Documenti per la storia'	'Documenti per la storia ecclesiastica e civile di Roma', ed. E. von Ottenthal, *Studi e documenti di storia e diritto*, VII (1886), pp. 101–22, 195–212, 317–36, and continuing
Forcella	*Iscrizioni delle chiese e d'altri edifici di Roma dal secolo XI fino ai giorni nostri*, ed. V. Forcella, 14 vols (Rome, 1869–84)
Gattola, *Historia*	*Historia abbatiae Cassinensis per saeculorum seriem distributa*, ed. E. Gattula, I (Venice, 1733)
Kehr	*Papsturkunden in Italien*, ed. P. F. Kehr, 6 vols (Rome, 1977)
LC	*Le Liber Censuum de l'église romaine*, ed. P. Fabre and L. Duchesne, 3 vols (Paris, 1905–10)

Liberiano	G. Ferri, 'Le carte dell'archivio Liberiano dal secolo X al XV', *ASRSP*, XXVII (1904), pp. 147–202, 441–9, and continuing
LF	*Il 'Liber Floriger' di Gregorio di Catino*, ed. M. T. Maggi Bei, I (Rome, 1984)
LL	*Liber largitorius vel notarius monasterii Pharphensis*, ed. G. Zucchetti, 2 vols (Rome, 1913–32); vol. 1 (documents nn. 1–945); vol. 2 (nn. 946–2155)
LP	*Le Liber Pontificalis*, ed. L. Duchesne, 2 vols (Paris, 1955)
Manaresi	*I placiti del 'Regnum Italiae'*, ed. C. Manaresi, 3 vols (Rome, 1955–60)
Marini	*I papiri diplomatici*, ed. G. Marini (Rome, 1805)
MEFRM	*Mélanges de l'École française de Rome. Moyen âge*
MGH	*Monumenta Germaniae Historica* (*SS*: *Scriptores*; *SRG*: *Scriptores rerum germanicarum*)
Orsini	Archivio Storico Capitolare, Archivio Orsini
Papsturkunden	*Papsturkunden 896–1046*, ed. H. Zimmermann, 3 vols (Vienna, 1985–9); vol. 1 (for documents nn. 1–325); vol. 2 (nn. 326 onwards)
Pflugk	*Acta pontificum romanorum inedita*, ed. J. von Pflugk-Harttung, 3 vols (Tübingen, 1881, Stuttgart, 1884–6)
PL	*Patrologiae cursus completus, series latina*, ed. J.-P. Migne (Paris, 1844–55)
QFIAB	*Quellen und Forschungen aus italienischen Archiven und Bibliotheken*
Regesta Hon. III	*Regesta Honorii papae III*, I, ed. P. Pressutti (Rome, 1880), Appendice, II, pp. LI–CXXIV
Regesta Inn. III	*Innocentii III regesta sive epistolae*, ed. in *PL*, CCIV–CCVI; hitherto partial re-ed. in *Die Register Innocenz' III*, ed. O. Hageneder et al., 10 vols continuing (Graz, 1964; Vienna, 1979–). Where the numbering in each edition is different, I cite Hageneder's and add *PL*'s in brackets.
RF	*Il Regesto di Farfa*, ed. I. Giorgi and U. Balzani, 5 vols (Rome, 1879–1914); vol. 2 (documents nn. 1–448); vol. 3 (nn. 449–601); vol. 4 (nn 602–996); vol. 5 (nn. 997–1324)
RS	*Il Regesto Sublacense del secolo XI*, ed. L. Allodi and G. Levi (Rome, 1885)
S. Agnese	I. Lori Sanfilippo, 'Le più antiche carte del monastero di S. Agnese sulla Via Nomentana', *Bullettino dell' 'Archivio palaeografico italiano'*, NS, II–III (1956–7), II, pp. 65–97
S. Alessio	A. Monaci, 'Regesto dell'abbazia di Sant'Alessio all'Aventino', *ASRSP*, XXVII (1904), pp. 351–98, and continuing
S. Anastasio	I. Giorgi, 'Il regesto del monastero di S. Anastasio ad Aquas Salvias', *ASRSP*, I (1878), pp. 49–77
S. And. Aq.	*I documenti di S. Andrea 'de Aquariciariis', 1115–1483*, ed. I. Lori Sanfilippo, Codice diplomatico di Roma e della regione romana, 2 (Rome, 1981)

SCD	P. Fedele, 'Carte del monastero dei SS. Cosma e Damiano in Mica Aurea, secoli X e XI', *ASRSP*, XXI (1898), pp. 459–534, XXII (1899), pp. 25–107, 383–447, republished as and cited from a book with the same title, ed. P. Pavan, Codice diplomatico di Roma e della regione romana, 1 (Rome, 1981). For after 1100, see ASR SCD.
S. Cecilia	E. Loevinson, 'Documenti del monastero di S. Cecilia in Trastevere', *ASRSP*, XLIX (1926), pp. 355–404
S. Gregorio	*Il regesto del monastero dei SS. Andrea e Gregorio ad Clivum Scauri*, ed. A. Bartola, 2 vols, Codice diplomatico di Roma e della regione romana, 7 (Rome, 2003), vol. 2
S. Marcello	I. M. Albarelli, 'Septem bullae ineditae ad ecclesiam Sancti Marcelli Romae spectantes', in *Monumenta ordinis Servorum Sanctae Mariae*, ed. A Morini and P. Soulier, II (Brussels, 1898), pp. 191–211
SMCM	*Cartario di S. Maria in Campo Marzio (986–1199)*, ed. E. Carusi, Miscellanea della Società romana di storia patria, 17 (Rome, 1948)
S. Maria in Monasterio	P. Fedele, 'S. Maria in Monasterio. Note e documenti', *ASRSP*, XXIX (1906), pp. 183–227
SMN	P. Fedele, 'Tabularium S. Mariae Novae ab an. 982 ad an. 1200', *ASRSP*, XXIII (1900), pp. 171–237 (documents nn. 1–31);, XXIV (1901), pp. 159–96 (nn. 32–56); XXV (1902), pp. 169–209 (nn. 57–84); XXVI (1903), pp. 21–141 (nn. 85–170)
SMT	Archivio Storico del Vicariato, Archivio del Capitolo di S. Maria in Trastevere, n. 532; unnumbered are from n. 35, a seventeenth-century cartulary, entitled *Copia simplex instrumentorum ac bullarum contentam in libro primo authentico venerlis ecclesie S. Marie Transtyberim, extracto mense Iulii, Anno Dni 1654.*
SMVL	*Ecclesiae S. Maria in Via Lata tabularium*, ed. L. M. Hartmann and (for vol. 3) M. Merores, 3 vols (Vienna, 1895–1913); vol. 1 (documents nn. 1–80); vol. 2 (nn. 81–146); vol. 3 (nn. 147–279)
SMVL, Baumgärtner	I. Baumgärtner, 'Regesten aus dem Kapitelarchiv von S. Maria in Via Lata (1200–1259)', *QFIAB*, LXXIV (1994), pp. 42–171, LXXV (1995), pp. 32–177
S. Pancrazio	C. Colotto, 'Il "De monasterio Sancti Pancratii et Sancti Victoris de Urbe", unico testimonianza superstite di un archivio medievale romano perduto', *ASRSP*, CXXVII (2004), pp. 5–72
S. Paolo	B. Trifone, 'Le carte del monastero di S. Paolo di Roma dal secolo XI al XV', *ASRSP*, XXXI (1908), pp. 267–313, and continuing
S. Prassede	P. Fedele, 'Tabularium S. Praxedis', *ASRSP*, XXVII (1904), pp. 27–78 (documents nn. 1–21); XXVIII (1905), pp. 41–114 (nn. 22–90)
SPV	L. Schiaparelli, 'Le carte antiche dell'Archivio Capitolare di S. Pietro in Vaticano', *ASRSP*, XXIV (1901), pp. 393–496 (documents nn. 1–30); XXV (1902), pp. 273–354 (nn. 31–83), and continuing
S. Sisto	*Le più antiche carte del convento di San Sisto in Roma (905–1300)*, ed. C. Carbonetti Vendittelli, Codice diplomatico di Roma e della regione romana, 4 (Rome, 1987)
S. Sil.	V. Federici, 'Regesto del monastero di S. Silvestro de Capite', *ASRSP*, XXII (1899), pp. 214–300, 489–538, and continuing [after 1100, the registers in the edition have been checked against ASR, fondo Clarisse in S.Silvestro in Capite (cassette 38–38 bis)]

Senato	*Codice diplomatico del Senato romano dal MCXLIV al MCCCXLVII*, I, ed. F. Bartoloni (Rome, 1948)
Tivoli	*Regesto della chiesa di Tivoli*, ed. L. Bruzza (Rome, 1880)
Velletri	E. Stevenson, 'Documenti dell'archivio della cattedrale di Velletri', *ASRSP*, XII (1889), pp. 63–113
Volpini	R. Volpini, 'Per l'archivio pontificio tra XII e XIII secolo: i resti dell'archivio dei papi ad Anagni', *Rivista di storia della chiesa in Italia*, XXXVII (1983), pp. 366–405

A Note on Names

Almost all personal names in this book are rendered into modern Italian from Latin, thus Cenci di [son of] Leone. The exceptions are the names of popes and emperors, which are in English, plus two figures who are very well-known in their English version, Hildebrand (the future Gregory VII) and Matilda of Tuscany.

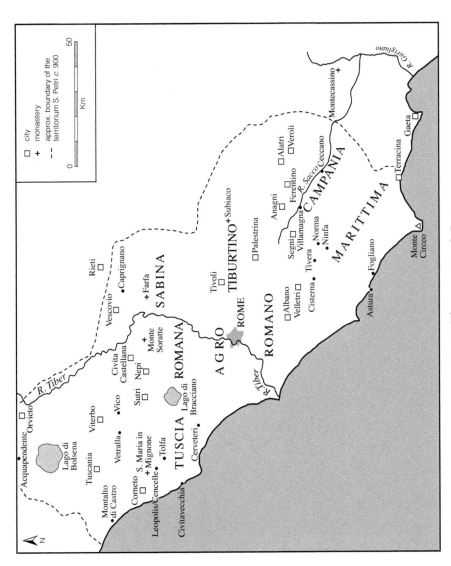

Map 1. The *territorium S. Petri*.

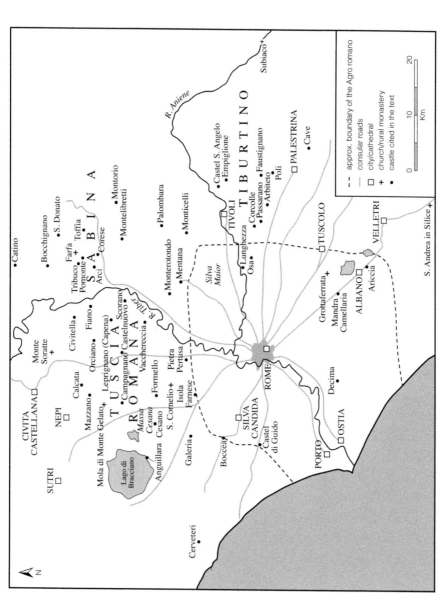

Map 2. The land of castles.

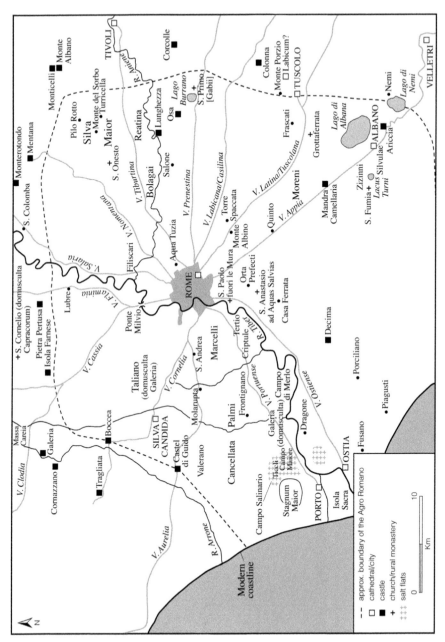

Map 3. The Agro romano.

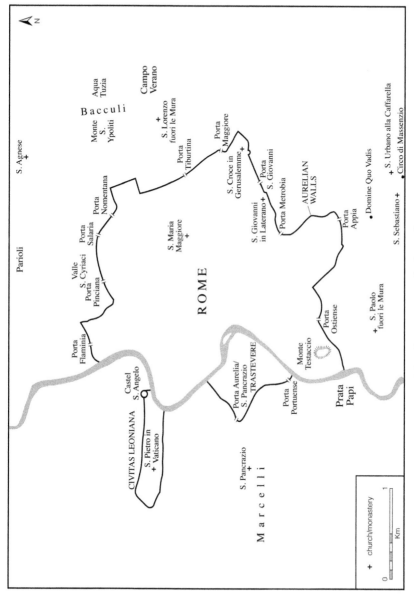

Map 4. Rome outside the walls.

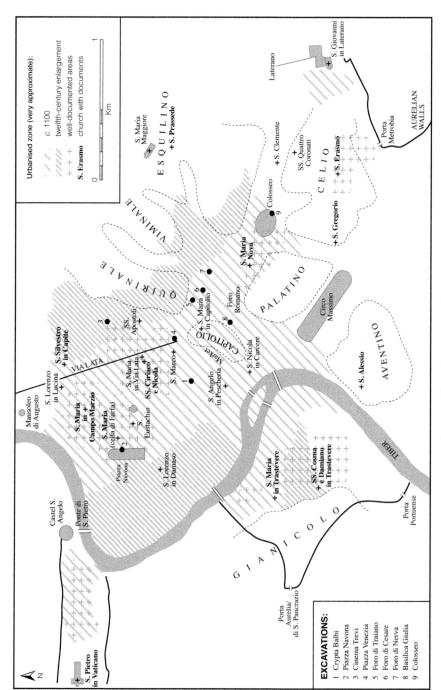

Map 5. The urban centre of Rome.

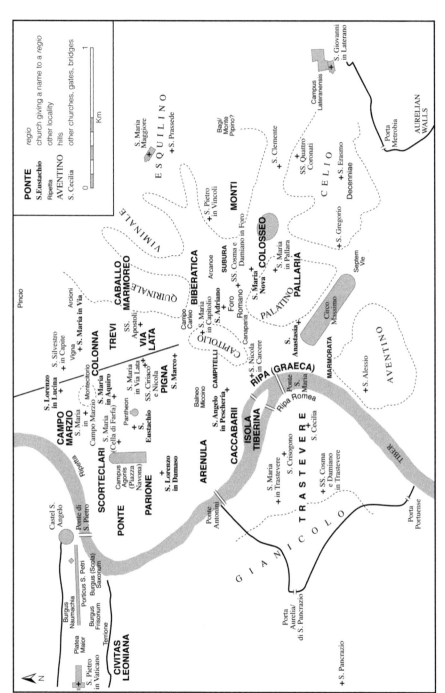

Map 6. The regions of Rome.

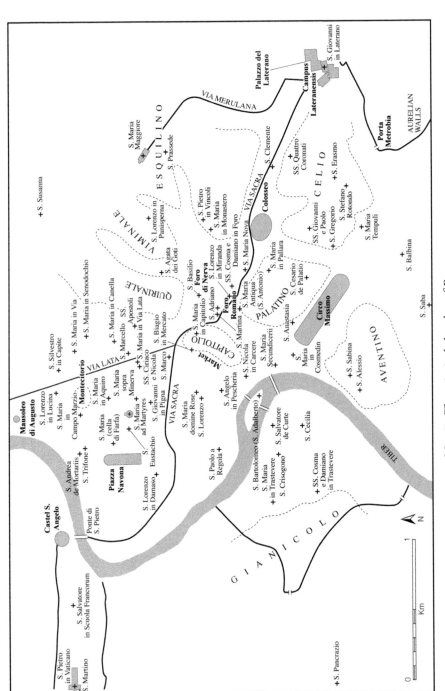

Map 7. The principal churches of Rome.

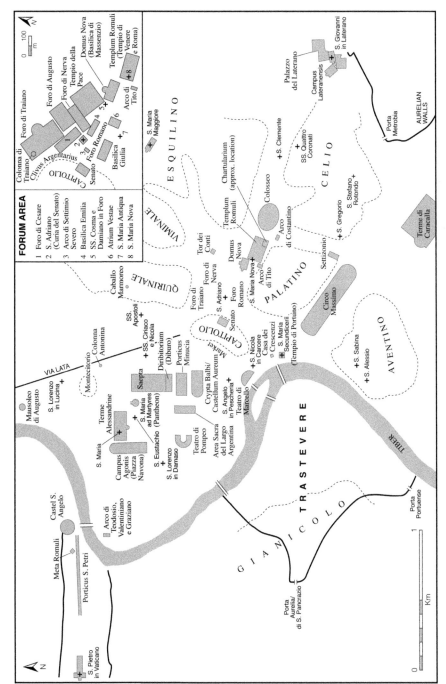

Map 8. Classical and secular buildings.

FORUM AREA

1 Foro di Cesare
2 S. Adriano (Curia del Senato)
3 Arco di Settimio Severo
4 Basilica Emilia
5 SS. Cosma e Damiano in Foro
6 Atrium Vestae
7 S. Maria Antiqua
8 S. Maria Nova

Colonna di Traiano
Clivus Argentarius
Foro di Traiano
Foro di Augusto
Foro di Nerva
Tempio della Pace
Domus Nova (Basilica di Massenzio)
Templum Romuli (Tempio di Venere e Roma)
Arco di Tito
CAPITOLIO
Senato
Foro Romano
Basilica Giulia
S. Maria Maggiore
ESQUILINO

S. Maria Maggiore

Chartularium (approx. location)
Colosseo
S. Clemente
SS. Quattro Coronati
CELIO
S. Stefano Rotondo
S. Gregorio
Templum Romuli
Arco di Costantino
Settizonio
Circo Massimo
PALATINO
S. Maria Nova
Domus Nova
Foro di Nerva
Foro di Adriano
Senato
S. Maria Secundicerii
S. Nicola in Carcere
Casa dei Crescenzi
S. Maria (Tempio di Portuno)
S. Maria in Pescheria
S. Angelo in Pescheria
Teatro di Marcello
CAPITOLIO
Mercati
VIMINALE
Tor dei Conti
Palazzo del Laterano
S. Giovanni in Laterano
Campus Lateranensis
Porta Metrobia
AURELIAN WALLS
Terme di Caracalla
S. Sabina
S. Alessio
AVENTINO

Caballo Marmoreo
QUIRINALE
SS. Apostoli
SS. Ciriaco e Nicola
Diribitorium (Diburo)
Porticus Minucia
Saepta
Colonna Antonina
Montecitorio
VIA LATA
Mausoleo di Augusto
S. Lorenzo in Lucina
Terme Alessandrine
S. Maria
Campus Agonis (Piazza Navona)
S. Maria ad Martyres (Pantheon)
S. Eustachio
S. Lorenzo in Damaso
Teatro di Pompeo
Area Sacra del Largo Argentina
Crypta Balbi/ Castellum Aureum

Castel S. Angelo
Arco di Teodosio, Valentiniano e Graziano
Meta Romuli
Porticus S. Petri
S. Pietro in Vaticano

TRASTEVERE
GIANICOLO
TIBER
Porta Aurelia/ di S. Pancrazio
Porta Portuense

N
0 100 m

N
0 1 Km

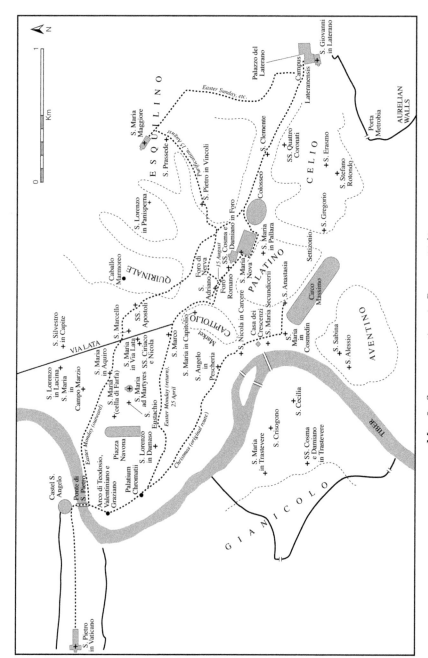

Map 9. Some processions in Rome, c.1140.

1

Grand Narratives

THE PROBLEMATIC

Rome too often hides under the light. Its past lies about you as you walk its streets; its imperial traditions and papal centrality are too obvious to develop, and often seem too obvious for hard scrutiny to be needed. As a result, the city seems to many to have a destiny far greater than a mere local politics. Paolo Brezzi, author in 1947 of the most acute and deft of the traditional narratives of the medieval city, could write 'Roma è tale solo quando si alimenta ad un'idea universale', Rome is fully itself only when it nourishes itself with a universal idea—in this case the eleventh-century papal 'reform' movement. Brezzi was in fact here seeking to combat the idea that the reform papacy was antithetical to a 'real' Romanness; in a delicate argument, he managed to claim that the former in fact underlay the key secular change of the immediately succeeding period, the autonomous city commune, itself.[1] But in Brezzi, quite as much as in the historians he was criticizing, we find a recurrent opposition, in which Rome as a city is simply seen as a constraint. Generations of historians have claimed or assumed that, for popes (in particular) to gain their 'natural' international role, they had to subdue or reject or ignore the city they were actually bishops of. For some, the Romans were simply too corrupt, too factional, too spiritually impoverished to be worthy of the destiny of the city (this was also, of course, the view of any number of medieval writers, particularly non-Romans); for others, including Brezzi, the Romans had it in them to rise to that destiny, but they often did not manage to do so and had to be coerced from outside.

This debate has been pushed in different ways in the past 150 years, with different shades of Catholic historiography fighting against a Protestant tradition more critical of papal power (though just as romantic about Gregory VII or Innocent III[2]), and an often anticlerical Roman tradition (strongest in the period 1870–1929, when the popes rejected the legitimacy of the Italian state) which argued for the 'Roman revolution' that established the Senate in 1143–4 in the teeth of papal opposition as the real turning-point in the city's history. But the majority of writers, from whichever tradition, have posited Rome as somehow special, whether especially good or especially bad (or often both), and anyway *different*—and separable, in particular, from the history of the rest of Italy. People

---

[1] Brezzi, *Roma*, pp. 223–4.
[2] See, for example, Gregorovius, *History*, IV.1, pp. 254–60, V.1, pp. 101–5.

write about Rome in a different way to that in which they write about Florence or Milan, as we shall see in a moment; this seems to me pointless. And Rome is seldom prominent as a case study in surveys of Italian social or political development, for it is seen as too atypical to contribute much to a specifically Italian history; this seems to me simply mistaken.

I wish in this book to face squarely the problems of these assumptions. I have a twofold aim in writing it. The first is simply to take up the challenge of writing a structural urban history. I want to approach the problem of the history of Rome as a city, across a longish period—the 250 years between the end of Carolingian rule in the ninth century and the bedding-down of the commune of Rome, the Senate, in the second half of the twelfth—so as to see how economic, social, and religious/ cultural structures intermeshed and acted on each other in a period of substantial political change. Rome was in demographic terms the largest city in Latin Europe, and (for most of the period) second only to Constantinople in Europe as a whole, before it was overtaken by Milan, perhaps around 1100 (below, p. 112); and in spatial terms it was and remained far larger than anywhere else, with a complicated urban geography which writers in both the twelfth century and the twentieth have spent some time unpicking: it was a complex stage for the structural interplay I wish to describe, and was entirely absorbing for the Romans, as we shall see. I want to reconstruct the changing parameters of that absorption.

In so doing, I will consistently focus on the aims and strategies, needs and constraints, of the Romans. And not, it must be stressed, of the various external figures who sought to control the city—whether German emperors, or the various German, French, or north Italian ecclesiastics who were prominent in the papal Curia after the mid-eleventh century. This is not because I wish to minimize, or polemicize against, the considerable changes in ecclesiastical government, both in Rome and in the whole of Latin Europe, that took place after 1050; but, rather, because the way those changes played out in the city was quite different to the way they played out in Canossa, or Clermont, or Clairvaux. I am personally pretty neutral about the advantages and disadvantages of these changes (in the charged atmosphere of 'reform' historiography, neutrality is already a political stance, but there is no help for that), but the important issue for the book is what they, and their bearers, meant for the Romans themselves, and this is the direction the argument will focus on. Some well-known popes will therefore vanish from the book, or nearly (Urban II, most notably), some less well-known ones will be more prominent than usual (Benedict VIII, the eleventh-century Clement III, Innocent II)—though Gregory VII will retain his traditional centrality. This seems to me to reflect the purchase each of them had on the city.

My second aim is to situate, as much as possible, the history of Rome inside that of Italy. Here, I wish to explore both similarity and difference. Rome is, as already noted, assumed to be different without sufficient attention; what has often been missing is any sort of approach linked to systematic, interregional, comparison. This is not really an Italian strength, it has to be recognized. The regional fragmentation of scholarship in the peninsula produces many strong scholars whose research experience hardly goes outside a single city territory. It is also the case that the period I am focusing on is not one in which there have been very many detailed monographic studies on other Italian cities either, so there are few interpretative models (though exception should always be made for the various collective histories, such as *Storia di Milano, Napoli, Venezia, Bergamo*, some of which are of good quality, and a few of which are recent enough to be good guides to current scholarship). Rome is not, in fact, at all badly off in its local historiography, even when set against other relatively well-studied cities such as Milan and Florence. The context from which Rome is missing is, rather, the general narrative which culminates in the early city communes as a whole. This narrative has as its basic underpinning a history of the failure of the Kingdom of Italy, that is to say northern and north-central Italy; Rome was outside that kingdom, so its parallel development tends to remain unconsidered. It may be added that the history of the southern Italian principalities (itself lacking a good monographic synthesis) has seldom recognized the strong similarities that the Roman region—roughly present-day Lazio, then somewhat generically called the *Patrimonium* or *territorium S. Petri*—had with Benevento, Naples, Capua, or Salerno, at least in the first half of the period covered by this book.

I am conscious of these southern comparators, and I will use them on occasion (see e.g. below, pp. 455–7). But one of the main turning points in this book will be the breakdown of traditional government in the wars of the late eleventh century, and its substitution at a local level by new political structures which were invented locally; and this means that the main points of comparison have to be northwards, with the larger cities of communal Italy—'larger', because it seems to me that only cities of a reasonably substantial size and complexity are proper comparators here. I shall focus when making such comparisons on two modern regions, Lombardy and Tuscany: the former because of a particularly strong post-war historiography (headed by but by no means restricted to Cinzio Violante, Hagen Keller, and François Menant, and for a slightly later period Paolo Grillo), the latter for similar reasons, but also because I myself know it best.[3] I shall range wider in comparison than this, when it seems relevant and helpful, of course. Conversely, though, it does also have to be said that this is a study of Rome, not of Italy as a whole. Rome cannot be understood except comparatively, but the other cities will appear as comparators, not as free-standing actors.

Rome is thought to be different because of its unique status as the 'papal city'. Its sovereigns were not kings or dukes or princes, as in other Italian cities, but bishops, who were, furthermore, not hereditary: there were only a few exceptions to these statements in our period, most importantly the rule of Marozia *senatrix* and

---

[3] Violante, *La società milanese nell'età precomunale*; Keller, *Adelsherrschaft* (here cited from the Italian translation with an important new introduction, *Signori e vassalli*); Menant, *Campagnes lombardes* and *Lombardia feudale*; Grillo, *Milano in età comunale*. See further, for the period before 1200, among others, *Storia di Milano*, III; Dilcher, *Die Entstehung*; *Milano e il suo territorio*; Rapetti, *Campagne milanesi*; *Storia economica e sociale di Bergamo*; De Angelis, *Poteri cittadini* (now the key analysis of the early commune of Bergamo). For Tuscany in our period, the best recent single-city monographs are Cortese, *Signori, castelli* and Faini, *Firenze* for Florence; Delumeau, *Arezzo*; Ronzani, *Chiesa e 'civitas' di Pisa*; and Savigni, *Episcopato e società* for Lucca.

Alberico *princeps* in *c*.925–54 and the hereditary succession of three successive Tuscolano popes, Alberico's second cousins, in 1012–44/46. Rome is also seen as different in that, as I have already said, it was a supposed drag on the attainment by the popes of their world-historical role as the leaders of the western church. This has produced a curious double vision in Italian historiography: whereas the eleventh-century uprisings against—say—the archbishops of Milan tend to be seen in a positive light as harbingers of the moment in which the Milanesi took over their rightful rule in the city in the *primo comune*, similar uprisings in Rome against eleventh- and twelfth-century popes are seen as selfish and localist moves against the achievement by popes of their international role. Even the anticlerical strands of the historiography of Rome, which have often been strong, have seldom sought to rehabilitate any of those moments, except the dramatic foundation of the Senate itself in 1143–4.

These do not seem to me to be helpful historical viewpoints; and they also seem to me to misrepresent what actually made Rome different. That Rome was ruled by bishops was not particularly unusual; in the eleventh century, Milan, Cremona, Ravenna, and any number of other northern cities were as well. The latter were, of course, not fully autonomous, unlike popes—they were the local representatives of the king/emperor. But it cannot be said that the emperors actually intervened in the local affairs of most northern cities all that often; and they intervened, often choosing popes, quite as often in Rome too, even though the latter was not technically part of their kingdom. The common travails of an episcopal politics, in particular at the moments of the selection of new bishops, link Rome to the north of Italy quite closely.

More important as a difference was that the governmental infrastructure that ruled Rome was remarkably complex. At times it included three separate official hierarchies, military, judicial, and clerical, as we shall see in Chapter 4. This complexity, inherited from the Byzantine empire (and the Roman empire before that), was greater than that found in the governing hierarchy of any other western polity, including that of Carolingian Francia at its height. This alone was enough to make the politics of Rome compelling to insiders, and also incomprehensible to outsiders. It contributed very greatly, too, to the institutional solidity of Rome, including in the time of its greatest political crisis in our period (and for a long time before and after), the late eleventh and early twelfth centuries, as we shall see in Chapter 7. It was backed up by a notably dense ritual and processional landscape, which potentially involved, as it appears, the entire urban population, and which united a physically sprawling city into a cohesive whole, as we shall see in Chapter 6.

The second main way in which Rome was atypical is still more important: in its wealth. Rome was unusually large and unusually economically active by all western standards before the twelfth century, and by the standards of all but a few Italian boom towns well into the thirteenth. It was full of artisans, who are better documented in our period in Rome than anywhere else, as we shall see in Chapter 3. It also took a higher percentage of the agricultural surplus of the countryside around it than any other city did, and developed a set of agrarian specialisms in that countryside earlier than almost any other city, too: this agrarian dominance seems to me the fundamental underpinning of Rome's economic exceptionality, and it is why Chapter 2, on the countryside, is the first of my main monographic chapters. Except in some very recent works by historians in Rome, this wealth has been misunderstood, and sometimes even denied, but it is clear to any reader of the sources who has an eye to a comparative perspective.

Rome was big, rich, and politically complex, then. But it was also inhabited by people who were not, economically or socially or culturally, all that different from the inhabitants of the rest of Italy. The overall changes in the economic history of the city from a tenth-century baseline have close parallels elsewhere, apart from the fact that Rome was initially more precocious. Changes in aristocratic and non-aristocratic society, which were considerable from the eleventh century onwards, as we shall see in Chapters 4 and 5, also had considerable analogies to those of other Italian cities. Here, we have to articulate the similarity of the history of elites, for example, against Roman difference: the unusual complexity of the political structures that they operated (or sought to operate) inside. The same is true for the greater complexity in Rome of its artisanal structures, or its processional practices, even though equivalent artisans and processions existed everywhere. And it is, overall, my aim in this book to set out that articulation—between similarity and difference—more widely. It is not my aim at all to make Rome seem *just the same* as Milan, or any other northern city, or for that matter Naples, which had certain elements in common with it too. Rather, it is to explore how its differences can really be understood. Italy is always made up of differences; its unity is always a patchwork of diversity. To get Italy's history straight in any period, we must get the nature of those differences right, and also the parallels which are always there, and not get trapped in false or rhetorical oppositions, as regionalist politicians did in our period, and still do today. I hope this book will contribute to that.

THE PROBLEM OF SOURCES

Historians of Rome in our period, 900–1150, are accustomed to lament the poverty of its narratives, so inferior in quantity and quality as they are to the dense papal biographies in the eighth- and ninth-century sections of the *Liber Pontificalis*, or to the detailed chronicles of the eleventh-century South. That is indeed so, even if it is equally the case that other Italian cities are even more devoid of good accounts before the twelfth century, with the single and important exception of Milan. Rome has one chronicle, the sketchy and incoherent work of Benedetto of Monte Soratte, which focuses on the early tenth century; it has a fragmentary and heterogeneous set of annals, the *Annales Romani*, for the years 1044–73, 1100–21, and (after our period) 1182–7; it also has a revived set of papal biographies written by two cardinals, Pandolfo in the 1130s and Bosone in the 1160s–70s, which are extensive for the twelfth century only: not a lot, indeed.[4]

---

[4] Benedetto, *Chronicon*. Of the later texts the *Annales Romani*, Pandolfo (from Gregory VII to Honorius II) and Bosone are all ed. by Louis Duchesne in *LP*, II, pp. 331–50, 282–328, 353–446, but

These texts are backed up, it is true, by a remarkably long list of non-Roman sources, some of which appear very immediate, from Liutprando of Cremona at the start of our period to John of Salisbury at the end. Events in Rome seemed important to much of Latin Europe, in particular from Leo IX onwards, but often before as well.[5] These, however, were written by men who were (with few exceptions) ill-informed about the wider context of either papal politics or the city of Rome, and were (with no exceptions) concerned above all to moralize; the city, in particular, is almost never seen except in the most negative light. They have to be used with considerable caution.

Recent decades of historical scholarship have, of course, taught us that even the best-informed and most detailed narratives are problematic guides to 'the truth'. The open prejudice and disregard for context of a Liutprando or a Benzone of Alba or a Bonizone of Sutri would not necessarily mean that their works were less useful than the apparently more circumstantial accounts of the *Annales Romani* or Pandolfo. They are guides to rhetorical strategies in the framework of circum-scribed genres, as much as or more than to what we would call reportage. But this does not mean we should trust Benzone more; it means we should trust Pandolfo less. The latter's careful account of the degrading travails of Gelasius II, who was taken prisoner by the Frangipane family in 1118 and in the end fled Rome in despair, or of the fixed election of Honorius II in 1124,[6] are no less constructed, for all their informative details about local alliances, than are the most clichéd denun-ciations by outsiders like Bernard of Clairvaux.

Which is to say: I do not base this book very tightly on the surviving narratives. They can be mined for prosopographical detail (again with care); they are valuable for the mindsets of writers, and for guides to the way that Rome (and, especially, the aspects of Rome relevant for papal politics) was understood and could be written about. Sometimes their collective voice, despite their extreme heterogen-eity, is so consistent that their presuppositions seem trustworthy: the unusually prominent role of money and treasure in Roman politics is an example.[7] But a narrative-based account risks taking us straight back to the heightened and moralistic historiography I complained about at the start of this chapter, which is, indeed, focused on those narratives, and borrows their censoriousness, often pretty uncritically.

It is also a striking feature of all these narratives that they home in on only a few events. The pontificate of Gregory VII (1073–85), for example, was unusually

---

a better and fuller version of Pandolfo on Paschal II, Gelasius II, Calixtus II, and Honorius II, discovered after Duchesne did his edition, is ed. in *Liber pontificalis Dertusensis*, ed. March and *Liber pontificalis*, ed. Přerovský; for those popes I will cite him in the latter, the latest, edition. Note that March, pp. 41–60, did not consider Pandolfo to be the author of the lives; the argument for Pandolfo seems more plausible to Přerovský, I, pp. 111 ff., and to me. The basic critical commentary on the *Annales* is Whitton, 'The *Annales Romani*'.

[5] Liutprando, *Antapodosis* and *Historia Ottonis*; John of Salisbury, *Historia pontificalis*. The complete list of non-Roman sources is vast; see the bibliography for those used here.

[6] *Liber pontificalis*, ed. Přerovský, II, pp. 731–41, 750–4.

[7] See Wickham, 'The financing', and below, pp. 172–4.

momentous, and nearly every chronicle in Europe paid attention to it. It is therefore curious that, before the emperor Henry IV took Rome in 1084, our narratives tell us nothing about Gregory's Roman experiences except his poor relations with a Roman aristocrat named Cencio di Stefano, who briefly kidnapped Gregory during Christmas 1075, and whose brother Stefano killed Gregory's urban prefect Cencio di Giovanni in 1077 (see below, pp. 233, 422).[8] Even the Monte-cassino chronicle, which is a long text written by three authors between the 1100s and the 1150s, and which is attentive to Rome (only some 120 km away) and its politics, only tells us about a set of standard events. For the period after 1060, besides papal elections, it only discusses Gregory VII's imprisonment by Cencio, the attacks on Rome by Henry IV and the Normans in 1084, the failed attempt by Pope Victor III (Abbot Desiderio of Montecassino itself) to hold Rome in 1087, Henry V's capture of Paschal II in 1111, and the disputed election of the urban prefect Pietro in 1116—except for Victor's career, which the Cassinesi had a special interest in, these are the same events that every other chronicle relates.[9] It is as if the narrative history of Rome consisted of isolated blocks of data, which were told to and chewed over by half of Europe, but which are separated from a wider narrative context in every source, even those from Rome itself. Rome's internal political history is reduced in these texts to a set of *exempla*, valuable in their own terms but limited—and not to be taken too seriously—as a guiding framework.[10]

The core of the evidence-base for this book is therefore documents. This has been my major evidence in my other Italian studies, too;[11] and I have offered defences of the use and validity (and problems) of this sort of source elsewhere.[12] Roman documents survive from the period of this study from around thirty ecclesiastical archives, to which must be added the multifarious locations of later copies of individual papal bulls to Roman churches, almost all of them tracked down at the start of the last century by Paul Kehr. The archives are fully listed in three of the most significant Roman studies of the last forty years, by Pierre Toubert, Étienne Hubert, and Tommaso di Carpegna Falconieri. They are also almost all edited, mostly in the two great periods for Roman document editing, 1885–1925 and 1980 to the present.[13] Of the *inedito*, there survive before 1200

[8] See esp. D'Acunto, 'Il prefetto Cencio'.

[9] *Chronica Casinensis*, III.36, 50, 53, 66–9, IV.35–40, 60–1.

[10] See in particular Frugoni, *Arnaldo di Brescia*, for a case study.

[11] e.g. Wickham, *The Mountains*; *Community and Clientele*; *Courts and Conflict*, the book whose focus links best with this one.

[12] e.g. Wickham, *The Inheritance*, pp. 15–16.

[13] Toubert, *Les structures*, pp. 3–37; Hubert, *Espace urbain*, pp. 9–16; di Carpegna Falconieri, *Il clero di Roma*, pp. 309–21. Kehr, *Italia pontificia*, I, also described Rome's archives in great detail, although, a century later, some of his information is out of date. The major charter editions are all cited in the bibliography and the list of abbreviations. Papal documents are the only ones that regularly present problems of authenticity, which Kehr and his successors (notably Zimmermann, in his edition of *Papsturkunden*) dealt with well enough; I will express disagreement when necessary, but it will be only occasional. Papal confirmations are also often regarded as being highly unreliable guides to the real properties owned by beneficiaries, but for Rome only one (more or less) authentic text, *S. Paolo*, n. 1 (a. 1081), is really suspicious in its claims. More serious is that they often also use out-of-date terminology.

not so many: the twelfth-century documents for SS. Cosma e Damiano in Trastevere, around eighty in number, are the largest group, plus around twenty texts for
S. Maria in Trastevere, a dozen more from the eighteenth-century Galletti manuscripts in the Biblioteca Apostolica Vaticana, around twenty-five originals and copies
in the Archivio Segreto Vaticano, and a rather smaller number of charters surviving in
the Archivio di Stato di Firenze (for S. Giovanni in Laterano), the Archivio Storico
Capitolino in Rome (a few texts from the Orsini archive), and the Archivio di Stato di
Roma (isolated texts for several churches).[14] If there are other such documents
remaining to be found, which is certainly likely enough—particularly in the trackless
archives of pre-1870 *eruditi* preserved in the Archivio Segreto, who recorded many
texts now lost to us—I am hopeful that there must by now be relatively few.

There are around 1300 documents for tenth- to twelfth-century Rome, of which
two-thirds are for the period up to 1150. Roman documents hardly exist for the
eighth and ninth centuries;[15] but they get off the ground in the tenth, and are
reasonably generous in number from around 950 onwards. They cover both the
city of Rome and its immediate hinterland, the Agro romano (see Chapter 2); about
40 per cent are for the city itself, a high percentage by Italian standards, and those
for the countryside overwhelmingly involve city churches, and often lay citizens as
well, which is also unusual in Italy. This gives us material to deal with; there is quite
a lot that one can say about Rome as a result. (I only discuss the period up to 1150
here, but I looked at documents systematically up to 1200, and even later in the
case of one or two collections, to get a sense of subsequent developments.) But it
has to be recognized from the outset that Rome is not as well provided with
documents as some other cities are. For the same three centuries, Lucca has some
6000 documents, and Milan has nearly 3000. Rome has enough documents for
quite an extensive analysis of the socio-economic structures of the city after 950 or
so, in a way that is not possible earlier on the basis of written evidence (the *Liber
Pontificalis* of the Carolingian period is a marvellous resource, but it only offers us a
very limited range of data). But restrictions in its evidence-base must be reckoned
with all the same.

Roman documents in our period are almost all single-sheet parchment originals.
The main exceptions are most papal documents, which overwhelmingly survive
only in later copies (including the *Liber Censuum* cartulary of 1192), and three
other cartularies: from the rural monasteries of Subiaco and Farfa, each of which has
numerous documents for the city, and from the urban monastery of S. Gregorio sul

---

[14] Respectively cited as (see the list of abbreviations), ASR SCD; SMT; BAV; ASV; ASF
Rocchettini di Fiesole; Orsini; and ASR with *fondo* title. The archive of S. Giovanni in Laterano in
the Archivio Storico del Vicariato now has a complete register, Duval-Arnould, *Le pergamene*; it has
nothing unpublished for Rome in our period. The long-closed Colonna archive, now open and housed
in Subiaco, also has no charters for our period; I am grateful to the Soprintendenza Archivistica per il
Lazio for letting me see the register of the Colonna documents housed in its offices in Rome.

[15] For Rome, there are two full texts for the eighth century and fifteen for the ninth, mostly
surviving in the *Regesto Sublacense* (*RS*), plus some thirty-five abbreviated leases for the eighth century,
surviving in Deusdedit's late eleventh-century *Collectio canonum*, III.241–58 (= *LC*, I, nn. 71–3).
Non-*RS* charters before 900 are *S. Sil.*, nn. 1, 2; the fragmentary *ChLA*, LV, n. 4; *SPV*, n. 2; *Liber
instrumentorum monasterii Casauriensis*, ff. 74v–75r; *I papiri diplomatici*, n. 136.

Celio. The single-sheet documents almost all survived in the archives of Roman churches and monasteries; the only lay archive that begins before 1200, of the Orsini family, is very small for this period. This is typical for Italy. No serial sets of documents exist in Italy before the notarial registers of Genoa start in 1154, and five Genoese registers are the only ones surviving in more than fragmentary form anywhere in the peninsula before the thirteenth century. This means, however, that our Roman source-base depends on the archival strategies of those thirty churches; what was not in the field of interest of those establishments does not survive. Furthermore, it must be added, any type of activity that was not regarded as important enough to pay a *scriniarius* (the commonest word for notary in Rome in our period) to record in full on a parchment will also not survive. Notarial registers, once they begin to be preserved, document, in highly abbreviated form, very many ephemeral transactions, such as sales of movable goods and short-term credit deals, which were not significant enough to set out at length in a more permanent take-home version; full records on parchment were reserved for relatively important agreements, nearly all of them involving land—the sale, lease, pledge, or gift to the church of urban house-plots and rural estates, or disputes about their rightful possession. Parchment collections thus only illuminate a part of the economic and social activities of the people who made them; an important part, but—particularly in a city, where economic activity was artisanal or commercial, not agrarian—not always the most important part. And they overwhelmingly privilege ecclesiastical involvement; lay men and women who did not transact with churches mostly do not get recorded.[16]

If there was one city where an ecclesiastical bias to our evidence might not matter, it is Rome. Indeed, quite apart from the political importance of church institutions there, Rome was the only city in Italy in which virtually all land, both urban and rural, seems to have belonged to churches (see below, pp. 53–9), so that everyone, rich or poor, had potentially to deal with ecclesiastical landlords, who could sometimes keep apparently extraneous documents as a result. But, although thirty separate ecclesiastical archives might seem a wide range, there were over three hundred churches (plus dozens of monasteries and hospitals) in the twelfth-century city,[17] most of which are hardly documented at all, so substantial swathes of the city remain outside any possible analysis; and most of those thirty archives give us only small handfuls of texts. It is also the case that 1300 documents cover the ground rather sparsely. In Lucca or Milan, the scale of our documentation means that separate archives overlap; the same lay person may appear in several

---

[16] See the insightful comments in Esch, 'Überlieferungs-Chance', pp. 532–9, and, for ecclesiastical mediation, Cammarosano, *Italia medievale*, pp. 49–61. Notarial registers of some kind (*dicta*) already existed in Rome by 1075 (*S. Gregorio*, n. 18), but the earliest fully surviving are fourteenth-century; for the first (short) Roman register, on a roll from the late twelfth century, see below, p. 281.

[17] See the lists in Cencio's *Liber Censuum* of 1192, *LC*, I, pp. 300–4 (churches), 309 (monasteries), and the similar but more articulated modern lists of di Carpegna Falconieri, *Il clero di Roma*, pp. 226–34 and Passigli, 'Geografia parrocchiale', pp. 78–86. Note that these lists, long though they are, understate the total numbers; there are a number of small churches in the 1186 S. Lorenzo in Damaso bull, for example (this chapter, n. 19), which they do not include.

different collections, gaining depth of focus as he (or, more rarely, she) does. This is less common in Rome, where the micro-geographical fields of the major document collections are more focused, and do not overlap very much—a problem exacerbated by the physical size of the city's landscape. Roman material lacks a certain density as a result.

The result of all this is that in Rome, more than in some other cities, our clearest knowledge is restricted to particular urban regions. These regions are seven in all: the Celio hill, illuminated by the documents of the monastery of S. Erasmo sul Celio, a dependency of Subiaco (these texts run out after around 1020); western Trastevere, illuminated by SS. Cosma e Damiano in Trastevere, and to a lesser extent by S. Maria in Trastevere; the Civitas Leoniana, illuminated by S. Pietro in Vaticano; the *regio* of Scorteclari north and east of piazza Navona, illuminated by Farfa (these texts run out around 1090); that of Campo Marzio to its north-east, illuminated by S. Maria in Campo Marzio and to a lesser extent S. Silvestro in Capite; that of Pigna to the south of Campo Marzio, illuminated by SS. Ciriaco e Nicola in Via Lata (these are the only three documented regions even to touch each other physically); and finally the area between the Palatino and the Colosseo, illuminated by S. Maria Nova.[18] These are the richest archives we have for the city (the richest three by far are SS. Cosma e Damiano, S. Maria Nova, and SS. Ciriaco e Nicola), but they only cover around half its inhabited area. In particular, most of the area of the Tiber bend, the heart of the later medieval city, and also the politically important market and river-port area between the Teatro di Marcello, the Capitolio, and the Aventino, the old Foro Boario, are almost wholly undocumented: a chance-surviving papal privilege to the important super-parish church of S. Lorenzo in Damaso in 1186, in the middle of the Tiber bend, lists sixty-six subordinate churches, almost none of which have any prior evidence.[19] (For all this, see Map 5.)

We thus find that 'Rome' is, in the documents at our disposal, in reality seven separate regions in our period, with only small document collections and isolated chance survivals covering the areas in between. (The countryside around the city is similarly attested, with a small number of well-documented areas and big gaps between them, though the main document collections are not identical here.[20]) Two separate conclusions follow from this. First, that when generalizing about the development of 'Rome', we must always keep, at least at the back of our minds, an awareness of the undocumented spaces in the city; indeed, some of the sharper apparent changes in the city's history may just be the by-products of one document

---

[18] Documented respectively in *RS*; *SCD*, ASR SCD, and SMT; *SPV*; *RF*; *SMCM* and *S. Sil.*; *SMVL*; *SMN*. Note that *SMVL* has in this period only a small number of documents from the titular church of S. Maria in Via Lata, from which the archive is named; it is above all the archive of the neighbouring female monastery of SS. Ciriaco e Nicola in Via Lata, which was absorbed by S. Maria in 1435–57 (Cavazzi, *La diaconia*, pp. 263–4). In this book I shall refer to the latter as S. Ciriaco.

[19] Ed. in Fonseca, *De basilica S. Laurentii*, pp. 250–5.

[20] The main rural document collections, in addition to those listed in n. 18 (of which *SMCM* has few for the countryside), are *S. Alessio*, *S. Gregorio*, *S. Prassede*, and *S. Sisto* (which collects the charters of S. Maria Tempuli). See in general Wickham, 'La struttura', and below, Chapter 2.

set drying up and a different one coming on stream—as when, for example, around 1020, S. Erasmo's documents for the relatively ruralized Celio stop, and S. Maria Nova's and S. Ciriaco in Via Lata's sets for built-up *regiones* begin to be dense. I shall write about Rome quite explicitly in terms of its seven best-documented areas as a result. The second conclusion is that, inside each of these areas, we must be aware that we are the prisoners of the interests of one single church, or at the most two. What we really have at the core of our urban documentation are the interests, strategies, social and economic choices, and lay clients of less than ten Roman churches and monasteries, which might rise to fifteen if we added churches with a largely rural economic interest. Our evidence is biased towards monasteries, too, though at least it includes one major papal basilica, S. Pietro, a major *titulus*, S. Maria in Trastevere, and a very well-documented *diaconia*, S. Maria Nova (see below, p. 307, for this terminology). We will have to reconstruct an entire secular social and economic urban fabric, and an entire—and sharply changing—political and institutional superstructure, from building blocks originally destined for quite other purposes. We can do this, but it requires us to be aware of the interpretative steps involved. When previous historians have been unaware of them, or have forgotten them, the force of their argumentation has been diminished.

Historical reconstruction from documents is not straightforward anywhere, particularly when one moves away from very locally focused socio-economic history. (It is, from this standpoint, not wholly surprising that historians can sometimes, still today, get swept into trusting acceptance of narratives, which seem to give them more of what they want.) But at least Rome does provide us with some different *sorts* of material, which can sometimes pluck us away from the tramlines of analysis which are inescapable in other cities. One is a certain quantity of atypical written sources. There is a large amount of religious polemic, from nearly the whole period, which at least gives us an idea of the state of mind of (perhaps small) sections of the clergy. Rome also, perhaps more usefully, has several liturgical and procedural encyclopaedias, which tell us about the offices and ceremonials in the major churches; the modern edition of one of these, the *Liber Censuum* from 1192, collects together three separate twelfth-century accounts of the major ceremonies of the ritual year in the city, including substantial information about processions.[21] I will argue later that the regularity and complexity of this processional practice was one of the major things that held the city together.

The *Liber Censuum* was a more ambitious encyclopaedia than that, too, for, besides providing us with its main content, a set of major twelfth-century papal documents and a list of some of the forms of papal revenue, plus the processional *ordines* just mentioned, it also includes a version of one of the best examples of another Roman literary speciality, accounts of the secular and antique monuments of the city.[22] Rome's classical monuments are dominant enough now; they

---

[21] See in particular Andrieu, *Les ordines romani*, II–V, and, *LC*, I, pp. 290–314, II, pp. 90–159.

[22] *LC*, I, collects all these; pp. 262–73 for the *Mirabilia urbis Romae*. For the earliest version of the same text, from *c.*1140, see Valentini and Zucchetti, *Codice topografico*, III, pp. 3–65; the four volumes of this publication collect all the various *Mirabilia* texts.

were far more dominant a thousand years ago. A Roman self-awareness of the ancient past of the city is quite widely attested, and it is one of the most particular aspects of the city's culture—it is also visible in some of the city's unusually substantial corpus of inscriptions from this period, most notably the long and plangent portal inscription of the so-called Casa dei Crescenzi, a twelfth-century tower-house with reused and imitative classical elements beside one of the Tiber bridges (see below, pp. 235–8).[23] Romans had an articulated and explicit sense of the city's monumental and symbolic geography, structured by processional routes past buildings both secular and ecclesiastical. This can often also serve as a real counterpoint to sometimes-monochrome documents recording ecclesiastical leases or sales of one-storeyed urban houses, and I shall use it as such, particularly when looking at the area between S. Maria Nova and the Colosseo (below, pp. 292–303).

Finally, and not least, I shall pay attention to archaeology. Rome's medieval urban archaeology is among the most active in Italy, and Rome is also one of the few Italian cities that have so far provided us with significant excavations from the central Middle Ages, my focus in this book: here the Crypta Balbi and the Fori Imperiali excavations stand out, but are flanked by a considerable number of smaller recent excavations, in piazza Venezia, just south of the Trevi Fountain, on the Foro Romano side of the Capitolio, in the Colosseo, outside S. Paolo fuori le Mura, and others again (see map 5).[24] These are backed up by numerous surviving secular buildings, some evident, others rather more hidden, and, of course, a rich network of churches, with some major early twelfth-century rebuildings. This material evidence shows more clearly than anything else how Romans appropriated the past physically, and, of course, how they changed it.[25] And it also gives us the most direct evidence we have for the sophistication and commercialization of artisanal products, which we need to understand if we want to understand the city's economy.

Rome's evidence thus allows us to create a picture of the tenth to twelfth centuries that is far from one-dimensional. It is certainly heterogeneous; and the operation of putting chalk and cheese together always requires care, and a critical awareness of which connections can (and which cannot) legitimately be made. But I hope to give a sense both of the range of material we have for the city, and of the complexity of conclusions we can draw from it. All these types of source have their problems, but as long as we are aware of them we can get past them.

---

[23] Forcella, XIII.1339–41. Forcella is the basic collection of Roman inscriptions, and is nearly complete, but only begins in the year 1000.

[24] See above all, up to 1000, Meneghini and Santangeli Valenzani, *Roma*; for later, see esp. Saguì and Paroli (eds), *Archeologia urbana a Roma*, V; Meneghini and Santangeli Valenzani, *I fori imperiali*; Serlorenzi and Saguì, 'Roma, Piazza Venezia'; Insalaco, *La 'Città dell'Acqua'* (a booklet available at the site, in vicolo del Puttarello, 25); Rea, *Rota Colisei*; Spera (ed.), *Lo scavo 2007–2009*.

[25] See in general Krautheimer, *Rome*.

THE PROBLEM OF THE HISTORIOGRAPHY

Here, it is necessary to be quite clear: Rome's historiography is, overall, rich and of high quality. It privileges some areas too much (Otto III; most popes and many cardinals; the establishment of the Senate), others too little. But the long-standing attraction of the city—and of its numerous foreign academies—has brought many outsiders in to do work on Rome, some of whom have done their best work there; and the strength of by far the largest university in Italy, the Sapienza, now flanked by two others, also highly active in this field, plus the country's Istituto Storico per il Medio Evo and a venerable and important school of palaeography, have provided firm bases for a dense body of work by Romans on their own city. When I worked on Lucca, I usually knew by name every person who had even cursorily looked at any given document before me, and it was sometimes as few as two or three, after the archivists and text-editors who had arranged them to start with. For Rome, nearly every document has been studied, often in detail, often dozens of times. There are few new discoveries, except in archaeology; the best one can hope for is new insights.[26] But, notwithstanding this overall quality and density, Roman historiography remains fragmented, until at least the world of Innocent III, and maybe later. A fuller list of the works on the city will, of course, be found in the bibliography. Here, I want to characterize some of the main approaches that have structured them, and, at times, also limited them. The arguments I wish to make here will, it is necessary to state at the outset, be familiar to those who currently work on the social history of the city, particularly in the later Middle Ages (the fourth strand of recent work on Rome discussed below, p. 19); but they may not be to others, and it is therefore necessary to set them out as clearly as possible here. They will make clearer what I want myself to achieve in this book as well.

A high percentage of the work done on Rome in the period 900–1150, especially in the last century of that period, has been in the framework of the papal grand narrative. This is true even of the first major scientific historian of medieval Rome, Ferdinand Gregorovius, Protestant and heavily opposed to the politics of Pius IX in the 1850s and 1860s; of course, narrative histories then all focused on rulers, and thus here inevitably on popes, but Gregorovius also offered a compelling model for later historians of all persuasions, and his basic storyline underpins Paolo Brezzi too.[27]

That story-line began with the supposed moral degradation of the early tenth-century age of the Teofilatto rulers of Rome, until the emperor Otto I saved the city by conquest in 962; followed by a confused period of family rivalries punctuated by

---

[26] For example, one of the Roman documents with the most recent scientific publication date (1996), an 1177 text for the Colosseo area ed. Augenti, *Il Palatino*, p. 188, was already known to Gregorovius (*History*, IV/2, pp. 404–5). But finds do still appear, as with ASV, Arm. XXXVII, vol. 8, ff. 364r–9r, an early modern MS transcript of an important text of 1125 for the coast near the Tiber mouth, signalled in Passigli, 'Per una storia', fig. 13 verso (a modern edn is planned by Marco Vendittelli)—see below, pp. 67–8; or BAV, CVL 8044, ff. 4–16 (a. 1145)—see below, pp. 269–71.

[27] Gregorovius, *History*, vols III–IV.2; Brezzi, *Roma*.

Ottonian intervention, in the Crescenzian period, which lasted up to 1012; then the stable but still degraded Tuscolano papacy. Emperor Henry III again saved Rome at the synod of Sutri in 1046, when he overthrew three rival popes and installed a period of foreign pontiffs, first German, then Italian and French, which continued until 1130. The 'reform' papacy began here too, first under imperial patronage (Leo IX most notably), then increasingly independently of the emperors, until Gregory VII dramatically broke with them in 1076. War and papal schism followed until 1100, when a 'reform' pope, Paschal II (1099–1118), took the city back, and until 1122, when Calixtus II (1119–24) made peace with the emperor. Trouble began again with a new schism in 1130, this time between two Roman popes, Anacletus II and Innocent II; after Anacletus died and Innocent returned in 1137–8, the city was increasingly resistant to papal power, and the Senate was born violently, against Innocent, in 1143 as a result. The Protestant version of this story has tended to point up Sutri and the German popes as the great moment of 'reform', with Gregory VII as a powerful but tragic figure who deviated the movement by breaking church from state;[28] the Catholic version has seen Gregory as taking 'reform' to new heights, by freeing the papacy not only from the aristocratic corruption of the Roman *Adelspapsttum*, but also from the chains of state and lay power.[29] Both of these versions, of course, faithfully reflected the intense polemics of the late eleventh century, published by the *MGH* editors in the *Libelli di lite* in the 1890s.

By now, the Catholic version has largely won out; the central position accorded to Gregory in the work of Anglican historians such as John Cowdrey is a clear sign of it.[30] But what unified both sides in this long dispute was the role Rome as a city played in their storylines, which was uniformly negative. A church controlled by Romans (as, usually, before 1046) was seen as not just degraded but narrow-minded, and careless of the universalist obligations of popes. Hence the importance of the 1059 election decree, which, however seldom followed thereafter, institutionalized the principle that popes did not need to be elected in Rome. Romans thereafter were simply trouble: avaricious, they still had to be bought off, over and over, by 'reformers' who wished to rule the city; factious, their endless struggles undermined the authority of well-meaning popes like Paschal II and Gelasius II, and the very legitimacy of their successors, Honorius II and the papal rivals of 1130. As Bernard of Clairvaux put it, 'What should I say of the people? It is the Roman people . . . What is better known to the world than the impudence and obstinacy of the Romans? A people unaccustomed to peace, accustomed to tumult, unpeaceful

---

[28] See e.g. Tellenbach, *The Church in Western Europe*, pp. 141–253 (a very good survey in itself).

[29] See as a classic traditional example Fliche, *La réforme grégorienne*. Note that I will use the phrases 'reform' and 'reform papacy', in inverted commas, for ease of reference to the period after 1046. They are problematic words, in that they take the standpoint of Leo IX, Gregory VII, etc. for granted (and also because 'reform' was not actually then a very common word: see Tellenbach, *The Church in Western Europe*, p. 160 and Barrow, 'Ideas', pp. 361–2), but they are convenient labels.

[30] Cowdrey, *Gregory VII*. Robinson, *The Papacy*, begins the book at 1073 and skips the Sutri period altogether. But see also the recent critique by Miller, 'The crisis', as a sign that paradigms in this field can still shift.

and intractable to this day...'—Romans are simply Romans, you can't deal with them.[31] This view, a cliché in the eleventh and twelfth centuries, remains one today. The estimable series of papal biographies published since the 1970s by Anton Hiersemann Verlag, plus similar biographies published by the *MGH* and elsewhere, tend to have a short chapter in each entitled 'Rom', which details the (often futile) attempts by whichever pope to bring order to the city, alongside rather longer and more enthusiastic sections on Germany, France, Spain, etc. Rome becomes simply an Other in this tradition. Papal government, from Leo IX onward, properly looked outwards, to Latin Europe; its precarious local base was only an embarrassment. Even when Klaus-Jürgen Herrmann offered a partial rehabilitation of the Tuscolano popes in 1973, he did so by stressing their internationalist reforming credentials, too, with little discussion of their Roman rule at all.[32]

It is of course the right of every historian to choose his or her subject of study; and the analysis of major changes in papal institutions, as part of a wider ecclesiastical history, is not only an obviously legitimate historical field, but a very well-documented and thus satisfying one. I am very happy to leave it to its experts to study it. But it is a pity, all the same, that this tradition tends to neglect one of the longest-standing functions of the bishop of Rome, which was to rule his own diocese. This is what bishops are supposed to do everywhere, and the pope was not any less the ecclesiastical head of Rome because he often had an international role as well. Furthermore, since Hadrian I in the 770s at the latest, the pope was also the secular ruler of the city, and of most of what is now called Lazio as well. The way that rule was exercised is not an unimportant part of a rounded view of any given papacy. From Innocent III onwards into the thirteenth century, and still more in the sixteenth and seventeenth, papal historiography does not usually neglect it. By contrast in our period, particularly with the internationalization of the papacy after 1046, how Rome was actually ruled has remained opaque in this tradition, and is clearly to most authors in this tradition relatively unimportant.[33] But Rome did have to be ruled, of course. To understand how it was, we will have to turn elsewhere.

In the 1870s, Rome was not governed by a pope for the first time since the eighth century, with the exception of a few intervals: Marozia/Alberico and Otto III/Giovanni di Crescenzio in the tenth and early eleventh, the Senate several times in the twelfth, Cola di Rienzo in the mid-fourteenth, Napoleon for five years in the early nineteenth century. In 1878, a newly founded journal, the *Archivio della Società romana di storia patria* (*ASRSP*), still the major journal for Roman history in our period and later, took as one of its main aims the publication of early Roman

---

[31] 'Quid de populo loquar? Populus Romanus est.... Quid tam notum saeculis, quam protervia et cervicositas Romanorum? Gens insueta paci, tumultui assueta, gens immitis et intractabilis usque adhuc...': Bernard of Clairvaux, *De consideratione*, IV.2.

[32] See, among others, Cowdrey, *Gregory VII*, pp. 314–29; Becker, *Urban II.*, pp. 98–113; Servatius, *Paschalis II.*, pp. 69–85; Schilling, *Guido von Vienne—Papst Calixt II.*, pp. 467–71. For the Tuscolani, Herrmann, *Das Tuskulanerpapsttum*, pp. 5–24.

[33] Halphen, *Études*, is the clear exception here.

documents, up to 1200 and often beyond, and in the years around 1900 some of the best palaeographers in Italy dedicated themselves to that task, Pietro Fedele and Luigi Schiaparelli at their head.[34] Their aim was essentially the creation of a documentary base for the study of the history of the city, which could thus be seen independently of the papal narrative. This took them into the reconstruction of Roman noble families in the tenth and eleventh centuries, as the structuring element in local politics, and often a truly difficult challenge—there are at least three rival versions of the genealogy of the Crescenzi, for example (see below, pp. 197–202)—and also into a rehabilitation of the rule over Rome by the Teofilatto family in the tenth century.[35] (In both these fields they were also ably backed up by German and Austrian scholars.[36]) But above all it took them into the study of the origins of the Senate of Rome.

Most of the leading medievalists in the city in the early twentieth century, from Fedele on, dedicated major research articles to the 'Roman revolution' of 1143–4 and its scarce documentation. No other Italian commune, except perhaps Pisa, has such a dense historiography focused on its origins, in fact, which also partly excuses the near-total absence of any comparative element in their work. Was the 'revolution' aristocratic or popular, or somewhere in between? Did the city have any autonomous secular government before 1143, and how did it relate to the senatorial moment? What was the intellectual and cultural underpinning of that moment? These are significant questions, of course; they will recur here in Chapter 7. But what is equally striking is how much they *mattered* in this tradition, up into the early 1950s in fact, when Antonio Rota's 110-page article on the first two years of the Senate and Arsenio Frugoni's whole book on the fragmentarily attested activities of Arnaldo of Brescia beat the field into submission for a generation. For Brezzi in 1947, who clearly wished to reconcile the papal and Roman historiographical traditions in his influential narrative, the years of the foundation of the Senate were its 'heroic age', the summation of the 'autonomous Roman history' of the previous centuries, a moment 'justly exalted' by its historians.[37] The extra-historical aims of this tradition are seldom as clear in other writers as they are in Brezzi, but this enthusiasm for Roman 'heroism' is quite as visible in duller and more positivist authors. The storyline, however, marked Roman failure as well. The commune did not last; its autonomy and eventually its institutions were destroyed by papal and baronial machinations. The origins of the commune, the Senate, are all the more wrapped in romanticism as a result.

---

[34] See Ignazio Giorgi's programmatic statement in *ASRSP*, I (1878), pp. 47–8. For Fedele and Schiaparelli see esp. (but not only) *SCD*, *SMN*, and *SPV*.

[35] See for example Bossi, 'I Crescenzi'; Fedele, 'Le famiglie' and 'Sull'origine dei Frangipane'; and, for the early tenth century, Fedele, 'Ricerche', with Falco, *La santa romana repubblica*, pp. 222–40, slightly more negative.

[36] See for example Sickel, 'Alberich II.'; Kölmel, *Rom und der Kirchenstaat*; Gerstenberg, *Die politische Entwicklung*.

[37] See among many Fedele, 'L'êra del Senato'; Bartoloni, 'Per la storia del Senato'; Solmi, *Il Senato romano* (a controversial text); Frugoni, 'Sulla "Renovatio Senatus"' and *Arnaldo da Brescia*; Rota, 'La costituzione originaria'; and for the quote Brezzi, *Roma*, p. 317.

Between the romance of Gregory VII and the romance of the 'Roman revolution' there may seem little to choose. But at least this second tradition dealt with the city, and took it on its own terms. Similarly, even the less value-laden studies of the post-1046 papal Curia in the past generation or so are, in general, of less centrality for this book, precisely because its membership was so rarely of Roman origin;[38] on the other hand, the revived interest in the origins of the Senate in the 1980s, notably in a short and important monograph by Laura Moscati and an influential article by Girolamo Arnaldi, are of direct relevance here. Moscati in particular will be much cited in this book.[39] There has also been a significant revival in the palaeographical and diplomatic analysis of Roman documentary and other scriptorial traditions, which has not only produced a raft of new editions but has also enforced new ways of looking at the act of writing in the city.[40] Rome has also, however, been approached from new historical directions in the past generation as well, which I have found of rather more use than most of the foregoing. Here, schematizing somewhat, I think that four separate strands of analysis can be identified. Let us look at them in turn.

The oldest is an interest in Roman topography, which indeed goes back to the nineteenth century, and has been a feature of the *ASRSP* from its inception. It gained particular purchase because of the existence of so many medieval accounts of the significant buildings of Rome, which were edited in four substantial volumes between 1940 and 1953, and have been widely commented on both before and after, not least in the framework of an interest in the classicizing culture of the twelfth century (see below, Chapter 6).[41] Separately, work on the standing buildings of medieval Rome produced the huge and rich corpus of church architecture associated with Richard Krautheimer, and some later and less complete attempts to catalogue the secular tower-houses of the city. Krautheimer synthesized a lifetime's work in his *Rome: Profile of a City* in 1980, which also summed up and surpassed the Roman topographical tradition.[42] Most of what has followed since in the field of topography has been little more than updating of detail, but recent archaeological work has produced a major re-examination of the period up to 1000 by Roberto Meneghini and Riccardo Santangeli. After 1000, there is no current synthesis of Rome's archaeology, but Étienne Hubert's document-based study of urban development between then and 1300 takes the story on in forceful and

---

[38] For earlier scientific studies, see e.g. Jordan, 'Die Entstehung'; Jordan, 'Zur päpstlichen Finanzgeschichte'; later important works include Fried, 'Die römische Kurie'; Hüls, *Kardinäle, Klerus*; and the insightful Laudage, 'Rom und das Papsttum'. Much more attentive to the city are some works in the English tradition, esp. Whitton, 'Papal policy'; Twyman, *Papal Ceremonial*; and Doran, 'The legacy of schism'.

[39] Moscati, *Alle origini* (see the bibliography for her other works); Arnaldi, 'Rinascita'.

[40] Supino Martini, *Roma e l'area grafica romanesca*; Carbonetti, 'Tabellioni e scriniari', together with her other articles cited in the bibliography; and see in general the 'Codice diplomatico di Roma e della regione romana', begun in the 1980s and continuing, which supplements the old *ASRSP* editions at a more up-to-date technical level.

[41] See esp. Valentini and Zucchetti, *Codice topografico*; Cecchelli, 'Roma medioevale', sums it up.

[42] Krautheimer, *Corpus basilicarum* and *Rome*; an update of the former is in Claussen, *Die Kirchen der Stadt Rom*. For tower-houses, Katermaa-Ottela, *Le casetorri* (with caution); Pani Ermini and de Minicis (eds), *Archeologia del medioevo*; and Bianchi, *Case e torri*, I.

innovative ways.[43] Krautheimer's sharp separation between the *abitato* and the *disabitato* inside the city has in this recent work been considerably nuanced, as we shall see in Chapter 3. But no one has yet reworked Krautheimer's remarkable evocations of the different faces of Rome's *regiones*.

A second strand is a greatly developed understanding of the city in its regional context. The topography of the Campagna Romana is one aspect to this, one however almost devoid of synthesis, from Giuseppe Tomassetti in the late nineteenth century to (the enormously more scientific) Jean Coste in the late twentieth; the political and institutional history of Lazio has some good traditional studies, too, from Giorgio Falco or Peter Partner.[44] Most recently, Valeria Beolchini's important study of Tuscolo is a model combination of documentary and archaeological work. But it was Pierre Toubert's monumental *thèse* on the Sabina and eastern Lazio in 1973 that marked the step change here.[45] Toubert placed everyone's understanding of the history of settlement, society, and the economy in Lazio on a different, integrated footing; his book has been a model for all subsequent work on the rural history of medieval Italy (and not only Italy). *Les structures du Latium médiéval* was avowedly not about Rome, and its socio-economic conclusions do not work for Rome's immediate hinterland, as we shall see in Chapter 2; but Toubert's careful structural analysis also allowed him to entirely refigure the history of papal power in Lazio, and, as an integral part of that, the structures of papal authority in the city as well. His pages on the pre-1050 *Adelspapsttum* and on the judicial system of Rome up to 1100 are the best there is. Rome is here lit by an external light, to great effect. And Toubert owed very little to the two traditional grand narratives of Roman history—indeed, he could barely hide his lack of interest in them. He argued for a largely stable and bureaucratized city government, seen best through its judicial structures, lasting throughout the often sharp changes in Rome's leadership, right up to its dissolution at the end of the late eleventh century, to be substituted in the twelfth by newly formed institutions, more attentive to Roman law.[46] These are views that I accept in all but detail; I develop some of them further in Chapter 7. But, to repeat, the social structure of the city was not in his remit, and was barely mentioned except in a handful of footnotes.

A third strand is a network of recent work on Rome's use of classical traditions. Some of this is an extended analysis of the classicizing imagery associated with the early Senate, part of it in the tradition of the *Geistesgeschichte* of Percy Schramm, whose 1929 account of the imperial ideology of Otto III and his predecessors and

---

[43] Meneghini and Santangeli Valenzani, *Roma* (and this chapter, n. 24; for later work, a good updated survey is Augenti, 'Roma tra la tarda Antichità e l'alto Medioevo'); Hubert, *Espace urbain*; an important correction to Krautheimer is Coates-Stephens, 'Housing'.

[44] Tomassetti, *La Campagna romana*; Coste, *Scritti di topografia* (and see further Chapter 2, n. 9); for Lazio, see e.g. Falco, *Studi sulla storia del Lazio*; Partner, *The Lands of St. Peter*. The best synthetic work on our period in Rome's hinterland is Lenzi, *La terra e il potere*; for the immediately succeeding period, Carocci and Vendittelli, *L'origine della Campagna Romana*.

[45] Beolchini, *Tusculum II*; Toubert, *Les structures*.

[46] Toubert, *Les structures*, pp. 1191–257, 1314–48.

successors is still the starting point for the study of Rome's pre-'reform' cultural history; and part of it located in the intellectual framework of 'twelfth-century Renaissance' studies. Some of this has a rather romantic tinge as well, and the '*renovatio*' imagery of the Senate was smartly critiqued in 1987 by Ingrid Baumgärtner.[47] More solidly based and useful has been the substantial recent work on the revival of classical Roman law in the city, particularly that by Giovanni Chiodi and Emanuele Conte; this has indeed transformed our understanding of legal practice there, even if the impact of Justinianic law was more paradoxical and inconsistent than has been recognized.[48] Rome is seen by scholars such as Conte not in the negative, as a drag on the historic potential of its rulers, but rather as a model for other cities, in its development of complex law and bureaucratic government. This is certainly a set of discoveries that this book will build on.

The fourth strand is the extension backwards of a substantial body of sophisticated work on the thirteenth-century city. (Note that there is less of an equivalent extension forwards into the tenth century of the equally sophisticated work currently done on Carolingian Rome, both in Italian by the school of Paolo Delogu, and in English.[49]) Scholars such as Sandro Carocci, Marco Vendittelli, Jean-Claude Maire Vigueur, Matthias Thumser, and indeed Étienne Hubert again, look back at the twelfth century with eyes trained to a thirteenth- and fourteenth-century problematic, the network of power and ceremonial attached to a truly powerful papacy and the newly established baronial families, and to a much more commercialized city than previous scholarship recognized, and they seek its origins in the post-1050 'reform' period.[50] This has the potential to overturn, in particular, some of the core elements in the grand narrative of senatorial origins, particularly when used together with Moscati's parallel work on an earlier period; indeed, both Carocci/Vendittelli and Maire Vigueur have sought to do precisely that, in ways I shall be happy to follow.[51] I would add here Tommaso di Carpegna Falconieri's excellent study of the city clergy, 700–1200, the only work of ecclesiastical history for my whole period that pays proper attention to Rome's urban society, for the

[47] Schramm, *Kaiser, Rom* (Schramm, *Kaiser, Könige*, III and IV.1 collects his other Roman articles too); subsequently, Benson, 'Political *renovatio*' and Claussen, '*Renovatio Romae*' are good guides to 'Renaissance' imagery, as are also the more speculative Gramaccini, 'La prima riedificazione' and Strothmann, *Kaiser und Senat*. The recent Petersohn, *Kaisertum und Rom*, is far better, and the best place to start. For Baumgärtner, see esp. 'Rombeherrschung'—see the bibliography for her other works.

[48] Chiodi, 'Roma e il diritto romano'; Conte, '*Res publica*' and 'Posesión y proceso', among others; see further Padoa Schioppa, 'Il ruolo'; Wickham, 'Getting justice'. See below, pp. 336–75, 403–8.

[49] See e.g. Paroli and Delogu (eds), *La storia economica*; Delogu, 'L'importazione di tessuti'; Marazzi, *I 'patrimonia'*; Noble, *The Republic of St. Peter*; Goodson, *The Rome of Pope Paschal I*; Leyser and Costambeys, 'To be the neighbour of St. Stephen'. The exception here is Girolamo Arnaldi, whose Roman work covers our whole period; and a new direction is also shown by Leyser, 'Episcopal office', which links the ninth century and the tenth.

[50] Carocci, *Baroni di Roma*; Carocci, *Il nepotismo*; Carocci (ed.), *La nobiltà romana*; Vendittelli, 'Mercanti romani'; Hubert (ed.), *Roma nei secoli XIII e XIV*; Hubert, *Espace urbain*; Maire Vigueur, *L'autre Rome* (a substantial synthesis; see the critical commentaries with Maire Vigueur's reply in *Storica*, L, 2011, pp. 103–42); Thumser, *Rom*.

[51] Carocci and Vendittelli, 'Società ed economia'; Maire Vigueur, 'Il comune romano'; Maire Vigueur, *L'autre Rome*, pp. 305–70.

author's training was in the later medieval environment of the Sapienza as well; this book is all the more valuable in that through it one can see how the Curia actually related to the city's own ecclesiastical structure, which allows one to avoid the temptation to ignore the papal court altogether.[52] Again, this is not a mistake anyone who reads about the thirteenth century (for example in the work of Robert Brentano and Agostino Paravicini Bagliani[53]) could make, and it is a recognition that anyone studying the period 1050–1150 needs to keep hold of.

This rapid survey of recent and earlier work shows the wealth and density of current scholarship, which, to repeat, is not surpassed for any other Italian city. But Rome as a structural whole, at least in the period 900–1150 which is my focus here, does not emerge from it with full clarity. No general synthesis of any depth has been written since Brezzi; Maire Vigueur's recent and ambitious survey starts just as my period ends. Perhaps it would be enough to synthesize all these strands, but that would be a dull task. It seems to me more effective, and certainly more satisfying, to start again: to try to figure Rome structurally in this period from scratch, bouncing off the secondary literature dialectically rather than depending directly on it. Notwithstanding my great respect for so many of the scholars cited in the last few pages, this is what I have tried to do. The society of the city, and the overarching economic structures that made it work up to 1150, are at the centre of my attention, as they are not for any of these writers except Moscati. On the basis of this, a ceremonial analysis like Twyman's, a topographical analysis like Krautheimer's, an urbanistic analysis like Hubert's, an institutional analysis like Toubert's, a legal analysis like Chiodi's, a social analysis like that of Carocci and Vendittelli, will, I hope, fit together as a whole. Such, anyway, is my aim.

A POLITICAL FRAMEWORK FOR ROMAN HISTORY

The intention of this section is simply to offer a fairly rapid narrative of the history of the city of Rome, from slightly before my period starts until slightly after it ends. This is partly so as to introduce that history to readers who may not have a clear idea who Giovanni di Crescenzio was or why Calixtus II has a relatively good press, as an essential background to the more monographic analyses that follow; partly, however, it is an initial attempt to distance myself from the grand narratives of the past century and a half, for it has quite a distinct storyline from those characterized earlier, although it is indebted, in particular, to the insights of Pierre Toubert.[54] Some of its cruxes will be defended and discussed in more detail in Chapters 4 and 7; but here they are set out in a simple chronological format, with a minimum of footnoting.

---

[52] Di Carpegna Falconieri, *Il clero di Roma*.
[53] Brentano, *Rome before Avignon*; for Paravicini Bagliani, e.g. *Il trono di Pietro*; *La vita quotidiana*; and the series he edits for Viella editrice, 'La corte dei papi'.
[54] Toubert, *Les structures*, esp. pp. 960–1038.

Let us begin with the very active late Carolingian papacy of Nicholas I (858–67) and his immediate successors. The city was run then, and had been for a century or more, by a network of aristocratic families, all of whom obtained status and power through the occupation of official posts, the underpinnings of papal government, in three separate hierarchies: as one of the seven palatine judges and administrators, such as the *primicerius* or *nomenculator* or *arcarius*, plus the influential and more specifically financial office of the *vestararius*; as military leaders, headed by a *magister militum* or *superista* (for all this see below, pp. 186–90); or else as clerical officials. The latter were either the bishops of neighbouring sees (many of whom resided in Rome), or the priests of the twenty-plus *tituli* of the city, the churches with early baptismal rights, or the deacons who became progressively more closely associated with the *diaconiae*, originally poor-relief centres, which became the alternative foci for the ecclesiastical regions of the city. (These were to become the three components of the college of cardinals. See below, p. 307, for more detailed discussion.) In the eighth century, most popes had previously been deacons; in the ninth, more had been priests of *tituli*; popes who had been bishops of another see only began with Marinus I in 882 and were highly controversial for a generation.[55] The aristocratic families of the city spread easily across all these separate hierarchies. Popes themselves were, even if not universally, usually from the same range of families too.

The important point is not that Rome was controlled by its aristocracy. All Italian cities were. More important is that that network of aristocrats was so closely tied to such a complex system of office-holding. It structured the city's political procedures. It also dominated a clientelar structure which extended far down into the rest of the city's population, for Rome's numerous churches had many subordinate priests, who could be members of much less influential families; there were many levels to the papal administration (notably a whole range of *iudices* and *scriniarii*); and the city's *militia*, divided into *scolae*, was extensive and ceremonially important (indeed, probably more important ceremonially than it was militarily). The structural attachment of rich and poor alike to the political system centred on the pope was also underpinned by the fact that aristocratic and non-aristocratic landed wealth, in the city and its hinterland, was held overwhelmingly in lease from Roman churches. Such a statement can only fully be justified by tenth-century sources, as we shall see in Chapter 2, but all the signs are that it was true of the ninth as well. This landowning pattern seems to have become established in the third quarter of the eighth century, in fact, for it was in that period that the popes finally established their full independence from the Byzantine empire, while simultaneously avoiding absorption into that of the Franks. A new papal sovereignty over Rome entailed a new papal ownership of former imperial lands as well, and these were most probably very extensive, adding substantially to the pre-existing landed

---

[55] See in general Toubert, *Les structures*, pp. 1194–229; Toubert, 'Scrinium et palatium'; for the judges, Halphen, *Études*, pp. 37–52, 89–146; for the ecclesiastical networks, di Carpegna Falconieri, *Il clero di Roma*, pp. 103–36, 195–226. For Marinus, Bonaccorsi, 'Marino I'; for the controversiality of moving sees, Leyser, 'Episcopal office'.

resources of the church, which were already large. The popes, by now hugely wealthy (as indeed their ninth-century building programmes attest) then gave this land out, not to the lay aristocracy, but to the churches of the city and its immediate surroundings, which provided both a firm and a wide basis for a solid and long-lasting ecclesiastical dominance in the city, continuing throughout the period of this book and later as well. (For all this see below, pp. 53–9.)

This solid political structure was the stage for intense and violent rivalry. There were conflicts at every papal election (almost all air-brushed away by the *Liber Pontificalis*), and some prominent ecclesiastics, such as Anastasio *bibliothecarius* and Formosus bishop of Porto, could go dramatically in and out of favour, with show trials and subsequent political reintegrations. Both of these had been papal candidates too, and Formosus in 891–6, in his seventies, finally made it to pope, in a period that had become more sharply charged because of John VIII's murder in 882, and which was also marked by Arab attacks in Lazio, which became more serious from John's reign (872–82) onwards—among other things, they sacked and occupied the rich monastery of Farfa in the Sabina in *c*.898.[56] Formosus had been controversial under John VIII, however (he was formally condemned in 872, and again in 876), and was also a bishop already, which was unacceptable to many of his enemies; after his death his corpse was famously subjected to a trial by his successor Stephen VI (896–7), who was then himself murdered; the ideological and factional battle between Formosans and anti-Formosans, with a substantial corpus of religious and political invective surviving from the Formosan party, continued into the 910s.[57] Factional violence had thus escalated to the murder of popes; it had become mixed up with a theological polemic which allowed little basis for compromise; and the Arabs were settling in the countryside around Rome, with little opposition from the established powers elsewhere in Italy, the heirs of the Carolingians, whether kings or the marquises of neighbouring Spoleto and Tuscany, who were tied up in their own civil wars. The period of this book thus starts with a crisis.

It is nonetheless significant that Rome's political system did not then break down. The popes of the ten years after Formosus had short reigns and hardly visible activities, but by 905 two bulls of Sergius III (904–11), to the bishop of suburban Silva Candida and the female monastery of S. Maria Tempuli, granting lands north-west and south of the city, refer explicitly to a restoration after Arab devastations; and our narratives, though brief and problematic, converge in the claim that the Arabs were in retreat from the sections of the interior of northern and eastern Lazio under their control, thanks to Roman and Lazial military action, well

---

[56] For John, see most recently Arnold, *Johannes VIII*. Formosus does not have a full study, but see Brezzi, *Roma*, pp. 86–92; Arnaldi, 'Papa Formoso'; Sansterre, 'Formoso'; and citations in the next n. For the Arabs in Farfa, Ugo of Farfa, *Destructio farfensis*, pp. 29–32. The Arab threat was very visible to John VIII, who used it rhetorically throughout his letter collection; an 876 trial of his opponents (see Chapter 4, n. 20) accuses many of the defendants of inviting the *Sarraceni* into Rome, in tones reminiscent of Senator Joe McCarthy.

[57] See for Formosan tracts esp. *Auxilius und Vulgarius*, ed. Dümmler, and the *Invectiva in Romam*, a still-angry text from after 914. For the 'synod of the corpse', see e.g. Liutprando of Cremona, *Antapodosis*, I.30; *Auxilius und Vulgarius*, pp. 71–4; *Invectiva*, pp. 138–40; and the full bibliography in Sansterre, 'Formoso'.

before the big campaign of 915 which saw an alliance of central and southern Italian powers, from Rome, Naples, Capua, Gaeta, and the Byzantine provinces, expel the Arabs from the Garigliano valley. The 915 alliance is documented among other things by a surviving treaty between these powers which was brokered by Rome: by Teofilatto, Giovanni *senator Romanorum*, five of the seven palatine judges, and six other aristocrats, all acting for Pope John X (914–28).[58] John was, almost uniquely in this early period, not Roman; he seems to have been Bolognese and had been archbishop of Ravenna. He too was killed in the end, but had the longest papacy for seventy years before him and nearly two hundred after. John X had probably been put in by Teofilatto, who was the real architect of this renewed stability: he was *gloriosissimus dux, magister militum*, and *vestararius* already under Sergius III by *c.*906, perhaps *senator* later, and was clearly, from our few surviving texts, the major lay player in the city from then on, up to his death in *c.*925. Teofilatto has been plausibly associated genealogically with the Teofilatto *nomenculator* and his sons who were condemned in an 876 show trial, and anyway he certainly came from the old Roman official aristocracy; he was also allied from the start to Alberico marquis of Spoleto, who had put Sergius on the papal throne and who married Teofilatto's daughter Marozia.[59] Under Teofilatto, the Formosan dispute must finally have quietened down, if he was close both to the violently anti-Formosan Sergius and also to John, who had been a bishop elsewhere. The many-levelled crisis of the mid-890s was in fact over at the latest by 915 and maybe already by 905.

Teofilatto has generally been seen as the architect of a new regime in Rome, based on his own family, and this is not false either: his wife Teodora *vesterarissa* or *vesteratrix* is unusually prominent in our scarce sources, with (among other things) a praise-letter written to her by Eugenio Vulgario and an attack on her by Liutprando of Cremona; their daughter Marozia *senatrix Romanorum* ruled the city after Teofilatto (*c.*925–32), bringing down John X when he and his brother tried to oppose her; Marozia's son Alberico overthrew her in 932 and ruled as *princeps atque omnium Romanorum senator*; Alberico's son Ottaviano—an unusual classicizing name, hinting at the ancient shift from republic to empire—succeeded in 954, and in 956–64 was also Pope John XII.[60] The family did not need to have

---

[58] *Papsturkunden*, nn. 22, 23 for Sergius III; Benedetto, *Chronicon*, pp. 157–8; Ugo of Farfa, *Destructio farfensis*, pp. 31–2; cf. Toubert, *Les structures*, pp. 311–12, 970–3. For the Garigliano, see Vehse, 'Das Bündnis', who edits the 915 text at pp. 202–4; Fedele, 'La battaglia del Garigliano'; Venni, 'Giovanni X', pp. 36–53.

[59] For Teofilatto, Toubert, *Les structures*, pp. 967–74 is the best starting point, with Brezzi, *Roma*, pp. 97–109. For *gloriosissimus dux* etc., see e.g. the future Pope John X's letter to him and his wife when still archbishop of Ravenna, which also gives an idea of the patronage relationship between the two, in Loewenfeld, 'Acht Briefe', p. 517; for the date and ascription of the letter to John, see Fedele, 'Ricerche', pp. 205–6, 75–115. Note that the title of *senator* is assumed by historians on the basis of the list of participants in the 915 text, but that text says *senator Romanorum*, referring to an otherwise unknown Giovanni, not *senatores*, which would have unequivocally included both Teofilatto and Giovanni.

[60] For Marozia, only the recent study of di Carpegna Falconieri, 'Marozia', is of any real use. Alberico has several accounts, notably Sickel, 'Alberich II.'; Arnaldi, 'Alberico di Roma'; Toubert, *Les structures*, pp. 974–98. See also as an overview Wickham, 'The Romans'.

prominent popes, at least between John X's death and 956; even John XI (931–6), Marozia's own son, had no visibility in the city after his brother Alberico's coup, and Marinus II (942–6), if we believe the words of the extremely unreliable chronicler Benedetto of Monte Soratte, 'did not dare touch anyone without Prince Alberico's order'.[61] Alberico's princely title was, indeed, a clear imitation of the hereditary princes of the south Italian states; and already before him Marozia's dominance over the city, outpacing all the gender assumptions of the century— other female rulers were widows of their predecessors, not daughters and heirs[62]— shows that the Teofilatto family were already claiming authority by hereditary right, something that had no prior history whatsoever in post-imperial Rome. When we add the novelty of the other titles of the Teofilatto family, notably *senator/senatrix*, but also *gloriosissimus*, which is not attested earlier in Rome but had been attached to Carolingian emperors in northern Italy and to Beneventan rulers,[63] the sense of a new regime becomes even clearer.

But this sense of novelty must be recognized as being incomplete. For a start, the Teofilatto family were not at all consistent about their titles; they were taking up a range of past images without settling for any one on a permanent basis, which indicates that they themselves were not sure of the bases of their potential legitimacy. Alberico put his name on coins, but his (few) surviving documents are dated by his popes. And, above all, Alberico's decision on his deathbed to ask the Roman *nobiles* to swear to accept Ottaviano not just as his successor but as the next pope shows that the project of creating a lasting principality of Rome had failed, even in the mind of its originator. As Toubert remarks, 'there was no place in Rome for two masters at once'.[64] Rome's traditions of legitimacy made it impossible even for an unprejudiced innovator like Alberico to turn the pope into a mere bishop on a permanent basis. And, once one recognizes this, the other highly visible elements of continuity in the Teofilatto period fall into place too. The seven palatine judges are as prominent in the tenth century as they had been in the ninth. The non-office-holding aristocrats of the city, generally called *consules et duces* in the ninth and early tenth centuries, are much more visible now than they had been before 900, thanks to the appearance of more land documents in the tenth; but officials and non-officials alike maintain the same basic names as in the ninth, Graziano, Adriano, Stefano, Gregorio, Sergio, and there is no reason to think that most of them came from new families. Teofilatto and his heirs simply stabilized an old political and

---

[61] Benedetto, *Chronicon*, p. 167.

[62] Widows as rulers, always ruling for their young children, included Æthelflæd in Mercia, Theophanō in East Francia, and Ol'ga in Rus'; only Æthelflæd's young daughter Ælfwynn, very briefly 'lady of Mercia' in 918 before being overthrown, has any parallel to Marozia—see e.g. Stafford, *Queens*, pp. 140–74.

[63] *Gloriosissimus*: see e.g. *Ludovici II. Diplomata*, nn. 3, 4, 9, 10, 16, 19, 21, 22, 66; and, for Benevento, just as samples across the eighth and ninth centuries, *Regesti dei documenti*, nn. 265–92, 522–39, 1070, 1093, etc.

[64] 'Il n'avait pas place à Rome pour deux maîtres à la fois', Toubert, *Les structures*, p. 998. Note that our source for Alberico's request is Benedetto of Monte Soratte (*Chronicon*, p. 172), whom we do not trust for anything else he says; but the point would still be valid if it was Ottaviano himself who chose to make himself pope in 956.

institutional system which had a strong landowning basis but had temporarily come apart; the only novelty was that they imposed themselves as a single ruling family, over and above the older institutional framework. And this worked. If we set aside the death of John X and the coup of 932, both by-products of the fact that Marozia as a woman was in a structurally weaker position, we can see the four-generation period 906–63 as the longest stable period in Roman history across the entire Middle Ages, until the end of the Avignon schism.

Alberico did introduce some novelties. His monastic refoundations, many done with the help of Odo of Cluny, are famous. He seems to have revived the office of urban prefect, who would soon become the head of the city's judicial system. He had a handful of men around him without formal offices who were clearly essentially courtiers, benefiting from *Königsnähe* (or *Fürstennähe*), such as Benedetto Campanino (who is, significantly, called *gloriosus dux* in 943), some of whom may well have been from new families—as well as men like Ingebaldo di Ingelberto, a Frank married into a Roman family, who is the first known person to have held the increasingly important office of *rector* of the Sabina, in 939. This latter is, furthermore, only one sign out of several that Alberico had a sense of how to re-establish territorial control over the whole of the *territorium S. Petri*, through non-hereditary local officials answering to him.[65] But these were developments out of a system that otherwise remained little changed. One particularly notable sign of this lack of change is the fact that the churches of Rome maintained their monopoly over landowning in the city and its hinterland. If there was a period in which Roman aristocrats might have thought it worthwhile to try to turn their long-term emphyteutic leaseholding into full property, it might have been the troubled years around 900. But it is precisely in the tenth century that the appearance of documents allows us to argue that aristocratic land was overwhelmingly held on lease. In addition, even the land disposed of by Alberico was emphyteutic in origin, and so was that of his cousins, daughters of Marozia's sister Teodora, and their heirs the Tuscolani. Even the ruling family did not patrimonialize their leases; and still less did they create local rural power-bases for themselves. Not yet, anyway.[66]

The newly crowned Saxon emperor Otto I overthrew John XII in 963–4, and ushered in nearly forty years of renewed instability, until 1002. Not one of the eleven popes across these years lived out their reign without being either deposed or at least temporarily exiled. Three popes did in fact rule for twenty-seven of those years, John XIII (965–72), Benedict VII (974–83), and John XV (985–96), so some consistency of government was maintained (each of the three was exiled once, but not for long). The popes themselves were, for the most part, clearly the rulers of Rome again. But Otto I intervened in papal politics several times, subjecting John XII to a show trial at a synod in 963, besieging the city in 964, and hanging insurgent leaders when he restored John XIII in 966, the most traumatic intervention of the

---

[65] Toubert, *Les structures*, pp. 978–97; pp. 981–3 (and esp. *RS*, n. 35) for Benedetto, pp. 377 and 993 (and esp. *RF*, n. 372) for Ingelberto.

[66] Wickham, '*Iuris cui existens*'; p. 16 for the Teofilatto/Tuscolani family.

three. So did Otto II in 974, and his widow Theophanō in 990.[67] And so, most famously and unluckily, did Otto III in 996, when he chose as pope his relative Gregory V, and then again in 998–1001, when he killed his Roman opponents and sought to rule from Rome itself, based in his newly founded palace on the Palatino, until the Romans revolted and drove him out. Otto III's doomed attempt at a *renovatio Romani imperii* fascinated German historians throughout the twentieth century: it seemed alternately so stupid, and so innovative and grandiose, with his new titles for offices such as *prefectus navalis* and various signs of classicizing commitment.[68] 'Stupid' in my view wins out; the eighteen-year-old Otto was living out a fantasy. But had Otto ever succeeded in getting his hands on the landed wealth of the Roman churches, which was immense, he would have had a resource that could have rivalled his other major economic power-bases, Saxony and the central Po plain: that was not stupid, and the Romans when they drove him out may have been aware of it.

As Toubert has stressed, the government and political society of Rome was rather more stable than the last paragraph implies. Many of the lay *primates* participating in Otto I's synod which overthrew John XII in 963 were members of John's and his father Alberico's entourage, including the *illustrior* of the Roman *optimates*, Deme-trio di Melioso.[69] The network of Roman aristocrats in documents later in the century does not show much further change, and the same official hierarchies continued to dominate formal judicial and political action. Indeed, Alberico's cousins continued to monopolize the titles of *senator* or *senatrix*, even though they did not hold any direct power as far as we can see; the first documented non-Teofilatto to hold the title, Crescenzio di Crescenzio (Crescenzio 'II'), did not do so until 988, and the Teofilatto/Tuscolani family seem fairly clearly to have remained the premier family in Rome. Otto III's new *prefectus navalis* was none other than Gregorio of Tuscolo, son of Alberico's cousin Marozia 'II'. This is often called the 'Crescenzian' period, because of the supposed dominance of a family of that name. As we shall see later (pp. 197–202), the close kinship of all the various supposed 'Crescenzi' is in some doubt, and the late 980s, which saw Crescenzio 'II' as *omnium Romanorum senator* and his brother Giovanni with the revived title of *patricius*, are the earliest moment when some form of Crescenzian hegemony seems likely.[70] Crescenzio *senator* did certainly control the city by the 990s; it was his

---

[67] See in general Toubert, *Les structures*, pp. 998–1015; Brezzi, *Roma*, pp. 137–48. For the trauma of 966, Benedetto, *Chronicon*, pp. 185–6, an authentic lament, and *LP*, II, p. 252. Gerbert of Aurillac in 984 wrote to a Roman friend that 'tota Italia Roma michi visa est', meaning all Italy was by now as bad as Rome (Gerbert, *Epistulae*, n. 40); it might better be said that all Italy faced the same local destabilization by German intervention that Rome did—see in general Cammarosano, *Nobili e re*, pp. 310–21.

[68] See esp. Schramm, *Kaiser, Rom*, pp. 87–187; Görich, *Otto III.*, pp. 187–267; Althoff, *Otto III*, who normalizes Otto more than anyone else has managed to do.

[69] Toubert, *Les structures*, p. 964 n; for Demetrio in 962–3, Liutprando of Cremona, *Historia Ottonis*, chs 6, 9; see further below, pp. 190–4.

[70] For the titles for the brothers, see *Historia*, ed. Gattula, I, pp. 115–16 (a. 986); BAV, CVL 12632 (formerly ASV, Indice 224), pp. 313–17, and Falco, *Studi*, p. 411 (a. 988); *RF*, n. 401 (a. 988, the least certain citation); and cf. their joint appearance as *illustrissimi viri* in *Regesta Hon. III*, pp. cxx–cxxi (a. 988).

Rome that Otto III invaded, and also he whom Otto beheaded, besides mutilating his pope John XVI (996–8), after Otto besieged and captured Castel S. Angelo in April 998. That moment was never forgotten by the Romans, and the monument was often called the *castellum Crescentii* in the centuries to come.[71] It also cemented Crescenzian rule after Otto was expelled, for the *senator*'s son Giovanni di Crescenzio was clearly Rome's ruler (*senior*) for a decade or so up to his death in 1012, with the titles of *patricius urbis* or *patricius senatus* or *patricius Romanorum*.[72]

The late tenth century does show two significant changes, however. One may simply be the result of the greater density of documents: it is the visibility of a hierarchy of families among Rome's leading aristocrats. The Tuscolani were clearly at the top, and then four more families stand out: the already-mentioned brothers Giovanni and Crescenzio, sons of Crescenzio 'I' di Teodora; the heirs of Demetrio di Melioso; Hildebrand and his wife Imiza and their heirs (called the *de Imiza* in some documents and by modern scholars); and Giovanni *de Primicerio* and his heirs.[73] The second and fourth of these were certainly important in Alberico's time; the other two may have been as well. It is likely that there was always such a hierarchy back into the ninth century and the eighth, but now, at least hesitatingly, we can track it, which helps our understanding of the city's social structure, as we shall see in Chapter 4.

The second change is that aristocratic power can sometimes be located more firmly in specific rural territories, for the first time. One good example is Stefania *senatrix*, Alberico's cousin, and a probable collateral ancestor of another of the families called 'Crescenzi' by historians, who received a three-generation lease of the city of Palestrina and all its *publica datio et functio*, its public resources and powers, from John XIII in 970; the 'Stefaniani' still had Palestrina as a power-base in 1014. Historians assume that Tuscolo was ceded to Gregorio di Marozia 'II' (Stefania's sister) in roughly the same period, for Gregorio is only called 'of Tuscolo' from 999, and he and his heirs are very regularly so named from then on; I would propose that they, too, held it by emphyteutic lease.[74] This was the great age of *incastellamento*, with aristocrats of all types founding small-scale power-centres all over Lazio (though not in the Agro romano: see below, Chapter 2). This was significant for the localization of power, and would become more so.[75] But handing over public powers for whole cities was an operation on a different political level, and it potentially led to autonomous lordships of considerable size. Palestrina and Tuscolo also blocked the way into the Val di Sacco, the modern Ciociaria (the province of Frosinone), then called *Campania*, which slipped away

---

[71] See Romeo, 'Crescenzio Nomentano' for an overview of Crescenzio's rule in the 990s. For the *castellum Crescentii*, see Chapter 6, n. 50.

[72] See most recently di Carpegna Falconieri, 'Giovanni di Crescenzio'; the evidence for Giovanni and the decade of his rule is, however, sketchy.

[73] See for the last two respectively Görich, 'Die *de Imiza*'; and, more fleetingly, Toubert, *Les Structures*, p. 1224n. See further below, pp. 192–5.

[74] See for Palestrina *Papsturkunden*, n. 205, and Ugo di Farfa, *Exceptio brevis relationum*, p. 67. For Tuscolo, Beolchini, *Tusculum II*, pp. 55–60, 389–92, etc.; Wickham, 'La struttura', p. 218n.

[75] See classically Toubert, *Les structures*, pp. 303–54 and *passim*.

from Roman control from now on for the first time. The Sabina, on the other hand, did not; despite its dissolution into castle territories, the *rectores Sabinenses* looked to Rome for another century.[76] Notwithstanding its variety of pacing, it is clear that the possibility of localized power from now on existed. All the same, its holders continued to live in Rome, and Roman politics remained their focus. Only political losers left the city, and even then for as short a time as possible.

The rule of Giovanni di Crescenzio was followed at once by the solid victory of the Tuscolani family, who took over the papacy in 1012 and turned it into a stable autocracy, for the first time since John XII. Gregorio of Tuscolo's sons Benedict VIII (1012–24) and John XIX (1024–32), and then their nephew Benedict IX (1032–44/48), ran a regime with no contestation until the very end.[77] Giovanni di Crescenzio did not leave direct male heirs, so there were no immediate rivals to the Tuscolani; the main political intervention that marked Benedict VIII's early years was the removal in 1014 of the 'Stefaniani' from their position in Palestrina and as *rectores Sabinenses*, and from some (not all) of their Sabina castles as well. Interestingly, the new *rectores* were the family later called the Ottaviani, from a Rieti family patronized by Alberico, for they were also heirs of Giovanni di Crescenzio's sister Rogata, who had married into the family. Benedict thus uprooted a family who were almost certainly his own (step-)cousins, in favour of a family closely linked to his rival and predecessor.[78] This may simply show that female-line family connections crossed the whole of the Roman ruling class, which they did, but it also counters any firm sense of regime change in 1012. So does the considerable continuity of office-holding in the 1010s.[79] Indeed, more widely than just a continuity in personnel, all the basic patterns of Roman government which had begun in the Carolingian period (at the latest) survived without change into the 1040s, in an *ancien régime* lasting up to three hundred years. The only change that can be traced, and it may not be any more than the chance result of documentary survival, is a decrease in the number of formal court case records after *c*.1020 (see below, pp. 392–3). Court records are good guides to political structures—I shall rely on them a lot in this book—and their absence leaves the last half of the Tuscolano period harder to read. But other than that, the family rebuilt the peaceful Rome which had not been experienced between Otto I's arrival and Otto III's departure.

The Tuscolano period does, all the same, seem to show one major social change, one which is harder to see, partly because of the gap in court case records. (It will be discussed in detail in Chapter 4, for it is important for the argument there.) That is a tendency for the major Roman families to drop out of city politics. More and

---

[76] Toubert, *Les structures*, pp. 1024–31, 1274–87, and Falco, *Studi*, pp. 424–30 for Sabina and *Campania*. What happened in northern Lazio, west of the Tiber, is much less clear. Note that throughout this book I shall put *Campania* in italics—i.e. in Latin—to distinguish it from the modern region of Campania further south; I shall do the same with *Marittima* (roughly the modern province of Latina) to match it.

[77] Toubert, *Les structures*, pp. 1022–38; Herrmann, *Das Tuskulanerpapsttum*, pp. 5–24.

[78] Ugo of Farfa, *Exceptio brevis relationum* is the main primary source.

[79] See Chapter 4, n. 80.

more, members of the most important older families are less visible in the city, and appear more often associated with cities and castles elsewhere in Lazio. This might be simply the result of the stability of the Tuscolano regime, as it would have been clear by the 1020s that a shift in political leadership was not going to happen soon; but it is also notable that the only really powerful new family patronized by the Tuscolani, the counts of Galeria, were put into a rural castle, and never had any visible urban presence.[80] As already in the late tenth century, this trend towards the *contado* on the part of major aristocrats has close parallels in other cities. So does the slow emergence of new elite families inside the city, which is visible in the early eleventh century for the first time—this being the period when our documents first shed light on a wide range of Rome's social strata, whether artisans or *rentiers*; a 'new aristocracy' was forming, based on less extensive landholding, probably more commercial interest, and an urban political focus that persisted. The scene was set for the first significant shift in Rome's ruling class that can reliably be documented since the eighth century, and, again judging by what happened in other cities, this would have happened even had Tuscolano rule continued.

What actually went wrong at the end of Benedict IX's reign is unclear (see below, p. 245), but it is at least certain that he faced serious armed opposition inside the city from 1044, with a rival but temporary pope, Silvester III, in 1045, and that he resigned his papacy later in 1045 to Gregory VI, though he subsequently sought it back.[81] Emperor Henry III cut this short in December 1046 by deposing everybody in a synod at Sutri, north of Rome, and installing the first of a set of five German popes, most of them short-lived; after the failure of Benedict X in 1058–9, their opponent, no Roman pope would be elected again until 1130. This was a real period of trouble in the city. The second half of the 1040s sees an abrupt drop in the number of surviving documents to half the average of the Tuscolano period; and we see from now on for the first time a real political cleavage between city and country, with the rural *comites* (as our sources call them) systematically opposed to the new papal regime, notably the Ottaviani rulers of the Sabina and the counts of Galeria, who were now joined by the Tuscolani themselves, driven to base themselves for the first time in Tuscolo.[82] The new regime also saw itself very clearly as being the bringer of transalpine and, increasingly, north Italian ecclesiastical 'reform', under the aegis of the empire. We have extensive and often intimate texts from the entourage of the German popes, particularly the most forceful and longest-lasting of them, Leo IX (1049–54), which show (in, above all, the letters of Pier Damiani) a group enthusiasm about and commitment to far-reaching change which recalls the early years of the Russian Revolution.[83] Already in this initial period, however, Rome as a city began to be seen as a problem: full of enemies of 'reform', and a difficult basis for a new model of papal activity.

---

[80] See esp. Whitton, 'Papal policy', pp. 217–23, 227–33, 236–44; see further below, pp. 217–18.
[81] *Annales Romani*, p. 331; cf. Herrmann, *Das Tuskulanerpapsttum*, pp. 151–6; Borino, 'L'elezione', pp. 176–252; Zimmermann, *Papstabsetzungen*, pp. 120–3.
[82] See e.g. *Annales Romani*, pp. 331, 334–5, with Beolchini, *Tusculum II*, pp. 70–84.
[83] Pier Damiani, *Epistulae*, e.g. nn. 48, 49, 57, 72, 75.

The late 1040s thus opened the great crisis for Roman government of the whole medieval period. Initially, this may not have been obvious. Most of the leaders of Rome's new elite stratum, such as Cencio Frangipane, Giovanni Tignoso, Giovanni Bracciuto, and Leone di Benedetto Cristiano (the ancestor of the Pierleoni), supported the new regime most of the time; and their support was focused by the appearance in the 'reforming' group in 1049 of Hildebrand, a Tuscan who had been brought up in Rome and had been Gregory VI's chaplain; he acted from this time onwards as the bridge between the Roman lay elite and the outsiders in the papal court in the Laterano. By 1059 at the latest Hildebrand was archdeacon of the Roman church and leader of the city's clergy. Under two popes who remained bishops of sees in Tuscany, Nicholas II and Alexander II (1059–73), Hildebrand effectively ran the city, and so when he himself became pope, as Gregory VII (1073–85), he could be seen as bringing the papacy, newly refigured, back into a Roman political context: all in all, he gave Rome over two decades of consistent government.[84] The court cases from this period show that this regime had potential staying-power. They were by now headed by cardinals, as they had not been before, and the aristocrats who participated were by now from the new elite, not the old— the prosopography of Rome's 'new aristocracy' is particularly clear in a major court case concerning the castle of Arci in the Sabina in April 1060—but the urban prefect and the palatine judges still ran that case and others, just as they had done for a century and more. Gregory's urban prefects were from Giovanni Tignoso's Trastevere family, and they were certainly loyal to the new regime; Pier Damiani was a serious fan of the religious commitment of Cencio di Giovanni Tignoso, before he was killed in 1077 by a member of the main new family unconvinced by Hildebrand's political system, that of Cencio di Stefano.[85]

'Reform' spoke with many voices, however, and already in the 1060s began to be divided, between a group more attached to imperial leadership and a group closely attached to Hildebrand's popes; this was visible in the imperial-backed papal candidacy of Cadalo bishop of Parma as Honorius II in 1062–4, and blasted out into the open when Gregory VII fell out with Henry IV in 1076. Henry chose his own pope Clement III, formerly Guiberto archbishop of Ravenna, in 1081, named after Henry III's first pope Clement II (just as Hildebrand had named himself after Henry III's most prominent victim); and in 1084, by force of money and arms, Henry IV had both himself and Clement crowned in Rome. Gregory, besieged in Castel S. Angelo, appealed to the Normans of southern Italy for help; they freed him and took him safely to Salerno, burning parts of the north and far south of the city as they did so—less than writers claimed, but a traumatic event for all that.[86] Clement III ruled Rome for most of the period from 1084 to his death in 1100, though he had to face several attempts by 'reformist' rivals to displace him, and after

---

[84] Toubert, *Les structures*, pp. 1316–19; Cowdrey, *Gregory VII*, pp. 37–58, 314–29. For the new families, see below.

[85] Arci: *RF*, n. 906 and below, pp. 221–2; Cencio: Pier Damiani, *Epistulae*, nn. 145, 155, with D'Acunto, 'Il prefetto Cencio', and below, p. 390.

[86] For the Norman sack, see above all Hamilton, 'Memory, symbol and arson'. For the political history, Cowdrey, *Gregory VII*, pp. 221–32 is a convenient account.

1098 he had little purchase in the city; he died in Civita Castellana north of Rome, and miracles were attested at his tomb.[87]

This was, in fact, the period when the political crisis of the city was at its most serious, in ways the city did not fully recover from for another half-century. The revived urban institutions of the Hildebrandine/Gregorian period faded away, never to be recovered. Rome's new elite also turned out to be not quite so uncompromisingly attached to the Hildebrandine wing of the 'reform' movement. Cadalo in 1062–4 garnered some Roman support; Clement III had quite a lot, from the *filii Baruncii*, the Sant' Eustachio, Cencio di Stefano's son Tebaldo, and even the Frangipane on occasion.[88] This was not by any means unparalleled; the elites of most northern Italian cities had divided loyalties in the decades of civil war after 1081, which disrupted and displaced traditional political legitimacies every-where. What made Rome's allegiances seem more unstable and dishonest to outsiders (and to modern historians) was that the rewards offered by and for rival popes were almost invariably not in land, as elsewhere in Europe, but in money or treasure. It seems likely that this was not a new feature of the 'reform' period, too, although our narrative accounts are much sketchier for the previous century. We will look at the reasons why Rome's economy favoured monetary gifts in return for political loyalty later (pp. 171–4). But these gifts are the only respect in which the city's disunity is any different from the disunity shown elsewhere.[89]

When the papal schism ended, in 1100–5, the new north Italian pope Paschal II (1099–1118) found Rome hard to govern. We can see the public legal system of the past continue in an increasingly incoherent format under Clement, but under Paschal it had entirely gone.[90] The palatine judges were by now beginning to lose their wider political importance, and more and more in the twelfth century were just the senior legal experts of the city, their members no longer recruited from the top aristocracy (see below, pp. 248, 274). The main surviving secular office, the prefect of the city, remained of great importance, and a real political focus, but it was increasingly monopolized by a single family, the Corsi (the future Prefetti di Vico), and when Paschal tried to prevent a prefect from succeeding his father in 1116 he set off an urban uprising.[91] Rome's politics had become the focus of clear factional rivalry, with the Frangipane, based around S. Maria Nova, apparently

---

[87] Ziese, *Wibert*, is still the best account of Clement III, though the procedures of his Roman rule are not discussed much (cf. below, pp. 393–8, 423–5); see now above all Longo and Yawn (eds), *Framing Clement III*. For the miracles, see Chapter 7, n. 99. Note that I do not use the term 'antipope' in this book; it ill-serves a pope with as long-term a power-base as Clement (cf. Ziese, *Wibert*, pp. 275–9), and even in the case of more ephemeral popes (whose birth-names, as with Cadalo, I use more often), the term simply implies history written by the eventual winners. It is inconvenient that two popes are called Clement III, but it will be clear who is meant from the context, as they ruled a century apart.

[88] Cadalo: esp. *Annales Romani*, p. 336; Benzone of Alba, *Ad Heinricum*, II.3. Clement: e.g. *RF*, nn. 1097, 1115; *SMVL*, n. 121.

[89] See Wickham, 'The financing', for all this.

[90] As is shown by the ad hoc procedures in e.g. *CF*, II, pp. 230–3 and ASR, SCD, n. 109; for analysis and other texts, see below, pp. 398–9.

[91] Halphen, *Études*, pp. 16–27, 151–6; Pandolfo, *Liber Pontificalis*, ed. Přerovský, pp. 717–20; for the Corsi, see below, pp. 226–8.

seeking dominance, and other families, the Corsi, the Pierleoni, the Normanni, opposed to them. Paschal did not manage to control this network of rival powers, and nor did most of his successors: Gelasius II was imprisoned by the Frangipane in 1118, was then attacked by them again, and fled the city; Honorius II was imposed by the Frangipane in 1124; so was Innocent II in 1130, though that time their opponents had a Pierleoni candidate, Anacletus II, who held Innocent off until his death in 1138.[92] Our major source for the period, Pandolfo, is hostile to the Frangipane, so may well overdo the seriousness of this, but tensions inside the new elite, which were already visible in the 1080s, by no means slackened off in the years when a single pope ruled the city. Only one pope, Calixtus II (1119–24), managed to maintain a measure of dominance in the city over all factions; it was also he who finally made peace with the German emperor in 1122, but his government was no more institutionalized than that of Paschal.[93]

These families were relatively new; but their struggles for power were not. We saw the latter already in the Carolingian period. There were two principal differences by now, however, both of them products of the crisis years after 1046 and especially after 1084. One is that the Curia, the new name for the ecclesiastical entourage (with its own separate institutions) that crystallized around the popes from Paschal onwards, was overwhelmingly foreign, and had little to do with the Romans at all except as a source of demand for food and goods; Roman aristocrats attended the papal court, but remained external to it as well.[94] The second is that the rivalry between different families was no longer fought out through secular office-holding. Families had informal power only, as with (for example) the favour apparently shown by Calixtus II to Cencio Frangipane and his *masnada* or armed following.[95] Of lay offices, only the urban prefect maintained his institutional centrality. The instability of the early twelfth century, so much stressed by our narrative sources, seems to have been in large part because the informality and uncertainty of the political structures of the period gave so much scope for the simple application of force. There was a crisis of legitimacy after the civil war period, which took a generation to resolve. It is, in particular, not surprising that the papal office itself should be so clearly a prize for rival families from 1124, for so few other offices still had power in the city, and if one controlled the pope one could make up for—perhaps even reverse—the dominance of non-Romans over the Curia. In 1130, in fact, both rival popes were Roman, and there was a chance of a return to the more local politics of the 1040s. But the city's government remained very informal, far more than it had ever been in the centuries up to Gregory VII.

Other Italian cities faced this same problem in the early twelfth century: the collapse of Carolingian traditions of collective government in the civil wars, and the need to construct something new from scratch. They moved towards the early city

---

[92] See above all Pandolfo, in *Liber Pontificalis*, ed. Přerovský, pp. 727–56; for 1130, Palumbo, *Lo schisma*, and Stroll, *The Jewish Pope*.

[93] Stroll, *Calixtus II*; Laudage, 'Rom und das Papsttum'.

[94] See above all Jordan, 'Die Entstehung'; Hüls, *Kardinale, Klerus*. Roman aristocratic attendance: Laudage, 'Rom und das Papsttum', pp. 28–30.

[95] *Liber Pontificalis*, ed. Přerovský, p. 753.

commune: increasingly formalized groups of leading citizens, united by oaths and claiming to represent the *populus* of each city (the *populus* was often the urban elite here, not any wider group, but was definitely not the old top-down hierarchy of king/emperors and local counts); such leaders were becoming known as *consules*, and changed annually. The two generations after 1080 or so was the period they began in most places; in a very ad hoc way to start with, and then with greater clarity after—in many cases—the 1130s, although it took a century for the powers and institutions of these communes to become fully formalized. Rome saw a similar development, as we shall see, with an apparently self-selected group of *consules* already documented in 1088, and after *c.*1125 a steady sequence of urban aristocrats using the old Tuscolano title of *consul Romanorum*.[96] It may well be that Rome's medieval use of the title *consul*, which had never entirely ended, was the model for its adoption in Pisa and then elsewhere. In the absence of formal institutions, that is to say, there are signs that Roman elites were drifting in the same direction as elites of other cities. By the 1130s, a peaceful crystallization of a commune could well have been close.

Innocent II's triumphant return in 1137–8 changed matters. Innocent was one of the key popes of the twelfth century in his development of the international appeals system for ecclesiastical disputes, and his centring of them on the Roman Curia; he had developed this during his exile in Pisa, and he developed it further in the five years he ruled in Rome before his death in 1143. The papal court thus became the institutional focus of an increasingly vast traffic of litigation, with bribes attached, which helped to keep the Roman church afloat financially for centuries. The Roman aristocracy followed him with as much enthusiasm as they could as a result. But he also wished to exclude Romans from the Curia, and he expelled all the cardinals who had ever supported Anacletus, Roman and non-Roman alike. Although Innocent was from the city—from the Papareschi family of Trastevere—and a keen nepotist, tension mounted, particularly when the Romans won a difficult war with Tivoli in 1143 and Innocent made his own peace.[97] As Innocent was dying in the same year, the Roman *populus* created a Senate, based in the secular political centre of the Capitolio, and defended it against three successors until Eugenius III (1145–53) fully recognized it in 1149, inaugurating a decade of a balance of power between pope and Senate. In August or September 1144 the era of the *renovatio sacri senatus* began, a uniquely precise and self-conscious date for a new commune, even if a year later than it might have been (a fact that has occasioned much debate). The city's secular government henceforth focused on the Senate for over two hundred years; already by 1148–51 we have our first court cases heard by senators, and other senatorial institutions slowly came in across the rest of the century and after.[98]

---

[96] *RF*, n. 1115 (a. 1088); *SMN*, n. 42. For a fuller discussion of *consules romanorum*, see below, pp. 436–7.

[97] For Innocent and Rome, the most recent study is Doran, 'The legacy of schism', pp. 73–88. For the Tivoli war, Fedele, 'L'êra del Senato', pp. 589–95.

[98] See for all this the works cited this chapter, n. 37. First court cases: *Senato*, nn. 12–13.

The first known leader of the Senate was Giordano Pierleoni, *patricius* and (by 1149) *vexillifer*, brother of the late Anacletus II. For all that, the early senators were mostly not from the 'new aristocracy' which had dominated the city since the 1040s, but from lesser strata, including some artisans (see below, pp. 447–52). The higher aristocracy, such as the Frangipane and the rest of the Pierleoni, stuck with the popes, and only came on board at the end of the century.[99] By then, the Senate had had over a generation to establish itself, in particular in the period 1159–88, when the popes were almost never in Rome. Not until 1188 did the pope, another Clement III (1188–91), only the second Roman pope since Innocent II (although the first of five successive powerful popes from the city or its immediate environs), make peace with an eager Senate and return to the city. As in the 1150s, but now stably and for a long time, the city had two recognized rulers, Senate and pope, and two rival political systems. If the Senate thought they could keep the upper hand, however, they were wrong. In the 1190s they perhaps managed to do so, but Innocent III (1198–1216) was as forceful inside the city as he was everywhere else, just as his namesake Innocent II had been, and with less backlash. It was Innocent III and his successors who created the most recent new aristocracy of Rome, the *baroni*, richer than any had been before them in the Middle Ages.[100]

This book will end with the first senatorial decade; later developments have anyway a good recent historiography. I shall thus restrict myself to the problems of pre-communal Rome, which are sufficient to be getting on with. It can already be seen that I would downplay the crisis years around 900 as a break, but, conversely, I insist greatly on the importance of the late eleventh century as the turning point for Rome's government. The crisis of the 1040s was perhaps stabilized by Hildebrand, but the crisis of the 1080s–90s was not stabilized at all until city government was reconstructed—in, ominously, two rival forms, Innocent II's Curia and the Senate—in the 1140s. Rome henceforth had two masters again, as under Alberico. How that interplay would work in the future is not a focus of this book; but how Romans got to that point certainly is. The radical informality of city government in the early twelfth century is one of the major elements we will have to take into account as we track how city society, led after 1000 by ever newer sets of elites, steadily changed. How this played out in detail will be seen in later chapters.

---

[99] Thumser, *Rom*, pp. 107–8, 181–2, 205–10.

[100] For the Senate's institutionalization of judicial procedures, see most recently Wickham, 'Getting justice', which cites previous bibliography. For the *baroni*, Carocci, *Baroni di Roma*. For Innocent III, see most recently the collective volume Sommerlechner (ed.), *Innocenzo III*. For the commune across the whole span of its history, Maire Vigueur, *L'autre Rome*.

2

The Countryside and the City

The city is the focus of this book, but it cannot be understood without a proper analysis of its immediately surrounding area, the plains and low hills, largely given over to sheep pasture, which are still just visible behind the ribbon development and new shopping precincts as one comes into Rome from Fiumicino airport or down the Intercity train line through Settebagni.

'Just visible' is the key phrase here. In Italy, only Milan and Naples match Rome in the extent of the destruction of the city's medieval and modern agrarian hinterland. But, even before that destruction (essentially begun after 1950), the twentieth-century Roman landscape was a misleading guide to our period. Unlike around any other major city, the hinterland of Rome was, after a ring of specialist vineyards and orchards, a few kilometres deep, often pastoral in the modern era. This pastoral specialization, immortalized in the paintings of Claude Lorrain, was the product of a sophisticated exchange economy of foodstuffs: secure in their ability to buy grain from outside, the Romans were prepared to let out part of their extensive lowlands to flocks of sheep from the Appennines, mostly from the Abruzzo, for winter pasture. Those lowlands were divided into blocks of land, fairly even in size (mostly varying from 1 to 5 km² each), called *casali*; whether pastoral or agricultural, they tended to have a single estate-centre, also called a *casale*, and only itinerant, salaried estate workers, who were sometimes from outside Lazio, and sometimes artisans in the city for part of the year.[1] Rome was thus surrounded by a landscape not only partly pastoral but everywhere relatively empty of people, with very few substantial permanent settlements for the first 25 km out of the city. None of this, however, apart from the ring of vineyards, was true of the period before 1150; indeed, the pattern of *casali* did not gain its solidity and its empty aspect until after the Black Death, and it remained above all focused on grain production for longer still. If we wish to understand the Roman countryside in the earlier and central Middle Ages, we have to base our investigation on different criteria.

We need to make that attempt, as well. Even if we are only interested in urban, or papal, history, we cannot avoid studying what was, before the development of

[1] For later medieval *casali*, see Maire Vigueur, *L'autre Rome*, pp. 73–115, the best introduction; Maire Vigueur, 'Les "casali" des églises romaines'; Montel, 'Un casale de la Campagne Romaine'; Cortonesi, *Ruralia*, pp. 105–18; Cortonesi, 'L'economia del casale romano'; Esposito, *Archittettura*; for origins, Carocci and Vendittelli, *L'origine della Campagna Romana*. For lists, see Coste, 'I casali della Campagna di Roma all'inizio del Seicento', and Coste, 'I casali della Campagna di Roma nella seconda metà del Cinquecento'.

the city as the nation's capital after 1870, its principal source of wealth: its agrarian hinterland. Medieval Rome had a wider range of sources of income than that, wider than most cities in our period: the money brought by pilgrims and, after *c.*1140, by litigants before the city's church courts; later, after the popes returned stably to Rome in 1188, increasingly regular revenues from the international Catholic church and from the steadily crystallizing 'papal state' of central Italy would add further to that. Rome's artisanal community was highly active too, as we shall see in Chapter 3. But all this was outweighed by agricultural wealth, as in every pre-capitalist society. Rome, always a large city, needed to be fed, principally with grain; and it was fed from its hinterland from the eighth century at the latest into the late Middle Ages. Who controlled the lands around Rome, and how that control was exercised in detail, therefore mattered greatly to its inhabitants, and matters greatly to us as we seek to understand them. Indeed, the patterns of power in the Roman countryside had a direct effect not only on the economy but on the society of the city, as we shall see later in this book.

One respect in which Rome was highly atypical in our period, and indeed had been for long beforehand, was in the very size of its hinterland. For a start, Rome was traditionally at the centre of the *territorium S. Petri*, the heir of the Byzantine duchy of Rome, which included most of the present region of Lazio; this inde-pendent territory, of some 14,000 km^2, was still under the city's direct control in the tenth century (see Map 1). This put Rome among the southern principalities, such as Benevento and Salerno, and distinguished it from the cities of the centre-north, which were part of the *Regnum Italiae*, and whose control was generally restricted to their dioceses and/or counties (these two territorial systems were not identical, but mapped closely onto each other). Rome lost full control of much of the *territorium* in the later eleventh century, and did not regain it for a century and more, until after our period ends in 1150. But the city still remained the political centre of gravity for some 6000 km^2 of landscape, from Sutri in the north to Velletri in the south, most of it, except in the mountains east and north of Tivoli, relatively low and fertile. This distinguished it from other major cities very considerably. Milan, whose territory was roughly 2500 km^2, was surrounded by urban rivals, Como, Bergamo, Lodi, Pavia, and Novara, which it would have to conquer physically if it were to increase that territory further. Florence, whose territory stood at around 3500 km^2 (but much of this was wooded hills), faced Prato, Pistoia, Siena, and Arezzo. Rome, for particular historical reasons, did not have a diocese that stretched into the countryside, but it dominated all of the dioceses around; indeed, it had no serious rivals for over 80 km in any direction except Tivoli. Of the numerous cities, or at least bishoprics, in its immediate hinterland—these were by the tenth century, clockwise from the lower Tiber, Porto, Silva Candida, Sutri, Nepi, Civita Castellana, Vescovio (for the Sabina), Tivoli, Palestrina, Labicum (later Tuscolo), Velletri, Albano, and Ostia—again only Tivoli was a substantial population centre, and Silva Candida and Vescovio were literal 'cattedrali nel deserto', isolated in open country. The elites of centres such as Nepi or Albano often lived in Rome; so, even more unusually, did some of the bishops, and seven heads of these suburbicarian sees were regarded as part of the Roman clergy and became the cardinal bishops of the Roman Curia.[2] One would have to travel out to Corneto (modern Tarquinia), Viterbo, Rieti or Anagni to find other centres that did not automatically look to Rome, and, with the exception of Viterbo, none of these were effective opponents either. It is no surprise to find that the Romans particularly hated Tivoli, as also the rather smaller Tuscolo when it tried in the twelfth century to establish itself as a political player; but it is also interesting, and unusual in Italy, that they do not seem to have hated anyone else—all other rivals were too far away to engage with. The huge hinterland of the city was therefore Rome's to exploit: at least in principle.

'In principle' does not in any way mean 'in practice', however. Two elements got in the way of the full economic or political dominance by Italian cities over their *contadi*, in the tenth to twelfth centuries, and indeed later. The first was the existence of powerful rural lordships, which fragmented city territories, and which cities sought to reconquer or otherwise reabsorb into the urban political framework in the twelfth or thirteenth centuries. These developed everywhere in north-central Italy, focused on the castles which were their political centres, above all in the eleventh century. They represented the Italian version of the process of privatization of political and judicial power which the French call the 'feudal revolution'. They were usually less powerful than French *seigneuries banales*; territorial *signorie* in Italy were often relatively restricted, both in the economic weight of signorial rights and in the political power over the peasantry exercised by lords.[3] Cities often eventually abolished them or took over their management, with relatively little difficulty. In Tuscany, for example, lords in the territory of Lucca largely lived in the city, and/or held lands and rights throughout the Lucchesia, not just in single blocks, which meant that their interest in resisting the hegemonic power of the city was relatively restricted; Lucca took over most of its diocese/county with brief periods of violence in the middle decades of the twelfth century.[4] In Florence, it was harder, partly because its large county (two dioceses, not one—Fiesole, the other diocesan capital, was not an autonomous power) was geographically quite fragmented into separate valleys divided by hills, partly because in the years around 1100 Florence's diocesan-wide aristocracy itself fragmented into smaller, more local lordships, which often had to be reconquered by force, into and beyond the thirteenth century. It is true that no one ever doubted the city's military power, and only a few centres actively resisted Florence's political strategies by the end of the twelfth; but the city was not in full control of its *contado* for another century.[5] Put another way, even in dioceses with relatively weak signorial

[2] Nepi: see e.g. *LP*, I, p. 468. Albano: see *Papsturkunden*, n. 226; *RS*, n. 79; and Görich, 'Die *de Imiza*', p. 10, for Giovanni duke of Albano in the mid-tenth century; and more generally Wickham. 'Albano'. Bishops of Silva Candida and Porto in Rome: *Papsturkunden*, n. 569. Suburbicarian bishops more generally: see di Carpegna Falconieri, *Il clero di Roma*, pp. 104–9. See in general on Lazial cities Toubert, *Les structures*, pp. 657–73; among the few case studies for our period is Vendittelli, *Sutri*.

[3] See in general Provero, *L'Italia dei poteri locali*, pp. 129–82; Menant, *Campagnes lombardes*, pp. 395–485; Dilcher and Violante, *La signoria*; Spicciani and Violante, *La signoria rurale*; *La signoria rurale in Italia nel medioevo*.

[4] Bratchell, *Medieval Lucca*, pp. 27–47, sums up and nuances previous work.

[5] See e.g. Cortese, *Signori, castelli*, pp. 209–48; Magna, 'Gli Ubaldini del Mugello'.

territories (Lucca), there was always at least half a century, coinciding also with the uncertain crystallization of the early urban commune, in which the city had difficulty in imposing itself over a wide area. In many cities (Florence), however, this process took a lot longer, and was not fully complete even in 1300.

The second reason why cities might not dominate their territories was because of the structure of landowning. In a world in which signorial rights were not very remunerative, and before city taxation developed (which was invariably after 1150), the only way in which the fruits of agricultural labour could be taken systematically from the producers was by landlords taking rent from dependent tenants. Rents were generally fairly high in Italy, taking substantial proportions of agricultural surplus from tenant cultivators. By the eleventh century at the latest, however, at least in the immediate hinterlands of cities, the apportionment of rents between different levels of non-cultivators (all holding leases and subleases from the real proprietor) could be complex; and, although many of these non-cultivators lived in the city, not all did by any means. Furthermore, not all peasant cultivators were tenants. There was, and had always been, a substantial stratum of peasant propri-etors in most of Italy, a stratum which only became weaker, even relatively close to cities, in the late Middle Ages, and which remained strong in some more distant rural areas (such as much of the northern Appennines) for much longer. Land was also highly fragmented in most of Italy, the product of centuries of partible inheritance, and was often divided up field by field. This gave plenty of opportunity for peasant owners to continue, in the interstices of larger fractioned estates, as also for tenants, to keep hold of or acquire a few fields in full property, besides holding rented land from their landlord—or, usually, from several landlords.[6]

The social consequences of this fragmentation, and of peasant property-owning, are not our concern here. One important economic consequence, however, was that land owned by peasants sent no rent into the city; and the rents from lands held by non-cultivating owners or tenants who lived in villages—village elites, most characteristically, or small rural aristocrats if there were any—also, very substan-tially, stayed in the countryside. Agricultural wealth thus did not all come directly into cities. Marketable surplus did, of course; cities needed to be fed, and were the obvious first and most profitable market for anyone, rich or poor, who had grain, wine or animals (or wool, leather, etc., for the city's artisans) to sell. But taken as a whole, cities had to pay for this; it was not wealth that came into the city gratis as a result of rural exploitation, to make citizens or urban churches rich. In most Italian cities, there were enough rich urban landowners that much agricultural surplus did indeed roll into the city gates directly. But a substantial percentage would only do so if it were paid for, which certainly limited the city's power to exploit the countryside; and much was, of course, consumed locally and did not come to the city at all.

---

[6] See for Tuscan case studies, Conti, *La formazione*, I, pp. 133–217; Wickham, *The Mountains*, pp. 238–56; Wickham, *Community and Clientele*, pp. 19–28. For later survivals of peasant owners in the Appennines, see e.g. Cohn, *Creating the Florentine State*.

Rome was different here, and in many respects very different. Exactly how these differences worked will be discussed in detail in this chapter. In brief, however, they operated in both of the arenas just characterized, inside the city's effective 6000-km² territory. For the first 20–25 km around Rome, there were no signorial territories, and indeed, in our period, few castles; Rome's dominance over this wide zone, called here the Agro romano (the term is now a fairly common one, but is not medieval), was and remained unmediated. Rural *signorie* were, it is true, normal further away; after the mid-eleventh century, their lords did not by any means all look to Rome, and had to be coaxed back or brought back by force. The city's political hegemony was however re-established fairly quickly in the mid-twelfth century and early thirteenth, by Hadrian IV and then Innocent III, over all or most of the great block of land from Sutri to Velletri, and indeed increasingly beyond. That was the same process as elsewhere in Italy, with a time frame somewhere between Lucca and Florence, although on a much larger geographical scale than either; but it was never necessary inside the Agro romano itself, where the city was always hegemonic. And, even more important, all (or virtually all) the land in the Agro, and much of it further out as well, was also owned by the churches and monasteries of the city of Rome. They then leased much of it out, to aristocrats and (after 1000) to lesser elites, but these too overwhelmingly lived inside the city's walls. Land was never very fragmented as a result; and a landowning peasant stratum, so significant elsewhere, is invisible in the Agro romano, and almost certainly did not exist. Indeed, the Agro romano seldom even had village territories to give some structure to peasant society; these only began once one passed the 20–25-km limit outside the city. All these features came together to mean that the surplus from a wide swathe of the countryside came directly into the city, without needing to be paid for, apart from the costs of transportation. This made Rome's economy unique, and it is this direct underpinning for the active city economy and society that is the subject of later chapters: Rome's prosperity rested on the back of an unusually complete exploitation of the countryside in all periods, both before 1150 and later, into the age of the *casali*.

This intensity and directness of exploitation only adds to the points about the geographical scale of Rome's control, made earlier, though these need to be refined further. Many Italian cities had a zone around them in which castles and signorial rights were few or non-existent. Around Lucca, the territory was formally defined from the eleventh century as the Sei Miglia, the land within a six-mile (10 km) radius of the city, inside which castles were banned; although in practice castles began to appear about 8 km out, most of them did not have signorial rights attached.[7] In the rest of Tuscany, which has been systematically studied from this point of view, Pisa was similar; for Florence and Siena the area was a little smaller; of the major cities only Arezzo had no area free of castles at all, although even there those closest to the city were relatively small and short-lasting.[8] Around Rome, the

---

[7] Wickham, *Community and Clientele*, pp. 15–17, updated in Quirós Castillo, *El incastellamento*, pp. 133–50; Cortese, 'Castelli e città', pp. 209–14.

[8] Cortese, 'Castelli e città'.

Agro romano, similarly castle-free, extended two to three times as far, covering between four and ten times as much territory: nearly 1500 km² in all, in itself the size of some whole city territories in Tuscany and the Po plain. This entire zone was, as already noted, owned nearly completely by city churches, and was dominated by them and by their tenants, generally lay citizens, with no mediation. It was then bounded by another zone, three times as big, in which Rome and the Romans usually dominated politically, but castle/fortified-village societies and local landowners existed as well. The size of Rome's economic and political hinterland was so much larger than the norm, and the intensity of the city's control over the Agro romano was so much greater than that of any other city, even over its most immediate hinterland, that not only did far more surplus arrive regularly into the city, but a quite different sort of rural society developed too.

Rome's territory has been extensively studied. The topography of the Agro romano was first confronted systematically a century ago by Giuseppe Tomassetti, and was turned into a modern science by Jean Coste and his pupils and followers in the years since 1975. Even without the help of village territories, most rural properties in our documents can be located fairly accurately as a result, and some zones, along the via Tiburtina for example, have been studied in considerable depth for not only their topography but their socio-economic structures as well.[9] Although our documents are very few indeed before 950, the detailed work on papal properties possible for earlier periods on the basis of the *Liber Pontificalis* and Deusdedit's *Collectio canonum* has been carried out by, in particular, Federico Marazzi. The leases (emphyteuses and *libelli*; after 1050/1100, *locationes*) of our period have a detailed recent analysis by Mauro Lenzi. The origins of late medieval *casali* have been confronted brilliantly in a monograph by Sandro Carocci and Marco Vendittelli, who are particularly attentive to macroeconomic issues; their subsequent development, after our period, has been extensively treated by Jean-Claude Maire Vigueur.[10] And, of course, the castles outside the Agro romano have the huge, definitive study by Pierre Toubert, the model for the numerous regional *thèses* on different parts of Italy by French scholars of the past generation, and the book which, more than any other, has created an image of the region of Lazio as one of the standard subtypes of European rural development in this period.[11] Toubert did not deal with the Agro romano, whose development was notably different, but his picture stands as an account of the wider hinterland of Rome. This array of studies makes Rome and its territory unusually well analysed. All the same, some of

[9] Tomassetti, *La Campagna romana*; Coste, *Scritti di topografia*. For those influenced by the latter, see e.g. Mari, *Il Lazio tra Antichità e Medioevo*; Delogu and Esposito, *Sulle orme di Jean Coste*. For the Tiburtina, see Coste, *Scritti di topografia*, pp. 91–132, 269–365; Carocci and Vendittelli, *L'origine della Campagna Romana*, pp. 41–58.

[10] Marazzi, *I "patrimonia sanctae Romanae ecclesiae"*; see also the important topographical study of de Francesco, *La proprietà fondiaria nel Lazio*; Lenzi, *La terra e il potere*; Carocci and Vendittelli, *L'origine della Campagna Romana*. For Maire Vigueur and other authors, see this chapter, n. 1.

[11] Toubert, *Les structures*. For later work on the land of castles as a whole see Barceló and Toubert, 'L'incastellamento'; Hubert, 'L'incastellamento dans le Latium'; Hubert, 'L'"incastellamento" en Italie centrale*; and below, pp. 42–8. A good illustration of Toubert's paradigmatic influence is Fossier, *Enfance de l'Europe*, pp. 465–7, where he provides the only Italian case study in Fossier's core chapter.

the comparisons I have just made, however sketchy, have not been made before, at least in print; and some of the specific foci of my interest in the rest of this chapter have been pursued relatively little. In general, as observed in the introduction, the comparative method often shows Rome in a new light, and this is true of the countryside as much as it is of the city itself.

*

The size of Rome's hinterland, and the absence of village territories for a long way out from the city, made topographical identification very particular during our period. It was standard until the mid-eleventh century to identify properties by their distance in miles from the city walls along the main consular roads, and road identifications without mileages lasted for the rest of our period. These roads had their own ancient names, still used in our period, although actually more common was to name the gate out of which they ran: *foris Porta S. Pancratii* for the via Aurelia, *foris Porta S. Iohannis* [in Laterano] for the via Tuscolana, and so on. They ran regularly from the city like spokes on a bicycle, as they had since the Roman republic, and still do today, with in most cases only minor shifts in route: again clockwise from the Tiber, the Portuense, the Aurelia, the Cornelia (a minor road), the Cassia, the Flaminia, the Salaria, the Nomentana (also minor), the Tiburtina, the Prenestina, the Labicana (now called the Casilina), the Latina/Tuscolana, the Appia, and the Ostiense.[12] I too shall use them extensively as topographical markers in what follows, and I shall often refer to the sectors bounded by them, the slices of the cake, as well.

Leaving by any of these roads, one passed in our period through three separate agrarian belts, ringing the city. All three have been mentioned already. First, for the first 3–5 km from the Mura Aureliane (though sometimes rather less), one traversed a belt of specialist vineyards and orchards. This was a zone of (generally) very fragmented ownership, although once again overwhelmingly ecclesiastical. The vineyard belt had often also been (particularly to the east and south-east of the city) a zone of rich suburban *villae*, many of them imperial, during the Roman empire;[13] this settlement was mostly abandoned, and is not often referred to, but to an extent it meant that the extra-urban vineyards were an extension of the wide area of *disabitato*, unsettled or abandoned land, inside the walls as well, which was also often planted with vines. That said, however, it must be stressed that the vineyards beyond the walls are in general rather better documented, and were perhaps more attractive to hold, than those inside the city. Second, between the 3–5 km and the 20–25 km mark, came the great area of open land, mostly cultivated for wheat and other types of grain, the Agro romano. As I have already argued, this was the most atypical part of the city's hinterland, and also in many respects the most important; it will be discussed in most detail here as a result. Third came the wider lands of the castles of Rome and Lazio, where settlement was usually, after the tenth century,

---

[12] Tomassetti in *La Campagna romana* covered the whole territory road by road, and is still the most complete starting point for the medieval period.

[13] Coarelli, 'L'*urbs* e il suburbio', pp. 35–58; our information for the late empire is transformed by Pergola, et al., *Suburbium* and Spera, *Il paesaggio*, but a synthesis is not yet clear.

concentrated inside the walls of fortified villages called *castra* and *castella*. These essentially lie outside the remit of this book, but need to be characterized briefly, in order to point up what made the Agro romano special. The three belts all had very different economies and societies, and need to be treated separately; I shall do so here starting with the castles, and moving in towards the Aurelian Walls. Only two zones disturbed the neatness of these three concentric circles: the territory of Albano down the Appia, specializing in wine but on the outer edge of the Agro romano, and the salt pans on the Portuense and (to a lesser extent) the Ostiense. These two, well outside the city in each case, were exploited in much the same way as the vineyard belt, and will be discussed with it. Taken together, the analysis of these three agrarian belts will give us an insight into social relations in the countryside, at least from the standpoint of the city, whose optic indeed dominates all our sources for a long way out from its walls.

The traveller leaving Rome today will find that the vineyard belt is almost wholly lost to housing (except for around Albano, further out) and by now can only be imagined. Much of the Agro romano has gone too; but in most directions, perhaps 10 km out, sometimes more, one comes upon the rolling open land that has always been here, mostly cleared of woodland in protohistoric times. This is tufo country, soft volcanic lava. Where the land is slightly higher, as to the west of the city, streams have cut through the lava, creating valleys and promontories that, although not high, are often steep; this is less the case in the flatter eastern plain. To the south-east, however, the plain is broken by the old volcano which now makes up the zone of the Castelli Romani, in our period the territories of Tuscolo to the north and of Albano to the south; but this too was and is heavily settled and cultivated on its lower slopes. North of that, the land changes rather more, for Tivoli marks the edge of the great limestone region that will soon become the Appennines; already above Tivoli, and still more sharply above the Sabina villages north of it, the mountains rise up from the plain.[14] When we reach the mountains, we reach the edge of the remit of this book. Essentially, our territory is lowland, together with the gentle volcanic hills that punctuated it. Communications were always easy here, and made still easier by the roads. As a result, although each sector of the hinterland of Rome has its own identity, its own feel, they can be discussed together, as long as one respects the triple zoning already mentioned. Further differentiation would be for a different sort of book.

THE LAND OF CASTLES

The first private castles in Lazio appeared in the tenth century. They only had a few predecessors: old walled settlements that had always been called *castra* or *castella*, or sometimes *oppida*, such as Albano and Ariccia, maybe Tuscolo, and Catino in the Sabina.[15] The first references to *castra/castella* around the monastery of Farfa

---

[14] A good geographical introduction is Toubert, *Les structures*, pp. 135–67.
[15] For the uncertain evidence for early Tuscolo, see Beolchini, *Tusculum II*, pp. 23–30; for Albano and Ariccia, see Wickham, 'Albano'; for Catino, see Toubert, *Les structures*, pp. 381–2 (he seems to

in the Sabina and north into the Rietino date to the 930s: Montorio in 934, Bocchignano in 939, Toffia in 940; the Farfa cartularies are by far the largest collections of documents for our period in the whole of Lazio, and the Sabina is thus by far the best-documented part of the castle zone. In the Tiburtino, Subiaco is the first, in 937; in Tuscia Romana to the west of the Tiber, Mazzano Romano is the first, in 945, although already in the 950s two castles in the Sutrino are referred to as *desertum*, 'abandoned'. These were all almost certainly recent foundations.[16]

From here on, references to castles steadily increase in number, and by the 980s they were becoming common throughout Lazio, outside the Agro romano; Toubert argues convincingly that most of the main initial wave of castle foundations was complete by 1050.[17] On the edge of the Agro, we have three tenth-century documents that describe the actual foundation of castles, from 946 and 966–7, for the castles, both short-lived, of Monte Calvelli south of Velletri and Arbiteto south of Tivoli (see Map 2). In each case the block of land on which the castle was founded was leased out by a church or monastery (the bishop of Velletri for the former, the monastery of Subiaco for the latter) to a lay aristocrat who undertook to set the castle up, to build its walls and collect together (*aggregare* or *amasare*) its inhabitants (*populus*), and (in 946) to create vineyards and orchards around it on the slopes of the hill (*mons*) where the castle was to be. We do not know anything about the entrepreneurs who founded Arbiteto, but Monte Calvelli was the work of a leading Roman aristocrat, Demetrio di Melioso, who was a follower of Prince Alberico in 942, but had jumped ship by 963, when he participated in the deposition of Alberico's son Pope John XII.[18] To these foundations, cornerstones of Toubert's reconstruction of the *incastellamento* process, can be added the attempted foundation of Mandra Camellaria on the via Appia, only some 15 km out of Rome, by the equally urban and aristocratic *de Imiza* family, on land of the monastery of S. Gregorio sul Celio, in 994; here, however, as S. Gregorio claimed in a court case in 1018, they wholly failed to build the walls, *populare* the site or *congregare* its inhabitants, but only built 'three tiny houses with a bit of wall in the upper circuit, and nothing in the lower circuit', so the monastery claimed it back, eventually with success. The *de Imiza* had become close to Otto III during his regime in Rome in 998–1001, and perhaps therefore unpopular with the 'Crescenzi' rulers whom Otto supplanted violently and who returned after his own expulsion; Mandra Camellaria was also too close to Rome, too fully part of the Agro romano. Both of these were probably reasons why, as the *de Imiza* counter-claimed, although they did indeed build houses there and brought inhabitants in, the *senior* of Rome, who must be Giovanni di Crescenzio (*c.*1002–12), ordered the castle to

---

exclude an early origin for Catino, which I, on the other hand, see as clearly implied in Ugo of Farfa, *Destructio farfensis*, pp. 31–2).

[16] Respectively, *RF*, nn. 348, 372, 373; *Papsturkunden*, n. 77 (with Toubert, *Les structures*, pp. 408–9); *S. Gregorio*, n. 68; *SCD*, nn. 3, 6.

[17] Toubert, *Les structures*, e.g. p. 338. The whole long section of his book on *incastellamento*, pp. 303–447, is basic for what follows.

[18] *Velletri*, n. 1; *RS*, nn. 200–1 (see Toubert, *Les structures*, pp. 322–3n. for a list of *incastellamento* charters, which I follow in part); for Demetrio, see Chapter 4, n. 31.

be destroyed. Either way, they lost out, however; since there were no inhabitants, the cession was void.[19]

These texts set out many of the main features of documented early castles. They were conscious foundations, which needed quite elaborate planning—including some land clearance, for most (although not Mandra Camellaria) were on wooded hilltops. They involved bringing people in; we cannot be sure from where— perhaps usually just from the territory already designated for the new castle, although probably sometimes from a little further afield (in the similar tenth- century documents for S. Vincenzo al Volturno, further south in Molise, some- times from 100 km away, but this must have been rare). They were, from the start, village foundations, not simply the construction of fortifications. Indeed, although the walls were important for the identity of these *castra/castella*—and were in stone in 966–7, unlike the houses of Mandra Camellaria which were in wood (a textual observation which has amply been confirmed by archaeology)—the primary pur- pose of most of these castles does not appear to have been military. They were interventions in the settlement pattern of Lazio, and if they were not successfully populated they failed.[20]

Pierre Toubert argued in 1973 that castles of this type were indeed typical of the 'révolution castrale', and he characterized them in further detail. He stressed the reorganization (*aménagement*) of the landscape, best documented in a slightly later foundation charter from 1038, for Castel S. Angelo (today Castel Madama) above and to the east of Tivoli, but with parallels elsewhere, and he linked the whole phenomenon to a general process of land clearance and economic growth, which post-dated the period of Arab attacks on Lazio.[21] The Arabs had pene- trated deep into Lazio in the last two or three decades of the ninth century, and had taken Farfa itself, expelling the monks, maybe with the support of the *latrunculi christiani*, 'Christian brigands', of Catino, in *c*.898. In a sequence of unclear events, the Arabs were forced out of the Sabina and the territory of Nepi, and back to their redoubt in southern Lazio, at the mouth of the Garigliano, from where they were expelled in a coordinated campaign by Romans and south Italians in 915. Our source for much of this is the highly unreliable Benedetto of Monte Soratte, writing after 965, but two bulls of Pope Sergius III from 905, to the bishop of Silva Candida and the Roman female monastery of S. Maria Tempuli, refer to the destruction of the *paganica infestatio* as over, which does indeed indicate that the troubles of the Arab settlement had already receded in our region. This enabled Toubert to argue that *incastellamento* in Lazio, which was all later than 915, essentially had socio-economic, not military, causes, an argument that still holds good for the most part. He saw the process as

[19] *S. Gregorio*, nn. 130, 126 (for the quote). See for the political context Görich, 'Die *de Imiza*', pp. 36–8. The monastery then leased the estate (by now called a *casale*) to 'new aristocrats' from the Colosseo area, who still held it a century later: *S. Gregorio*, nn. 131, 134, 136, 145, and below, p. 293.

[20] See for S. Vincenzo, Wickham, *Il problema dell'incastellamento*, pp. 31–2. For archaeology, see e.g. Hubert, *L''incastellamento'*, pp. 48–52, and this chapter, n. 23.

[21] *RS*, n. 34, cf. n. 36; see Toubert, *Les structures*, pp. 311–38.

dominated by lords, the product of signorial entrepreneurship in an age of economic growth.[22]

The impact of Toubert's work was huge, and it is not an exaggeration to say that his intellectual interests have structured a high proportion of subsequent historical research on the countryside of Italy in the central Middle Ages, certainly including my own—and perhaps an even higher proportion of its active archaeology. But this has led to a good deal of nuancing of his overall model, in two main respects. First, the sharpness of the settlement break marked by *incastellamento* has been contested. There is written documentation for the prior occupation of the sites of at least some castles, and more recently there has been archaeological confirmation of at least small-scale hill-top occupation in some cases (the best instance is S. Donato, the eighth-century Cicilianus, close to Farfa). This is so for some later foundations too; the archaeological site of Caprignano, again in the Sabina, shows a new settlement of the tenth century that was unwalled until the twelfth; here the concentration of settlement (*accentramento*) preceded *incastellamento* in the strict sense, its fortification.[23] In other archaeologically attested cases, the fortification preceded the village. Étienne Hubert, who has done the most work on the medieval archaeology of the Sabina, remarks that the new planned walled settlements attested in foundation documents have not yet been found archaeologically (although Castellaccio above Mola di Monte Gelato in Tuscia Romana is, in my view, a probable eleventh-century example), and are at best only one, and the most abrupt, model of settlement change in the land of castles.[24] All the same, the broad lines of Toubert's narrative, which hinges on the absence of concentrated hill-top settlements before the early tenth century and their omnipresence by the late eleventh, have been supported by the archaeology of the Sabina, as also of Tuscia Romana (however simple and often 'un-signorial' they appear as yet to have been in material terms). Central Lazio thus looks different to the south of Tuscany, where hilltop villages of some size were widespread in the ninth century and often well before that, and were simply walled in the tenth and eleventh, as a host of recent excavations demonstrate.[25]

---

[22] For sources and bibliography for all this, see Chapter 1, n. 58; for the specific case of Farfa, Ugo of Farfa, *Destructio farfensis*, pp. 31–2; for Sergius, *Papsturkunden*, nn. 22, 23. Toubert, *Les structures*, e.g. p. 367, argues the non-military point.

[23] Written documentation: see e.g. Wickham, *Il problema dell'incastellamento*, pp. 54, 61; for S. Donato, see Moreland, 'The Farfa survey'; Moreland and Pluciennik, 'Excavations at Casale San Donato'; Moreland et al., 'Excavations at Casale San Donato, 1992' (pp. 197–8 for Cicilianus); Patterson, 'Rural settlement', pp. 150–1 gives a neat and up-to-date synthesis, and on pp. 148–9 and 155 develops the parallels for the area west of the Tiber, where there are other examples of small-scale pre-*incastellamento* hill-top occupation. For Caprignano, see Bougard et al., 'Du village perché au *castrum*'; the generalization of stone building is not common before the twelfth century elsewhere too—see Hubert, 'L'incastellamento dans le Latium', pp. 593–4; Molinari, 'Siti rurali', pp. 135, 139, and, for the rest of Italy, the whole volume of *AM* in which that article appears.

[24] See Hubert, 'L'incastellamento dans le Latium', pp. 590–3. For Castellaccio, see Potter and King, *Excavations at the Mola di Monte Gelato*, pp. 170, 181–8 (D. Wilkinson). In the Volturno valley there is a parallel case studied in Hodges et al., 'Excavations at Colle Castellano': an imperfect site, but one which shows a major and apparently systematic building intervention in the mid-tenth century.

[25] The best synthesis of Tuscany remains Valenti, *L'insediamento altomedievale*, although there are several more recent similar sites as well. Molinari, 'Siti rurali', is now the best overall synthesis for Lazio;

Secondly, more detailed work on the documents for some areas argues for greater diversity of choice on the part of lords. In the immediate hinterland of the monastery of Subiaco, its early castles were small and strategically/defensively placed, and the wider population remained more dispersed for rather longer, well past the late eleventh century; Subiaco only moved energetically to concentrate the population of its territories further away from the monastery, towards Tivoli, whose bishops were its rivals. The former of these patterns may also fit some of Hubert's upland Sabina sites where the fortification preceded the village.[26] Even the Farfa documents show that lords in some places, such as Pomonte and Montelibretti, monastic castles to the south of Farfa, did not immediately put all the inhabitants of their territories into the castle, although they certainly did elsewhere.[27] Sometimes this may show peasant resistance to the process of *congregatio hominum* (to use a modern phrase not actually present in our sources), which was transparently a mechanism for exerting control over them; sometimes it probably simply shows that lords did not always commit to a full-scale reorganization of the population and the landscape, which was, after all, a considerable organizational and even financial investment. Conversely, however, there are a handful of examples of castles apparently constructed and settled by peasants, not lords, a model explicitly denied by Toubert. Strenuous efforts by historians (including myself) to identify such castles have nonetheless never produced more than three or four in Lazio; the best examples are probably Formello and Cesano in Tuscia Romana, immediately north of the Agro romano near the via Cassia. In these cases, peasants were presumably resisting a trend to aristocratic control by copying its most character-istic form, the fortified village.[28]

One element that has not been fully explored is the degree to which a prior concentration of landed property into a single block affected the way *incastella-mento* worked, making the process easier to arrange. Subiaco held much of its land in large units, a product both of its location in the mountains, where such units were commoner, and of the papal (i.e. fiscal) origin of much of the property concerned.[29] It is less easy to be sure about the case of Farfa; some of its lands were large blocks, often the result of early gifts by the eighth-century dukes of Spoleto, but in many places, even close to the monastery, the fragmentation of its

---

note that pp. 133–7 surveys some of the recent work on larger open settlements in Lazio in the eighth and ninth centuries (such as the important site of Villamagna: see Fentress and Goodson, 'Villamagna' and 'Structures of power'), and indeed later, but they are in lower-lying areas, unlike in Tuscany.

[26] Delogu and Travaini, 'Aspetti degli abitati medievali', pp. 19–26; Delogu, 'Territorio e cultura', pp. 35–42; Travaini, 'Rocche, castelli', pp. 68–9, 79–80, 89–90; Hubert, *L'incastellamento*, pp. 292–5.

[27] Wickham, *Il problema dell'incastellamento*, pp. 64–5 for Pomonte; for Montelibretti, documented as a *castellum* by 1000 (*LL*, n. 441), extensive open settlement is shown in *LL*, nn. 627, 628, 839, 969, 983, 988, 1116, 1127, 1190, 1272, 1304, 1168 and *RF*, nn. 1313, 1320, a sequence which goes up to the year 1120.

[28] Wickham, 'Historical and topographical notes', pp. 155–65, 90–1; Wickham, *Il problema dell'incastellamento*, pp. 72–3. Even Formello had a papal-controlled *castrum*, however, although it does not appear in our documents: *Liber Pontificalis*, ed. Přerovský, p. 753.

[29] *RS*, n. 18; *Papsturkunden*, nn. 57, 72, 77, 92, etc.

property dealings seems to indicate that its lands were interspersed with those of others, whose properties it must have dominated but did not fully eradicate. Probably this explains the fact that Farfa kept (and thus perhaps made) no foundation charters for castles, for the completeness of the reorganization of the terrain seen at Monte Calvelli or Castel S. Angelo needed single blocks of land-owning to make it effective. If Farfa did not have any single blocks, lay powers in the Sabina (whose archives do not survive) were even less likely to; this is relevant, because we can be sure that many of the Sabina castles were the autonomous foundations of lay lords, including one of the first documented, Bocchignano—although the probable founder there was Ingebaldo di Ingelberto, who was the first *rector* of the Sabina for Alberico and his pope in the 930s, this property was apparently privately owned.[30]

One sector of the castle zone where large single blocks of land are relatively clearly documented is, however, closer to the border with the Agro romano. Monte Calvelli and Arbiteto are already examples of this, over to the east; to the north, Farfa's southernmost castle, Montelibretti, is probably another, and so may be Mentana, property of S. Paolo fuori le Mura. West of the Tiber, the same seems to be true for the castles of Pietra Pertusa, a papal property, Isola Farnese of the monastery of SS. Cosma e Damiano in Trastevere, Boccea of S. Pietro in Vaticano, and Castel di Guido of S. Gregorio sul Celio.[31] These western castles were all right on the edge of the Agro romano, and are also, with a couple of exceptions to which we shall return (p. 60), the closest castles to the city. They were stably held by Roman churches and monasteries, however, and in most respects behaved more like the estates of the Agro than like the more politically ebullient centres further away; we will come back to them in that context. The nearest castles that looked to Rome but had an independent politics were Galeria to the north-west and, above all, Tuscolo to the east. The first was probably a papal castle, ceded to the counts of Galeria; Girardo di Ranieri, founder of the main family of counts and son of the marquis of Tuscany, was appointed by the Tuscolano popes.[32] Tuscolo itself, an old settlement, and called *civitas* as well as *castellum* in our sources even though the bishopric of Labicum was not transferred there until the 1060s, may have been a substantial papal property, ceded in emphyteusis to the Tuscolani. If so, it was before 999, the first reference to the settlement in connection with Benedict VIII's and John XIX's father Gregorio, but probably not long before; as we have already seen, it may parallel the three-generation emphyteusis of the city of Palestrina by John XIII to Stefania *senatrix*, aunt of Gregorio of Tuscolo, in 970.[33] Tuscolo was an exception to nearly every rule, but not, probably, to the rule that land in and near the Agro romano tended to be owned and held in large blocks; it is very

---

[30] *RF*, n. 372; see Toubert, *Les structures*, pp. 377, 993–5.

[31] These statements are essentially based on the absence of any other owners in our documentation. First references to the churches owning each castle: *LL*, n. 441; *S. Paolo*, n. 1; Deusdedit, *Collectio canonum*, III. 194; *SCD*, n. 12 with *Papsturkunden*, n. 419; *SPV*, nn. 2, 11, 47; *S. Gregorio*, nn. 18–19.

[32] See Whitton, 'Papal policy', pp. 217–54, and below, pp. 217–18; for Galeria as papal, see Wickham, 'La struttura', p. 207n.

[33] See Chapter 1, n. 74; for Labicum, Beolchini, *Tusculum II*, pp. 80–1.

striking how little land is ever documented in or around the city/castle, which implies that the Roman churches whose archives survive never acquired anything, whether big or small, here.[34]

By 1050, castles characterized the landscape of nearly the whole of Italy north of the Byzantine territories of Puglia and Calabria. Central Italy, from north of Siena to Capua and beyond, was however particular, in that the great majority of castles there were not only fortifications, but full-blown fortified villages. Toubert's models continue, in large part, to hold for their origins; but they do so even more for their development. These fortified villages represented economic reorganization and political control; but also, above all, they led to active local societies, with militarized village elites (*boni homines* or *milites castri*) who were themselves not easy to control as the eleventh century wore on.[35] This was especially so if one family had emerged as locally dominant, perhaps leasing the castle itself from Farfa or Subiaco or the bishop of Tivoli; but the monasteries and other major lords had to deal with the military stratum, the lesser aristocracy, as political players even if the former continued to control much of the castle lands and let them directly to peasants. This village society and castral politics had some direct parallels in its novelty to the 'feudal revolution' in France, as has already been suggested; here, however, the new military stratum lived side by side with those whom they would often seek to dominate, inside the *castra* or *castella* whose territories divided up the countryside.

Even more than in France, and much more than in Tuscany and the Po plain, signorial rights, notably private justice (*placitum et districtum*), were explicitly associated with castles around Rome from the start: this early date has unclear reasons, but was quite possibly a spin-off of the substantial settlement changes that many castles represented. The bishop of Velletri conceded them for Monte Calvelli in 946; Subiaco conceded them for Arbiteto in 967—as early, in fact, as that monastery is recorded as holding them for the castle of Subiaco itself, for the first concession (by the emperor Otto I) of the latter's '*constricto*' *et placito* was only a month earlier. The (probably) normal content of this privatized justice is in one case made explicit already in the tenth century: in a lease of 978 from the monastery of S. Andrea in Silice near Velletri to Crescenzio *illustrissimus vir* di Teodora, father and grandfather of the rulers of Rome in the 990s–1010s, of rights in *castrum* Vetus in the Velletrano. In this text, uniquely, the monastery kept the rents of the castle, the *glannaticum et herbaticum* (see below), and the judicial rights over civil disputes concerning land, but ceded high justice (*bandum sanguinis et forfacture*), and judgements concerning roads and army service. From then on, justice was a regular part of the appurtenances of castles, and is also casually referred to by a lay castle-

---

[34] Wickham, 'La struttura', p. 218n, based in large part on the texts in Beolchini, *Tusculum II*, pp. 387–436. The only owner with much documented land in the territory was the local monastery of Grottaferrata: see esp. 'Documenti per la storia', n. 2 (a. 1116), which, against Kehr, *Italia pontificia*, II, p. 43, seems to me essentially authentic.

[35] Toubert, *Les structures*, pp. 1113–26, 1285–313.

holder, the *illustris femina* Purpura, for Faustignano in the Tiburtino, already in 1019, the first of a substantial (though never huge) documentary set.[36]

Judicial rights were not yet a universal feature of castle-holding. Farfa is not recorded as having them before 1014, when Pope Benedict VIII ceded it the *placitum et districtum* of Bocchignano, which a papal army had just taken by force from the 'Stefaniani' counts of the Sabina. The monastery held these rights, as it stated in a text of four years later, *ut homines ad placitum duceret, sicuti comites de comitatu Sabinensi antea facere solebant*, 'so that they should bring men to the *placitum*, as the counts of the county of the Sabina were previously accustomed to do', a clear indication that Benedict had simply handed over an element of the local public powers of the counts, along with the castle itself. The nature of the justice is also specified here, even more carefully than at *castrum* Vetus: it covered homicide, wounding, theft, arson, betrayal of the castle, and adultery with a married woman or a nun if committed inside the castle. This was a standard set in later centuries, but is unusual anywhere in Europe so early; all the same, the casual way the document attests it lets us be confident, even more than for the *castrum* Vetus text, that it was regarded already as normal in the Sabina. To this was added the collection of *fodrum, guaita* (the duty of castle guard), and labour service for building/repairing the castle. But from here on our evidence for justice in the Sabina is more and more associated with Farfa and its representatives, and the counts are not recorded as holding courts after 1046. The Sabina still had local judicial officials, *iudices*, who held courts into the 1090s, but Farfa's castles had courts too, where the monastery dominated. As Toubert showed, the private judicial rights attached formally only to Bocchignano had come, by the end of the century, to cover all or most of Farfa's castles.[37] It would not be implausible, or controversial, to argue that by 1100 there were few castles in the wider territory of Rome whose holders did not have local judicial rights too.

Signorial rights in Lazio hardly extended further than justice in our period, all the same. Castle guard and repair were doubtless typical outside Bocchignano too, though rarely attested. The only other dues at all commonly associated with rights of justice in our texts were *herbaticum* and *glandaticum*, the right to take dues from peasants for their pasturing of animals in fields and woods. The other standard signorial rights, found in different combinations elsewhere in Italy (and still more outside Italy)—mill rights, tolls, the tying of peasants to the land, forced hospitality, dues owed at marriage and death—are simply absent in our period. Sometimes an ill-defined *datio* (or, occasionally, as at Bocchignano, *fodrum*) is attached to this

[36] See above, n. 18 for Monte Calvelli and Arbiteto; *Ottonis I diplomata*, n. 336 for Subiaco; *Statuti della provincia romana*, pp. 3–9 for *castrum* Vetus; *S. Gregorio*, n. 5 for Faustignano. See for this paragraph and the next three the more detailed study in Wickham, 'The origins of the signoria', with, for the twelfth century and later, Carocci, 'La signoria rurale nel Lazio'.

[37] For Bocchignano, *RF*, nn. 491, 513. It is discussed in detail by Toubert, *Les structures*, pp. 1309–1311n. For later in the century, see Toubert, *Les structures*, pp. 1274–13; Wickham, 'Justice', pp. 222–34.

list: miscellaneous dues owed to lords.[38] The political and economic aspect of local private power in Lazio, however, remained essentially justice, and even this was not wholly under the control of lords, for *la justice castrale*, in Toubert's terminology, was actually exercised by local *milites* and other *boni homines*—only the profits, not the transactional power, of private justice went to Farfa or Subiaco. Up to 1100 and indeed later, signorial rights were simply a spin-off of whatever power accrued to any castle-owning or castle-holding lord, and were probably (as in much of Italy, indeed) rather restricted in their economic weight.

Signorial rights were also tied, very closely, to the land of castles in a geographical sense. We have a handful of papal immunities from the Tuscolano period that extend into the Agro romano, but they are very particular. The clerics of the bishop of Porto in 1018 were granted immunity from papal *placitum et districtum*; so were the inhabitants of the newly fortified cathedral of Silva Candida in 1037 (as also were that bishop's clerics, but only in one place, the castle of Galeria). These were immunities from a papal justice which was represented implicitly as otherwise universal, and, as can be seen, they were highly restricted. So, still more so, was the concession of an immunity from papal justice on one small estate of the monastery of Grottaferrata in the territory of Albano, Cucuruzzi, and not any other of the monastery's lands, in 1037. This immunity was important enough to be stressed again in a papal confirmation of monastic land in 1116, and even then, still only Cucuruzzi was so privileged.[39] But these restricted concessions were essentially outside the land of castles. Here we are in the Agro romano, and the universal presumption of these texts is that a city-based judicial system was still omnipresent. Even this low level of immunity was not added to by any later pope. The politics of private power simply did not exist in the Agro romano, except, on a small scale, in Silva Maior on its north-eastern edge (below, pp. 70, 76). This has close parallels in the castle-free zones around cities in northern Italy and Tuscany, too, but, to repeat, the Agro romano was a far larger territory. We will return to this point later.

As already stated, the land of castles was not fully under Rome's control in the last century of our period. In the tenth century and early eleventh, the counts and rectors of the different sectors of Lazio—Tuscia, Sabina, Tivoli, *Campania* and *Marittima*—were more or less firmly dependent on whoever ruled the city, prince or *patricius* or pope. We see some cracks in this pattern when, for example, Benedict VIII had to conduct a military expedition against the counts of the Sabina to take back the Farfa castle of Bocchignano in 1014, as already mentioned. However, it was only with the breakdown of comital power in the decades after

---

[38] For *datium/fodrum*: *Papsturkunden*, n. 608; *RF*, nn. 513, 1160; with Toubert, *Les structures*, pp. 1070–2 for Roccantica and Montasola in 1060, both papal castles. Compare for Lombardy the model study of Menant, *Campagnes lombardes*, pp. 395–485, and for Tuscany Wickham, 'La signoria rurale in Toscana'.

[39] Respectively, *Papsturkunden*, nn. 522, 608, 607; 'Documenti per la storia', n. 2. Note also SMT, n. 7 (a. 1079), in which the family of Giovanni Tignoso, a 'new aristocrat' of Trastevere (below, pp. 224–6), has land at Valerano *cum omni suo districto*; this was right on the western edge of the Agro, close to Castel di Guido.

the 1040s that the Sabina turned into a network of potentially autonomous castle territories—some still controlled by the counts, like Arci, which Farfa wrested from them with papal support in 1060–1, or Palombara and Monticelli, which they held until the late twelfth century; many owned by Farfa, though the monastery had trouble holding on to some of them; others held by local lords. By the 1130s, the Sabina had disintegrated into a set of castle territories, and little more.[40] The Sabina is only the best-documented example of a Lazio-wide pattern. The popes responded to this breakdown creatively, by buying up castles directly from their lords, or else 'persuading' them to cede them to the pope and receive them back in fief. This process is already visible under Nicholas II around 1060, and popes pursued the creation of a network of *castra specialia* of the Roman church whenever they could after that. We can see some signs of renewed papal territorial protagonism with Calixtus II and Honorius II in the 1120s in parts of southern Lazio, but it did not really extend far until Eugenius III and especially Hadrian IV in the 1150s in the lands north of Rome, and then again in the south as well.[41] Only the sector dominated by Tivoli remained outside this strategic process, and, in the far north, that around Viterbo. The latter would be absorbed later, under Innocent III, who turned this network (back) into something resembling a state.

The Lazio that the popes effortfully constructed in the twelfth century went well beyond the 6000 km² territory around the city described earlier; in *Campania* (now the province of Frosinone) it extended past Anagni to Alatri and Veroli; in *Marittima* (now the province of Latina) it extended without a break to Terracina; in Tuscia Romana it extended north of Sutri even before Innocent III absorbed Viterbo. This wider Lazio recreated the *territorium S. Petri* of the eighth to tenth centuries, whose borders had remained recognized as the zone of the (at least potential) exercise of papal authority. Its existence, and eventual reconstruction, allowed the new Roman baronial families of the thirteenth century and onwards to expand their property-owning and political power very widely, across the whole of Lazio. Indeed, overall papal supremacy and government in that period did not prevent—did not wish to prevent—the establishment of territorial *signorie* with networks of local rights and exactions which were far more intense and exploitative than anything visible in the tenth to twelfth centuries.[42] The increased weight of local signorial lordship in the thirteenth century inside, rather than opposed to, the formation of regional states has, for that matter, plenty of parallels, in southern Italy and even in Tuscany.[43] The commitment of Roman aristocrats to this very wide network of property-owning and local power contributed, in fact, to the development of a larger geographical scale for the exercise of the power of the city at all levels. The political practices of the land of castles were the same around Veroli and Viterbo as they were closer into the city, after all, so there was no need to see *Campania* or northern Lazio as separate once the popes had absorbed them into the

---

[40] See in general Vehse, 'Die päpstliche Herrschaft', esp. pp. 144–52; for Arci, *RF*, nn. 903–6.
[41] See the survey in Toubert, *Les structures*, pp. 1068–79.
[42] Carocci, *Baroni di Roma*, pp. 247–70.
[43] See Casini, 'Signoria e società rurale nella Toscana nordorientale'.

'papal state'. Before 1100, however, apart from at the level of longer traditions of papal and princely government, Roman interest did not extend so far. As will be explored in Chapter 4, we see leading Roman aristocrats playing castle politics in the Sabina and around Velletri, and taking over Palestrina, Tuscolo, and Cerveteri; we see Roman churches and monasteries owning land in and around Sutri and Nepi and (above all) Albano; but we do not often see them active north of Sutri or in *Campania* and *Marittima* (with the exception of Terracina on occasion). Only in the later eleventh century did even the Tuscolani, no longer a city family, begin to expand their interests in the west of *Campania* and *Marittima*; only in the early twelfth do we find the urban Corsi family in north-west Lazio, and, by the 1140s, the Frangipane in *Marittima*; other city families did not follow them until well after 1150.[44]

In our period, therefore, the Lazio that potentially looked to Rome, and which the Romans regarded as their actual or potential territory, seldom extended beyond the 6000 km² block from Sutri to Palestrina. And it also has to be recognized, as we shall see in more detail in Chapter 4, that only the greater 'old aristocratic' families of the city in the late tenth and early eleventh centuries had more than an occasional interest outside the Agro romano. Many Roman churches had possessions, and eventually fortified villages, in the land of castles, particularly in Tuscia Romana, but they almost universally had trouble keeping control of them.[45] Castles were a risk: to move into the world of castles, one had to move a step up in the game, and begin the expensive politics of military commitment. Not everyone was successful at that game, and many did not wish to try—and that went both for churches and for lay elites in the city, before, at any rate, the popes around and after 1200 increased so massively the potential resources (and reduced the risks) for their favoured families. For that matter, even the Tuscolani only played the castle game with any enthusiasm when they lost their authority in Rome, after 1046, and the 'old aristocracy' as a whole for the most part abandoned Rome when they committed more to castle politics in the same period. These are all reasons why the land of castles will not, from now on, figure much in this book. The elective terrain of most Roman economic and political action was the Agro romano. But that was already large enough for a real commitment, on the part of a host of secular and ecclesiastical powers.

THE AGRO ROMANO

I have already briefly characterized the original features of the Agro romano; here let us look at some of them. We will examine in turn the distribution of landowning, the patterns of settlement, what can be said about the nature of peasant society and economy, and the management of estates. These will give us some insight into how

---

[44] Beolchini, *Tusculum II*, pp. 75–90; see below, pp. 226–31 for the Frangipane and Corsi.
[45] e.g. *S. Gregorio*, n. 7; *S. Paolo*, nn. 2–7; ASR, SCD, cassetta 16, nn. 109, 118.

this zone's peculiarities actually worked out on the ground. (See Map 3 for this section.)

The patterns of property-ownership

I have argued elsewhere that all the signs are that the Agro romano was overwhelmingly owned by churches and monasteries up to at least 1050, and that this was only beginning to change very slowly by the end of the period, in the later twelfth century.[46] It was not a unitary Church that owned the land, but a large range of individual churches; they were nearly all from Rome or immediately outside its walls. The only major exceptions to this were the bishops of Silva Candida and Porto (who anyway both generally lived in the city, on the Tiber Island) and the rural monasteries of Farfa, Subiaco (both of whom ran their Roman lands from intramural monasteries too, respectively S. Maria in the Terme Alessandrine and S. Erasmo sul Celio), and Grottaferrata. This certainly defuses any sense that the Agro romano was some sort of monolithic block, but the church dominance over landowning nonetheless had some important consequences, as we shall see throughout this book.

Our documentary evidence for Roman landowning, as we saw in Chapter 1, all comes from ecclesiastical archives.[47] It is therefore only to be expected that the best-documented landowners would be churches and monasteries, as is true throughout medieval Europe in the early and central Middle Ages. But Rome in the tenth century is unusual in Italy in the surviving number of lay donations to the church and other lay alienations (elsewhere in the peninsula the tenth century is usually a fallow period of lay gift-giving, between the two high points of *c*.750–830 and the eleventh century). These lay documents, for lands throughout the Agro romano, overwhelmingly make it clear that the land alienated in the texts was held in lease from a church; that is to say, it was the church that held full property rights (called *ius* in this period) in the land, not the lay men or women who were ceding it away. Before 980 or so, it was normal to name the ecclesiastical owner, as when in 913 Domnina *nobilis femina* sold land to Giovanni *consul et dux*, 60 *modii* of land at Filiscari (now Prato Fiscale) on the Salaria, *iuris monasterii S. Viti*, and 10 *modii* of meadow beside the Ponte Milvio, *iuris sancte Romane ecclesia* (i.e. the papacy). Even in the tenth century, however, much land was simply identified as *iuris cui existens* or variants, which is best translated as 'whoever's property it is', a much vaguer formulation that simply made clear that the alienator of land explicitly denied claims to full property rights. This latter phrase took over in the late tenth century, and dominates our lay texts until the 1070s.[48] In several cases we can prove that the proprietor of land held *iuris cui existens* was a church, and we can safely assume it in the other documents where it appears. Conversely, in all the tenth-century documents we have, of all kinds—for the Agro romano, the inner vineyard belt, and the city of Rome itself—only one charter clearly attests to a lay full proprietor, a gift to

---

[46] Wickham, '*Iuris cui existens*'; 'La struttura'.   [47] See Chapter 1, n. 13, for guides.
[48] Wickham, '*Iuris cui existens*', pp. 6–14; for 913, *RS*, n. 115.

Subiaco in 959 of a salt pan in the via Portuense salt flats by Marozia *senatrix omnium Romanorum* (Marozia 'II' as she is generally called), the cousin of Prince Alberico and the ancestor of the Tuscolano family. Marozia was hardly a typical landowner but, conversely, it does have to be recognized that even Alberico and Marozia 'II', and the Tuscolani after them, held land *iuris cui existens* in surviving documents for the most part. The next land demonstrably held by a lay man or woman in full property is not until 1007 (a mill outside Albano), and there are barely half a dozen more examples before 1075, when, as part of the sharp change in formulae for writing documents in Rome in the last third of the eleventh century, the phrase *iuris cui existens* drops out of the documentary record.[49] Before that date, other lay land was in nearly every case explicitly held in lease from the church. Before 1000 or so, documented lessees tend most of all to be Roman aristocrats or near-aristocrats, *consules et duces* or *viri illustrissimi* or *viri magnifici* or *nobiles viri/feminae*; only after 1000 do less prominent figures, such as urban artisans, and the wide social stratum (both rich and poor) generically labelled in texts as *viri/feminae honesti*, appear as such landholders, although even they, as we shall see, were rarely the actual cultivators of the land.

Leases to aristocrats and other urban *rentiers* are a common feature of ninth- to eleventh-century ecclesiastical practice in Italy, and, quite often, the church land-owner never got the land back. Rome was, however, a city where a consciousness of the difference between full property (*ius*, the classical *proprietas* or *dominium*) and possession (*possessio*), a key distinction in classical Roman land law, had never gone away, and churches display, for example in court cases, a clear determination not to lose their ultimate property rights. Up to 1075 at least, they seem to have succeeded. Aristocrats did not try to turn possession into full property, or, if they did so (usually simply by not paying rent, which, if not contested for thirty years, would result in de facto proprietorial rights), could be brought before courts run by their peers and rivals, who always, in surviving texts, judged against them.[50] Churches seldom sought to keep court documents for cases they lost, so our sample is not representative, but then again we also do not have texts claiming lay propri-etorship as long as the *iuris cui existens* phraseology lasted, so the balance between church property and lay possession seems to have remained. Aristocrats in Rome had to resign themselves to having possession of their lands, not full property, and so did everyone else. Even after 1075 this did not change quickly, except occasionally in the castle zone, where aristocratic tenants of castles did sometimes succeed in dispossess-ing church proprietors; a particularly good example is Poli north of Palestrina, lost by S. Gregorio sul Celio in the early twelfth century despite a long and public court case in the city in 1139–43, a loss made permanent when Oddone of Poli gave his castle to Pope Hadrian IV in 1157 and received it back in fief.[51]

---

[49] Full property to 1075: *RS*, n. 64 (Marozia); *SMCM*, nn. 2, 4; *SMN*, nn. 9, 15, 21; *SMT*, n. 5; for Alberico and the Tuscolani, see Wickham, '*Iuris cui existens*', p. 16.

[50] Examples: *RF*, nn. 428, 457, 637; *S. Gregorio*, n. 14; *SMN*, n. 42.

[51] *S. Gregorio*, n. 7; *LC*, I, nn. 101–2 (a.1157); *Reg. Inn. III*, VII.133 (a.1204) shows a failed later attempt by S. Gregorio to get it back.

In part, Roman aristocrats could easily deal with not being full proprietors because this had long been the case, and they found it normal (the pattern went back to the long-term leases held by senators on imperial lands in the late Roman empire). In part, too, it is because this form of land right did not greatly inconvenience them. Aristocrats all knew that what churches of all kinds, from the pope's to the smallest *diaconiae*, would normally do with most of the lands they owned was, precisely, to cede them out, very often to aristocrats, in long-term emphyteutic lease: for three generations (the Romans often called the lease a *tertium genus*), and for a low rent.[52] We will come back to the economics of this later; but these leases offered very stable possession, and aristocrats in practice treated them as if they were full tenure—they founded churches and monasteries on them, and, outside the Agro romano, castles as well.[53] And they also gave them to other churches in pious gift, for the benefit of their souls, more so, as already noted, than in most parts of Italy after the mid-ninth century, and not less in the eleventh, when other regions began the process again.

Pious gifts of this kind were doubtless very laudable; but in and around Rome they were also in every case illegal. Every emphyteusis contained as a standard element in its formulary the statement that the leased land could be alienated (saving the rights of the proprietor) to anyone except to *piis locis vel publico numero militum seu bando*—churches or army detachments—who evidently, if they got their hands on such land, would be less likely ever to give it back. The army detachments hardly existed any longer; the phrase shows the conservativeness of the formulary, for this is the terminology of the sixth to eighth centuries (indeed, the first surviving document for Rome, from 758, uses the phrase).[54] The churches definitely did, however, and the caution shown in these documents with regard to the good will of ecclesiastical colleagues seems amply to have been justified. New and/or rising churches and monasteries, of which there were many in the tenth century and later, needed to accumulate land from lay patrons (unless they were lucky enough to have papal patronage), and that meant taking over the lands already owned by other churches. We have a number of court cases in which the original proprietor sought, often only with partial success, to get back such land, now in the hands of another church.[55] This was for long one of the principal means, indeed, by which property rights seem to have changed hands, for churches so seldom alienated them of their own free will.

Churches did not strictly need to cede lands in emphyteusis. They could, and did, also farm them more directly. A well-known precursor of this was the set of around ten *domuscultae*, founded in the Agro romano by Popes Zacharias and Hadrian I in the 740s and 770s–80s respectively, which seem to have been manorial estates, managed directly by papal officials, and inalienable—excluded from the normal run of emphyteuses, that is to say, which are documented for other'

---

[52] Lenzi, *La terra e il potere*, pp. 48–66; for *tertium genus*, see e.g. Ugo of Farfa, *Exceptio brevis relationum*, p. 63.

[53] Wickham, 'Iuris cui existens', pp. 24–8.   [54] *RS*, n. 111.

[55] e.g. *S. Gregorio*, n. 126; *RF*, nn. 504, 506; *S. Alessio*, n. 6.

eighth-century popes. We know this practice was unpopular in the city, for in 815, when Leo III was dying, the *proceres Romani* (the Roman aristocracy) supposedly had all of them burnt; however true this account might or might not be (it does not have any support in the archaeology), there is no trace of them after the 840s, and some of them visibly passed out of papal hands to other churches or to lay tenants again.[56] Less controversial was the cession of such land in shorter-term lease and for higher rents, in a second type of contract, the *libellus*. The *libellus* allowed the church, rather than an aristocratic emphyteusis-holder, to gain much of the economic surplus from the land; I say 'much' only because even these leases were not usually to cultivators, although they could be. *Libelli* were most frequently for land in the city or the vineyard belt, or else for the latter's outliers in the salt flats or the Albano vineyards, but they can be found in the grain lands of the Agro romano too, and they show that ecclesiastical proprietors were capable of making choices about how their land was exploited.[57] Such choices, and a lasting concern for control over even emphyteutic leases, are also shown in the numerous texts we have in which tenants ceded leases back to their landlord, often for substantial pay-offs, before the term of the lease (generally it was an emphyteusis) ended.[58] Even when churches stuck to emphyteutic leases, which was very often, they could also choose whom to lease to after the three lives were up. This made possible the steady drift in the eleventh century towards more and more lessees from Rome's 'new aristocracy' and 'medium elite', rather than from its 'old aristocracy'; churches could indeed make the fortunes of new families by sympathetic leasing, and doubtless exploited the political possibilities involved as much in 1000 as they did in the better-documented thirteenth century. This contributed substantially to Rome's political/social fluidity. But there was so much land available that these choices did not undermine the dominance of older families, if these stayed afloat for other reasons. And aristocrats, too, knew that they could benefit from the rights of churches to choose whom to lease to. It is probable that the potential advantages attached to a church monopoly on property-ownership outweighed the risks in the minds of the lay powerful; this will have reinforced the stability of the system.

I am setting out a snapshot of time here, focused on the tenth and eleventh centuries; but the longer history of this dominance of church property deserves at least a brief survey. The papacy, and several other Roman churches, benefited dramatically from the gifts of the emperor Constantine I after 312, and by the end of the western Roman empire the popes were doubtless already the largest private

[56] The most recent study is Marazzi, *I 'patrimonia sanctae Romanae ecclesiae'*, pp. 235–61; pp. 259–60n for burning. No such traces of burning have been found in the excavations of two major centres of the *domusculta* Capracorum, ed. in Christie, *Three South Etrurian Churches*, and Potter and King, *Excavations at the Mola di Monte Gelato*, although in each case the material record from that period is pretty fragmentary. The *domusculta* Galeria on the Aurelia was in the hands of the Vaticano monasteries already by 854; Galeria on the Portuense ended up by 1018 with the bishop of Porto; Capracorum was held by a lay aristocrat by 1041 at the latest: see Wickham, 'La struttura', pp. 198, 208–9; Wickham, 'Historical and topographical notes', pp. 173–7.

[57] Lenzi, *La terra e il potere*, pp. 13–48.

[58] Examples: *RS*, nn. 29, 66, 114; *S. Gregorio*, nn. 75, 151; *SCD*, n. 47; *SMVL*, n. 83.

owners in Lazio, with lands across most of the western Mediterranean.[59] The major change to the local resources of the church must, however, have been in the later eighth century, when the popes established full political autonomy for themselves as rulers of the *territorium S. Petri*, because when they did this the fiscal land of Lazio, previously under imperial control, automatically accrued to them: most plausibly between *c.*745 (the date of a gift by the emperor Constantine V to Pope Zacharias of two estates held *iuris publici* in *Marittima*, at Norma and Ninfa) and 782 (the date of a gift by Pope Hadrian I of public land outside Ravenna: for if popes disposed of ex-imperial land even here, one could hardly doubt they did so closer to Rome). This change in papal resources has no other documentation, and has not been much stressed by historians, except by Federico Marazzi; but it was an inevitable consequence of the replacement of the emperors by the popes as the sovereign power in Lazio, and must have been of major economic importance—quite possibly enough even to outweigh the better-studied imperial confiscation of the rich papal lands in Sicily and elsewhere, not long before. We do not know how much of the Agro romano (and, indeed, the future castle zone) had been imperial land, but the indications we have are that this land was very extensive indeed, and also organized in many cases in large blocks of territory.[60] I would suppose that this was the moment when the church gained control of the majority of the Agro romano, and, probably as a result, the political dominance necessary to take over whatever remained in private hands (a process we can sometimes see eighth-century popes engaging in).[61] This initially benefited one church only, the *sancta Romana ecclesia* itself. Popes will then, probably soon, have distributed much of this land among the network of Roman basilicas, monasteries, *scolae*, palatine offices, *tituli*, and *diaconiae*, for these are the bodies who we find owning the land in the tenth century, although the popes must have kept a considerable slice in their own hands as well. All this land was then available for emphyteutic and other leases to the laity, as indeed imperial land had been before 750, but the ultimate property rights had changed decisively. As a result, the ninth to eleventh centuries signal the high-water mark of church landowning in Lazio, out of two millennia of history.

Exactly how this process worked politically at the start will forever be in the realm of hypothesis, given that barely twenty Roman documents survive for the period before 900. All the same, one might well link to it the huge papal gifts of gold and silver and church decorations recorded in the *Liber Pontificalis*, the notable ambition and expense of early ninth-century church building,[62] and, overall, the striking political protagonism of the popes of the century from Hadrian I onwards,

---

[59] Early imperial gifts: see *LP*, I, pp. 170–202, cf. 232–4. For papal lands around 600, see e.g. Recchia, *Gregorio magno e la società agricola*, pp. 11–12.

[60] The best analysis of this process is Marazzi, *I 'patrimonia sanctae Romanae ecclesiae'*, pp. 274–80; the two cited texts are *LP*, I, p. 433 and *Le carte ravennati dei secoli ottavo e nono*, n. 7. For the loss of the Sicilian lands, the most recent study is Prigent, 'Les empereurs isauriens', pp. 571–94; at pp. 587 and 594 he sees the papal takeover of imperial land in central-northern Italy as a possible direct response to the southern confiscations, which I am less sure of—they seem to me different sorts of process.

[61] *LP*, I, pp. 434–5, 501, 505, 509.   [62] See below, Chapter 3, n. 142.

for popes will have been the undivided centre of attention of every political actor in the city, ecclesiastical or lay, as long as they were distributing ex-imperial land to church proprietors and lay lessees. Perhaps also the end of large-scale building by 850 or so, notwithstanding the continued political centrality of both Nicholas I and his less effective successors, also shows the end of the territorial dominance of the papal church, now that other churches had taken over much of that land.

This set of hypotheses cannot be developed further here, for they precede the period of this book; what is not in doubt, however, is the stability of the system that resulted. The major crisis of the Arab attacks at the end of the ninth century, coupled with the contemporary breakdown in the unity of the papal political structure at the time of the Formosan controversy, which seriously split the clergy and Laterano bureaucracy, had no effect on the solidity of church landowning: for it was precisely in the aftermath of these crises that the best evidence for the dominance of ecclesiastical property rights first appears, in our tenth-century charters. We might have supposed that the rule of Teofilatto, Marozia 'I', and Alberico as secular rulers of Rome in the first half of the tenth century, culminating in Alberico's use of the title of prince, and the temporary relegation of popes to the position simply of bishops, would be accompanied by the secularization of church land, but nothing of the kind occurred then either. Instead, the Teofilatto family were happy to dominate a stable, largely bureaucratized, and above all wealthy political system, and indeed to re-establish its unity after the Formosan period. As we have seen, they were content to hold even most of their own family land *iuris cui existens*. Their interest in monastic foundations will have redirected other church properties to these, but a secularization process is here invisible.[63] The *Adelspapsttum* that followed Alberico for a century (itself not that different from the papacy of the ninth century, which was also controlled by Roman aristocrats) simply carried the process on. Aristocrats indeed had to seek to dominate the papal bureaucratic apparatus: in an agrarian world in which the church owned all the land, power lay nowhere else.

A far greater crisis for the coherence of church landowning came in the late eleventh century. As sketched out in Chapter 1, and as we shall amply see in Chapter 7, the combined effect of the coup of 1046, the internationalization of papal interests and senior clerical appointments after the 1040s, and the civil war of the 1080s–90s had a seriously negative effect on the government of Rome. The solidity of church property rights depended substantially on a political regime that Roman landholders could buy into, and the clerical side of the hierarchy of rewards was henceforth largely cut out of that; the crisis in government also meant the collapse of the traditional judicial system after the 1070s, and there then followed a fifty-year period with little institutional structuring for rule over Rome at all (below, pp. 393–403). Roman elites thus simultaneously had less of a stake in the system, and will have found that there were fewer controls against bad behaviour. It would not be surprising if church property-ownership began to slip under these

---

[63] Hamilton, 'The monastic revival'.

circumstances, and we begin to get signs of it. It is a pity that we cannot track this exactly, for this is precisely the moment when the *iuris cui existens* formula drops out of the texts. All the same, there is some anecdotal evidence for it: this includes two charters from 1059–60 for the female monastery of S. Ciriaco in Via Lata, in which the nuns each time buy out tenants (one of them the heirs of a senior palatine official, Giorgio *arcarius*) who had held land illegally and without paying rent, for substantial sums of money; or Clement III's characterization in 1084, in a church vs. church court case this time, of the judicial failings of five 'reform' popes in settling an apparently simple case of dues unpaid to S. Marcello since 1025; or the case of the laywoman Bella, who died around 1105, leaving to the monastery of SS. Cosma e Damiano in Trastevere her lands in Isola Farnese, which had once been that monastery's property, but had been lost because no rent had been paid on them for at least fifty years; or the complicated proceedings around the *massa* Careia on the via Clodia, which S. Maria Nova had great difficulty getting back from the counts of Galeria in 1124–6. In each of these cases, the church did indeed obtain a recognition of proprietorship, because otherwise we would not have the documents, but the trends are new.[64]

It would be wrong to conclude from this that large-scale church landowning became suddenly threatened from the late eleventh century onwards. Most land in the city seems to have remained ecclesiastical (below, pp. 122–4). Even in the fourteenth century, Jean-Claude Maire Vigueur has calculated that over half of the *casali* of the Agro romano were ecclesiastically owned.[65] But half is still not as much as the whole; and it was from *c.*1080 onwards that it first began to be possible for lay possessors of land to turn that possession into full property. Churchmen, too, began to be aware that long-term leases might lead to the loss of the land; as Pope Alexander III remarked in 1166, sales had a *magna similitudo* with leases—he used the word *locatio*, the multi-purpose lease that had replaced both emphyteusis and *libellus* in the late eleventh century.[66] The balance had shifted, and foot-dragging over rent-paying from now onwards could become part of strategies aimed at the transfer of rights. Even though church land remained overwhelmingly dominant throughout our period, these new fears for the loss of property rights underpin some of the new landowning directions of the twelfth century, as we shall see.

I have been stressing that aristocratic and other lay lessees of church land were not greatly disempowered by not owning in full property; but there were some consequences which do matter to us. One is that the fragmentation of land that was a normal consequence of partible inheritance did not take place in the Agro romano, simply because land owned by the church was never inherited, and thus never had to be divided. This is clear enough on the level of property-owning; but it might have been different on the level of the leases held by the laity. These, particularly when they were held for three generations, were indeed inherited,

---

[64] *SMVL*, nn. 87–8; *S. Marcello*, n. 1; ASR, SCD, cassetta 16, n. 109; *SMN*, n. 42, a case not resolved in 1126 (see e.g. n. 68).

[65] Maire Vigueur, 'Les "casali" des églises romaines', p. 66.

[66] *S. Marcello*, n. 7. See in general for this process Wickham, '*Iuris cui existens*', pp. 28–38.

sometimes by several heirs; heirs shared such land equally, in theory male and female heirs alike, as Rome lived by traditional Roman law. We have very many examples of heirs holding land together in our documents, and there might well have developed pressure on lessors to divide leases between them. Since leaseholders of all types of lease also had the right to sell or pledge the land or parts of it, a right we can often see them exercising, we might well have seen a fragmentation of a single lease among a range of unrelated people which a church might find hard to hold together. Such developments were normal elsewhere in Italy, where a tenant-holding might well only be a collection of scattered fields, and they can be found in the vineyard belt and the city of Rome as well. But they are much less visible in the Agro romano. It is true that tenth-century leases are more often for whole estates (*fundi* or *casalia*) or parts of them, and those of the eleventh century and twelfth are more often for *pedicae* of land—that is to say, in the eleventh century at least, the land which a pair of oxen could plough, or roughly a tenant-holding. But a tenant-holding is not that small a unit, and around Rome single *pedicae*, sometimes groups of *pedicae*, could often be solid parcels of land, with their boundaries listed in the lease. Divisions of *pedicae* can certainly be found too, but they do not dominate our texts. It thus becomes clear not only that the temporary nature of leases (even long-term leases) could have allowed church landowners to reconstitute land-blocks at the end of them, but that this was a right they must often have exercised. These blocks would be fairly easily put back together again in the thirteenth century, as late medieval *casali*.[67]

The solidity of the blocks of land in the Agro romano itself had implications. In particular, it contributed to a geographical framework for the zone which remained firmly anchored to property boundaries; and it contributed to the social and economic marginalization of the peasantry of the hinterland of Rome. We will explore these issues later in this chapter. But it is important to recognize that these are consequences not only of the fact that the churches owned the land, but also of the fact that they continued to exercise choices about how to exploit it. They could indeed have allowed inheritance and alienation to break their lands up, and let them be distributed among different sets of tenants in smaller and smaller pieces; but here they chose not to, and as a result there was a minimum of fragmentation beyond which the lands of the Agro romano did not go. We can track a very rough geography of church landowning around Rome in the tenth to twelfth centuries: of the lands, at least, of the best-documented churches. City churches and monasteries often owned land above all in the sector of the Agro romano closest to the part of the city where they were located; so the Trastevere churches (of which the best documented is SS. Cosma e Damiano) mostly owned land along the Portuense, which runs from Trastevere to the salt flats, the Vatican monasteries owned huge tracts in the sector west and north of the Civitas Leoniana, S. Gregorio sul Celio owned a set of linked estates on the Appia, which ran out from under the Celio, and S. Paolo fuori le Mura owned much of the Ostiense sector, between the monastery

---

[67] Wickham, 'La struttura', pp. 188–93, 202, 232–5; for the size of a *pedica* in our period as land sufficient for *lavorandum unum parium de bobum*, see *SMVL*, nn. 64, 65; *S. Prassede*, n. 8.

and the sea. The bishops of Porto and Silva Candida also owned most of the land around their respective cathedrals. But the vagaries of legal and illegal cessions blew many holes in this neat division, and anyway there were many churches in the centre of Rome that could look in any direction. In addition to these churches, therefore, we find S. Ciriaco in Via Lata owning two substantial estates along the Portuense, a smaller one up the Flaminia, and a very large tract of land along the Tiburtina, close to the border with Tivoli; S. Gregorio owning another block at the western edge of the Agro, between the Aurelia and the coast; and S. Prassede owning a solid estate by the Lago Burrano on the Prenestina, flanked by more land of S. Paolo.[68]

This list is obviously not exhaustive. It does seem faithfully to represent the main landowning interests in the Agro romano of these particular churches, but it does not help with respect to the churches whose archives do not survive. It is interesting, however, how few large geographical gaps there are in our knowledge of the landowning of the Agro romano. Almost no one is attested as owning land in the eastern sector of the Agro along the via Labicana, and I think it likely that this is where the papacy, the *sancta Romana ecclesia* itself, kept the great bulk of its property, ungranted to other ecclesiastical bodies, for this is the sector closest to the Laterano palace.[69] The Salaria is also relatively ill-documented, and so is the (almost certainly underpopulated) sector east of the Ostiense. But one can move down the Portuense, Aurelia, Tiburtina, Prenestina, and Appia, and be fairly sure at each step who owned the land around. And some sections of it, in particular Marcelli of SS. Cosma e Damiano on the Portuense, Taliano of the Vatican monasteries on the Cornelia, Silva Maior of S. Ciriaco on the Tiburtina, and the Appia estates of S. Gregorio, were owned in blocks that were really huge, 20 km² in each case, and double that in the case of Silva Maior.[70]

These vast properties were as much a feature of the Agro romano as were the more contained (but still substantial) estates along, for example, the Prenestina. They make one wonder where the land could have been for the host of churches whose archives do not survive. But it is also noteworthy that another group of urban churches with good archives, such as S. Maria Nova and S. Maria in Campo Marzio, did not really own all that much in the Agro romano beyond the vineyard belt (and Albano); and when we have twelfth-century papal confirmations or inventories of the lands of even some of the major churches, S. Maria Maggiore, S. Croce in Gerusalemme, and S. Giovanni in Laterano itself, the same seems by that century to be true for them. (All three of the last-named had been richly endowed, including in the Agro romano, in the fourth or fifth centuries, with lands that were no longer claimed by them in the twelfth; the hidden history of papal power over the lands of the greatest churches may well explain this shift.)[71] It thus

---

[68] See Wickham, 'La struttura', for a more detailed analysis of each of these.

[69] Wickham, 'La struttura', pp. 217–18.

[70] Wickham, 'La struttura', pp. 194–201, 206–7, 210–15, 218.

[71] For these three churches see *Liberiano*, n. 22; Kehr, IV, pp. 226–8; Pflugk, III, n. 142 with Lauer, 'Un inventaire inédit'. For the fourth and fifth centuries, respectively, *LP*, I, pp. 233, 180, 173–4.

seems to be the case that even important churches in the city could sometimes own just a group of houses inside the walls, a substantial set of vineyards in the belt around the city and near Albano, some salt pans, and only a few blocks of land in the grain lands of the Agro romano. Most of the smaller, newer ecclesiastical foundations of the twelfth century doubtless had less, sometimes perhaps little more than the land they were built on.[72] This leaves much of the Agro romano as the preserve of maybe as little as two dozen churches, and we have at least some documents for most of these. This is convenient for the security of our reconstructions. It might also have led to the establishment of real rural power blocks, political foci that might have played an autonomous part in the politics of the city, as the lay centre of Tuscolo did, on the edge of the Agro to the east. But the churches did not do that with their lands, and nor did their lay tenants. The fate of Mandra Camellaria (see p. 43), a little closer in than Tuscolo, and founded by a less powerful family than the Tuscolani, is a marker for why this did not happen; the city's rulers would not permit it. But churches, too, were not obviously keen on such power centres for the most part; the land was enough for them, and power centres such as castles (which would usually have been run by lay lessees) risked slipping out of their control. The Agro romano simply remained a network of estates as a result, both in our period and after.[73] It was an economic, not a political, power-base. But its economic role was very important, as we shall see shortly.

Settlement

The really disorientating feature of the Agro romano, at least to the eyes of anyone used to other regions of medieval Italy—indeed medieval Europe—is the absence of villages. This was true right up to 1950, in the famous emptiness of the landscape of the *casali* before Rome's building boom began; but it was an abiding feature of our period. Indeed, it was older than that, for it was inherited directly from the Roman empire. In the Roman West, village territories are rare in our evidence for the imperial period, and we overwhelmingly get references to landed properties as identification markers: *fundi*, groups of *fundi* (called *massae*), as also divisions of *fundi*. The Roman jurists recognized that *fundi* could be large or small, divided or undivided, grouped or single, but ownership remained the key marker for the location of properties in the countryside; the *fundus* network became the basis for land-tax calculations, too, which will have maintained its structure.[74] This changed in the post-Roman West, in Francia or Lombard Italy, where villages and their territories came to define the rural landscape. In Byzantine Italy, such as Rome or Ravenna or Sicily, *fundi* survived, however. The great papal *patrimonia* of the early

---

[72] See for example Kehr, IV, pp. 450–1 (a. 1104), Pflugk, II, n. 300 (a. 1128), and (for an eleventh-century foundation, S. Trifone) *Papsturkunden*, n. 424, with Pflugk, III, n. 430, for papal confirmations of relatively little land.

[73] Carocci and Vendittelli, *L'origine della Campagna Romana*, pp. 93–107.

[74] A good survey is de Neeve, '*Fundus* as economic unit'.

Middle Ages were all made up of *fundi*, in larger or smaller groups.[75] In some parts of Lazio, landowning was relatively fragmented, and *fundi* could simply become geographical markers, devoid of any real internal structure after the end of the land tax; but in the Agro romano, as we have just seen, the extremes of this geographical breakdown did not occur, and the estate-based identification network survived. In the land of castles, one clear result of the *incastellamento* process was that the territories of the new fortified villages imposed themselves at the expense of the old *fundus* pattern; we can already see this process in the tenth century, and by the end of the eleventh it was effectively complete.[76] In the Agro romano, however, estates simply continued.

Our period did, certainly, see changes. *Fundi* (also by now known as *casalia*) could be divided, and their divisions were also called *casalia*; this amœba-like segmentation implies that some property units became smaller. We have also seen that it became common to lease, not whole *fundi*, but *pedicae* of land in them. In this context, the terminology of *fundi* and *casalia* became rather more inconsistent, and *locus* became a common synonym for *fundus*: one instance is a *pedica* of land leased out in 1024 by S. Erasmo sul Celio *in locum Quinto* on the Appia, bounded by another *pedica* and three *casalia*; Quinto itself was also termed the *casale S. Erasmo in Quinto* in 1005, and the *fundus ad S. Herasmum* in 1034.[77] By the end of the century, the word *fundus* itself became rare, and *casale* almost non-existent, except in papal confirmations of rights, which always used an anti-quated terminology. In the twelfth century, the large area of the *fundus* Marcelli west of Trastevere, property of SS. Cosma e Damiano, was called a *fundus* only twice in the nearly twenty private documents for the territory, and a *locus* twice more; other texts simply locate land *in Marcelli*.[78]

It could be argued that Marcelli, one of the larger blocks of land in the Agro romano at some 20 km², as we have seen, had indeed become only a geographical marker. SS. Cosma e Damiano might have seen it as more of an integrated estate, however; this is quite likely in fact, though it is difficult to tell for sure. But what it emphatically was not was a village territory. No one is ever identified as *de Marcelli*; and in the three dozen texts for our period as a whole there is not a single reference to a house. Peasant cultivators must inevitably have lived inside this enormous territory, but we do not know where, and it was never necessary to specify. We could suppose that their houses were scattered across Marcelli, and were quite possibly attached to single *pedicae* of land; there are enough documents for the territory to allow one to feel that had they been aggregated in a single settlement, we would have had at least casual reference to it. I would indeed conclude this. But we do not, and cannot, know for sure; and archaeology will never help, for the area is now one of the recent housing estates on the new western edge of Rome.

---

[75] Wickham, *Framing*, pp. 470–3, 487–8, 510–14; for Lazio and the popes, Marazzi, *I 'patrimonia sanctae Romanae ecclesiae'*; for the Romagna, Castagnetti, *L'organizzazione*, pp. 171–9; for Sicily, Vera, 'Massa *fundorum*'.

[76] Toubert, *Les structures*, pp. 330–8.

[77] *RS*, n. 106, 108; *Papsturkunden*, n. 421 (a. 1005).

[78] Wickham, 'La struttura', pp. 189–91; see further Lenzi, 'Per la storia dei *casalia*'.

This is where the disorientation characteristic of the Agro romano comes into play in particular. The Romans of our period did not refer to houses in their lease documents for rural properties. House leases are standard inside Rome and Tivoli, and references to *domūs* can also be found in the old quasi-cities of Porto, Ostia, and Albano; but not in the countryside.[79] In Tuscany and the Po plain, it was normal to alienate, or lease out to peasants, *casae massariciae*, that is to say tenant houses (and their attached holdings), and this terminology was normal even in documents which do not themselves have peasants as actors; even in the Sabina, tenant houses/holdings (here just called *casae*, or else, confusingly, *casalia*) are a common unit in our sources, including outside castles. But in the Agro romano all that was leased was land. A *pedica* may have been a peasant holding, and the dependant who cultivated it is sometimes named in documents, but a *pedica* is never mentioned as having a house, and we cannot ever automatically assume it, however likely it actually was.[80] Where people lived was, that is to say, simply irrelevant to the makers of documents for the Agro romano. This was not simply a formulaic convention either, for one sector of the Agro, Silva Maior, did have settlements (*villae*) that are well documented, as we will see in a moment, and in that territory they constantly crop up, including in casual references. Elsewhere, though, habitation could be ignored, for the most part. This was a key element in the general lack of interest our documents show for the peasantry as a class, which I shall come back to in the next section. But it must also indicate that settlement was not organic enough to become anything that landowners and non-cultivating tenants needed to transact in. Houses were probably casually scattered, and a social identity attached to living in them would probably have been weak, if not non-existent. Units of property-owning, even if no longer called *fundi*, were the only markers people needed.

We do sometimes find, particularly in papal bulls, occasional references to houses attached to *fundi/casalia*, often in formulaic possession-clauses: they are called *casae* or, sometimes, *coloniae*. Examples include Taliano on the Cornelia in 854 and 1053, Monterotondo near the Salaria in 1013, and Galeria and Palmi on the Portuense in 1018.[81] All these tell us is that these estates did indeed have cultivators who lived there, which is reassuring, but we had presumed it already; and papal bulls were also, of all our documentary sources, the texts most likely to be anachronistic. In one unusually specific example, a bull for Silva Candida from 905 in which Sergius III gives the bishop the *massa* Cesana and its *fundi*, *coloniae*, *casae*, and *casalia*, he lists fifteen separate *coloniae*, each with its name. This decision,

---

[79] See below, nn. 87, 223 for Albano (and nearby Ariccia) and Porto; *SPV*, n. 79 for Ostia. *Domūs* appear in some smaller concentrated settlements too: the castle of Boccea (see below, n. 85) and the *burgus* of Lubbre on the Flaminia (*SMVL*, n. 137). Note that *RS*, n. 93 (a. 963), for the *fundus* or *casale* Papi near Tivoli, explicitly shows that that estate had inhabitants, but here we are firmly outside the Agro romano.

[80] For the Sabina, see above, n. 27. The *criptis, monumento, parietibus* in the two *pedicae* at Moreni on the Appia in 1128, *S. Gregorio*, n. 136, are most likely to have been classical ruins.

[81] *SPV*, nn. 2, 16; *RF*, n. 638; *Papsturkunden*, n. 522. Another example is Arcioni near Silva Candida in *Papsturkunden*, n. 569; the cathedral of Silva Candida also had inhabitants living around it once it was walled in the 1030s—see *Papsturkunden*, n. 608.

possibly linked to the stated motive of the gift—the desire to recompense Silva Candida for the devastation of the Arabs and the fact that the bishopric's *plebes atque casilia* [i.e. *casalia*] are now *pene absque agricolis et habitatoribus*, 'almost without cultivators and inhabitants'—at least lets us know that in the territory of this *massa* (probably north of the later castle of Cesano near the Cassia, so outside the Agro romano in the strict sense) the settlement was indeed dispersed. But this is the most explicit text we have. References to rural churches, which arguably might imply some gathering of the faithful (the *massa* Cesana had one *infra massa*, for example), are not all that much more common. Another indicator is probably references to *vineae* in texts for the Agro, for concentrations of vineyard cultivation are likely to be associated with housing too, but these are not so very many either.[82] We are left again with the generic sense that *fundi* did indeed have houses on them, but that it did not matter to any landed document-maker how they were articulated; and anyway only a minority of estates are ever described as having them. Indeed, it is not clear that *fundi* in our period even had an estate-centre—for the collection of rents, say, or for the at least occasional reception of a bailiff—with any regularity.

There is a limit to how much one can say about absences as total as this. I am here assuming that the bulls, however anachronistic, are at least providing us with a rough model which can be extended to later periods. Another solution, however, might be to conclude that there was never any significant permanent settlement in the medieval Agro romano, and that in our period, as certainly was the case from the end of the Middle Ages onwards, settlement was temporary, based on a seasonal and maybe paid workforce, and also relatively limited demographically. There has indeed been some discussion of such a pattern in our period.[83] Essentially, this argument would propose that the major break from a settled agrarian landscape in the Agro romano was not the fourteenth century, with the drop in population following the Black Death and a development of exchange sufficient to allow for an essentially salaried rural workforce, but, rather, at some point in the early Middle Ages—presumably, subsequent to the development of the formularies used in papal bulls. This seems to me not to work. Our rural leases (in Marcelli, for example) do sometimes mention stable subtenants, even if they do not say where they lived; these were not temporary labourers.[84] It is difficult to hypothesize the development

---

[82] *Papsturkunden*, n. 22. See Wickham, 'Historical and topographical notes', pp. 156–7, with a few misunderstandings. For rural churches as estate-centres, see below, p. 81. For the few *vineae* in the eleventh-century Agro romano (there are none in the tenth), see *SMVL*, nn. 40, 64–5; *S. Gregorio*, n. 17; *RF*, n. 1026; *SMT*, n. 7, for, respectively, *sacco* Olibolesi on the Salaria, Lubbre on the Flaminia, Molarupta on the Aurelia, *massa de* Vestario Domnico on the Salaria, and Cancellata on the Aurelia. Thanks to Sandro Carocci for ideas on this point and useful discussion of what follows.

[83] See Santangeli Valenzani, 'Forme dell'insediamento', who discusses the excavation of an apparently temporary site from (probably) the tenth or eleventh century at Torre Spaccata, east of Rome; he cautiously proposes that this might have been a norm in the lands closest to the city, along the lines of modern-period patterns, which he extends even more cautiously as a model back to the sixth century in 'Vecchie e nuove forme di insediamento'. For a relatively low population, see also Maire Vigueur, *L'autre Rome*, pp. 79, 81.

[84] For Marcelli, *SCD*, n. 35; *SMT*, n. 7; ASR, SCD, cassetta 16, n. 142; and below, p. 72. One area of the Agro romano did have temporary settlement, the salt pans of Porto; here at least it is explicitly referred to in documents (below, n. 204), in a terminology which we never find elsewhere.

of a temporary and/or salaried workforce in the early Middle Ages in the absence of any evidence; the abandonment of current economic models for the period, which stress relatively simple economic relationships (even for Rome), would need more reason than this. The evidence we have that the majority of the Agro romano was always exploited agriculturally, an exploitation which was extended with the clearance of Silva Maior and Reatina (see below, p. 85), also indicates to my eyes a relatively intensive pattern of cultivation, which temporary settlement, in early and central medieval conditions, could not guarantee over wide areas. I note this solution, therefore, so as to set it aside—although I would not exclude a version of it in more limited areas, as we shall indeed see for Reatina later.

It may be more useful to set out the exceptions to our general absence of evidence, see how they may be explained, and see how they shed light on the rest of the Agro romano. There were four or five tracts of genuine village settlement around the city, each with its own individual characteristics, which deserve some attention if we want to get a sense of how the landscape of Rome's hinterland was articulated. Let us look at them briefly in turn (and see also Map 3).

The first point to be made is that the Agro romano was not entirely devoid of castles. Two areas show them in our documents, the strip of land along the western and north-western edge of the Agro, including Castel di Guido, Boccea, Isola Farnese, and Pietra Pertusa; and another strip between the Prenestina and the Aniene, including Lunghezza, Osa, and maybe Salone. The first, already mentioned above, is easier to explain; it was simply the border of the land of castles, the line where fortifications were beginning to seem normal. It is only appropriate to include it in the Agro because these castles did not obviously have signorial rights, or any real autonomy, and they were also all on substantial blocks of church land. Boccea and Castel di Guido by 1201 had local customs (*consuetudines et usus*), along the lines of their neighbours Tragliata and Galeria, more fully part of the castle zone, but this is as much as we can say about village society here. All the same, it is at least possible to be pretty sure in these cases where cultivators lived.[85] Lunghezza and Salone are more surprising, because they are more fully inside the Agro romano, next door to one other. They first appear in a papal bull for S. Paolo in 1081, which includes more suspicious claims to land than any other document from our period; but Lunghezza, at least, remained a S. Paolo property in the later Middle Ages, and had documented inhabitants in the late twelfth century. Salone did not, and was a *castellarium* with a tower (*turris*), probably already a *casale* of late medieval type, of S. Maria Maggiore by 1176, so it may never have been a real castle of S. Paolo; conversely, though, the next S. Paolo estate along the River Aniene, the

---

[85] For Boccea, see esp. *SPV*, nn. 11, 39, 47, 53, 56, 64 (nn. 11, 53 for *domūs*); for Castel di Guido, esp. *S. Gregorio*, nn. 18, 19, 21–4. For 1201, *Senato*, n. 55; see in general Montel, 'Le "casale" de Boccea'. For Isola and Pietra Pertusa, Wickham, 'Historical and topographical notes', pp. 149–53, 168–70. Another isolated and probably temporary example is Frontignano just north of the Portuense, which had a *castellum* in one text (Pflugk II, n. 284), but not in the few other citations of the locality (*Papsturkunden*, n. 419; SMT, n. 4).

massa S. Iuliani, had acquired a castle, the *castrum* of Osa, between 1081 and 1130, which is attested in a much more reliable bull. S. Paolo thus put a castle in at least two, possibly three, of its estates along the Aniene, quite close to the city. Perhaps S. Paolo decided to do this because it was itself fortified, by John VIII in 880–2— the fortification is occasionally called Iohannipolis in our sources (cf. also p. 68 for Decima); perhaps, too, the city let it do so because the monastery had no political or signorial pretensions. Either way, the south bank of the Aniene shows a relatively structured settlement pattern.[86]

Albano and Ariccia were the centres of another zone of comprehensible settlement. These were old settlement nuclei dating back to the late Roman empire, with some institutional identity in the tenth century, for both of them had dukes. People certainly lived in both, for we have references both to houses and to inhabitants of each, and to a variety of churches there too.[87] The two centres were the foci for a specialist vineyard zone which will be discussed separately, but all the vineyards were at accessible distances from one or the other of them. Even then, however, we have some references to inhabitants living out in the countryside as well, at S. Eufemia (the modern S. Fumia) and S. Cecilia, and it may be that other rural churches, of which half a dozen are known in the sources, had small settlements linked to them as well.[88] The *territoria* of Albano and Ariccia were thus, in our whole area of study, one of the zones with the most 'normal' settlement pattern. They were on the edge of the castle zone too, but in these two territories all the signs are that this pattern pre-dated *incastellamento*. They were also close to Tuscolo, an important castle on the fringe of the Agro romano with imperial-period antecedents, which has been partially excavated. The Spanish archaeological team found in the lower town, on top of the abandoned forum and theatre, a number of reasonably well-built buildings in reused stone, plus an extramural church, dating to the eleventh and twelfth centuries, the period in which Tuscolo appears in the documents as well. The upper town or *rocca* has not yet been excavated, but earlier Italian survey work showed an even thicker settlement.[89] This may provide a material correlate for what Albano and Ariccia, too, looked like in our period, although they were considerably smaller.

The section of the via Ostiense closest to the sea is almost devoid of documentation, but one text stands out. It is a lease of 1125 from the monastery of S. Saba to Giovanni *iudex* for the foundation of the *locus* Piagusti as a settlement, *ad homines ibi congregandos, domosque inibi inedificandas*, in a territory bounded by the sea, marshes, woods, serpentine columns (presumably from the seaside villas of the

---

[86] *S. Paolo*, n. 1 (a. 1081), *PL*, CLXXIX, cols 692–6, n. 4 (a. 1130) for the bulls; *SMVL*, n. 192, 281 for Lunghezza, and *SMVL*, Baumgärtner, n. 95, for its territory (*tenimentum*) in 1215; *Liberiano*, n. 21 for Salone; for Iohannipolis, *Inscriptiones Christianae*, II.1, pp. 326–7 (a. 880–2); *S. Paolo*, n. 1. For the late medieval estates of S. Paolo, see Adams, 'A history', pp. 188–378.

[87] Albano: for the period up to the twelfth century, see R. Martorelli, *Dalla 'civitas Albona' al 'castellum Albanense'*, pp. 139–69; Wickham, 'Albano'. Ariccia: for churches, *SMVL*, nn. 14, 25, 168–9; for *domūs*, *SMVL*, nn. 20, 25, both just outside the *castrum*.

[88] S. Fumia and S. Cecilia: *RS*, n. 129; *SMVL*, n. 7 with n. 47.

[89] Beolchini, *Tusculum II*, pp. 111–318.

classical period—Pliny the Younger had one nearby, and several have been excavated), and the *communitates* of Dragone and Fusano. This remarkable text echoes
the *incastellamento* charters of a century or more earlier, but without the fortifications. The word 'community', also unique, indicates that at least two other such
villages existed here too, and, although Piagusti no longer survives, the other two
do; a third, Porciliano (now Castel Porziano) is also implied in the text. Dragone
was a *fundus* of S. Paolo in 1081, and held by the monastery continuously
thereafter; it is evident that this *fundus*, at least, was a real village, and so also
perhaps was Decima, just beyond Castel Porziano, which S. Paolo called a *castellum*: S. Paolo may just have walled a pre-existing village in this case.[90] Piagusti itself
was a failure. It may conceivably have been the short-lived twelfth-century archaeological site found on top of the ancient Vicus Augustanus, published by Amanda
Claridge, for that site was certainly inside the (wide) bounds of 1125, although if so
it resembled a rather later *casale* more than it did a village, with its tower, courtyard,
church, and just two arrays of rooms—a very different form of settlement, far from
the intentions of the 1125 text. But the intention of bringing inhabitants together
in a single unfortified settlement, flanked by other villages, is nonetheless clear in
the document. So is the heavily silvopastoral nature of the landscape; S. Saba kept
hold of its wood-rights and herds of pigs in the *silva* there. The wood was to be sold
in Rome, where the need for it must have been extensive and remunerative, given
that so little of the Agro romano was wooded; we know that nearby Ostia, still
called a *civitas* but no more than a large village itself by now, also dealt in wood (as
well as salt, from salt pans between Ostia and Dragone).[91] Piagusti—and probably
the other settlements—was an economically specialist site, then; this will have
added to its atypicality.

The other zone of villages was Silva Maior, property of the monastery of
S. Ciriaco in Via Lata, and we can say rather more about them; they have also
been studied extensively, in particular by Jean Coste, Sandro Carocci, and Marco
Vendittelli.[92] From our earliest documents around 1100 for this very large tract of
land—it was in the hills north of the via Tiburtina, just west of the boundary of the
land controlled by Tivoli itself—we find references to houses, and a court case
about Silva Maior in 1124 characterizes it as consisting of five *villae*, two named
casalia, and eight rural churches.[93] By the end of the twelfth century there were
only three *villae*, Monte del Sorbo, Pilo Rotto, and the less important Turricella,
but they were evidently real settlement centres. People are described as being from
them, and in the early thirteenth century they had village territories, here *territorium* or *tenimentum*, in which there are a few signs of more scattered settlement as

[90] ASV, Arm. XXXVII, vol. 8, ff. 364r–9r; cf. Passigli, 'Per una storia', pp. 27–36. I can see no
reason to doubt the authenticity of this text, even though it is unique in format and only survives in a
seventeenth-century transcription. See further *S. Paolo*, n. 1; Adams, 'A history', pp. 271, 269, for
Dragone and Decima.

[91] Claridge, 'A date for the medieval settlement'. For the salt and wood, see below, nn. 200, 229.

[92] Coste, *Scritti di topografia*, pp. 91–132, 269–365; Carocci and Vendittelli, *L'origine della
Campagna Romana*, pp. 41–58.

[93] *SMVL*, n. 123 (a. 1099) refers to a rural *casa*; for 1124, *Bullaire Cal. II*, n. 500.

well. In 1191, a land lease for part of the area required the tenant to live in Pilo Rotto or else the lease would be made void: a standard feature of much of Italy, but a unique requirement in the Agro romano.[94] When in 1201 there was a major court case about Silva Maior and the neighbouring territory of Reatina between S. Ciriaco and S. Paolo fuori le Mura, for which three rolls of witness interrogations survive (they are the best single evidence for the nature of rural society in the Agro romano, even though they date to half a century after the end of our period, and we will return to them), one of the local witnesses refers casually to the discussions, *communiter*, that his father had with other 'elders of his house and community' (*antiquos de domo et vicinia sua*), about S. Ciriaco's rights. This reference to a standard type of village sociability—standard, that is, anywhere else in Italy—puts into relief how much we are missing for the rest of the Agro romano.[95]

Silva Maior was, however, a land clearance zone. Its very name implies it; and, although it was evidently largely cleared (mostly for grain-fields) by the twelfth century, it still had *forestarii* in 1201 who controlled local wood rights, and defended them by force. This may well explain why we find proper villages here: land marked for clearance arguably developed more concentrated forms of settlement, as we have seen on the Ostiense.[96] The 1201 documents are such an attractive and detailed source, as we shall see in the next section, that one could well be tempted to see them as the tip of an iceberg of peasant social action in the Agro romano, which could well have parallels elsewhere too. Nor would I wish to deny that, in part. But it is worth stressing that the other documents for Silva Maior are unusual too; *villae* and rural housing consistently recur in them, as they do not anywhere else. When we use these texts, we have to remain aware of the atypicality of the micro-society that produced them, and cautious about the way we generalize from them.

The zones of the Agro romano with villages in them thus appear exceptional in other ways as well. Some were products of *incastellamento*, which focused settlement on the edge of the Agro and also in one tract along the Aniene. Two were products of large-scale land clearance, which clearly came with different presuppositions about how to order rural territories—but land clearance on this scale is not otherwise attested in our period. And the land around Albano looked to local settlements largely because Albano was an old centre, still technically a *civitas*, though now reduced to the size of a large village, and Ariccia was similar; Porto and

---

[94] The three *villae* are named together in *SMVL*, n. 262 (a. 1199), which also cites their inhabitants, and in the text which begins the 1201 court case over the area, *SMVL*, Baumgärtner, n. 12. For 1191, *SMVL*, n. 237. For *tenimenta*, etc.: e.g. *SMVL*, n. 257 (Monte del Sorbo), *SMVL*, Baumgärtner, n. 33 (Pilo Rotto). Scattered settlement: *SMVL*, n. 250; *SMVL*, Baumgärtner, nn. 33, 70, 98. But references to inhabitants and houses in these *villae* are too many to cite. See Coste, *Scritti di topografia*, pp. 318–24, 345–8; Carocci and Vendittelli, *L'origine della Campagna Romana*, pp. 42–6.

[95] *SMVL*, n. 281, testimony of Crescenzio; the other two rolls are n. 280 and *SMVL*, Baumgärtner, n. 14.

[96] This is the opposite development to that discussed by Toubert, *Les structures*, pp. 339–48, who showed that *incastellamento* in the Sabina and Tiburtino preceded and facilitated land clearance (generally of a fairly small-scale type).

Ostia, too, may have played a similar role, although they were more isolated, between the salt flats and the sea. The great bulk of the Agro romano, the land of long-occupied *fundi*, was not like these. The only other agglomerations we find there are *burgi* along the consular roads looking north (and, in the thirteenth century, looking east as well), which were reception centres for travellers rather than agricultural settlements.[97] Elsewhere, we have to assume settlement; we cannot study it. But the *villae* of Silva Maior prove to us that the Romans of our period knew perfectly well what villages were; it must be the case that they did not see the (presumably) scattered settlement in *fundi* in the same way. That settlement, to the eyes of Roman landholders and notaries, did not ever crystallize into social realities that were worth mentioning, let alone into ordered *villae* with their own customs, gossip networks, or potential political protagonism.

This is also a context for the absence of signorial territories in the Agro romano. Signorial powers are over people; if owners/lessees had so little interest in the peasantry on their lands that they never even mentioned where they lived, then they certainly did not claim political or judicial powers over them. It is no coincidence that it is only in Silva Maior that we ever have references to any form of signorial rights, apart from the fragmentary judicial immunities mentioned earlier (p. 50). The signorial rights held over Silva Maior did not belong to S. Ciriaco, but to the Ottaviani lords of Monticelli (now Montecelio) and Monte Albano, just north of Tivoli in the castle zone. They are very vaguely characterized, as *consuetudines* or *consueta servitia*, and were beyond doubt less important than the cut of S. Ciriaco's rent that the Ottaviani also took. They may have included some labour service and a small death duty of $1/37$, for these are part of the *consuetudo loci* which S. Ciriaco, who had taken over the Ottaviani rights by then, claimed from Pilo Rotto in 1202.[98] They did not, as far as we can see, include private justice, the major signorial perquisite in Lazio in our period. But even these minor rights were exercised over people; and people appear in the Silva Maior documents, as they hardly appear anywhere else. In most of the Agro romano, owners did not seek domination, but only rent, and the peasantry could thus almost completely disappear from our sources.

In the late twelfth century, this pattern would start to change, with the slow beginnings of the agricultural reorganization associated with late medieval *casali*. We will look at this later, at least briefly (pp. 86–8) but it is relevant here to note that these new patterns of estate management were associated with at least some form of settlement focus. 'Towers', *turres*, appear in a sprinkling of documents for the mid- and later twelfth century (the clearest early example is from 1131); exported from the city, where tower-houses first become common two generations earlier, they visibly represent estate-centres for almost the first time in the medieval Agro romano, and a number of them still survive—Daniela Esposito calculates that

---

[97] Carocci and Vendittelli, *L'origine della Campagna Romana*, pp. 35–9.
[98] The rights are referred to extensively in the 1201 witness rolls, above, n. 95; for 1202, *SMVL*, Baumgärtner, n. 24.

25 per cent of surviving towers are from the twelfth century.[99] In this context of *proto-incasalamento*, some other texts from the end of the century and later begin to refer to *sedimina* and other generic housing terms, as also to Salone's 1176 *castellarium*, and once, on the Portuense in 1184, to a *villa* of S. Ciriaco which contained monastic servants and animals.[100] These were not, as far as we can see, settlements for the local peasantry; they were essentially estate-centres. But they could become larger settlements; the wave of new castles built on the outer edge of the Agro romano that is a feature of the thirteenth century, and which also saw a small number of new *villae*, future or ex-castles in each case, do often seem to have been genuine agglomerations.[101] Few of these settlements survived as such; in the late Middle Ages, they became isolated estate-centres again, as the *turres* of the twelfth century doubtless had been, and many of these *casali* still exist. But this whole process points up the novelty of the agrarian reorganization of the mid- to late twelfth.

The peasant economy, and the society of Silva Maior

The huge majority of the inhabitants of the Agro romano were peasants; indeed, they would have outnumbered the inhabitants of the city too, on any normal medieval population projection. But we know almost nothing about them; they are almost invisible in our documentation, and only appear in casual and often ambiguous references. I say 'ambiguous', because there is hardly any identifier that marks out peasant cultivators in our sources without any question. Cultivators were often called *laboratores* or *lavoratores*, but this was a term which at the end of the twelfth century was also used for the elite tenants of early *casali*.[102] In the Porto salt pans, salt workers and salt entrepreneurs also fade seamlessly into each other (below, pp. 100–5), and even in the vineyard belt, where cultivators are slightly more visible, we cannot assume that they included all *quartarini* by any means (below, pp. 92–7). So the best we can do is generalize. Detailed accounts of peasant society can hardly be offered; the only areas with some relatively dense

[99] Up to 1200: *Bullaire Cal. II*, n. 227; *S. Gregorio*, n. 137 (a. 1131); *SMVL*, nn. 157–8; *S. Prassede*, nn. 25, 28; Pflugk, III, n. 142; *S. Sisto*, n. 3; *SMVL*, n. 192; *S. Alessio*, n. 19; *Liberiano*, nn. 21, 22; ASV, A. A. Arm. I–XVIII, 5006, n. 3; *SMCM*, n. 62; *SMVL*, nn. 250, 251; *SMN*, nn. 159, 162; *Regesta Inn. III*, II.94 (102), II.144 (153). See in general Carocci and Vendittelli, *L'origine della Campagna Romana*, pp. 18–20, 69–74, 95–6, and 216–21 (D. Esposito); and Esposito, *Architettura*, pp. 25–63 (p. 62 for the figure).

[100] *Sedimina*: *SMVL*, nn. 246, 247 (cf. 268 for *trulla*) for the Criptule area on the Portuense, n. 251 for Bolagai on the Tiburtina, with 209 for *casae* on the Flaminia; *Liberiano*, n. 21 for Salone; *SMVL*, n. 225, for 1184 (differently interpreted in Carocci and Vendittelli, *L'origine della Campagna Romana*, p. 129, who see it as a village; and it is true that the *puer* who was harmed in an attack on the *villa* could be a child of a peasant family rather than a servant).

[101] Carocci and Vendittelli, *L'origine della Campagna Romana*, pp. 23–33, 56–68 (lists); Maire Vigueur, *L'autre Rome*, pp. 82–6.

[102] *Laboratores* or *laborare* as meaning entrepreneurs (and their work) in the late twelfth century: *SMVL*, nn. 229, 247, 268; *SMN*, n. 160 (and, earlier, e.g. *SMVL*, n. 40; *SMN*, n. 13). References to peasants which I see as certain include *RS*, nn. 129, 93, 86, 106; *SMCM*, n. 2; *SMVL*, nn. 50, 65, 280–1, *SMVL* Baumgärtner, n. 14; *S. Prassede*, nn. 4, 13; *SMN*, nn. 9, 138, 151. See Lenzi, *La terra e il potere*, pp. 83–4 for other examples.

information are, once again, Silva Maior, and a couple of vineyard estates just north of the city which will be discussed in the next section. But we can make some very broad statements about the peasant economy.

Peasants rarely made written leases in the Agro romano. Emphyteuses were (mostly) for aristocrats and other elites, but even *libelli* were almost never visibly for cultivators, and the *locatio* which replaced both in the late eleventh century was not different in that respect. We do have a handful, but they are all unusual in one way or another. The three-generation *libellus* to ten *laboratores* in 963 for a rent in kind by the Roman aristocrat Caloleo was a clear, and early, lease to cultivators, but it was in the Tiburtino: controlled by Rome, but outside the Agro romano. At Isola Farnese, a local inhabitant leased a mill for a grain rent in 989, and the same man seems to have renewed it for the same rent forty years later; this was a miller, not a direct cultivator, but he was almost certainly the worker of the mill, not a middleman. All the same, Isola was a castle, and again just beyond the edge of the Agro.[103] Inside the Agro, it is likely that the three-generation lease from 1139 in which SS. Cosma e Damiano conceded to four cousins a vineyard in Marcelli, which their uncle had previously held as security for a loan of 14 *solidi*, and which was now converted into a lease for an extra 10 *solidi*, was to cultivators; 24 *solidi* was not a trivial sum, but the lease goes out of its way to stress that the tiny annual rent they will owe is not to be regarded as typical, and other *agricole* there should pay their quarter in rent according to their own contracts (*locationes*), and *in suo statu permaneant*, 'keep their own status'. The implication is that this family was one of *agricolae* or *agricoli* as well, that is, cultivators, although this was in a wine zone, not far from the vineyard belt around the city, where cultivator contracts were more common. In 1146, a layman in Boccea (probably a tenant of S. Pietro in Vaticano) leased a site for a mill to a family without rent because they had let him have three horses which he did not want to return; in 1183, an uncle and nephew renounced a lease on the Portuense to S. Ciriaco in return for a small annual pension of barley and wine: these two disparate and atypical contracts are also so small-scale that the tenants may well have been cultivators. In 1177, senators had a record made of the rent in grain due by two men, clearly cultivators, to Rufavelia, a middleman tenant of S. Ciriaco, in an unnamed place (but without doubt in or near Silva Maior), after a dispute—although here there is no sign that the two cultivators had a written lease, and the implication is that they did not. But we are scrabbling for information here; the rest of the time, the world of the written agreement was one for elites, rich or less rich urban entrepreneurs. We can assume, as Mauro Lenzi has argued, that the terms that cultivators held land by were otherwise generally unwritten and customary.[104]

Cultivators were called *laboratores* or *agricoli*; more rarely *coloni*, a more antiquated word which mostly appears in papal bulls; twice, *massari*.[105] They were, as

---

[103] *RS*, n. 93; *SCD*, nn. 12, 33.

[104] ASR SCD, cassetta 16, n. 124; *SPV*, n. 41; *SMVL*, Baumgärtner, n. 5; *Senato*, n. 31 = *SMVL*, n. 210; Lenzi, *La terra e il potere*, pp. 44–7, 113–18.

[105] See above, n. 102 for *laboratores*. For *coloni*: *Papsturkunden*, nn. 22, 77, 92, 134, 419, 569, 598; *S. Alessio*, n. 1; *S. Gregorio*, n. 85; *SMN*, n. 21; *S. Paolo*, n. 1; *PL*, CLXXIX, cols 692–6; CVL, 8044, ff. 4–16. *Massari*: *SCD*, n. 60; *SMVL*, n. 158.

far as we can see, by now all legally free. Outside generic papal confirmations, unfree tenants are by now only attested for the territories of Sutri and Nepi; in the Agro romano itself, *servus* or *famulus* are words that already are coming to mean (free) servant; it is thus apparent that peasant unfreedom, well-documented in the eighth and ninth centuries in the Sabina, had by now become vestigial, and, nearer to Rome, had entirely gone.[106] The *laboratores* and *agricoli* are, however, simply invoked casually; they are sometimes mentioned as the subtenants of the holder of a lease, or, more occasionally, used as a marker for size, like the *terra* of SS. Cosma e Damiano in Tertio on the Portuense which was described as 'as much as a *massaro* holds *ad laborandum*', ceded back to the monastery in 1060—this was the equivalent of a *pedica* (see above, p. 60), which was elsewhere also often held by a named person *ad laborandum*, though here the image was expressed in an unusual phrase.[107] As far as we can guess, peasants simply paid rents in kind; we do not have many details of these rents, but *libelli* were often for rents in kind very early, and it would be unreasonable to propose that peasants were more involved in the market than non-cultivators. The standardization of customary rents in grain is shown by a 1073 lease to a non-cultivator from S. Gregorio sul Celio, for land in Orta Prefecti (now Grotta Perfetta near the Roman suburb of EUR), for the rent of a *modius* of wheat and one of barley 'at the *modius* by which your [the monastery's] *agricoli* pay you'.[108] But there are also clear signs that these standardized rents were normally a quarter of the crop. The term *quarta* is often used as a generic term for the rent paid by cultivators, as at S. Primo on the Prenestina in 1060, or Lubbre (now Prima Porta) on the Flaminia in 1109; and, most significantly, it is sometimes used as a term for rent even when the actual rent paid was explicitly less, or else a fixed quantity.[109] This level of rent, which was, even more clearly, the standard rent paid on vineyards too (below, p. 92), would be high when it was paid by middlemen, but it is relatively low as one paid by cultivators—a third was not uncommon in the grain lands of northern Italy, for example, and a half in vineyards.[110] It is a sign that, throughout our period and beyond, the attraction of the Rome produce market and the involvement in leasing of the city's entrepreneurs did not yet lead to a more 'commercial' attitude to the details of estate management—that would be a feature of the late twelfth century and later, as we shall see.

The ecclesiastical landowner or lay lessee of the land collected the rent by sending a *ministerialis* or *superista*, an agent or bailiff, whom the peasants had to feed when he came. This was described as *victure a vino et a fenum* (for the horses), as a lease of

---

[106] For unfreedom, see in general Toubert, *Les structures*, pp. 510–13; Lenzi, *La terra e il potere*, pp. 84–5. For *servi* and *famuli* around Sutri and Nepi see (among others) *SCD*, nn. 19, 93A; *S. Gregorio*, n. 4; *SMVL*, n. 34. In *RS*, n. 144 and *SMVL*, n. 151 the words clearly denote free men.

[107] *SCD*, n. 60.

[108] *S. Gregorio*, n. 133.

[109] *S. Prassede*, n. 8; *SMVL*, n. 137 (see also below, n. 190); for the term coming to mean any rent, see Lenzi, *La terra e il potere*, pp. 85–7; see further Toubert, *Les structures*, pp. 541–2.

[110] e.g. Fumagalli, *Coloni e signori*, pp, 73–6, with ninth-century data; in Lombardy in the thirteenth century, a quarter of the grain crop was standard, rising to a third of the wine, but rent levels had been higher earlier: Menant, *Campagnes lombardes*, pp. 325–33.

1036 for Lubbre put it; in Albano in 1142, the *superista* and his horse were to be given to eat and drink 'as is the custom of Albano *agricoli*, and to other *superistae* of the Romans'.[111] Peasants were not expected to bring rents into Rome themselves, except occasionally for the Porto salt pans, and the wood-rent owed to the pope from Ostia.[112] This may well indicate that they were normally separated from the city's markets, too. They were kept at arm's length by the landowners and lessees who took their surplus, and only *ministeriales* interacted with them at all regularly. We have so little information about the process that we cannot be entirely sure here, but it certainly looks as if these *ministeriales* were sent directly from Rome, a further sign that there was often no permanent landlordly presence, or any estate-centre, on the land, at least before the reorganization and slow crystallization into *casali* of the later twelfth century. Even bailiffs, then, may not have seen peasants that frequently. Maybe this helped to create an autonomous sociability for each *fundus* or *casale*, given that the peasants so seldom had to do with landlords and their agents; it would be logical to think so; but we have absolutely no evidence of it for the great bulk of the Agro romano, and we cannot assume it.

A little more information about peasant economy and society is available from Silva Maior, and Reatina to its south. Here, several of the witnesses who gave evidence in the 1201 court case were peasants, and they do not obviously show the isolation and silence that is implied by the last couple of paragraphs. The grounds for S. Paolo's claims against the female monastery of S. Ciriaco in Via Lata for Silva Maior and Reatina were derived from the gift to the former monastery of most of his landed property by Giovanni of Monte Albano, who died without heirs at the end of 1199 or shortly after; Giovanni, one of the last Ottaviani (see below, p. 199), had also held half the family's non-proprietorial rights in Silva Maior, though he ceded his half of these to S. Ciriaco on his deathbed, and he also added the pledge he held from his cousin for the other half. S. Ciriaco's task was thus to show that these rights of the Ottaviani had only ever been held by them in *feudum*, as monastic vassals (so, implicitly, they could not have been willed as property to S. Paolo), and that after Giovanni's death they had been formally taken over by S. Ciriaco, thus establishing the latter monastery's rights to claim them. Hence the detailed descriptions of what peasants owed and to whom in the 1201 witnessing, for S. Ciriaco built its case on them. (We do not have S. Paolo's side of the story, but it must have lost; Monte Albano appears in a papal confirmation for the latter monastery in 1203, but not Silva Maior and Reatina.[113])

The core of the Ottaviani rights was rent; they took one-fifth of the produce of Reatina (the property most discussed in the case), whereas S. Ciriaco only took one-sixteenth until Giovanni's death. This totals just over a quarter, which seems from

---

[111] *SMVL*, n. 65; *SMN*, n. 54 (see below, p. 98).

[112] See *SMCM*, nn. 27, 30; *SMVL*, nn. 175–6 for rare examples; below, pp. 103, 106 for Porto and Ostia.

[113] For Giovanni's gift, *SMVL*, nn. 261–2; for S. Paolo's claim, *SMVL*, Baumgärtner, n. 12; for the witnessing, *SMVL*, nn. 280–1 and *SMVL*, Baumgärtner, n. 14; for the 1203 S. Paolo bull, *Regesta Inn. III*, VI.88. See in general, for the 1201 cases and their context, Carocci and Vendittelli, *L'origine della Campagna Romana*, pp. 41–52.

these texts to have been the standard peasant payment, on grain land in this case, as elsewhere in the Agro romano. The Ottaviani and S. Ciriaco collected this together from the *laboratores* who worked the land, the *ministri* and *milites/scutiferi* of Giovanni of Monte Albano collecting together with the *nuntii* and *vicecomites* of the nuns—except when either Giovanni or S. Ciriaco pledged out their rights to creditors, when the latters' *nuntii* took their place.[114] The formal procedure seems to have respected S. Ciriaco's rights over both payments, before the Ottaviani took the bigger cut. Although this might have been S. Ciriaco's deliberate spin in a court case context, we have a pledge by the nuns for Reatina's rents from 1186 (it was paid back in 1201 with money left by Giovanni of Monte Albano) which simply refers to the Ottaviani as the people who 'work' (*laborant*) the land.[115] It is likely that the case concentrated on Reatina because it was only there that rents were taken directly by the area's two lords; the lands of the *villae* of Silva Maior, by contrast, were largely leased out in standard contracts to non-cultivating middle-men.[116] Reatina seems to have been only recently cleared, and also seems not to have had any permanent settlement. Its cultivators came from the *villae* of Silva Maior or else from Lunghezza just across the River Aniene, both of them (just) close enough to make such cultivation feasible. None of the witnesses who said they worked there claimed to have cultivated there for more than a short time, however; Reatina was in some ways a small frontier or colonial zone, without permanent commitment from a peasant population, perhaps similar to the underexploited *demani* of southern Italy, which peasants cultivated when and where they chose, paying a fixed partiary rent. But it was all the same, as an area of direct management, profitable for its lords, particularly the Ottaviani, until S. Ciriaco leased it out as a proto-*casale* in 1210, for a sizeable rent.[117]

The social picture the witnesses presented of Silva Maior and Reatina was of a society with stable rules, reinforced by recognized rituals (when S. Ciriaco took over the Ottaviani rights in 1200, the monastic *yconomus* or economic manager came in person to plough in public there), although also underpinned by violence.[118] One of the most detailed witnesses, Bentivoglio, when asked about the other signorial rights that S. Paolo claimed the Ottaviani had had in Silva Maior, labour services and recognitive gifts, said that he knew nothing about such rights, but, since the lords were *viri potentes*, they indeed sometimes *violenter extorquebant* goods from

---

[114] See *SMVL*, nn. 280–1 and *SMVL*, Baumgärtner, n. 14, *passim*. (For *SMVL*, Baumgärtner, n. 14, I was able to use Jean Coste's photograph of the original, BAV, Fondo S. Maria in Via Lata, varia 1–150, perg. 133, through the kindness of Susanna Passigli, during the period of closure of BAV in 2007–10; I thank her equally for texts of several of the other Latin documents which lie behind Ingrid Baumgärtner's summaries in German.) Note *SMVL*, n. 177 for a *quartarinus* in Monte del Sorbo in 1151.

[115] *SMVL*, n. 229; *SMVL*, Baumgärtner, n. 10.

[116] e.g. *SMVL*, nn. 190, 249–50.

[117] *SMVL*, Baumgärtner, n. 71. Reatina did have one church in it, S. Sinforosa, which had been there since at least 1124: *Bullaire Cal. II*, n. 500. For southern Italian *demani*, see Carocci, '"Metodo regressivo" e possessi collettivi'.

[118] Ploughing: *SMVL*, n. 280, *SMVL*, Baumgärtner, n. 14, testimony of Bentivoglio, Bartolomeo, Giovanni *Rubeus*, Giovanni Agmelli.

people, *sicut potentiores consueverunt a debilioribus extorquere*, 'as the more powerful were accustomed to extort from the weaker'. They had tried to extort a cow from him, but he himself could fight them off, *quia potens erat*, 'since he [himself] was powerful'.[119] Bentivoglio was here seeking to argue that if such dues were ever exacted by the lords, they were 'violent', that is illegal, rather than being a demonstration of the Ottaviani's and thus S. Paolo's legal rights. All the same, as an image of ad hoc rural oppression, this is as clear as we get in our period, even if it needs to be stressed again that the Ottaviani, however oppressive in casual ways, did not actually take very much in signorial dues.

Bentivoglio is also important because he shows an unexpected flexibility in the society of Silva Maior: he may have been a local *potens* in the 1190s, but he remembered back into the 1160s, and as a boy (*parvulus*) he used to work in Reatina *tamquam cultor*, as a cultivator, and paid his rent like other *laboratores*. Being a local *potens* probably meant that he was by now a local middleman for S. Ciriaco, collecting rent from the real cultivators on the basis of his own written lease; we do not have such leases for him, but he was a local monastic representative in 1181, and an occasional member of S. Ciriaco's witnessing group, including in the city.[120] Viviano of Pilo Rotto—evidence for whose leases does survive, so we know him to have been such a middleman—in his witnessing said that he too had worked in Reatina once, when there was a 'great famine', which evidently had forced him to take, and work, extra land to survive.[121] It looks as if it was possible to start as a cultivator, or be one part-time, but end up as a non-cultivating middle-man: for Viviano's leased lands were very substantial by 1200 or so. Silva Maior's lands were largely in the hands of Roman lessees (below, pp. 284–90), but there were several other locals like Bentivoglio and Viviano who were significant players in the area, such as Giovanni *Rubeus*, another 1201 witness, who had a substantial lease in the 1190s–1220s, or the Metones family, who leased all across Silva Maior, and had had a run-in with S. Ciriaco some time in the 1180s.[122] Any of these could have started out as a cultivator, or have been one in their youth before their father died, or have had less successful relatives who still were. Here, at least, there was no unbreakable barrier between *cultor* and *potens*.

This is a pattern that is not uncommon throughout Italy. There are, however, grounds for thinking that, in the context of the Agro romano, it might have been specific to Silva Maior. This was as we have seen, with Albano, the only well-documented zone with a real village society, and thus a plausible context for people both staying put locally and rising socially. The unpopulated lands of Reatina also

[119] *SMVL*, n. 280.

[120] *SMVL*, nn. 215 (a. 1181), 221, 276, *SMVL*, Baumgärtner, n. 7; he held land on the boundary of the land documented in *SMVL*, n. 249.

[121] *SMVL*, n. 281 for Viviano's witnessing; for Viviano's leasing, see *SMVL*, Baumgärtner, nn. 16, 21–2, 33, and Carocci and Vendittelli, *L'origine della Campagna Romana*, pp. 47–8.

[122] Giovanni: *SMVL*, Baumgärtner, n. 14 (witness), *SMVL*, nn. 249, 254, *SMVL*, Baumgärtner, nn. 17, 93, 125; Metones: *SMVL*, nn. 249–50, 254, 257, 280 (referring to earlier violent disputes, *controversias seu imbrigamenta*, between S. Ciriaco and the family), *SMVL*, Baumgärtner, nn. 25, 47, 94, etc.

gave unusual opportunities for locals who were, for whatever reason, temporarily short of resources. It is hard to see how it could have worked in places like Marcelli, with its invisible housing, or Campo di Merlo down the Portuense on the Tiber, whose leasehold middlemen were so firmly associated with the rising 'medium elites' of the city (see below, p. 83); the mechanisms for peasants rising socially there were not in place. But it is also worth remembering that the city will always have been a great magnet for migration. Every medieval city depended on immigration even to keep its population stable, and Rome's was expanding in this period, particularly after the 1130s (see Chapter 3); a high proportion of that immigration must have been from the Agro romano. A Bentivoglio from Marcelli or Campo di Merlo could simply have gone into the city as a late adolescent, and then, if he made it, have re-emerged as a local middleman in later life, but now from an urban, not a rural, base. We cannot track this, and it must have been rare, but it is a legitimate hypothesis. It does something to reduce the social distance between the Roman and the local entrepreneurs in Silva Maior, too, for it is very easy to imagine circumstances in which some of each had similar origins. The simple proximity of the city must have given more opportunity to the peasant society of the Agro romano than we can normally see in any of our documents, apart from the 1201 witness rolls.

If Reatina had no stable inhabitants, we might imagine that it was worked at least in part by wage labour, hired in by the year by S. Ciriaco and the Ottaviani; this would fit the temporary cultivation claimed by the 1201 witnesses, and, given the dominance of temporary salaried labour in late medieval and modern *casali* as we have seen, far greater than in most of Italy, it is worth wondering here again whether it had begun already. But the witnesses in 1201 were unanimous that they only paid rent, in a context in which it would have been natural to mention wages had they ever been given any. Similarly, a detailed document of 1202, in which Viviano's former *tenimentum* in Pilo Rotto was leased to a family of city dealers, simply describes a set of rents (and also labour service, apparently part of the Ottaviani signorial package). Anyway, even later, in all the documents of the thirteenth century, Carocci and Vendittelli have only found one reference to wage labour, from 1255. They see this, doubtless correctly, as the tip of an iceberg, for the world of salaried labour hardly gets a mention even in notarial registers, let alone the single-sheet parchments which are so far our only source.[123] But I am convinced by its absence in the 1201 text; I conclude that wage labour had not yet begun to be a presence in Rome around 1200, and still less, presumably, in 1150. It is part of later, highly market-orientated, developments. We cannot prove this, and indeed can prove almost no statement about the Roman peasantry beyond reasonable doubt, given the paucity of the evidence; but I can see no reason to doubt it.

---

[123] SMVL, Baumgärtner, n. 24 (a. 1202); Carocci and Vendittelli, *L'origine della Campagna Romana*, p. 184; cf. also Carocci, *Tivoli*, p. 450.

Estate management

By contrast, we can say something about how Roman landowners managed their estates, for this is what our leases explicitly tell us about. Mauro Lenzi has worked most fully on this subject, and I base myself quite largely on his detailed treatment. He shows very clearly the difference before *c.*1050 between the emphyteusis (often called a *conductio* in our texts) and the *libellus*, and how in the dissolution of formularies of the late eleventh century both ended up replaced by a more generic *locatio*, which took elements from each but was by no means the same.[124] All these forms of written lease were, as we have seen, above all contracts between churches and non-cultivators: aristocrats and members of Rome's 'medium elite', and indeed some entrepreneurial artisans. How these leaseholders then ran their holdings is far less clear, for this takes us into the obscurities of the peasant economy, just sketched out. But it is of some use to see how the lay elites took their own leases all the same, for this certainly had an impact on the economy of the city as a whole.

The emphyteutic lease was, as we have seen, of extremely long standing, and its (rather wordy) formulary scarcely changed until the last such contract known, in 1065. It was essentially a three-generation concession for a very low rent, only a few *denarii* in most cases. It was often for a large tract of land, a whole estate in effect, and in the tenth century the typical lessee was an urban aristocrat or other relatively high-status figure, a *consul et dux* or *vir magnificus* (in the eleventh century, as we have seen, lessees were often less prominent). It gave full rights of possession in the technical Roman-law sense, and nearly full rights of alienation.[125] In the Agro romano, it is the commonest form of surviving lease, into the mid-eleventh century. What was it for? It has tended to be assumed that such leases had an exclusively political function, given that they were so unremunerative for churches: they created a network of powerful clients, which the church or monastery would need in order to navigate the dangers of urban power politics. And there must have been a strong element of that, of course. But it creates a problem, all the same; several, in fact. If a church ceded the great bulk of its land out for almost no rent, how did it get any usable resources? Why choose such an unremunerative arrangement for so long (especially as it was not the only contract available before 1050)? What use would political support be if one's economic situation was already so parlous? Why, if emphyteuses produced so little, did churches bother to seek, largely successfully, to hold on to them? And, although it is fairly straightforward to see how a *consul et dux* could be politically useful, what political use would have been—to take an example at random—Giovanni *vir honestus* di Gianna, who leased a *casale* and other land in the *fundus* Palmi on the Portuense from SS. Cosma e Damiano, for three lives at a rent of 4 *denarii* per year, in 1003, who was probably from the 'medium elite' or artisan stratum of Trastevere like most of that

---

[124] See Lenzi, *La terra e il potere, passim*.

[125] See Lenzi, *La terra e il potere*, pp. 48–66, for a full analysis; also Theisen, *Studien zur Emphyteuse*, pp. 220–73 (note also pp. 13–24, for classical Roman law being uncertain about whether emphyteuses carried possessory rights; but *RS*, n. 112, in particular, makes the latter explicit for our period). For 1065, *SMVL*, n. 93.

monastery's other clients?[126] This is certainly a way for a monastery to build up a clientele, but it is a very expensive one.

Emphyteuses in the Sabina were not given out free; they included *entraturae* or entry-fines, payments the tenant made to enter the lease, which could often be substantial.[127] *Libelli* in the Agro romano, if they were not for substantial rents, had a sizeable entry-fine as well. As we shall see, this became normal in the twelfth century for every kind of lease. There are also occasional signs of entry-fines in the context of emphyteutic contracts, when we have supporting documents. In 992, S. Gregorio sul Celio made an emphyteutic lease for three lives to Gregorio *presbiter* and *medicus* of part of one of the monastery's big estates down the Appia, at Moreni, for a standard and low 5-*denarii* annual rent. On the same day the same transaction was repeated, but this time was *libellario nomine* for twenty-nine years only, and for an entry fine of six pounds of silver, a very substantial sum. Two Subiaco leases from 1035 to Salomone, a city smith (*malleator*), for the same land at Prata Decii just south of the Aurelian walls, are a close parallel: one is a normal emphyteusis, for a 4-*denarii* rent for three lives; the other is a *libellus* for twenty-nine years, for the same rent, but adding a *libellaticos* (an entry-fine) 'for this *libellus* and for the *chartam enphitheuseos*' of five pounds of silver, which is payable again at the renewal of the *libellus*. These two doublets are sufficiently similar in their terms, well before the breakdown in formulae which came after the mid-eleventh century, that they give us the clue here: Gregorio and Salomone wanted the stability of the emphyteusis, but the monasteries wanted the money. But it is also clear that the formulae of an emphyteusis, unchanged as they had been for a long time, could hide a substantial pay-off, and if we had only had the first document we would never know it.[128] These texts seem to me most plausibly interpreted as the tip of an iceberg of rather more remunerative leasing. It is less clear whether having a three-life emphyteusis as a cover for a renewable *libellus*, as in these two cases, was normal, and perhaps it was not: an easier recourse would simply have been to require a larger lump sum at the beginning of the three-life lease, which would be equally hidden because the formulary of the charter of emphyteusis in Rome had no provision for it. This would have been what negotiation would have been over, with the political advantages of the lease relationship traded off against the economic needs of both lessor and lessee, in variable ways. The result would have been a somewhat irregular resource for churches, with big sums coming in only every three generations (or every twenty-nine years), but at least it would mean that landlords could make real economic calculations about how to use their land.

---

[126] *SCD*, n. 20; cf. Lenzi, *La terra e il potere*, pp. 59–60n; see below, pp. 278–82 for Trastevere and SS. Cosma e Damiano.

[127] Toubert, *Les structures*, pp. 521–33; Lenzi, *La terra e il potere*, p. 56, notes however that the *entraturae* are not cited for Roman lessees in the Sabina.

[128] *S. Gregorio*, nn. 128–9; *RS*, nn. 98–9; a parallel is *SMVL*, n. 75, which is a *libellus* for 29 years, but which says that the huge entry-fine of £27 is *pro hunc libellum et uno empfiteussis chartae*—this is presumably the same sort of double contract, with the emphyteusis not surviving. See for these texts and a few others Lenzi, *La terra e il potere*, pp. 21–2, though he interprets them differently, and also p. 55 for hidden sales.

The *libellus* itself is an easier contract to interpret, for here the entry-fine (regularly called *libellaticum*) was always present in normal leases; if the rent was low, the entry-fine was high, and vice versa.[129] There were not huge numbers of them for the Agro romano (they were more often a lease for vineyards, salt pans, and city property), but we have a certain number, starting to be numerous around 1020, and continuing up to the decline of the contract in the later eleventh century. They largely reflect the growing division of the *fundi* of the Agro into *pedicae* and other relatively small units, which not only shows the breakdown of the *fundus*, but also, in some places at least, the concern of churches to exploit its sections more tightly, in nineteen-year or twenty-nine-year leases with more regular rents and *libellatica*. The tenants were generally non-aristocratic but prosperous Romans, including some artisans and *negotiatores*, who were presumably putting their profits into rural land; quite a number of such contracts involved small-scale investment, to turn marshes into agricultural land or grain-fields into meadows.[130] These interventions only begin to get into our documentation in the early eleventh century, and probably reflect a growing church (and non-aristocratic lay) interest in the urban produce market; but that market, as we shall see, had always been there, and always been strong. A concern for exactness marks many of our contracts. From the 1030s, this was reflected among other things by the appearance of a clause that allowed tenants not to pay rent if they were affected by the 'three *plagae*' (as it says in some texts, but there were sometimes four, or two): hail, attacks of mice or rats (*sorices*), and the (plundering of the) royal army. Army plundering would continue to be an image in our texts, and by 1165 it was differentiated, with imperial, papal, and communal armies invoked. Either way, however, this sort of provision appeared early in Rome, and marks once again an interest in precision which goes with an interest in profit.[131]

We have already seen that rural estate-centres are rarely documented in the Agro romano. It is possible that they had long been uncommon. *Domuscultae* had them in the eighth century, and one has been excavated: it shows a church and a substantial set of outbuildings, presumably largely for the storage of products. But *domuscultae* were, as noted earlier (p. 55), exceptional. They seem in fact to have been manors, of a north Italian type, with a demesne cultivated by labour-service and tenures, a highly organized estate structure that is to say.[132] That structure certainly did not survive into our period. We only have a couple of references to labour-service (*opera*) in all the documents for our period, from the early eleventh century (the next citations are not until the late twelfth), and the

---

129 Lenzi, *La terra e il potere*, pp. 31–40.

130 The first surviving *libelli* for the grain-lands of the Agro romano are *S. Gregorio*, n. 128, just cited; *SMVL*, n. 40 (a. 1018). Investment: e.g. *SMVL*, n. 50 (a. 1025). One explicit, though late, example is the *expendium agri* in *SMCM*, n. 46 (a. 1154).

131 The first example is *SMVL*, n. 63B (a. 1035); for 1165, *S. Sil.*, n. 28. See Lenzi, *La terra e il potere*, pp. 27–8; cf. for Lucca, where such clauses are rare before the twelfth century, Wickham, *Community and Clientele*, p. 20.

132 Christie, *Three South Etrurian Churches*, pp. 175–86; Wickham, 'Historical and topographical notes', pp. 173–7; Marazzi, *I 'patrimonia sanctae Romanae ecclesiae'*, pp. 235–66 is more cautious.

labour required was simply a week's ploughing, a symbolic due; and no references exist to demesnes.[133] The easy divisibility of *fundi/casalia* into smaller *casalia* of the same structure, or into tenant holdings, also indicates a relatively inorganic estate structure; presumably, most estates just consisted of a set of leased peasant tenures. It is in this context that it was possible to do without estate-centres, with rents just going straight into Rome.

Only in a handful of cases do we seem to see more than this: in particular, where estates were associated with a rural church or monastery. S. Primo on the Prenestina was one, a monastic foundation of 1030 which perhaps gained material force because it was on the site of the ancient and abandoned city of Gabii; by 1060, no longer a monastery but still a church, its *clausura maiore* was the focus for at least eight *pedicae* of land, and the church had at least a limited capacity (*secundum possibilitatem loci*) for the reception of the representatives of its proprietor, S. Giovanni a Porta Latina.[134] Other examples were S. Natolia on the Isola Sacra at the Tiber mouth in 936; S. Cornelio, a rural monastery just outside the Agro romano on the site of the former *domusculta* Capracorum, in 1041; and the *curtis* Galeria with the church of S. Maria and associated 'rooms' (*caminatis, cubiculis*) in 1018, that too the site of a former *domusculta*. S. Cornelio was an autonomous rural monastery with an independent history up to 1188, so it, at least—unusually—will have operated as a real economic focus in its territory.[135] S. Primo already by 1060 was no longer autonomous, and it is far from clear that it still acted as an active estate-centre; by 1135, the monastery of Grottaferrata, which held part of it in emphyteusis, was leasing land directly inside its bounds with no reference to the church. It was, however, reconstituted as an estate by a third ecclesiastical landlord, S. Prassede, between 1148 and 1187, and is from then on sometimes called a *tenimentum* (S. Prassede even put a castle there by 1225)—it is in fact a prime example of an early *casale* of late medieval type, and the unity of that *casale* had hardly been broken up since 1030.[136] We might expect to see parallels to this sort of continuity in other ex-*fundi* with churches. But, to reiterate, rural churches are not so very common in the Agro romano, and most estates were, as it would appear, not much more than groups of tenures paying rent directly to Rome. Only the long-standing coherence of church landowning prevented them from complete break-up.

Twelfth-century leases were different again. In the Agro romano almost none were for nineteen or twenty-nine years (only S. Ciriaco in Via Lata used them at all,

---

[133] Labour-service: *SMVL*, n. 57 (a. 1030—a unique text, however; see below, pp. 89–91); *SMN*, n. 9 (a. 1038); it begins again with *SMVL*, n. 209 (a. 1175), S. Cecilia, nn. 1–2 (a. 1184).

[134] *S. Prassede*, nn. 5, 8 (recent fieldwork and excavation at Gabii by a team led by Nicola Terrenato has not so far shown anything medieval there in its *Fasti* interim reports: <http://www.fastionline.org/micro_view.php?)item_key=fst_cd&fst_cd=AIAC_2234>, accessed 7 February 2012).

[135] For S. Natolia, *SPV*, n. 3; for S. Cornelio, *SCD*, n. 45 (for the excavation, Christie, *Three South Etrurian Churches*, pp. 188–99; for S. Cornelio references, Wickham, 'Historical and topographical notes', p. 177); for Galeria, *Papsturkunden*, n. 522 (cf. *LP*, I, p. 502, and Marazzi, *I 'patrimonia sanctae Romanae ecclesiae'*, pp. 252–3, 262; de Francesco, *La proprietà fondiaria nel Lazio*, pp. 263–9). Lenzi, *La terra e il potere*, pp. 77–83, gives other examples.

[136] *S. Prassede*, nn. 18, 21, 24, 26, 34 (*tenimentum*), 40, 41, 58 (a. 1225).

in fact); they were either for two lives or, increasingly, perpetual.[137] Lessees still tended to be middling figures from Rome, as far as we can tell. The new *locationes* had substantial entry-fines, or else, as with *libelli*, high rents, in money and in kind, or often both.[138] When formularies change as much as they did in the late eleventh century, bringing substantially different forms of tenure with this change, however strong the pressure from tenants, the new forms must have also reflected what landlords could live with; and it is therefore significant that high entry-fines, long leases, and low rents remained an acceptable economic model for them. This in my view supports the reasoning set out earlier about the hidden payments behind emphyteuses. But we are now in a period in which proprietors could no longer be sure that they could keep full control over long-term leases, and it is therefore also interesting that entry-fines are often, from around 1100 onwards, called *pretium*, 'price' (an early example of such a lease even calls itself a 'sale').[139] The logic here is that, if everything went wrong, if the *locatio* ended up too like a sale, as Alexander III put it (above, p. 59), then the owner had at least got a substantial price for it.

The other extra payment that proprietors got was the *comminus*, a word that first appears in 1092 in the city (1103 in the grain-lands), though the practice goes back over half a century. This was the money due to the owner when the land was sold by its tenant to a third party, who would take over the tenure. It was specified carefully in nearly all twelfth-century leases, and, in our numerous lay alienations in the century, it is often explicitly paid. In a world of an active land-market, this was not an insignificant resource for owners (30 *denarii* was a common figure); and it helped to focus their attention on keeping hold of their lands.[140]

There is another consequence of the developed logic of the high entry-fine and the low rent: this is that leases became more similar to pledges. Pierre Toubert first noticed this. Loans of money in return for the temporary possession of the land until the pledge is repaid are, like *locationes*, new in our documentation in the late eleventh century. They were generally long-term and stable contracts; the interest on the loan was simply, and often explicitly, seen as the fruits that could be taken by the creditor from the land. (Shorter-term and more obviously 'commercial' pledges are only common in our surviving documentation after about 1170.)[141] Pledges, like entry-fines in leases, provided capital for churches and monasteries; and they were redeemable at the will of the ecclesiastical debtor, unlike the process of buying back leases, which required the consent of the lessee. Pledges therefore had some advantages for churches, as long as the initial lump sum was the most important economic benefit to the proprietor, for pledges of course did not involve the rent

---

[137] See in general Lenzi, *La terra e il potere*, pp. 108, 119. S. Ciriaco short-term leases: *SMVL*, nn. 165, 188, 209, 226, 259.

[138] Lenzi, *La terra e il potere*, pp. 109, 120–3, 127–30.

[139] *SCD*, n. 87 (a. 1079) for the lease/sale (see Lenzi, *La terra e il potere*, p. 124); but the real beginning of the frequent usage of *pretium* in the Agro romano is with *SMVL*, n. 134 (a. 1106).

[140] First explicit reference: *SMN*, n. 29; ASR, SCD, cassetta 16, n. 104 for 1103; first example of the practice: *SCD*, n. 51 (a. 1047); see Lenzi, *La terra e il potere*, pp. 17–18n, 51, 111, 122.

[141] Toubert, *Les structures*, pp. 608–12; pp. 612–19 for shorter-term pledges. First clear examples in Rome: *SPV*, n. 27 (a. 1083); *SMVL*, nn. 126 (a. 1102), 129 (a. 1104), 145 (a. 1116); and the undated but late eleventh-century *SMN*, n. 169.

that leases guaranteed. It would be impossible to imagine that churches could base any form of long-term economic strategy on pledges, but as a short-term expedient they could be useful, and were demonstrably popular; they gave added flexibility to landowners, and were often mixed together with leases with some detachment.

An example may make this point clearer. At the start of the dealings of S. Ciriaco in Via Lata in 1135–8 with a certain Grisotto di Ingizello (he seems to have been a 'medium-elite' dealer from Trastevere) over lands in Campo di Merlo on the Portuense, Grisotto was a monastic creditor, holding nine *pedicae* of land in pledge for £26; in 1138 the monastery redeemed all nine, and pledged three back to Giovanni Sarraceno, a nephew of Pope Innocent II. As for the other six, S. Ciriaco leased them back to Grisotto in 1140, in a lease which in 1148 it could prove in court to be phony, a defence against the acquisitiveness of Innocent and his nephews, so S. Ciriaco got the lease reversed. In 1149, however, it re-leased the same land to Grisotto's son for life, this time for a substantial rent (15 *solidi* and 12 *modia* of grain per year), and after Grisotto died in the same year it renewed another lease to his son for the same rent, but now including a large entry-fine of £10, nearly as much as the pledge (of £12) on the same lands twelve years earlier. These documents are well known, because of the complexity of the long-drawn-out court cases between S. Ciriaco and the *filii Grisotti*, which went on for another half-century; but they point up the similarity between pledges and leases. Grisotto moved easily from one to the other, for sums of money that were pretty similar. The monastery would of course have preferred to keep his fat rent of 1149, but the family often did not pay it; and when Grisotto was a creditor, he could be removed from the land at will, whereas as a lessee this was a long and often difficult process.[142] S. Ciriaco anyway resorted to pledging away land very frequently, elsewhere as well, in the twelfth century, and seems not to have lost out in so doing. The monastery's large estate of Bolagai, next door to Silva Maior, was another which was as much exploited through pledges as through leasing in this period.[143] Pledges were more dangerous if churches ran into systemic debt, which many did in the later twelfth century, for they were harder to redeem. S. Ciriaco itself faced a considerable debt crisis in the 1180s (in large part as a result of the expense of the Campo di Merlo disputes), and the pledges it engaged in then, often simply to find the money to pay off other pledges, came to include higher percentages of monastic land, which was clearly a risk.[144] But S. Ciriaco always had enough land to get rents from some estates and capital from others. It did not lose control of either Campo di Merlo or Bolagai in this period, and, as far as can be seen, had no less land in 1200 than in 1100.

---

[142] *SMVL*, nn. 160–2, 172, 175, 176 are the texts up to 1149; after that, the major ones are 178, 194, 216, 225 with 228 (= *Senato*, nn. 34–40), 258, 266, *SMVL*, Baumgärtner, n. 66. See for commentary Carocci and Vendittelli, *L'origine della Campagna Romana*, pp. 127–30; Wickham, 'Getting justice', pp. 108–11; Wickham, 'La struttura', pp. 203–5.

[143] Pledges; *SMVL*, nn. 145, 208, 227, 227A, 251; leases; 123, 134, 180, 212, 255. Cf. ASR, SCD, cassetta 16, n. 124 (a. 1139), for Marcelli on the Portuense, which shows a pledge being turned directly into a lease.

[144] *SMVL*, nn. 227, 227A, 229, 242, 244–5, 251.

Given that we know so little about what and how the actual cultivators of land paid, our extensive information about leasing and its changes may seem simply to be about games-playing, over how global rural surplus should best be divided up. The absence of information about cultivators might be thought to imply that owners and lessees were not very interested in maximizing the profits from agriculture that come with closer control over cultivation; but it is worth remembering that we do not know much more about the details of surplus extraction on late medieval *casali* either, and they certainly saw considerable, focused, investment[145]—cultivators, as noted in the previous section, were simply outside the arena of formal agreements expressed in writing. On the other hand, if, as seems likely, standard expectations of rents from cultivators in our period were a quarter of the crop, they were not as high as peasants could pay. The essential point, it seems to me, is that nearly all the surplus from the Agro romano, and much from beyond it, flowed straight to Rome in every period. This direction for the surplus of some 1500 km^2 (including salt pans and vineyards) meant that the agricultural products coming gratis into the city were so enormous in scale that proprietors and lessees in our period could afford not to exploit the peasantry as tightly as was theoretically possible. We can also presume that a high proportion of the goods were destined for the produce markets of the city, for urban demand remained very high, as we shall see in Chapter 3, and to that had to be added the food necessary to feed the pilgrim quarter between S. Pietro and Castel S. Angelo (see below, pp. 137–40). The issue was, therefore, who got that surplus, and thus the opportunity to sell it (or, of course, consume it directly), and on what terms. This is what the history of the forms of leasing in our period tells us most about.

Before 1050, from the standpoint of proprietors, the choice was between emphyteuses and *libelli*. In the tenth century (and probably earlier), when lessees were above all aristocrats, the strategic advantage of ecclesiastical landowners was probably less than it was later, for their ability to choose whom to lease to was more limited; the eleventh century, which saw a much larger array of lessees from the artisanal stratum of Rome, must have given more power to proprietors, for by now they had more flexibility, and their lessees were less routinely powerful—even if Roman citizens from the 'medium elite' were not always straightforward to manipulate either, as the *filii Grisotti* show. Emphyteuses were for money, and, even if they involved hidden entry-fines, were still for money. Their lessees thus got all the surplus produce from the land, and must have sold it directly, after taking out the food needed to support households large or small. In the case of *libelli*, churches still got a substantial amount of money (particularly in entry-fines), but produce too, for rents in kind appeared early in Roman *libelli*. Here, it is less clear who used the market most, for rents in kind will have been partly used to feed ecclesiastical establishments, but it is likely that both proprietors and lessees sold some of the surplus on. The only alternative to emphyteuses and *libelli* that was theoretically available, that is to say the direct management of estates, with proprietors leasing

---

[145] See for the thirteenth century Carocci and Vendittelli, *L'origine della Campagna Romana*, pp. 69–92, 135–47, for investment in buildings.

directly to cultivators and taking all the rent, was hardly exercised in Rome, except at Reatina, as we have seen, and on some vineyard estates (see below, pp. 92–6). This option was perfectly common on church estates elsewhere in Europe; but elsewhere in Europe aristocrats owned their own land too, and were not dependent on ecclesiastical proprietors for all their resources. When the popes had tried direct management on a larger scale on their *domuscultae*, they had faced a serious backlash.

Given the geographical restriction of *libelli* to, for the most part, the vineyard belt, we can divide out the effective market involvement of ecclesiastical proprietors and lay lessees in terms of types of produce. Lay lessees must have controlled the grain supply of Rome, for the grain-lands of Agro romano were mostly leased by emphyteusis. Wine, fruit, vegetables, and oil from orchards, and salt, which were leased by *libellus*, were divided between ecclesiastical owners and lay *libellarii*. It is less clear who profited from wood, for it is never the subject of leases; there are hints that profit may even have gone to the local inhabitants of woodland areas, notably the coastal lands running north and south from Ostia and parts of Silva Maior; but church owners took their cut here in *silvaticum*.[146] The major absentee is any information about animals. There were some specialized meadow-lands around the city, such as Prata Papi just south of Trastevere, which could plausibly be seen as an area where incoming animals were fattened up for the city markets; and pigs were certainly run in the coastal woodlands.[147] But there are no documented areas of open pasture-land in the Agro romano, apart from the fallow lands and occasional tracts of temporarily unused land that are part of any agricultural economy; and, although animals will certainly have been run on the fallow at least, they were not required in rent. The pastoral specialization of much of the late medieval Agro romano is, in fact, invisible in our period; and I think we must conclude that animals were often brought into the city from rather further out, from the higher lands of northern Lazio, the Sabina and Tiburtino, and indeed the Appennines. This is important for our understanding of the economy of Rome and its region; we certainly know enough about the Agro romano as a whole to be sure that our sources are not misleading us here. The Agro was grain-land, above all. Indeed, it became still more so as a result of the small amount of documented land clearance we have for the twelfth century, when Silva Maior was mostly turned to agricultural land by the first half of the century, and then Reatina was cleared by, probably, *c*.1160, these being the last documented areas of woodland apart from the coastal strip.[148] As we shall

---

[146] *S. Gregorio*, n. 20; ASV, Arm. XXXVII, t. 8, ff. 364r–9r; *LC*, n. 117; *SMVL*, n. 280.

[147] *RS*, nn. 39, 52–3; *S. Alessio*, n. 5; *Bullaire Cal. II*, n. 227 (all for Prata Papi); ASV, Arm. XXXVII, t. 8, ff. 364r–9r (the coast); see also *SPV*, n. 39 (a. 1144) for a *societas* for *vaccae* in Boccea, a unique reference in this period.

[148] Silva Maior seems largely agrarian by the time of *Bullaire Cal. II*, n. 500 (a. 1124) and *SMVL*, nn. 157–8 (a. 1134); Reatina does not appear in our sources until *SMVL*, nn. 192 (a. 1161, still unnamed) and 229 (a. 1186). They could, of course, both have been cleared earlier, but the huge size of the block of land S. Ciriaco got here, probably from the Tuscolano popes (Wickham, 'La struttura', pp. 210–15), plausibly indicates that it was uncultivated into the eleventh century at least. There was also woodland along the Tiber, up the Salaria north of Rome (*SMVL*, n. 143), but it is hardly

see (pp. 144–5), the archaeology of Rome shows that the animal bones found in the city in our period are principally of pigs and sheep, rather than cattle. Pigs could be bred in the city itself, and otherwise, as just noted, in the coastal woodlands; it was probably above all sheep (and their wool) which were brought in from further away, with cattle imports relatively unimportant—they will have been used for traction in the fields (this we can certainly show) rather than for selling in the city.

After 1050, as we have seen, all forms of lease changed, which means that proprietors had a chance to reshape them in ways that suited them best (as long as they could get lessees on those terms). The risks of losing property rights slowly grew as well; but, as we have seen, long-term leases did not by any means become less common, which shows that churches were less preoccupied with those risks than one might expect. We shall shortly see that they continued to get reasonably high rents in wine from the vineyard belt, on an ever greater scale indeed, which must indicate that church owners were committed to its sale, whether to citizens or to pilgrims and other incomers. The rents from grain-land were by now often in kind, or else mixed, part in money, part in grain, which indicates an entry by ecclesiastical landowners into the grain market of the city too, alongside their tenants.[149] But otherwise the balance of interest in the market potential of different sorts of produce does not seem to change dramatically, as we move into the twelfth century. There was a certain stability here, notwithstanding the considerable changes in types of lease available. What did change was the steady expansion after 1000 of the range of lay social strata who wished (or were allowed) to participate in the division of the surpluses from ecclesiastical land, by taking leases. We shall look at them in Chapters 4 and 5, when we analyse the changing structures of urban society. But these newly landholding social strata, which came to make up the new elites that crystallized in the eleventh and twelfth centuries, were evidently happy to establish relationships with ecclesiastical proprietors which were at least analogous, and often close to identical, to those which had long existed. The wagons of grain and wine probably rolled in through the city's gates in much the same way in 1150 (or later) as in 900 (or earlier).

The twelfth century did nonetheless bring some agricultural changes in the Agro romano. One sign is a limited degree of land clearance, as we have just seen. A second, crucial for the future, is the start of the investment in estate-centres already mentioned (p. 70), the appearance of *turres* and other buildings, which begin to be visible in the first half of the century and are decidedly commoner in the second half. This indicates the beginning of the idea that rural reorganization might bring advantage—presumably via greater profit, since political control was so weak an aspiration in this area. By the end of the twelfth century, we also begin to find, increasingly often from c.1185 onwards, a new type of lease, in which an urban

documented. Maire Vigueur, *L'autre Rome*, pp. 104–15, shows how the importance of pastoralism, although growing, was still limited even in the late Middle Ages.

[149] Lenzi, *La terra e il potere*, pp. 129–30.

layman, generally of at least 'medium elite' status, leased a substantial tract of ecclesiastical land called a *tenimentum*, or, from *c.*1200, *casale*.[150]

The word *tenimentum* just meant 'holding' or 'territory' (it was a common word for the territory of a castle already at the end of the eleventh century, or for a village territory in Silva Maior); but increasingly it came above all to denote these new large estates. They were not yet all single blocks of land, although they could be, as with the *casale seu tenimentum* leased out by S. Ciriaco at Criptule on the Portuense in 1200.[151] Into the thirteenth century, however, in the *incasalamento* process (as historians now often call it), such big blocks became increasingly normal; they slowly became, that is to say, the network of *casali* of the modern period. They were formed out of the separate *pedicae* (themselves not so very small, as we saw, p. 60) and *petiae* of grainfields which had been the main focus of twelfth-century leases; and by now they all had estate-centres at their heart. It is important to add that leases of *tenimenta* increasingly often required substantial rents, usually in kind. In Criptule in 1200 it was 20 *ruglos* (5000 litres) of grain, to be delivered to S. Ciriaco on 15 August, plus 10 *solidi* on the feast day of the saint (8 August); for the *tenimentum* at Lubbre on the Flaminia in 1198 it was 20 *ruglam* of grain, 1 of beans and chickpeas, and 20 *solidi*, all in August, and 6 *saumas* of wine, or else 30 *solidi*, in September.[152] These were substantial cessions, which would result in stable returns for the church that leased them, and a framework for whatever future investments the lessee wished to make.

The process of *incasalamento* would be a long one, as the work of Sandro Carocci and Marco Vendittelli above all shows.[153] Lay lessees did not visibly change their strategies immediately. Estate-centres and annexed buildings for storage were the most visible novelty for a long time; they could indeed develop in size quite considerably, with simple towers in the twelfth century developing in some areas into full-blown castles, *castra* or *castella*, later in the thirteenth, as we have also seen, locations for a genuine concentration of settlement, at least for a time—they emptied out again after the Black Death, when isolated estate-centres and by now temporary seasonal settlement by estate workers became the norm. Watermills could be attached, and even fulling-mills (*gualcae* and equivalent words)—although there are few signs of the latter before 1200.[154] Mills had

[150] *Liberiano*, n. 21 (a. 1176); *S. Prassede*, n. 38 (a. 1180); ASR, SCD, cassetta 16 bis, n. 154 (a. 1186); and then *SMVL*, nn. 227, 237, 242, 250, 257, 260, 268 (*casale seu tenimentum*, a. 1200), 269; ASF Rocchettini di Fiesole 11 giug. 1189; *SPV*, n. 81.

[151] *SMVL*, n. 268.

[152] *SMVL*, n. 260. For the size of the *rugla* or *ruglum* (*rubbio*), see e.g. Maire Vigueur, 'Les "casali"', p. 123.

[153] Carocci and Vendittelli, *L'origine della Campagna Romana*, passim. See further, for the internal structure of late medieval *casali*, Carocci, *Tivoli*, pp. 433–54, which has to range well outside even notarial registers to get a full sense of the complexity of how they worked.

[154] Carocci and Vendittelli, *L'origine della Campagna Romana*, pp. 89–92. For a fulling-mill at Domine Quo Vadis in the vineyard belt in 1081, see *S. Paolo*, n. 1, and Spera, *Il paesaggio*, pp. 72–3, 427–9.

always existed throughout the Agro romano, one should note; they appear from our earliest texts, and were a normal part of the rural economy throughout our period. Their presence on its own is not a mark of infrastructural development, and there are not all that many documents in our period attesting new rural mills. In the twelfth century, there were in fact rather fewer new mills than in some parts of Lombardy or Tuscany; the main investment in mills, on a large scale, was instead along the Tiber in the city, which was more convenient for Rome's grain market and bread shops (see below, pp. 150–2). But when estate-centres began to crystallize, it was logical for mills, too, to become associated with them if watercourses were convenient.[155]

There was thus, by the early thirteenth century, a complex network of buildings at the centre of each new *casale*, which were a focus for a tighter control over its exploitation than either proprietors or lessees had been concerned to establish hitherto, and for the beginnings of steady investment. We may also imagine that the rents of cultivators rose as a result, although it is very difficult to tell. We have no further information about structural change, however, until the rise of a new system of agricultural production based on a salaried labour force, which only becomes visible in the mid- and later fourteenth century. The newly named *tenimenta* of the late twelfth were at the origin of what would in the long run be genuinely new ways of organizing the countryside, but they were not as yet, in 1200, so very significant a break with the past. All the same, this is in large part because an interest in sale to the city's markets had always been important in Rome. Lay entrepreneurs had always concerned themselves with the most effective ways of achieving it, and ecclesiastical proprietors had always been alert to the best ways of keeping as much control over surpluses as was practicable, too. The *tenimentum* or *casale* of *c*.1200 came to seem the most solid and stable way of satisfying both parties. This in itself meant that it would be the focus of future innovation, even if that innovation was not as yet in 1200 (and still less in 1150) very organic. The fragmentation of *fundi* into smaller tenures, which was never a very thoroughgoing process in the Agro romano, unlike elsewhere in Italy, was steadily reversed, a process that had certainly begun before 1150, at least on some estates.[156] Rome's large agrarian hinterland, always systematically exploited, was beginning to be so in more ordered forms, and to the advantage above all of the greater and medium lay elites of the city, who will be the protagonists of much of the rest of this book, in one way or another.

---

[155] New mills: for 900–1050, *Papsturkunden*, nn. 284, 522; *SMCM*, n. 2; *SMN*, n. 7. For 1050–1200, Pflugk II, n. 152; *SPV*, n. 41; *SMVL*, nn. 165, 250, cf. 254. This is all the documentation we have for the land outside the city. Compare Menant, *Campagnes lombardes*, pp. 176–93, implicitly, for Lombardy; Wickham, *Courts and Conflict*, pp. 188–99—with p. 189n for further bibliography—for Tuscany.

[156] Wickham, 'La struttura', pp. 205, 232–7.

THE VINEYARD BELT

Ortulani

In April 1030, a unique document, later kept in the archive of S. Ciriaco in Via Lata, establishes a *scola ortulanorum* in a private contract and sets out its regulations. In it, eight *ortulani* (orchard-men or gardeners), all *viri honesti*, that is, standard free men of non-aristocratic status, chose Amato *magnificus vir* as its *prior* for life, saying that they had made the *scola* with him. His powers were to arbitrate in disputes between the members of the *scola*; to ensure that they did not usurp the *libelli* of each other at the end of the lease (i.e. take on a lease which a fellow *ortulanus* expected to renew); and to ensure that no *dominicalis* done by a *scola* member (some form of labour service) damaged the *ortus* of another—and if it did, the *lex ortulanis* would be applied by the whole *scola*. Members of the *scola* would give 6 *denarii* to it if they bought leases from each other 'for joy' (*propter gaudium*, i.e. willingly, not out of obligation), and if they won money in disputes inside the *scola*, it was to be kept communally; Amato personally got one *denarius* in twelve from such cases, and was also entitled to one week of labour service from each of the *ortulani* every year. The *scola* was being set up as a tight collective corporation (Ludo Moritz Hartmann, who first edited the text in 1892 and was an active Social Democrat, called it a *Genossenschaft*, in effect a cooperative). It was not the only one; if Amato could not solve internal disputes on his own, the charter envisaged that he would consult with other *priores ortulani*.[157] The cooperative was presumably being set up between the *libellarii* of one of the specialist areas of *orti*, orchards or gardens, around the city; but, although this document is unique, and remarkably early, its references to other *priores* and to the *lex ortulanis* show that it fitted into an already established Roman pattern, of formal customary procedure and local proto-guild collective action, in the world of orchard cultivation around 1030. The *ortulani* were principally worried about competition and dispute between themselves. There is not a word about who their cooperation was against, so it is quite plausible that they simply did not want to see their rough equality undermined. I conclude from this that the terms of their *libelli* could well have been standardized, or at least not so harsh that they needed to defend themselves against landlords.

The location of the orchard/garden area of the 1030 text can be pinpointed; it was on the via Portuense, four to five miles (7–8 km) outside the walls of Trastevere. We can conclude this because one of the *ortulani*, Giovanni 'called *tabellio*', took a nineteen-year lease in 1025 from S. Ciriaco of a section of marsh four miles out along the road at Pantano di Cicimanno, presumably close to the Tiber, to make into an *ortuus* and grain-fields; and two of the other *ortulani* of 1030, Urso and Gaudioso, held *ortui* on its boundary, as did Amato, who in 1025 is called *vir honestus*. Amato appears again (as *vir honestus*) holding land slightly further down the Portuense at Criptule in 1037; his title of *vir magnificus* could

---

[157] *SMVL*, n. 57; previously, Hartmann, *Urkunde einer römischen Gärtnergenossenschaft*.

thus plausibly be seen as an honorific given to him by other members of the *scola*, and not used outside it.[158] The Pantano di Cicimanno is not referred to again—presumably it was indeed drained—but S. Ciriaco had a specialist orchard/garden area at Criptule by the 1190s, and it is very probable that it was this area, or land close to it, that was the location of the cooperative a century and a half earlier, and that the 1030 *ortulani* were all S. Ciriaco's tenants. In Criptule in the 1180s–90s, S. Ciriaco expected rents in vegetables—onions, beans, pumpkins, herbs, mustard—from some of its lands (they are the only vegetable rents we have in our twelfth-century documents for Rome), and it is significant that almost the only eleventh-century example of such a rent is Giovanni *tabellio*'s 1025 lease.[159] This is evidently what an *ortus* in Criptule could be expected to produce, unlike the olive oil, apples, and figs that were common orchard rents elsewhere. Giovanni *tabellio* was not necessarily a professional scribe, for *scriniarii* were by now the standard scribal group in Rome (the old tradition of scribes called *tabelliones*, or *scriniarii et tabelliones*, did still exist, but the word *tabellio* was rare by now in city documents; it continued to be used above all in other Lazial cities, such as Sutri, Nepi, and Tivoli[160]); he was perhaps simply marked out by his peers as literate. He was not himself a cultivator, however, for his land reclamation in 1025 was to be carried out by his own *lavoratores*. The *scola ortulanorum* of Criptule (or environs) was thus probably a cooperative of middlemen, although it is not to be excluded that some of them were cultivators, given that they took no precautions in their founding charter against the improper behaviour of *lavoratores*.

The 1030 document is well known to historians (apart from Hartmann, the best-contextualized study is by Laura Moscati), and it has played its part in the old and unhelpful debates about whether or not medieval guilds descended from classical Roman *collegia*.[161] More relevant to us is that Rome had already before 900 numerous religious associations (whether of clerics or laity), and also secular militias, called *scolae*, which must have been at least the terminological model for the associations of craftsmen, salt-workers, fishermen, boatmen, and occasionally agriculturalists that are documented in a dozen Roman texts from our period, starting in the 970s. The only other strictly agricultural references are to the *prior* of the *olerarii*, olive-workers, who witnesses a document for Isola Farnese in 1029, and another *prior ortulanorum* who witnesses for Monte Albino, south of the city, in 1120.[162] We will encounter the other *scolae* later (pp. 103–5, 152–4); but it is at

[158] *SMVL*, nn. 50, 66.

[159] Vegetable rents: *SMVL*, nn. 50 (a. 1025), 226, 259, 279 (all for Criptule), and *SMCM*, n. 16 (a. 1072, for Orta Prefecti south of the city). See also *RS*, n. 118 (a. 966) for an early *ortus cucummerarius* outside Porta Maggiore.

[160] The word *tabellio* was still used in the city of Rome in *RS*, nn. 98–9, 57; *SCD*, n. 42; *SMVL*, n. 67, all for the 1030s, but these few texts are a small proportion of Roman documents for the decade, and the proportion drops still further later. See for the basic recent points of reference the focused but diverging analyses of Toubert, *Les structures*, pp. 108–13, and Carbonetti, 'Tabellioni e scriniari'.

[161] Moscati, *Alle origini*, pp. 58–9; Hartmann, *Urkunde einer römischen Gärtnergenossenschaft*, pp. 16–19. For the debates see for example Hartmann, *Urkunde einer römischen Gärtnergenossenschaft*, pp. 4–12; see below, Chapter 3, n. 137.

[162] *SCD*, n. 33; *SMN*, n. 40. See also the rural *scolae* referred to casually in CVL 8044, ff. 4–16.

least clear that already by 1000 such professional associations, whether tightly or loosely organized, were normal in Rome in all economic environments—and rather better documented than in most other Italian cities, too. Their leaders were regularly called *priores*, and those closest to the papal court had ceremonial roles in the twelfth century.[163] The *ortulani* of 1030, though their *scola* was new and their statute unique, thus fitted entirely with a standard Roman associative and cooperative tradition in their period; and, as we shall see shortly in the context of the salt-working and fishing at the Tiber mouth, the sorts of rules that were set out in 1030 were put actively into practice by *scolae* elsewhere.

The existence of growing numbers of *scolae* of *ortulani* shows something else of importance: *orti* were evidently an organized operation around the Rome of 1030. They were producing food for the city, and their products must largely have moved straight into the urban food markets.[164] It is for this reason that we find certain zones specializing in *orti*. Criptule was one, as we have just seen, dominated by S. Ciriaco in Via Lata. Orta Prefecti by the via Ostiense, now Grotta Perfetta northeast of EUR, was another; first documented in 954, it was a focus for the landowning of many churches. Nine are documented before 1150, above all holding *orti*, though some vineyards and *terra seminativa* as well, in an area of only 2–3 km², judging by the size of the sixteenth-century *casale* there.[165] Not far to the south, Casa Ferrata (now Ferratella and Casale S. Sisto), entirely the property of S. Maria Tempuli, was a third zone of *orti*, which in the late twelfth century were divided into *quatrae*, each separately leased. In both of these latter areas, rents were above all in money; the *ortulani* here were probably sufficiently active middlemen that they took produce directly to the urban markets, and paid in rent only a restricted proportion of their profits.[166]

These were the main zones of orchard/garden specialization that are attested in surviving documents. There could well have been others; as there was also at least one zone of specialist meadows, Prata Papi, just south of Trastevere on the Tiber, a good spot for fattening animals from elsewhere, as we have seen (p. 85). *Orti* were also interspersed with vineyards elsewhere, as for example at Monte Albino near the via Tuscolana, where we saw a *prior ortulanorum* witness in 1120.[167] But the main product of the belt of land inside three miles of the city walls was beyond doubt wine, from the myriad *vineae*, particularly to the north and south-east of the city. I have begun here with the *orti*, because of the interest of the 1030 document, but the vineyards were certainly dominant. Romans evidently wanted more wine to go with their bread than they wanted fruit and vegetables (or even, perhaps, meat).

[163] Twyman, *Papal Ceremonial*, pp. 189–93. See Chapter 3, n. 138, Chapter 6, n. 36.

[164] Lenzi, *La terra e il potere*, pp. 46–7. For the high degree of specialization of many *orti* around late medieval Tivoli, see Carocci, *Tivoli*, pp. 470–3.

[165] To 1200, *S. Gregorio*, nn. 124, 133; *Papsturkunden*, n. 148; *Liberiano*, nn. 10, 17; *SMCM*, nn. 16, 30, 39, 42–3, 50–1, 62–3; *S. Prassede*, n. 11; *S. Alessio*, n. 17; *SPV*, n. 79. For the early modern *casale*, see Tomassetti, *La Campagna romana*, V, pp. 123–9.

[166] For 1150–1200, *S. Sisto*, nn. 2–4, 6–7, 9–11, 13–15—as can be seen, this was the main rural landholding of S. Maria Tempuli.

[167] Monte Albino area: *Papsturkunden*, nn. 419, 564; *SMN*, n. 40, 55; *S. Prassede*, n. 41. Note also the *orti* specializing in olive production outside Porta S. Paolo in 1051, *SCD*, n. 56.

So let us look at the vineyards next, focusing on some particularly well-documented vineyard estates and generalizing out from them; then we will look again at the parallel specialist vineyard area around Albano and Ariccia; and, finally, finish with the salt flats north-east of Porto. What unifies all these with the *orti* we have begun with here is an evident concern with the urban market.

Aqua Tuzia, Albano and the vineyard economy

Aqua Tuzia lay in the valley now occupied by the Stazione Tiburtina, just beyond the Campo Verano; it was part of the area called Bacculi, which also included the hill to its west, Monte S. Ypoliti (roughly the zone of the modern piazza Bologna: see Map 4). Aqua Tuzia had been given to the nearby S. Lorenzo fuori le Mura by Constantine in the fourth century, but by the late tenth century it was in the hands of S. Maria in Capitolio, who leased the *casalecclo* there in 987 to lay aristocrats; these gave the land to S. Maria Maggiore, who sold it on in 998 to three monasteries; two of these leased out part of it in 1010, by when it was being turned into vineyards.[168] Aqua Tuzia is thereafter not documented for a century, but this rapid turnover of church ownership and possession had stopped by 1116; by then, and throughout the twelfth and thirteenth centuries, Aqua Tuzia had become stably the property of S. Prassede, which owned almost the whole area, now (from 1160) often simply called the Valle S. Praxedis. It was overwhelmingly a vineyard area, and half of S. Prassede's entire surviving twelfth-century document collection relates to it: it must have provided a high proportion of the church's agrarian resources, matched only by the S. Primo estate up the via Prenestina (see above, p. 81).[169]

In the twelfth century, Aqua Tuzia was simply divided into a large number of *petiae vineae*, or *terrae ad vineam pastinandam*, in a constant process of vineyard refurbishment. Rents were overwhelmingly in wine, consisting of a quarter of the crop (*quarta*), and the tenants were routinely called *quartarini*; additional dues usually included 2 *denarii* for *vascaticum*, apparently the rent for the wine-press or *vasca* which was attached to many of the vineyard parcels, and a barrel (*canistrum*) of grapes, both of which were standard additions to the *quarta* rent around Rome. The tenants tended to hold water-rights in local wells and *fontanae* in common with

---

[168] *S. Prassede*, nn. 1–3. For the location of the area: first, the texts universally say that it is one mile outside either Porta S. Lorenzo or Porta Nomentana, and *S. Prassede*, n. 60 (a. 1226) shows that it touched the via Tiburtina, on whose northern side it must therefore have been; *LP*, I, p. 182, the Constantinian gift, says it is *ad latus* to *Veranum fundum*; also, the name shows that it is in a river valley, and the only one here is the branch of the Acqua Mariana which runs north to the Aniene, along which the railway line now runs. Bacculi, its other name in tenth-century documents, is also used in later Monte S. Ypoliti documents such as *SMN*, nn. 60, 122, and the catacombs of S. Ippolito are just above the Stazione Tiburtina.

[169] *S. Prassede*, nn. 13–17, 19–20, 22–3, 27, 29 (first reference to Valle S. Praxedis), 30, 33, 35, 39, 42, 45–6 is the twelfth-century set up to 1200. These mention up to ten other churches as owners as well (cf. also *Liberiano*, n. 22), but S. Prassede was clearly the main one by far in the twelfth century. The nearby church of S. Agnese was one (*S. Prassede*, nn. 13, 17, cf., earlier, 2), but the property never appears in S. Agnese's own documents.

other *quartarini*.[170] Leases were perpetual, and after 1140 no entry-fines were exacted by S. Prassede; presumably the stability of the *quarta* rent was enough for the church. The tenants sold their leases to others fairly often, with S. Prassede taking a regular *comminus* (see above, p. 82), which, here too, was an extra ecclesiastical resource.[171]

The tenants seem to have constituted a fairly stable group. They often witness each other's documents, or else sell to each other, and Aqua Tuzia was not a territory in which a single tenant accumulated vineyards on any scale; the same sort of network of tenants held land in 1200 as they did in 1110, and this indeed did not change much into the thirteenth century. Nicola of Fogliano (he came from the coast of the Pontine marshes, if *de Foliano* refers to the place, rather than to a father with an otherwise-unattested personal name) was a tenant here in the 1130s–40s, as three leases show; after he died his two surviving daughters Siginetta and Dulchiza negotiated a division in 1153 with their brother-in-law Romano di Trotta, which shows a small-scale landscape bounded by *vascae* and fences. That negotiation was agreed by three arbiters, at least one of whom was the son of a *vitulator*, who appears as a witness elsewhere in these texts; Siginetta and Dulchiza were themselves active into the 1170s. The 1153 arbitration shows the same sort of collective problem-solving that was legislated for so carefully in the 1030 *scola ortulanorum* document; the *vitulatores* or *quartarini* of Aqua Tuzia seem to have operated as a community.[172]

I proposed that the *ortulani* of Criptule were a group of urban middlemen. This is less likely in the case of Aqua Tuzia. The *quartarini* of the estate barely appear elsewhere, and certainly none of them have any wider profile. It is true that S. Prassede's document collection is not that large, and does not include the sort of urban property-dealing that some churches, such as S. Maria Nova and S. Maria in Campo Marzio, engaged in, but it is striking that an Aqua Tuzia *quartarinus* appears only once as a witness for any of S. Prassede's other transactions: they were not visibly part of a stable witness community attached to the church.[173] Although Aqua Tuzia is only 3 km away from S. Prassede, half an hour's fast walk, and only a kilometre or so from the walls, making it highly likely that it was cultivated by people who lived in the city, there is at least reason to think that these tenants did not live around the church. And, although as usual our documents are not explicit as to who actually did the work on the land, there are a series of signs that imply that it was the *quartarini* themselves.

None of these signs are conclusive on their own, but, put together, they have a cumulative effect. One is that there is no evidence, as just noted, that any of the Aqua Tuzia tenants were urban dealers, even though the zone was so close to the city; another is the apparent tightness of the community. The rhetorical phrase in a

---

[170] Good guides to the above include *S. Prassede*, nn. 13–15, 19–20, 23, 33, 35. *Quartarini*: e.g. nn. 19, 22, 33, 35–6.

[171] *Comminus*: *S. Prassede*, nn. 22, 35, 39.

[172] *S. Prassede*, nn. 19–20, 23, 27 (a. 1153), 29–30, 35. For Fogliano, see e.g. *RS*, n. 51.

[173] *S. Prassede*, n. 37 (Pietro di Giacintello, cf. nn. 29, 35, 39).

1116 lease that the vineyard should be held *prout bonam vineam decet et boni laboratores laudent*, 'as is fitting for a good vineyard and as good workers determine', also seems to put the tenant of that lease, Vassalletto, into the category of a *laborator* or direct cultivator. The right of the wife and heirs of Marmanno to press wine in the *vasca* of two other tenants was separately safeguarded in lease sales of 1165 and 1183; Marmanno's son Giovanni took out a separate lease in 1162; it looks as if Marmanno's family, who were standard leaseholders, were doing their own wine-pressing. Neither here nor anywhere else are dependent agricultural workers mentioned. Conversely, in 1212, a tenant sold on a lease of a *vinea deserta* because 'it had gone into abandonment and we did not want to work it because of our poverty' (*propter onus paupertatis*), which certainly implies prima facie that this tenant family worked the land directly. Two of the twelfth-century tenants were artisans, a roofer in wood (*scandolarus*) and a smith (*ferrarius*), but these could have been part-time trades. I conclude that the Aqua Tuzia lessees were mostly cultivators, at least for part of the year (assuming they were city-dwellers with other occupations); and, as such, they shed—unusually for the hinterland of Rome—some light on the nature of the economy as it functioned on the ground.[174] At Aqua Tuzia that society was apparently stable, although not static (there was one family of probable immigrants, and the sale of leases was commonplace, as one would expect for city-dwellers); the constant movement of vineyard parcels did not, all the same, prevent S. Prassede from keeping hold of its quarter of the wine produced for two centuries.

The small scale of Aqua Tuzia society is also emphasized in negative by the documents we have for Monte S. Ypoliti, only half a kilometre to the west, which show a rather different social profile. This area was mostly the property of S. Maria Nova, and it was, from its first attestation in 1051, overwhelmingly a vineyard area as well.[175] The Aqua Tuzia *quartarini* do not appear here, even though the two areas were so close. But more of S. Maria Nova's tenants were people with visible social status, too: a family of *dativi iudices* in 1051 and 1063; the son of a bishop of the Sabina in 1063; the Frangipane, S. Maria's long-term tenants and patrons in the church's own power-zone between the Foro Romano and the Colosseo (below, pp. 292–303), in 1071; a century later, the rising aristocrat Giovanni Capocci in 1197, only a year after he had been the single senator in the city. Some other tenants seem to have been dealers elsewhere in the city too.[176] The leases (two-generation until 1140, then perpetual) were much the same as those for Aqua

---

[174] Cited examples: respectively, S. Prassede, nn. 13, 33, 39, 30, 52; artisans: nn. 16, 33. That cultivators could indeed make written leases in the vineyard belt is made explicit in CVL 8044, ff. 4–16, an 1145 court case, which contains references to *locationes* for vineyards on the Gianicolo made to *coloni*, and held *colonario nomine*. At Aqua Tuzia the term *coloni* is never used, but the pattern is analogous.

[175] The texts are *SMN*, nn. 14, 20–1, 23, 35, 48, 60, 63–4, 122, 125, 156–7, plus *SMVL*, n. 147 and *Liberiano*, n. 22.

[176] See, respectively, *SMN*, nn. 14, 21, 20 (cf. 21 for the Sabina), 23, 156 (cf. Thumser, *Rom*, p. 242); other examples include Nicola di Giovanni di Gentile (nn. 125, 156) who reappears as a landholder on the Pincio in ASR, SCD, cassetta 16 bis, n. 248; and a *scriniarius* who appears as a landholder in *SMN*, n. 14.

Tuzia, if slightly less generous in small-scale agricultural detail, but they were clearly not automatically to cultivators. The rent was the same as it was in S. Prassede's valley just below, so S. Maria Nova did not suffer by it; we must assume the existence of a *laborator* stratum which here actually cultivated the vines and paid more to the middlemen, one that is certainly documented elsewhere.[177] But Monte S. Ypoliti's social profile is so marked that its absence at Aqua Tuzia is all the more striking.

If we move west from the Stazione Tiburtina, and look at the equally complex network of vineyards outside the Porta Pinciana, in and around the modern Villa Borghese and north to Parioli, we can see similar contrasts. The Valle S. Cyriaci, the section of this network owned by S. Ciriaco in Via Lata, was all vineyards by the mid-eleventh century at the latest, when the documents start, and *quarta* contracts are once again standard, as are sales of them among tenants.[178] One court case from 1057 shows Maria, widow of the late Mugeffo, and her children and her new husband, the weaver Farulfo, unsuccessfully contesting their rights to a vineyard leased from S. Ciriaco, for it turned out that Mugeffo had given his lease as a pious gift to another church, S. Angelo. In a pay-off, Maria accepted from the latter church some money and the movables attached to the vineyard, consisting of grain, wine, onions, and agricultural tools: the scale of the operation is so small that we must here be dealing with cultivators, previously leasing from S. Ciriaco.[179] Others of that monastery's tenants were, however, more obviously small-scale urban entrepreneurs, most notably Giovanni di Bona (fl. 1098–1110), who was a regular witness for S. Ciriaco and evidently part of its clientele, for he was also a monastic tenant for land in Pigna in the city and his death was recorded in its necrology (see below, p. 283). Giovanni di Bona was significant enough for one of his leased vineyards to have on it in 1106 not only the standard *vascae* but also half a *palatium*—presumably meaning a surviving classical building or ruin, but it must have been an impressive one, for the word was otherwise almost exclusively used for important political centres like the Laterano and Palatino.[180] S. Ciriaco did not have any Pincio tenants of the political prominence of the Frangipane, but it clearly leased to city middlemen and cultivators alike, and we cannot normally tell which.

What seems to be an abiding feature of most of the vineyard belt was that it was a fairly loose and flexible society: Aqua Tuzia's relative tightness may have been less common. Indeed, S. Prassede's tenurial dominance there may have been relatively unusual too; we do have clear concentrations of property held by a single owner elsewhere, such as S. Maria Tempuli's Casa Ferrata on the Ostiense, or the

---

[177] Leases: *SMN*, nn. 35, 48, 63, 122, 156–7. For *vindemiatores* or *laboratores* elsewhere who were not the holders of the surviving leases, see e.g. *RS*, n. 79 (for the city in 976); *SMN*, nn. 40, 151.

[178] For the set to 1200, *SMVL*, nn. 62, 85–6, 118–19, 132–3, 138, 146, 173 (= *Senato*, n. 12), 198 (a. 1162, first reference to Valle S. Cyriaci), 234, 238, 248, 271–2, 278.

[179] *SMVL*, n. 85, cf. 86.

[180] Giovanni: *SMVL*, nn. 132 (a. 1106), 138, and, slightly to the west, 136; he holds in Pigna in 131, and is a monastic witness in 122–3, 127, 134. Another city tenant in the Pincio vine-lands, this time of S. Silvestro in Capite, was Giovanni 'cum zocculis' (with clogs) in the 1160s, for his house was listed in the *Liber Censuum* as being on the papal ceremonial way through the city centre, somewhere near the Largo Argentina: *S. Sil.*, nn. 29, 31; *LC*, I. p. 300.

eponymous Valle S. Cyriaci, but usually the land was fragmented and owned by a myriad of city churches (and even, by the twelfth century, the occasional layman or laywoman[181]). Inside that network, city dealers frequently took leases, to bulk out their urban possessions with vineyard profits, and also pledges of land from city churches (on the Pincio, there are some for S. Silvestro in Capite). By the twelfth century, they bought and sold them sufficiently frequently to create a market in leases, around Rome just as around other cities.[182] But between the changing leases of these richer citizens, there were clearly leaseholding cultivators as well, even though we get evidence of them only in scattered references. In 1008, Benedetto and his wife Ursa, who took a lease from Subiaco to create a vineyard outside the Porta Metrobia, are called *laboratores*; in 1158, the papal *camerarius* Bosone leased a set of vineyards outside the Porta S. Giovanni gate in Clusa Pape to nine tenants on the same day, all of whom witnessed each other's charters, so were evidently a small community, none of them attested elsewhere; in 1189, Tuttadonna widow of Biagio di Mabilia sold off a vineyard in the Valle S. Cyriaci to pay for her daughter's dowry, 'since in the possessions of the said minor there are no other goods, movable or immovable, less useful', and got extremely bad terms for it as well.[183] These tenants were by no means members of urban elites, and we can legitimately conclude that they worked the land. There are not many of them, and only a handful of other, less certain, examples can be added to them, but they do confirm the supposition that the leaseholding tenants of suburban vineyards could as easily be cultivators as middlemen.

It is necessary to stress this point, for it has been doubted. Mauro Lenzi, who convincingly argues that grain leases in the Agro romano were not to cultivators (see above, p. 72), explicitly extends this to the vineyard belt, particularly before the late eleventh century, but, more cautiously, in the twelfth century as well. He lists a number of holders of *locationes* of vineyards who were certainly urban dealers, and he could have mentioned others.[184] But it is always easier to identify members of relatively high-status families than cultivators, for they are better documented in general. Aqua Tuzia and the handful of other references just cited seem to me to offer us a counter-demonstration. Still, the main point is perhaps a different one. It is not that these leases offer us a clear sight line to an at least partially peasant society—in the whole territory of Rome, only the 1201 Silva Maior court case does that—but rather that everyone, from the Frangipane, through the urban 'medium elite' and artisans (who will often have been part-time cultivators), down to a few full-time peasants, participated in the process of taking leases from urban churches for vineyards *ad quartam*. There was no social preclusion here, and a considerable flexibility at all social levels. That flexibility extended to where tenants lived, for,

---

[181] One instance seems to be *SMVL*, n. 156.

[182] *S. Sil*, nn. 30, 51. See for a parallel to the lease market Esch, *Lucca*, ch. 1.

[183] *RS*, n. 86; 'Documenti per la storia', nn. 5–7, with ASV, A. A. Arm. I–XVIII, 4999, nn. 7–8; *SMVL*, n. 234.

[184] Lenzi, *La terra e il potere*, pp. 43–4, 113–18; he does recognize that lessees in documents can sometimes be cultivators, however. His whole section, pp. 101–18, 137–40, is the best guide to the rent system of the vineyards.

although leases for the vineyard belt are quite as vague about housing as these for the *fundi* further out, here at least the vineyards were accessible from the areas of urban settlement documented within the walls. Even full-time peasants, not to speak of part-time cultivators and higher-status *rentiers*, could have lived in the nearest urban *regio* to each vineyard area.

Vineyard leases become much more numerous with the appearance of *locationes* at the end of the eleventh century. This does not show that vineyards themselves became so much more numerous then; most of the best-documented areas around the city already show a wine specialization earlier in the eleventh century. Before 1000, however, there are too few documents for the lands close to the city for us to be sure when they began. It is interesting that a 945 list of ninth- and tenth-century episcopal leases from the immediate environs of Tivoli already shows a notable concentration of vineyards around that city; this might be a sign of a similar concentration around Rome.[185] But the *vineae* of the tenth century in Roman documents, although numerous, concentrate overwhelmingly in Albano, and to a lesser extent inside the city walls. It is thus probable that the first vineyard belt was inside the city, which (unlike Tivoli) had plenty of space, and that a vineyard specialization outside the walls was a later development, although already in operation in the early eleventh century, when our suburban texts begin to appear.[186] This also matches the *ortus* specialization reflected in the 1030 *scola* document. From then on, however, the extramural belt must have become steadily more intensively specialized, a specialization which was very substantial by 1100 or so. The well-documented expansion of vineyards in the thirteenth century thus had long roots in Rome. This must reflect a steady expansion in the city's market across the eleventh century, and probably its population as well, as we shall see in Chapter 3; for suburban vineyard specializations of this kind invariably had a commercial function.

This was of course already true of Albano and Ariccia, the earliest documents for which bunch in the middle decades of the tenth century.[187] Here, a vineyard specialism was fully established from the start, and, strikingly, in the forty or so documents from this territory in the tenth century there is only one reference to grain-land.[188] As we have seen (p. 67), Albano had a clear structure for its settlement, with most people living in Albano and Ariccia, though some living near rural churches in the first two or three kilometres down the hill from these two centres. It would be unheard-of in this period for the Albanesi to be buying in grain from outside, and we have to assume that they cultivated grain-land as well in every period, as indeed is implied by our evidence for several rural mills, concentrated above all between Albano and the Lacus Turni (the modern Quarto Laghetto, now drained), in an area called Silvulae or Butte; by the twelfth century, we find more

---

[185] *Inventari altomedievali*, XII, pp. 249–75. The place names recur on the map of the area around Tivoli in the late Middle Ages in Carocci, *Tivoli*, at the end of the book.
[186] e.g. S. Prassede, n. 3; SMVL, nn. 45, 52, 62; RS, n. 84, 86, 100, 106.
[187] For what follows see the more detailed treatment in Wickham, 'Albano'.
[188] *RS*, n. 125.

references to grain-fields as well.[189] Albano's vineyard specialism was, above all, in the rents due from the land, and was less complete in terms of what was actually produced. All the same, vineyards were what chiefly interested landowners in this area, and fifteen churches, overwhelmingly Roman, are documented as owning them here already in the tenth century, with another eleven added in the eleventh, and seventeen more in the twelfth: every major Roman church had land there. As elsewhere, they leased these vineyards out to the laity, mainly urban aristocrats (including the Teofilatto-Tuscolani family), officeholders, and artisans. In Albano, documented rents were mostly in money for a long time, for the tenth-century leases were mostly emphyteuses, so vineyard profits were, as in the Agro romano, largely made by the urban laity; Albano leases began to move to the standard *quarta* pattern relatively late, in fact, not until the 1130s, and that pattern never became wholly dominant.[190] The small group of pre-twelfth-century leases with rents in kind were largely granted to explicitly local inhabitants, who doubtless had less easy access to city markets. Some of these were clearly cultivators, too, such as the *laboratores* of leases of 964 and 1011. So, too, presumably, were Ansone and his wife Urza in 965, and Amato and his wife Pretia in 1001, who, even though Ansone was a *vir magnificus* from Albano and Amato was a priest of S. Pietro di Ariccia, were paying a very high 50 per cent rent, too high to permit any subletting.[191] Later on, in the twelfth century, as we have already seen, a S. Maria Nova lease of 1142 to the three sons of Pietro *vaccarius*, for a *quarta* rent, required that they give food and drink to the church's *superista* and his horse 'as is the custom of Albano *agricoli*, and to other *superistae* of the Romans': the text clearly invokes a world in which it was normal for peasants to be dealing directly with bailiffs sent out from the city. We have seen this already for the grain estates of the Agro romano; once again, Roman ecclesiastical owners often did not have local estate-centres. Only one is documented, a rural church which in 1116 was an estate-centre for S. Alessio sull'Aventino.[192] But the situation for tenant cultivators was different in Albano: they probably had several different landlords, for the fragmented vineyards in this zone could be very small; and they had their own local society, focused on the twin *castra* of Albano and Ariccia, which made them potentially more autonomous from their lords.

The society of Albano in our period can be partially reconstructed, unlike any other rural society around Rome except Silva Maior. This is not the place to do so in detail, but some of its elements can be sketched out here. Tenth-century Albano and Ariccia had their own local elites. Each had a *dux*, documented once in the

[189] e.g. *SMN*, n. 33; *SMCM*, nn. 26, 29, 44, 58; *S. Gregorio*, n. 152; *S. Alessio*, nn. 16, 22. For mills, *SMCM*, nn. 2, 20, 62; *SMN*, n. 9.

[190] First *quarta* in wine: *SMVL*, n. 108 (a. 1080); they become regular from *SMCM*, n. 33 (a. 1133)—though cf. n. 29 (a. 1118) for a grain rent already called *quarta*.

[191] Early rents in kind: *RS*, nn. 129 (with *laboratores*; redated to 964 by Hamilton, 'The monastic revival', p. 58), 142 (Ansone); *SMVL*, n. 25 (Amato); G. Gullotta, 'Un antico ed unico documento'; *S. Prassede*, n. 4. For *laboratores* see also *SMCM*, n. 2.

[192] *SMN*, n. 54 (a. 1142, for the quote); *S. Alessio*, n. 12 (a. 1116), for which see de Francesco, 'S. Eufemia'.

century, although these were not necessarily from the area: the *dux* of Albano before 973 was a member of the Roman *de Imiza* family.[193] But a set of *iudices* and *nobiles viri* who appear in a linked set of documents in the 970s–80s certainly seem local— for example, Mercone *natione de Albano* who, on becoming a monk of Subiaco in 985, gave the latter a church in Albano, S. Pietro, and whose son Lupo was a *castaldio* in Ariccia in a 980 court case. How these elites related to Roman landowners, or whether they owned any land themselves (not inconceivable, as we shall see in a moment), is not easy to see; they witnessed documents more often than they made them. But Giovanni Peroncio, who made or bought two leases near Ariccia from S. Ciriaco in Via Lata in 978, had Ariccia notables witnessing for him, so may well have been one himself; and anyway, given the overwhelming domin-ance of Roman churches as landowners in the zone, none of them could have avoided being city tenants for much of their land.[194]

In the eleventh century, even this rather circumscribed elite fades from our documentation. But it had not gone away, for an interesting text of 1104 suddenly illuminates some of the things that had been going on in the meantime. In it, Pietro of Albano gave himself and a set of lands to the Roman church of S. Maria Nova; the lands (five fields of unspecified sizes) were situated around Albano, and to them were added his own *domus maior* in the town. Pietro seems to have owned his own land outright. He was not the first known lay proprietor in Albano, for there had been a few in the eleventh century—it is not surprising that a territory with as fragmented an ownership structure as Albano should have had a few lay owners early—but he is the first known who seems to have been local. He stated that he was from the *genealogia* of the Dimidia Maza on his father's side, and that of the Carucini on his mother's; this is still fairly early for surnames even in Rome, and must indicate a considerable claim to status in Albano. Pietro's family were not exclusively Albano-based, and we shall encounter them later in a Roman context; for a Giovanni Dimidia Mazza is recorded as leasing land near S. Maria Nova in 1052, the same church that Pietro joined, and the Carucini were legal professionals in the city from now on into the 1160s (see below, p. 268). But Pietro's own base was certainly local, and the Carucini kept their Albano interest too.[195]

It is not surprising that we should find an Albano leadership drifting to the city of Rome; Rome would have been so much more attractive a location for a career, and links with the city were tight. Even when local elites stayed, they are hard to track, for they tend to vanish among all the church leases to obscure and often clearly non-local tenants. Some form of local protagonism must have existed, on the other hand, for only that can explain the choice of the *Albanenses* to side with Frederick Barbarossa and the lords of Tuscolo in 1166–7, which led to the Romans sacking the town in 1168.[196] All the same, Albano was not Tuscolo. It had no local lord;

---

[193] *Papsturkunden*, n. 226; *RS*, n. 79. For his family see Görich, 'Die *de Imiza*', esp. p. 10.
[194] *RS*, n. 138 (a. 985; cf. n. 142); *SMVL*, nn. 7–9 (a. 978), 10 (a. 980), 14, 16.
[195] *SMN*, n. 33 (a. 1104), 15 (a. 1052).
[196] See, for the events of 1166–8, *LP*, II, pp. 415–16, 419 (Bosone's contemporary account of the destruction of Albano, stating that *eorum civitatem funditus destruxerunt*, though the town's later history shows this was an exaggeration); *Annales Ceccanenses*, p. 286.

even its bishop is hardly visible in our sources—startlingly invisible in fact, given the wealth of Albano texts after 900; episcopal land is never mentioned at all in any of them—until the pope gave jurisdiction over the town to its bishop in 1217. Ariccia was more of a political pawn, for Paschal II ceded it to the Tuscolani in 1099, who held it at least until 1116, and Alexander III ceded it to the Roman Malabranca family in 1171, who held it until 1223; but Albano remained free of any lay control until the Savelli took over later in the thirteenth entry.[197] Conversely, it was wholly part of Rome's economy, as its oldest large-scale source of wine, and its territory was dominated tenurially by all the city's churches. It had no chance of any real political autonomy, given that, and it never, except maybe in 1166–8, ever thought of trying for some. Albano is a guide to the very circumscribed limits of political protagonism in Rome's hinterland, and to the risks that immediately became visible when these limits were tested. But, of course, the systematic destruction of Tuscolo in 1191 would be a far clearer guide—and warning—than whatever damage the Romans did to Albano in 1168.

Albano was thus not quite the same as the rest of the Agro romano, but also not fully different. Its territory was owned by Roman churches, and overwhelmingly leased to members of Roman elites; nor can we be sure what the tenurial base of local elites was—they might have held from Albano or Ariccia churches, for example, for some of these are attested as landowners,[198] and after 1100 or so (and maybe before) some of them will have matched the full proprietorship of Pietro Dimidia Maza, but they almost certainly all held from Rome too. Either way, however, they were dwarfed by the Roman-focused tenurial structures that surrounded them. Already in the tenth century, the dominance of Albano wine in the city had led to the total absorption of the territory into the Roman commercial supply network. By 1100 one might wonder if that dominance was so complete, for the suburban vineyard belt was fully in operation; but Albano's vineyards certainly did not diminish. Furthermore, the importance of vineyards here led to an early fragmentation of tenure and of exploitation which had no parallel in the Agro romano in the tenth century, and little parallel in the twelfth.[199] This could give space to a local society, and evidently did so, but also restricted its coherence and autonomy quite considerably.

Salt

The salt pans of the Tiber lay on the left and right banks of the river, just above Ostia and Porto. By far the most important of them lay on the Porto side;

---

[197] *Italia sacra*, ed. Ughelli, I, cols 257–8 (a. 1217; the text implies that the cession had already been made by Innocent III, but we have no independent record of that). For Ariccia, Sigebert of Gembloux, *Chronica*, p. 369; *LP*, II, pp. 303, 344; and then, for the Malabranca, Kehr, II, pp. 358, 366–7; *Codex diplomaticus dominii temporalis S. Sedis*, I, n. 31; *LC*, I, n. 203; Thumser, *Rom*, pp. 126–8. See Carocci, *Baroni di Roma*, p. 415–18, for the Savelli.

[198] *SMCM*, n. 2; *SMVL*, nn. 122, 168–9. See in general for Albano's churches Martorelli, *Dalla 'civitas Albona' al 'castellum Albanense'*, pp. 189–255.

[199] Wickham, 'La struttura', pp. 191–2.

references to Ostia *salinae* make up quite a small minority of our documentary evidence before 1150, or even later.[200] This had probably always been the case; although Livy in the first century claims that the Ostia pans were developed by Rome first, in the seventh century BC, once the right-bank pans were taken with the conquest of Veii in the fourth century BC, he simply calls them the *Romanae salinae*.[201] Anyway, the salt specialization of these areas was old in the tenth century. The Porto salt pans were a major source of revenue until the late fourteenth century, after which they became harder and harder to exploit, apparently because of a build-up of river alluvium; by the late fifteenth their importance was marginal, and by the eighteenth only the Ostia pans survived.[202] Throughout our period, all the same, they were active and remunerative. It is not easy to work out their complex geography, for the landscape has changed so much that the place names are all lost. The Porto pans were, however, certainly situated between the last hills before the coastal plain, above the fosso Galeria, and a large lagoon, the *stagnum maior*, on the modern site of Fiumicino airport, which was important for fishing. The main salt zone was called the Campo Maiore (or just the Campo Salinario); two sometimes separate zones were called Burdunaria and Serpentaria. These were in turn divided into *pedicae*, each with its own name: Vetere, Ticcli (these two are the most often cited), Nova, Fossato Maiore, Cerasia, and others.[203] Every *pedica* was made up of a large number of *fila*, artificial basins which were filled with seawater and dried out, leaving the salt to be collected. *Fila*, or groups or portions of *fila*, were the basic units of ownership and rental in the Campo Salinario, together with their attached canals (*fossata*), dykes (*andita*), and temporary huts (*tuguriola, attipla*) for the salt-workers, who only worked seasonally—here, at least, we know that they lived on the spot, but not on a permanent basis.[204]

The Porto salt pans were as popular as the Albano vineyards as sources of revenue, already in the tenth century and throughout our period. Some twenty-five churches and monasteries (mostly urban, but with a prominent place for

[200] Toubert, *Les structures*, pp. 681–3 gives an almost complete list of the eighty-odd texts for the salt pans up to 1200; to them should be added *S. Gregorio*, nn. 127, 50–1, 20; *Papsturkunden*, nn. 522, 608; *SMN*, nn. 12; *SMVL*, nn. 88, 97–8, 205, 243; *SMT*, n. 9; Kehr, IV, pp. 450–1; Pflugk, II, n. 276; *S. Pancrazio*, nn. 14, 12; ASR, SCD, cassetta 16, nn. 129, 146 (third text on roll), cassetta 16 bis, n. 163 (eighth text on roll); Ratti, *Genzano*, nn. 1, 2; *Liberiano*, n. 22; *SPV*, n. 74 (and the forged n. 1); *Reg. Inn. III*, II. 94 (102). For Ostia, the full set seems to me to be *RF*, n. 1280; *SMN*, n. 36; Pflugk, II, n. 276; *SMVL*, nn. 202, 243; *Liberiano*, n. 22; *SPV*, n. 74: all except the first three postdate 1150, although the last refers to a ninth-century gift. The basic studies of the *salinae* in our period are Toubert, *Les structures*, pp. 641–51; Maggi Bei, 'Sulla produzione del sale'; Passigli, 'Per una storia', pp. 110–11 and *passim*; there is need for a focused and long-term account.

[201] Livy, *Ab urbe condita*, I. 33, VII. 19; see Lanciani, 'Il "Campus salinarum romanarum"'; Morelli et al., 'Scoperte recenti'.

[202] For the fate of Porto salt, see esp. Montel, 'Un *casale* de la Campagne romaine', pp. 51–64; and also the documents cited in Tomassetti, *La Campagna romana*, VI, pp. 419–28. For Ostia, Fea, *Storia delle saline d'Ostia*, although those who say this pamphlet is an essential text have evidently never opened it.

[203] Maggi Bei, 'Sulla produzione del sale', gives the references.

[204] Good sample texts with these details are *SCD*, n. 23 (a. 1011) and *S. Gregorio*, n. 54 (a. 1063). The *attipla* and *tuguriola* were normally mentioned in terms of a space being set aside for them to be constructed—i.e., given that the *fila* were usually well established, the huts must have been temporary.

Subiaco, Farfa, and the bishops of Porto and Silva Candida) are recorded as owning there, nearly as many as in Albano, and the salt pans were a much smaller area. A papal confirmation of 1018 shows that the bishop of Porto claimed much of the Campo Salinario, which might seem to fit the fact that in the later Middle Ages the *casale* of Porto, which included the salt pan zone and also the woodland tract between the *stagnum maior* and the sea, was divided between S. Pietro in Vaticano and the bishopric; but this later dominance by a dual landlord was not a feature of our period. Many of the sectors claimed by Porto in 1018 were, indeed, routinely registered as the properties of other churches in other tenth- to twelfth-century documents.[205] As elsewhere in the Agro romano, there is no reason to think that the laity were often proprietors in the Campo Salinario; there is only one visible exception, a *filum salinae* owned by the *senatrix* Marozia 'II' in 959, as we have seen. Pierre Toubert argued that one could assume a substantial range of lay ownership here, but there is no good evidence for it.[206] In one papal cession, to Benedetto bishop of Porto in 1005 (it is a gift of half of a smaller lagoon, the *stagnellum Maledictum*, between the Campo Maiore and the *pedica* Ticcli, which had been converted into salt pans and which the pope therefore renamed *Benedictum*, presumably in part as a compliment to the bishop), the pope also ceded half of the rent (*pensio*) and *publica functio* that was due from the lagoon, which may imply that the pope claimed dues from the whole salt pan area. This fits with the dues that were collected by the pope's *castaldiones* in Burdunaria as part of their *castaldionaticum*, which a later pope ceded to Bishop Benedetto in 1018. How much the popes got out of such dues is unknowable; if it had been a large sum, they might not have ceded it away so easily. But a public (i.e. by now papal) right over the Campo Salinario would at least fit with the long-standing rights that public powers in the classical period had had over salt extraction.[207]

As with the Albano vineyards, the Porto salt pans were leased immediately out to the laity. But there were differences. One is that the social range of lessees was much wider from the start; top aristocrats like the *de Imiza* and palatine officials are attested, but also priests and *mansionarii* (sacristans of urban churches), and artisans and other members of the commercial strata: a smith in 988, two merchants in 1015–16, two goldsmiths in 1036, a doctor in 1039, and so on.[208] Lessees have a decisively urban feel, as elsewhere; although—again as elsewhere—we cannot be sure of the origin of ill-documented lessees, they were certainly not local, for no one lived in the Campo Salinario, and all food would have to have been brought in. The other is that rents were high. Leases (nearly all *libelli*) were for nineteen or twenty-nine years, with substantial sums for renewals, and *pensiones* were in large amounts of salt: 43 *modia* of salt and a *modius* of *flos* (fleur de sel, flake salt) was a common

[205] *Papsturkunden*, n. 522; for one of the sectors claimed by the bishop, Ticcli, see for other owners *Papsturkunden*, n. 419; SMT, n. 9; *SMN*, n. 57, 90, 103–4, 167.

[206] RS, n. 64 (see above, p. 54); cf. Toubert, *Les structures*, pp. 645–6.

[207] *Papsturkunden*, nn. 420, 522; cf., for the Roman empire, Rostowzew, *Geschichte der Staatspacht*, pp. 412–15.

[208] For the artisans: RS, n. 68; RF, n. 500; LL, n. 2055; S. Gregorio, n. 53; Liberiano, n. 8.

annual rent in Subiaco leases, for example.[209] The churches clearly on this occasion wanted much of the salt themselves; and we have a couple of leases that show that lessees had to bring salt into the city—in one case by road, with *bestiae*, although we can scarcely doubt that the nearby river was the normal route.[210]

Toubert is inclined to play down the importance of Rome's salt production ('Rien que de modeste, au total. Rome n'était pas Venise . . .').[211] The cumulative weight of all our surviving salt documents (over sixty before 1150) is, however, quite striking, and has no parallel in Italy in our period, except indeed for the very substantial and atypical Venetian evidence. Salt extraction is much less well evidenced, for example, in the sea marshes next to Lucca and Pisa, even though for these two cities our documentation is very extensive.[212] It is at least evident, once again, that the urban market for salt must have been large and stable, to maintain such a dense exploitation of the Campo Salinario and to justify such high rents; and that, this time, the ecclesiastical network was intent on taking a substantial profit for itself—although the city's elites and artisans must have shared in it, or otherwise they would not have been so interested in the leases. How much Rome exported salt is less clear; it had no equivalent to the major inland urban market in the Po valley that Comacchio, and then Venice, had. But one enigmatic late twelfth-century text shows that the Frangipane were involved in a substantial salt trade through Terracina: perhaps to southern Lazio as Toubert supposes, but equally plausibly to larger southern markets such as Naples, which did not have a salt production of any scale on its own.[213]

The *salinarii* of the salt pans had their own *scola* (or *ars*), which we see documented in a dispute arbitrated by the *prior* and *rectores* of the *scola*, and by a *paterens* and a *prior fossati*, in 1118–19, and also in several arbitrations surviving from the period 1217–29—by which date the collectivity was no longer called a *scola*, but still had *priores*, *consiliarii*, and a *paterens*.[214] This collectivity can be set beside another active in the same area, the *scola piscatorum stagni*, of the fishermen in the *stagnum maior*, who in 1115 tried unsuccessfully to prevent S. Gregorio sul Celio from claiming its half of the *stagnum* on the grounds that they held rights only from the pope; the *scolenses* leased S. Gregorio's fishing rights by 1158, however, for a rent of a ninth of the catch, and their descendants, again no longer called a *scola*, still held the lease in the late thirteenth and fourteenth centuries.[215]

The *scola piscatorum* was clearly led by members of the urban 'medium elite' of the twelfth century. The *prior* in 1115, Alberico di Fuscone, was succeeded by 1158 by his son Ottaviano (and his own three sons were due to inherit it); we

[209] *RS*, nn. 68–72, 75.   [210] *S. Gregorio*, n. 53; *Liberiano*, n. 14 (*bestias*).

[211] Toubert, *Les structures*, p. 651.

[212] For the remarkable Venetian evidence from our period, see the survey by Hocquet, 'Le saline'. For Tuscany, see the brief survey in Wickham, 'Paludi e miniere', p. 463; documentation concentrates on Vada Volterrana and Grosseto, not in the Lucca–Pisa area.

[213] *SMN*, n. 152 (Terracina), cf. Toubert, *Les structures*, p. 650; in Naples, ships from Rome had to pay a tax in salt in 1018 (Carrero, *Napoli*, p. 90).

[214] See *SMN*, n. 37, and Carbonetti Vendittelli, 'La curia dei *priores*'; see further below, p. 400.

[215] *S. Gregorio*, nn. 34, 55, and, for later texts, 43, 44; for an analysis, see Vendittelli, 'Diritti e impianti di pesca', pp. 409–22.

cannot be sure of their wider status. However, the next name on the list of 53 *scolenses* in 1158 was Pietro di Cencio di Guido, whose brother was a *consul* in 1148, and whose family, then and earlier, are found acting with the rapidly rising Papareschi of Trastevere (see below, p. 311); these two families are also the principal *genologiae* who still leased the lagoon in 1296. Most of the other fifty-odd names in 1158 are much more obscure than that (although one near the top of the list is Astaldo *scriniarius*, clearly a qualified figure, and writer of a handful of surviving documents from around 1160, mostly for Trastevere; another, Nicola di Rustico, third on the list, is perhaps the father of a senator of 1151), but the social standing of the *scola*'s leaders is nonetheless clear.[216] The leaders of the *scola salinarum* were less prominent; most of them are unknown outside the court documents themselves. Duro di Giovanni di Caritia, *prior* in 1119 (his brother Stefano was a *rector* in the same year), is recorded as a lessee of a salt pan in 1116, which indicates a certain professional commitment, but if Ottaviano di Obizzo, *paterens* in 1119, is the same man as the homonymous *tutor* for a householder in the Colosseo area in 1127, then we are dealing with urban *rentiers* again, just as many of the salt leases imply from the start.[217] The 1217 *priores et consiliarii* include one certain member of a family from Trastevere, the *filii Summeragi* (see below, p. 280), and several more who have other links with properties along the Portuense and so could well be Trasteverini as well. This certainly fits later salt documents, which are overwhelmingly associated with Trastevere middlemen.[218] It also fits later fishing documents, for which the same is true, and one person in the 1217 salt case indeed was from the same family, the *de Rubiis*, as two of the *scolenses* who leased fishing rights in 1158.[219]

The leading *salinarii* and *piscatores* of the tenth to twelfth centuries were thus usually visibly urban-based, and increasingly often from Trastevere. This fits the picture of rural profits being run by urban middlemen, which we have seen for the grain-fields and vineyards of the Agro romano as well. But it is also worth noting that very many other members of the *scolae* cannot be identified at all, and the *scola piscatorum* was very large by the 1150s; it is far from impossible that these collective groups included both entrepreneurs and the salt-workers/fishermen themselves. It is significant that the 1220s salt court cases refer to the *paterens salinariorum sive laboratorum Campi Salini*: 'of the *salinarii* and of the [salt-] workers'.[220] This is where we can begin to think of these collectivities in terms of guilds, which controlled access to the profession and its internal labour process, linking everyone

---

[216] Pietro di Cencio di Guido's family: see esp. *S. Gregorio*, nn. 20, 7, 43 (a. 1296); *SMVL*, n. 172 (a. 1148). Astaldo: *LC*, I, nn. 101–2; *SMVL*, n. 194; ASR, SCD, nn. 135, 146 (eighth text on the roll). Rustico di Nicola di Rustico: *Senato*, n. 12.

[217] *SMN*, nn. 36 (a. 1116), 45 (a. 1127).

[218] Carbonetti Vendittelli, 'La curia dei *priores*'; Montel, 'Un *casale* de la Campagne romaine', p. 61.

[219] Compare Carbonetti Vendittelli, 'La curia dei *priores*', p. 140, with *S. Gregorio*, n. 55; other references to the family are ASR, SCD, cassetta 16, n. 146 (thirteenth and sixteenth documents on the roll), cassetta 16 bis, n. 163 (seventh document on the roll)—in typical Trastevere contexts.

[220] Carbonetti Vendittelli, 'La curia dei *priores*', pp. 139, 141. Cf. Vendittelli, 'Diritti e impianti di pesca', pp. 417–18, 424.

involved in salt, rich and poor alike. Whether one could work one's way up, from a youth spent drying salt to a prosperous middle age spent organizing the salt work of others, is wholly unclear, but not inconceivable; this would have parallels not only in city trades but also in the experience of agricultural workers in Silva Maior (see above, pp. 75–6). Since no one lived on the salt pans all year round, it is also conceivable that they were all, rich and poor, based in Trastevere (or indeed in other parts of the city with easy access to the Tiber, particularly before Trastevere expanded in the twelfth century). As usual, when we come to the actual labour, we are back to hypotheses. But that people made money out of salt is nonetheless very clear; salt-working was indeed important enough to generate its own tribunal, which dealt with small claims just as the *scola ortolanorum* of 1030 planned to—and charged a lot for judgements.[221] The Campo Salinario was economically important throughout our period; and this meant not only that urban demand was consistently high, but that there was a good deal of money and resources associated with it.

Porto and Ostia were easily the closest settlements to the salt pans, but they had other sources of wealth. The city of Porto was less than 5 km away, and its bishop had substantial rights in the area. The city is not itself, however, connected to the Campo Salinario in any text; the most we can say is that a salt storehouse is perhaps attested in a 1022 reference to a *domum terrinea* [one-storeyed house] . . . *que vulgo salario dicitur*.[222] Porto also had a fairly substantial population in this period, with at least eight churches; we only have around twenty documents for the city, but they included several references to *domūs*, some of them *solaratae* [two-storeyed], following the standard terminology for urban housing in Lazio, and in 1005 even a tower, *turris*. There may have been shops there, as references to *tendiae* may imply.[223] And there were forms of local organization; Benedetto *prior scole militie Portuensis* is attested in 974, which indicates some political structures modelled on those of Rome (see below, p. 263); the city's inhabitants also included at least two *curiales* by 1018.[224] The pope controlled Porto, as he put it in his 1018 cession to the bishop, as part of his *publicum*. In that cession he gave the bishop his *castaldionaticum* over all dues not only from the salt of Burdunaria but also from the *portis* and *navibus* of the city; but he kept other *dationes* from, and judicial rights over, all Porto's inhabitants except the two *curiales* and also two *piscatores*, whomever the bishop chose to exempt. These *piscatores* were probably not those of the *stagnum maior*; the old imperial harbour had significant fishing in 992, controlled by the bishop, and the Tiber delta had fishing too, some of which belonged to the Vatican monasteries.[225]

---

[221] Carbonetti Vendittelli, 'La curia dei *priores*', pp. 140–1—implying a court fee of 50 per cent of the value of the goods claimed.

[222] *SCD*, n. 27; a papal confirmation to S. Maria in Trastevere in 1123 also lists the church's lands in Porto and its *fila de salinis* one after the other: Pflugk, II, n. 284.

[223] *Domūs*, etc.: *SCD*, nn. 9, 14, 27, 57 (with *tendia*); *Papsturkunden*, nn. 419 (*turris*, belonging to the bishop), 522; ASR, SCD, cassetta 16, nn. 103 (*tendia*), 122.

[224] *SMVL*, n. 6B; *Papsturkunden*, n. 522.

[225] *Papsturkunden*, n. 312; *SPV*, nn. 3, 16.

Porto remained part of the pope's *dominatus* for a long time; it was one of the main *regalia* safeguarded to Clement III in the civic accords of 1188. No matter what the pope conceded in 1018, he still kept rights over taking tolls from ships that came through Porto, for Victor II in 1055–7 lifted them from Montecassino's *naves*.[226] It looks as if Porto's prosperity still largely derived from its port, and its role as the place where goods were transferred from sea-going to river-going ships; this was significant, given that Rome's international commercial role has been partially revalued (see below, pp. 165–8). Fishing perhaps came second here, and salt would have come a distant third—although the 1022 text means that we certainly cannot exclude that some salt-workers could have lived in Porto, which seems to have been, together with Albano, the largest settlement in the Agro romano. The late medieval decline in its population, apparently begun by the 1230s and total by the fifteenth century, is not visible in our period.[227] Half a dozen Roman churches owned land in the city: like the salt pans, and the vineyards of Albano, its port was a source of profit, which was divided up quite carefully. At the very least, Porto adds to the evidence of the salt documents, that there was money to be made in the Tiber delta, all through our period.

Ostia adds to it too; but here our evidence is much poorer, and hardly exists until the end of our period. The pope had the city as part of his *regalia* in 1188 too, and one text from 1192 shows us three *domūs* in the city and house-plots outside its walls as well.[228] But the main text that illuminates Ostia is an agreement between the *Hostienses cives* and Pope Hadrian IV in 1159, in which their *procurator* and his five *socii concives* promised to send the pope two barge-loads (*plactatae* or *platratae*) of wood every year; this *contractus* was then taken to Ostia and approved by 56 members of its *populus*, which implies a population of at least 300 people.[229] Ostia's community had clearly by now developed, along twelfth-century lines, into a quasi-commune, unlike the more traditional patterns shown by Porto's tenth-century *militia*—it is a pity that we do not have twelfth-century texts for Porto, but they probably would have shown a social structure similar to Ostia's. The Ostia littoral was hardly populated, and one of the most substantial wooded areas in the whole Agro romano (cf. above, pp. 67–8); it therefore makes sense that wood-rights would be an important papal interest. It would be reasonable to assume that wood can be added to salt and fish as intensively farmed specialities of the Tiber mouth. If it is hardly documented, this might be most of all because large-scale wood-rights did not always come into the category of the sort of private property that was normally alienated or leased—like mining rights, they were often held publicly, or as part of signorial powers. Given the absence of local *signorie*, this may imply a substantial papal control over the surviving woodlands of the Agro, and we have already seen that in the case of Silva Maior.

*

---

[226] *PL*, CXLIII, n. 18, cols 831–4 (confirmed in 1105 in *PL*, CLXIII, cols 144–8); *Senato*, n. 41.

[227] See Montel, 'Un *casale* de la Campagne romaine', pp. 50–3; already in 1236 Gregory IX could say that Porto 'in solitudinem pene devenerat, et vix paucissimis tunc, sicut et nunc, incolebatur habitatoribus', i.e. that it had by now very few inhabitants at all: *Italia sacra*, ed. Ughelli, I, cols 130–2.

[228] *Senato*, n. 41; *SPV*, n. 79.   [229] *LC*, I, nn. 117–18; cf. p. 9.

Cities needed a secure supply of a wide variety of foodstuffs and other raw materials. What is clear from the Roman evidence is that certain specific areas provided the resources for this particular city. Garden and orchard produce came from the vineyard belt; wine from the same belt, at least after 1000, from the city itself, and from Albano in all periods; salt from the Porto (and Ostia) pans; wood from the Ostia woods. These territories do not present the analytical problems that the great grain area of the Agro romano does: if it is difficult even here to be sure that we are ever dealing with the people who did the work on the land, it is not quite impossible. And we can at least guess in these cases where cultivators and workers lived, for all these territories are accessible from known settlements—except for the salt-pans, which were not, however, areas of permanent occupation. The only major resources for the city that cannot be tracked are animals and metals, which must have been partly sourced from further afield (see pp. 85, 144). But it is the intensity of specialization that strikes one most, as one reads through the documentation discussed here. This is already visible in the tenth century for Albano and for the Porto salt pans, and extends to most other sectors by the early eleventh. This is early for Italy, and it marks Rome out. The point will be developed further in the final section of this chapter.

CONCLUSION

Many cities in Italy saw a sharp increase in agricultural specialization, and an integration of the rural and urban economies, in the twelfth century. In Tuscany, this is quite clear for Lucca, where around 1100 the long-standing tendencies for grain to be grown in the Plain of Lucca and wine/olive oil in the hills above it became very sharp indeed, at least on the level of rent-taking. This went together with a growing dominance of rents in kind, which began in the later eleventh century (earlier than in most of Tuscany), and which show a landlordly interest in urban sales; this is further underlined by the growing importance of the grain measure of the *classo salaiolo*, the city's grain market, in documents for the lands around Lucca. By the mid-twelfth century, as Arnold Esch has shown, a steady inflation in land prices affected properties close to the city more completely than those further away, and there is evidence of calculations of rental values in land-investment decisions, which resulted in regular profits of 4–6 per cent on capital outlay by the end of the century. The years 1050–1100 were the start here for a steady process of the commercialization of the rural hinterland along lines drawn by the urban market.[230]

This was the date of similar signs of agrarian development in eastern Lombardy, too, the hinterlands of Bergamo, Brescia, and Cremona. Here, François Menant points to the late eleventh and twelfth centuries as the moment of take-off for systematic irrigation, the development of vineyards on cleared land, the

---

[230] Wickham, *Community and Clientele*, pp. 23–4; Esch, *Lucca*, ch. 1; for 4–6 per cent, Esch, *Lucca*, pp. 45–51, 77, 83–6.

development of transhumant pastoralism, and, later in the twelfth century in the Cremonese, linen.[231] For Padua, the late twelfth century was the period of clearest development, with the best evidence for wine specializations on the Colli Euganei (though this was beginning earlier), and a similar expansion of both olive-growing on the hills and linen on the eastern plain.[232] Only around Milan can we see some earlier signs of economic change: a price rise in agricultural land already in the late tenth century, which matched that for city housing; land clearance which started then or even earlier, and went on into the twelfth; though even there it was not until the twelfth century that irrigation began in any organized way.[233]

For these cities, then, with the partial exception of Milan, the late eleventh and even the late twelfth centuries were moments in which the pull of the city's markets began to affect agrarian specializations. Not every city is well enough documented—or well enough studied—to allow us to make such statements, but we have here evidence for some of the larger cities of our period, and others would show changes rather later in time. The Agro romano is not exactly comparable to these central-northern areas in the pacing of its agrarian history: it experienced less land clearance in our period than did the Po plain, and did not live through the earlier rise and decline of the *sistema curtense*, the manorial system, except in the short-lived experiment of the *domuscultae*. All the same, this general focus on the twelfth century as a moment of decisive change for the commercialization and specialization of agriculture throws into relief the early date of similar processes in Rome. The Albano area was a clear focus for a vineyard specialization already in the mid-tenth century at the latest; the Porto salt pans were already highly active at the same moment. We cannot place any other city's specializations so early, except the Venetian salt pans (which supplied the whole Po plain), and the tendency for vineyards to concentrate close to city walls in the Po plain in every period.[234] This must mark the long-standing size and stability of Rome's urban market by any Italian (let alone European) standards; even Milan only began to move in the same direction at the end of the tenth century.

After this early start, however, Rome's agrarian development moved more slowly. The early eleventh century did see a further specialization, the development of the vineyard and orchard belt around the city, which was established effectively by 1100, and was already much larger than that around any northern city, and unusually clearly organized, as our scattered but illuminating documentation for *scolae* shows. After this, however, the process slowed down for a hundred years. The twelfth century did see some changes, but much less than in the North. The second half of this century saw the beginning of the crystallization of *tenimenta*, the future *casali*, with an expansion in the number of rural estate-centres and the earliest block leases; but it would not be until well into the thirteenth that these would show any

[231] Menant, *Campagnes lombardes*, pp. 172–93, 225–6, 244–9, 255–97.

[232] Rippe, *Padoue*, pp. 557–74.

[233] Violante, *La società milanese*, pp. 99–117; Rapetti, *Campagne milanesi*, pp. 38–42, 83–90, 99–109; Grillo, *Milano*, pp. 89–98.

[234] e.g. Torelli, *Un comune cittadino*, pp. 279–80 (Mantua); Rippe, *Padoue*, pp. 555–6; Pini, *Vite e vino*, pp. 78–9 and map opposite p. 64 (Bologna).

major organizational shifts, even in the size of tenurial units, for these had always been unusually large around Rome.[235]

We could figure this relative lack of change in the twelfth century in terms of it being the end of the period in which Rome was far larger and more active than any other Italian city. This is probably true, in fact; we shall see other signs of it when we come to the urban economy in Chapter 3. But this did not mark any retreat in Rome's own economic complexity; it was more a question of other cities catching up and moving on. Rome shows us an essential continuity in its complexity, and in the generalized subordination of the economy of a huge agrarian hinterland to the needs of the urban market, which no northern city could match before 1100. This economy indeed went way back. As we shall see (pp. 154–5), there are some grounds for cautiously seeing tenth-century Rome as more economically active than the city was in the ninth, but even then the low point for Roman economic complexity (probably the eighth century) was less low than anywhere else. Under these circumstances, looking for substantial change is arguably not the point.

Another reason why it is not the point is that Rome was also already dominant over its hinterland, the Agro romano, the first 20–25 km outside the city gates, to a degree that other cities could only dream of. This was the core argument of the second main section of this chapter. The Agro romano all belonged to churches, which were either based in the city or (in the case of Subiaco and Farfa) had urban subsidiaries. There was no visible lay landowning, and above all no peasant or other rural landowning, except to a small extent in Albano. The tenants of this land who appear in the documents for the Agro romano were also, above all, city-based, in all the cases we can see, except sometimes for Albano and Silva Maior (to which we must doubtless add Tuscolo). The peasants who actually worked the land are hard to see in our sources, but it is anyway evident that the overwhelming proportion of their rents went to the city, to be then divided up between ecclesiastical proprietors and lay lease-holding middlemen, according to the type of lease agreement they had made. The urban food market was thus supplied by, and operated to the profit of, urban-based figures, almost exclusively: no profit went back to the countryside, until the slow beginnings of investment in estate-centres after 1150. No other city matched this overwhelming dominance of the city over the countryside. One of the results was that Romans did not need to try so hard, when in the twelfth century other urban communities can be seen making changes. We have seen (p. 73) that one result was that rents from peasants were not as high as they could have been, and were elsewhere. It is true that when *quartarini* were Roman *rentiers*, we do not know how much more than a quarter of the crop they extracted from the real cultivators; all the same, overall, the Roman elites were getting so much already that they could afford to be lax.

Rome's dominance over the Agro romano was also political. We have seen that there were no *signorie* there, and almost no castles. Indeed, there were also almost no villages or coherent rural settlements, and thus very few autonomous centres for

---

[235] The vineyard belt expanded further in the second quarter of the thirteenth century too; for Tivoli parallels (the work of Roman landowners) see Carocci, *Tivoli*, pp. 415–19.

rural sociability; and the absence of owner-cultivators meant that the only thing that grouped most peasants together would have been the stability of their subjection. The only major exceptions here were Albano, Silva Maior, and probably also Porto and Ostia; we should also again add Tuscolo, though the role of that centre as a tiny political/military rival to Rome itself makes it wholly unusual—and Tuscolo is in fact in strictly agricultural terms rather ill-documented. Over everywhere else, Rome's dominance was unmediated; and it was not all that limited in any of these exceptions (except Tuscolo) either.

I have cautiously suggested that there was scope for a certain flexibility in personal careers, even for members of as subjected a rural society as the Agro romano must have been. We see some signs of it in Silva Maior (see above, p. 75), where locally powerful people had sometimes been cultivators earlier in their careers; but Silva Maior had more local society than did most places. I also postulated it for the *salinarii* of the Porto salt pans (see above, p. 105). The latter proposition was made possible by suggesting that the salt-production *scola* was, in effect, a rural version of an artisans' guild; so one could make urban-type suppositions about career paths. Perhaps the *scola ortulanorum* of Criptule (see above, p. 89) offered similar opportunities. But the structuring of the whole rural economy by the city may mean that this model had a wider application. Peasants were kept apart from the city, but they could migrate there without difficulty; the roads were straight, and the distances not insuperable. Rome must have absorbed constant immigration, indeed. If there was little sociability in the countryside, beyond the level of the family holding, perhaps there was less to keep people there. And if such immigrants survived in Rome at all, a tiny percentage could have made enough to buy into some of the churches' leases in the countryside again. The Agro romano operated as a giant resource for the city at all levels, providing it not only with surplus but with people as well. The flexibility of urban society would certainly have been far greater than in the countryside, but its very existence increased that of the countryside as well.

Rome's rural society was unique, up to the boundary of the Agro romano. Outside it, Lazio of the castles was much more like many other places, particularly in central Italy, but also, in the effervescence of local society, the North. Rome's wealth certainly meant that, even after the city (and the papacy) lost control of much of Lazio in the mid- to late eleventh century, it was not so difficult to regain it a century later. The attraction of the city pressed on small rural lords of the Sabina or *Campania* or *Marittima*, as much as it did on peasants of the Agro romano; not a few of them (the Conti di Segni, for example) ended up in the city too. But here, too, Rome was less exceptional, for exactly the same process can be tracked for plenty of other cities. The exceptionality of the city lay in the completeness of its control over the Agro romano, and the unusually large size of that periurban territory. Rome's unusual wealth, in our period, hung on that. The next chapters will confront the issue of what the city did with it.

3

The Urban Economy

As with its political and ecclesiastical institutions, Rome's urban fabric and economy has too much ideological baggage attached to be seen straight. Its surviving classical buildings and huge late antique churches towered over the Romans of our period; and those other numerous buildings which had fallen out of use since the fourth century, when the city still had maybe half a million people, made much of the land inside the Aurelian Walls an immense field of ruins. Outsiders could marvel at the *mirabilia* of the city, and did so in numerous writings praising the statues, palaces, and arches of the ancient world,[1] or—in a more surreal Arab tradition—the bed of the Tiber paved in copper so that ships could not anchor there, the thousand baths, the lead roofs resembling the sea, the thirty thousand columns for stylites, the twelve thousand markets, and so forth.[2] Conversely, they could focus on the ruins and on the failure of the Romans to live up to their former glories, as with the *Versus Romae*, perhaps a Neapolitan text, in the late ninth century; or, alternatively, on the superiority of Christian poverty to pagan splendour, as in the poems of Hildebert of Lavardin around 1100.[3] What the Romans themselves thought of their material past (a substantial amount, in fact) we will see in Chapter 6; but it certainly got in the way of all sensible analysis by anyone else, both in our period and later, up to nearly the present day. Rome's economy is hardly better understood. The image of the city as essentially unproductive, except on a small scale, and living off its countryside and the papal court, survives even in the recent work of analysts of the calibre of Philip Jones, not to speak of papal historians without economic experience, who can still write that there was 'virtually

---

[1] The *Mirabilia* text of the Englishman, *magister* Gregorius, is most recently ed. in Nardella, *Il fascino di Roma*.

[2] See Guidi, 'La descrizione di Roma', pp. 176, 177 (al-Idrīsī in the twelfth century, also trans. as *Géographie d'Édrisi*, II, here pp. 251–2, rather more fanciful than he is for other Italian cities), 181, 183 (Yāqūt's thirteenth-century compilation of earlier work; this is given rather more credence than I would by McCormick, *Origins*, pp. 622–4—Rome's roofs were, for example, not made of lead but mostly of tile or wood). Ibn Hawqāl in the tenth century, following the slightly earlier al-Istakhri, was more measured, and a lot more brief: Ibn Hauqal, *Configuration de la terre*, I, p. 197. A substantial set of Arabic accounts, including these, has also been retranslated in De Simone and Mandalà, *L'immagine araba di Roma*, pp. 65–94. The entire tradition is discussed briefly in Nallino, 'Un'inedita descrizione araba di Roma', pp. 296–7 (useful lists); in De Simone and Mandalà, *L'immagine araba di Roma*, pp. 11–63; and in Di Branco, *Storie arabe di greci e di romani*, pp. 223–30, who shows how these fantasy descriptions of Rome were originally based on an equally fantastic description of Constantinople. The Hebrew description in Benjamin of Tudela, *The Itinerary*, pp. 6–7, is more measured and more accurate.

[3] Ed. respectively in *MGH*, *Poetae*, III, pp. 554–6; and Hildebertus, *Carmina minora*, nn. 36, 38.

no industry' in the twelfth-century city.[4] We will see that this is about as accurate as were the Arab geographers. Faced with this, we have to start again.

The work of starting again is already under way. The international merchant activity and the active urban redevelopment of the thirteenth century are clear in work by Marco Vendittelli and Étienne Hubert, and their links back to the very clearly attested artisanate of the years around 1100, analysed among others by Laura Moscati, are evident. The quality of Roman-made glazed pottery from as early as the eighth century, and its complexity from the tenth, has long been known to archaeologists. A picture of a thriving city is now easy to see, throughout our period, in fact.[5] But it presents us with one basic problem, which needs to be confronted. Rome in the tenth century was by far the biggest city in Latin Europe, with a population plausibly estimated by Riccardo Santangeli Valenzani at 20–30,000 inhabitants (after a fall from a sixth/seventh-century level of maybe double that). It had a complex economy, and its elites were capable of innovative planning, as we shall see. In the eleventh and especially the twelfth century we can see it expanding further, with new urban building, including some ambitious churches; by 1300, Étienne Hubert and Jean-Claude Maire Vigueur would see, again on plausible grounds, a population of 40,000 or even 50,000.[6] But by then it was by no means the largest city even in Italy. Milan was at least three times as big, with Venice, Florence, and Genoa not much less; Rome was by now in the middle range of Italian cities, along with Verona, Bologna, Pisa, Siena, and Palermo. Rome's evident expansion did not match that of other Italian cities, then; Milan, the biggest and oldest of the new metropoleis, perhaps indeed surpassed the city on the Tiber already by 1100.[7] Rome's early size and wealth was measured by the much more modest parameters of the early Middle Ages; it did not adapt to the more commercial world of the central medieval Mediterranean with as much brio. We must, therefore, balance the city's considerable urban activity against a knowledge that it might in theory have become still more active; and we have to ask why. This issue will underlie the whole chapter, and we will come back to it at the end.

THE URBAN FABRIC

Richard Krautheimer has given us the fullest and most evocative account of what Rome looked like as a city in our period, and we can do no better than start with his

    [4] Jones, *The Italian City-State*, pp. 271–2; Sayers, *Innocent III*, p. 31; another recent example is Petersohn, *Kaisertum und Rom*, p. 237.

    [5] See esp. Vendittelli, 'Mercanti romani'; Vendittelli, 'Élite citadine'; Hubert, *Espace urbain*; Moscati, *Alle origini*, pp. 29–65; for ceramics, pp. 146–50 below; and for a general overview Carocci and Vendittelli, 'Società ed economia'.

    [6] Meneghini and Santangeli Valenzani, *Roma nell'alto medioevo*, pp. 21–4; Hubert, 'L'organizzazione territoriale', p. 174, with Hubert, 'Rome au XIVe siècle'; Maire Vigueur, *L'autre Rome*, pp. 36–8.

    [7] See in general Ginatempo and Sandri, *L'Italia delle città*, except for Rome itself; Paolo Grillo accepts 150–200,000 for Milan around 1300 (*Milano*, p. 39). The date of 1100 is my guess, assuming a population for Milan of 15,000 in 1000, and a geometric growth curve. See further for Milan below, pp. 178–9.

picture. Krautheimer was very influenced by the early modern watercolours and maps of the city which showed a sharp division between the *abitato*, the thickly populated city on the low land of the Tiber bend and the regions around via Lata, and the *disabitato*, the rest of the city inside the vast third-century Aurelian Walls, which was not resettled until the late nineteenth century. There was in the sixteenth century a clear edge to the settled part of the city, which did not get past the Trevi fountain and piazza SS. Apostoli to the east, the Capitolio and the Teatro di Marcello to the south, to which beyond the Tiber were added a few parallel streets in the northern part of Trastevere and the agglomeration of the Civitas Leoniana, Leo IV's new walled suburb of the 840s, by now called the Borgo. The Forum area and all the hills except the Capitolio were empty of settlement, apart from ruins, isolated churches, and small concentrations around the major basilicas of S. Giovanni in Laterano and S. Maria Maggiore, and also (not on a hill) S. Maria Nova near the Colosseo. The *abitato*, which is still visible in Rome's urban fabric, was thus little more than a quarter of the geographical size of the ancient city, and rather smaller an area than that included inside the walls of late medieval Milan. Krautheimer saw its formation as being as early as the late sixth century, and Rome's population thus as being concentrated in the river plain for the whole of the Middle Ages.[8]

This picture has been modified in the last two decades, thanks to recent archaeological investigations and also some dedicated topographical work on the basis of early medieval written sources, in two separate ways. The first is a much clearer realization of how much more settlement there was in the so-called *disabitato* for much of the Middle Ages; the second is a strong argument for a much more scattered settlement in the river plain until the late eleventh century at the earliest, with a set of in effect separate groups of houses connected by fields, and relatively little occupation of the Tiber bend west of piazza Navona before 1100 or so (the latter point, in fact, Krautheimer argued already). These two arguments, taken together, would diminish very substantially the difference between *abitato* and *disabitato* before 1100, and they create a clear image of a largely ruralized urban landscape, with no 'compact urban nucleus'.[9] They need to be taken separately; the first is fully convincing, but it seems to me that the second needs nuancing. (See Map 5 for what follows.)

The argument that the hills of Rome were by no means abandoned yet in our period has by now a good deal of evidence behind it. One element in this evidence, going back to the eighth century, is the location of the city's *diaconiae*, which were initially poor relief centres, though often thereafter slowly gaining parish status (below, p. 307). These churches must have been founded in then-inhabited areas for their role to have had any sense, and it is therefore striking that only four of the eighteen are located in the river plain, as opposed to seven in and around the wide Forum area, which was outside the *abitato* by the late Middle Ages, and seven on the hills.[10]

---

[8] Krautheimer, *Rome*, esp. pp. 271–326, with p. 68 for the sixth century.

[9] Krautheimer, *Rome*, pp. 271–2; Hubert, *Espace urbain*, p. 75 for the quote.

[10] Meneghini and Santangeli Valenzani, *Roma nell'altomedioevo*, pp. 76–91 (map at p. 78); Bertolini, 'Per la storia delle diaconie', pp. 370–88. For churches and the changing structures of early medieval habitat, see most recently Spera, 'Le forme della cristianizzazione'.

That distribution pre-dated our period, and might be seen to represent a different distribution of settlement to that which we face after 900; but another element, certainly chronologically relevant, is the fairly regular information we have for the birthplaces of popes, who were generally from the city's aristocracy, and also for the houses of some lay aristocrats. In the period 900–1046, before Henry III's coup, Leo VIII was from the Clivus Argentarius on the Capitolio, Benedict VI from nearby, John XV from the *regio* Gallina Alba, probably on the Viminale, John XVII from the *regio* of Biberatica on the slopes above the Fori Imperiali, John XVIII from right out by the Porta Metrobia beyond the Celio: all these are outside the later *abitato*.[11] As for lay aristocrats, Prince Alberico was born on the Aventino and subsequently had a house by SS. Apostoli, where the Tuscolani were later based as well; a Crescenzio active in the 960s was known as 'from Caballus Marmoreus' and thus lived on the Quirinale, near the statue of Castor and Pollux and their horses; some of the *de Imiza* family were based on the eastern edge of the Palatino, and another lived near S. Agata on the Quirinale. Less well-known but nevertheless elite members include Gregorio *de Abentino* and Giorgio *de Cannapara* (just south-west of the Foro Romano) in 942, Pietro *de Canaparia* in 963 and 966, Farolfo *a S. Eustathio* (S. Eustachio west of the Pantheon) in 999 and several other notables from the same region in the 1010s and onwards, Crescenzio *sub Ianiculo* (the lower slopes of the Gianicolo in Trastevere) in 1002, Stefano from Campo Marzio in 1011, Duranto from the via Lata (the great classical main north–south street, the modern via del Corso) in 1012, Gregorio *de Ripa* (a palatine judge, from the Tiber port south-west of the Forum area) in 1013, Graziano *a Balneo Miccino* just to its north in 1017, and Andrea *de Coloseo* in 1019. If we accept that major lay monastic and church foundations were generally in or near the residences of founders, we might add Benedetto Campanino's SS. Cosma e Damiano in Trastevere, rather south of the main run of Trastevere housing, in perhaps the 940s, Alberico's cousins' SS. Ciriaco e Nicola in via Lata in the same period, Pietro *medicus*' S. Maria in Pallara on the Palatino before 977, and Crescenzio the urban prefect's S. Trifone in Campo Marzio shortly before 1006.[12]

[11] *LP*, II, pp. 250, 260, 265, 266. Benedict X (1058–9), the last pope in the Tuscolano tradition, was similarly from the S. Maria Maggiore area: *LP*, II, p. 335.

[12] See, respectively, Ugo of Farfa, *Destructio*, pp. 39–40, with *RS*, n. 155 and *RF*, n. 637 (Alberico and Tuscolani); Liutprando, *Historia Ottonis*, ch. 9 (Crescenzio); *S. Gregorio*, n. 151 with *Papsturkunden*, n. 226 and *RS*, n. 79 (*de Imiza*; see Görich, 'Die *de Imiza*', pp. 1–10); *RS*, n. 155 (Gregorio and Giorgio); Liutprando, *Historia Ottonis*, ch. 9 and *RS*, n. 118 (Pietro 'de Canaparia'); Manaresi, n. 254 (Farolfo; cf. *RF*, nn. 616, 657, *SMVL*, n. 75, and below, pp. 231–2 for the S. Eustachio group); *S. Alessio*, n. 1 (Crescenzio); *RF*, n. 657 (Stefano); *RF*, n. 658 (Duranto); *S. Gregorio*, n. 126 (Gregorio); *RF*, n. 504 (Graziano); *S. Gregorio*, n. 14 (Andrea 'de Coloseo'). For monasteries, *RF*, n. 439 (Benedetto); Hamilton, 'The monastic revival', pp. 52–4 and Hamilton, 'The house of Theophylact', pp. 202–8 (cousins of Alberico: these articles are the best account of tenth-century monastic foundations, but some of their ascriptions to founders are hypothetical); for S. Maria in Pallara, Fedele, 'Una chiesa', p. 349 (for the 977 date) and *passim*, Augenti, *Il Palatino*, pp. 65–6, and Marchiori, *Art and Reform*, pp. 3–7 (plus, perhaps, *S. Prassede*, nn. 1, 2, 3, for they are to another monastery founded by Pietro *medicus* called S. Lorenzo, which could well be the same place); *Papsturkunden*, n. 424 (S. Trifone). Parallel lists are in Krautheimer, *Rome*, p. 363; Hubert, *Espace urbain*, p. 290; Coates-Stephens, 'Housing', pp. 239–41.

This is a heterogeneous set of citations, but half are for the hills of Rome (usually their lower slopes), almost a quarter for the Forum area, and less than a third from the future *abitato*. Krautheimer knew most of these references, but he saw them as signs that aristocrats simply preferred fortifiable locations with more space to expand. This is misleading. These were not rural castles (there is no sign that any of them were fortified); they were urban residences, and they would have attracted merchants and artisans just as aristocrats always did, to create a network of small *quartieri*, some contiguous, some not. So, indeed, would the biggest residence of all, the Laterano palace, which was even further from the river plain.[13] The patterns of aristocratic housing in this period match those of the *diaconiae* slightly earlier, and are, like them, best seen as attesting to a considerably wider spread of settlement than Krautheimer recognized. As we shall see in a moment, references to private housing on the Celio, the only well-documented Roman region before 1000, point in the same direction. And this would continue, to some extent at least: the 'new aristocracy' of the eleventh and twelfth century did not live on the hills (except the central Capitolio), but, out of the thirteen families discussed in Chapter 4, three lived in the Tiber bend, with four in Ripa, four in Trastevere, and two in the Colosseo area—half, then, were still based outside Krautheimer's *abitato*.

A third element is based on archaeology, and here we need to be cautious, simply because excavations tend to be unplanned, taking advantage of rebuildings, demolitions, new metro stations, and the reorientation of roads, and large sections of the city have never seen detailed medieval archaeology. (See Map 5 for major published sites.) All the same, the picture of a rather more geographically extensive urban fabric has been amply confirmed by recent work. Robert Coates-Stephens has tracked signs of early medieval housing in older excavations on a variety of sites on the hills; inevitably scrappy, these show at least some settlement across as much as two-thirds of the ancient city. But the clearest instance is the detailed set of excavations by Riccardo Santangeli and Roberto Meneghini in the Fori Imperiali, once again largely beyond the edge of the later *abitato*. Here, two-storeyed stone buildings have been found in the Foro di Nerva from the ninth century, abandoned around 1100; in the Foro di Cesare, smaller tenth-century houses have been found, apparently a planned group, surviving into the eleventh; in the Foro di Traiano, another tenth-century planned development survived longer, and developed further in the thirteenth. To the south, into the Foro Romano, traces of more two-storeyed houses from the ninth century have been found in and beside the Basilica Emilia, and the Atrium Vestae further up the via Sacra had an early medieval building in it, excavated in the 1880s, which contained an important hoard of tenth-century coins from Anglo-Saxon England.[14] Occupation in this sector

---

[13] Krautheimer, *Rome*, pp. 254–5.

[14] Coates-Stephens, 'Housing' (p. 249 for the Atrium Vestae, with G. B. de Rossi's contribution to Lanciani, 'L'atrio di Vesta', pp. 487–97; the hoard dates to *c*.945, and later occupation there was not discovered). For the Fori, the most convenient overview by the excavators is Meneghini and Santangeli Valenzani, *I fori imperiali*, esp. pp. 115–55, with Meneghini and Santangeli Valenzani, *Roma nell'altomedioevo*, pp. 45–51, 127–9, 157–88 (pp. 165–7 for the Basilica Emilia). Santangeli Valenzani, *Edilizia residenziale*, sets these data in a wider Italian context.

continued later, too, as we shall see (below, p. 126). The Foro di Augusto and Tempio della Pace seem to have been converted to gardens, but the rest of the Forum area, far from being abandoned, seems to have been switched to housing, once the marble paving of most of it had been stripped in the ninth century. This housing was clearly interspersed with agricultural land, but it is attested across all this great former public area, right up to the well-attested medieval *quartiere* around S. Maria Nova and the Colosseo. Sections of it went in and out of use; if the houses in the Foro di Cesare failed in the eleventh century, to be replaced by agricultural land, new houses a little to the south-west on the edge of the former Basilica Giulia were built not long after, in the twelfth century.[15] But the Fori clearly remained occupied. Indeed, it would be better to say that, from the ninth century onwards, this area of enormous monumental buildings was given over to permanent human habitation for the first time.

Settlement of different types thus extended some way beyond the river plains of the late medieval city. Riccardo Santangeli and Ilaria de Luca have called attention to an account of a prodigy, dated to 921 in the later tenth-century *Chronicon* of Benedetto of Monte Soratte, in which a woman living near S. Susanna by the Porta Salaria was unable to move a cooking pot (*olla*) containing millet porridge from its marble shelf, despite the help of neighbours, *vicini et proximi*, 'all running', and eventually a whole crowd of clerics and lay people, until enough prayers were said to get it moved; the miracle is an unusual one, and has importance for students of house furnishings, but the image is also one of an active *quartiere*, even though S. Susanna is far from any other documented settlement area.[16] And a set of tenth-century documents preserved in the Subiaco cartulary show an equally active *quartiere* on the Celio, around the monastery of S. Erasmo sul Celio (acquired by Subiaco from the pope in 938 on the instruction of Prince Alberico) and south down the hill to Porta Metrobia, as well as a smaller but contiguous group of houses out at the Porta Maggiore, and another at the Septem Vie at the eastern corner of the Circo Massimo.[17] Let us look at the former for a moment.

The Celio settlement, called Decenniae, is hardly visible in the fairly substantial archaeological work done on the hill. Nonetheless, it had a dozen houses in texts from 857 to 1017, mixed in with several large late antique and ninth-century churches, vineyards, *orti* with tree crops, and some grain-fields (we have leases to cultivators for two new vineyards on such fields from 967 and 978), and

---

[15] For the Basilica Giulia, see Maetzke, 'La struttura stratigrafica', pp. 103–22, 192–3, with Paganelli, 'Area N-O del Foro Romano' for the previous period. Medieval occupation in the Colosseo has been partially excavated too: Antonetti and Rea, 'Inquadramento cronologico', pp. 305–17.

[16] Benedetto, *Chronicon*, pp. 163–4, cited in Meneghini and Santangeli Valenzani, *Roma nell'alto medioevo*, p. 215, and in de Luca, 'Ritrovamenti', pp. 106–8.

[17] For the Porta Maggiore houses, see above all Coates-Stephens, *Porta Maggiore*, pp. 111–26 (with, as a probable *terminus ante quem* for abandonment, the rural landscape in Kehr, IV, pp. 226–8, a. 1166); for their contiguity, see e.g. *RS*, n. 122 (a. 952), referring to three *domora iunctas*. For Septem Vie, *S. Gregorio*, nn. 151, 79, 21; *CDC*, n. 70. For 938, *Papsturkunden*, n. 85; see in general Camobreco, 'Il monastero di S. Erasmo' and Lori Sanfilippo, 'I possessi romani', pp. 26–39, for background.

a functioning aqueduct.[18] This sense of a partly ruralized community, scattered between the Celio's churches, is tempered however by the existence of some prosperous *rentiers*, Leone priest of SS. Quattro Coronati and his family in 953–65, who had a two-storeyed house with a marble staircase (much like one of those found in the Foro di Nerva), or Crescenzo Murcapullo (documented 978–1003), a dealer both inside and outside the Porta Metrobia, who lived just inside it in a one-storeyed house—or indeed the future Pope John XVIII (1004–9), who came from the same area, as we have seen.[19] The witness lists of the charters also include a substantial set of artisans, particularly bleachers or dyers (*candicatores*) and wool weavers. We know that bleaching was carried out in the mills at Domine Quo Vadis, 2 km to the south outside the walls on the via Appia, in 1081, so this edge of town was clearly a cloth-making area; it is likely that the bleachers of the Decenniae area—who were organized enough to have a *prior*, implying a *scola*, in 978—got their water from the above-mentioned aqueduct, still in this period called the Forma Claudia.[20] We do not know who they were selling cloth to, but it is not at all impossible that these are signs of the effect of the demand of the Laterano palace, just over 500 metres away, on its immediate hinterland. We also cannot say what happened in Decenniae after the Subiaco documents give out in the 1010s; after a gap in our evidence, the fragmentary documentation for the twelfth-century Celio tells us about nothing except churches. These may already by then have been as isolated among the fields as they certainly were in the early modern period, as is also hinted at by the daunting solidity of the apse of SS. Quattro Coronati on the edge of the Celio, rebuilt by Paschal II in his reconstruction during the 1110s (see Chapter 6, Figure 6.7). The Norman sack of the city in 1084 was not as serious as was then claimed, but one area that was certainly devastated was that around the latter church.[21] This may indeed have marked the end of the Celio settlement. But a century earlier, the Celio showed a certain density of settlement by both rich and poor, agriculturalists and artisans alike. Only the interspersed vineyards and grain-fields distinguished it from more central urban regions.

---

[18] *RS*, nn. 59, 85, 87, 88, 89, 90, 114, with *Papsturkunden*, nn. 57, 85, and (with caution) Pflugk, II, n. 105; see Hubert, *Espace urbain*, p. 77. The Forma Claudia was probably kept in repair in large part to support the Laterano: cf. Pflugk, III, n. 289 (a. 1179). For archaeology, see most recently Pavolini, 'Aspetti del Celio', pp. 428–31, which does however recognize some signs of artisanal activity on the Celio in our period.

[19] *RS*, nn. 89, 90 (Leone), 59, 84, 91, 82 (Crescenzio Murcapullo—he may well have been an immigrant from the Galeria area, where his nickname was a place name: *SPV*, n. 7).

[20] Artisans: *RS*, nn. 89 (generic *opifices*), 59 (*prior candicatoris*), 91 (*lanistae*—cf. this chapter, n. 106; one was 'de Alefanto', from the Ripa Graeca region), 82 (*opifex, candicator*), 85 (*calzulario*), with *tessitores* from the area around S. Gregorio: *S. Gregorio*, nn. 79, 173. Compare *S. Paolo*, n. 1 for Domine Quo Vadis, together with with the partially-surviving central medieval fulling-mill identified by Lucrezia Spera, *Il paesaggio suburbano*, pp. 72–3, 427–9; and, much later, the *walkeria* or fulling-mill at S. Maria in Cosmedin (again on the Ripa Graeca) in 1208, *Reg. Inn. III*, XI.83. Bleaching is often an edge-of-town or rural operation: see e.g. Menant, *L'Italie des communes*, p. 294.

[21] For the Norman sack and the Celio, Hamilton, 'Memory, symbol', pp. 393–4, 397–8. For SS. Quattro Coronati, see Forcella, VIII.717; Kehr, I, pp. 417–18; Krautheimer, *Corpus basilicarum*, IV, pp. 1–36; Barelli, '*Ecclesiam reparare*'; for an up-to-date introduction, Barelli, *Il complesso monumentale*.

This pattern has some analogies with the top of the Esquilino, around S. Maria Maggiore, too. Settlement continued longer there, throughout our period and beyond (although with fewer attested artisans in our poorer sources).[22] There is no good reason, in fact, given the distribution of aristocratic housing mentioned earlier, not to postulate similar patterns for most of the city, extending from the lowlands and the Forum out past the great papal palace complex at the Laterano, as far as the Walls, perhaps everywhere except the far north, the far south, and parts of the far east of the city: a network of urban villages, with smaller and bigger agglomerations separated by vineyards, the occasional grain-field, and (of course) ruins. There were probably fewer such villages in the twelfth century than the tenth, but some survived then too.

This picture of a half-urban, half-rural landscape has been extended into the future *abitato*, too, at least before 1050 or so. Krautheimer already assumed it, although without giving any evidence. Hubert stresses it as well, but most of his evidence is taken from the hills, as in the last few paragraphs here, not from the river plain; at most, he notes some references to *terra vacans*, open land, among the houses of Campo Marzio.[23] And the archaeologists have perhaps stressed it most of all. The other classic medieval excavation of recent years, the Crypta Balbi, focused on a block of land on the river plain not far west of the Capitolio, shows a constantly changing set of medieval structures built inside the ancient Porticus Minucia and Teatro di Balbo, including, among other things, workshops, a burial ground and a huge rubbish pit in the sixth and seventh centuries, two churches in the fifth to ninth, a limekiln in *c*.800, a substantial wall in the late tenth, a small house and a bath complex in the eleventh and onwards, a late eleventh-century 'palazzo' with a tower, expanding in size later, and several stone houses and smaller houses in the twelfth—the whole also accompanied by an unbroken ceramic sequence. But the overall impression given by the recent survey of the site by its principal excavator, Daniele Manacorda, is one of abandonment and agricultural infill until the building expansion of the twelfth century, an impression reinforced by the always-compelling Inklink pictorial reconstructions in the text.[24] The same is true of the Foro di Nerva houses (again supported by Inklink reconstructions, although of a somewhat more 'urban' style: see Figure 3.1). Although the latter are among the most elaborate early medieval private houses yet excavated in Europe, surpassed only by the occasional Carolingian or Asturian palace or the ninth-century houses on the Morería site at Mérida, in al-Andalus, Santangeli has referred to the 'marked "rural" quality of the landscape' there.[25] In his more recent writings

[22] Houses in the S. Maria Maggiore area: *Papsturkunden*, n. 226; *RS*, n. 120; *S. Agnese*, n. 4; de Rossi, 'Atto di donazione'; *SMVL*, n. 82; *S. Prassede*, nn. 10, 37; *Liberiano*, n. 22—an interestingly heterogeneous set.

[23] Krautheimer, *Rome*, p. 249; Hubert, *Espace urbain*, pp. 74–5, 79–83, 127, 141–2 (p. 82: *terra vacans*).

[24] See in general Manacorda, *Crypta Balbi*, pp. 48–69 (pp. 45, 65 for Inklink pictures); for the bath complex, Saguì, 'Lo scavo', pp. 15–63. The clearest survey of recent work is in Ricci and Vendittelli, *Museo nazionale romano—Crypta Balbi*, I, pp. 9–22. I am most grateful to Alessandra Molinari for guidance here.

[25] Santangeli Valenzani, 'Residential building', p. 111. For the Morería, see Alba Calzado, 'Apuntes sobre el urbanismo'; Alba Calzado, 'Diacronía de la vivienda', pp. 179–87.

Figure 3.1. The Foro di Nerva in *c.*900, as reconstructed by Inklink.

this rural imagery has largely disappeared, as he and his collaborators have become more impressed by the 'interventi di "urbanizzazione"' in the tenth-century Fori Imperiali (see below, p. 126), of which, it is important to stress, *orti* for vines and fruit trees make up a structured part. But the impression of a rarefied habitat often remains; Daniele Manacorda has even seen it as potentially concentrated inside isolated intra-mural fortifications, although this hypothesis has not been taken up by the historiography.[26]

One thing is certain: pre-twelfth-century housing was, as a whole, all less impressive and less dense than it would be later. Houses (*domūs*) were described in documents as one-storeyed (*terrinea*) or two-storeyed (*solarata*), with, usually, a courtyard (*curtis*) in front leading onto the street and often an *ortus* at the back.[27] This loose pattern certainly fits the archaeology of the Fori, and it gave ample space for greenery around houses. Houses also, even though they were mostly not built in wood (as in much of pre-twelfth-century Italy), were very simply constructed out of reused stone and brick, and look crude to our eyes, dwarfed by the classical monumental buildings around them; small wonder that still-habitable bits of those buildings, called *cryptae* in our sources, were almost as popular for housing as was new construction. The tower-houses and terrace-houses which became

[26] Manacorda, '*Castra e burgi*'; cf. the caution in Meneghini and Santangeli Valenzani, *Roma nell'altomedioevo*, p. 44 (and p. 48 for 'interventi di "urbanizzazione"'), and in Di Santo, *Monumenti antichi*, pp. 27–9, 32.

[27] See above all Hubert, *Espace urbain*, pp. 172–6. Typical early examples, taken at random, are *RS*, n. 82 for *terrinea* and n. 90 for *solarata*.

increasingly important between the end of the eleventh century and the end of the twelfth were more solidly constructed, and allowed a much greater population concentration, as Hubert accurately shows.[28] But this picture of houses with courtyards is still different from a picture of isolated houses or groups of houses, separated by tracts of vineyards. Such a picture is valid for the hills of Rome, as we have seen. But it is remarkably difficult to substantiate for the main areas of pre-twelfth-century settlement, around the via Lata, west to piazza Navona, and south into Ripa and the Forum area. We have hardly any tenth-century documents for this core area, it is true—and also, unfortunately, even less archaeology than on the hills, apart from the two major sites just mentioned. There were undeniably open spaces, as is shown for instance in a small piazza Venezia site, which reveals a settlement gap between the mid-ninth century and the twelfth in a central area. But by the early eleventh century, in the areas we have texts for, we find a regular run of courtyard houses, with only the occasional *terra vacans* or field, in the great bulk of our documented regions: Scorteclari, Campo Marzio and Pigna around the Pantheon, S. Maria Nova in the eastern Forum area, and northern Trastevere and the eastern Civitas Leoniana beyond the Tiber. We do not see any great open areas at all here, although I would not wish to doubt that the Tiber bend west and south of piazza Navona was indeed as yet fairly little occupied, as the historiography universally assumes. (I would only remark here that we hardly have any evidence for this region at all before the late twelfth century, either positive or negative, and it is far from impossible that there was more housing here, too, than people have proposed.) This was indeed the heart of Rome, and there is a case for seeing the via Lata–piazza Navona–Ripa–Fori quadrilateral as a genuine urban nucleus throughout our period, acting as an economic and social focus for the more scattered urban villages on the hills.[29] It was not yet a political focus, for Rome was always in the early Middle Ages poised between the two great power centres on opposite edges of the city, the Vaticano and the Laterano; but when the Romans did look for their own political centre, their choice of the Capitolio, a steep fortifiable hill near the middle of this urban core, which also overlooked the principal market east of the Tiber, was not just classicizing sentiment.

Let us look a little more closely at those different parts of this urban nucleus which have good documentation, to see how they were articulated. I shall here focus on a long eleventh century, 980–1150, the first period in which we can say much about the fabric of our documented regions, as a point of reference. The end of this period was also one of renewed urban expansion and rebuilding, as discussed by Étienne Hubert (and clearly photo-documented in Krautheimer: the standing secular buildings of Rome in effect begin in the early twelfth);[30] we will see signs of this expansion as we move from region to region in the city. But I will discuss the issue of the pacing of expansion as a whole, briefly, at the end of the next section.

[28] Hubert, *Espace urbain*, pp. 142–7, 172–213.
[29] See already for the ninth century Goodson, *The Rome of Pope Paschal I*, p. 55 (correctly criticizing an earlier view of mine). For piazza Venezia, see below, n. 63.
[30] See below, n. 153. For the photographs, see Krautheimer, *Rome*, pp. 279–308, and Figures 3.3 and 4.1–2 here.

Before we do so, two preliminary points need to be made. First, a word on terminology. It will already be evident that Rome had names for a long list of urban *quartieri*: so much so, in fact, that it is usually easy to locate land and buildings mentioned in charters, at least approximately, and people as well, when they are recorded in texts as *a Campo Martio, a Colossus/Coloseo, a macello sub Templo Marcelli*, etc.—'*de*' is used as well, but '*a*' is exclusively used for people from localities in the city, and not the countryside, in texts from the 950s onwards.[31] Clearly, Romans identified with particular areas in the city, and thus presumably always had a sense of their participation in local communities of some type. Hubert has tracked how the twelve or fourteen numbered *regiones* of the tenth century (II for the Celio, III for the far east of the city, IV for Colosseo, IX for the area around the Pantheon, XIV for Trastevere, etc.) dropped out of usage in the eleventh century. They were replaced, in built-up areas at least, by many more named *regiones*, at least thirty in number: Scorteclari, Campus Martis (Campo Marzio), Pinea (Pigna), Ponte, Tribii (Trevi), S. Maria Nova/Colosseo, Pallaria (Palatino), and so on, which were also mostly much smaller, and were increasingly themselves subdivided into *contradae* (see Map 6). These were essentially the crystallization of pre-existing local identities, which may well go back to well before the end of the larger numbered *regiones*. They will be key points of reference in the rest of the book, as they were for Romans themselves throughout our period, as documents extensively show.[32]

In the twelfth century, conversely (the first reference is from Pandolfo's biography of Gelasius II, and relates to events in 1118), we begin to get renewed references to twelve Roman *regiones* again. When the city acted as a single body, in war, in ceremonial, or, later, in the choice of senators, the building blocks of the city were seen as twelve (plus Trastevere, which was the thirteenth *regio* by 1313 at the latest, and probably already so a century earlier). These twelve/thirteen 'super-regions' were made up of between one and three of the *regiones* of the eleventh century, but, confusingly for us, used the same regional terminology. The 'super-regions' were clearly seen as groupings of smaller *regiones*; in 1188, one is called 'Monti, Biberatica and Colosseo', another 'Arenula and Caccabarii', another 'Ponte and Scorteclari'.[33] The smaller *regiones* were real urban quarters, and often real

---

[31] Tenth-century instances are *Papsturkunden*, nn. 134, 155; *RS*, n. 118; *S. Gregorio*, n. 77; Gullotta, 'Un antico ed unico documento'; *RS*, n. 141; Manaresi, n. 236; *RF*, n. 428; Manaresi, n. 254; *SMVL*, n. 24A—taking off in the 990s.

[32] See in general Hubert, *Espace urbain*, pp. 70–4, 83–4, 86–96, 365–8, with, earlier, Halphen, *Études*, pp. 10–15. 'Twelve to fourteen' numbered *regiones*: there may well have been twelve left-bank Roman *regiones* throughout, as arguably shown for the tenth century by *LP*, II, p. 252, which records the twelve '*decarcones*' hanged by Otto I (see further below, p. 449); but, although no *regio XIII* is ever cited, *regio XIV Transtiberim* has several citations in the early eleventh century, *Papsturkunden*, n. 419; *SCD*, nn, 34, 35; SMT, n. 2.

[33] The 1118 reference is in *Liber pontificalis*, ed. Přerovský, p. 734; for 1188, 'Documenti per la storia', nn. 14, 15, 17. (Contrast the sixteen *regiones* whose *scole* met Henry IV in 1084: Benzone of Alba, *Ad Heinricum IV*, I.9–12. These were clearly representatives in some sense, but Benzone may not have been exact.) Note also that the *contradae* who swore peace to Eugenius III in 1149 (*Senato*, n. 8), that is to say subdivisions of 'super-regions', were almost certainly the *regiones* of our documentary collections, not the smaller *contradae*, subdivisions of the documentary *regiones*, which only appear later in the century: the first of the latter appears in 1164 (*SMN*, n. 91), and the first clear instance is 1171 (*SMCM*, n. 55).

communities, whereas the 'super-regions' were more artificial political districts. It was the latter which would dominate in later centuries, and would become the set of late medieval and modern *rioni* ('Monti, Biberatica and Colosseo' would thus become the *rione* of Monti). But in this chapter, and more generally in this book, it is the smaller *regiones* that are referred to throughout. The twelve political *regiones* will be referred to, when necessary (here and in later chapters), as 'super-regions'. The word *rione* will not be used.

It is, I would add, also necessary to stress quite how small some of these regions were. One passed from the *regio* of Campo Marzio up through the *regio* of S. Lorenzo in Lucina and back to the *regio* of Colonna (Antonina) in the twelfth century by walking half a kilometre. This micro-localization of identity is also one reason why Rome had such a bewilderingly large number of churches, since every tiny *contrada*, and sometimes every prominent family in it, wanted its own (for the major ones, see Map 7). The main local areas of the city in our period are marked on Map 6. They were clearly contiguous by the twelfth century, if not overlapping—the *regio* of S. Maria in Via Lata of the eleventh century seems to have been taken over by Colonna and its subordinate *contrada* of Vigna in the twelfth; S. Maria Nova and Colosseo were synonyms; and how anyone could have really known they were crossing from Campo Marzio to S. Lorenzo in Lucina cannot be said.[34] This form of localization also seems to have made identification by street names unnecessary; not many regularly appear, apart from the via Lata and its extension into the Forum as the via Sacra, although some piazze (*campi*) in more built-up areas were beginning to get their own names, the Campo Carleo around the Colonna di Traiano or the Campo Camilianus near S. Ciriaco in Via Lata.[35] So: regions mattered to people, and they appear in our earliest detailed documents for the city, in the 950s and onwards. As we shall see in Chapter 5, the degree to which they acted as the basis for a fully organized community was probably quite variable, but some of them were very organized indeed.

The second point concerns the ownership of land. We have seen that there is no evidence for significant lay proprietorship in the Agro romano in our period (above, pp. 53–9) and, indeed, almost no evidence of any kind for it before the late eleventh century. It is important to stress that this includes the city. We would of course expect ecclesiastical archives to privilege the ownership of land by churches and monasteries, but in the city, as in the countryside, almost all references to the alienation of land by the laity, before charter formularies changed in the 1070s, say it is the *ius* of a given ecclesiastical institution, or else the vaguer *iuris cui existens*, which, as we have seen, at least means that the alienator is not the proprietor. There

---

[34] *Regio S. Maria in Via*: *SMVL*, nn. 90, 96 (aa. 1063–70); this area is *retro Columpne Antonini in loco Vinea* in 1163 (*SMVL*, n. 201), which is *in regione Colupma in contrada de le Vinge* in 1171 (*SMCM*, n. 55; cf. *SMVL*, n. 236 and *S. Sil.*, n. 54). See Hubert, 'Patrimoines immobiliers', pp. 137–40. S. Maria Nova and Colosseo as the same *regio*: see *SMN*, nn. 69 and 70 (a. 1153), for the same property.

[35] *Campo Carleo*: from *SMVL*, n. 26 (a. 1004). *Campo Camilianus*: *SMVL*, n. 115 (a. 1086). First refs. to other *campi* before the latter date are *RS*, n. 79 (*Campo S. Agathe*); *RS*, n. 89 (*Campo Decennias*); *LL*, n. 279 (*Campus de Agonis*); *SCD*, n. 30 (*Campo S. Blasio*). A few ascending streets were still called *clivus*, too: *Argentarius, Scauri*, etc.

are some exceptions to this generalization. In 868, Pietro di Karolo *consul et dux* sold his large town house, held *iuris mei*, to the emperor Louis II for 800 pounds of silver; in 1052, Gregorio *illustris vir* di Gregorio di Michele leased out a house plot in the Basilica di Massenzio, *iuris vestri* [Gregorio's] *dominii*; in 1073, Franco di Sera seems to have owned the riverbank in Trastevere that he gave to S. Maria there. These imply that aristocrats and other members of urban elites, including entrepreneurs like Franco, could gain full property rights on occasion—in the first case, conceivably from a pope who knew that an emperor would not want to buy a lease. But their rarity is still striking, among all the other clear indications of aristocrats and others holding leases in the city. Indeed, even after the 1070s, when it seems to have become slowly easier to own land outright, it is remarkably hard to find clear signs of it in the texts. I have found only one more before 1150, another house plot in the *regio Colosei* in 1146; then, before 1200, a house in Colosseo, a house plot in Pigna, a house in Campo Marzio, and a group of vineyards on the Esquilino.[36] We have many lay transactions preserved in the city for the twelfth century in our ecclesiastical archives; nearly half are explicitly for land held in lease; the rest usually do not make ownership explicit. We cannot assume that the latter were held in full property. It seems to me that lay property rights, though they undoubtedly existed, made only slow inroads into the established ecclesiastical monopoly of land.

This is my only serious disagreement with Étienne Hubert's picture in his remarkable book on the city's urban fabric. Hubert interprets *iuris cui existens* as meaning proprietorial ownership, and thus feels entitled to assume that land is lay-owned unless the opposite is demonstrated. This is a misreading, as I have argued elsewhere. Even then, Hubert argues for a decline of small property-owning into the thirteenth century, with only aristocrats maintaining substantial lands under their direct control, among the large stretches of church land. This seems to me a convincing picture; but I would see it, rather, as marking a slow trend by aristocrats to gain full title over their urban possessions, and also as marking an increase in evidence (after our period ends) which shows that non-elites, mostly, did not gain such title. We would not, I think, disagree over the high percentage of ecclesiastical landowning in 1150/1200; it is just that Hubert sees it as increasing (from the eleventh century), and I see it as slowly decreasing.[37] The key issue for what follows

---

[36] Texts cited, in turn: *Liber instrumentorum monasterii Casauriensis*, ff. 74v–75r; *SMN*, n. 15; *SMT*, n. 5; *SMN*, nn. 58 (a. 1146), 66 with 109; *SMVL*, n. 186; *SPV*, n. 67; and the Bagi-Monte Pipino vineyard group, *SMN*, nn. 89, 131, 138, 147, 155, 161. I have excluded two other texts: *RF*, n. 651 (a. 1011) describes lay control of a Tiber riverbank as their own *ius*, but then uses possession (not property) formulae in the rest of the text; the lay *domibus propriis* in the Porticus S. Petri in *SPV*, n. 16 (a. 1053) also seem to be ultimately or originally leasehold (below, n. 90); see also n. 54 below. *SMN*, n. 58, already cited, is odd, too: the text firmly claims full property rights for the lay lessors, *iuris nostri dominii*, but S. Maria Nova collected rent from it in the same year and continuously thereafter, as dorsal notes show. Either the owners immediately gave the land to the church in a lost text, or else even explicit claims to full property are not always accurate.

[37] Hubert, *Espace urbain*, pp. 270–89. On pp. 265–70, developed also in Hubert, 'Gestion immobilière', he shows that thirteenth-century lessees also normally owned the houses they erected on church land, although this is only explicit from the late twelfth century, and the distinction is much vaguer in our period (one possible example is *SMVL*, n. 67A, already in Nepi in 1038, although the case is unusual). For my views on property, see Wickham, '*Iuris cui existens*'.

in this chapter and the next two is whether we can assume that land alienated in a document by a layman or laywoman after 1050, which gives no indications about property rights, is really held in full property. I do not think we can make that assumption, although I would be very cautious about claiming that we can show it was *not* held in full property, and I have tried not to do so in what follows. The main point for the whole of the book, however, is the overwhelming dominance of ecclesiastical property in the city, which has socio-political as well as economic implications, as we shall see.

We begin our tour of the central areas of the city at the Colosseo, a major Roman monument partially turned in our period into a huge housing block, far and away the largest in the city (as it still would be if it was occupied), and inhabited for some time after, as both archaeology and written documents show. From here it was only a 200-metre walk west to S. Maria Nova (modern S. Francesca Romana), a ninth-century *diaconia* built into the Tempio di Venere e Roma, whose documents are the main source for this *regio*. In the S. Maria Nova texts, classical buildings are prominent: houses were built inside the latter temple (in our period called the Templum Romuli), as also inside the Basilica di Massenzio (by now called the Domus Nova), right beside the church, fronting the via Sacra, which ran through the region. There were also houses around the two large arches which still stand there, the Arco di Costantino (by now called the Arcus Maior Triumphalis or the Arcus Traso) and the Arco di Tito (by now called the Arcus Septem Lucernarum from the seven-branched candlestick sculpted on it—booty from Titus' sack of the temple of Jerusalem).[38] (For these and other classical buildings in the city, see Map 8.) Many habitations in this tightly built-up area were clearly simply reusing other classical buildings, too: there were several *criptae*, mostly *cum sinino*, vaulted roofs, and two with two storeys. But most houses were standardly, as elsewhere, called *domus terrinea* or *solarata*: they were built in and against the omnipresent classical masonry. They were also added to, often enough; in the twelfth century, in particular, there are clear signs of the infilling of housing, with new ones built in courtyards, or on occasional tracts of vacant land. The dense building of this zone thus steadily became denser at the end of our period. The 1192 list of decorated arches, described by Cencio *camerarius* in 1192 on the processional route from the Vaticano to the Laterano, includes over forty houses in this zone, all presumably located along the via Sacra (below, pp. 295–6).[39]

---

[38] Colosseo: see in general Rea, *Rota Colisei*. It was not fully occupied for housing in any period, but such occupation began by the ninth or tenth century, and extended past the thirteenth. Templum Romuli: from *SMN*, n. 1 (a. 982) onwards, with, later, *Mirabilia*, p. 57; see also Castagnoli, 'Il tempio di Roma'. Domus Nova: from *SMN*, n. 11 (a. 1039); Arcus Maior/Traso: from *SMN*, n. 17 (a. 1060) and n. 102 (a. 1173) onwards; Arcus Septem Lucernarum: from *SMN*, n. 19 (a. 1062) onwards—cf. *Mirabilia*, p. 57. Not far south of these was the Settizonio, fortified by the 1080s: below, n. 159. Note that the Palatino-edge site excavated in recent years just south-east of the Arco di Tito showed very little material from our period: Saguì, 'Area delle "Terme di Elagabalo"', p. 151.

[39] *Criptae*: e.g. *SMN*, nn. 4, 5; with two storeys, nn. 62, 72. New housing: nn. 44, 47, 51, 58, 65 (a new *cripta*). 1192 arches: *LC*, I, p. 300.

S. Maria Nova owned most of the region around the church, including many of the classical buildings, as is clear from its numerous surviving leases; it is at least plausible that it was given them by Leo IV around 850, when he built the *diaconia* on its present spot to replace the probably earthquake-damaged S. Maria Antiqua, further into the Foro Romano, for the pope would have had sovereign rights over former public buildings. It did not own everything, however. The Colosseo was only in part the church's property. The Chartularium, a papal archive into the eleventh century, situated between the Colosseo and the *diaconia*, perhaps inside the temple, was probably not transferred to the church either, for it does not appear in S. Maria Nova's charters.[40] The church also did not own much north of the classical monuments, towards the Trivio Cambiatoris, the crossroads of the money-changer, an area which seldom appears either, and into the old Subura, today the *rione* Monti.[41] This incomplete proprietorial control over the area must explain another absence from these charters, the tower-houses of the Frangipane. The *regio* of S. Maria Nova/Colosseo was the power-base of this family, and we can track the close links between family members and the church from as early as the 1030s (see below, pp. 230, 293); they had tower-houses and *palatia* in this area, as we know from other sources, particularly narratives; but none were leased out by S. Maria Nova, at least in surviving texts.[42] We cannot exclude that by the twelfth century the Frangipane owned some of their land in full property. They could well, however, also have held papal leases; a reference in the 1192 list of arches to one put up by the *familia Fraipanorum de Cartularia* indicates an association between the family and that papal building, and indeed Oddone Frangipane had housed Alexander III there in 1167. But the Frangipane, however militarily strong—popes could be defended against their rivals in the family's *firmissima munitio* near S. Maria Nova, as Urban II was in 1093–4, and both Innocent II and, as we have just seen, Alexander III benefited from similar protection later—were not the only powers in this zone, and their possessions, fortified and not, were interspersed with those of others.[43] Most of the *regio* of S. Maria Nova was much more standard

[40] Foundation by Leo IV: *LP*, II, pp. 145, 158. *LP* does not mention an earthquake here, but there was one in 847 (*LP*, II, p. 108), which fits the unusual move. S. Maria Nova was often in the eleventh century called *olim Antiqua nunc Nova* or similar (e.g. *SMN*, nn. 3, 6). Colosseo: see Chapter 5, n. 96, for papal ownership; *SMN*, n. 128 shows S. Maria Nova owning there, but n. 97 shows the property of S. Maria in Pallara. C(*h*)*artularium*: Deusdedit, *Collectio canonum*, pp. 191–4; *Mirabilia*, p. 57; Rodríguez López, 'La Torre Cartularia'. S. Maria Nova charters refer to it a couple of times in the thirteenth century as a place for the redaction of texts: Rodríguez López, 'La Torre Cartularia', p. 325. A section of the Domus Nova was also held in 1052 by a member of the elite in full property: *SMN*, n. 15 (cf. above, n. 36).

[41] Trivio/contrada Cambiatoris: *SMN*, nn. 15, 114.

[42] Frangipane towers/*palatia*: *Liber Pontificalis*, ed. Přerovský, p. 739; *Mirabilia*, p. 56; and n. 43 below. One further south, on the Circo Massimo, was leased from S. Gregorio: *S. Gregorio*, n. 152 (a. 1145).

[43] *LC*, I, p. 300; *LP*, II, p. 416 (with Maragone, *Annales Pisani*, p. 43). For Urban, see Geoffroy of Vendôme, *Œuvres*, pp. 288–90, with *Die Chroniken Bertholds und Bernolds*, p. 509. For Innocent, see *LP*, II, p. 380 among others. For the Frangipane and their power-base see in general Thumser, 'Die Frangipane'; Rodríguez López, 'La Torre Cartularia' (which disposes of the common view that the Cartularia was a tower); Augenti, *Il Palatino*, pp. 89–110 (with topographical notes on the whole area); Gargiulo, 'La torre del Circo Massimo'; Di Santo, *Monumenti antichi*, pp. 95–114; Maire Vigueur, *L'autre Rome*, pp. 65–8.

domestic housing, which would have adapted itself to the Frangipane towers in much the same way as it did to the Colosseo and the Domus Nova; and this was largely owned by S. Maria.

If we move west from S. Maria, we immediately enter the Foro Romano complex, which has few documents, but will have shown the same mixture between classical monuments and private housing that we have just seen, given the archaeology already described, although certainly not always as tightly packed as around S. Maria. S. Adriano in Foro was chosen for the tense discussions prior to the papal election of 1130 despite all the *munitiones*, presumably tower-houses, around it, which had to be handed over to the cardinals during the meeting. In 1192, there were two houses charged with raising arches for processions between the Arco di Settimio Severo and the portico of SS. Cosma e Damiano 200 metres away, those of Gozo and Nicola di Ferro. There was housing around the arch in the 1190s too, for a bull of 1199 from Innocent III to SS. Sergio e Bacco, on the Foro side of the Capitolio, tells us that full ownership of the Arco di Settimio Severo was divided between this church and the heirs of Cimino (regrettably, an otherwise unknown family), and that the arch had towers on top—as early modern drawings also show—and constructions all around it. Some of these constructions were excavated in the late 1980s, and showed themselves to be fairly small and modest houses, but consistently placed from the twelfth century along the road down from the Capitolio.[44]

If we then go around the Capitolio to the east, we enter the Fori di Cesare and di Traiano, already described. Riccardo Santangeli has tentatively attributed the small tenth-century planned houses of the Foro di Cesare to the future Pope Leo VIII (963–5), who had formerly been a *protoscriniarius*, one of the palatine judges, and who came from near this area. More securely, he attributes the contemporary planning of the Foro di Traiano to Caloleo, one of Alberico's associates in the 940s and still alive in 963, for the whole area was by 1004 called after the *campo de quondam Kaloleoni*—later in the Middle Ages the Campo Carleo—in its centre, and the name is very uncommon.[45] That planning did not give so much explicit weight to classical buildings, however; the only one that regularly appears in texts is the Colonna di Traiano, which was the contested property of at least three churches until S. Ciriaco in Via Lata won out in 1162.[46]

The Capitolio or Campidoglio overlooks this entire area, but it is ill-documented before the creation of the Senate in 1143. By the late eleventh century it was a stronghold of the Corsi family, but it was also becoming a clearly defined place of power in other respects, and as such it is best dealt with in a later chapter (p. 339). All the same, we should cross over it here, because the other, western side of the Capitolio was the

---

[44] 1130: *Historia Compostellana*, III.23 (p. 456); 1192: *LC*, I, p. 300. For Innocent, *Reg. Inn. III*, II.94 (102); for the excavations, Maetzke, 'La struttura stratigrafica', pp. 192–3. For a tower on the arch, see Krautheimer, *Rome*, p. 321. Note also *SPV*, n. 31 (a. 1103) and *S. Sisto*, n. 5 (a. 1160), for other houses *in Foro*, although it is not clear exactly where.

[45] Meneghini and Santangeli Valenzani, *Roma nell'altomedioevo*, p. 48; Meneghini and Santangeli Valenzani, *I fori imperiali*, pp. 150, 153. For Caloleo, *RS*, nn. 155, 93; for the *campo*, *SMVL*, n. 26.

[46] *SMVL*, nn. 26, 60A, 60B, 63C, 196.

city centre's major market, extending from the saddle at the top of the hill (the modern piazza del Campidoglio) northwards down to the river plain beneath, where S. Biagio di Mercato is, and then westwards along the few hundred metres to the river port, south of the Teatro di Marcello, where a meat market existed by 998 and a fish market (at S. Angelo in Pescheria) by the twelfth century at the latest.[47] This area, too, is ill-documented; we do not have the archives of major churches of this zone such as S. Maria in Capitolio (now in Araceli), or S. Marco in what is now the Palazzo Venezia, or S. Nicola in Carcere on the river, which was to the Pierleoni family what S. Maria Nova was to the Frangipane. Indeed, but for a bull of Anacletus II to S. Maria in Capitolio from the 1130s, surviving because it was copied into the register of Innocent IV in 1252, we would not know about the main market at all in our period, with its *domos, casalinas, cryptas,* and *ergasteria* (shops), despite its evident importance.[48] We do not even know whether the market was daily or weekly—by the fourteenth century it was a Saturday market, but we cannot assume the same earlier.[49] Our ignorance about important issues such as this is a marker of the dangers involved in assuming too readily that our main archives reflect the whole city in our period.

Ripa was the name of the Tiber port area; to be exact, the east side was the Ripa Graeca, called Marmorata at its southern end under the Aventino, and the west side, in Trastevere, was the Ripa Romea. The eastern port extended north from the Aventino up to the Isola Tiberina, which made navigation impossible for large boats (and the mills on the island would have made it harder still: below, p. 150), though some river traffic did run further upstream, to the port at the Scola Saxonum in the Civitas Leoniana and the left-bank port in Campo Marzio, where the via di Ripetta still is.[50] Casual references confirm this picture systematically without allowing it to be filled out much: the popes received *ripaticum* or *teloneum* from all the ports, for example (John XVIII conferred that for the Ripetta on the newly founded church of S. Trifone in 1006, which may imply that this

---

[47] For the main market, see n. 48. Teatro di Marcello: *macellum sub Templo Marcelli,* Manaresi, n. 236. S. Angelo in Pescheria first gets variants of that name in the late twelfth century (*ad Piscivendulos* in 1173, *SMN,* n. 100; *Piscium Venlium* in 1192, *LC,* I, p. 301); but, given the evidence of a *tabella* entitled 'Il mercato del pesce' in the Area archeologica del Portico d'Ottavia, which cites an unpublished excavation of a shop in the church portico with many clam and oyster shells of the 'epoca altomedievale' (consulted 17 October 2012), it is plausible that it was already a fish market in the early Middle Ages. It is badly attested earlier, despite being an eighth-century *diaconia,* but was generally just called S. Angelo (e.g. *Regesto degli Orsini,* pp. 29–30, a. 1149). For the fourteenth century, see Lori Sanfilippo, *La Roma dei Romani,* pp. 337–74, esp. p. 367; Maire Vigueur, *L'autre Rome,* pp. 136–47.

[48] *Bullarum . . . collectio,* ed. Cocquelines, III, p. 329 n. 28. The market extended north into the plain at least as far as S. Biagio di Mercato (*LC,* I, p. 301), which is near the foot of the S. Maria in Araceli steps: see Hülsen, *Le chiese di Roma,* p. 218; S. Giovanni di Mercato, further north, is not known until the late Middle Ages (Hülsen, *Le chiese di Roma,* p. 273).

[49] Lori Sanfilippo, *La Roma dei Romani,* pp. 126–8; Maire Vigueur, *L'autre Rome,* pp. 159–60.

[50] See in general Hubert, *Espace urbain,* pp. 99–102. The Scola Saxonum port is called *maior* in 955 (*Papsturkunden,* n. 134), but it is hard to believe that a port upstream from the Isola Tiberina could have been more important than the two long-standing Ripae; it is most likely (as is the Ripetta) to have been a port for the smaller number of boats coming down the Tiber.

northern port was pretty small). Similarly, the pope could in 1159 choose whether his annual dues in wood from Ostia were to be landed at Marmorata or at Ripa Romea—though this may not have mattered much: one of the Tiber's three medieval bridges, the Ponte S. Maria below the Isola Tiberina (destroyed in the sixteenth century by floods, it is today the Ponte Rotto), connected the two ports directly.[51] What is interesting about the east bank, however, is its evident economic and political importance. It is an area where reinterpretations of 1930s' excavations have allowed the recognition of networks of eighth- and ninth-century buildings, hard to read but doubtless connected to the port, including a bath house; it is also an area where the street level has hardly risen since the classical period, a clear sign of an unbroken continuity of occupation.[52] And, in the early twelfth century, it appears as the location of the principal residences of a number of the main families of the 'new' urban aristocracy. The Pierleoni were based near S. Nicola at the northern end (and also on the adjacent Isola Tiberina across the next Tiber bridge) by 1099; both the Normanni family and Pietro Latrone of the Corsi family lived 200 metres further south near S. Maria Secundicerii, the former Tempio di Portuno, in 1118 (as just noted, other members of the Corsi had been based on the Capitolio, just above S. Nicola, in the 1080s), and between these two neighbouring foci, beside the road leading to the Ponte S. Maria and opposite the Tempio di Portuno, still stands the elaborate early tower-house known as the Casa dei Crescenzi, which was possibly erected by the *filii Baruncii* family, and, even if not, was certainly a residence of a leading family (below, pp. 235–8).[53] This focusing of such a substantial percentage of the major families of the period after 1050 on the land just behind the port is a sure sign of the continuing centrality of Ripa, and it makes it even more unfortunate that no archives survive for the churches of the area. All we have to go on for what the area looked like is the Casa dei Crescenzi; but, given its aristocratic neighbours, who had their own towers, its decorative ambition may not then have been unique.

Crossing the bridges to Trastevere brought one to as active a suburb, if a less high-status one. Trastevere had aristocrats too—probably Benedetto Campanino in the tenth century, certainly the newer families of Giovanni Tignoso and the Bracciuti in the eleventh, and the Papareschi in the twelfth—though not, for the most part, as powerful a set as lived in Ripa; and also the first documented tower-

---

[51] See for our period Hartmann, 'Grundherrschaft', pp. 148, 154; Hubert, *Espace urbain*, pp. 102–4 (with citations of later sources too); Palermo, *Il porto di Roma*, pp. 13–29 (but this book is really focused on the period after 1350). For 1006, *Papsturkunden*, n. 424; for 1159, *LC*, I, n. 117. Popes also had the right to dues at city gates: see e.g. *S. Sil.*, n. 2 (a. 844), and the possibly inauthentic Pflugk, II, n. 105 (a. 1050).

[52] See above all Meneghini and Santangeli Valenzani, *Roma nell'altomedioevo*, pp. 194–200; there are also useful points in Campese Simone, 'Fra l'*Ara Coeli* e Piazza Bocca della Verità'.

[53] Pierleoni: *LP*, II, p. 294 (a. 1099), with *CF*, II, p. 232 (a. 1103); for the Isola Tiberina, *Liber Pontificalis*, ed. Přerovský, p. 728; and note the Pierleoni among the *dependentes* of Ripa and Insula in 1189 ('Documenti per la storia', n. 20). Normanni and Pietro Latrone: *Liber Pontificalis*, ed. Přerovský, pp. 738–9; for S. Maria's location, Meneghini and Santangeli Valenzani, *Roma nell'altomedioevo*, p. 195. Corsi on Capitolio: *LP*, II, p. 290. See Chapter 4 for all these families.

houses in the city, in 1069–73.[54] But most houses were one-storeyed well into the twelfth century, and it is both accepted and likely that Trastevere's densely occupied area did not extend very far away from the river—and not yet as far south as Benedetto's monastery of SS. Cosma e Damiano, the source of most of our local documents, which was initially an area of vineyards.[55] This would change by the end of the twelfth century, a period in which Trastevere saw a good deal of enlargement.[56] But it is significant, in terms of our sense of the region, that the major detailed written evidence we have for any Trastevere buildings is for the mills along the Tiber. Trastevere had some prestigious churches, one of which, S. Maria in Trastevere, was rebuilt on a large scale in our period by the Trasteverino Innocent II, in the years just after 1140 (below, pp. 358–61). But it was always slightly marginal as well. The Romans could not decide if it was part of the city or not. It was still the *regio XIV* in 1037, and its leading men played a full part in city politics thereafter, furnishing two eleventh-century prefects and some twelfth-century senators too, but there are too many narrative references to the *Romani et Transtiberini* for us to think that either group saw the region as a fully integral sector of the city. It was Mestre or Brooklyn, not the Rive Gauche. But it was a potent basis for political opposition as well, and could not safely be ignored.[57]

Moving back across the Tiber, the *regio* to the north of the Capitolio, Pigna, is by contrast much more easily visible, for in it was the female monastery of SS. Ciriaco e Nicola in Via Lata, called S. Ciriaco here, whose archive is larger even than that of S. Maria Nova.[58] This was another built-up area for the whole period after 1000, when our documents start, but not one where classical monuments dominate our descriptions of properties. Only one is named, in fact, the Arcum Divurio, which gave its name to the *locus* Diburo in other texts; this must have been part of the hall of the Diribitorium, in the porticoed courtyard for voting known as the Saepta in antiquity, but, if so, not much of it physically survived into our period.[59] Instead,

---

[54] Benedetto: *RF*, n. 439 (a text that says he founded SS. Cosma e Damiano *in sua proprietate*, but this is a Sabina commentator, and full property rights were normal there); Bracciuti, family of Giovanni Tignoso and Papareschi: see below, pp. 224–6, 242. Tower-houses: *SCD*, n. 70; *SMT*, n. 5.

[55] The only *domūs solaratae* in Trastevere before 1150 are in *SMT*, n. 2 (a. 1037) and ASR, SCD, cassetta 16, n. 126 (a. 1145). SS. Cosma e Damiano owned the whole southern half of Trastevere according to John XVIII's confirmation in 1005 (*Papsturkunden*, n. 419), and it only seems to have had a few *domora* and *criptae* in it then.

[56] Building on SS. Cosma e Damiano's land was already beginning in the eleventh century, as *SCD*, n. 34 (a. 1029) shows, but *casarini* are particularly common in the later twelfth century, especially in the 1170s: ASR, SCD, cassetta 16, nn. 140, 144, 145, 146 (several of the twenty-four charters on this single sheet); *SMVL*, Baumgärtner, n. 3. See Hubert, *Espace urbain*, p. 138, and pp. 128–31 for *casarini* meaning building plots.

[57] For *Transtiberini* as separate from Romans, see e.g. *LP*, II, p. 331; *MGH, Constitutiones*, I, n. 94; *Liber Pontificalis*, ed. Přerovský, p. 734; *Chronica Casinensis*, III.68; Maragone, *Annales Pisani*, p. 43 (a. 1168). Giovanni Tignoso and his son Cencio were prefects for Nicholas II, Alexander II, and Gregory VII: Halphen, *Études*, pp. 149–51. Trastevere senators: e.g. *Senato*, nn. 42–3 (aa. 1188–91).

[58] *SMVL* is the archive of S. Maria in Via Lata, which incorporated the neighbouring S. Ciriaco in the fifteenth century, but most of its documents in our period are for S. Ciriaco or its dependencies: see Chapter 1, n. 18.

[59] *Arcus*: *SMVL*, nn. 29, 105, 115; *Papsturkunden*, n. 608; Hülsen, 'I *saepta* e il *diribitorium*', p. 142 (a fragmentary text from Paschal II's reign in a seventeenth-century cartulary; this whole article is the

we simply find networks of houses, around the monastery and across the via Lata to the Trevi area, only a few of which seem to be built inside classical buildings. There are not even many tower-houses, the best signs of prosperous elites, despite the powerful presence just east of Pigna of the palace of Alberico and the Tuscolani; only two towers are documented in the S. Ciriaco collection, in the late eleventh century (one is associated with an *arcum antiquum*, probably the Arco di Diburo again).[60] This was not a very grand region, then, very unlike its present status, situated as it is at the mouth of the via del Corso.

If not grand, however, the area was certainly expanding. A priest and his family are documented setting out land near the monastery of S. Ciriaco for house-building as early as 1017 and again in 1031, and by 1019 S. Ciriaco itself was branching out into the Trevi area a little to the north-east, where it divided up orchards near S. Maria in Senodochio into plots of similar sizes, each 12 metres wide, for houses; other churches can sometimes be found doing the same; and later, in the late twelfth century, we also find several references to *casarini*, building plots, in Pigna, via Lata, and Trevi.[61] A small excavation under the Cinema Trevi gives us an idea of how some of this building might have looked: here, two twelfth-century houses, roughly 8 metres wide, were built on the first floor of a substantial classical town house, using the cement ceiling, by now presumably at ground level, as a foundation. (There was some earlier occupation here, for Forum Ware jugs from the ninth or tenth centuries were found, but it is otherwise archaeologically invisible.[62]) All this probably shows an expansion eastwards of the densely settled area of the city, for references to the *regio* of Trevi only begin after 1150; but it is worth repeating that excavations on the via Lata in piazza Venezia, on the main road 250 metres south of S. Ciriaco and even closer to the Capitolio market, have shown a period of partial abandonment for a row of early medieval shops there between *c.*850 and a large-scale twelfth-century rebuild.[63] If there was tenth- and eleventh-century abandonment even here, then there was certainly room for growth in Pigna. In the twelfth century, this growth is clear, but we shall also see (p. 143) that this area was full of artisans in the eleventh century; however unmonumental, it had a complex society.

Moving a little further north, into the *regio* of Campo Marzio and its neighbours, S. Lorenzo in Lucina and Colonna, we find a similar picture. This too was not a major area for classical buildings, although the Colonna Antonina remained a crucial point of reference, giving its name to the twelfth-century *regio*—it had

most detailed topographical analysis of the area); *locus* and similar: *Papsturkunden*, n. 608; *SMVL*, nn. 38, 59, 129.

[60] Houses in classical buildings: *SMVL*, nn. 44, 81 (both near S. Maria in Senodochio in the Trevi area). Tower-houses: *SMVL*, nn. 115 (with the arch, a. 1086), 121 (a. 1094).

[61] Respectively, *SMVL*, nn. 38, 59, 41–3 (S.Maria in Senodochio; see further 74, 81, 90 later), 61A, 63C (S. Salvatore ad Duos Amantes doing the same); for the late twelfth century, 181, 185, 186, 191 (up the hill to the Quirinale), 199, 232 (all *casarini*).

[62] See Insalaco, *La 'Città dell'Acqua'* for all this, plus the permanent exhibition under the Sala Trevi at vicolo del Puttarello 25.

[63] *Regio* Trevi refs. start with *S. Sil.*, n. 26 (a. 1163), but cf. *SMVL*, n. 185 (a. 1155). Excavations: Serlorenzi and Saguì, 'Roma, Piazza Venezia', pp. 188–9.

belonged to the nearby monastery of S. Silvestro in Capite in 955, though they had apparently lost it by 1119 (a dated inscription survives in S. Silvestro saying so, and cursing any abbot who leases it away and any layman who in future appropriates it).[64] Campo Marzio was on the northern edge of the settled area. The nearby Mausoleo di Augusto was part of S. Silvestro's great block of property stretching from the Pincio to the Tiber, probably given to the monastery by its founder Pope Paul I in 761, but, imposing though it remains, it was not part of the cityscape, and is hardly ever mentioned—it was just north of the inhabited area of the city, in an area not built up until the sixteenth century.[65]

Although Campo Marzio was on the edge of the city, it was nonetheless bustling. The Ripetta port on its north-west side may have been relatively small, but it attracted inhabitants, including Giovanni the river boatman (*sandalarius*), who already in 1010 had enlarged his shop, on the street to one of the river gates.[66] It was an artisanal area from then onwards. It was largely built up in the eleventh century already, with little open land mentioned in charters; but in the twelfth, both the monastery of S. Maria in Campo Marzio, whose archive is the best source for the area, and also S. Silvestro in Capite and S. Ciriaco, were leasing out *casarini*, building plots, presumably as infill, as with the plot (*sedium*) of *terra vacua* destined to become an *argasterium*, a shop near the northern river gate, in 1128. Actually, in Campo Marzio in particular we have some evidence that *casarini* were occupied already, sometimes having wooden or at any rate impermanent huts (*tendiae*), so it may well be that much of this building was the improvement of housing, not its increase; some was also restoration, as with the *casarinus* that had once been a wine shop (*cervinaria*) in 1134.[67] By the 1150s the word seems here to denote any plot of land, inhabited or not, as with the 1155 division between half-brothers of their mother Oresma's lands which included a *domus maior*, a *domus* with stable, a *casarinum* with a *cervinaria* in it, a *casarinum* where a tenant lives, and three other *casarini* with *orti*, all situated around the tower-house (*turris*) of a certain Pietro on the Mons Accriptorum, the low hill now called Montecitorio (see below, p. 274).[68] By 1194, S. Maria in Campo Marzio had 154 *domūs* in a papal confirmation, spread across some 700 metres, mostly close to the monastery (but also in five other separate parishes). Housing was by now tightly packed; by the 1190s, in fact, we begin to get disputes and agreements about the sharing of living space and water drainage, which presume unbroken housing. This is after our period ends, but they are the first such cases in Rome. Campo Marzio may have been the first *regio* fully to resemble the dense *abitato*

---

[64] *Papsturkunden*, nn. 134, 155; Forcella, IX.149.

[65] *Papsturkunden*, nn. 134, 155; for its imposingness, see esp. *Mirabilia*, pp. 47–8. Krautheimer, *Rome*, p. 255, saw Stefano di Agusto, urban prefect in 1002 (*SCD*, n. 19), as based here; this is wrong, for Agusto is not a toponym, but, explicitly, the name of his father.

[66] *Papsturkunden*, n. 424 for the port; *SMCM*, n. 3 for the *sandalarius*, cf. also *SMVL*, nn. 79–80.

[67] Open land: only *SMCM*, n. 5 (a. 1030). For the 1130s onwards, see Hubert, *Espace urbain*, p. 139. For 1128 text: *SMVL*, n. 150. Inhabited *casarini*: *S.Sil.*, n. 20; *SMCM*, n. 49, and n. 35 (a. 1134).

[68] *SMVL*, n. 185.

documented so clearly by Krautheimer and analysed so well for its thirteenth-century landed economy by Hubert.[69]

Campo Marzio was never, in our period, a major location for the city's leaders, less so even than Pigna. There were a number of tower-houses there, but they are not associated with people of any obvious prominence; one was held by a smith in 1117. At most, what I call the 'medium elite' (see below, Chapter 5) lived in the area, notably the Cerratani, who held the first tower documented here, in 1076, and who were local dealers and small-scale public figures for the next century; and, later, the Parenzi, heirs of Giovanni di Parenzo, who rose fast in a judicial career in 1145–88, and whose sons and grandsons indeed became leaders: city senators, and *podestà* elsewhere in central Italy, throughout the early thirteenth century.[70] In our period, however, S. Maria in Campo Marzio had no tenants or associates even remotely resembling the Frangipane or the future Parenzi, and its practical concerns were, above all, economic. This reflected the wider concerns of an essentially artisanal and commercial quarter.

Just a little further south-west, however, the social climate shifted again. West of the Pantheon, perhaps five minutes' walk from S. Maria in Campo Marzio, was the *regio* of Scorteclari, a word of uncertain derivation (*scortum* means both 'hide', hence 'tanners', or 'prostitute', hence 'pimps'); whichever skin trade went on here, parts of the area were rather grander than those we have just seen. Close to the Pantheon was a large classical bath complex, the Terme Alessandrine (named for the emperor Severus Alexander), today long demolished but still largely standing in the eleventh century; this extended westwards to the old Stadium Domitiani, in our period the open Campus Agonis (it is today piazza Navona). Inside the bath complex, in the western range, in the location now occupied by the church of S. Luigi dei Francesi, was the *cella* of S. Maria, property of the great rural monastery of (S. Maria di) Farfa in the Sabina; from the late tenth century to the late eleventh, with a particular density in the 990s and 1010s, the *Regesto di Farfa* preserves a substantial set of documents for the zone.[71]

These documents, more than any others in Rome, even those of S. Maria Nova, stress the omnipresence of classical buildings (see Map 8). A high percentage of them show bits of older structures in the eleventh-century fabric of houses: often Farfa simply leased out or bought back *cryptae*, but the *domūs* had classical walls too, as with the *domus maior solorata*, the great two-storeyed house, in 1012, 'surrounded by an ancient wall' (*a muro antiquo circumclusa*), beside the Campus Agonis; or a year later the *domum soloratam in ruinis positam*, placed in ruins, with

---

[69] *SMCM*, n. 62 (a. 1194), nn. 61, 66 (space disputes and agreements); see Hubert, *Espace urbain*, p. 144, and *passim* for the thirteenth century.

[70] *SMCM*, nn. 28 (a. 1117), 17 (a. 1076); for the Cerratani and the Parenzi, see below, pp. 267–71.

[71] Basic for the Farfa properties and local topography is Fiore Cavaliere, 'Le terme alessandrine', although I do not follow it in every detail, especially for lay ownership. Cecchelli, 'Roma medioevale', p. 312, excludes the sexual derivation for *scortum* too easily. For the Campus Agonis, see for the documents Vendittelli, 'Il *Campus Agonis*'; the eastern and northern side of it seems from recent archaeological work to be hardly occupied in our period until the twelfth century, although its southern end shows longer-term occupation: see Molinari, 'Gli scavi al n. 62 di Piazza Navona'.

'ancient walls', *parietinis antiquis,* and a bath (*terme*) behind, now a hayloft (*fenile*), extending to two *columnas marmoreas* at the back; or in 1017 a plot of land with *parietinis antiquis* including an *arcu* and two *triclinea*—in the classical period, dining or reception rooms, but here apparently just habitable units, for one had a domed roof, and the other was a *domus et curtis,* house and courtyard. Most of the houses were two-storeyed here, unlike in Pigna or Campo Marzio, and many of them had marble staircases, doubtless using the raw materials to be found in the zone. Houses with their gardens (with fig or apple trees) thus studded the old fabric of the baths and the stadium, reusing it with a certain degree of enthusiasm, at least as creatively as the builders of the Foro di Nerva houses and perhaps even more so.[72]

Farfa controlled the *cella* of S. Maria (and two other churches, S. Benedetto and S. Salvatore) by *c.*898, for some of its monks lived there in the period from then up to the 930s and later when the monastery in the Sabina was occupied by the Arabs and then left in ruins for a generation. It is unclear whether Farfa was given the *cella* by a pope, or took it in lease from the neighbouring *diaconia* of S. Eustachio, just to the south of the baths; S. Eustachio certainly claimed the latter to be the case in 998. Although the priests of S. Eustachio lost the resultant court case before Otto III, they tried to reopen it in 1011 before Giovanni di Crescenzio, and they certainly owned much other land inside the bath complex, as Farfa had unwillingly to recognize in a third case which it lost in 1017; so the *diaconia* may have originally held more rights than Farfa claimed.[73]

Farfa leased out its land to a clearly defined clientele, which often had links to the Sabina and was generally of quite high status (below, p. 232). Only a few artisans appear in the Farfa documents, whatever the etymology of Scorteclari.[74] Men called *a Sancto Eustachio* also seem to have had social status, and the late eleventh-century aristocratic family of that name can be tracked back to at least 1011 (below, p. 231). But this may just be Farfa's particular landowning politics. The occasional texts for the eleventh-century *regio,* which do not survive in the monastery's cartularies, all have artisans as witnesses, and one 1092 text for S. Pietro in Vaticano (surviving, sadly, only in seventeenth-century notes) has that church leasing a *domus* and *porticus* and a first-floor balcony for doing commerce (*preforulo ad faciendum negotia*) in Scorteclari. This may have been along the via Sacra or via Pontificalis from S. Pietro, through the Forum area, to the Laterano; that road passed through the southern edge of Scorteclari, and S. Pietro had other

---

[72] *RF,* nn. 652–3 (*casa cum cripta*), 658 (a. 1012, cf. 657), 667 (a. 1013), 506 (a. 1017), 616 (another *domus solarata*), 669, 506 (trees).

[73] Ugo of Farfa, *Destructio,* pp. 31, 33, 35, 37 for the monastery's *cella* in Rome, with vague dating. He also does not specify where it was; it is a modern supposition (which I share) that S. Maria and the other churches (first referred to as a trio in 998, Manaresi, n. 236), with their *cellae,* are the same place. The 998 text was S. Eustachio's first attempt to get the property; for later cases, *RF,* nn. 616, 506 with 504.

[74] Artisans: *RF,* nn. 667–8 (Guido *calcararius*), 669 (Benone *negotians*), 710 (Azone *negotians qui residet ad Terme,* Benedetto *calcarius*), 761 (Giovanni *textor*).

land along it in 1027.[75] So we gain the sense of the Terme Alessandrine zone as rather a posh area, which was surrounded by at least some more ordinary people behaving in ways more similar to those of Pigna and Campo Marzio. And the latter would be more numerous as time went on. The Farfa texts are also mostly very early; they precede the large-scale move to fill up the Tiber bend west and south of piazza Navona, which was getting under way in the late eleventh century (the aristocrat Cencio di Stefano had tower-houses in Parione and Ponte by then, one of them on the Ponte S. Pietro leading to Castel S. Angelo), and proceeding, as far as we can see, with considerable speed in the twelfth, with new church foundations common from the 1110s onwards. This would transform the social makeup of this part of Rome, a process apparently largely complete by the 1180s.[76] But that is late for us, and these developments are anyway nearly invisible in the sources, which are very poor for the Tiber bend. What stands out for us is the extent and quality of the reuse of the classical fabric between the Pantheon and piazza Navona, and the relative wealth of the *rentier* stratum who lived there.

Once one crossed the Ponte S. Pietro to the major papal fortification of Castel S. Angelo, one had left Rome proper. The Civitas Leoniana was not in fact reckoned to be fully part of the city of Rome until the sixteenth century, and it had an economy, focused on the reception of pilgrims, that was quite distinct as well. We shall look at it in detail at the start of the next section. Here it is only necessary to stress that its urban fabric was all medieval, for in the classical period there was little here except tombs, until Constantine built his vast basilica at the top of a set of steps, against the Monte Vaticano. The two main tombs were those of Hadrian—the Castel S. Angelo itself—and the nearby 'tomb of Romulus' or Meta, a tall pyramid, demolished in the sixteenth century, which is a prominent feature of early drawings of the *civitas*, and which turns up occasionally on the boundaries of buildings in our period (as Castel S. Angelo, important but separate from the main street, never does).[77] But the main spatial framing for the *civitas* was entirely medieval: the Leonine Walls themselves, built in 848–52 and still largely standing today, forming a long rectangle between the Castel S. Angelo and the hill behind the basilica; the Porticus S. Petri, running along the middle of this rectangle between the bridge and the Platea Maior S. Petri; and the Platea itself, the prototype for the modern piazza S. Pietro, with the basilica steps to its west, a Carolingian palace probably on the northern side, and the eighth-century papal

---

[75] *SMVL*, n. 49; *SPV*, nn. 9, 23–5, 29 (a. 1092). *Preforulum* as balcony: Hubert, *Espace urbain*, p. 209; it is otherwise only found in the Civitas Leoniana in our period (*SPV*, nn. 10, 13; *SCD*, n. 88). Via Sacra: *SPV*, n. 9, cf. *RF*, n. 506 (*via pontificalis*).

[76] Cencio di Stefano's towers: *LP*, II, p. 337; Bonizone of Sutri, *Liber ad amicum*, VII (pp. 603, 605, 606); see further below, n. 156. Housing in the late twelfth-century Tiber bend: *SPV*, n. 52; *SMVL*, n. 205; *S. And. Aq.*, nn. 2, 3. Church foundations: see the inscriptions in Forcella, XI.321, IX.1007, XII.539. For a very long list of the subsidiary churches of S. Lorenzo in Damaso in 1186, Fonseca, *De basilica S. Laurentii*, pp. 250–5. See in general, for the build-up of housing here, Krautheimer, *Rome*, pp. 271–2.

[77] The Meta is clear on fifteenth-century drawings: see e.g. Krautheimer, *Rome*, pp. 262–3. For references, see *SPV*, nn. 16, 40. Other tombs are referred to in *SPV*, nn. 1 (a mid-eleventh-century forgery), 16.

palace on the south (though a new papal palace existed by 1151 to the north as well). The basilica was, obviously, late antique, but the dozen or so churches and monasteries around it were early medieval as well.[78]

We finish our tour of Rome, then, with at least one essentially medieval monumental landscape. S. Pietro was mostly backed by open land (as it still is), and, south of the piazza, the zone called Terrione seems to have been relatively empty too.[79] But, between the piazza and the bridge, the long Porticus was the location for the lodging, feeding, fleecing and burying of Rome's never-ending stream of pilgrims. Not yet known as the Borgo, it contained three *burgi* by the eleventh century, the Burgus Frisonum, Burgus Saxonum, and Burgus Nauma-chiae—*burgus* being by then a standard word for an extramural city suburb, which they were, but also for a major stopping point on the via Francigena, the pilgrim route down from France. The Porticus was, furthermore, the location for nearly all Rome's documented *ergasteria* or shops in our period.[80] This was Rome's real reception area for outsiders, from emperors to *pauperes*, kept somewhat separate from the older city beyond the Tiber with its classical buildings and other great churches—which the outsiders would certainly visit, usually marvel at, always pray in, but not stay too long in. The Civitas Leoniana, with its monumental church and wholly medieval infrastructure, not too big as well (the Porticus was under a kilometre long), was indeed also a more familiar location to most visitors, for that was closer to what cities elsewhere were like.

And this is one of the crucial points about Rome, taken as a whole, that must be stressed here: other cities were indeed not like it. We have not looked at the whole city; only the sectors of it that are best documented. For other sectors—the Palatino and the other hills, or the southern part of the Tiber bend, up to the Ponte S. Pietro—the interested reader should consult other surveys, which will be definitive until the archaeologists tell us more.[81] But even given the spatial restrictions of our evidence, it must be recognized that we could not possibly do a similar tour, even one as summary as this, of any other eleventh-century city. In Constantinople, it might have been possible had any documents survived for it, but not in the West, even for very well-documented cities like Milan or Lucca. The classical walls of Lucca, which bounded most of the city's inhabitants before a (fairly unambitious) twelfth-century expansion, covered an area about the size of

---

[78] Leonine Walls: see the exhaustive analysis in Gibson and Ward-Perkins, 'The surviving remains'. Porticus, etc.: good surveys are Krautheimer, *Rome*, pp. 261–9; Pani Ermini, '*Forma urbis*', pp. 317–23 and plate XVI; Meneghini and Santangeli Valenzani, *Roma nell'altomedioevo*, pp. 217–21. The best discussion of the palaces is Brühl, 'Die Kaiserpfalz' (he correctly observes, pp. 4–12, that there is no good evidence that Charlemagne built the imperial palace which was called *palatium Karoli* by 1017, *RF*, n. 504, although it existed by at least 872, *Ludovici II. diplomata*, n. 57); the 1151 text is in ASV, A. A. Arm. I–XVIII, n. 117.

[79] Terrione: *LL*, n. 112; *SPV*, nn. 6, 54.

[80] First references to houses in *burgi*: *SPV*, n. 12 (*Saxonum*): *SMVL*, n. 72 (*Naumachiae*); *SPV*, n. 13 (*Frisonum*). For the word *burgus* in general, see Hubert, *Espace urbain*, pp. 85–6; Settia, *Castelli e villaggi*, pp. 315–25. See this chapter, n. 86 for *ergasteria*.

[81] The Palatino is authoritatively covered in Augenti, *Il Palatino*. For other areas, Krautheimer, *Rome* and, more generically, Cecchelli, 'Roma medioevale', are guides.

Pigna plus Scorteclari, so we would expect less spatial articulation, but we do not find there anything resembling the wealth of microtoponyms that survive for the heart of Rome, and most buildings were simply located with respect to the nearest church or city gate, or the extramural Perilascio (amphitheatre), until carefully bounded parishes came in in the twelfth century.[82] Much the same is true for Pisa, which was slightly smaller before its fast expansion after 1050 or so; only in the new suburbs outside the old walls was toponymic detail more generous.[83] Milan's churches and gates were similarly the major location points for the city, although in this fast-expanding city smaller *contrade* were also prominent by 1200.[84] Rome had the advantage of its huge classical buildings, whether standing or ruined, which made regions like S. Maria Nova or Scorteclari particularly dense in spatial points of reference, but the range of topographical identification we see was not restricted to them. And, above all, the differentiation between regions which we can see for Rome had no parallel whatsoever elsewhere. Eleventh-century Rome had a highly complex articulation between its different sectors, rich and poor, monumental and workaday, densely settled and villagy, which in other cities would not be visible for two or three more centuries, and which underlay all its political and social developments. We will come back to the point in most detail in Chapter 5.

THE URBAN ECONOMY

Arnold Esch has remarked in a lapidary phrase, much cited, that our documentation 'makes the Middle Ages still more agrarian than it was already', for the tendency of our texts to deal with the ownership and leasing of land privileges agricultural information at the expense of data about artisanal or commercial activity.[85] This was less true in Rome, however, than in any other Italian city before 1150. Artisans and merchants appear in our sources with an insistency that can be matched nowhere else; and at least an outline of a complex urban economy can indeed be delineated. For now, one simple reason for this needs to be held in mind: the unusual scale of the economic control the city had over the Agro romano, as explored in Chapter 2. All the surplus of Rome's hinterland came along the consular roads and into each of the city's gates, as well as both up and down the river to the city's ports, heading for the storehouses of the churches, monasteries, 'old' and 'new' aristocracies, and (after 1100) rising urban elites, who controlled them. The grain, wine, orchard products, and wood of the Agro romano, and also

---

[82] Lucca: Belli Barsali, 'La topografia', pp. 542–51, with Nanni, *La Parrocchia*, pp. 145–54, for the twelfth century. Belli Barsali's data from the contemporary written sources are clear, although her map (n. 4) shows many more toponyms, presumably from later periods. One street is named, the Classo Salaiolo, part of the central market.

[83] Pisa: Garzella, *Pisa com'era*, esp. pp. 155–9.

[84] Grillo, *Milano*, pp. 65–71, 485–93; earlier, Salvatori, 'I presunti "*capitanei* delle porte" di Milano', pp. 41–2.

[85] 'Urkundliche Überlieferung macht das Mittelalter noch agrarischer, als es ohnehin schon ist': Esch, 'Überlieferungs-Chance', p. 536.

animals from further away, were then used to feed a very large population by early medieval standards and a substantial one by those of the twelfth century, including the ever-growing papal entourage and the always considerable pilgrim community; and the presence of a large productive urban population, providing rich and poor alike with consumer goods, is all the more plausible as a result. How all this may have articulated together we will see in the final section of this chapter. Here, I shall concentrate on setting out the data for the complexity of the Roman urban economy, including examples of regional specialization and local intervention.

Artisans and tradesmen

This time, we should start with the Civitas Leoniana, whose Porticus and Platea Maior were almost certainly the most commercialized part of the whole city. As already noted, before 1150 nearly all Rome's documented *ergasteria*, shops, were located here. In 1041, for example, Wilielmo the merchant (*negotiens*) bought the lease of a *domus* on the Porticus (in the Burgus Saxonum) with two *ergasteriis ad preponenda negotia*, for commercial activity, and a canopy (*pergula*) in front of them; much the same phraseology recurs in a lease of *argasteria* in 1043 by one of the Vatican monasteries.[86] These leases were, as usual, from churches. The Civitas Leoniana was overwhelmingly owned by S. Pietro or its associated monasteries, which were by the mid-eleventh century increasingly run as a single group by the canons of S. Pietro, themselves subjected directly to the pope. Altar offerings in S. Pietro by pilgrims, and dues sent to S. Pietro from abroad (from England, for example), were an extremely large resource for the papacy, and even more so once Leo IX and Gregory VII centralized them out of the hands of S. Pietro's *mansionarii*, 'semi-lay' church managers who had taken half the profit until then. Thereafter, we have quite a lot of documentation as to how they were to be distributed, as with the tenth of the offerings that Leo IX handed back to the basilica in *c.*1053 for building repairs and lighting, or the substantial dues from the altar to which a large set of church officials were by the 1140s (at the latest) entitled every time they performed a nocturnal vigil in S. Pietro.[87] The church recouped money from visitors in other ways too. When pilgrims died, the church where they were buried was entitled to their goods, and this again mattered financially. In 1053 Leo IX set out the protocols for this in a long bull to S. Pietro, which owned all the burial churches: no one must hide the sick or persuade them to leave the city; no one must hide the goods they left; they are all to be buried in S. Salvatore in the Scola

---

[86] *Ergasteria*: *SPV*, nn. 12 (a. 1041), 13 (a. 1043), 16, 35, 40; *SMVL*, nn. 36, 152; ASR, SCD, cassetta 16, n. 146 (ninth text on roll). Elsewhere in the city there are only two such citations: see above, nn. 48, 67, for the Capitolio and the Ripetta. For the Platea in the thirteenth century, see Hubert, *Espace urbain*, p. 120, with two important texts in *Senato*, nn. 76, 108 (aa. 1233–44), which show Roman communal regulation of selling in this extramural territory.

[87] For the *mansionarii*, see below, Chapter 7, n. 71. Tenth: *SPV*, n. 19. Standard dues to officials: see below, p. 346. The bishop of Silva Candida (whose diocese may theoretically have included the Civitas Leoniana) had claims to some altar offerings too: *Papsturkunden*, n. 569. For other dues to S. Pietro, see Jordan, 'Zur päpstliche Finanzgeschichte', pp. 70–80.

Francorum, S. Pietro's lodging house for visitors from beyond the Alps, except the Frisians who were lodged in the Scola Frisonum, the English who were in the Scola Saxonum, and the Italians who were in the Scola Longobardorum, who would each be buried locally.[88]

Pilgrims also spent money, above all in the Porticus area, and around the Platea Maior. That was what the shops were for. Their inhabitants had an effective monopoly over the pilgrim trade which was not moved against until 1235, when Rome's single senator enacted that pilgrims could lodge and buy food where they wished.[89] In our period, it was so remunerative to live in the Civitas Leoniana, and 'to lodge pilgrims and sell essentials', as Leo IX's bull put it, that its inhabitants had made an agreement—supposedly in the presence of Leo IV, that is, when the city was built in the late 840s—which ceded to the Vatican churches the right to take all the goods of anyone living there permanently (i.e. any non-visitor) who died without legitimate children. No one would have agreed to such an extreme death duty, one otherwise only known in the heaviest private signorie elsewhere in Europe, if the advantages of living in the Leonine city were not equally great. Not surprisingly, however, this duty was also unpopular; in 1123, first in the First Lateran Council and then later that year in a bull to the *civitas* inhabitants, by now called Porticani, Calixtus II abolished it, calling it a *prava consuetudo*, a depraved custom, and citing *Codex Iustinianus* I.2.1 on the right of free disposition of goods. By then, the recipient of the goods was the urban prefect, who had evidently taken over the role, on the pope's behalf, from the Vatican churches, even though the Civitas Leoniana was not technically part of the *urbs*.[90]

Not only pilgrims spent money, too. The emperor, when he came to Rome once a reign to be crowned (and more often if there was trouble), was based in the Civitas Leoniana, and brought a substantial entourage, who were likely to buy generously in the food shops and *tabernae* of the Porticus. This was in part papal security: the advantage of having an imperial palace beside S. Pietro was that the emperor did not mix so much in strictly Roman politics (unless he was Otto III, who pointedly moved to the Palatino). The violence with which many emperors dealt with Rome, including frequent brawls with the latter's inhabitants even during ostensibly peaceful visits as in 1014, 1027, or 1111, not to speak of armed assaults as in 963–6, 1083–4, or 1166–7, also impacted on the Civitas Leoniana, where much of the fighting took place; it is not surprising, then, that a sublease of a house beside the piazza in 1030 (three years after one such brawl) contains a clause in which the lessor agrees to repair the woodwork of the house if the emperor's men break it, and

---

[88] See the forged *SPV*, n. 1 and especially *SPV*, n. 16. Burying was assigned to S. Salvatore already in 854: *SPV*, n. 2.

[89] *Senato*, n. 86.

[90] *SPV*, n. 16 (there is no hint of this in Leo IV's own bull, n. 2, and the *locatio*, the term for the agreement in n. 16, is anachronistic and anyway highly unlikely in this form); *Conciliorum oecumenicorum decreta*, p. 168 (= *MGH, Constitutiones*, I, n. 401; canon 11); *Bullaire Cal. II*, n. 410. Calixtus in the latter claimed that the *prava consuetudo* had led to a population decline. This is rhetorical, but it may well be that the troubles of the past forty years had impacted on the prosperity of the Porticus, which would have made the custom seem more of a financial imposition.

to recompense the lessee if he has to vacate the house because of an imperial presence.[91] But, dangerous or not, such a presence would have brought still more money to the *civitas* as well.

One result of this is that it was not only S. Pietro that had an interest in ground rents. S. Ciriaco in Via Lata and SS. Cosma e Damiano in Trastevere both kept leases for the Porticus area. They may have leased directly from S. Pietro or its monasteries, but S. Ciriaco in 1042 actually leased a room in the Burgus Naumachiae to one of those monasteries, S. Martino, renewed twenty years later, which would be unusual if the real proprietor was the Vaticano.[92] It is most likely that the commercial attraction of the Civitas Leoniana encouraged other churches to get what they could there too, one way or another, for example in gift from lay tenants of the Vaticano. The Porticani themselves were envisaged as sometimes living *in domibus propriis* by 1053, even though their supposed agreement with Leo IV was a *locatio*, lease, and it may be that they were sometimes by now appropriating or buying out their tenures.[93] But these inroads on S. Pietro's landed rights were all due to the fact that the tenures were so remunerative. The leases we have, starting in 1015, were mostly for nineteen years only, and were all for substantial entry-fines on each renewal. Unusually, most of them were for high rents as well. The 1042 lease just mentioned, and its renewal, were for a 22–40 *solidi* entry-fine and 6 *solidi* annual rent, for a single room in a house; and S. Martino, the lessee, must have charged even more to the actual occupant. This was at a time when whole houses in Pigna and the Campo Carleo were being leased for a 2 *solidi* entry-fine and 3 *denarii* rent, under a tenth as much.[94] House rents of more than a few *denarii* were almost unheard of in the rest of Rome up to at least the late twelfth century; but they were quite normal in the Porticus S. Petri. This is as clear a marker as any of the profits that could be made there.

What was being sold in the Civitas Leoniana? Food and drink, for sure; sex, doubtless, though it is not documented; lead and tin seals with portraits of the apostles Peter and Paul by 1199 at the latest, and so presumably the same array of religious trinkets that one can buy in and around piazza S. Pietro today.[95] Our documents mention several *negotientes*, as actors or witnesses, as one would expect; a *cambiator* or money changer in 1083; and several food sellers of different types.

---

[91] *SPV*, n. 10 (a. 1030; note that the text says that money is paid for the lease as *prestitum*, i.e. a cession in return for a pledge of money; but there is no reference to repayment, and I think this must be a mistake for a *pretium* or entry-fine). Brawls: see Chapter 6, n. 46. *Tabernae* are not cited as such, but *tabernarii* appear in *SPV*, n. 16.

[92] See above, n. 86, and below, n. 93; the leases to S. Martino *post hecclesiam S. Petri* are *SMVL*, nn. 72, 89. Other church landowners or landholders were Farfa, for non-commercial land (*LL*, n. 112); S. Gregorio (*S. Gregorio*, n. 172); S. Maria in Cannella (Kehr, IV, pp. 450–1); and maybe S. Paolo, though only its most suspect bull (*S. Paolo*, n. 1) claims so.

[93] *SPV*, n. 16; cf. also *Bullaire Cal. II*, n. 410, *in domo sua.*

[94] *SMVL*, nn. 36, 72, 89, 152; *SPV*, nn. 10, 13, 40, 65; *SCD*, n. 88; ASR, SCD, cassetta 16, n. 146 (ninth text on roll). Pigna in the early eleventh century: e.g. *SMVL*, n. 60B.

[95] *Reg. Inn. III*, I.534 (536); cf. the *fiolarii*, sellers of glass phials for incense, lamps, and candles, in *LC*, I, pp. 299, 306, who in the former citation clearly lived in the Porticus.

Only a few artisans appear: workers in metal and cloth.[96] This was, then, a commercial suburb, more than a productive one. The basilica gained the right not only to sell seals in 1199 but to have them made, but it is likely that their *fusores*, who actually made them, lived on the other side of the Tiber.[97] We have no direct evidence in our period, all the same, about how any goods sold along the Portico actually got there. We will look again at this issue at a more general level later (pp. 168–71).

The Porticani were evidently a highly prosperous group; but it is, finally, striking that they did not visibly make it into the elite strata of Rome in our period. No aristocrat is recorded as living here. The *mansionarii* of S. Pietro, who were locally based and (for a long time) well off, appear often enough in the eleventh century, but not in major roles.[98] Similarly, although we have two references to tower-houses, both of them are linked to *argasteria*, so they were substantially commercial; and, uniquely, one of them, a lease from 1129, forbids resale by the lessee except to *mediocri persone equalis vos*, 'lesser people like you'.[99] I doubt that there was any preclusion against the Leonine city's inhabitants rising socially on the basis of commercial profit; there certainly was not elsewhere in Rome (the Pierleoni are the classic example). One inhabitant of the Porticus, Franco di Sera, expanded out of the *civitas* and had begun to deal in mills in Trastevere by 1073; his family seem to have been active there and down the via Portuense since the 1040s, and he was rich enough to give a substantial section of his mills to S. Maria in Trastevere in pious gift in 1073.[100] This family was elite by any economic definition, and could easily have become part of the rising strata of Rome's 'medium elites' after the end of the century (see below, Chapter 5), though we cannot track them later and they may simply have died out. Franco's family does, however, show the sort of path others could have followed: the investment of money from the Civitas Leoniana elsewhere in Rome, and the use of the new area as a future base. This is not documented for others, but it is likely enough.

The Civitas Leoniana was a special case in a variety of ways, and its extensive evidence (by the standards of the period) for selling has no parallels elsewhere, but it was not the only commercially active sector of Rome by any means. The documentation for artisans in particular is generous across almost all the city's regions, from the end of the tenth century, when they begin to appear in witness lists, onwards. It is somewhat less generous after the formulae for documents change in the later eleventh century, after which the occupations of the actors and witnesses in

---

[96] *Negotientes*: *SPV*, nn. 5, 6 (with Schiaparelli's note), 7, with *LC*, I, p. 299; *cambiator*: *SPV*, n. 27; food sellers: nn. 35 (a female *fornarius*), 51, 57; cloth: nn. 13, 14; metal: *LC*, I, p. 299 with *SPV*, n. 83. These citations include witnesses to *SPV* charters for the entirely rural diocese of Silva Candida: see below, n. 101.

[97] See n. 95.

[98] *SMVL*, nn. 72, 89, for the Civitas Leoniana; outside, S. Pietro's *mansionarii* appear in *RS*, nn. 42, 92, 97, 105, 134; *Papsturkunden*, n. 134; *SMVL*, nn. 32, 56; *SMT*, n. 2; *SPV*, n. 11; *S. Agnese*, n. 4; *RF*, n. 664; see also Chapter 7, n. 71.

[99] *SMVL*, n. 152 (a. 1129); ASR, SCD, cassetta 16, n. 146 (ninth text on roll).

[100] *SMT*, nn. 5, 8; cf. Crescenzo Sere in *SCD*, nn. 52, 60; Carbone di Sera in *SCD*, n. 74. (Sera is an otherwise unknown name.)

texts are mentioned less often; we therefore have a fuller snapshot of artisanal activity for the eleventh century than for the twelfth, although occupations continued to be listed after 1100 in one region, S. Maria Nova. Notwithstanding the political crisis in the city in 1050–1100, which had clear economic reflections (see below, p. 156), this contrast cannot reflect a real decline in activity, for it is still visible in the late twelfth century, when Rome's economy was certainly moving. Rome's exceptional evidence for artisans is largely, that is to say, the result of formulaic conventions: Roman *scriniarii*, for a time, saw occupations as relevant to mention in documents, in a way that notaries in other cities did not; and those same *scriniarii* in most regions of the city became less concerned to mention them as time went on. Why this should be is problematic to explain, and does not make easy either comparison across time or comparison with other cities, at least in terms of intensities of economic activity. But it at least means that we have enough data to create snapshots of artisanal activity and specialization in our well-documented regions in Rome, in the eleventh century and sometimes even the twelfth. Let us follow them, to see what we can discover.[101]

Before the late twelfth century, slightly over a hundred trades are recorded in our documents for Rome. They included workers in leather, metal, cloth, wood, ceramics, glass, and soap (in descending order of frequency); also food preparers and sellers, dealers and transporters of animals, workers in transport and building, doctors/pharmacists, moneyers/money changers, and the omnipresent *negotiatores* or *negotiantes*, merchants. This is the basic range of trades that marked any later medieval city; what marks out Rome here is the very early date we can attest it, by not long after 1000 in many cases. Rome also shows an early division of labour in a classic Smithian sense, between separable parts of the same profession. Sometimes this may be a false impression; the numerous *calzolarii* and *sutores* of the city were probably not different types of shoemaker, only different words for the same occupation, and our single reference to a *callicularius*, technically a bootmaker, in Balneo Miccino just south of Pigna in 1033, is almost certainly not to a separate trade either.[102] But when, in the iron-working sector, we find *maniani*, locksmiths,

---

[101] I should note that I have amalgamated, with the direct evidence for our regions, the witnesses to rural charters from the main urban collections—in particular, as usual, S. Ciriaco in Via Lata, S. Maria Nova, SS. Cosma e Damiano in Trastevere, and S. Maria in Campo Marzio. As long as these were written in Rome, they were normally written in or around the church concerned, and the witness community is thus most likely to reflect that of the region in which the church was situated. (Witness communities around churches are well documented; we shall look in more detail at examples in Chapter 5.) This adds to the number of references to artisans that we have; and the addition of witnesses also means the inclusion of people who were not necessarily prosperous enough to transact directly, or even indirectly, with the churches that kept all our documents, which adds to the social range we are dealing with. It is true that charters for rural areas could equally, of course, have witnesses from the locality; rural neighbours turn up often enough as witnesses, even when the document is (at least nominally) written in Rome. But we have seen how weak most communities were in the Agro romano (above, pp. 62–7), and few were capable of supporting a set of urban-style artisanal occupations. I therefore, for the most part, feel justified in assuming that artisanal witnesses in these cases were urban; I excluded all cases I felt doubt about.

[102] *Sutor* in Rome meant a clothworker, not a shoemaker, by the fourteenth century, in a shift from standard classical usage: Lori Sanfilippo, *La Roma dei Romani*, p. 255. Pier Damiani still uses the word to mean a sewer of leather (i.e. for shoes) in our period, however (*Epistolae*, n. 153, p. 59), and I follow

scudarii, shieldmakers, and *maniscalci*, farriers, as well as standard words for smith, *malleator, faber*, and (by far the commonest) *ferrarius*, it does seem to me that we are looking at specialization. This specialization was most marked in the food-selling trades, where sellers or preparers of wine, oil, bread, fish, meat, and *pulmentarium* or *companaticum*, the standard cooked vegetable accompaniment to bread in medieval Italy (the ancestor of pasta and pizza sauces), were all separate by the eleventh century.[103]

The different trades spread all across the city. Food sellers can be found everywhere, a demonstration that, whatever the availability of *orti* and vineyards throughout Rome, before housing became dense in the late twelfth century, and however sparsely settled the outlying areas of the city, there was not a full agricultural economy inside the walls—many or most people, that is, had to buy food, not grow it for themselves. This is also so for the major artisanal sectors; no region was entirely void of leatherworkers, clothworkers, or metalworkers. But there were some significant concentrations as well, which show the articulation of the city more clearly.

Trastevere specialized in leather and ceramics, and to a lesser extent iron. Some fifteen shoemakers are attested there, one of the largest concentrations in the city, and twelve ironsmiths. But it is, above all, the potters (*figuli*) who mark the region out; for not only were they numerous there (nine are documented), but they are also unknown in any other documented region of Rome. By the eleventh century, I think we can be sure that a large part at least of Rome's substantial ceramic production was focused west of the river. We can say quite a lot about it, thanks to archaeology, and I shall return to its scale shortly, but its concentration in Trastevere needs to be stressed here. The *figuli* certainly made pots, it is worth stressing; one lease from 1047, from SS. Cosma e Damiano to Romano *figulus*, of a *cripta* in the region, bordering on the *cripta* of another potter, has a rent in *laguenae*, jars (probably for wine)—a phenomenon which is very rare indeed in western European documentation; up to this period, I have only seen such contracts in late Roman Egypt.[104]

---

that meaning. The *sutor vestimenta* of *SMVL*, n. 66 (a. 1037) marks the beginning of the change; but it is significant that it is necessary in this period to state that he was working in clothing. *Callicularius*: *SMVL*, n. 61A. See in general for all this Moscati, *Alle origini*, pp. 29–41. A hundred trades for the tenth to mid-twelfth centuries compares well with the 130 in the possibly complete list in the great Pisa oath of 1228: Salvatori, *La popolazione pisana*, p. 142 (pp. 141–78 for a full analysis); I have also excluded professionals such as *iudices, scriniarii*, etc., included in that Pisa list.

[103] *Maniani*: *SCD*, n. 32; *SMVL*, n. 62; *S. Alessio*, n. 7. *Scudarii*: *SMVL*, nn. 92, 144; ASR, SCD, cassetta 16, n. 121; *S. Gregorio*, n. 55. *Maniscalcus*: *SMN*, n. 120. *Supulmentarius*: *SMVL*, n. 69. *Conpanadius*: ASR, SCD, cassetta 16 bis, n. 163 (fifth text on roll).

[104] *Figuli*: SMT, n. 1; *SCD*, nn. 51 (a. 1047), 57, 83; ASR, SCD, cassetta 16, nn. 111, 146 (second text on roll). Another *figulus* clears a vineyard outside Porta Flaminia, north of the city, in 1021, *SMVL*, n. 45; it is not known where he lived. For *laguenae*, see examples in Niermeyer, *Mediae latinitatis lexicon minus*, p. 579; in *SMN*, n. 13 (a. 1042), they are certainly wine jars. For Egypt, Wickham, *Framing*, pp. 763–4. Outside the walls of Rome, there is also a reference to kilns 'ubi lutea [clay] vasa coquuntur' in, probably, the Circo di Massenzio on the Appia, in *S. Paolo*, n. 1 (a. 1081); cf. Spera, *Il paesaggio suburbano*, pp. 63, 428 for a kiln find (of uncertain date, but medieval).

Pigna specialized in different sorts of iron goods. It had numerous *ferrarii*, and it was the major region for Rome's shieldmakers. It also had over a third of the city's documented carpenters, most of them wheelwrights (*rotarii*).[105] Campo Marzio had a smaller number of trades in our documents, which reflects the smaller size of the S. Maria in Campo Marzio archive, but clothmakers, especially in wool (*lanistae*), stand out here, and secondly ironworkers, the latter having a *scola* in the nearby *regio* Colonna.[106]

S. Maria Nova was the central location of Rome's *erarii* or bronze-workers. They are virtually only documented here, and appear in large numbers in the eleventh century (not, however, the twelfth); they are documented in families, and by 1025 at the latest there was a *scola erariorum* in the region, whose *prior* was prosperous enough to lease vineyards in Albano from S. Maria Nova. The region also had an even larger number of shoemakers, particularly in the twelfth century, and was furthermore, after 1100, home to Rome's only substantial documented community of pelterers or furriers (*pelliparii*, *pelliciarii*)—although another, smaller group is visible later in Scorteclari, perhaps at the start of the concentration of the leather trades in Pigna which is visible by the fourteenth century. There were a few woolworkers and woodworkers in S. Maria Nova too, but this region was very much a bronze and leather area; one had to go up to the Celio to find a really high proportion of textile-workers, at least in the tenth century, as we have already seen.[107]

It does not take long to set out the regional balance of trades in the city of Rome (or at least in its best-documented regions) in our period. We cannot do the micro-regional analyses which the late fourteenth-century notarial registers allow for historians of that period, for we have a much less fine-grained evidence-base. But even that has important implications for us. One, a simple one, is that regional differences entail exchange. Trastevere needed to get its bronzework from S. Maria Nova, and S. Maria Nova needed to get its pottery from Trastevere. Given the poverty of the evidence we have for the city's market under the Campidoglio, we cannot tell how much of this exchange was organized centrally in our period, rather than by buyers personally crossing the city, but it is at least plausible that both

---

[105] *Rotarii* in Pigna: *SMVL*, nn. 11, 51, 52, 93 (from the Quirinale), 119A. In the fourteenth century, Pigna had workers specializing in cloth and leather: Lori Sanfilippo, *La Roma dei Romani*, pp. 150, 297, 300, 305.

[106] *Ferrarii Columpne*: *LC*, I, p. 304, 306. *Lanistae* in Campo Marzio: *SMCM*, nn. 7, 9, 11, 22. I translate '*lanistà*' as 'woolworker', aware that 'butcher' is a popular alternative (e.g. Lenzi, *La terra e il potere*, pp. 144–5); we cannot really be sure here, but Rome has *macellarii* anyway, but no *lanaioli* or similar term apart from this one—and wool must have been the city's main cloth (linen-making, in particular, is never cited, in strong contrast to Naples—see Feniello, *Napoli*, pp. 197–202; nor is flax cultivation documented in Rome's hinterland).

[107] *Erarii*: *SMN*, nn. 4, 5, 6 (*scola*), 8, 16, with *RS*, n. 102 for the nearby Celio. Note that Moscati, *Alle origini*, p. 60, sees these as public officials or moneyers, from *erarium*, treasury; there is no basis for this reading, given their association with other artisans. In fact, *erarium* was not a standard word in Rome in our period (although it was in the Frankish and Ottonian court), and *erarius* is the standard classical word for copper- and bronzesmith (and not for treasury-worker), as in, for example, Paul's *Second Epistle to Timothy* (4. 14). *Pelliparii*, etc.: *SMN*, nn. 62, 78, 109, 119, 121, 124, 126, 168, and Augenti, *Il Palatino*, p. 188; compare for Scorteclari *SPV*, n. 52; *S. And. Aq.*, n. 2. For the fourteenth century, see above, n. 105.

forms of internal exchange were mediated by local *negotiatores*, who are particularly well documented (apart from in the Civitas Leoniana) in Trastevere, which had the river port, and in and around Pigna, just north of the main market.[108]

A second point is that fairly mundane trades, focused on a potentially wide market, are by far the best documented here, not luxury craftsmen, unlike in many other cities. There are fewer than ten goldsmiths in all our Roman evidence, and fewer references still to glass-workers, silk-workers, or marble-workers.[109] The rich metals and clothing attested in so many papal sources, and the complex mosaic work, involving glass and gold, on the major prestige churches of the early twelfth century, S. Clemente and S. Maria in Trastevere—as well as the marble decoration in many others of the same period, S. Lorenzo in Lucina or SS. Giovanni e Paolo sul Celio or S. Crisogono in Trastevere[110]—did not generate anything remotely resembling the quantities of artisans that shoemaking or wool-weaving did, notwithstanding the greater visibility today of the luxury markers from the past. But, of course, even the papal court used far more woollen clothes and shoes than it did gold and silk vestments, which were restricted to popes and cardinals, not their huge entourage. The productivity of Rome, as of nearly every city in every period, was determined by the scale of bulk, not luxury, production.[111]

A third issue is raw materials. Lazio was not strikingly rich in iron, but it had some, for example around Alatri; the ironworkers who are prominent in the Sabina castles and the cities of *Campania* doubtless got their materials locally too. The same may at least in part be true of Rome, whose hinterland was so extensive. It may be the case, however, that some of the city's iron was already being imported from further away, such as from the mines of Elba, which took off by 1100 at the latest—they were under Pisan control, but the Pisans had close Roman links in the early twelfth century.[112] The leatherworkers and woolworkers, for their part, derived most of their raw materials from animals, presumably the same animals whose meat was sold by the city's *macellarii*. Excavations in the city that have published animal bones are relatively few, but they indicate (as do almost all Italian sites from the period) a clear predominance of pigs, with sheep next (but sometimes overtaking pigs after the eleventh century), and cattle relatively uncommon, a pattern which is particularly clear in the eleventh- to thirteenth-century levels analysed in the Colosseo excavations, that is, in the leatherworking *regio* of

---

[108] *Negotiatores* (and equivalents) in Trastevere: *SCD*, nn. 16, 17, 20, 45, 46, 65, 76; in Pigna, *SMVL*, nn. 13, 26, 36, 55, 56A, 60B, 61A, 104. For the fourteenth-century registers, see above all Lori Sanfilippo, *La Roma dei Romani*, pp. 95–389; Maire Vigueur, *L'autre Rome*, pp. 121–63.

[109] *Aurifices*: S. Gregorio, nn. 53, 169; *SCD*, n. 32; *SMVL*, n. 63; *SMN*, nn. 31, 53, 57; *SPV*, n. 58. *Bitraroli*: *SMVL*, n. 39; *SMN*, n. 30. *Setarius*: *SPV*, n. 9. *Marmorarii*: *Papsturkunden*, n. 577 (in Tuscolo); *SMN*, n. 142. See Moscati, *Alle origini*, pp. 67–72.

[110] See for example Claussen, *Die Kirchen der Stadt Rom*, s.vv.

[111] Cf. Wickham, *Framing*, pp. 696–700.

[112] For Lazio, Toubert, *Les structures*, pp. 229–31, 671. General context for Tuscan iron: Cortese and Francovich, 'La lavorazione del ferro'; Corretti, *Metallurgia medievale*, pp. 12–13, 43–4. Note that the mines of the Tolfa region, above Civitavecchia, are never attested in our sources, and Roman economic involvement here is ill-documented before the late Middle Ages; field survey in this area showed no link between settlement and more than localized mineral extraction in our period (Nardi Combescure, *Paesaggi d'Etruria meridionale*, pp. 57, 112–13, 135).

S. Maria Nova.[113] Sheep and cattle were presumably brought into the city from outside, often from a long way outside, in our period (above, p. 86). Pigs, however, are less easy to transport, and thrive in urban environments. The court-yards and open lots of the city were almost certainly generously occupied by pigs in our period, and half the references to members of the animal-handling trades in our sources are to *porcarii*. But, if these *porcarii* were responsible for funnelling meat to butchers and skins to shoemakers and pelterers, they were relatively centralized as well; they are, above all, documented in and around Pigna, again not far from the central market.[114]

Finally, how rich were these artisans? They are mostly not obviously either socially or economically prominent. Nearly half the artisans and tradesmen called *viri magnifici* before the title drops out after *c.*1075 were *negotiatores*—with two *aurifices* and a *setarius* (silk-worker), luxury craftsmen, among others.[115] The title *vir magnificus* was certainly a claim for prestige, but by no means had to signify what we would call 'aristocratic' status (cf. below, p. 195); given that, what this title's usage here most probably indicates is that only a few artisans apart from merchants were as yet part of what would become the 'medium elite' in the first half of our period. (For definitions, see pp. 182–4 and Chapter 5.) Later, artisans could become more prominent, and early senators included a *pictor* and a *sartor* (in 1151, just before occupations dropped almost totally out of the documents); all the same, this does not automatically mean that they were rich and/or had 'elite' status, for our evidence for the Senate at its origin, however problematic, at least indicates that its membership was relatively wide (below, pp. 447–52).[116] And when artisans are recorded as dealing in land, the scale they were operating at was mostly fairly restricted: single houses in the city, a couple of vineyards outside it, particularly in Albano, and quite often *fila* of salt at the Tiber mouth. They were clearly not (or very seldom) cultivating that extramural land themselves (for some probable exceptions, see p. 94), but they were acting as *rentiers* on a pretty small scale. It is easy to list all the dealing we see on a larger scale than that: a *monetarius*, son of another *monetarius*, who sold 25 *modia* of land just outside Porta Maggiore in 936; a *magnificus aurifex* who leased several *mansiones*, probably warehouses, at the south end of the port under the Aventino in 1025; another *vir magnificus aurifex* whose ward conceded an estate on the Portuense to S. Ciriaco in 1034; and a *ferrarius* who

---

[113] See esp. Bedini, 'I resti faunistici' (Crypta Balbi); Bedini, 'I reperti faunistici' (Colosseo); de Grossi Mazzorin, 'Il contributo dei reperti archeozoologici' (S. Paolo); de Grossi Mazzorin and Minniti, 'Lo studio dei resti animali' (Rome in general). For Italy as a whole, Salvadori, 'Campioni archeozoologici italiani', pp. 123–42, 251–9, is basic.

[114] *Porcarii* in Pigna, etc.: *SMVL*, nn. 29, 29A, 31, 52, 60, 60B, 92, 105, 268, 273.

[115] In chronological order: *RS*, nn. 130–1 (*negotiator*); *SPV*, n. 5 (*negotiens*); *SCD*, nn. 16–17 (*negotiens*); *S. Gregorio*, n. 85 (*sartore*); *RF*, n. 500 (*negotians*); *RS*, n. 136 (*negotiator*); *RF*, n. 710 (*negotians*); *Liberiano*, n. 4 (*malleator*); *SCD*, n. 27 (*negotiens*); *S. Gregorio*, n. 169 (*aurifex*); *SMVL*, n. 52 (*porcaro*); *SPV*, n. 9 (*setario*); *SMVL*, n. 57 (*ortulanus*); *S. Prassede*, n. 6 (*sartore*); *SMVL*, nn. 60 (*porcario*), 63 (*aurifex*), 64 (*maleator*); *SCD*, n. 45 (*negotiens, sutor*); *RF*, nn. 761 (*hortulanus*), 771 (*calcararius*); *SCD*, n. 56 (*negotiator*). Note that Moscati, *Alle origini*, pp. 31–5, argues that *ferrarii* were the elite artisans; I do not find her arguments convincing here. Contrast, however, the prominence of *ferrarii* in Naples: Feniello, *Napoli*, pp. 80–2, 219–23.

[116] *Senato*, nn. 12, 13.

bought a quarter of a tower-house in Campo Marzio in 1117.[117] All except the last were clearly on the high-status end of the artisanate.

Some rising artisans had children who dropped their father's profession and established themselves as *rentiers* and moneylenders. They cannot have been uncommon. Even the soon-to-be-'aristocratic' Frangipane probably had a *sutor* among family members in the early eleventh century, although certainly not later. Others, probably more normal, included the Maccii, who began as artisans in Trastevere in the early eleventh century but by the second half of the century had an early tower-house; and the family of Sassone *macellarius*, a well-documented butcher in S. Maria Nova in the early twelfth century, for he had locally prominent children who do not claim in their charters to follow their father's trade.[118] These last two show that it was straightforward to use artisanal prosperity to get into the 'medium elite'. The evidence we have for the 'medium elite' as a whole, as we shall see in Chapter 5, also makes it reasonably clear that its members, regional leaders, could include active artisans without difficulty, presumably the most successful ones. But we are here restricted to noting generalized patterns and probabilities. How many active artisans, and how many ex-artisanal families, ended up as regional leaders, must remain hypothetical. All we can say is that the great majority of artisans did not do so, and remained at a much less prosperous economic and social level.

What we can therefore say about the Roman artisanate as a set of social strata (we cannot easily say a 'class') is that many of them were prosperous enough to benefit from the agricultural labour of others; that some of them made it through to the 'medium elite' and even beyond; and that, when they did so, they often (but not always) stopped being artisans. We cannot, however, easily distinguish between rich entrepreneurial artisans and poor salaried artisans—a bourgeoisie and a proletariat, that is to say. The *scolae* of artisans, which were numerous, do not (yet) show this sort of class hierarchy, as we shall see in a moment. The sense I get is that most artisans worked with their own hands, in family workshops, for much or most of their lives, with the exception of some rich dealers. Merchants were different. As we shall see, the Pierleoni, who started as merchants (p. 223), and several other members of the urban 'new aristocracy', continued to engage in mercantile and credit activities, indeed on an international scale; even if they did not call themselves *negotiatores*, those activities continued to bring real wealth. But most of the productive sector of Roman society remained, throughout our period, considerably more modest.

Conversely, there were a lot of artisans in Rome. Even if they each worked in individual workshops, this must have resulted in production on a considerable scale, particularly in regions with a concentration on a single craft, such as ceramics or bronze. This can be tested for one product above all, ceramics, for this is the

---

[117] *RS*, n. 43; *S. Gregorio*, n. 169; *SMVL*, n. 63; *SMCM*, n. 28.
[118] Sutor: *SMN*, n. 13; see below, p. 229. For the Maccii and Sassone, see below, Chapter 5, pp. 266–9.

Figure 3.2. Forum ware (*ceramica a vetrina pesante*) jug (*brocca*), ninth or tenth century, Foro di Nerva.

product that is overwhelmingly the best-documented and best-studied in archaeological contexts. It is worth pursuing this, for the evidence is quite clear as a result of the past twenty-five years' work, and relevant for us as a result.

Rome's pottery production was on an unusually large scale by Italian standards in our period. At the top of the market, from the eighth century, the city developed what was arguably the first new fine pottery type in the early medieval West, and certainly the most complex type for the period: *ceramica a vetrina pesante* or Forum Ware, a brown- or green-glazed ware, often with applied petals, probably following models from Constantinople (see Figure 3.2). This pottery type expanded production in the ninth century and again, massively, in the tenth. By the end of the tenth century, it was beginning to lose the full glaze that marked the early period, and it is now usually called *ceramica a vetrina sparsa* or Sparse Glaze Ware. This version of the type was highly standardized, and had a high-quality *depurato* fabric; by the eleventh century it can be regarded as mass-produced. Most Roman glazed pottery consisted of jugs (*brocche*); there were some open forms, plates, basins (*catini*), and bowls (*coperchi*), but Romans probably ate their food most regularly off wood or metal.[119] Beside this fine pottery, excavations regularly show up undecorated two-handled jugs (*anforette*) in, again, high-quality *acroma depurata* fabrics, which continue throughout the period, and which by the late twelfth century were sometimes red-painted, following a south Italian aesthetic; and

---

[119] See for a clear overview Paroli, 'La ceramica invetriata', updated to 1000 in Romei, 'Produzione e circolazione'. (There is more debate over the origins of the ware, but this does not concern us here.) The type-site, here as everywhere for ceramics, is the Crypta Balbi: for post-1000, see Paroli, 'Ceramica a vetrina pesante'; Ricci and Vendittelli, *Museo nazionale romano—Crypta Balbi*, I, pp. 28–43.

cooking-pots, usually *olle* (but also some bread-cookers, *testi di pane*), in a coarser but still good-quality fabric.[120]

This is a more articulated set of productions than was normal for single cities in Italy in our period.[121] It is striking for a number of reasons. First, its stability and scale: these ceramic types continued for four centuries without major change, except that their production became steadily larger-scale and more systematic. (New types, particularly of glazed wares, only came in after 1200.[122]) Marco Ricci has recently proposed that by the eleventh century at the latest the three main types, glazed wares, *anforette*, and cooking wares, were made by three separate sets of workshops, for they had developed sufficiently different artisanal traditions; if this (plausible) argument is confirmed by future work, such a specialization again marks the size of Roman ceramic production.[123] Second, its consistency: all recent excavations in Rome have simply confirmed and replicated the ceramic sequences first worked out before 1990 on the Crypta Balbi site, which shows that a single set of ceramic types was available, across Rome, in much the same percentages, throughout our period.[124] Third, its spread. Forum Ware is found in small quantities across the whole of central Italy, and on sites on the Tyrrhenian Sea from Provence to Sicily. Much of this was locally produced, in imitation of Roman productions, but Roman fabrics are attested in Sardinia, Tuscany, and Liguria, as well as parts of central Lazio. Sparse Glaze Ware seems, for all the size of its production, to have extended less fully into the countryside around Rome; local productions had by now developed sufficiently for more fine wares to be produced outside Rome (though following urban models). But Roman fabrics have been identified at Albano in the eleventh century, and maybe also alongside local wares north of Rome around Capena and at Tarquinia.[125] Although it is relatively

[120] See the various articles in Manacorda et al., 'La ceramica medioevale', and in Saguí, *L'esedra della Crypta Balbi*, pp. 215–484; more recently, esp. Romei, 'Produzione e circolazione', de Luca, 'Ritrovamenti dei secoli IX–X' (Fori Imperiali), and Ricci as in n. 122 below. *Testi di pane* imply household baking, which balances the evidence of Rome's documented bakers (*pistores, pistrinarii*): *SMVL*, n. 77, 112; *SCD*, n. 83; *S. Sisto*, n. 6. For red-painted ware, which was never as popular in Rome as elsewhere, see most recently Panuzzi, 'Ceramica dipinta in rosso'.

[121] Compare Brogiolo and Gelichi, 'Ceramiche, tecnologia', for the Po plain. For Tuscany, see now Cantini, 'Dall'economia complessa' and Cantini, 'Ritmi e forme'; Grassi, *La ceramica, l'alimentazione*, pp. 14–38, 56–9, which all show an increasingly developed ceramic network across the region as a whole, but no single cities with the complexity of Rome.

[122] Molinari, 'Le ceramiche rivestite'.

[123] Ricci, 'I reperti archeologici', generalized in Ricci, 'La bottega delle olle acquarie', and replacing his earlier survey in 'Appunti per una storia'.

[124] See Ricci, 'I reperti archeologici' (Colosseo); de Luca, 'Ritrovamenti dei secoli IX–X' (Fori Imperiali); Annis, 'Ceramica altomedievale a vetrina pesante' (San Sisto Vecchio); Paganelli, 'Produzioni ceramiche' (Foro Romano); Pentiricci, 'Palazzo della Cancelleria'; Mandarini and Paganelli, 'Note preliminari' (S. Clemente); Smiraglia and Zanotti, 'Ceramiche medievali' (via Ardeatina); Fresi and de Santis, 'Reperti ceramici' (S. Paolo).

[125] See in general Paroli, 'La ceramica invetriata' and Romei, 'Produzione e circolazione'; with for Lazio, esp. Camilli and Vitali Rosati, 'La ceramica a vetrina pesante' (Capena and northwards); Barbini, 'Ceramica invetriata' (Albano); Bartoloni and Ricci, 'Produzioni ceramiche' (Tarquinia); Romei, 'La ceramica medievale' (Scorano near Capena); Nardi Combescure, *Paesaggi d'Etruria meridionale*, p. 113 (Tolfa region). In Tuscolo, petrological analyses have not yet been carried out, and the excavators think that local productions are most likely, but it is very striking how the entire ceramic corpus there

straightforward for an experienced artisan to build a pottery kiln anywhere, if the right clay is available, the city's dominance over production extended not only throughout the urban area but also to some places outside it, and, on the level of taste, throughout almost the whole of Lazio and indeed beyond.

These are clear patterns. They will, of course, be refined in future work; but the only major issue currently left obscure is the location of the workshops, for kilns have not yet been identified in Rome in the medieval period, before one from the thirteenth century apparently present in via S. Paolo a Regola in the Arenula region, on the other side of the Tiber from the north of Trastevere (this region was one of the main potters' quarters by 1500).[126] As we have seen, Trastevere clearly specialized in ceramics already in the eleventh century, but we cannot be absolutely sure that it was the only one in our period, given the weakness of our documentation for half the city (including the *regio* Arenula). But if Ricci is right about the three groups of workshops, then one, at least, was in Trastevere; the *laguenae* that are attested in 1047, given that the word is used elsewhere for wine jars, could well be the *anforette* of the archaeologists.

We thus get, in the case of this product, a detailed material correlate to the data in the written sources; and one that was already present in 900 and before, earlier than any of our document collections. But the archaeology takes us much further than that: it gives us clear guidelines as to scale. It is, indeed, evident that ceramics were produced in Rome on an unusually large scale for the period. This shows that the city (and, to a lesser extent, its hinterland) was a market which was large enough and stable enough to allow artisans the security to mass-produce. I have proposed elsewhere that aristocratic demand was the major cause of developed ceramic production under early medieval conditions, and that is likely here too (counting Rome's numerous churches, led by the papacy itself, as part of the stratum of rich buyers);[127] but the size of Rome as a city, and the homogeneity of the ceramics found on a wide variety of Roman sites, both ecclesiastical and lay, are good arguments in favour of a mass urban demand for these products as well. It does not seem hard, that is to say, to see pottery production as both large-scale—sets of linked workshops, probably what David Peacock has called 'nucleated workshops'[128]—and available on a regular basis to the city's population in general.

matches exactly that of Roman productions across the eleventh and twelfth centuries: Beolchini, *Tusculum II*, pp. 323–62 (326 for production perhaps being local). Roman wares did not reach the Sabina mountains: Lecuyer, 'De la ville à la campagne', pp. 423–5. The end of Roman fabrics in the countryside with the start of Sparse Glaze Ware is particularly clear in Patterson, 'La ceramica a vetrina pesante', pp. 428–31 (Tuscia Romana); Romei, 'La ceramica a vetrina pesante', p. 440 and Romei, 'La ceramica medievale', p. 127 (Scorano). The furthest Forum Ware is known to have reached is Moravia (Poláček, 'Ninth-century Mikulčice', p. 508).

[126] For the late Middle Ages, see above all Güll, *L'industrie du quotidien* (pp. 49–85 for the geography of the workshops—note that Trastevere was less important by then, but took off again in the sixteenth century, pp. 63–4, 76–9); I did not, however, find reference to kiln wasters in Quilici, 'Roma, via di S. Paolo alla Regola'. More recently, see the fifteenth- or sixteenth-century potter's workshop and kiln found in the Foro di Traiano: Meneghini, 'L'attività delle officine'.

[127] Wickham, *Framing*, pp. 535–6, 706–7.

[128] Peacock, *Pottery*, pp. 9, 38–43.

And if this was so for pottery, it is likely to have been so for iron, leather, and woollen cloth as well. We have to adjust our vision. Roman artisans were already prominent in eleventh-century sources, but we need to recognize that many of them were not just the local craftsmen for a *regio*, but mass-producers for the whole city. They could do that without increasing the scale of individual workshops, which could well have remained family-based; their density and interconnection, and the stability of demand, were enough to allow for consistent productive patterns.

We cannot track that density in our written documents for most trades, but there is one exception: milling. The floating mills of the Tiber are well known to historians, for they crop up in plenty of published documents, and there are drawings and photographs of them right up to the late nineteenth-century embankment of the Tiber. By the start of our period, Roman mills were almost all on the river; the mills on the Forma Traiana, as that aqueduct came down the Gianicolo, though they were restored in the 830s, are referred to as abandoned in a document of 1005.[129] And there were a large number of these floating mills; over twenty documents mention them before 1150, and, given their references to multiple mills, we have evidence for over thirty of them along the Tiber inside the city walls. They clustered around the Scola Saxonum, at the north-western edge of Trastevere, along the Ripa Graeca, and above all around the Isola Tiberina; but they probably existed everywhere around the Tiber bend in smaller densities.[130]

The papacy may have originally owned the river banks, but in our period the lands attached to these mills were owned by other churches, and the mills themselves were also owned for the most part by churches. Although the regions along the Tiber banks are not well documented, with the exception of north-western Trastevere, a dozen churches and monasteries are attested as controlling urban mills, including all those with more than a handful of documents except S. Maria Nova; so, in the tenth century, are Benedetto Campanino and the *de Imiza* family, leading aristocrats, and in the mid-eleventh the Pierleoni. The mills of Rome were from the start a productive resource which everyone influential wanted a part of;

---

[129] Forma Traiana (or Sabbatina): *LP*, I, pp. 503–4, II, p. 77; *Papsturkunden*, n. 419; see Coates-Stephens, 'The walls and aqueducts', p. 172, and Lohrmann, 'Schiffsmühlen auf dem Tiber', pp. 284–6, an article which only cites a small part of the documentation. Overall, Krautheimer, *Rome*, pp. 240–2, although only a few lines long (plus pictures), and Meneghini and Santangeli Valenzani, *Roma nell'altomedioevo*, pp. 129–32, are the clearest surveys for our period of a well-known but hardly studied topic, with, for the fourteenth century, Lori Sanfilippo, *La Roma dei Romani*, pp. 320–32. There were also still a few mills not on the Tiber in our period. S. Giovanni had and leased out several on a lake just outside the Porta S. Giovanni (Pflugk, II, n. 152, III, nn. 142, 289; *LC*, I, p. 8); S. Paolo had three and S. Maria Nova had one on the Marrana di Caffarella not far outside the Porta Appia (*S. Paolo*, n. 1; *SMN*, nn. 107–8). These areas continued to have mills: Lori Sanfilippo, *La Roma dei Romani*, pp. 322–3.

[130] It is worth giving a complete list of the documents known to me, in chronological order up to 1200: *SCD*, n. 1; *Papsturkunden*, nn. 134, 155; *S. Gregorio*, n. 4; *S. Agnese*, n. 1 (all tenth century); *Papsturkunden*, nn. 419, 424; *RF*, nn. 651, 666, 665; *SMVL*, n. 54; *SCD*, n. 38; *SMVL*, n. 92; *S. Gregorio*, n. 17; *SCD*, n. 73; SMT, n. 5; *S. Paolo*, n. 1; SMT, n. 8; *SMVL*, n. 109; *Bullaire Cal. II*, n. 227; Pflugk, II, n. 284; Kehr, II, pp. 348–50; Fonseca, *De basilica S. Laurentii*, pp. 250–5; *Liberiano*, n. 22; *SMCM*, n. 62; and the undated BAV, CVL 8051, f. 33 for S. Maria in Trastevere.

indeed, although we have so few tenth-century documents for the city, we already have several citations of mills.[131]

The construction of floating mills, probably the most substantial wooden buildings in the city, was quite complicated. They had a wooden base (*ligamentarium*), which was tied up at the bank, sometimes to wooden bollards (*staffiles*), but often also brick or stone *monumenta*, to give greater solidity. The bollards were sunk into river mud, which may not always have given sufficient purchase; this is doubtless the reason for Franco di Sera's explanation in 1073, in a gift of a mill and its attached Lungotevere to S. Maria in Trastevere, the single most detailed description of a mill we have, that he had the right to insert *staphilia ac retinacula ad liganda ligamina* into the Trastevere city wall itself, where it met the river. The mill, with its *ferramenta* and *conciatura*, its internal machinery, was then built on the floating section. They were expensive: the same Franco bought half a mill in the same area in 1082 for the huge price of £9; another mill leased in the same year off the Isola Tiberina was valued at £4 and 5 *solidi*—this being a period in which the lease of an urban *domus*, whether *terrinea* or *solarata*, could be sold for anything between 10 *solidi* and £3.[132] They were major investments. We can thus see why the 1082 lease, from S. Ciriaco to a certain Ruscio di Beno di Setto, after giving us the value, makes it clear both that Ruscio is liable for maintenance, and that he can pay £4 and 10 *solidi*, more than its value, if he wants to buy the mill itself—for, of course, mills could be floated away by their lessees, even if it has to be said that, if they were removed illegally, they would have been hard to hide. But mills were built, quite often; we have a number of references to new ones.[133] The reason is that profits from them could be very substantial. Ruscio had to pay 17 *solidi* in entry-fine for a nineteen-year lease (which went on mill maintenance), but then 4 *modia* of grain in rent, not per year as was usual elsewhere, but per month (unless the river was too high or too low). Our only other mill lease, from 1072, also for the Isola Tiberina, was very similar: an entry-fine of only 2 *solidi* for nineteen years, but then 56 *sexstaria* of grain (probably the equivalent of 3.5 *modia*) per month.[134] The millers must have milled much more in order to pay on this sort of scale.

---

[131] Aristocrats: esp. *S. Gregorio*, n. 4; *Papsturkunden*, n. 419 (cf. *RF*, n. 439); *SCD*, n. 73. A lay-owned mill and riverbank is implied in SMT, n. 5; see above, n. 36.

[132] SMT, n. 5 (note that this faded parchment has two good early modern MS transcriptions, in SMT, n. 35, ff. 109r–11v, and BAV, CVL 8051, ff. 13–15); for 1082, SMT, n. 8, and *SMVL*, n. 109. For house prices in the period, see *SMVL*, nn. 84, 104, 114A; *SMCM*, n. 14; *SPV*, n. 25; *SMN*, n. 27.

[133] *SMVL*, n. 109. For mill-building: *Papsturkunden*, nn. 134, 155, 424; *RF*, n. 651; *SCD*, n. 38; SMT, n. 5; Kehr, II, pp. 348–50.

[134] *SMVL*, n. 109; *SCD*, n. 73. (Four other leases are for low rents, because they are part of wider transactions or because they are emphyteuses: *SMVL*, nn. 54, 92; *SCD*, n. 38; *S. Gregorio*, n. 17.) But how much was a *modius*? The classical *modius* was around 8.6 litres, not a lot. At least one can say that, in general, medieval (and also modern) *modii/moggi* were much larger than this. Devroey, *Économie rurale*, p. 71, estimates the Carolingian *modius* at 40–55 litres. Menant, *Campagnes lombardes*, p. 802, gives figures of 142–320 litres for a Lombard *modius* after 1050. Palermo, *Mercati del grano*, I, pp. 157–60, sees the problem of assessing measures in and around Rome in the fourteenth century as insurmountable, but his grain prices for *rubbi*, the measure used by then in Rome, set against those for *salme* (½ *moggio*) in Corneto (pp. 356–7, 371), taking into account differences in currency (p. 353), imply that a Corneto *moggio* was about four times a Roman *rubbio*, i.e. about 800 kg. (cf. Palermo, *Mercati del grano*, I, p. 157; and also Maire Vigueur, 'Les "casali"', p. 123), which would be around

Individual Romans could easily have had their own hand mills; in a city, no restrictions on private milling are documented or would have been enforceable. But grain was overwhelmingly brought into the city by prosperous or rich tenants of ecclesiastical estates, not by small dealers, so on a large scale (above, pp. 85–6). The similarly large scale of the Tiber milling operation matches this, and it at least hints at a relative centralization for the most important element in the food supply of Rome, as grain went to the Tiber mills to be turned into flour, before fanning out to the city, either to the city's *pistrinarii*, bakers, or directly to households and their *testi di pane*. The interest of Rome's major churches in the mills, and of many of its aristocrats too, is thus easy to understand. It went with the extensive interest of both in the Porto salt pans and the Albano vineyards as well (above, pp. 97–103): all three were crucial parts of the city's food supply, and there were major profits to be made from them, already in the tenth century, and consistently thereafter.[135] The picture we gain from all this is more impressionistic than that from the archaeological evidence for ceramics, but the net elements are, once again, scale and potential centralization—and the possibility of consistent profit. This again points to the size and stability of the urban market, taken as a whole.

Artisans and other trades were grouped into *scolae*. We have seen such collectivities in specialized rural areas already, the several *scolae* of *ortulani*, and those of the *salinarii* and *piscatores* of the Porto marshes, which visibly had a complex articulation and their own customs, which were regulated semi-judicially by their leaders (above, pp. 89–91, 103–5). In the city, *scolae* were certainly prominent as well: we see them or their head (usually called a *prior*, once a *patronus*) cited for *candicatores* in 978, the *errarii* of S. Maria Nova in 1025, *fullones* in 1034, *sandalarii* (with all the *scolenses maiores et minores*) in 1115, *muratores* in 1120.[136] As noted earlier (p. 90), these must have been modelled on the *scolae cantorum, mansionariorum, defensorum*, etc., of the ecclesiastical establishment—and also the various *scolae militiae*, the army in its ceremonial and processional role, which are documented from the eighth century through to the twelfth, whether welcoming emperors or acting as corporations to lease land. Although we cannot automatically assume that artisanal associations were old, these latter *scolae* undoubtedly had Byzantine origins; *scolae* for palatine officials were a standard feature of late Roman and Byzantine Constantinople. It is also not chance that the only other city in Italy where artisanal *scolae* were prominent was Ravenna, another major ex-Byzantine

1000 litres. One such *moggio* would feed two well-nourished people, or three ill-nourished ones, per year (Maire Vigueur, 'Les "casali"', p. 123; the figures for England are comparable: Dyer, *Standards of Living*, p. 114). If the fourteenth-century Corneto *moggio* is any guide, the mill rents alone of the 1072–82 leases would generously feed nearly ninety people a year, and the mills would have processed grain for far more. There are far too many uncertainties for us to be able to commit to this figure, but it gives us an idea of magnitude.

[135] Vineyards also existed in large numbers in the city, of course, but they seldom receive the same attention in our documents as do those of the *suburbio* or of Albano. They are more likely to have been used for subsistence. One exception by the late twelfth century is Monte Pipino and Bagi, two linked areas apparently on the Esquilino: *SMN*, nn. 89, 131, 138, 147, 155, 161, cf. *Liberiano*, n. 22.

[136] Respectively, *RS*, n. 59; *SMN*, n. 6; *RS*, n. 108; *RF*, n. 1215; *SMN*, n. 40. Moscati, *Alle origini*, pp. 51–65, and Lori Sanfilippo, *La Roma dei Romani*, pp. 57–63, have similar lists.

city, where by the tenth century at the latest *piscatores*, *negociatores*, and *callegarii*, shoemakers, had them.[137] When Cencio in the *Liber Censuum* in 1192 listed seventeen *scolae* (mostly unattested elsewhere) who were paid money by the papal Curia at Christmas and Easter, many of them still came from the ecclesiastical and palatine world, for example the *adextratores* or grooms, or were related to trades associated with it, as with the *fiolarii* who made/sold glass incense phials and lights, or the two *scolae* of *bandonarii*, flag-makers. But there was nonetheless a crossover into a wider lay society as well, for in 1192 the *ferrarii* of Colonna, the *calderarii*, the *carbonarii*, and the two *scolae* of *muratores* were ordinary artisanal groups.[138] This list of *scolae* thus goes further to stress the close links such artisanal associations had with the ceremonial of the papal court, which spread so far into Roman society, as we shall see in Chapter 6.

How important were artisanal *scolae* really, though? The only *scolae* that can actually be seen generating their own regulations and judging trade-related dis-putes, or indeed that seem to have a substantial size and internal articulation, are all rural. In theory, one could make a case for saying that urban *scolae* were hardly more than ceremonial groups; we certainly have no evidence to prove that any of them were either large or socially active. We can regard them as 'guilds' by now; they certainly fulfilled the basic roles of guilds. But we cannot yet see them as acting as later guilds would, controlling the terms of trade and the internal work relations of a hierarchical community. Nor can we see them as acting politically, unlike the *artes* during and after Rome's first *popolo*-based government, that of Brancaleone degli Andalò in the 1250s. Indeed, how the *scolae* turned into the *artes* of the later thirteenth century (which they certainly did in some cases; the word *ars* is used occasionally as a synonym for *scola* already before 1150, as we saw for the *salinarii*) is exceptionally obscure.

All the same, we can say some more positive things for our period. The normality of these professional associations is striking. Men who were a *prior scole*, as with Giovanni of the *scola errariorum* in 1025, flanked by his brothers, *nobiles viri errarii*, and other unrelated bronze-workers as well, were clearly proud to be heads of their professional association, which may also have had an established headquarters, as the *scola callegariorum* certainly had in Ravenna.[139] They add to the sense one equally has, looking at these trades or guilds as a group, that individual and independent artisans worked together, collectively, to make up more than the

---

[137] Early examples of welcoming: *LP*, I, pp. 496–7, II, pp. 6, 88. As landowners, maybe *SMVL*, n. 6B, and certainly *S. Alessio*, n. 14. Byzantine parallels: see for example Haldon, *Byzantium in the Seventh Century*, pp. 391–4. Ravenna: *Le carte del decimo secolo*, nn. 48, 77, 78, 213, 248, 276. Lori Sanfilippo, *La Roma dei Romani*, pp. 15–38, traces the over-schematic historiography concerning the supposed continuity or discontinuity of Roman *scolae* from the collective bodies of the late Roman and Byzantine empires.

[138] *LC*, I, pp. 304–6. See Twyman, *Papal Ceremonial*, pp. 189–93.

[139] *SMN*, n. 6 (a. 1025; cf. also the articulation of the *sandalarii* in *RF*, n. 1215). Ravenna headquarters: *Le carte del decimo secolo*, nn. 213, 248, 276; *Le carte ravennati del secolo undicesimo*, I, n. 33. For *scola* and *ars* in 1118, *SMN*, n. 37. For the mid-thirteenth century, Lori Sanfilippo, *La Roma dei Romani*, pp. 67–8.

sum of their parts. None of the city *scolae* may have been as large as that of the *salinarii* or *piscatores*, but it is highly likely that they all had similar semi-judicial roles, to cover sectoral disputes: it would be perverse, given what we know about the political articulation of the city and its absence in the countryside, to propose that only rural *scolae* were powerful enough to act in this way, particularly given the strong Trastevere links that both the *salinarii* and *piscatores* had. In the city, they may well also have contributed to the quality control necessary for separate workshops to produce the sort of standardized well-made products that we can see in the ceramic sector. And, although one should not get too enthusiastic about proto-communal associative forms here, for the early Senate was certainly not based on *scolae* (below, p. 306), their internal structures did contain elements that could be, and were, developed in the more communal world of the 1140s.[140] Artisans were, after all, genuinely important in the city; however low-key their professional associations, these will have been important too.

The pacing of the Roman economy

In the rest of this section, we will look at the evidence we have for changes in the economy of the city across our two and a half centuries. We should expect them; cities are never static. There are quite a number for Rome, all the same, particularly at the end of the period, and, put all together, they have important implications. I shall separate out three periods: the tenth and early eleventh centuries, the longest period but that with the most fragmentary evidence; the late eleventh and early twelfth, arguably a period of crisis; and the mid-twelfth, which shows clear indicators of economic movement.

The first sign of change in our period has already been discussed: it is the development of the Foro di Cesare and Foro di Traiano in the tenth century, which Santangeli has in each case associated with mid-century aristocrats, respectively the future pope Leo VIII and Alberico's associate Caloleo. As noted earlier (p. 126), the second association seems to me stronger than the first, but even one such association is significant: around 950, a Roman aristocrat was putting money into developing a block of urban housing, in which a formerly open area was repaved in crushed stone, with river-pebbled streets across it, and houses laid out between them, with some earth brought in for *orti*—an area subsequently named after him. Why did he do it? This is not the same as building a monastery, as Alberico and his entourage often did, for piety and political display; this is large-

---

[140] One intriguing example is the use of the term *paterens*, a characteristic office in the *scola salinariorum* by 1119 (*SMN*, n. 37), and usually only documented in that context in Rome (see further for the thirteenth century Carbonetti Vendittelli, 'La curia dei *priores*'—note that *patarentes* are also by 1178 lay patrons of churches in Trastevere as well, ASR, SCD, cassetta 16, nn. 147–8), to describe an official of what was arguably the early commune of Sutri (*S. Gregorio*, n. 89, a. 1142; though cf. Vendittelli, *Sutri*, pp. 62–74, who dates an organized commune here to later). This is hardly enough to show a direct influence of *scolae* on communes! But it at least indicates parallelisms.

scale, but by no means flashy, and in fact fairly low quality. It can best be seen as a construction for profit, that is, subletting out to others for money.[141]

This was not an entirely new development. Indeed, historians have been accustomed to see the late eighth and early ninth centuries as the high point for urban interventions in early medieval Rome, and the period from the late ninth to the late eleventh as one of relative stagnation. And it is true that the biggest surviving new churches between the sixth century and the twelfth were all built in the former period, in particular between the 800s and the 840s, plus Leo IV's Civitas Leoniana walls around 850, which were the only formal extension of the city between Aurelian in the 270s and the town planning of the post-1870 period. This is filled out by the long and remarkable lists of other new churches, roof repairs of older churches, rich gold, silver and silk refurbishments of all churches, and the restoration of aqueducts and the like, which appear in the *Liber pontificalis* in the same period. These certainly attest to the very great wealth of the papacy in the early Carolingian period, and to the preparedness of popes to spend that wealth very ambitiously. Earlier, I connected this, above all, to the overwhelming dominance the popes had over landowning, in Rome and the Agro romano, in the first generations after the papal takeover of imperial fiscal land.[142] But, after the troubled period of Arab attacks and the Formosan crisis, the half-century of stable Teofilatto rule did allow for public ambition again, as shown by the Alberician monasteries (less visible to earlier generations of historians because they mostly do not physically survive) and other non-papal church foundations and rebuildings.[143] Similarly, the sort of practical intervention in the urban landscape associated with early ninth-century popes like Leo IV could be renewed as well, now attached to influential aristocrats like Caloleo. When a pope rebuilt a city wall or an aqueduct, however, it still looked like a monumental intervention, however useful to the population. Developing an urban quarter for profit was different: precisely because it was less spectacular, it responded to new needs, more economic than political. Caloleo may thus be more significant for Rome's economic development than were the papal builders of a century earlier.

These lay interventions were then picked up by the church, in association with the laity. We do not have enough tenth-century documents for us to know when this began, but, after the millennium, we have seen S. Ciriaco in Via Lata laying out building plots in the Trevi region in the 1010s; S. Salvatore ad Duos Amantes did the same in Campo Carleo and Balneo Miccino in the 1030s; and the 1020s show recently built houses on church land in several other locations. Étienne Hubert

---

[141] Meneghini and Santangeli Valenzani, *I fori imperiali*, pp. 144–55. Caloleo is also the lessor of land in the territory of Tivoli in 963 (*Tivoli*, n. 93), an exceptionally rare example of a lay lease to cultivators before 1100 (see above, p. 72).

[142] For the ninth century, see, among many, Delogu, 'The rebirth of Rome'; Delogu, 'L'importazione di tessuti preziosi'; Delogu, 'Rome in the ninth century' (more downbeat); Krautheimer, *Rome*, pp. 109–42; Goodson, *The Rome of Pope Paschal I*. For greater continuities than those recognized by Krautheimer, see Coates-Stephens, 'Dark age architecture in Rome'. For land, see above, pp. 56–8.

[143] See for lists Hamilton, 'The monastic revival'; and now, especially, Coates-Stephens, 'Dark age architecture in Rome', pp. 204–22.

argued that these interventions were new, but that was before the archaeology; the continuities from the tenth century now seem rather more evident.[144] The active commercial leasing in the Civitas Leoniana in the same period fits with this as well, although that region, as we have seen, was something of a special case. We can see the early eleventh century as a period in which a steady urban expansion is visible, at least in fragmentary form, in many places in the city, and it seems to have started by the mid-tenth.

This expansion is much less visible in the late eleventh century and early twelfth. In part, this is simply because our documents are much less numerous between 1046 and the 1130s, with only a brief upturn in the 1060s; but this already, as we have seen (p. 29), marks crisis. Hubert shows that the period is marked by several negative indicators: a decrease in references to new houses which is sharper than the drop in documents; a decrease, indeed, in all references to the alienation and leasing of houses; and, in particular, a drop in house prices.[145] The supposed Norman sack of the city in 1084 is invisible in our documents, except for the inscriptions concerning Paschal II's rebuilding of SS. Quattro Coronati on the Celio in 1111–16, and it is likely, given our narratives, that it mostly affected the Laterano–Celio area in the south and the northern Campo Marzio between Porta Flaminia and Ponte S. Pietro. In the south, the Celio suburb probably suffered, as we have seen, but even there problems were discontinuous. S. Clemente shows no fire damage; the Colosseo does, in some of its recently excavated vanes; but nearby S. Maria Nova's late eleventh-century documents show no sign of trouble.[146] It is probably more significant that S. Maria in Campo Marzio in the north kept no documents for the city between 1075 and 1117, that no one else did for the *regio* in the period either, and that the major nearby church of S. Lorenzo in Lucina was rebuilt between before 1112 and 1130.[147] More important than single acts of war would, however, have been the general climate of insecurity and the weakness of city government, particularly from the late 1080s onwards (see below, pp. 393–403).

Similar trends are visible if we look for evidence of immigration, that is to say references to city dwellers with a toponym attached which indicates that they came from elsewhere, Sabbatino *Albanese* or Teodoro *de Anquillaria* or Giovanni *Cremonensis*.[148] These are not hugely numerous in Rome, it has to be said. One reason was doubtless the weakness of rural settlement structures up to 25 km around the city (above, pp. 62–71); there were simply not many major identification markers in the single most important reserve of urban immigration, the city's

[144] See this chapter, n. 61, for Pigna and its neighbours; with *S. Gregorio*, n. 169; *SCD*, nn. 30, 34. See Hubert, *Espace urbain*, pp. 135–7, 274.

[145] Hubert, *Espace urbain*, pp. 137–8, 337–9, 350–1.

[146] See in general Hamilton, 'Memory, symbol', pp. 393–4; Yawn, 'Clement's new clothes', and below, pp. 354–7, for S. Clemente; Antonetti and Rea, 'Inquadramento cronologico', p. 313, for the Colosseo; above, n. 21 for SS. Quattro Coronati.

[147] For S. Lorenzo, see Forcella, V.341–3; Krautheimer, *Corpus basilicarum*, II, pp. 161–86; and especially Claussen, *Die Kirchen der Stadt Rom*, III, pp. 261–309 (D. Mondini); cf. Hamilton, 'Memory, symbol', p. 397.

[148] Respectively, *S. Gregorio*, n. 170; *SCD*, n. 52; *S. Sil.*, n. 47.

immediate hinterland—a hinterland that must have supplied the city throughout, given that in no medieval city did births ever exceed deaths.[149] The rest of Lazio and sometimes further afield is, however, consistently attested after 1000. From the pool of references to Lazio incomers we have, Albano, the only well-attested location from the Agro romano, and *Campania* were clearly the most consistent sources of immigrants throughout our period; conversely, Tivoli provided relatively few (but perhaps they simply did not want to betray their origin) and so did the Sabina.[150] Further afield, some came from the Naples–Capua area, fewer from Tuscany, and, after our period, there was a very considerable immigration of 'Lombardi', presumably from the Po plain as a whole, after 1180. This doubtless reflects Rome's enduring attraction to a wider geographical region than most cities had (the only surprising near-absence is the Abruzzo, the great source of immigration into the city in the century after 1870).[151] Here, too, however, the late eleventh and early twelfth centuries see a clear drop in references (a drop faster than the decrease in the number of documents), and the period between 1080 and 1100 has none at all; there was no real pickup until the 1140s, though from then on we find a steady set of examples. These data are very labile, and have to be treated cautiously, but it is again significant that the late eleventh century may have seen trouble of some kind; the data here at least fit those for the stall in house-building.

This downturn was then reversed from the 1130s onwards. House sales became more frequent, house prices began to rise, in some regions at least, and these increases would continue for 150 years; immigrants are documented again. In general, references to building plots, *casarini*, became generalized across the city; they are prominent in all the regions we have good documents for, as we have seen, and they also appear regularly in our poor evidence for the Tiber bend.[152] This is when the most densely populated area around and north of the Capitolio lost the rest of its empty spaces, and expanded both west to the river and east up some of the hill slopes, the Quirinale and Esquilino. This was mostly a development subsequent to our period, but it had clearly started beforehand. I would not seek to be too apocalyptic about the economic crisis of the late eleventh century, precisely because it was so clearly and consistently reversed. That was also not a crisis visible in our best archaeological marker, ceramic production. But it is at least quite clear that the city was expanding again at the end of our period.

---

[149] Though Galeria, Ostia, and Lunghezza, among the few real rural settlements in the Agro romano or on its edge, do appear: Galeria: *RS*, nn. 82, 86; *SPV*, n. 7; Ostia: *S. Alessio*, n. 23 (a late reference); Lunghezza: *SMVL*, n. 126. So also, above all, does Albano: see n. 150.

[150] Albano has too many references to list; up to 1100, *RS*, nn. 102, 108, 107; *S. Gregorio*, n. 171; *SPV*, n. 12; *SMVL*, nn. 82, 90; *SMN*, n. 14. *Campania*: e.g. *SCD*, n. 65; *SMVL*, n. 140. Tivoli: *SMVL*, n. 97.

[151] Naples–Capua: e.g. Manaresi, n. 236; *S. Gregorio*, n. 81; *RF*, n. 524. Tuscany: e.g. *SMVL*, n. 131 (Arezzo). *Lombardi* begin with ASR, SCD, cassetta 16, n. 129 (a. 1161, second text on document). The only references to the central high Appennines are *Senato*, n. 12 (a. 1148), in which the first known *scriba senatus* is 'Boiani natus' (Boiano in present-day Molise), and ASR, SCD, cassetta 16 bis, n. 163 (third text on roll, a. 1191: Amiterno west of L'Aquila; cf. also perhaps *SMN*, n. 123, a. 1184).

[152] Hubert, *Espace urbain*, pp. 138–47, 340–5, 351–5.

If we focus on this, we can also see some new urbanistic and commercial patterns, which were changing Rome's economic structure in durable ways. Let us here look at the middle third of the twelfth century, and concentrate on three elements of this: types of housing; ecclesiastical leasing policies; and the rise of credit and of our evidence for international commerce. All three took shape by the mid-century in ways which would characterize the city for the rest of the Middle Ages.

The twelfth century was the period when Rome's characteristic late medieval house-types appear. It is hard to date the reused brick that marks most of Rome's earliest surviving private houses before the beginning of the use of *tufelli*, small but regular stone blocks, along with brick at the end of the twelfth century; but there are enough surviving two-storeyed houses, sometimes with porticoes, or else with an external stair across the street front, to show that this was a period in which front courtyards were being filled in, to create the narrow streets Rome is full of, as Étienne Hubert can also show on documentary grounds (see Figure 3.3 for an example).[153] It was also, in general, the period when two-storeyed houses came to be lived in by not just the rich, and when the main entrance was increasingly up the stairs onto the first floor.[154] *Domus terrineae* remained common; Rome's streets were not as dark and overhung as they would be later; but the housing stock became steadily denser.

Aristocratic and elite housing also became taller, a process which began before 1100. The clearest material example of an early medieval aristocratic house complex in Rome is that excavated in the 1920s in the Area sacra di Largo Argentina, and reconstructed on the basis of photos and descriptions by Riccardo Santangeli; it seems to have been based on a tufa-built house of a Foro di Nerva type, but also contained a set of accessory buildings and a (probably ninth-century) church, all enclosed by a substantial external wall. Presumably this would have resembled one of our best early descriptions of an aristocratic house, the one sold to the emperor Louis II in 868 for the giant sum of 800 pounds of silver: *solarium abitationis mee*, a two-storeyed house where I live, *cum area*, with *curte, sala, capella . . . S. Blassi, balneo, viridario* [garden], all in a single block (*insimul se teniente*). In this and other early examples, into the early eleventh century, the emphasis was very much on the horizontal.[155] But from the 1060s, things begin to change in our documents. The

---

[153] Hubert, *Espace urbain*, pp. 142–7, 162–4, 174–6. For dating brick buildings, the essential starting point is now Montelli, *Tecniche costruttive murarie medievali*; an important predecessor is Barclay Lloyd, 'Masonry techniques', who worked only on churches. One well-dated example is the late eleventh- and twelfth-century 'palazzo' excavated as part of the Crypta Balbi excavations: Ricci and Vendittelli, *Museo nazionale romano—Crypta Balbi*, I, pp. 18–22. Pani and de Minicis, *Archeologia del medioevo a Roma*, discusses groups of tower-houses which seem to be from the twelfth and thirteenth centuries. For photos, see Krautheimer, *Rome*, pp. 279–308. For some new bricks and tiles, see below, n. 160.

[154] Hubert, *Espace urbain*, pp. 209–13. Stairs as entry: an example is *SMN*, n. 83 (a. 1161).

[155] See for the excavation Santangeli Valenzani, 'Tra la *Porticus Minucia* e il Calcarario' (he then hypothesized, pp. 82 ff., that it was a monastery) and now the more convincing secular proposal in Meneghini and Santangeli Valenzani, *Roma nell'altomedioevo*, pp. 41–4; *Liber instrumentorum monasterii Casauriensis*, ff. 74v–75r (a. 868). For the horizontal, Hubert, *Espace urbain*, pp. 181–4; Santangeli Valenzani, 'L'insediamento aristocratico a Roma'.

Figure 3.3. Twelfth- or thirteenth-century house on via S. Angelo in Pescheria.

first documented example of a medieval tower-house in Rome is from 1069, when Gerardo di Romano of the Maccii family, a member of Trastevere's 'medium elite' with one of the first real surnames in the city (see below, p. 267), renewed his lease of the *turricella solarata tegulicea* [i.e. with a tiled roof] *cum scala marmorea*, in which he lived. Clearly this tower was simply an extension upwards of a standard two-storeyed building. This is followed in 1073 by a reference to a *turris* of the Bracciuti, a more prominent Trastevere family, and in 1076 by a description of a *turris* of the Cerratani family, of the 'medium elite' of Campo Marzio, which was built above an ancient vaulted *cripta*. In the same period, the aristocrat Cencio di Stefano is said in narratives to have had a *turris mire magnitudinis*, 'of striking size', on the Ponte S. Pietro, which he used to take tribute from people crossing the bridge until it was destroyed in 1075, and another *turris* where he kept the kidnapped Pope Gregory VII at Christmas of the same year; this and others were soon destroyed as well.[156] The first documentary references to towers show that they were already status markers for Rome's 'medium elite' and upwards; Cencio's towers show that they could already be elements in a militarized local politics. This is even before the civil war period; thereafter, they became steadily more prominent, crucial elements in 'reform' papal struggles and in the family political projections of Frangipane, Pierleoni, Corsi, and many others, as we shall see in later chapters.

None of this is surprising in the least. This is exactly the period in which tower-houses appeared everywhere in Italy. In Pisa, the earliest legislative pronouncement in the name of the city, in *c.*1090, was about them: this, the so-called *lodo* of Bishop Daiberto, enacted that no tower in the city should be higher than those of Stefano di Balduino and Lamberto (or, south of the Arno, that of Guinizone di Gontolino), with two exceptions, whose inhabitants could henceforth no longer climb to the top. A number of eleventh-century Pisan tower-houses still survive, in fact. Rome was also entirely typical in its earliest documentary attestations of them; the earliest known for Lucca is from 1059, and for Milan from 1043.[157] It is certainly arguable that early towers in Rome were often decorative elements in aristocratic residences that remained for some time more spacious and, as with the Frangipane, more dispersed than in other cities; the competitiveness of the Casa dei Crescenzi (whatever its date: see below, p. 237) was more in its design than in its defensive function. This would soon change, all the same. The Frangipane towers could certainly also be defensive, as we have seen; and a twelfth-century inscription, evidently originally on such a tower, inserted into the later Tor dei Conti, adds

---

[156] Respectively, *SCD*, n. 70; *SMT*, n. 5; *SMCM*, n. 17; and, for Cencio, *LP*, I, p. 337 (a. 1062); Bonizone of Sutri, *Liber ad amicum*, VII (pp. 603, 605, 606); Paul of Bernried, *Vita Gregorii VII*, chs 45–57.

[157] Rossetti, 'Il lodo del vescovo Daiberto'; Garzella, *Pisa com'era*, pp. 62–3; Redi, *Pisa com'era*, pp. 200–4 and figs. 12–13, 85–93. Some surviving towers in (among other cities) Arezzo and Padua are also plausibly eleventh-century: Mini, 'Le torri urbani di Arezzo'; Chavarría, 'Case solarate', pp. 26–33. Lucca: *Regesto del capitolo di Lucca*, I, n. 277; Milan: *Gli atti privati milanesi*, II, n. 303. Settia, 'Lo sviluppo di un modello', sees the eleventh-century development of tower-houses as the result of a ninth- and (especially) tenth-century privatization of the towers on city walls.

a military challenge wholly absent on the Casa dei Crescenzi: 'This house (*domus*) belongs to Pietro... the vigorous, faithful and very strong knight (*miles*); look, citizens (*quirites*), ... how strong it is inside and how very solid outside, more than any of you can say.' By 1202–4, towers were explicitly erected in military competition with each other. And already by the mid-twelfth century they were extremely common; they are by now attested all over the city.[158] Classical buildings—themselves much larger and more solid military defences, as with the Settizonio, which Henry IV failed to take in 1084—sprouted towers too. The cityscape thus became militarized, in a way that it had not been earlier in the Middle Ages. And this militarization added to the sense of height that was beginning to appear everywhere. Surviving twelfth-century towers are often clearly part of street frontages, as in the case of the Casa dei Crescenzi, the side and front of which are decorated down to street level.[159] To this must be added not just large rebuilt churches, but their omnipresent twelfth-century campanili too.

Housing was thus a solid element in the city's economic structure by the mid-twelfth century. Indeed, the beginnings of newly fired brick date from the twelfth century too, even if it was no more than a decorative speciality until the fourteenth;[160] here, the developments in Rome's built environment led straight back to the articulated artisanal world already discussed, despite the fact that *muratores* are far from the most commonly mentioned artisans in our written documents. Ownership of urban land with houses on was also a crucial part of the resources of the city's major landowners, the churches. What they did with them was lease them out, to rich and poor alike. It is not easy to be sure how this worked financially, it has to be said. Except for mills and in the Civitas Leoniana, rents were low, a few *denarii* each; this was not enough for any landowner to profit from. One extra income was the *comminus*, the money taken by the proprietor when leased land was sold (see above, p. 82); this was higher, but only by one or two *solidi*. Thus S. Maria in Campo Marzio, a high percentage of whose landed wealth was tied up in the 154 houses it had around the monastery by 1194, did not get much out of the sale of a lease of one of its tower-houses in 1192: only 6 *denarii* in *comminus* (and 1 *denarius* annual rent) from a price of as much as £12—480 times the *comminus*.[161] The main economic advantage that churches got from their property was, as with rural property, the entry-fine payable at the beginning of

---

[158] For the Tor dei Conti and for the quote, see Delfino, 'L'epigrafe di Pietro dalla Torre dei Conti'. For 1202–4, *Gesta Innocentii III*, chs 135–41. For the overall development of tower-houses in Rome, Hubert, *Espace urbain*, pp. 184–200, is basic; see further di Carpegna Falconieri, 'Torri, complessi e consorterie' (which I do not follow in all its arguments); a neat survey is in Maire Vigueur, *L'autre Rome*, pp. 61–4. For numbers, see the somewhat schematic figures in Kattermaa-Ottela, *Le casetorri medievali*, p. 70; for some emblematic detailed studies without synthesis, Bianchi, *Case e torri*, I; Pani and de Minicis, *Archeologia del medioevo a Roma*.

[159] For the Settizonio, see *S. Gregorio*, n. 151 (already in 975 seen as a potential fortification) and *LP*, II, p. 290; cf. Augenti, *Il Palatino*, pp. 95–8.

[160] Montelli, *Tecniche costruttive murarie medievali*, pp. 63n, 109–23.

[161] *SMCM*, nn. 62 (houses in 1194; it also had two rural estates, five tenant holdings, and forty-four vineyards), 60 (a. 1192—the *comminus* percentage was higher a few decades earlier, in nn. 49 and 53, aa. 1154–66, but still only a thirtieth of the sale price). See Hubert, *Espace urbain*, pp. 313–17; the *comminus* became more of an economic resource after 1200.

the lease, which Étienne Hubert calculates as between a third and a half of the average price in house sales in the mid- to late twelfth century. S. Maria in Campo Marzio's average here between 1134 and 1171 was 25 *solidi*, in a period when house prices in Campo Marzio varied between 20 and 80 *solidi*, which fits Hubert's global figures. Paradoxically, as Hubert and Mauro Lenzi have both shown, the nineteen-year *libellus* leases for houses, which were commoner in the eleventh century, tended to become longer-term when the *libellus* was replaced by the *locatio* in the late eleventh, and by the mid-twelfth two- and three-generation, and even perpetual, leases were standard in the city. Enough new leases with entry-fines survive to show that churches could indeed continue to gain some resources here, presumably because families died out regularly enough; but even here the global scale was not huge.[162]

The most substantial set of surviving urban leases is that for S. Maria Nova in the Forum area, for which thirty-one twelfth-century leases for houses survive (for S. Maria in Campo Marzio, it is only five), only two for anything less than two generations. Rents were never over 6 *denarii*, and usually only one or two. They were collected regularly; S. Maria Nova, almost uniquely, recorded annual rents paid on the dorse of some of its charters, but this was doubtless as much to establish the church's legal rights as to gain real profit. In the forty years from 1123 to 1164, the average entry-fine was 18 *solidi* and the average *comminus* was 1½ *solidi*, in a period in which the average sale price for houses in the region was 72 *solidi*. This is lower than S. Maria in Campo Marzio's figures, indicating a more somnolent economic practice, but S. Maria Nova would recover its enterprise after 1175: for the last quarter of the century its entry-fines averaged 55 *solidi*, when average house prices were almost identical, 56 *solidi*. Once S. Maria Nova began to realize how to manage its property, it could gain as much from initial leasing as people did from selling leases, and still keep its ultimate property rights. This was another church whose resources were above all urban, so it needed to get this right, and eventually did so. Given the low profits that seem to have come with urban renting, careful management was essential.[163]

By the mid-twelfth century the urban land-market was active anyway. As Hubert has remarked, the same (ruined) house near S. Maria Nova was sold for £6 and 3 *solidi* in 1152 and resold in 1176 for £8, some 30 per cent profit, even though it was and remained in such a poor state that the original owner had been unable to rent it—and even though average house prices, as we have just seen, were not rising in these decades in the *regio*; we see entrepreneurship here. Times had changed from the situation in 1120, when Stefania di Giovanni sold a house in the same region for 18 *solidi* and used the money to buy a vineyard, 'since it is of more profit

---

[162] For entry fines, *SMCM*, nn. 35, 38, 46, 52, 55. Hubert's calculations: see *Espace urbain*, pp. 304–9. For *libellus* to *locatio*, Lenzi, *La terra e il potere*, pp. 119–36; Hubert, *Espace urbain*, pp. 298–317.

[163] *SMN, passim*. Shorter-term leases, for 19 years: nn. 51, 80. Annual rents are recorded on the dorse of nn. 35 (for different properties from that in the charter), 55, 58, 70, 119; see for another parallel ASR, SCD, cassetta 16, n. 140 (a. 1170), with the comment in Carbonetti Vendittelli, 'Scrivere e riscrivere', p. 46n, and pp. 42–7 for the basic analysis of the phenomenon.

(*meliorem lucro*) for me than such houses and *orti'*. In 1184, Carafiglia and her son Angelo could sell a house in Campo Marzio for 100 *solidi* and invest this in other land (*in re inmobili*—it was not necessarily urban) with two other people, 'at the latter's risk (*eorum periculo*)', which shows that they were looking to profit from the arrangement. The idea of investing money in this way—usually dowries—appears in other texts from the 1160s onwards too. The urban laity were evidently hard-headed about what they could get out of land, perhaps more so than the church was.[164]

We saw in Chapter 2 (pp. 182–3) how widespread the practice of pledging land for loans of money was. Our first documents for it are from around 1070, and they increase geometrically from here to 1200, the furthest I have taken them. Most such examples indeed come from the countryside around Rome, not the city, and, as was explored earlier, can best be seen in a continuum with leases for a large entry-fine, for the standard interest on the loan was the profit from the land; that goes for the smaller number of pledges for loans that survive for urban property as well.[165] But in a chapter on the city economy, it is worth noting that Rome had plenty of people who could put up the money for deals of this kind, as, for example, Romano Cerratanus, from the *regio* of S. Lorenzo in Lucina (see below, p. 270), who appears in four unrelated documents between 1158 and 1182 loaning money for pledges in land both north and south of the city for a total of over £40.[166] Many Romans, probably most of them, simply dealt with credit as part of their regular economic and also social dealings: with laymen, certainly, but also with churches, as we shall see in Chapter 5; many of the entourage of S. Ciriaco in Via Lata were its creditors, for example (below, pp. 284–6). Everyone, indeed, needed to loan or pledge land at some point in their lives. From the 1130s, it was standard for husbands to take over the money their wives brought in dowry, *dos*, and to pledge whatever land was needed to make up the value in the future, as a guarantee that at the husband's death the wife or her heirs could have it back; this sort of arrangement, a product of the revival of Roman law marriage agreements (below, p. 316), will have aided the generalization of credit deals as a standard practice in the city.[167] But the real underpinning of the considerable expansion of credit was the papal court. This takes us well beyond the scale of operation we have been looking at in the last few

---

[164] Hubert, *Espace urbain*, pp. 331–2, with *SMN*, nn. 66, 109—note that this house, unlike most houses sold, was held in full property, not on lease; n. 39 (a. 1120); *SPV*, n. 67 (a. 1184), with, for investment and risk, *SMCM*, n. 53; *SMVL*, n. 221; *SMN*, n. 133.

[165] See in general Toubert, *Les structures*, pp. 608–19. Pledges of urban land for loans begin in 1080 (*SMVL*, n. 106); three follow before 1150 (*SMVL*, n. 129; *SMCM*, n. 28; *SPV*, n. 35), with then a slowly rising curve in the following decades. Commercial letters of credit do not survive for Rome in the twelfth century.

[166] *S. Sil.*, nn. 23, 27; *SMCM*, n. 54; *SMVL*, n. 216; the local base of the family is clear from *SMCM*, n. 17, and *S. Sil.*, n. 20.

[167] *Dos* pledges start in 1133 with *SMVL*, n. 155 and *SMCM*, n. 32. Such pledging was seen as a standard Roman practice in Tuscolo in 1168 (ASV, A. A. Arm. I–XVIII, n. 3655), when Rainone of Tuscolo, in a document making the fiefs of his dependants hereditary, explicitly allowed them to be pledged as a result of marriage to Romans.

pages, but it was certainly part of the urban economy, so it needs to be dealt with here.

When in 1120 the Genoese leaders Caffaro and Berizone came to the papal court of Calixtus II, their aim was to give gold and silver to (we would say bribe) whomever they could in order to persuade the pope to rescind the right of the archbishops of Pisa to consecrate bishops in Corsica, which was against Genoese interests. They succeeded, although it cost them the equivalent of nearly £1800 in silver marks and gold *unciae* in gifts to the pope and his entourage and several lay aristocrats, as we shall see later (pp. 173, 401). What is important here is that Caffaro and his colleague evidently underestimated the giant cost of getting Roman ecclesiastical privileges (this one was probably particularly expensive, as the Genoese were overturning a right Pisa had had since 1077), so had not brought enough money with them. They had to borrow from *Romani* the equivalent of £384, *cum labore de quattuor cinque*, which must mean 'at an interest of five for four', 25 per cent, and even then they had not yet paid off everyone in full when Caffaro wrote his memorandum for Genoa which describes all this. Two of the Roman lenders are named, Guilielmo Cilloblanco and Gilio Romano; we cannot track them elsewhere. Doubtless they were recommended by the churchmen and aristocrats whom the Genoese had to pay off, but they could have come from anywhere in the city.[168]

After 1046, Rome's papal connections increasingly offered a considerable opportunity to rising commercial strata with spare silver. The cost of Roman ecclesiastical justice, or of favourable papal privileges, was very great, and not everyone had the immediate cash to pay up. In the decades of civil war and papal schism, windfalls like the Genoese delegation may have been relatively few, but when Innocent II returned to Rome in 1137–8 he brought with him a Curia increasingly used to hearing international canon law appeals on a large scale (below, pp. 402–3), and the opportunity to loan money to supplicants and litigants grew rapidly. It never went away from now onwards. By the early thirteenth century, Roman moneylenders can be tracked in papal registers, and also the account-rolls of countries like England, as Marco Vendittelli has shown. They were not normally from the highest urban aristocracy, but they were from prominent families for all that; they are called *viri nobiles* or *domini*, and once 'in urbe nobiles et potentes'. And by now they had fanned out through Europe to find their clients, where—in a phrase rare in Rome itself—they were simply known as *mercatores Romani*.[169] As for the highest urban aristocracy, they lent money to the popes themselves. The Corsi and Frangipane were already doing so in the 1140s and 1150s; and we have particularly clear evidence of it from the reign of Alexander III (1159–81), who

---

[168] *Codice diplomatico della Repubblica di Genova*, I, n. 31 (also ed. in *Annali genovesi di Caffaro*, I, pp. 20–1), cf. I, n. 32 for Calixtus' bull; for Pisa's rights, *Gregorii VII Registrum*, V.2, 4, VI.12. Honorius II restored Pisa's ecclesiastical control over Corsica in 1126, however, and, in 1133, Innocent II divided ecclesiastical rights over the island between Pisa and Genoa: *Regestum Pisanum*, n. 302; *Codice diplomatico della Repubblica di Genova*, I, n. 65.

[169] See Vendittelli, 'Mercanti romani' (p. 110 for the quote); Vendittelli, 'In partibus Anglie'; Vendittelli, 'Testimonianze sui rapporti'; and especially Vendittelli, *Mercanti del tempio*. Innocent III calls them *mercatores Romani* in 1204: *Reg. Inn. III*, VII.15.

usually had little access to his financial base in Rome and often needed money very badly indeed. Here, the Malabranca and Frangipane came to his rescue, and the scale of their loans could be very great. Malabranca, the founder of the former family, got the whole of Ariccia in pledge for £100 in 1171–2, which remained unpaid—Malabranca's sons as a result got Ariccia in fief in 1179 and the family kept it until 1223; even more remarkably, Malabranca and three other men got all the altar-gifts from the *confessio* of S. Pietro in return for a loan of £630, which Alexander at least partially repaid in 1175. The Frangipane, for their part, loaned £250 in return for three-quarters of the papal revenues from Benevento for three years, repaid in 1178.[170] These financial dealings are so large-scale (and also late in time) that they take us away from the arguments of this chapter; however, they serve to remind us that the credit dealings around the papal court could extend out from the medium elite of the city into its leading aristocratic strata.

Moneylending and international commerce went closely together, as the word *mercator* shows. Here, Romans were active early, as a series of isolated (and much-cited) documents makes evident. In 1076, Gregory VII wrote a letter of introduction to al-Nāṣir, ruler of *Mauretania Sitifensis* (he actually ruled most of modern northern Algeria from the Kalâa des Béni Hammad, south of Sétif), recommending the representatives of two of his *familiares*, Alberico and Cencio, who had grown up in the Laterano. Cencio was plausibly a Frangipane (this is the most likely of the possible identifications); Alberico was not a Pierleoni, as has often been claimed, but was at least from the rising 'new aristocracy' of the city, for he is almost certainly Alberico di Pietro di Leone Cece, who had been in the Tuscolano entourage in 1068, but who leased a mill outside the Porta S. Giovanni from Alexander II in 1072, and witnessed, with Cencio Frangipane and others, Countess Matilda's gift of her allods to the papacy in 1074/1081. Both men were clearly planning some sort of link with the North African coast which can hardly have been other than commercial. This indicates that the well-known extension of Pisan and Genoese maritime activity throughout most of the central Mediterranean in the eleventh century had a Roman element too.[171]

---

[170] Before Alexander III, see *LC*, I, nn. 166 (Innocent II pledging Civitavecchia to Pietro Latrone for £200), 93 (Eugenius III pledging half of Tuscolo to Oddone Frangipane for £30), 167–8 (Hadrian IV pledging much of Civita Castellana and other lands to the urban prefect Pietro 'III' and his family for 1030 marks). Alexander: Kehr, II, p. 358, and *Codex diplomaticus*, ed. Theiner, I, n. 31 for Ariccia (cf. Thumser, *Rom*, pp. 126–30 for the Malabranca); 'Documenti per la storia', nn. 8, 27 for the *confessio* and Benevento. Other loans to Alexander are in 'Documenti per la storia', nn. 9–11 and Volpini, nn. 7, 8; cf. 'Documenti per la storia', n. 25, for a pay-off to the Frangipane for war expenses, and Volpini, n. 4 (a. 1168), in which the Frangipane themselves take a loan of £100, apparently for the pope. See in general Schneider, 'Zur älteren päpstlichen Finanzgeschichte', pp. 1–14.

[171] *Gregorii VII Registrum*, III.21; see, above all, Ait, 'Per un profilo dell'aristocrazia romana'. Cencio could also, however, be Cencio di Francolino, or Cencio di Giovanni the urban prefect, or Cencio *primicerius*. For Alberico di Pietro di Leone Cece, see Gattola, *Historia*, I, pp. 233–4; Pflugk, II, n. 152; *Die Urkunden und Briefe der Markgräfin Mathilde*, n. 73, a text of 1102 repeating the 1074–1081 gift (registered as *Die Urkunden und Briefe der Markgräfin Mathilde*, Deperdita n. 37); for his family, see below, p. 238. Lopez, 'À propos d'une virgule', and Ait, 'Per un profilo dell'aristocrazia romana', p. 325, make the Pierleoni claim, but it was clearly refuted already by Fedele, 'Le famiglie di Anacleto', pp. 417–19 (followed by Brezzi, *Roma*, p. 260). Lopez sought to introduce a comma into the Matildine gift before 'Cece', making Alberico simply the son of Pietro di

Rome was playing two roles here, as twelfth-century sources show: as the southern analogue to Genoa and Pisa, and as the most northerly of the Lazial–Campanian trading cities. In the former role, the Roman Senate made trade treaties with Genoa in 1165–6 and Pisa in 1174, with the Roman *consules mercatorum et marinariorum Urbis* ratifying—in 1174, actually making—the agreements; the Romans in 1165 were guaranteeing the coast of Lazio from Corneto (Tarquinia) down to Terracina, and the treaties were in principle between equals. One of the 1165 *consules mercatorum*, Cencio *scriniarius*, became very close to the Genoese, and was given trading privileges in that city in 1179 as a *quasi Ianuensis civis*.[172] By 1191, Romans had penetrated north to the Champagne fairs, and can be found in the Rhineland by the 1200s, so were part of the international luxury trade network from the Mediterranean into the heart of northern Europe.[173] In the latter role, Genoa grouped Roman merchants with Gaetans, Neapolitans, Amalfitans, and Salernitans in a list of customs dues in 1128; and we have some more detailed evidence of Roman dealings with Gaeta. In 1124, the Roman Bello di Bobone made a formal agreement with the commune of Gaeta, after a dispute in which Calixtus II himself had weighed in on Bello's side, in which he paid the city £9 (of which £1 was returned as a sweetener) to get his ships back, together with a Gaetan agreement to restore his goods. In (probably) 1127, the aristocratic leadership of Rome (see below, p. 437) formally agreed that Montecassino's ships, including those from Gaeta, should travel freely, presumably in Roman waters. This latter agreement was matched by similar concessions to Montecassino by Tolomeo I and II of Tuscolo in 1105 and 1130, the first of which envisions that monastic ships and their *marcimonia* could travel between Gaeta and Sardinia. Simple geography ensures that Gaeta is Montecassino's most obvious port, but the Cassinesi had also been using the Roman ports since at least 1057–9, for Victor II and Nicholas II lifted port dues for monastic ships in two bulls from those years.[174] This network of texts show that the Rome–Gaeta route was a frequent one, and it therefore may not be chance that the Frangipane took care to get hold of rights in Monte Circeo and Terracina, key points along the sea routes, in 1143–5 (the latter of which the Pierleoni had also tried to get in 1124); they kept Terracina for a long time.[175]

Leone, but this is an unnecessary reading, given our knowledge of Alberico Cece. Pietro di Leone of the Pierleoni, who died between 1124 and 1130, was anyway too young to be the father of an adult in 1076.

[172] *Senato*, nn. 23–5 (slightly more fully in *Codice diplomatico della Repubblica di Genova*, II, nn. 8–10, 12–13; cf. 122, a. 1179, for Cencio); for Pisa, *Senato*, n. 29.

[173] See Vendittelli, 'Élite citadine', p. 189, with references.

[174] Respectively, *Codice diplomatico della Repubblica di Genova*, I, n. 51; *CDC*, nn. 302 (see Moscati, '"Una cum sexaginta senatoribus"'), 312; *Chronica Casinensis*, IV.25; Hoffmann, 'Petrus Diaconus', n. 4 (these two are separately ed. in Moscati, 'Due documenti'); *PL*, CXLIII, cols 831–4, 1305–9.

[175] *LC*, I, n. 172 for Circeo; cf. Falco, *Studi*, II, pp. 461–4. For the bad behaviour of the Frangipane in Terracina in the late twelfth century, see Contatore, *De historia Terracinensi libri quinque*, pp. 52–7. In 1185, the Frangipane planned to exchange Terracina and Circeo for half of Tuscolo, in a deal which seems never to have been ratified: 'Documenti per la storia', n. 30. Pierleoni in 1124: *Liber pontificalis*, ed. Přerovský, pp. 753–4.

These two roles point, however, in different directions. Romans were active from North Africa to England, as were the Pisans and Genoese, and were undoubtedly players at the highest international level, aided at every stage by papal support (Innocent III, for example, intervened in favour of Roman merchants in trouble in both Liège and England in 1204), but not dependent on it.[176] But it is also likely that the bulk of the maritime exchange Romans dealt with was, as was that of the Campanian ports, in the central Tyrrhenian Sea, in the triangle between Pisa, Salerno, and Sardinia. There is no sign that Roman merchants broke into Sicily on any scale in the wake of Norman conquest, as the Pisans and Genoese did; nor did they take any trading benefit from the Crusades—even though, had they wished or been able to, we can assume that they would have had papal support.[177] Ceramic imports from the Islamic world are not frequent in Rome before the late twelfth century (in Pisa they begin in the late tenth); even after that, such imports to Rome are more commonly from Campania.[178] Rome's size and artisanal vitality—and the fact that it was the only coastal city of any size between Pisa and Naples—ensured it was the commercial hub of the central Italian sea routes, and there is no doubt that its ports, both at the Tiber mouth and at the city's heart, were active and profitable. But the major context in which we can see its *mercatores* extend further than that was as facilitators for loans to Europeans dealing with the Curia and the international church. There were a lot of such loans, particularly in the century after our period ends, and people could get rich and powerful as a result. But it is likely that the large-scale international dimension, however profitable, was only a limited part of Rome's economy as a whole in our period: less not only than Pisa and Genoa but also, probably, than Naples.[179] It was profitable enough to attract Alberico Cece and Cencio Frangipane out of the eleventh-century 'new aristocracy', but in the twelfth Bello di Bobone and the Frangipane seem more interested in Gaeta. I would guess that the *consules mercatorum et marinariorum* were too. They evidently also looked north, as far as Genoa; but everyone in the Tyrrhenian Sea dealt with Genoa. Probably the major good that pulled them north on a stable basis was Pisa's—Elba's—iron.

This international exchange, like its international money-lending, was thus a spin-off of Rome's own internal economic vitality, not a cause of it. And this would mark the rest of the Middle Ages for Rome. Around 1400, Luciano Palermo's reconstruction of the maritime traffic of Ostia and the Ripa Romea on the basis of the Datini archive shows some imports from the whole of Europe, as one would expect for the period, but the main traffic was with the ports from Genoa to Gaeta, and especially Pisa.[180] This was Rome's low point for commercial activity, it has to

---

[176] *Reg. Inn. III*, VI.214 (215), VII.15, cf. IX.168 (169).

[177] Note the low volume of Roman commerce recorded in Genoese notarial registers in 1191, Abulafia, *The Two Italies*, p. 182 (and the few references to Rome elsewhere in the book: pp. 175, 188); cf. also Schaube, *Handelsgeschichte*, pp. 43–8.

[178] Contrast Molinari, 'Le ceramiche rivestite', pp. 358–73, and Molinari, 'Dalle invetriate altomedievali', with, for Pisa, Cantini, 'Ritmi e forme', pp. 115–16.

[179] See for Naples Feniello, *Napoli*, pp. 163–210; Carriero, 'Napoli', pp. 78–94, 125–33.

[180] Palermo, *Il porto di Roma*, pp. 108–37; see also p. 193, a little later, when Genoa was more important. Grain was by then imported above all from Pisa; there is only one sign of this in our period, see below, n. 181.

be said; it is not a guide to the intensity of exchange that we have seen in the twelfth, let alone the thirteenth, century. But it is significant that the main geographical range of that exchange was still that just tracked in twelfth-century material. This was the point Rome had reached by 1150, and, for the most part, it stayed there.

MACROECONOMIC PROBLEMS

The data we have for Rome's economic activity, indeed prosperity, in the period 900–1150 are pretty solid, as the previous section has aimed to demonstrate. But when we try to put them together, to create a picture of how the economy of the city worked as a whole, we come up with a series of questions, not all of which can be answered except hypothetically. We have, all the same, to try to do so, for, if we are to make any sense of the data presented in the previous section, at least a hypothetical model for Rome's macroeconomy is vital. It seems to me most useful to start simply by posing bald questions, and then to do my best to answer them. So here they are: How was the agricultural surplus that sustained Rome distributed, and to whom? How was the pilgrim quarter fed, and where did the profits go? What was the role of coined money in the city's economy? How coherent was the economy of the city, taken as a whole? Who were the city's artisans selling to, and how wide was their reach in geographical terms? What, more widely, was the real economic relationship between Rome and its wider hinterland? And, finally, why did Rome's economic prominence in the tenth century not continue in as accentuated a form into the twelfth? Let us have a shot at answering each of these in turn.

We have seen numerous signs that Rome in our period was recognized as a sufficiently strong market that investment in its supply was worthwhile. The huge interest by churches and their lay tenants, aristocratic and not, in the Albano vineyards, the Porto salt pans, suburban vineyards and *orti*, and the urban mills on the Tiber (above, pp. 92–103, 150–2) are clear signs of this, already in the tenth century. So is the evident involvement of most strata of the city's aristocracy in taking the grain of the Agro romano (above, pp. 85–6). Some of this will have been for private, non-commercial use, of course; but a substantial percentage must have been for the urban market in the most general sense. Specializations on this scale are rare before 1100 in most other cities that have been studied (above, pp. 107–8), over a century after they are first visible in Rome, so Rome's demand must have been unusually developed for the period. I say 'market in the most general sense', because this food could have been distributed directly among the thousand streams of small-scale retail outlets in the city, with the help of clientele networks and the city's numerous *negotiatores*. But it seems most likely that it was in large part centralized, including (but not only) in the Capitolio market, simply because this would have been easier and more convenient for most food importers. The Tiber mills, in particular, would have pulled grain for milling into the city centre, and milling grain into flour is normally only done shortly before it is turned into bread and sold.

I would therefore envisage that grain and wine came in through all the city's gates, and that salt came up to the river ports (paying tolls at both gates and ports); then some of it went straight to the household of its owner or his/her dependants, some to neighbourhood tradesmen, and much to the warehouses of the main dealers in foodstuffs for the city. One further alternative is likely: the other dealers who supplied the lodgings and food shops of the Civitas Leoniana, that is to say, for the pilgrim population. The *burgi* of the Porticus S. Petri had their own river port, and probably also separate systems of supply—perhaps from some of the sectors of the Agro romano west of the Tiber, whose road traffic could easily go to the Civitas Leoniana first. It is not essential to suppose an independent supply system for the pilgrim trade, but it is easier than postulating that the traders of the Porticus regularly went across to the Capitolio and other urban markets—not least because this would then have been a relationship that could easily have been disrupted for political purposes, and we never hear this from our narrative sources. Indeed, we do not yet hear of food-supply problems, except in the most generic way—famine caused by imperial armies rampaging around the city, for the most part—which indicates that the normal methods of moving food around inside the city in general were not, in this period, easily disrupted.[181] Rome did not need Constantinople's *Book of the Eparch*, which spends so much time discussing the rules for food retailing, or the scale of the *politica annonaria* of the thirteenth-century cities of the North; it was not big enough for that.[182] The Agro romano was not only profitable, but also generally sufficient for the city's needs in our period.

Thus far we have hypotheses, but not particularly speculative ones. The relationship between the profits from the Civitas Leoniana and the main city presents more problems. Pilgrims, above all, came with money. It would have taken a remarkably dogged (and lucky) pilgrim to make it across Europe and the Alps and down the via Francigena inside Italy just on charity, and anyway not all were poor, as with the aristocratic saints whose hagiographies retell pilgrimages to the city (Gerald of Aurillac, to name but one, supposedly went seven times).[183] They gave to the altars of the Vaticano and other churches; they bought food and, often, lodging; they bought souvenirs and other goods. This money, as we have seen (pp. 138–9), largely went to the Vaticano in ground rent and oblations, and also to the tradesmen of the Porticus and Platea S. Petri. The former was a crucial resource for popes; the latter was the basis for local commercial prosperity. Tradesmen who

---

[181] e.g. Benedetto of Monte Soratte, *Chronicon*, p. 181 (Otto I); *LP*, II, p. 341 (Henry V). The clearest early examples of non-imperial famines are that of 1138 (*LP*, II, p. 383), perhaps relieved by grain from Pisa (see *Senato*, n. 29, a. 1174, a reference to a toll on Pisan wheat in, apparently, 1145), and that of 1196 (*Epistolae pontificum Romanorum ineditae*, n. 421), in which Pope Celestine III hoped for supplies from Sicily. The first evidence of a *politica annonaria* seems not to be until the late 1260s: see Palermo, *Mercati del grano*, I, pp. 173–81, 197–206, for the years 1269–1340; and imports seem still to have been the exception rather than the rule.

[182] *To eparchikon biblion* for Constantinople; good recent studies of the *politica annonaria* of thirteenth-century cities are Grillo, *Milano*, pp. 535–9; Day, *Florence before Dante*; and for laws see Peyer, *Zur Getreidepolitik*. The latter shows that quite small northern cities had such laws; but they also had far smaller territories than Rome, so were more in competition with their neighbours.

[183] Odo of Cluny, *Vita sancti Geraldi*, II.17.

lived in the Civitas Leoniana did, however, have to pay for the food and artisanal goods they sold. This must have been how money got over the river and into the city proper: either through direct sales in the Capitolio and other markets, or via whichever merchants and artisans in Pigna or Trastevere or Ripa the Porticus tradesmen had particularly close dealings with; or, if the Civitas Leoniana was supplied separately with grain, by direct payments to Rome's aristocratic holders of grain-lands, who did not live in or near the Porticus. An alternative hypothesis would be that rich Porticus tradesmen transferred themselves to Rome proper and did their selling through middlemen, which could sometimes have happened, and which would thus have directly transferred profits east of the Tiber—as was also the case when Roman churches owned shops in the Civitas Leoniana, which we know occurred.

Here, we are building hypothesis on hypothesis, but some model of this kind seems to me necessary: for, if money spent in the Porticus S. Petri had largely stayed there, the local tradesmen would have become sufficiently rich to be powerful independent players in Roman city politics in our period, which there is no sign at all that they were (above, p. 140). Although the Civitas Leoniana had a largely separate economic system, it cannot have been totally independent of Rome, or there would undoubtedly have been even more violence, with attempts by Rome to take it over, than there was. (Rome was uncompromising in its desire to dominate Tivoli and Tuscolo, far less wealthy centres in all likelihood.) The profits of the Civitas Leoniana must, therefore, have been absorbed into a wider city economy, seamlessly: that is to say, without any need for an organized intervention that could also have been disrupted. Rome, in other words, must have participated in the supply of the pilgrim market west of the Tiber, and have profited systemically from the sales to it, much like Mestre today does from the tourist market of the central Rialto in Venice, although Mestre, like Rome, also has other outlets for its production.

Other sources of high demand were internal to the city: the households of the richest aristocrats and biggest churches, the court of Alberico near SS. Apostoli for a few decades, and of course, above all, the palace of the Laterano. The Laterano, at a city gate, probably also had partially independent supply lines; it had its own lands, and thus, like any aristocratic family but on a far greater scale, could have largely fed itself non-commercially.[184] In all these cases, artisanal needs would probably have been supplied by trusted craftsmen, in aristocratic or ecclesiastical clienteles, although even these were presumably mostly paid to order—we have no evidence in our extensive papal sources from the thirteenth century of craftsmen kept in the papal *familia* on any scale, whereas food providers certainly were.[185] After 1046, however, the internationalization of what would soon become the papal Curia meant that there were numerous incomers in and around the Laterano; this had

---

[184] The Basilica Laterana did not have a huge landed base in our period (Pflugk, III, n. 142; Lauer, 'Un inventaire inédit'), but the papacy as an institution plausibly owned much of the eastern sector of the Agro romano, outwards from the Porta S. Giovanni: Wickham, 'La struttura', pp. 217–18.

[185] Paravicini Bagliani, *La vita quotidiana*, pp. 99–116.

increased markedly by the time of Calixtus II at the latest, and would do so again when the international appeals court developed under Innocent II and onwards. These incomers were far richer than most pilgrims, and could well have lodged throughout the city, but they and their entourages spent much time in the geographically separate palace quarter, and it is likely that specialist providers fed and sold goods to them too. We have very few documents for the Laterano and its *suburbium*, so we cannot confirm this, but it would be likely enough that it was, by the twelfth century at the latest, in economic terms a smaller version of the Civitas Leoniana.[186] If so, the previous two paragraphs, on the organization of supply and the distribution of profit, would apply to the Laterano region too by 1100.

This aspect of the model puts a lot of stress on the transfer of money, or at least treasure—items of wealth that were valuable enough to be practically portable by pilgrims and visitors, that is to say—from one part of Rome to another. And indeed there is a good deal of written evidence that Romans could own and deal in an unusually large amount of money, which fits this assumption. This brings us to a structural problem, however, because this money is not at all visible in our major material evidence, that is to say archaeology; there is thus a problem of interpretation here which we need to confront head on. Here, I shall therefore depart from hypotheses for a few pages, though we shall be returning to them soon enough.

The written evidence for money in Rome is twofold: references to money in legal documents, and accounts of its use in narratives. The documentary history of money is indeed fairly clear. Rome had its own silver currency which dominates tenth-century transactions in coined money, and which continues to be invoked in a handful of eleventh-century examples up to 1042, although the last pope in whose name surviving coins were minted was Benedict VII, minting with Otto II, who both died in 983–4. After that, there was no Roman mint for two centuries, until the Senate began to strike coins in the 1180s; the first document to cite them probably dates from 1182 and certainly 1186, which fits the likely date of the first surviving senatorial coins we have.[187] Rome never, however, abandoned the use of silver; unlike in the Sabina and further inland, there are almost no references in urban charters to money equivalents, payments *in valente*.[188] There are plenty of references to apparently uncoined silver (in *librae* and *unciae*) up to the 1050s,

---

[186] See, for example, the account of Hariulf of Oudenburg's visit to the Curia in 1141, ed. in Müller, 'Der Bericht', p. 101: 'prima die visitavit ... basilicam beati Petri apostoli. Die secunda transiit in palacium Lateranense ...' Some pilgrims came here too (Pflugk, II, n. 300, a. 1128), and left oblations (Pflugk, III, n. 142, a. 1154; Augenti, *Il Palatino*, p. 188, a. 1177).

[187] See above all Toubert, *Les structures*, pp. 561–601, for all that follows. The last 'Roman' coins cited in documents are in *RS*, n. 100 (a. 1021, still *novos*) and *RF*, n. 762 (a. 1041). The earliest senatorial coins are cited in *S. Gregorio*, n. 93 (a. 1182; it is just possible that in this late cartulary *sen(ensis)* was misread for *sen(atus)*) and *SMVL*, n. 229 (a. 1186). Toubert, *Les structures*, p. 583n, cites two texts of 1177 and 1184 which refer to 'new' or 'subsequent' Provins *denarii*; it is not clear that we can be sure that these are really senatorial coins. Carocci, 'Pontificia o comunale?', p. 155, prefers a date of 1184–8 for the first surviving senatorial coins, on the basis of unpublished work which I have not seen; Day, 'Antiquity, Rome', p. 240n, narrows that down to 1186–7.

[188] Money equivalents are cited in *S. Paolo*, n. 2 (= Carbonetti Vendittelli, 'Vaccareccia', n. 1); *LC*, I, n. 102; and *SMVL*, n. 192. The first two are transactions for castles outside the Agro; the third is clearly exceptional.

sometimes more than to coins, but they stop abruptly after that as well, and from then on silver *denarii* are close to universal in our references to methods of payment.[189] Rome had always accepted non-local currencies (there are four tenth-century coin hoards in the city from Anglo-Saxon England, for example[190]), and in the two centuries it lived without a mint it relied on them. *Denarii* from Pavia dominate the documents until the late 1140s; the first reference to them is in 1041, and there are only a handful of citations to other currencies (almost all from Lucca; a couple from Milan) for the next century. In the 1150s, Lucchese *affortiati* became the commonest currency, but they too are replaced in our documents after 1160 or so by *denarii* from Provins in Champagne. The late twelfth century saw *Provenienses* dominate, with Pavese *denarii* increasingly restricted to more formalized penal clauses; it was Provins *denarii* that provided the model for the senatorial coinage.[191] But Lucca, Milan, Pisa, Genoa, Siena are all still documented as sources for coins; and it was common in leases from 1148 onwards for one currency to provide the entry-fine, another the rent—indeed, in a handful of documents there were three currencies, with a third providing the *comminus* (and often still with a penal clause in *unciae* of gold).[192] The senatorial coinage slowly made headway against this complex pattern, but the complexity continued for a long time.

Pecunia and analogous terms are also common in our narrative sources. Above all in the political strife of the century after 1046, the Roman aristocracy were regularly persuaded to back one side or another by gifts of money; sources both from the city and outside it are uniform in their references to it. Here are the citations in the *Annales Romani*, a heterogeneous group of short narratives but certainly urban in origin: in 1046 the exiled pope Benedict IX 'divided the Roman *populus*' with *praemium* and took back the papacy; in 1058 Benedict X gained the fidelity of 'the majority of the Roman *populus*' and the *comites* around the city, *data pecunia*; in 1059 Hildebrand sent *pecunya* to Rome to Leone di Benedetto Christiano, the ancestor of the Pierleoni, so that the 'Roman *populus* was divided' against Benedict X; in 1062 Hildebrand and Leone distributed *pecunia per urbem* 'all night long' to prevent the coronation of Cadalo of Parma as pope the next day; once Cadalo ran out of money (*pecunia deficiente*) his backers left him, so he had to return to Parma. The *Annales* break off shortly after this, but they restart with Paschal II, who used 1000 *unciae* of gold to get Clement III out of Rome in 1099, paid off the Tuscolani with another £100, and gave *pecunia* to Giovanni di Oddolina to get the latter to

---

[189] Silver is universal except in penal clauses, which are often in *unciae* of gold up to 1200 and beyond; penal clauses in Italy often use out-of-date currencies. The *marcae* of Caffaro's 1120 dealings (above, n. 168), and *LC*, I, nn. 167 and 178–83, were doubtless ingots: Spufford, *Money*, pp. 209–24; note also the *unciae* of gold in real transactions in *S. Prassede*, n. 32; *LC*, I, n. 166 (aa. 1164–93).

[190] See G. B. de Rossi's contribution to Lanciani, 'L'atrio di Vesta', pp. 487–97, summarized in Keary, 'A hoard', with, in particular, Metcalf, 'The Rome (Forum) hoard of 1883'; O'Donovan, 'The Vatican hoard'; and, for the other two hoards, one lost and one partially surviving, Blunt, 'Anglo-Saxon coins', pp. 159–63. All four date from *c*.900–*c*.950.

[191] First Pavese reference: *SCD*, n. 46. For all this, see Toubert, *Les structures*, pp. 577–83, with references. In the 1160–70s, two Lucchese or Provins *denarii* were worth one Pavese *denarius*: ASR, SCD, cassetta 16, nn. 145, 146 (eighth text on the roll); *SMN*, n. 99.

[192] Three currencies: e.g. *SMN*, n. 81; *SMVL*, n. 201; ASR, SCD, cassetta 16, n. 145.

withdraw support from Alberto bishop of the Sabina during the latter's attempt at the papacy in 1102; but he failed to give sufficient *munera*, gifts, to other Romans (we have this in a letter from Paschal himself), so another papal rival, Silvester IV (Maginulfo *archipresbiter* of S. Angelo in Pescheria), gained a good deal of support in 1105, and only failed because 'when Maginulfo's *pecunia* ran out, all that *coniuratio* left him', so, like Cadalo, he had to flee the city in 1105.[193]

All the accounts of papal politics in this period tell stories like these. A rhetorical trope as widely spread as this attests to assumptions about Roman political rules which were very deep-rooted indeed, and they were shared by the Romans themselves, who presumably did know how they themselves dealt. When the accounts are of opponents of the party their author favoured, they stress corruption, the buying of support, the avarice of the Romans; when they are of the activities of supporters, the *pecunia* is seen as honourable gifts, which serve to counter the nefarious acts of opponents. But there is no doubt that political support in Rome could be obtained with *pecunia*, and that it was regularly needed and used. This was not necessarily coined metal, and sometimes it definitely was not, as with the 700 pounds of silver and nine of gold which one near-contemporary source says Matilda of Canossa sent to Gregory VII to help him combat Clement III. Indeed, whenever gold is invoked, as it often is in these texts, it was certainly not coined money. All the same, when Geoffroy of Vendôme helped Urban II to buy entry to the Laterano palace in 1094, he says he paid 13,000 *solidi* to do so in gold, silver, money, mules, and horses, so coins were certainly involved in part.[194]

I have discussed these sources in more detail elsewhere, so it is not necessary to cite all the other examples of the use of *pecunia* here.[195] What a political practice based so heavily on transfers of gold and silver tells us about how Rome worked politically is an issue we will return to in Chapter 7 (below, pp. 417–19). But Romans, or at least powerful Romans, were certainly used to gifts of money or treasure in return for political support. And this was also the case in other well-documented contexts, as with Caffaro's gifts to Calixtus II, his officials, and several Roman aristocrats, already cited, which were in *marcae* (ingots) of silver, *unciae* of gold, and silver *denarii* of Pavia, the money here being a minority of his gifts; or Diego Gélmirez's huge *benedictiones* of gold and silver treasure to a succession of popes, but particularly Calixtus, to gain and stabilize archiepiscopal rights for the church of Compostela.[196] The culture of giving substantial gifts to the pope and his entourage in return for papal privileges or favourable judicial decisions started long before our period began and continued long after it ended, but it certainly added to

---

[193] *LP*, II, pp. 332, 334, 336–7, 345–6—and, for Paschal, with the addition of three other sources (two of them also Roman): *Liber pontificalis*, ed. Přerovský, pp. 708–9; Sigebert of Gembloux, *Chronica*, p. 369; *Udalrici codex*, n. 124 (Paschal's letter).

[194] Donizone, *Vita Matildis*, p. 385n (a contemporary gloss to Donizone's poem, the text of which has the alternative figure of 200 pounds of silver); Geoffroy of Vendôme, *Œuvres*, pp. 288–90.

[195] Wickham, 'The financing', with citations of other sources. Note that this sort of use of *pecunia* is not wholly unique to Rome; *Landulphi Iunioris Historia Mediolanensis*, chs 38–9, 58–9, uses similar imagery for Milan in the 1110s and 1130s.

[196] Caffaro: above, n. 168; *Historia Compostellana*, II.4, 10, 16, 20, etc.—see Fletcher, *Saint James's Catapult*, pp. 196–212.

the availability of gold and silver in the papal court.[197] So did all the more regular international incomings of the papacy, Peter's Pence from England (plausibly the source of the surviving Anglo-Saxon coin hoards in the city), similar tribute from the Norman kings of Sicily and from kings in Spain in the twelfth century, dues from half the monasteries of Europe, and of course the offerings of pilgrims.[198] We can add to this ground rents from much of both the city and the Agro romano, and tolls at the city gates and the Tiber ports and the active urban markets. There was so much money, coined or not, visibly coming into Rome that it is hardly surprising that lay political actors wanted a cut of it whenever they could. And here, too, they did so regularly as well as irregularly. At papal elections, and every Christmas and Easter, by the 1140s at the latest, a series of payments was made to all the orders of clergy, and also the urban prefect, the palatine judges, *scriniarii* and other officials, and, soon, the city's senators. Senators and *populus* took substantial 'customary gifts' in return for their swearing of fidelity to incoming popes. The makers of the decorative arches along the route from the Vaticano to the Laterano every Easter Monday all got money, and money was thrown into the crowd during the procession.[199] In short, as we shall see in more detail later (below, pp. 346–8), the entire ritual life of the city used money as one of its major elements, by the twelfth century and often well before.

So one could easily say that there was a great deal of money in Rome, above all coming from a long way from Lazio; and that, although most of it went to the papal court, it was also in part directly distributed from that court to a wide swathe of the city's population at different times—as well as reaching an equally wide but perhaps different swathe as a result of the provisioning of the Civitas Leoniana and Laterano with food and artisanal goods, as already mentioned. This further fits the fact that non-Roman *denarii* dominate our documents for two centuries; maybe with all these incomings they were not necessary.

We cannot, all the same, rely too uncritically on those documents. For a start, as Toubert has already noted, there is a problem with the dominance of Pavia, and then of Lucca and Provins, over references to *denarii*: these three coinages were by no means what pilgrims, or indeed well-heeled foreigners who came to the Laterano, necessarily brought with them. The hoard of S. Paolo fuori le Mura, buried in the 1050s, had Italian, French (the majority), German, Hungarian, and English money, presumably reflecting pilgrim oblations at that basilica. The substantial numbers of eleventh-century coins found under the *confessio* of S. Pietro included a similarly wide set, and Danish and Spanish money as well—here, very many of the *denarii* were halved or quartered, in a manner more typical of northern European money usage, evidently in order to create the sort of small currency that pilgrims would need for shopping, *denarii* being too large, for example, for market food

[197] See for the thirteenth century Paravicini Bagliani, *La vita quotidiana*, pp. 107–11, 117–33.

[198] See in general Jordan, 'Zur päpstlichen Finanzgeschichte'; Pfaff, 'Aufgaben und Probleme'; Whitton, 'Papal policy', pp. 294–308.

[199] *LC*, I, pp. 291–2, 299–300, II, pp. 123–5, 146–8; *Senato*, n. 8.

purchases.[200] This makes sense; it is what one would expect. But what did Romans in the 1050s do with coins that were not from Pavia? They could not re-mint them, as there was no mint (it would be stretching the bounds of speculation way too far to imagine that they sent them to Pavia to be re-minted, or got Pavese moneyers to come to Rome). They might have engaged in the sort of complex exchange operation that now requires a computer, so as to calculate the value of *denarii* from London and Venice, or half-*denarii* from Cologne, in Pavese money. Perhaps this is what *cambiatores* (documented from 1009 onwards) did, maybe at the Trivio Cambiatoris north of S. Maria Nova, which is documented from 1052.[201] But it is also equally possible that the *cambiatores* just melted the metal down and weighed it out, perhaps in Pavese-multiple weights: this would have been arguably more useful. This is pretty certainly what Caffaro's *marcae* were, which he valued at 13 Pavese *solidi* each.

The other reason for worry is more directly archaeological: coins are exceptionally rare on sites in Rome between around 800 and the late twelfth century. This is actually true for most of Italy; it is only from then onwards that the silver mines of Tuscany and Sardinia and the Bergamasco produced metal on a large enough scale to allow for a really widely-available coinage. The Crypta Balbi excavations, the best-published, produced precisely four coins between 1000 and 1180: from Normandy and Pavia. Only after that were Lucchese *denarii* (by now debased, so a little more useful for minor purchases, and more easily lost) and senatorial *denarii* found in slightly greater numbers.[202] The issue of value is relevant: most coins in our period were too valuable not to be looked for if they were lost. So their absence from sites does not in any way show that coins were not in circulation. But if pilgrim-brought half- and quarter-*denarii* had been at all widely used, they might indeed have been dropped and lost, and these have not been found in excavations. There have never been any excavations in the former Porticus S. Petri, where we might expect to find the sort of fractional money discovered under the *confessio* of the basilica of S. Pietro; but money like that does not seem to have got across the bridge and onto any published urban site.

Rather than throw up one's hands and lament the inability of historians (or archaeologists) to find the right things, it seems to me more useful to return to hypothesis. I would propose that pilgrim coins were indeed melted down into ingots, before the Senate's mint began at least; and that these ingots, like the gold and silver brought in all kinds of forms by outsiders seeking to influence papal politics or papal justice, functioned as uncoined money in the Roman economic

---

[200] Toubert, *Les structures*, p. 578n. For the hoards, di S. Quintino, 'Monete del X e dell'XI secolo'; Apollonj Ghetti et al., *Esplorazioni*, I, pp. 225–44 (C. Serafini). I am very grateful in the latter case to Ermanno Arslan, who is studying the S. Pietro materials, for details on fractioned coins.

[201] Cambiatores: *RS*, nn. 53, 100; *SMVL*, nn. 66, 76; *SPV*, nn. 27, 57; *SMN*, n. 53; *LC*, I, n. 182. Trivio/contrada cambiatoris: see above, n. 41.

[202] Rovelli, 'Monete, tessere e gettoni', pp. 169–72, 185–9; Rovelli, 'La Crypta Balbi. I reperti numismatici', p. 66 (which lists two coins not mentioned in the preceding, one from an illegible Italian mint). More widely on Rome in our period, Rovelli, 'Monetary circulation', pp. 95–9; Rovelli, 'Emissione e uso della moneta', pp. 842–52; Rovelli, 'Nuove zecche'. I am very grateful to Alessia Rovelli for stimulating discussions on this issue.

system, or at least as part of that money. We do have some references to coins in our documents which are so specific that they show that Romans had at least seen and dealt with them: the *grossi* of Pavia, cited between 1063 and 1092, for example, or the Provins coins *de manganello*, current in the 1170s, and worth more than the *posteriores* by 1184.[203] But the way silver moved around Rome, and above all the way it moved inwards from the Vaticano and Laterano areas to the city centre, seems to me best explained in terms of silver weight, not coins. Before 1050, there are enough documentary references to weighed silver to make this less controversial, but I think the logic of the material evidence points to it in later periods too. We still have a means by which wealth could be distributed through the city, then, and it is certainly one that would not easily be picked up by archaeologists, for ingots would be almost never lost by accident. It would have been inconvenient for small transactions, but so were *denarii*: whole houses were sold for only a few hundred *denarii*, after all. Any society without small change uses credit for small transactions, and it seems inevitable to propose that Rome did too.

How coherent was Rome's economy, then? It would be hard to doubt that it would have run more smoothly if Rome had maintained its mint, which nothing prevented it from doing. But that apart, the city seems to have been effectively integrated as an economic unit. The provisioning of the city was decentralized enough not to be controllable for political purposes, unless an army occupied the Agro romano, but it does equally seem to have had elements of scale, deriving from the control of the lay elite over the grain-lands of the Agro, the systematic exploitation of specialist crops, and, inside the city, the centralization of the mills and probably the Capitolio market. The even availability of good-quality ceramics across the city argues in the same direction. Rome was full of artisans of all kinds who operated on a tiny scale, but we have seen that the ceramic patterns are arguably a guide to mass-production in other sectors too, even though from small workshops, once they were taken together—and linked by *scolae*. And I have also argued for a systemic link between the commercial demand of the pilgrim quarter (and doubtless the Laterano) and the food supply and artisanal production of the city's core. It is for all these reasons that the city held together economically, and was wealthy. It produced things people wanted to buy, it had buyers with sufficient resources to acquire them, it had a large hinterland with an impressively focused system of extracting agrarian surplus to the profit of citizens, and it operated on a large scale, in 900, 1000, 1100 (despite war and civil discord), and 1150 alike.

If the city produced objects en masse, how far away did it sell them? This is the hardest question of all to offer an answer to, for we are seriously short of evidence. The ceramic material is here contradictory. At the top end of the market, glazed pottery, Forum Ware made in Rome reached out into the Lazio countryside in the ninth and tenth centuries, and also, more as a luxury item, all along the coast of the Tyrrhenian Sea; but urban-made Sparse Glaze Ware, from the eleventh and twelfth

---

[203] *Grossi*: SMN, nn. 20, 21, 169 (which is misdated in the edition; it must be late eleventh century); *SPV*, n. 24; *SMVL*, n. 95; *SCD*, n. 92. *De Manganello*: SMN, nn. 99, 110; *S. Sil.*, n. 32; ASR, SCD, cassetta 16 bis, nn. 153 (a. 1184), 168.

centuries, although it was more evidently mass-produced, is found much more rarely. It is found sometimes in the Tuscan countryside; but if we go up the coast to the next large port, Pisa, we find that Lazial glazed imports failed to hold their place after around 1050, against the large range of prestigious alternatives by now available, particularly polychrome glazes from the Islamic world; this is perhaps comprehensible.[204] But why did Sparse Glaze Ware not have a greater impact on Lazio itself? The new local productions that replaced Roman-produced ceramics in the rural sites that have been excavated do imitate Roman wares, so some must have been available. But it does appear likely, although it is paradoxical, that the main market for Sparse Glaze Ware was the city itself—and also, very plausibly, the Agro romano immediately around the city, which had few centres that were likely to have generated serious competitors for Roman products. One centre that might have done, Albano, shows, in one of the very few excavations made in the countryside close to the city, Sparse Glaze of plausibly Roman production. There are signs that Roman glazes were available more widely than this, alongside local productions, presumably as prestige items; as we have seen already, a Tarquinia excavation provides one likely example.[205] I would expect more instances of this to appear in the future. But a dominance by urban productions, at least in ceramics, is unlikely to have extended much beyond the Agro romano after 1000 or so. That was not a small area, as we have amply seen, but it was limited. One could tentatively propose that this might have been equally the case for Rome's other major bulk productions, ironwork, woollen cloth, or leatherwork.

The highly uneven distribution and small scale of rural excavations in Lazio in our period makes this conclusion very uncertain. But we can equally ask who, exactly, we would expect to be buyers of Roman goods. Rome's extraordinary economic dominance over the Agro romano had a downside: it meant that there were not only few competitors to city production, but also few people with the means to buy products on any scale. As for the rest of Lazio, Toubert showed a generation ago that, east of the Tiber, although the society of the castles was active, urban development was very weak, so few centres would have been able to generate more than a small handful of elite buyers. The major exception, Tivoli, where no useful excavations have taken place, could well have developed an exchange relationship with Rome, despite the well-known antagonism between the two centres: let us say, hypothetically, with Tivoli buying Roman artisanal goods in exchange for silvo-pastoral primary products, which the larger city was short of.[206] We might suppose something similar for Viterbo and Corneto (Tarquinia), the two main urban centres in Lazio west of the river. But the overall weakness of urbanism in Lazio meant that Rome, while it had no serious political competitors, which was

---

[204] Cantini, 'Ritmi e forme', pp. 117, cf. 118–19 (and pers. comm.); see also Baldassarri et al., 'Analisi archeologiche ed archeometriche'.

[205] See above, n. 125.

[206] Toubert, *Les structures*, pp. 657–79. Note that documented exchange between Tivoli and Rome in the fifteenth century involved Rome exporting cheese above all, in return for paper, honey, and pomegranate juice (Carocci, *Tivoli*, pp. 318–22). I cite this, however, essentially to show that later medieval evidence is here of no help at all for understanding our period.

an advantage, also had no one to deal with economically, as potential rivals but also as markets. Rome's products thus would only extend as far as there were rural buyers who valued quality, or understood the status conveyed by urban products, more than they appreciated the convenience and cheapness of locally made goods. In the eleventh and twelfth centuries, this was probably not very far. The city's dynamism thus slowly, as it extended outwards, ran into the sands of the rather more traditional rural economies surrounding it. The major market for its goods was therefore, in all probability, Rome itself.

This did not matter in the early Middle Ages, up to 1000 say. Rome was the largest city in Italy, and the major market for its goods was clearly itself. In an age when aristocratic buyers were the essential motor of all economic complexity, the quantity of them in Rome—headed by the pope, probably the second richest person in Italy after the king in Pavia—was enough to create an active Roman economy. Forum Ware was for two centuries the only decent fine ware made in Italy, and it is not surprising that it was bought (and imitated) in a wide range of centres, but that range is only a sign of Rome's economic importance, not a cause of it. To put it crudely, agrarian wealth came into the city on a large scale; it fed a wide range of artisans and aristocrats; the artisans made products for themselves and the aristocrats; everything else was secondary.

Two centuries later, in 1200 say, high-end urban prosperity was structured differently. Let us here take Milan as an example, for it was the biggest urban economy in Italy, is well documented and well studied, and is a better comparator than port cities like Pisa and Genoa (still less Venice, which had no hinterland). Milan was a major cloth and metal producer; it specialized in low-cost woollen and fustian (cotton and linen) cloth, and arms and other iron goods. Not all the production focused on the city, however; basic iron-making centred on the Brianza, where the iron was extracted, fulling and bleaching was above all rural, and there were numerous subsidiary *burgi*, growing fast in the late twelfth century, such as Monza, which made cloth as well. Monza was inside 25 km from the city; other *burgi*, Meda, Busto Arsizio, Abbiategrasso, were at the 25–30 km mark, with Varese and Cantù a little further away. Milan was thus at the head of an urban hierarchy in its immediate political hinterland. It was also at the head of a set of larger rival cities, Como, Bergamo, Lodi, Cremona, Piacenza, and Pavia, all closer to Milan than Corneto is to Rome, which alternately fought Milan, competed with it (Cremona with linen, Piacenza with fustian, Bergamo with steel), and bought its products. It was this double network that produced the density of production and exchange that allowed Milan to become so large, perhaps 100,000 people in 1200 if it reached 150–200,000 a century later, and eventually to import raw wool from England and cotton from Sicily, and to export finished cloth and arms to northern Europe and the Mediterranean.[207] Milan had been the major city of the inland Po plain for centuries, and its *negotiatores* are already well documented in the tenth century; it is not surprising that it ended up at the top of this urban hierarchy. But

---

[207] See for all the above Grillo, *Milano*, pp. 209–34, with the wider bibliography in n. 208.

this was not at the expense of (most of) its rivals; Cremona remained large, and Piacenza and Pavia at least medium-sized; they benefited from the density of this production and exchange too.[208] So also, a century later, would Italy's thirteenth-century boom town, Florence, which developed out of much less than Milan and was equally set against rivals, Prato, Lucca, Pisa, Siena, Arezzo, but became nearly as big as the great Lombard city.[209]

Put like this, it is fairly clear what Rome did not have: a trading hinterland, and a set of rivals who would stimulate exchange and competition. Part of this was just the chance of geography; active neighbours simply were not there, and had never been there; significant competitors/rivals like Pisa and Naples were too far away. But part was the reflex of the very reasons why Rome had been so impressive in the tenth century. Milan in the eleventh–twelfth century (or Florence in the thirteenth) did not own its *contado*. In order to get enough food for the city, it had to buy grain, wine, and animals. (Eventually, such megalopoleis had to buy grain from well beyond their *contadi*, but that only adds complexity to the model; it does not alter it.) This meant that the transfer of wealth was not only one-way; it got back to the *contado* too. Hence the ability of towns like Cantù and Monza to expand and gain their own artisanal communities; hence also the ability of rural communities to buy urban products, and thus to expand the productive levels of the city. Rome, however, taken as a whole, did own nearly all its *contado*, right out to the 25-km mark; it did not need to buy its food (nearly all such buying went on between people living inside the city's walls), and therefore urban wealth did not need to go out to the countryside at all, except—very early—to develop specialist agricultural areas, Albano for wine or Porto for salt, again to the benefit of the city. This made the city very much richer and larger in the tenth century; but, although this situation did not change in our period, it made the sort of exchange that allowed Milan to expand so fast in the following period very difficult, if not impossible. Rome extracted too much out of its hinterland for the levels of exchange characteristic of the twelfth- and thirteenth-century Po plain to be practicable.

Rome is often regarded as parasitical on its *contado*, and on pilgrim-cum-papal demand. This is to misunderstand how urban economies worked in our period.[210] All cities extracted wealth (and people) from their immediate hinterland; all cities responded to the aristocratic (including ecclesiastical) demand within their walls. But Rome's very success in taking rural wealth meant that its demand-base *remained* inside its walls. The city still expanded, in size, in population, in artisanal activity. Its urban buildings were by 1200 not only more numerous, but much

---

[208] The best recent synthetic overview of this is Menant, *L'Italie des communes*, pp. 267–77; see further Franceschi and Taddei, *Le città italiane*, pp. 48–52, 71–87; the rapid but stimulating survey in Jones, *The Italian City-State*, pp. 189–92; Fennell Mazzaoui, *The Italian Cotton Industry*, pp. 31–2, 62–70; Epstein, *Freedom and Growth*, pp. 115–27 (for a later period); and, for Piacenza, Racine, *Plaisance*, pp. 293–357, 705–13. For Milan before 1000, see above all Violante, *La società milanese*, pp. 45–9.

[209] For Florence's urban expansion, see Day, 'The population of Florence'.

[210] Moscati, *Alle origini*, pp. 47–9, makes similar points to me against this argument, but comes from a different direction.

better built, and the same is true of the new rural estate-centres of the *casali*; in the thirteenth century, new fine-ware ceramic types would develop in the city too.[211] But it could not change the macro-structure of its exchange, for there were no new markets to be had. As a result, what looked grandiose in 950 looked mediocre in 1150, even after that expansion, at least to the eyes of Lombards, and soon to Tuscans as well. It was not mediocre by European standards (here it is Milan that was the exception, not Rome), but in the specific framework of the Italian economy its position had slipped. It remained a hyperactive early medieval city; and that was no longer enough.

Other cities would come to match Rome, in the thirteenth century and onwards, it should be added. They developed fiscal systems to tax the *contado* and thus to skim off rural wealth that was not already appropriated by urban landowners; urban owners in the fourteenth century and later bought up rural land too. In so doing, they too depressed the countryside, and thus rural demand for their own products.[212] That is to say, the generalized nature of all these developments—essentially, all autonomous cities exploited the countryside which was politically subject to them, with all the means at their disposal, as soon as they worked out how to do it—also means that the hyperdevelopment of a Milan or a Florence was unlikely to last; the temptation to drain away subject rural resources was too great. Rome reached the limits of its economic complexity very early; but, in doing so, it was once again a precursor.

This was for the future. In our period, Rome was doing pretty well. It was politically and economically dominant in its landscape; it was full of artisanal activity; its urban economy was generating wealth. The last section of this chapter has been devoted to showing how all the documented elements of this economy, urban building and leasing, artisanal and commercial activity, fitted together, to generate that wealth. They were not disrupted by the crisis of the late eleventh century, severe though it was, any more than the destruction of Milan in 1162 damaged that city's long-term development. That wealth was, then, the basis for the steady generation of new elite strata, a phenomenon which marks the two centuries and more after 1000, and which would change, and change again, the socio-political face of the city. Rome was in that respect not unusual at all; all cities saw the constant renewal of urban elites. But Rome's leaders were both rich and numerous, and we can say a fair amount about them, an unusual amount for Italy before 1150. These elites, and their clients stretching way down into the population, will be the theme of the next two chapters.

---

[211] See Esposito, *Architettura*, for the *casali*; Molinari, 'Le ceramiche rivestite', pp. 389–461, and Molinari, 'Dalle invetriate altomedievali', for the ceramics.

[212] Taxation: see e.g. Pini, *Città, comuni*, pp. 88–108; for the problem of cities misusing political control, see e.g. Jones, 'Economia e società nell'Italia medievale', pp. 328–72; Epstein, 'Cities, regions'.

4

Urban Aristocracies

In July 1118, Cardinal Pandolfo recounts in his papal biography, Pope Gelasius II went to the titular church of S. Prassede on the Esquilino to celebrate mass on St Praxedis' day, at the invitation of the cardinal priest of the *titulus*, Desiderio. This was not a peaceful period, for there was a rival pope in S. Pietro, Gregory VIII, backed by the emperor Henry V, and Gelasius also had aristocratic opposition from Leone and Cencio Frangipane, who had kidnapped him briefly at his election the previous January. Since S. Prassede was *in fortes Fraiapanum*, that is, in one of the Frangipane sectors of the city, Gelasius' allies were worried, and he was accompanied by Stefano Normanno, the pope's nephew Crescenzio, and their followers. This was wise, for the *milites* and *pedites* of the Frangipane attacked the church during mass. The pope fled as the fighting continued (he was later found outside the city, in tears), and, seeing that he was safe, Stefano called out to Leone and Cencio Frangipane: 'What are you doing? Where are you running? The pope whom you seek has already left, he has now fled. Now do you want to destroy us? For we are Romans like you, your relatives, if we can say so. I ask you, leave, so that we, exhausted, can leave too.' So the Frangipane, who were indeed his nephews, called the fight off, and everyone went home. The next day, Gelasius decided to flee the city permanently.[1]

This was one of the low points for papal authority in Rome, although we cannot say whether the event was really as degrading as Pandolfo depicts it: his whole narrative is highly crafted, and, as noted earlier, his hostility to the Frangipane structures most of his papal lives. Stefano Normanno's speech obviously cannot be regarded as reportage. But the imagery of 'Romans like you' (*Romani similes vobis*) and 'relatives' (*consanguinei*) is important all the same, as a rhetorical framing which Pandolfo could judge to be effective; so is the idea that even the Frangipane could back off once appealed to like that. A common Romanness marked the sensibility of the city's ruling elites, and was recognized at every stage, for all the interminable wheeling of the carousel of alliances, particularly in the century after 1050. Rome was divided, both socially (as we shall see in this chapter) and politically (as we shall see in Chapter 7), but never to the point of disintegration. This must be remembered throughout the rest of this book. This chapter, on Rome's leading aristocratic strata, together with the next, on the society of Rome's *regiones*, are in many respects the central chapters of the book, for in them I aim to set out the changing

---

[1] *Liber Pontificalis*, ed. Přerovský, pp. 739–40.

patterns of the social stratification of the city. Without a proper understanding of these, we cannot correctly interpret Rome's political developments, which we will come to in more detail later.

In this chapter and the next, various social strata will be analysed, which are identifiable to historians, but which do not have standard names in the literature. They were all members of a very wide urban elite, which became as a whole increasingly militarized and active as political protagonists, in the last half of our period. (For that militarization and its significance, see below, pp. 262–6.) This elite was not by any means homogeneous, however; and indeed several strata in it can be fairly easily identified. Here I will describe three wide strata, and each of them had identifiable subgroups, of greater and lesser wealth and influence, as well; it is of crucial importance for the whole of the rest of this book that we identify that stratification as clearly as possible. I shall call the three main strata discussed here the 'old aristocracy', the 'new aristocracy', and—the focus of Chapter 5—the 'medium elite', maintaining the inverted commas throughout the book to mark the fact that these are my divisions, not those explicitly made by our sources.

By the 'old aristocracy' I mean the ruling families of the eighth to early eleventh centuries; these were the families who traditionally provided the palatine judges or the prefect of the city or the priests of the major churches, who made up the immediate entourage of Alberico and the late tenth-century popes, and whose economic base seems to have been above all emphyteutic leases of church lands. This was not a closed elite, but it was certainly identifiable: notably by titles, in particular the generic title *consul et dux*, which marked no office in Rome in our period, but very common in the ninth and tenth centuries (it dropped slowly out of use from the 970s). This was the group that was called the *primates Romae* or *optimates* by Liutprando of Cremona in his eyewitness account of Otto I's takeover of Rome, culminating in Pope John XII's deposition at the synod of 963.[2] They dominate our evidence up to the early eleventh century, but slowly slip out of sight from then onwards.

As I have already implied, the 'old aristocracy' did absorb new families into it, whether from talented bureaucrats (both ecclesiastical and lay), from rising elements in the city, or from elsewhere in Lazio. But the newer families of the eleventh century are distinct, for they had a different relationship to political power. Only one can be tracked to before 1000, the Frangipane, whose ancestor Pietro Imperiola was at the 963 Rome synod too, but significantly called *ex plebe* and *de militia*, the only member of the *plebs* to be named. Others first appear as smaller-scale lessees of the land of Rome's churches in the early eleventh century, and/or as commercial figures, such as Leone di Benedetto Cristiano, ancestor of the Pierleoni. The 'new aristocratic' families emerge as political players from the 1010s, and above all after the 1040s, but they are not given titles such as *consul et dux* (*dominus* is common, but it extended as an honorific well beyond the 'new aristocracy'), and seldom held offices. They were more visibly attached to Rome's *regiones* than the 'old

---

[2] Liutprando of Cremona, *Historia Ottonis*, chs 8–9.

aristocracy' had been, and by the later eleventh century were building tower-houses in their power-bases inside the walls, but their political frame was the city as a whole. By 1100, when sources refer to *nobiles* or *proceres*, it is this 'new aristocracy' they mean; surviving members of the 'old aristocracy' by now were generally called *comites*, and were largely rural-dwelling. By 1050, too, this newer group was beginning to acquire surnames; as well as the Frangipane, the Corsi, the Normanni, and the Sant' Eustachio stand out, although not all leading families were surnamed, and, apart from the Frangipane, such names were not used consistently until past 1150.

The 'new aristocracy' are clearly distinguishable from the 'old aristocracy', but the boundary with the 'medium elite' was based on less formal criteria, and is not always easy to pin down in our sources. Indeed, the 'new aristocracy' seem, even more than their predecessors, systematically to have accepted newer members, from the richer and more solidly based of the next stratum of the elites of the city; by the 1140s, for example, as we shall see later in the chapter, the Boboni and Papareschi had joined the eleventh-century families, and, conversely, some eleventh-century leaders were beginning to drop out of the topmost urban stratum. This was an ever self-renewing elite, then; only after 1200 did the families who were by then dominant take the next step, in the great land-grab which marked the reaffirmation of papal power in Lazio and beyond, and become the *baroni* of the late Middle Ages, a clearly marked and super-rich aristocratic stratum.[3] The 'new aristocracy' of our period might therefore simply be seen as the leading edge of a large elite community in the city, whose internal similarities—in particular a diffuse militarized culture and practice: the 'new aristocracy' and the 'medium elite' are often grouped together as *equites*, for example—were greater than their differences.[4] That hypothesis, however, does not seem to me to work: the two strata became more distinct than that. By 1100, between ten and twenty leading 'new' families were clearly separated from the others; many of them are called *nobiles* in the sources, and they were often name-checked as a group, or singled out as political players in each political dispute inside the city.[5] There was also a clear contrast in political direction between these two strata, for the 'new aristocracy' were political players on a city canvas and associates of popes, whereas the 'medium elite' were much more attached to the churches of the *regiones* of the city. This for me justifies the distinction I am drawing inside the urban leadership of the late eleventh and twelfth centuries; it will be developed further in this chapter and at the start of the next. *Nobilis* is also the pan-European term that best translates as 'aristocrat(ic)' in modern terminology, and this is the reason why I use the term here too.

---

[3] Carocci, *Baroni*, pp. 17–66.   [4] For *equites*, see below, pp. 262–3.
[5] See for example *PL*, CLXXIX, col. 707, n. 18, a letter of the Romans to Lothar III in 1130, from 'viri illustres, . . . nobiles omnes, et plebs omnis Romana, capitanei et comites qui extra sunt'; or the mass meeting in support of Gelasius II in 1118, listing ten aristocrats or aristocratic families, each *cum suis*, and then the rest of the city: *Liber Pontificalis*, ed. Přerovský, p. 734. For other examples, see below, n. 160. For *nobiles*, see below, p. 26. Maire Vigueur, *L'autre Rome*, pp. 188–95, draws the same distinction between a 'nouvelle aristocratie' and the rest that I do, although he sees it as made up of fewer families.

We do need to pause a little on the terminology I am using here, all the same. The word 'aristocracy' has cultural baggage in any language; so does 'elite'. It is instructive that the recent eight-volume collection 'Les élites dans le haut Moyen Âge' does not attach itself to any conclusive definition, even in the final volume, which has a section dedicated to 'vocabulaire et concepts'; it problematizes definitions, rather than imposing them; at most it offers very wide characterizations of the word 'elite', such as Régine Le Jan's 'a minority which directs, and which concentrates wealth and prestige'. Such an openness is part of the attraction of that set of books, indeed, which give us a detailed understanding of how elites operated—transacted—in the changing world of the early Middle Ages, especially, but not only, in Francia. But it does not help us much if we try to counterpose, as I have just done here, two types of 'aristocracy' against other levels of 'elite'. I myself have attempted elsewhere to get around the problem of definition by proposing nine elements that might characterize an ideal-type aristocrat: ancestry, wealth, title and/or office, *Königsnähe* (personal closeness to the ruler—the Roman situation, in the absence of kings, requires different neologisms), legal or group definition (as with *nobilis* in twelfth-century Rome), peer recognition, prestige among the less powerful, display, and training or expertise (literary, military, or legal/administrative, as it might be).[6] The point of an ideal type is that it sidesteps definition; any given society will privilege a subset of these elements as characteristics of its aristocratic stratum or strata, and any given aspirant aristocrat will get some of them first before seeking others to stabilize his (very seldom her) position. This is useful when one is comparing aristocracies across a range of societies. But it, too, is more problematic when one comes to seeking differences between aristocratic (or elite) strata in a single society, which is the issue here. Historians do not tend to think that the 'old aristocracy' in Rome had many problems of self-definition; it was, in particular, highly engaged with offices and titles, as we shall shortly see. The 'new aristocracy' requires more care, because if one does not have clear criteria for what made someone 'aristocratic' in the century and more after 1050, one risks generating circular arguments; but one of the very points about the boundary between 'new aristocracy' and 'medium elite' is that it was porous, resisting easy characterization. We shall come back to this issue when we discuss the 'new' families in the second section of this chapter (below, pp. 247–51), but the problem underpins all the discussion here.

What are called here the 'new aristocracy' were anyway, by 1060 at the latest, the new secular leaders of the city, its upper elite. Beneath them there was a complex array of locally significant families, leading artisans, clerics and clients of the richer

---

[6] See above all Bougard et al., *Théorie et pratiques des élites*, the last volume of the series (p. 4 lists the previous volumes, two of which are web publications; Le Jan's definition, 'une minorité qui dirige, qui concentre les richesses et le prestige' is taken from <http://lamop.univ-paris1.fr/IMG/pdf/introduction.pdf>, accessed 5 August 2012); for a neat problematization of the standard terminology, Patzold, '"Adel" oder "Eliten"?'; for the ideal type, Wickham, 'The changing composition of early élites', developing Wickham, *Framing*, pp. 153–5 (the different terminology used in each of these last two, elite in the former, aristocracy in the latter, is a marker of the fluid terms of the debate).

tituli and *diaconiae*, moneylenders and merchants, who did not have such a prominent role in politics, but who were figures to reckon with in their *regiones*. This is the 'medium elite' as defined here, and they will be discussed in both Chapter 5, which deals with regional social structures, and Chapter 7 on post-1050 politics. In many cities, this group, more powerful collectively than any of its members could be individually, became a core element of the early commune, as it crystallized in the mid-twelfth century. This would by and large be true of Rome as well, particularly in the decades before the permanent return of the popes to the city in 1188, for that would be the moment after which the 'new aristocracy' took over communal leadership with some firmness.[7] But the typical history of the Italian city commune, *consolare* to *c.*1200, *podestarile* to *c.*1250, and intermittently *popolare* from then on, played itself out differently in Rome, not only because of institutional differences, but also because the 'new aristocratic' families had a different orientation to their equivalents elsewhere, and their baronial descendants, unusually wealthy, were even more different. The Senate, Rome's commune, did indeed largely belong to the 'medium elite' at the start.[8] But the relationship that stratum had with its richer aristocratic neighbours needs to be understood with some exactness before we can successfully explain why it was that the early Senate took the path it did, and much of the rest of this book will have that as one of its underlying problematics. To repeat, the social boundary between this stratum and the 'new aristocracy' was permeable, and it would be a waste of ink to spend too much time arguing whether, at the margins, family A was one rather than the other, or exactly when family B rose from one to the other. But we can pin down a different focus for each, all the same, as we shall see; and the fact of these differences in focus had a considerable effect on the way the commune developed in Rome.

Many of these observations will be familiar to any expert in the history of Rome in this period, and the distinction between the Frangipane/Pierleoni and their predecessors will be no surprise to anyone; it has long been a standard element in university course manuals. Nonetheless, these three strata need to be set out here as clearly as possible, because I shall be analysing their membership and their changing identity in turn. I shall look at each stratum family by family, while also seeking to analyse them as a whole. In so doing, I shall not aim at prosopographical completeness; that would require a different sort of book. Family reconstruction is also, by and large, fascinating only to the few (and those few may well feel that the analyses presented here are too lacking in completeness); balance is hard here. But we need to follow *enough* families to allow us to get a sense of each of these three elite groups, so at least some family reconstruction seems to me essential; anyway, much preceding analysis (quite a lot has been done) is unreliable.[9] In this chapter,

---

[7] Thumser, *Rom*, pp. 231–56, for after 1188; see in general for the wider military elite Maire Vigueur, *Cavaliers et citoyens*.

[8] For example Moscati, *Alle origini*, pp. 24–7. This will be developed further at the end of Chapter 7, pp. 447–52.

[9] Görich, 'Die *de Imiza*' and Thumser, 'Die Frangipane' are the only high-quality studies for the period before 1150; furthermore, Beolchini, *Tusculum II*, gives an effective survey of the relatively well-studied Tuscolani.

I shall look at the 'old' and the 'new' aristocracy in turn, and then, more briefly, compare their internal structures and interrelationships with those of other cities in Italy; in the next, the focus will switch to the 'medium elite'. After we have looked at the complexities of each, and their varying attachment to land, office, title, and the political world in general, and also at the clientelar links each stratum had with other secular players and with the churches that kept our documents, we will be able to gain a better sense of how Roman political society was articulated, and how that articulation changed. Because change was indeed constant, as the city slowly expanded demographically and economically, and as its political structures shifted. Change and complexity were always the key elements in what was Italy's largest and richest city until, maybe, 1100 (above, p. 112); and Rome's aristocratic strata were the most complex of any city in Italy for much longer than that.

THE 'OLD ARISTOCRACY' AND THE *ANCIEN RÉGIME* OF ROME, 900–1046

Before 1000, most of what we know about the society of Rome focuses on its aristocracy. This section thus contains most of the knowable social history of the tenth century (particularly the later tenth century) in Rome, and tracks the 'old aristocratic' families later as well, through to the effective end of their power in the city, which was in most cases already before the failure of Rome's *ancien régime* in the uprisings of 1044–5, and in the resultant German coup of 1046. Those families, at least up to 1000, and often for another generation, were very closely associated with the traditional governing structures of the city, focused on the popes and the (rather more stable) hierarchies of officials who ran the city from the Laterano palace. This section will therefore discuss aspects of Rome's government as well. But it is not intended to provide a political history. I sketched out a short version of one in Chapter 1, and that also contains references to longer ones elsewhere. Political and institutional developments will inevitably appear and be discussed here, because they are important for our understanding of how the 'old aristocracy' operated and changed, but they will not be at the centre of the analysis. Instead, we will look, first, at the nature and complexity of the official hierarchies of the *ancien régime*; then at the people who made up the leading families of the Alberician and post-Alberician period, up to 1012, at their titles and wealth, and their family structures; and finally at the newer families of the early eleventh century, and at the move of the leading members of the 'old aristocracy' out of city politics in the Tuscolano period.

In the ninth century, there were three separate official hierarchies in Rome: military, judicial, and ecclesiastical. Least is known about the military hierarchy, but men called *magister militum* or *superista* are attested off and on throughout the century; the papal *militia* had both military and ceremonial importance (see below, p. 333), and these were its leaders. There were clearly several such leaders at any one time, as the *Liber Pontificalis* makes clear in, for example, its account of the contested papal election of 855, and other senior military figures sometimes appear, such as Cesario (son of Sergio *magister militum*), *ordinatus super exercitum* in 849. A hierarchy of rank appears earlier in 855, when Daniele *magister equitum* accused Graziano, *eminentissimus magistro militum et Romani palatii* (or *Romanae urbis*) *superista*, clearly his superior, of disloyalty to the Carolingians, a charge he could not sustain.[10] Apart from this, however, the structure of the military side of Rome's aristocratic hierarchies is obscure to us. A set of military offices appear in a wide array of heterogeneous texts, but we cannot put them into a credible ordering. We can say, however, that it was normal to call senior military men *nobiles*, and Cesario di Sergio's case shows that they had hereditary elements; we shall see in a moment how complex links between families were by 876. The terminology just outlined becomes much less common after the beginning of the tenth century, perhaps because the supreme military leaders were by now Teofilatto and his heirs; but two people are called *superista* under Alberico, and Otto III briefly revived the office of *magister militiae*.[11] Formal military offices cease to be documented at all after that. All the same, military leadership, with or without titles, remained an important role for Rome's aristocrats.

Equally status-filled were the offices of the seven palatine judges, the *primicerius, secundicerius, primus defensor, nomenculator, arcarius, saccellarius*, and *protoscriniarius*.[12] These officials had specific roles in the papal administration: broadly, the first two and the last ran the notariate or *scrinium*, the third was the senior official among the managers of papal lands, the fourth ran papal charity, the fifth and sixth ran the treasury; but there was much overlap, and it is far from clear by the tenth century whether these long-standing bureaucratic roles were more important than their directive roles in the judicial system, the solid assembly-based civil justice of the Roman *placitum*, which is where we see them operate most often (below, pp. 387–93). Slightly separate was the office of *vestararius*, which was again a financial office; this official was not a standard judge. On the other hand, when the *vestararius* appears in court proceedings, he seems often to preside over cases, whereas the palatine judges run the court under him; although here, too, we do not have enough evidence to be sure of a firm hierarchy of office, *vestararii* seem to be political leaders of unusual importance.[13] There were also lands in the Agro romano attached to the office, which made it visibly remunerative.[14] It is thus

---

[10] For the 850s narratives, see *LP*, II, pp. 118, 134, 141–2. One ninth-century documentary reference is *RS*, n. 83 (a. 866), in which Leone *superista* and his wife lease land from S. Erasmo sul Celio. See in general Noble, *The Republic of St. Peter*, pp. 234–5, 248–9, and the judicious comments in Toubert, 'Scrinium et *palatium*', pp. 436–40.

[11] *Superistae*, aa. 921–54: *SMVL*, n. 1; *RS*, n. 155; *S. Gregorio*, n. 124; for *militiae magister*, Manaresi, n. 254. Thereafter, *superista* as a word declined in status, and means 'bailiff' in later Roman documents, starting with *SMVL*, n. 118 (a. 1088).

[12] Halphen, *Études*, pp. 37–48, and 89–146 for an authoritative list of office-holders (updated in Toubert, *Les structures*, pp. 1349–53); Toubert, 'Scrinium et *palatium*', pp. 440–55; Noble, *The Republic of St. Peter*, pp. 212–41.

[13] *RS*, nn. 155, 126, 118; *SMVL*, n. 10A; Manaresi, n. 254. Galletti, *Del vestarario*, pp. 31–51, collects citations fairly accurately. In 985 (*RF*, n. 402), a document is dated by Giovanni *vestararius*: cf. this chapter, n. 46.

[14] Teofilatto: see Chapter 1, n. 59. For the lands of the office (identified as *ius vestararii*), see Wickham, 'Iuris cui existens', p. 10.

significant that Teofilatto, Rome's effective ruler in the first quarter of the tenth century, was not only *magister militum* but also *vestararius* (and his wife Teodora *vestararissa*). *Vestararii*, together with *superistae/magistri militum*, seem to have marked the highest positions lay aristocrats could reach in Rome—even if, having said that, it is equally important to stress that we do not hear of either of them so very often.

In the tenth century the importance of the *vestararius*, although sometimes still very great, was by now intermittent; after 1000 references to the title vanish.[15] The new tenth-century political office that came to be of major importance was instead the revived position of urban prefect, which reappears in the middle decades of the tenth century after a long break, and it is very likely that it was Alberico who re-established the office. The prefecture was particularly central from 1000 onwards. This did not replace the office of *vestararius* in any simple way, for the prefect handled criminal justice and public order above all (under Otto III, indeed, the two officials appear together), but the prefect, too, would be a court president in the eleventh century, and his office was politically important, and clearly sought after, by then. Structurally, the prefect had, by 1010 at the latest, taken over from both the *vestararius* and the *superista* as the most prominent secular official in Rome. He even took the physical place of the *vestararius* at the back of major papal processions through the city.[16]

These were essentially secular hierarchies (although palatine judges could certainly be deacons, and even bishops on occasion).[17] They were set against purely ecclesiastical hierarchies, of the priests of the city's *tituli* and great basilicas, the deacons of the *diaconie*, and the bishops of the sees around Rome, the three components of the later college of cardinals; to these should be added a handful of more clearly ecclesiastical offices in the bureaucracy, notably the *bibliothecarius*, who was often a bishop.[18] These positions were, perhaps more often than the secular offices, available to talented men without an elevated family background, but most cases where we can track ecclesiastical families (usually, when one of their members got to be pope) show them to be aristocratic too. Indeed, as in every other period of medieval history, it was common for relatives to follow different career paths, one secular, one ecclesiastical: as with the two sons of Bishop Arsenio of Orte, one of whom was the *bibliothecarius* Anastasio, noted intellectual and failed papal candidate in 855, the other the apparently military and certainly secular figure Eleuterio, who had the particularly unpleasant notoriety of having murdered the wife and daughter of Pope Hadrian II in 868; or, earlier on, the deacon Adriano, from 772 Pope Hadrian I, whose uncle

---

[15] Galletti, *Del vestarario*, pp. 53–5, cited a certain 'Eiquocus' in *c*.1032, but in error; Bertolini, *Scritti scelti*, II, pp. 765–70, showed that this really referred to Prince Alberico.

[16] Halphen, *Études*, pp. 16–27, 147–56 (better than Paravicini, *Saggio storico* and Hirschfeld, 'Das Gerichtswesen', pp. 473–8); Toubert, *Les structures*, pp. 1208–9. For processions, see below, p. 328.

[17] See for example Halphen, *Études*, p. 116, for two *arcarii* who were bishops in 879–96.

[18] For the clergy, see di Carpegna Falconieri, *Il clero di Roma*, pp. 103–36; for the *bibliothecarius*, Bresslau, *Handbuch*, I, pp. 211–20.

Teodoto was *dux* of Rome and then *primicerius*, and one of whose relatives was again *primicerius*.[19]

We can see the complexity of these interconnections particularly clearly in the list of victims of a show trial of the opponents of John VIII (872–82) in 876. These included Gregorio *nomenculator* and Stefano *secundicerius*, sons of Teofilatto *nomenculator*; Giorgio *magister militum* and *vestararius*, son of Gregorio *primicerius*, who had married Pope Benedict III's niece and then lived with Gregorio *nomenculator*'s daughter; Sergio *magister militum*, son of Teodoro *magister militum*, who had married Pope Nicholas I's niece; and Gregorio *nomenculator*'s other daughter Costantina, who had married in succession the sons of Pipino *vestararius* and of Gregorio *magister militum*.[20] There was thus no structural opposition between ecclesiastical and secular hierarchies, and nor would there be until the apex of the ecclesiastical hierarchy was taken over by outsiders in the years after 1046.[21] They were intertwined; they regularly collaborated in ceremonial, governmental action, and military engagement; they divided out into factions along family rather than career lines, as in 876; and they were heavily involved, on varying sides, in the election of popes who were, normally, their relatives too.

These three hierarchies formed the government of Rome. It is not part of my aim here to track further the institutional structures of that government, which have been well analysed elsewhere;[22] rather, it is to point out their implications for the structure of the 'old aristocracy'. The aristocracy of Rome in the ninth and early tenth centuries (as also, as far as we can tell, in the eighth) focused their career paths, and their ambitions, on achieving positions for themselves and/or their relatives in one or more of these hierarchies. In the ninth century, almost no known political player in the city was not in one of the three. This may be a bias of our sources, for the *Liber Pontificalis* is so obviously an official chronicle, but even in the tenth century, when legal documents begin to be more numerous, these hierarchies were still important for aristocratic identity. Together, as Pierre Toubert noted (following Harry Bresslau), they made up 'un puissant "*Selbstverständnis*"' for the city's aristocracy. Although the standard aristocratic title *consul et dux* by the tenth century, unlike in the past, conveyed no formal official duties, it too marked a sense that aristocratic status was tied up with roles in Rome's government, perhaps even more than the title *iudex* did in the tenth-century cities of Italy's Centre-North.[23]

The parallelism with *iudices*, the generic office in northern Italian cities, gives us perspective on another essential aspect of these Roman hierarchies: they were

---

[19] For Arsenio's sons, a convenient account is Duchesne, *I primi tempi*, pp. 98–108; for Eleuterio, see esp. *Annales Bertiniani*, s.a. 868 (p. 92). For Hadrian I's family, *LP*, I, p. 486 with p. 514, II, p. 4 with p. 36.

[20] See the letter of John VIII, not collected in his register, edited as *Epistolae passim collectae*, n. 9; commentary in Arnaldi, *Natale 875*, pp. 20–8.

[21] See in general for post-1046 Hüls, *Kardinäle, Klerus*.

[22] Bresslau, *Handbuch*, I, pp. 192–229; Halphen, *Études*; Toubert, '*Scrinium* et *palatium*'; Noble, *The Republic of St. Peter*, pp. 212–55.

[23] Toubert, '*Scrinium* et *palatium*', p. 454. For *consul et dux*, Halphen, *Études*, pp. 28–36 (too institutional a reading); for *iudex* in the north, see e.g. Schwarzmaier, *Lucca*, pp. 293–328.

startlingly complex. Rome was the centre of an independent state, so one would expect more organizational complexity than in any individual northern city; but there was also more than in the capital of the *regnum Italiae*, Pavia, which had a relatively restricted array of public offices, and arguably even more than in Carolingian Aachen, as set out, schematically but usefully, in Adalard of Corbie's and Hincmar of Reims' *De ordine palatii*.[24] They were, that is to say, sufficiently complex to absorb the political ambitions of a substantial group of families; it was not necessary to go outside the major offices of the city to make a political career and to become powerful. This meant that rivalries inside the hierarchies could be murderously violent on occasion; but also that the system, as a whole, remained very stable. This must have been the main reason why Rome's political structure weathered the crisis of the 890s (above, pp. 22–3) without substantial change. The strongman who emerged to orchestrate the revival of political stability in the city, Teofilatto, was in himself proof of this, for, as we have seen, he held both of the top secular offices at once. His daughter Marozia was able to take over his power; she did not, as a woman, hold any formal offices to match those of her father, but the fact that she held on to power for nearly a decade (*c.*925–32) shows not only her own staying power but also the open recognition that her family's rule was by now hereditary (above, p. 24). Her son Alberico (932–54) invented his own southern-influenced title of *princeps*, which might imply a change in the bases of the family's authority. All the same, when our documents begin to become slightly more numerous, from the 940s, taking this regime out of the shadows, we see that the rule of Alberico and of his son Ottaviano/John XII (954–63/4) was almost as structured by the city's traditional hierarchies as was that of any ninth-century pope. That period will be our starting point here in our detailed analysis of the 'old aristocracy', for we can say too little about the aristocratic networks of the early part of the tenth century. It is clearly the heir of the ninth-century world I have just delineated, but it also shows some new developments.

We learn something about Alberico's entourage from a variety of (usually sketchy) narrative sources, but our best snapshot of it is a court case of 942, in which a dispute between the monastery of Subiaco and four inhabitants of Tivoli was heard and resolved *in curte principi Alberici* beside the church of SS. Apostoli in the centre of Rome, just west of the Quirinale; so let us start with that text. Bishop Marino of Bomarzo presided, perhaps simply acting for Alberico, for he was later, in 955–8, papal *bibliothecarius*; five of the seven palatine judges were there; so were, in order, Benedetto Campanino, Caloleo, the *dux* Giorgio *de Cannapara*, Teofilatto *vestararius*, Giovanni *superista*, Demetrio di Melioso (*de Umiliosum*), all more or less identifiable figures, and then nine other named *obtimates* whom I cannot trace elsewhere.[25] If one was to do a strict Kremlinology on this ordering, the status of

[24] See e.g. Mayer, *Italienische Verfassungsgeschichte*, II, pp. 178–89; Hincmar, *De ordine palatii*, chs 12–25 (pp. 54–78).

[25] *RS*, n. 155; for Marino, *S. Sil.*, n. 3 (=*Papsturkunden*, n. 134); *Papsturkunden*, nn. 139, 144, 148; *RS*, n. 20. For Alberico's rule the most detailed account remains the very traditional Sickel, 'Alberich II.'.

the *vestararius* and *superista* might have seemed to have slipped, behind not only the palatine judges but also some untitled aristocrats; but both sign together with the judges at the end, which restores their prominence, and anyway Teofilatto was (or would soon be) the husband of Alberico's influential cousin Marozia 'II', and father of the first of the Tuscolani, Gregorio of Tuscolo—he was certainly, then, a significant political player. Giovanni *superista*'s son Stefano was sufficiently important to be named first among the *primates Romanae civitatis* who participated in the 963 synod to depose Alberico's son John XII, so Giovanni was presumably a major player too.[26] For his part, Leone *protoscriniarius* would become Pope Leo VIII in 963–5; his father had been Giovanni, likewise *protoscriniarius*, active in 917–20. Giorgio *secundicerius* would become abbot of Subiaco in 964, apparently moving directly from one office to the other, and remained there, usually explicitly referring to himself as *dudum* [formerly] *secundicerius* (which points up the importance of the office to him), until 971–3.[27] These two were also, then, operating much as such officials would have done a century before; they both, together with two others of the 942 palatine judges, were present at the 963 synod too. But we also find non-officials with an apparently central role in 942. Giorgio of Cannapara (an area of Rome beside the Foro Romano, just south of the Capitolio) is not recorded elsewhere, but Pietro of Canaparia, conceivably his son, was present at the 963 synod and in a court case of 966. Caloleo is attested in 963 as owning land outside Tivoli, and, more significantly, has been argued on good grounds to have been the developer of the Foro di Traiano and the creator of an urban quarter there, around the eponymous Campo Carleo (above, p. 126).[28] Benedetto and Demetrio are more extensively attested, however, and deserve further attention.

Benedetto Campanino was from *Campania*, that is the modern province of Frosinone; he held lands there, and also held or acquired lands in Trastevere, around Tivoli, and probably down the Tiber to the sea and in the Sutrino— quite a wide range. He was an active associate of Alberico, who sent him on an embassy to Constantinople, and he was the founder of the important Trastevere monastery of SS. Cosma e Damiano, probably in the 940s (as well as a donor, including of land in *Campania*, to Subiaco in 952), in which respect he followed the family practice of Alberico and his cousins. Toubert denied forcefully that he was count of *Campania*, and I follow him here; *Campaninus* is simply a mark of his origin, and he is never titled *comes*.[29] But he did have a political and judicial role, for he is twice found presiding over court cases. In 943 he held a formal case, over land

---

[26] For 963, Liutprando, *Historia Ottonis*, ch. 9.

[27] For Leone and his father, see the references in Halphen, *Études*, pp. 140–2. For Giorgio, Halphen, *Études*, pp. 110–11; as abbot of Subiaco, *RS*, nn. 71, 26, 130–1, 166, 149, 142, 25, 67, 69, 200, 118, 46, 201, 88, 142, 127, 58, 186, a notable number of texts for the period.

[28] Pietro in 966: *RS*, n. 118; Caloleo in 963: *RS*, n. 93.

[29] See esp. Toubert, *Les structures*, pp. 981–3; cf. for example two people called *Kampaninus* as an ascription, i.e. necessarily geographical, in *Papsturkunden*, n. 516 (a. 1017). (Toubert, 'Scrinium et palatium', pp. 432–3n, seems to retract the argument in part, but I see no need to.) For Constantinople, Benedetto, *Chronicon*, p. 171; for the foundation of SS. Cosma e Damiano, *RF*, n. 439 (cf., for the probable range of his lands, *Papsturkunden*, n. 419, a. 1005, which lists the properties then owned by the monastery); for Subiaco, *RS*, nn. 110, 195.

just outside the city, in his own house in Rome (*domus*); here he is *eminentissimus vir et gloriosus dux*, serious and elevated titles. At an unspecified date he also, as *eminentissimus consul et dux*, ran a case in Alatri in *Campania*, in which he was authoritative enough to demand the presence of the litigants at a hearing where he sat with four bishops, Andrea *arcarius* from Rome, maybe a couple of other Romans, and an assembly of Alatri notables. This is of course the reason why Giorgio Falco saw him as the count of the territory, for the powers he had here were, precisely, comital ones; but it remains true that he was not called a count in the document, and his authority in Alatri does not seem different in type from that which he exercised in the 943 case in Rome. It is better to see him as having a substantial slice of delegated authority from Prince Alberico, which he could—probably at the latter's request—exercise anywhere.[30] Benedetto's de facto role was thus that often exercised earlier by the *vestararius* and later by the urban prefect, as the main secular representative of the ruler, but it may be significant that Alberico did not see it as necessary to give him a formal office. He was simply a high-ranking and rich aristocrat who came into the city and gained sufficient *Königsnähe* (*Fürstennähe*) to be politically prominent. He was probably dead before 963, as he does not appear in the Rome synod of that year, and his heirs cannot be traced.

Demetrio di Melioso also held no office, although he too was *eminentissimus consul et dux* by 946. He may have been a little younger than Benedetto, for he was active in 963; Liutprando then calls him the *illustrior* of the Roman *optimates*, when he was one of John XII's envoys to Otto I, just before the latter moved militarily against the pope, and the city's whole ruling class changed sides. In between, he is only attested as a witness, invariably to pious gifts by other major aristocrats, together with palatine judges and the like; here, he is *nobilis vir* or *dux*. His origin is unclear; his father's name is very uncommon, and is not attested earlier than this; another Demetrio—this name is not common either—was however *arcarius* in 926 and maybe *superista* before 921, and he might have been an office-holding grandfather. Demetrio di Melioso is also notable for being the lay protagonist of Lazio's first *incastellamento* charter, for the short-lived castle of Monte Calvelli in the Velletrano, in 946 (above, p. 43), the text calling him *eminentissimus*; this is however the only time we can track his landed activities, and the land was apparently newly leased to him.[31] Demetrio was probably dead by 977, when his son Giovanni *excellentissimus vir* leased the castle and lagoons of Fogliano on the Lazio coast from Subiaco, and certainly was by 987, when Giovanni, now, like his father, *eminentissimus consulus* [*sic*] *et dux*, together with two *nobilissime* sisters (married to a *nobilis vir* and a *consul et dux*), gave an island in the Tiber to SS. Bonifacio e Alessio sull'Aventino. Giovanni was still active as late as 1015 in the entourage of Benedict VIII, so there is also no reason to doubt that he is the Giovanni *illustrissimo et clarissimo viro*, son of 'Melioso' *consulus et dux* and Marozza

---

[30] For 943, *RS*, n. 35; the Alatri case is ed. in Falco, *Studi*, pp. 415–16, with comment at p. 402; Toubert, *Les structures*, p. 982n, corrects the edition.
[31] *Velletri*, n. 1 (a. 946), Liutprando, *Historia Ottonis*, chs 6, 9; *RS*, nn. 110, 122, 52, for witnessing; *RS*, n. 9 and *SMVL*, n. 1 for 921–6.

nobilissima femina, who in 1007 made a land deal in, probably, the territory of Cerveteri. The rarity of the name also means that the two sons of Crescenzio di Melioso, attested as tenants and witnesses west of the city in the 1060s, are likely to be a later generation of what I shall call the 'Meliosi'; one of them was a high-status *consul comunitatis boum* in 1088, in a radically different political environment (see below, pp. 394–8). As already noted, Demetrio as a name is not much commoner than Melioso, so it is also likely that the *consul et dux/Romanorum consul* of that name in 979 and the *illustris vir* of 1017–24 were somehow related as well; these aristocrats held land in Albano.[32]

In order to understand what Benedetto and Demetrio show us, it is worth looking slightly later as well, at the list of the other *primates Romanae civitatis* of the 963 synod. These are listed in Liutprando's text after twenty-five bishops, fourteen priests of *tituli*, three deacons, six of the seven palatine judges (the seventh would become pope in the same synod), thirteen *scriniarii*, and thirteen ecclesiastical officials. That is to say, in this unusually complete list of Rome's elite, it is the non-office-holders who were essentially characterized as *primates*.[33] There were twelve of them, three of whom we have met already; five others we cannot say much about. Of the remaining four, Crescenzio *Caballi marmorei* had links with the later group of aristocratic families we call 'Crescenzi', and we will return to him shortly (p. 199). Two more, Giovanni *Mizina* and Stefano *de Imiza*, have been shown by Knut Görich to be brothers, sons of Hildebrand *consul et dux* and his wife Imiza/Mizina, and members of the important *de Imiza* family. For the history of that family it is sufficient to cite Görich, but, to summarize: Giovanni was later *dux* of Albano before becoming a monk, before 976, and his probable son Gregorio was Rome's last-known *vestararius* in 999; Stefano, by contrast, had no known offices, and nor did his children, but they are attested into the 1010s, as *consules et duces, viri illustrissimi*, and similar titles. They were closely associated with S. Gregorio sul Celio, as donors and lessees, and Stefano was buried there. They held land in the city (between the Aventino and the Palatino, and on the Quirinale) and in the Agro romano, including profitable leases of salt pans and Tiber mills, and a failed castle at Mandra Camellaria on the Appia (above, p. 43).[34] The final member of the 963 group, Giovanni *de Primicerio*, was, as Toubert showed, probably son of Urso *primicerius* (fl. 932), for both held lands in the same sector of the territory of Albano, Zizinni. Giovanni was the son of an office-holder, but, like many of the *de Imiza*, not an office-holder himself. Nonetheless, like Benedetto Campanino before him, he reappears as a senior participant in court cases in 966 and 983; in the latter year he was also executor of the will of Stefano *de Imiza*, as *consul et dux*, together with the *arcarius*, three abbots of city monasteries, and a

---

[32] Respectively, *RS*, n. 51 (a. 977); *S. Alessio*, n. 2 (a. 987); *RF*, n. 502 (a. 1015); *SMVL*, n. 27 (a. 1007—the text cites the *territorio Cesense*, which is no known place and must be corrupt; *Cerense*, i.e. Cerveteri, is the most plausible alternative); *SCD*, n. 60 and *S. Gregorio*, n. 15 (aa. 1060–7); *RF*, n. 1115 (a. 1088); *RS*, nn. 125 and 143 (a. 979); *SMVL*, n. 39, 47 (aa. 1017–24).

[33] Liutprando, *Historia Ottonis*, ch. 9.

[34] See in general Görich, '*Die Imiza*'; one correction to the genealogy is in Santangeli Valenzani, 'L'insediamento aristocratico', p. 242n. For Stefano's burial, *S. Gregorio*, n. 4 (a. 983).

comes palatii. He lived in the south of the city, and, as noted, held land in Albano. His son Leone *illustris* is also attested in the 980s, in a court case and again in Albano, although evidence for the family ends here.[35]

The 942 and 963 assembly lists are the best sources for the mid-century Roman aristocracy, because the first is the only formal public document surviving for Alberico, so is the main guide we have to his entourage, and the second was clearly intended at the time to include the whole of Rome's political society, so as to mark Otto I's new regime (although the latter was not, in the end, a very permanent one). They are backed up, but not added to, by other public documents, such as court cases from 966 and 981, in which several of the above-named also appear.[36] The interesting thing is, indeed, how many of the same aristocrats appear reasonably regularly, and can be characterized at least approximately in their political and social actions, in our public documents. If one looks at the set of tenth-century Roman documents as a whole (mostly monastic leases to aristocrats, or sales and gifts of those leases, and mostly preserved in the cartularies of either Subiaco or S. Gregorio sul Celio), one finds a daunting array of almost anonymous urban notables, as with the witnesses to a 936 sale, Nicola, Baduaro, Pietro, Leone, and Romano, all described as *consul et dux*, or those to a parallel sale in 944, Adriano, Pietro, Benedetto, and Gregorio, all *nobilis vir*, plus Benedetto *illustris* and Giorgio *secundicerius*, or those to a lease of 961, Bonizone, Giorgio, and Crescenzio, all *nobilis vir*, plus Gregorio *consul et dux*. These common names, from a very restricted naming set, with generic titles, cannot be put into any plausible genea-logical network, and dozens of such people are identifiable in any given generation, well into the eleventh century.[37] But if one begins with the major assembly and judicial documents, then it is striking that the most prominent figures in them are much easier to track, and there are far fewer really important families on that list. A high percentage of lay actors in documents, too, are linked to one or other of these major families, to whom would be added the heirs of Teofilatto and Alberico themselves, after they lost political power in 963–4. Rome's 'old aristocracy' was large, but it seems to have had, in the mid-tenth century, not more than a dozen really powerful families: those we have looked at plus, doubtless, some other families more exclusively linked to ecclesiastical and lay office-holding. These latter are less well documented because, unfortunately, texts seldom tell us whom any given bishop or *arcarius* or *nomenculator* was son of; we therefore get a sense of their families only when their sons did not hold office but still alluded to it, as with Giovanni *de Primicerio,* or later, in 981, Pietro di Berta *de Vesterarius.*[38]

The same impression of an internal hierarchy in the aristocracy is created if one looks more closely at the most high-flown titles people used. *Consul et dux* and

[35] Toubert, *Les structures,* p. 1224n; for Urso and Zizinni, Halphen, *Études,* p. 96, *S. Sil.,* n. 3 (=*Papsturkunden,* n. 134), and *RS,* n. 137. Other references to Giovanni and his son: *RS,* nn. 118, 185; *S. Gregorio,* n. 4; *SMVL,* n. 10A; *S. Alessio,* n. 4.

[36] *RS,* n. 118; *SMVL,* n. 10A.

[37] Respectively, *RS,* nn. 43, 54, 139. See Hubert, 'Évolution générale', pp. 575–80, for the restricted naming set.

[38] *SMVL,* n. 10A.

nobilis vir are so frequent in the early and mid-tenth century that they simply denote generic aristocratic membership.[39] *Vir magnificus*, just as common, hardly even denotes that.[40] But we saw Benedetto Campanino and Demetrio di Melioso and the *de Imiza* using more glamorous titles too: *excellentissimus, glorios(issim)us, eminentissimus, illustris(simus)*; these are much rarer. *Excellentissimus* is only used by Alberico's cousins and their heirs, the Tuscolani, plus Demetrio di Melioso. *Gloriosus* is used by Teofilatto and Alberico as rulers (as a ruling epithet it goes back to the Carolingians), and then by very few aristocrats: Crescenzio 'II' as ruler of Terracina, two early eleventh-century urban prefects, some counts in Lazio, and Benedetto Campanino. *Eminentissimus* is used by Benedetto and Demetrio, by the latter's son, by Teofilatto *vestararius* husband of Marozia 'II', and by his grandson the Tuscolano Alberico 'III', so we can suppose that the half-dozen other people who used the title, less easily placeable, were major figures too.[41] *Illustris* was, however, perhaps the title that most clearly marked out the leading families of the 'old aristocracy', for it was commoner, and also more often applied to women, than were any of the other words just cited. As an elite title, it of course looks straight back to the late Roman empire (as indeed did most of the others)—it then meant the highest-ranking members of the Senate. Before 1000, it is used nearly forty times in surviving documents; over half of these are visibly for the figures we have just looked at or their close relatives, in particular the family of Teofilatto and Alberico, the *de Imiza*, the *de Primicerio*, the 'Crescenzi', and the wives and daughters of two *arcarii*; we could propose that many of the other half were on the social level of these families too.[42] Significantly, after 970, when the title *consul et dux* steadily becomes less common, it too by now focuses on the same families, in particular the *de Imiza*, the *de Primicerio*, the 'Crescenzi' and the 'Meliosi', before (from 1013) coming to denote the Tuscolani exclusively.

We are by now looking into the later tenth century, which is on the level of papal succession a relatively unstable period between the solid regimes of the Teofilatto family (up to 963) and of Giovanni di Crescenzio and the Tuscolani popes (after 1002; see above, pp. 25–8). That instability, as Toubert remarked, is much less visible at the level of the aristocracy; the families that are most prominent in 970 are still, for the most part, those most prominent at the end of the century.[43] The major novelty of this intervening period at the level we are looking at was the

---

[39] Toubert, *Les structures*, p. 964n, shows that the two titles were often synonyms. The vagueness of *nobilis*, in particular, in this period is well shown by two documents of April 1011 (*RS*, n. 85 and *RF*, n. 651), in the former of which a *nobilissima* is also called *honesta femina*, a title used by definitely non-elite people in the city, and in the latter two other *nobilissimae* are also called *illustrissima*, a very high-status title.

[40] For *vir magnificus*, see Chapter 3, n. 115; merchants and high-status artisans used the title, so it was a marker of a different category to that of *consules* or *nobiles*.

[41] Carolingians (and Beneventan rulers) using *glorios(issim)us*: see Chapter 1, n. 63. *Gloriosus* (excluding people already cited): *S. Gregorio*, n. 125; *SCD*, n. 93A; *CVL* 12632, pp. 313–17; *S. Alessio*, n. 1; *Papsturkunden*, n. 424; *RF*, nn. 616, 658, 1270; *eminentissimus*: *RS*, nn. 115, 97, 123, 52, 114; *S. Gregorio*, n. 125; *SMVL*, n. 24A; *RF*, n. 637.

[42] There are too many citations of *illustris* to list here. For the wives and daughters of *arcarii*, see *RS*, nn. 35, 81.

[43] Toubert, *Structures*, pp. 1220–5.

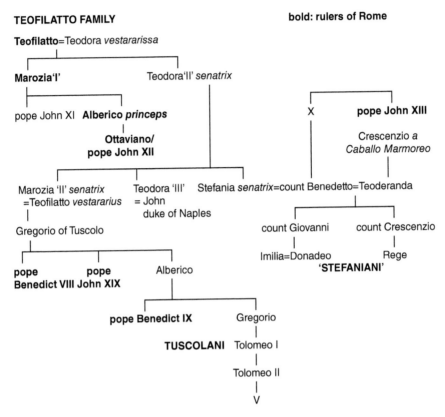

Genealogy 1

temporary return of the Teofilatto family to private life, in the form of Alberico's cousins Marozia 'II' and Stefania, daughters of Teodora 'II' and their heirs.[44] The

44 The family of Teodora 'II', the sister of the ruler Marozia 'I', is less controversial than most, and the links between its members are fairly secure. Marozia 'II' and Stefania are, in particular, explicitly stated to be her daughters in the only document which attests to a gift of land by Alberico and his brothers, sisters, and cousins: *S. Gregorio*, n. 68, a. 945. The only major link in it which is not clearly supported in the documents is the relation of Gregorio of Tuscolo, the first known holder of that city and ancestor of the Tuscolani, to Marozia 'II', who is generally accepted as his mother; for it hangs on the assumption that he is the same man as the Gregorio *illustrissimo viro filius Maroze senatrix* of *RS*, n. 109 (a. 980) who leases east of the city, and the Gregorio *Romanorum senator* of *SMCM*, n. 1 (a. 986). This is an identity which the Gregorio of Tuscolo texts (beginning with the Gregorio *excellentissimus vir qui vocatur de Tusculana* in Manaresi, n. 254, a. 999) do not make explicit. But Gregorio of Tuscolo's children included a Teofilatto and an Alberico, clear claims of family links with the older Teofilatto family, and the Tuscolani were patrons of S. Ciriaco in Via Lata, founded by Marozia 'II' and her sisters (see Hamilton, 'The house of Theophylact', pp. 203–8); furthermore, an epitaph of 1030 (ed. in Forcella, XII.3), found near Vacchereccia in Tuscia Romana, refers to Giovanni, son of Gregorio and nephew of Pope John XIX (and thus grandson of Gregorio of Tuscolo), as Prince Alberico's *nepos*. I see these, as do most historians, as strong arguments for the unification of the two Gregorios into one; the name is not at all rare, but these two are uniquely prominent in our documentation. Kölmel, *Abhandlungen*, pp. 160–2, following Bossi, 'I Crescenzi', p. 103 (who did not develop the point), however, took a more literal reading of *nepos* and saw Gregorio

latter were not any simple aristocrats, all the same. The title *senator/senatrix*, which was used by Teofilatto, Marozia, and Alberico as rulers, became the exclusive property of Marozia 'II' and Stefania, their sister Teodora 'III', and then of Gregorio son of Marozia 'II', the first Tuscolano, until Crescenzio 'II' di Crescenzio is found using it in 988 (the 'Crescenzi' continued to use it intermittently until 1013). It was less common in the eleventh century, but was still a Tuscolano privilege even after 1046; no one else claimed it as a specific title in Rome until the foundation of the Senate in 1143.[45] Similarly, as just noted, *consul* was by the 1010s an exclusively Tuscolano title, although it was being claimed by others by the 1080s (below, pp. 394–5). This family was thus marked out as Rome's super-elite family throughout the whole of our period, up to the middle of the eleventh century at the earliest, just as it would become in the next century Rome's major enemy, once it became clear that the family was never going to be able to get back to the city from Tuscolo. No other family matched their status at any time, except the 'Crescenzi' for perhaps twenty-five years.

The period 963–1012 is commonly known to historians as the 'Crescenzian period'. This is a misnomer, at least until the end of the 980s. Crescenzio 'I' di Teodora (d.984), the family's first major figure, was certainly an important political actor in the 970s (implicated in the death of at least one pope, as we shall see in a moment), but no sort of ruler in any source we have; and his two sons are thereafter, although indeed claiming important titles (*patricius, senator*), only intermittently hegemonic in any texts we have in the next years. Giovanni was *patricius* in 986 (a year in which a document is dated by him), and a thirteenth-century chronicle which may have an early basis claims that he put in Pope John XIV, who was consecrated in 985. Conversely, Crescenzio 'II' is first recorded as *omnium Romanorum senator* in 'my' Terracina in 988, which he claims to be ruling by papal and imperial concession—probably along the lines of the cessions of Palestrina and Tuscolo to major members of the Teofilatto family—rather than in Rome itself. Structured family power in Rome does not visibly begin until Crescenzio 'II' took control of the city more fully in the early 990s.[46] In a chapter about the aristocracy, however, it is crucial to stress that these men, although certainly prominent—and newly so in the 970s and onwards—are no more prominent until just before 990 in our documentary sources than are the *de*

---

of Tuscolo as a direct descendant of Prince Alberico, warning us (with unconscious irony, given his hypotheses elsewhere) against 'das freie Feld unkontrollierbarer Phantasie'. That theory creates far more problems than it resolves, but it is a marker of our uncertainties.

[45] *Senator/senatrix* after 945: *S. Sil.*, n. 3 (=*Papsturkunden*, n. 134, Alberico); *RS*, nn. 64, 124, 109 (Marozia 'II'); *Papsturkunden*, n. 205; *SMCM*, n. 1 (Gregorio); *S. Alessio*, n. 3 (Stefania); see the next n. for Crescenzio 'II' in 988; *RF*, n. 490 (Rogata di Crescenzio); Gattola, *Historia*, pp. 233–4, 235–6, with Hoffmann, 'Petrus Diaconus', n. 2 (Tuscolani in the 1060s).

[46] Gattula, *Historia*, I, pp. 115–16 (a. 986; this dating clause might look significant for rulership, but in 985 *RF*, n. 402 is dated by a *vestararius*; the period was a highly unstable one for popes); *Cronica . . . S. Bartholomaei*, p. 214; BAV, CVL 12632 (formerly ASV, Indice 224), pp. 313–17 (a. 988), an eighteenth-century transcription: see Falco, *Studi*, pp. 411–13. The 'Crescenzi' did not keep Terracina after their temporary fall in 998; it was given in *beneficium* to the Gaetans by Silvester II in 1000 (*Papsturkunden*, n. 393). See in general Kölmel, 'Beiträge'; Romeo, 'Crescenzio Nomentano'.

Imiza, the *de Primicerio*, and the 'Meliosi', and less than Benedetto Campanino had been. We could therefore see the later tenth-century 'old aristocracy' as (to be clichéd) a pyramid, with the proto-Tuscolani clearly at the apex, then these four families (with the 'Crescenzi' rising to the top around 990), then up to ten other main families of *illustres*, palatine judges, and counts of parts of Lazio; and below them a larger mass of less prominent but still aristocratic families, called *nobiles viri* and suchlike in texts. This hierarchy seems to be recognized in a court case of 993, which refers to *nobiliores homines magnis et parvis*, 'great and small'. Alberico probably created the 'Meliosi' as a particularly prominent family, as he would doubtless have created the 'Campanini' had the family survived; the other major families do not emerge into visibility until 963 (and the 'Crescenzi' later still), but could have risen under John XII, who is even less documented than his father. After that, however, this de facto hierarchy continued for several decades. Otto III is reputed to have attempted to change the rules in Rome, and he certainly marginalized Crescenzian power for three or four years, but his palatine judges remained unchanged, and most of his new grandly named officials (*prefectus navalis, palatii magister*) were either Tuscolani or *de Imiza*.[47] The same families stayed dominant. Real shifts did not come before the 1020s.

It can be seen that I wish to downplay the importance of the 'Crescenzi', except for the two decades or so up to 1012. But they do need attention here all the same, for exactly who was a Crescenzian has been hotly contested (it needs, always, to be remembered that 'Crescenzi' as a family name is not a contemporary usage—hence the inverted commas, more necessary for this family than for many—so it is up to us to decide whom we wish to count as one). I will therefore focus for the next pages on the problems of Crescenzian genealogy. This is not simply a genealogical debate, however; who was related to whom here matters if we want to understand both the nature of politics in the period and the patterns of family identity and loyalty. The Crescenzian family has in fact become one of the hardest to reconstruct, even in its main lines, out of all the leading families in our period. There are at least three versions of the family available; it seems to me that they are all mistaken at least in part, and that the idea of a unitary family at all is very questionable. Let us look at least briefly at the issues here, for they can serve as a case study for our understanding of the structuring of late tenth-century politics and the problems inherent in its analysis.

The basic things that we know about the 'Crescenzi' in the late tenth century fall into two major groups. Let us start with the easy one, the family of Crescenzio *illustrissimus vir* (or *consul et dux*) di Teodora, and his wife the *illustrissima femina*

---

[47] For the 993 text, *RS*, n. 78. For the titles, see esp. Schramm, *Kaiser, Rom*, pp. 112–15; the main text, Manaresi, n. 254 (a. 999), shows Gregorio of Tuscolo as *prefectus navalis*, Gregorio Miccino (probably a *de Imiza*) as *vestararius*, and Alberico di Gregorio (son of one or the other, very probably the former) as *imperialis palatii magister*. The only unknown, perhaps new, figure is Gerardo *imperialis militiae magister*, whom Otto also made count of the Sabina (Toubert, *Les structures*, pp. 1026–7). Giovanni the urban prefect continued in his office as well: Halphen, *Études*, pp. 147–8. For Otto's relations with the Roman aristocracy, see, apart from Schramm, Görich, *Otto III.*, pp. 250–67; Görich, '*Die Imiza*', pp. 29–38.

Sergia. Crescenzio 'I' (I use these numbers to avoid confusion) is most often called *de Theodora*, but his surviving epitaph also names his father as Giovanni; these names are exceptionally common in the period—as is the name Crescentius itself— and we cannot trace them further (there are, in particular, absolutely no grounds for saying that his mother was Teodora 'II', daughter of Teofilatto ruler of Rome, as Gaetano Bossi and Willi Kölmel thought, followed by Toubert). Crescenzio 'I' was a protagonist in the deposition and murder of Pope Benedict VI in 974; he leased the judicial rights over a castle in the Velletrano from the rural monastery of S. Andrea in Silice in 979, agreeing to fight for the monastery if necessary; he became a monk at S. Bonifacio sull'Aventino before his death in July 984, as his epitaph states.[48] His sons were called Giovanni and Crescenzio ('II'), as texts of May 984 and October 988 make clear (the latter shows they had controlled in some way S. Andrea in Silice itself); these two became, as already noted, major political figures as well, the former claiming the resonant title of *patricius*, the latter as ruler of Rome in the 990s. Crescenzio 'II', who was killed in 998 by Otto III, was the father of the *patricius* Giovanni di Crescenzio, who also ruled the city, and more stably, from *c*.1002 to his death in 1012, and of Rogata *senatrix*, who married Ottaviano, son of Giuseppe *rector* of the Sabina. This is the family that I refer to as the 'Crescenzi'; it is a simple three-generational group. Rogata and Ottaviano were the ancestors of the Ottaviani counts of the Sabina (the surname appears in the early twelfth century) who ruled the territory for much of the eleventh, with their power extended by Benedict VIII in 1014 and then reduced by Nicholas II in 1060; their descendants can be tracked in the southern Sabina up to 1199.[49] There is, however, no particular reason to extend the 'Crescenzi' name later to include the Ottaviani, in the phrase 'Crescenzi Ottaviani', as many do.

This is not a problematic genealogy, then; the problems come with other political figures. Abbot Ugo of Farfa recounted in the 1020s how Pope John XIII (965–72; Ugo just says *Iohannes maior*, but this must be the right John) married his nephew Benedetto to the *nobilis* Teoderanda, daughter of another Crescenzio, called *a Caballo marmoreo* (the Quirinale), whom we have seen active in the 963 synod of Rome; Benedetto was given the *comitatus* of the Sabina; and he had two sons, also called Giovanni and Crescenzio. Benedetto was a supporter of Crescenzio 'II', and had trouble from the regime of Otto III; his sons were supporters of the *patricius* Giovanni di Crescenzio after 1002, who (again according to Ugo) loved

---

[48] Epitaph: see the photograph in Brezzi, *Roma*, facing p. 160; it is ed. in *LP*, II, p. 256. Benedict VI: *LP*, II, p. 255; *Annales Beneventani*, s.a. 975 (p. 176); *Herimanni Augiensis chronicon*, s.a. 974 (p. 116). S. Andrea: *Statuti della provincia romana*, pp. 3–9. Romeo, 'Crescenzio de Theodora', is a reliable survey of the scarce sources. For the Teofilatto descent theory, see Bossi, 'I Crescenzi', pp. 65–9; Kölmel, *Abhandlungen*, pp. 28–9, 167; Toubert, *Structures*, pp. 1016, 1027, 1085–7.

[49] *RS*, n. 144 (a. 984); *Regesta Hon. III*, pp. cxx–cxxi (a. 988); for the next generation and the Ottaviani, among many, Bossi, 'I Crescenzi di Sabina'; Gerstenberg, 'Studien'; Brezzi, *Roma*, pp. 149–70; Toubert, *Structures*, pp. 1027–31, 1276–81; Whitton, 'Papal policy', pp. 103–83. In the twelfth century, the surname *Octavianisci* occurs in *CF*, II, p. 293; see for the period Schwarzmaier, 'Zur Familie Viktors IV.'.

them 'as beloved kinsmen' (*uti dilectos consanguineos*).[50] They still had comital power in the Sabina, until Benedict VIII removed them by force in 1014 and gave the territory to the Ottaviani; they kept lands in the Sabina after that, however (some of which Farfa claimed from them, hence Ugo's narrative), and are also recounted as holding *turres Penestrini montis*, most plausibly the fortification at the summit of the city of Palestrina. After 1014, they remained politically active still; Crescenzio di Benedetto was probably urban prefect in 1036, as we shall see; Rege, supporter of Pope Benedict X in 1059, who held the castle of Passarano in the diocese of Palestrina, was probably his son; but after that the family drop out of the record, and we can conclude that the events of 1014 did much to weaken their political influence.[51]

This account is not problematic either, apart from the overlapping of names with those of the family of Crescenzio di Teodora, which is confusing, but not so strange, given the frequency of the names in this period. (See the genealogies on pp. 196 and 203.) The problems are threefold. First, the *senatrix* Stefania, sister of Marozia 'II', appears in a 987 charter married to a count Benedetto; this would not mean much on its own, for Benedetto is a common name too, but Stefania had in 970 been granted public power over Palestrina for three lives by John XIII, and it is arguable that this power is what Giovanni and Crescenzio di Benedetto held there in 1014, and that they conceivably did so as Stefania's heirs; as a result, since Bossi's articles of 1915–18, the family has been called the 'Crescenzi Stefaniani'.[52] Second, Ugo uses, as we have just seen, the word *consanguineus* for the relationship between the *patricius* Giovanni di Crescenzio and the sons of Benedetto, which may imply that they too were relatives in some way: but in what? The third problem is that a host of historians have jumped to conclusions about the family relationships that can be supposed to underlie such apparent links. Bossi, Kölmel, and Toubert pushed the relationships to their extreme, and supposed not only that Crescenzio di Teodora was the son of Teodora 'II' (and thus brother of Marozia 'II' and Stefania of Palestrina), but that John XIII was as well (because he held land contiguous to that of Marozia in Albano in 961); Benedetto of the Sabina, John's nephew, could thus be seen as son of the Stefania and Benedetto of the 987 document, despite the fact that he must have married Teoderanda a long time earlier, before 972.[53] The two 'Crescenzi' families thus became cousins, and easily

---

[50] Ugo of Farfa, *Exceptio relationum*, pp. 62–5.

[51] Ugo of Farfa, *Exceptio relationum*, p. 67 (Palestrina); *LP*, II, p. 335 (a. 1059); for 1014 and its consequences, Bossi, 'I Crescenzi di Sabina', pp. 114–28; Romeo, 'Crescenzio, figlio di Benedetto'; Whitton, 'Papal policy', pp. 104–17, 154–66.

[52] Stefania: *Papsturkunden*, n. 205; *S. Alessio*, n. 3 (a. 987); for the name, Bossi, 'I Crescenzi di Sabina'.

[53] Bossi, 'I Crescenzi', pp. 57–9; Kölmel, *Abhandlungen*, pp. 28–9 (just citing Bossi); Toubert, *Structures*, p. 1027. (Zimmermann, 'Parteiungen', pp. 68–73, followed by Pauler, 'Giovanni XIII', p. 578, in a variant, has the hypothetical elder Benedetto as John XIII's brother, not brother-in-law.) The 961 document is *RS*, n. 124—note that nearly every major Roman aristocrat held land in Albano (see refs. in Wickham, 'Albano'). Bossi, 'I Crescenzi', pp. 69, 126, also launched a set of totally fanciful links between every Crescenzio of the early tenth century, making Crescenzio *a Caballo Marmoreo*, who has no documented link to any of these families apart from being Teoderanda's father, brother-in-law of Teodora 'II'; these have had some, but less, effect on the literature. (It is worth adding that Bossi

consanguinei, as well as cousins of the Tuscolani (all through the female line, a point we need to return to). The trouble is that these relationships are entirely gratuitous, and are based on the assumption that people in different documents, bearing some of the commonest names in the century, have to be the same person. Otto Gerstenberg, writing in the 1930s (and followed by Paolo Brezzi) denied that Crescenzio di Teodora and John XIII were related to Marozia and Stefania (or each other), but accepted that Stefania was the mother of Benedetto, John XIII's nephew (and also that Pope Benedict VII, 974–84, was Stefania's brother, another gratuitous claim).[54] Bernard Hamilton in 1960 thought there had to be two Stefania's, Stefania the sister of Marozia 'II' and her daughter, and that the daughter was Benedetto of the Sabina's second wife after Teoderanda had died. David Whitton in 1979 thought that Stefania was inevitably Benedetto's second wife, but that there did not have to be more than one of them (he was certainly right here); Stefania *senatrix* must have been in her sixties in 987, it is true, given that she was an adult in a text of 945, and Count Benedetto perhaps in his forties, but the marriage could easily be seen as political. Hamilton and Whitton complicated the question further by supposing that Crescenzio *a Caballo Marmoreo* and Crescenzio *de Theodora* were the same person, which would make Teoderanda, married around 970, the sister of Crescenzio 'II', and would restore the cousinage of the two families in the 1000s. This theory has been less influential than those of Bossi, because these two British authors argued their ideas in unpublished doctoral theses, but the latter argument is equally gratuitous.[55]

Any of these arguments are possible (although not, certainly, all of them at once). It would take many pages to set out the problems of each in full; and most of the authors I have cited here spent even more pages on their own reconstructions. I risk boring and confusing the uncommitted with these pages of discussion, and not convincing the committed. There is, however, really very little basis for linking these two families together, apart from the overlap in very common names, and apart from the *consanguineus* quote. But that quote says they were loved '*as*' kinsmen; although I would not want to lay too much stress on the commonest meaning of *ut* as an adverb, it certainly does not force us to look for real family links.

It can be added, finally, that the same is true for yet another Crescenzio, urban prefect in 1006–17, and thus across the transfer of power from Giovanni di Crescenzio to the Tuscolani popes. This Crescenzio is identifiable as the same

was very frequently wrong, but his articles are certainly scholarly; they would have been less influential otherwise.)

[54] Gerstenberg, 'Studien', pp. 1–7; Brezzi, *Roma*, pp. 150–4. Benedict VII is brought in because the rather later *Chronica Casinensis*, II.4, says (in one version) that he is a *propinquus* of Alberico, and *SMVL*, n. 10A, a. 981, says that a *comes* Benedetto is his nephew, who is taken, despite the frequency of the name, to be the count of the Sabina.

[55] Whitton, 'Papal policy', pp. 105–14, who also cites, at pp. 110–12, B. F. Hamilton, 'The Holy See, the Roman Nobility, and the Ottonian Empire', PhD thesis, University of London, 1960, pp. 217–20, 366. Whitton is, despite this latter hypothesis, easily the best current guide to the 'Crescenzi'.

man throughout because his brother Marino witnesses his documents; this is
Marino *de Turre* who gave some land to Farfa, probably on his deathbed, and
was still recording his brother as *olim prefectus*, in 1036. Brezzi and Toubert (but
not, for once, Bossi), supposed that this was the same man as the count of the
Sabina Crescenzio di Benedetto, despite the presence of a Crescenzio *comes*,
certainly that count, in two of the urban prefect's documents in 1011–12. (In
fact, as Bossi, Kölmel, and Whitton saw, if Crescenzio di Benedetto became urban
prefect, it was rather later, in the 1030s, as a text of 1036 more plausibly shows.)
Crescenzio brother of Marino cannot, in fact, be usefully attached to either
'Crescenzian' family; he was doubtless an aristocrat, for he had a serious directive
role, but probably not a major one if Marino says so insistently, for two decades,
that he is 'brother of the prefect', indicating that this was the core element of his
status. The urban prefecture seems to have been the highest office the family
achieved, and its members have to be kept separate from any other 'Crescenzi'.
We will come back to them in a moment.[56]

Of all these hypotheses, the only one that has a slightly stronger plausibility is the
marriage of Stefania *senatrix* to Benedetto count of the Sabina; she did at least
marry a count Benedict, and this would explain how her three-life grant of
Palestrina by John XIII in 970 was later controlled by Benedetto's children (by a
previous marriage, but emphyteuses were transferable if direct heirs were not
available). Even this hangs on a generous reading of Ugo of Farfa's narrative,
which sees Palestrina's *turres* as a metonym for control over the whole city. It
does, however, faintly justify the modern surname 'Stefaniani' for Benedetto's heirs,
which I will therefore use for convenience.

The reason why historians have come up with so many different versions of the
'Crescenzi' family is because they seem to belong, more than their contemporaries
do, to high politics, but on the other hand we do not really have any better evidence
for them than we do for (say) the 'Meliosi'. If they are disaggregated in the way
proposed here, then we can add an extra family to the small leading group of the
late tenth century, that of the 'Stefaniani', nephews of John XIII and married into

---

[56] For Crescenzio urban prefect and his brother Marino, see *RF*, nn. 616, 657 (active together with
Crescenzio *comes* di Benedetto: see below, p. 389), 658 (the follow-up to that case; here the prefect is
active together with Crescenzio *gloriosus comes*), 492, 506; he is *olim praefectus* in nn. 524 (June 1019),
587 (the 1036 text); he is *gloriosissimus* in *Papsturkunden*, n. 424 (a. 1006). For Crescenzio's career, see
esp. Halphen, *Études*, pp. 148–9 (who misses the 1006 text); this also shows that he had a career break
in 1015 when a certain Giovanni was prefect (*RF*, n. 502). For the supposed connection with
Crescenzio di Benedetto, see Brezzi, *Roma*, p. 194; Toubert, *Structures*, p. 1019n (though on
p. 1224n, in an evident lapsus, he also sees Marino as son of the *patricius* and ruler of Rome
Giovanni di Crescenzio). For Crescenzio di Benedetto as a different man but as prefect later, in
1036 (*RS*, n. 36, and cf. also *RS*, p. 245 for an account of a lost charter), see Bossi, 'I Crescenzi di
Sabina', pp. 148–9; Kölmel, *Abhandlungen*, pp. 158–9; Whitton, 'Papal policy', pp. 144–7. Kölmel
and Whitton argued that he had been prefect from as early as 1019; this is because in November 1019,
S. Gregorio, n. 14, has a Crescenzio as *urbis Romae prefectus*, but Crescenzio brother of Marino was
already *olim* in June. This is at once too positivist for me and, in its assumption of a single prefect ruling
without documentation across the whole period 1019–36, too hypothetical. Bossi, 'I Crescenzi',
pp. 119–20, thought Crescenzio brother of Marino was an Ottaviani; Kölmel saw him as 'offenbar
ein Crescentier' but stressed that there was no evidence for the link. See further below, p. 215.

'CRESCENZI'

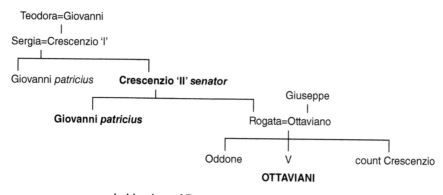

```
          Teodora=Giovanni
                 |
          Sergia=Crescenzio 'I'
       ┌─────────┴─────────────┐
Giovanni patricius      Crescenzio 'II' senator
                    ┌────────┴────────┐    Giuseppe
             Giovanni patricius       |       |
                                 Rogata=Ottaviano
                             ┌─────────┼─────────────┐
                          Oddone       V        count Crescenzio
                                   OTTAVIANI
```

bold: rulers of Rome

Genealogy 2

both the otherwise undocumented family of Crescenzio *a Caballo Marmoreo* and that of the proto-Tuscolani, who ended up later in the century with land not just in the Sabina, but also in Palestrina and Cerveteri (Pope Gregory V confiscated the last-named in 998).[57] They did not have the prominence in the city that the Crescenzi 'proper', the sons and grandson of Crescenzio di Teodora, eventually achieved, but they certainly operated on the level of the 'Meliosi' and *de Imiza*. We could add the Ottaviani, female-line descendants of the 'Crescenzi', too; but they were seldom documented in the city—their interests lay in the Sabina for the most part.

Many of these families came together in one of the most striking ecclesiastical success stories of the later tenth century, the development of the monastery of SS. Bonifacio e Alessio sull'Aventino in and after the 980s. Alexis was a new saint in the city, probably brought in from Syria by Bishop Sergios of Damascus (d.981), and his cult became very visible very fast; it was added to that of S. Bonifacio in the pre-existing monastery between 984 and 987. By 1000, the monastery, by now containing both Greek and Latin monks, became for a time a major focus of learning in Rome, and it trained the martyr-saint Adalbert of Prague, as well as Abbot Giovanni Canapario, who wrote a life of Adalbert. It was the only Roman church in our period to use relic miracles to buttress the development of its cult, doubtless because the cult was so new. We shall look at the significance Alexis had for ordinary Romans in more detail later (pp. 357–8). What is interesting for us here, however, is the range of support this cult initially had from Rome's leadership. Crescenzio 'I' became a monk here and was buried here in 984, as we have seen. In 987, both the 'Meliosi' and the Teofilatto/'Stefaniani' (in the persons of Stefania *senatrix* and her husband Benedetto *comes*) gave land to the monastery; in the same

---

[57] Ugo of Farfa, *Exceptio relationum*, pp. 64–5.

year, Leone di Giovanni *de Primicerio* sold land in Albano in a text that survives in
S. Alessio's archive, so it presumably soon ended up as a monastic gift too. In 1002,
Pope Silvester II (making a rare appearance in a Roman document), together with
Giovanni the urban prefect and a large set of slightly less important Roman
nobiliores homines, formally ratified a recently forged founding document for the
monastery. And the monastery even gained the support of the Ottonians: Otto II
came here already in 981; Otto III confirmed its properties in 996, and appears in
the monastic miracle collection giving a decorated cloak for the high altar; Giovanni
Canapario's *Vita* celebrates his arrival in Rome in 996. SS. Bonifacio e Alessio did
not keep this centrality after the 1010s, as far as we can see, but for a moment
it represented a religious aggregation which was not restricted to any faction in
the city's leadership. On the contrary: it showed the common identity of that
leadership, as a group that had the same essential reactions, expressed (doubtless)
competitively in its patronage, to an exciting new cult.[58]

There are three issues emerging from these discussions of the most influential
Roman families of the mid- to late tenth century that need particular attention,
before we move on: the changing role of titles and offices in their structure; their
wealth; and the role of women in their construction, which was unusually great by
contemporary standards—and by the standards of Roman history both before and
after. Let us look at them in turn.

The clear sense that one gains from a study of the land documents for Rome,
which (to repeat) begin to be less than occasional around 940, and reasonably
numerous around 960, is that office-holders became slowly less prominent as the
century ran on. Few palatine officials are found as actors in documents, selling or
giving land, or taking it in lease—the exceptions are *arcarii*, who perhaps gained
materially from their financial role.[59] The people who dominate these documents
were, as we have seen, from the half-dozen leading families of the city, but these are
no longer for the most part recorded as holding office, except, again, as rulers of parts
of Lazio (the Sabina, Albano), and except for a short period under Otto III. Instead,

---

[58] *S. Alessio*, nn. 2, 3 (a. 987), the 'Meliosi' and Teofilatto gifts, are the first references to
SS. Bonifacio e Alessio as the monastery's saints; n. 4 is the sale by the *de Primicerio* family; n. 5
(= *Ottonis III diplomata*, n. 209) is Otto III's confirmation; n. 1 is the 1002 ratification. The basic
analysis of the monastery in this period is Hamilton, 'The monastery of S. Alessio'; p. 271 for Otto II.
Duchesne, 'Notes sur la topographie', pp. 234–50, is still the most sensible analysis of the appearance
of the St Alexis cult in Rome, and its probable connection to the exiled bishop Sergios of Damascus,
whose epitaph in the church he publishes (p. 243); in *LP*, II, p. 256, he publishes that of Crescenzio 'I'
(d.984), a text that mentions Bonifacio but not Alessio, so is a probable *terminus post quem* for the
addition of Alexis. The refoundation of the monastery by Sergios, at the request of Benedict VII,
although likely, does not have contemporary support (*contra* Duchesne and the over-circumstantial
account in Hamilton), but was accepted by 1060: Pier Damiani, *Epistulae*, n. 72. For the miracle cult,
existing by the 1010s, see the *Miracula* (BHL, 299–300) in *AASS Jul.* IV, cols 258–61 (ch. 9 for Otto
III), and cf. Chapter 6, n. 63; for Adalbert, see Giovanni Canapario, *Vita S. Adalberti* (ch. 21 for Otto's
arrival), and Wood, *The Missionary Life*, pp. 207–15, who explores the tensions inside the monastery
shown by a comparison of the two latter texts. Note that I call the monastery 'S. Alessio' throughout
most of this book, for this is its familiar name, but will add Bonifacio in discussions of the late tenth
century, when the double name matters.

[59] *Arcarii: RS*, nn. 35, 81.

they held an elaborate array of titles, which marked them out from their aristocratic contemporaries, such as *illustris* or *eminentissimus*; at most, they were the descendants of officials, as Giovanni *de Primicerio* certainly was and the 'Meliosi' probably were. It thus seems as if the greatest aristocratic families were beginning after 960 or so to cut loose from the old official *cursus honorum* of the ninth century, and could by now operate more autonomously. Is this an optical illusion? After all, we certainly still find *vestararii*, prefects, and palatine judges in *placitum* documents and the like. But it does at least have to be said that, if we go back a century, of the seven ninth-century private documents with lay male actors, five feature an official (or, once, his son): a small sample, but a striking proportion.[60] I think we can see a change here.

Initially, as we saw, this may have been because Prince Alberico was happy to have some close associates acting as his representatives without formal office. But by a generation later, in the politically uncertain decades between 963 and the 990s, the leading families had grown into a fractious oligarchy who did not necessarily need office-holding to establish and represent social status. The great officials still had status as well; we shall see the heirs of several officials still acting as leading aristocrats in the 1020s–40s in a moment. But this may mark the very beginning of the slow decline in prominence of the palatine judges, who by the twelfth century were refashioned as professional judicial experts, by then drawn largely, as it seems, from the 'medium elite' (below, pp. 248, 274). One consequence of this shift is that status was no longer so dependent on the choices of the ruler, whether pope or *patricius*; these choices remained crucial, of course, but a family who lost formal power did not necessarily lose all social position, as is clearest in the case of the Teofilatto family. This change has plenty of Europe-wide parallels in this same period, and it is important to recognize that we can see it in Rome too. It did not at all mean that rulers could not menace and weaken such families. Benedict VIII did not destroy the 'Stefaniani' when he removed them from the countship of the Sabina in 1014, but he did their power much damage, just as, in Saxony in the same period, Henry II greatly harmed the power of Werner of Walbeck when he removed him from the marquisate of the Northern March in 1009, even though Werner remained a major magnate.[61] Total destruction of a family's social position remained conceivable as well, although we seldom see it in Europe, and do not see it in Rome. But, in its absence, families who lost office could still continue to be players, could maintain their respect, could sometimes bounce back, and could if necessary—though not yet in Rome—go it alone.

The titles of *eminentissimus*, etc., did, of course, show the importance of some sort of formalized status in Rome. Since we have no idea how or by whom the titles were conferred (or if they were conferred at all, rather than assumed), we cannot say exactly how that worked. But it is certainly significant that they existed, and that they conveyed something real when they were used; when, say, in 1007 Giovanni di [Demetrio] Melioso gave land to his *fidelis* Giovanni, it must have been relevant

---

[60] *RS*, nn. 55, 31, 87, 83, 6, 116; Marini, n. 136; exceptions are *RS*, n. 60; *Liber instrumentorum monasterii Casauriensis*, f. 74v–75r.
[61] Thietmar, *Chronicon*, VI.48–50, 90, VII.4–7.

that the lord was an *illustrissimo et clarissimo viro* and the dependant was simply a *novle* [*sic*] *viro* and the latter's son a *viro magnifico*: elite titles in a generic sense, but not necessarily high-status.[62] It is interesting, therefore, that most of the highest-status titles soon drop out of our documentary record as well. We have seen that *consul* and *senator* became restricted to the Tuscolani after the 1010s; likewise, the last reference to *eminentissimus* is 1013 (a Tuscolano reference); *gloriosus* is attested only once after 999 (a count of Galeria in 1058).[63] Only *illustris*(*simus*) survived in the eleventh century as a common epithet for top aristocrats. There was a certain simplification process here.

How rich were these aristocrats? This is exceptionally hard to tell. We have seen that churches owned effectively the whole of Rome's urban area and the Agro romano, but that they leased much of it back, precisely, to the 'old aristocratic' stratum we have been looking at. Aristocrats also had or obtained estates well beyond Rome's hinterland, often in full property, in the 'land of castles' all around the city, sometimes in the context of the ruling of territories on behalf of Rome and its rulers (the 'Stefaniani' and Ottaviani in the Sabina; Stefania *senatrix* in Palestrina; Crescenzio 'II' in Terracina, etc.). The least that we can say is that the richest families had many estates, and that these estates, leased from churches as they often were, were frequently large solid blocks of land, loci for the exercise of full economic domination, and (outside the Agro romano) of signorial rights as well.

We lack any full property lists for aristocrats in this period, unfortunately. When in 983 the executors of Stefano *de Imiza* gave a substantial set of lands (all held *iuris cui existunt*, i.e. on lease) to the monastery of S. Gregorio, this is evidently only the land he did not bequeath to his direct heirs, and not necessarily all even of that land. It did, all the same, consist of halves (in each case) of a castle and three estates, and a whole (small) lake, in Tuscia Romana, of an estate in *Campania*, of two castles south of Tivoli, of nine vineyards in Ariccia, and of lands in the city, including a house, a church, and a Tiber mill. If, then, we consider that Stefano had, as far as we can see, three children, and that it was not uncommon to hand over a maximum of a child's portion to churches in pious gift, then Stefano might have held a minimum of four times this gift, and more if he gave to more than one church.[64] A hypothetical minimum of twelve castles and twelve other estates, even if held in half-portions, is enough to live well on, and to support numerous military dependants, and as a result to be a serious player in the city, as the *de Imiza* family demonstrably was. This may give us an order of magnitude.

Another order of magnitude is offered us by the Tuscolani. Here, we have no snapshot of family possessions, however incomplete, to compare with that of the *de Imiza*; as we have seen, however, there is a case for arguing that the whole territory around Tuscolo had been leased to Gregorio of Tuscolo in perhaps the 980s, and the family kept it for two centuries. The lands they controlled directly there could

---

[62] *SMVL*, n. 27.   [63] *RF*, nn. 637, 1270.

[64] *S. Gregorio*, n. 4; cf. n. 151, an earlier gift by Stefano of part of the Settizonio monument; *RS*, nn. 67, 69, 71, 75 for salt pans; and Chapter 2, n. 19, for another estate. See in general Görich, 'Die *de Imiza*', pp. 19–27.

conceivably have amounted to a solid block of up to 100 km², over twice the size of S. Ciriaco's Silva Maior, and demonstrably a sufficient base for a regional-level military protagonism until the final Roman destruction of Tuscolo in 1191.[65] Outside Tuscolo, by contrast, the family is documented much less securely: a church and some land in the Velletrano, the castle of Mazzano in Tuscia Romana, vineyards and fields in Albano, and at Fiano and Scorano in Tuscia Romana, a salt pan at Porto, and land in and beside the city exhaust the list before 1100. This is a small set.[66] Although we cannot regard it as anything approaching a full sample, given the gaps in our documentation, it certainly implies that Tuscolo and its territory was by far the family's major resource; and, given that the Tuscolani seem to have been the principal family in Rome, it is likely that this is the outer limit of individual aristocratic wealth—it is maybe more than the *de Imiza*, but, if so, not overwhelmingly more. It can be added that the known lands of the 'Stefaniani' and Ottaviani—several castles in the Sabina and Tiburtino in each case, plus for the former the city of Palestrina and, more briefly, Cerveteri—are at the same order of magnitude as well, though this was complicated by a much more unstable history of gains and losses of land.[67]

It is clear that Rome's leading families extended their landholding well beyond the Agro romano, and that they dealt in castles as much as did any other ambitious aristocratic family in Italy—in Europe—in and around 1000. They could extend their political interests a long way north and east of the city, as far as Rome controlled politically, which, as we have seen (pp. 36–7), was far more than other northern and central Italian cities controlled. But, although they were unusually widely spread, and held land in many places (notably Tuscolo itself) in unusually large blocks, it is not transparent that they were unusually wealthy. In Tuscany, in the Fiorentino, the 'Suavizi'—a member of whom ceded her part of the family lands to the church of S. Pier Maggiore in Florence in 1067 and thus listed them—seem to have controlled twenty-three estates, usually with castles attached, even if many will have been smaller and more fragmented than estates in central Lazio; and the 'Suavizi' were by no means the dominant family in Florentine politics (that would be the Guidi, with several other families rivalling the 'Suavizi').[68] In non-urbanized southern Tuscany, the Aldobrandeschi in 973 already had at least forty-five castles and estates. We cannot say that the 'Suavizi' outmatched the Tuscolani or the *de Imiza* (indeed, I would doubt it, at least for the former), but the Guidi did by 1100, at the latest, and the Aldobrandeschi did

---

[65] Beolchini, *Tusculum II*, pp. 59–68, 78–82.

[66] *S. Gregorio*, n. 68; *RS*, nn. 64, 124, 126; *Papsturkunden*, nn. 481, 577; *SMN*, n. 71; Gattola, *Historia*, pp. 232–6; Hoffmann, 'Petrus diaconus', n. 2; *Velletri*, n. 6; *SMCM*, n. 1. In the twelfth century, they expanded substantially eastwards and south-eastwards from Tuscolo: see Beolchini, *Tusculum II*, pp. 82–4, and cf. below, p. 255.

[67] The best analysis is Whitton, 'Papal policy', pp. 125–54.

[68] ASF S. Pier Maggiore, 27 febb. 1066 [1067], cf. S. Pier Maggiore, 19 dic. 1066; see Cortese, *Signori, castelli, città*, pp. 36–43, 61–5 (including other parallel families and convenient maps), 98–100, 231–2, 356–65, and also below, p. 252. For fragmentation see classically Conti, *La formazione*, I, esp. pp. 133–43.

throughout.[69] And, it must be added, so did many of the baronial families of thirteenth-century Lazio, the Annibaldi and Caetani with some thirty castles each (often foci of large solid estates), the Colonna and Orsini with double that.[70] In our period, Roman families certainly dominated both the city's near and far hinterland, but they did it collectively, through their large number (if the less prominent aristocratic families, with a few estates each, are added to the leading few), rather than as individuals.

This is important, for it puts into perspective my prior remarks about the ability of leading Roman families to go it alone. In our period, this was already conceivable; a dozen castles are already enough for serious territorial politics, and the territory of Tuscolo still more so. Around Florence, this was a choice visibly made by local aristocratic families, particularly after 1100 or so: they largely separated themselves from the city, facilitated by a growing trend to territorial concentrations in the city's large *contado*.[71] But Florence was not a leading political centre (except briefly under Matilda), and was certainly not a major economic focus yet; it was not attractive enough to keep powerful political actors attached to urban politics if they had reasons to leave. Rome was an independent state, and far larger and richer. If its leading families held lands of the same rough order of magnitude as those of Florence (and often less), we might reasonably conclude that there would be less incentive to leave the city and adopt a purely rural politics; but they did so all the same, and two generations earlier. We will come back to the point shortly. It must be added, however, that there is a converse to these observations. The 'Crescenzi' may not have had time, in their brief periods of rule, to build up large landed endowments to which they could repair in more difficult times, but the Tuscolani did; and they did not take advantage of it. The basic block of Tuscolani possessions at the moment of their fall in 1044–6 does not seem significantly greater than it had been in the 990s. The Tuscolani popes had not bet on the establishment of a strong landed base for their relatives, unlike Roman popes in the thirteenth century; they had, rather, bet on the maintenance of family control over something still more important, hereditary power over the city itself. When they lost that, they were pushed back to the level of any powerful city-level aristocrat in Italy, and to well below the level of the Guidi or Aldobrandeschi. That was indeed defeat; and it would have been much less serious had they been as unscrupulous about family accumulation as Innocent III or Boniface VIII. But it shows how much they, at least, had been committed to a strategy that was overwhelmingly focused on the city.

Family identity is a difficult topic to grasp in this period, one without contemporary surnames to guide us (these are not documented before 1000, and are very rare before 1050); we cannot be sure what links individual family members thought were most relevant. But it is at least clear that female-line links were often regarded

[69] For the Aldobrandeschi, *Codex diplomaticus Amiatinus*, II, nn. 203, 206; cf. Collavini, 'Honorabilis domus', pp. 80–5; for the Guidi, Delumeau, *Arezzo*, pp. 384–410; Cortese, *Signori, castelli, città*, pp. 7–21; Collavini, 'Le basi materiali'. For non-Tuscan parallels, see below, pp. 253–4.
[70] Carocci, *Baroni*, pp. 312–16, 327–32, 353–64, 387–400, and the attached maps.
[71] Cortese, *Signori, castelli, città*, pp. 231–48.

as of significant importance. Over all, more than a third of people with recorded parents in tenth-century documents have matronymics; but, in particular, numerous aristocrats identify themselves with matronymics in our sources: Crescenzio *de Theodora*, Stefano *de Imiza*, and Gregorio *filius Maroze senatrix* are only the most prominent.[72] We know the names of the fathers of each of these, and they were in each case aristocrats as well. There was no intent to hide some form of disadvantageous or morally problematic alliance in these cases, or in any others we know of (for example, marriage to ecclesiastics—we have anyway half a dozen cases of men who claim to be bishop's sons in our documents).[73] We could possibly conclude that the status of the mother in these cases was greater than that of the father (Marozia 'II' *senatrix*, thanks to her cousinage to Prince Alberico, outranked her husband Teofilatto, even if he was a *vestararius*), but it would be unwise to assume this in all our examples. We can, conversely, conclude with some certainty that, in general, families who privileged descent from a mother rather than a father regarded mother's kin as at least as relevant as a source of political loyalty, and, perhaps, identity itself, as the kin of the father. The question is what this means for our understanding of aristocratic strategies.

The big debates about the changing structures of early medieval European aristocratic families are a generation old, and indeed more: it was Karl Schmid in the 1950s who first proposed that the early medieval aristocratic *Sippe* was a cognatic kin-group, which included female-line relations, and was relatively wide and flexible—and also less politically focused—by comparison with the central medieval patrilineal *Geschlecht* or lineage. The latter, in Germany, crystallized along Carolingian royal models, but only after the power of the state had notably weakened in the eleventh century and later, and families had to go it alone. Male-line inheritance, surnames, and a reduced and often ambiguous social role for women, thus went together with the growth of local autonomous power for these lineages. In the 1960s and 1970s, this theory was both criticized and refined, as it was pointed out (for example) that patrilineal links were more important before 1000 or so than Schmid thought, that cognatic links could survive later, and also that lineage consciousness could equally be found in strong central medieval states, such as England. The core of the model has survived, all the same; a more nuanced version of it can be found in Régine Le Jan's influential 1995 analysis of Frankish aristocracies, in which she argues that the fully cognatic *Sippe* was replaced in the tenth century by a bilateral pattern, in which 'power was transmitted in the paternal and nobility in the maternal line'.[74] It was different in Italy, however. Cinzio

---

[72] Hubert, Évolution générale', p. 593; di Carpegna Falconieri, 'Le trasformazioni onomastiche', p. 614 (the two have differing figures).

[73] *LP*, II, p. 252; *RS*, n. 130; *SMVL*, nn. 7, 39, 66; *RF*, nn. 420, 906 (the latest, in 1060); *SCD*, n. 48.

[74] Schmid, *Gebetsdenken*, pp. 183–244 (a republication of a 1957 article); among very many contributions to the debate subsequently, important points of reference include Duby, *Hommes et structures*, pp. 267–85, 406–16; Leyser, *Medieval Germany*, pp. 168–89; Stafford, 'Women and the Norman Conquest' (which highlights a more nuanced gender analysis of the issue than was common in the earlier continental debate); Le Jan, *Famille et pouvoir* ('la puissance se transmettait en ligne paternelle et la noblesse en ligne maternelle'; quote at p. 433).

Violante pointed out in 1977 that early medieval aristocratic family structures were particularly patrilineal in the Lombard parts of the peninsula, so did not change very substantially as one moved from the tenth century into the eleventh and twelfth, and the world of surnames. This survived even the introduction of Roman law in many of the cities of the Centre-North, for, as Manlio Bellomo showed, it reduced, very greatly, the amount of property granted to wives at marriage. This was not matched by an increase in the amount daughters could inherit, which was supposed in Roman law to match the rights of sons, because married daughters were simply excluded from inheritance. The male lineage remained dominant as a result.[75]

Rome fits these latter patterns only in part, because it always lived by Roman law. At the start of our period and for a long time, daughters were accustomed to inherit in ways analogous to sons, which will have helped the cognatic underpinnings of family identity; into the twelfth century, female inheritance in the city was much more extensive than it was in most of the rest of Italy. In the twelfth century, as we shall see later for the city as a whole (p. 316), female inheritance diminishes substantially in our texts. Although this was not yet universal—the aristocratic holders of Civita Castellana in 1195, for example, certainly included both sons and daughters of previous holders—by the thirteenth century the baronial houses excluded female inheritance even more fully than did the laws of the northern city-states.[76] Rome thus developed, eventually, in the same male-lineage direction as did the rest of Italy. All the same, throughout the period of this book, daughters had access to quite a lot of land, and, as late as the early twelfth century, even surnamed families seem to have been happy to see land move to families with different surnames without difficulty (as classical Roman *gentes* already did, and as modern British or Italian surnamed families do as well). This in the end complicated family identity under the Roman empire, as students of the fourth- to sixth-century imperial families and the *gens Anicia* know,[77] as it does also today. But what effect did it have on a tenth-century Rome without surnames? Were there, in fact, bounded concepts of family at all in that period? Or is it illegitimate for us, in the end, to use our customary terminology, Tuscolani, 'Crescenzi', 'Stefaniani', 'Meliosi', Ottaviani, or whoever else, which tends to privilege the male line, at least in our own reconstructions? Were our families, rather, simply Schmidian *Sippen*, although in a decisively non-Germanic context, with individuals seeking alliances with kin of different kinds, competitively, in all directions?

This latter view would have been very easy to accept when the opinions of Bossi and Kölmel, and later Toubert, dominated: that the Tuscolani and Crescenzi were all descended by male and female lines from exactly the same ancestors, in the early tenth century. But even if these views are corrected in the ways I have proposed,

[75] Violante, 'Quelques caractéristiques'; Bellomo, *Ricerche sui rapporti patrimoniali*, pp. 1–25, 163–85.

[76] *LC*, I, nn. 178–83 for Civita Castellana; for the thirteenth century, Carocci, *Baroni*, pp. 160–5. See Chapter 5, n. 128, for the bibliography on Roman marriage, inheritance, and family structures, which is not restricted to the aristocracy.

[77] See e.g. Brubaker, 'Memories of Helena'.

some important female-line connections impose themselves among the upper aristocracy. Most notably, the close link between Prince Alberico and his cousins Marozia 'II' and Stefania, which is explicit in the only land document for Alberico himself, from 945, and which is assumed also in the fact that the cousins called themselves *senatrix* thereafter, was entirely female-line, through their respective mothers who were sisters (Marozia 'I' ruler of Rome and her sister Teodora 'II', both already titled *senatrix*). This link was further stressed by Marozia 'II''s heirs the Tuscolani, who, as we have seen, claimed kinship with Prince Alberico and used both Alberico and Teofilatto as personal names.[78] Similarly, the Ottaviani picked up the personal name Crescenzio for family members immediately after Ottaviano di Giuseppe married Rogata, sister of the *patricius* Giovanni di Crescenzio. The 'Stefaniani' did not pick up names from their stepmother Stefania's side, but their own use of the name Crescenzio is plausibly taken from their maternal grandfather Crescenzio *a Caballo Marmoreo*. Naming and titles are an important part of identity, so these are clear signs that the female line was similarly important.

I am happy to accept this general point. It fits with the constant privileging of sisters alongside brothers as participants in public acts, as with the participation of Costanza abbess of S. Maria Tempuli along with her three brothers (who appear elsewhere as sons *de Imiza*) in a court case of 977 over their collectively held property claimed by S. Lorenzo fuori le Mura, even though Costanza had moved to the religious sphere; or of the son and two married daughters of Demetrio di Melioso, who gave a collective gift in 987 to SS. Bonifacio e Alessio.[79] This in itself fits with the wider evidence for the standard division of landed possessions between daughters and sons, already referred to, throughout this early period. Daughters/sisters clearly did not move into a wholly different social network when they married. All the same, we cannot easily extend that common sociability into the next generation, with female-line cousins; except for the Tuscolani, I have not found such patterns. The Ottaviani, for example, notwithstanding some Crescenzian names, followed the Sabina-focused politics of their paternal ancestors, not the Roman politics of the 'Crescenzi'. Furthermore, notwithstanding the frequency of matronymics, most families that can be constructed by us from the documents are in the male line; daughters are recorded, but we can seldom track their own heirs.

What I would argue, in fact, is for the importance of female-line links in a kinship system that was for the most part structured by patrilineality. In this reading, it would be the Tuscolani who were the exceptions, and the reason for it is clear: the strong desire of female-line kin to attach themselves to the unparalleled prestige of Prince Alberico, whose own male heirs, it is worth remembering, were extinguished with John XII's death in 964. What is highly likely is that there were very many more female-line genealogical links between the various leading Roman 'old aristocratic' families than we know. Indeed, we could scarcely doubt it, given aristocratic tendencies to endogamy (this is too early a period for us to find a large-

[78] *S. Gregorio*, n. 68; see further above, n. 44.
[79] *RS*, n. 120 (a. 977) with Görich, 'Die *de Imiza*', p. 9; for 987, *S. Alessio*, n. 2, and cf. *SMVL*, n. 27, for a division between the same siblings.

scale recourse to marriage links with extra-Lazial aristocratic families; that would be a twelfth-century trend). But, given that this means that the families we have looked at certainly did indeed intermarry, it is also significant that we know little about it. Stefano *de Imiza* wanted to tell us what his mother's name was, implying a connection with her birth family, but he never gives us any guidance as to who her relatives actually were. We can say interestingly little about marriage strategies in general, indeed, across our period. (It may be added that we also cannot say much about strategies by which families located extra male children in the church, or female children in nunneries, even though Rome's nunneries were fairly numerous, and often status-filled—S. Ciriaco in Via Lata was founded by the Teofilatto family itself—for the documents tell us too little about family affiliations here.) Women could certainly be politically and socially active in Rome, but I conclude that they did so in the framework of largely, even though not exclusively, patrilineal families. For this reason, the network of historians' names, Tuscolani, 'Crescenzi', etc., seems to remain reasonably sound, as long as they are used with care.

The eleventh century sees a change in the 'old aristocracy': a change that can be centred on the Tuscolano period. The regime change of 1012 did not result in any dramatic shifts in either the office-holders or the leading families of the city; the urban prefect Crescenzio, as we have seen, was the same man off and on from 1006 to 1017, Giovanni *primicerius* served from 1005 to 1013, Giorgio *arcarius* from 1011 to 1017, Gregorio *primicerius defensorum* from 998, under Otto III, until 1014—and these are minimum terms, simply following the documents that survive.[80] But across the third of a century of Tuscolano power (1012–44), the major families become slowly less prominent in our city documentation. This is not helped by a sharp drop in the number of court cases, our best source for the membership of political society, after *c.*1020, but the process is beginning to be visible already in the 1010s; furthermore, even in our private documents the families we have looked at become less clearly delineated, with the sole exception of the Ottaviani. Let us look at what we can say about them.

The 1010s mark the last (relatively) dense set of records of the *placitum romanum*, with their roll-calls of Roman political society; thirteen of them survive, as many as there will be for the rest of the century, until *placitum* documents fade out in the 1090s.[81] They show a slightly different social profile to earlier court case texts, in that new families are prominent in them. This in itself is not remarkable; most of the families we have just looked at were newly documented in the mid-tenth century as we have seen, and it was high time for new ones to appear. But there are now differences, all the same. Take the very formal tribunal that Benedict VIII set up in front of the castle of Tribuco in the Sabina in August 1014, part of his military campaign against the 'Stefaniani': here, the pope had evidently brought Rome's political establishment to back up his confiscation of the castle of Bocchignano from Crescenzio di Benedetto. Present were

80 Halphen, *Études*, pp. 148, 98, 119, 126. For the urban prefect Crescenzio, above, p. 201.
81 See Chapter 7, n. 5, for a list; see further pp. 387–95 for the *placitum* in general.

four of the palatine judges, five *iudices dativi* (judicial experts with less standing), five city abbots, and two *comites* (one an Ottaviani, present with his brothers); and then at least twenty-eight members of the non-office-holding urban elite. Some of these were related to palatine judges: Costantino and Crescenzio *de Arcario a loco Transtyberim* and Beraldo *filius Primus defensor de Cavallo marmoreo*. Others, however, were simply described as coming from the *regiones* of Rome (as these last-named also were): Stefano and Perinzo *a Sancto Eustachio*, Elperino and Roizone *a Via Lata*, Giovanni di Stefano *a Campo Martio*; or else have something which was uncommon in the previous century, nicknames or surnames: Leone Fragapane, Benedetto Boccapecu.[82]

When these men, and others in the 1010s' court cases, gain definition in our sources, they will emerge as a different social stratum, called here the 'new aristocracy'; I will come back to them shortly. They are relevant here, however, in that they show that something was already changing by the 1010s: these new families do not call themselves by the old titles, even *consul et dux*, never mind *eminentissimus*, and, when we see them in operation elsewhere, they are urban and suburban dealers, not castle-holders or large rural landholders. The last years of Giovanni di Crescenzio and the first of Benedict VIII saw Rome's rulers look to a less rich and much more urban social category for the first time. In another case, of 1015, in which Farfa faced off Pope Benedict's brother Romano *consul et dux et omnium Romanorum senator* (the future Pope John XIX) over some land near Tribuco, Benedict heard the case in his own room in the Laterano palace, together with—unusually—his *fideles*, that is, his personal dependants: they included his other brother Alberico and some officials, but also men from both the 'old' and 'new aristocracy'; Giovanni di [Demetrio] Melioso, but also men from S. Eustachio and SS. Apostoli, and Leone Cece, ancestor of a family of supporters of Gregory VII.[83]

The old families were clearly there, then, as yet; but what happened to them from now on? The Ottaviani, as already noted, are the easiest to track, for they took over control of the Sabina, and thus, thanks to Farfa's unusually extensive documentation, stay in the spotlight to an extent. They ruled in the Sabina until around 1060, when they lost power for a time, probably as a direct result of the actions of Nicholas II, and they also lost the castles of Arci and Tribuco in 1060–1 to Farfa; they were sometimes counts/rectors of the Sabina later, but the Sabina was by then itself losing coherence as a *comitatus*, and in effect fragmented into its myriad castle territories. The Ottaviani remained on extremely poor terms with Farfa (in 1119 some Farfa monks refused to have any member of the *Octavianisca consanguinitas* as abbot, the first time that our name for the family has any justification in contemporary sources), and they lost their lands in the central Sabina around the monastery; in the twelfth century their power was focused on the Sabina–Tivoli borderlands, in Palombara, Mentana, Monticelli, and Monte Albano, and their shift in focus eastwards and southwards is already shown by the election of one of their number as Abbot Giovanni III of Subiaco in *c*.1065.[84] All

---

[82] *RF*, n. 492.   [83] *RF*, n. 502.

[84] *Chronicon Sublacense*, p. 12. *Octavianisca: CF*, II, p. 293. For the Ottaviani as counts, see Vehse, 'Die päpstliche Herrschaft', esp. pp. 144–59.

the same, the Ottaviani remained active and powerful, less powerful in the twelfth century than the eleventh, but serious players in Rome's countryside; they held signorial rights in Silva Maior, not far from Monticelli, up to 1199 (pp. 70, 76). But that was also, by now, the closest they got to Rome. They do not appear in the papal entourage, or in any Roman documents after 1014. They probably supported the papal bid of Silvester III in 1044, bishop of the Sabina as he was, and certainly that of Victor IV in 1159, who was a member of the family, but neither pope gained much purchase in Rome.[85] They had never been closely linked to Rome, but by now had become an entirely rural family, focused on their castle-holding.

Something of the same process is visible for the 'Stefaniani'. Crescenzio di Benedetto was urban prefect in 1036, as we have seen; but after that his family, too, vanish from Rome. They kept castles like Empiglione, Castel S. Angelo, and Passarano, on the Tivoli–Palestrina border, and also probably held Monticelli until *c*.1060; they were also supporters of at least one pope, Benedict X (1058–9), hardly more successful a figure than Silvester III. Thereafter we cannot trace them, and so it would not be so easy to say that they had already become as rural-focused as the Ottaviani; they died out or failed only twenty years after holding a major city office, and had remained players in papal politics until the end. But they, too, no longer figure in Roman documents after the 1010s; and the *nobilissima comitissa* Imilia, widow of Crescenzio's nephew Donadeo, is explicitly stated in a Subiaco text of 1053 to be *habitatrice in Pelastrina*. The family had evidently kept a Palestrina connection, and some of them, at least, had transferred themselves there permanently.[86]

The 'Meliosi' are more shadowy still, and not as clear an example. Giovanni di Demetrio Melioso was a papal *fidelis* in 1015, as we have seen, and Gerardo di Crescentio di Melioso, if he was indeed a family member, had clear urban connections in 1088 (see above, p. 192 and below, p. 396). A case could be made for continued participation in the changing urban political system for this family. But it is at least worth noting that we cannot track them in the city in any public document between these dates. They appear in a few private documents, but they had lost their former centrality.[87] As for the *de Imiza* and the *de Primicerio* families, they vanish altogether after the 1010s; they were either marginalized or died out.[88]

Not all the newly visible families of the Tuscolano period were members of the 'new aristocracy'. As in previous generations, there were also (relatively) new families who operated by the old rules; they might simply be said to have stepped

---

[85] No surviving Roman document dates for the admittedly short pontificate of Silvester III; Victor IV is recognized in Rome in only two documents, ASR, SCD, cassetta 16, n. 135, and *S. Prassede*, n. 31, in 1162–3. For the family in the time of the latter, Schwarzmaier, 'Zur Familie Viktors IV'.

[86] See for the 'Stefaniani' n. 52 above. References to castles: *RS*, nn. 36, 34; *LP*, II, p. 335. 1053: *RS*, n. 41.

[87] For references, see above, n. 32.

[88] Görich, 'Die *de Imiza*', pp. 6, 12–13, tracks that family into the twelfth century, but the genealogical links are too hypothetical here.

into the places left by the families we have been focusing on. We can track them by their continued use of the word *illustris*, or when we find individuals, as we still do, who claimed descent from major officials. None of them are as prominent as the major tenth-century figures, but we can say a little about some of them, all the same.

One example is the urban prefect Crescenzio and his brother Marino *de Turre*, whom we have already met. Crescenzio founded the church of S. Trifone in the urban region of Campo Marzio in or just before 1006; a papal confirmation of that year shows that he had given land around the church too, even if not a huge amount. This means that Marino is almost certainly also the Marino *a Campo Marzio* in documents of 1013 and 1021, as the name is not so common; this must have been the family's urban base. Marino witnesses an urban lease of Farfa in the first of these, together (unusually) with his own *fidelis* Giovanni; in the second he held a vineyard outside Porta Flaminia. He was also active as an *adstans* in court cases from the 1010s, as we have seen, and donor to Farfa of a substantial piece of land in Ponticelli, near the monastery, in 1036. Marino calls himself *nobilis vir* in the latter document, and his wife and daughter are *nobilissimae feminae*. Where Turre, only cited in the 1036 text, was is unclear; it was almost certainly not in Rome; but that latter document has an entirely Roman—here, Pigna and Trevi— witness list, reinforcing the family's urban background.[89]

A second example is Leone *nomenculator* (possibly the holder of the office in 988–93, although our data for the office are incomplete, so he could be later). He had a brother Pietro Capolonga *nobili viro*, who co-held a salt pan with Leone's heirs in 1011; one of Leone's sons, also called Leone, witnessed a sale near the Colosseo in 1018; Leone's heirs held land on the Aurelia, west of Rome, in 1036; and Stefano *nobili viro* di Leone *de Nomiculatorem*, presumably the son of the 1018 witness, founded the rural monastery of S. Cornelio (the old *domusculta* Capracorum) in and before 1041. Only this last document gives any hint that the family was particularly prominent, but the tract of land Stefano gave in 1041 (held *iuris cui existens*, probably from the pope) was substantial, so we can at least say that they were well off.[90] A third example is Albino *arcarius*. He left a widow, Teodoranda *nobilissima femina*, who with her children sold to Farfa in 1012 half an estate at S. Colomba on the Salaria; her daughter Berta was married to Farolfo *illustris vir*. A fourth is Crescenzio *illustrissimus vir*, the son of another *arcarius*, who in 1020 leased an estate on the Aurelia from SS. Cosma e Damiano in Trastevere; this estate was bounded by two *silvae*, both co-held by the heirs of Leone *arcarius*, probably the long-serving holder of the office in 966–99, and the heirs of a certain Costantino. When we add that the Tribuco case of 1014 included as *adstantes*, as we have seen, Costantino and Crescenzio *de Arcario a loco Transtyberim*, it is not difficult to

---

[89] *Papsturkunden*, n. 424; *RF*, n. 666 and *SMVL*, n. 45; *RF*, n. 587 (a. 1036); for Crescenzio and Marino in public documents of the 1010s, see above, n. 56.

[90] Respectively, *SCD*, n. 23 (for Leone *nomiculator* [*sic*] see Halphen, *Études*, p. 133); *SMN*, n. 5; *SCD*, nn. 41, 45 (note that the monastery of S. Cornelio already existed in 1035, *SCD*, n. 40, despite Stefano's donation of the land on which the monastery stood in 1041, in a pattern quite common for monasteries).

recognize all these people as an elite Trastevere family, descended from Leone *arcarius*, who held really quite a lot of land on the Aurelia.[91] All these families seem to be operating much as did their predecessors a century earlier, leasing large blocks of land from the church and proclaiming their links to office-holders; unfortunately, none of them can be traced further with any certainty.

If we follow further the title *illustris*, the last indicator of high 'old aristocratic' status, we encounter several more people who seem to be, once again, from this same social stratum. One is Purpura *illustris femina* (or *nobilissima femina*), wife of Benedetto di Rogata, who between 1019 and 1030 willed a castle in the Tiburtino (complete with signorial rights) and an estate on the Prenestina to S. Gregorio sul Celio, leased part of an estate on the Portuense from SS. Cosma e Damiano, and leased a hill above the Vaticano from S. Pietro. Another is Guido di Bellizzo, *illustrissimum atque inclito comite . . . que appellatur de Anguillaria*, i.e. count of Anguillara (he was probably son of the Belizo *comes* of a court case of 1011), who in 1020 leased out fishing rights in the Lago di Bracciano. A third, Guido *illustrissimo viro*, who with his wife Stefania and son Ardemanno (not a very common name) ceded back to S. Ciriaco in Via Lata a lease on the Portuense in 1012, must have been the grandfather of the Guido di Ardemanno whose heirs, *illustrissimi atque nobilissimi viri*, sold the castle of Arci in the Sabina to Farfa in 1059.[92]

One family of this type is documented in slightly more detail. Giovanni *inlustrissimo vir de urbi Romen* [*sic*] di Giorgio and his wife Bona *inlustrissima femina* in 1030 founded (or re-founded) the rural monastery of S. Primo by the Lago Burrano on the Prenestina, and gave it a substantial estate between the lake and the River Aniene. The monastery did not last (by 1060 it was just a church), but this was not the only family focus. In 1049, the two founders appear again, with the same titles, this time giving a portion of Castel S. Angelo in the mountains above Tivoli to Subiaco (a new castle whose ownership they shared with the 'Stefaniani', as texts of 1036–8 show); in that text their co-donor is their son Giovanni, similarly called *illustris, habitator in castello Corcorulo*, that is to say Corcolle, 5 km east of S. Primo. Here, we have a clear demonstration of something that I postulated earlier for the 'Stefaniani' themselves: an urban aristocratic family moving out of the city. The 'Stefaniani' link remained in this case even after the family had pulled out of Castel S. Angelo; Giovanni di Giovanni witnessed Imilia of Palestrina's cession of part of the same castle in 1053.[93]

We cannot say that any of these just-cited families was actually created by the Tuscolani; their earliest prominent members almost all first appear before Benedict

[91] Albino: *RF*, n. 656. Leone's family: *SCD*, n. 25 (a. 1020); *RF*, n. 492 (a. 1014); cf. Halphen, *Études*, p. 118 for Leone.

[92] Purpura: *S. Gregorio*, n. 5; *SCD*, n. 32 (cf. nn. 31, 39); *SMVL*, n. 55. Guido di Bellizzo: CVL 8044, fos. 1–3; cf. *RF*, n. 616 for Belizo (who may be the same as the Bellizo *de Thalasu*—the lake?—in *RS*, n. 78, a. 993). Guido di Ardemanno family: *SMVL*, n. 31; *RF*, nn. 492, 903, 906 (note that the latter, a Farfa record, claims that Arci was given them by Otto III; but Farfa was *parti pris* here—it was trying to argue that the Ottaviani had no rights over the castle).

[93] See *S. Prassede*, nn. 5, 8, 9; *RS*, nn. 44 (a. 1049, Castel S. Angelo; cf. nn. 36, 34, and Toubert, *Les structures*, pp. 323, 380) and 41 (a. 1053).

VIII became pope. Nor can we be sure that any major officials of the Tuscolano period itself produced new families such as these we have just looked at, for the period is rather sparse in its evidence of their acts.[94] There is in fact only one major family who clearly owed their position to the Tuscolani, and that is the family of Gerardo *comes* of Galeria and his brother Sassone *comes de comitatu* of Civita Castellana. Galeria, on the edge of the Agro romano, seems fairly securely to have been a papal property in 1037, when Benedict IX ceded its brothel (*domus lupanaris*) to the bishop of Silva Candida, and it was a strong-point of some importance in the disturbances of the next generation; already in a text of 1026 there was a *comes Galerie*, Giovanni Tocco, one of the first *comites* in central Lazio not to be attached to an episcopal territory, and the inhabitants of Galeria are also called a *magnus populus* in the latter text, a Galeria court case—it was probably the largest settlement in the diocese of Silva Candida. Giovanni Tocco is only documented once, and exactly when Gerardo was put in is not clear, but the latter was authoritative enough in 1048 to preside over an important Farfa court case (a rather unorthodox one, but including Andrea *secundicerius* in the witness list), and the *Annales Romani* describe him as the leader of the *comites qui veniebant per montanam*, the rural lords, in support of Benedict IX in 1044. (Bonizone of Sutri, too, associates him with Benedict in a confused story.) Gerardo was clearly a Tuscolano appointment, then, perhaps put in in the 1030s; and this fits with his and his brother's consistent hostility to the 'reform' popes, which culminated in Gerardo's successful military defence of Benedict X against a Norman siege of Galeria in 1059.[95]

Gerardo was son of Raineri, whom David Whitton argues fairly convincingly to have been Marquis Raineri I of Tuscany (1014–27). Raineri was removed as marquis in favour of the Canossa family by the emperor Conrad II, but his family remained great lords in the territory of Arezzo (modern historians call them the 'Marchesi' or 'Marchiones'). More recent historians of the 'Marchiones' have not picked up on this genealogical connection, which hangs on a reading of one Farfa document; this at least shows that Gerardo and Sassone (a distinctly more shadowy figure) had transferred themselves totally to Lazio, leaving no Aretine links behind. There is no particular reason to doubt Whitton's argument, however.[96] The Tuscolani had in this case brought in an external aristocratic family, and implanted them in a strategic centre of Tuscia Romana (or two such centres, if Sassone's comital title is from the same period, which is entirely plausible), presumably as papal lessees. Gerardo had no prior Roman links (though his family did have

---

[94] Exceptions: *SMVL*, n. 58, and *SMN*, n. 9, both showing palatine judges taking land in lease in the 1030s.

[95] The best account of the family is Whitton, 'Papal policy', pp. 217–23, 227–33; the only alternative is Kölmel, *Rom*, pp. 159–60, very sketchy. Galeria as papal: *Papsturkunden*, n. 608. Giovanni Tocco: *Papsturkunden*, n. 568 (the only earlier rural *comes* documented is Guido of Anguillara). 1048: *RF*, n. 813. For Sassone and his sons, see *RF*, nn. 990, 1096–7. For the narratives, *LP*, II, pp. 331, 335; 'Vie et miracles du pape S. Léon IX', I.3; Bonizone, *Liber ad amicum*, V (p. 584); *Chronica Casinensis*, II.99.

[96] Whitton, 'Papal policy', pp. 218–21. For the Marchiones, Delumeau, *Arezzo*, pp. 307–20; Tiberini, 'Origini e radicamento'. The Farfa text is *RF*, n. 813.

independent links to Farfa), so his loyalty to the Tuscolani could be presumed. That presumption was a justified one; Gerardo's political alignment did not waver, even after 1046. But it is also striking that the only demonstrably new family under the Tuscolani are never found in Rome: they were put straight into strong-points in Tuscia Romana, and stayed there.

In synthesis: in the Tuscolano period there are fewer references to the 'old aristocracy'. There are fewer court cases to give snapshots of their prosopography. The leases we have privilege emphyteuses to their members much less, too; this is partly because the Subiaco register, which has so many, runs out in the 1010s, and because more archives from smaller Roman churches, which had fewer links with the main aristocratic families, begin around the same period; but it is also the case that the emphyteuses that still survive (including from S. Gregorio sul Celio, source for many tenth-century aristocratic documents) are also to less prominent people.[97] So, certainly, are the *libelli* of smaller blocks of land, which are increasingly numerous, as we saw in Chapter 2 (pp. 56, 80). We also have fewer aristocratic donations to Roman churches, which had in the tenth century been an important element of 'old aristocratic' activity, and this seems in itself to be a less ambivalent mark of social change: these families were less involved in the city's ecclesiastical patronage, and thus in the world of our documentation. And this is also the conclusion I draw from what we do know about the old leading families. The great tenth-century families either died out or moved to the countryside, with the probable exception of the 'Meliosi'. Their eleventh-century successors often did the same, most obviously Guido of Anguillara, the family of Giovanni di Giorgio, and of course the *comites* of Galeria, who never had an urban foothold at all. We certainly cannot say that they all did; we do not have enough information about the heirs of Leone *arcarius* or Purpura *illustris femina* to be sure what happened to them. But we cannot track with certainty a single family from those described in this section into the slightly better-documented urban politics of the period 1050–1150, and only the 'Meliosi' show any even probable continuity. They did not participate in the battles over papal 'reform', or, if they did, they did so as members of the 'counts who were around the city', in the words of the *Annales Romani*: as external, not internal, forces.[98] After 1046, their numbers were powerfully swelled by the defeated Tuscolani themselves, who henceforth operated from their own extra-urban power-centre. The Tuscolani, 'Stefaniani', Ottaviani, and the counts of Galeria led this group; and they did so from castles on the edge of or beyond the Agro romano.

I argued earlier that the attraction of Rome was rather greater than that of (say) Florence, to aristocratic families with a dozen or so castles who wanted to be political players. Actually, in many cities, large cities like Milan or medium-sized ones like Cremona and Lucca, some urban aristocrats continued throughout the eleventh century and beyond to involve themselves in urban politics, even if they had castles; and even in Florence the moment of social separation from the city

---

[97] *S. Gregorio*, nn. 131, 169, 52, 13.   [98] *LP*, II, pp. 331, 334.

was not until the early twelfth, after the chaos of the civil war period.[99] In Rome, by contrast, the families we are looking at left urban politics rather earlier, in the second quarter of the eleventh century, even though Rome was so rich and powerful; and it is hard to see why Monticelli or Corcolle or Palestrina might have been more attractive bases than the Quirinale or the Aventino. It is thus tempting to regard the ruralization of Rome's 'old aristocracy' as a direct mark of political failure, after the Tuscolani moved against the 'Stefaniani', and after Henry III moved against the Tuscolani. That was, indeed, a dominant interpretation in the twentieth century. It works for the Tuscolani; but not, it has to be said, for any other family: the Ottaviani were patronized by the Tuscolani, but still had little to do with the city; the 'Stefaniani' were back in favour in Rome by the mid-1030s, but were also shifting out of the city's orbit in the same period. Political failure does not, therefore, work as an overall explanation.

In the absence of dense evidence about the Tuscolano regime, there is no final answer to this problem. But three elements can be isolated, two certain, one more hypothetical, which can help us to understand how it was that 'old aristocratic' families left the city. One is that the 1010s already saw the first appearance of newer families, the leaders of Rome's *regiones*, in the relatively numerous *placita* of the period: families who were less rich and much more urban-focused. Both Giovanni di Crescenzio and Benedict VIII were widening their political base. They did not do that at the direct expense of the older families (indeed, it is likely, as we shall see in a moment, that the newer families eventually felt they did not have enough), but there was only so much patronage to go around. Secondly, slightly later on, the few public documents for the 1020s–30s also show a greater participation of cardinals, that is, in general, leading churchmen, in what was after all the solidest papal-dominated regime since the ninth century (below, p. 392). This tradition, of using ecclesiastical office-holders in secular public acts, would be taken further under Hildebrand in the 1060s–70s, but started here. We do not know the family background of most Tuscolano cardinals, but clerical careers were more likely than secular ones to be open to men whose origins were not from the 'old aristocracy'. The three-decade Tuscolano regime thus, quite plausibly, owed its stability to a slightly wider social base than did its predecessors. There would have been less space in their patronage networks for the traditional families as a result.

We also need to be cautious about the attractions of stability for the 'old aristocracy'. Rome's politics was not normally very stable in any period of the Middle Ages; indeed, it owed much of its attraction to the continual changes of regime every five or ten years, with each new pope. Families who were out of favour would scheme to return next time; families in favour would scheme to fix the decision-making mechanisms, so as to stay on top. All sorts of realignments in the pecking order of power could be planned for, and political actors both wanted and needed to stay in the city to achieve their ends. But it must swiftly have become clear who would succeed Benedict VIII, and that his brother Romano would not, as

---

[99] Keller, *Signori e vassalli*, pp. 173–207, 246–51; Wickham, 'Economia e società rurale'; Cortese, *Signori, castelli, città*, pp. 231–48.

John XIX, change the regime at all; nor would their nephew Benedict IX—who was younger, thus marking a possible generation change, but who was unlikely to change much initially, while his father Alberico *comes palatii* was alive.[100] This stability was already a feature of the Alberician period, without any sign that families were leaving Rome then; but now the appearance of castles and the possibilities of rural lordship created a political alternative which had not existed previously. The main families also had relatively concentrated zones of influence, around Palestrina or Tuscolo, or between Galeria and Civita Castellana, or in the Sabina; there was not here the scatter of holdings that kept some northern Italian dioceses together for rather longer. So: now that there was less to do politically in the city, it would have been easier than previously for 'old aristocratic' families to transfer their attention to the castles and provincial towns under the direct control of each, even while maintaining links to Rome. These links might thereafter, across three decades, have become ever more formal, perhaps restricted to major cere-monial moments of the year such as Easter.

This is the hypothetical part; for exactly how the older families did link themselves to John XIX and Benedict IX has no useful documentation at all. But we do know that several of them maintained Tuscolano loyalties into the 1050s; the counts of Galeria supported Benedict IX and then Benedict X; the Ottaviani may have supported Silvester III against the former, but certainly swung behind the latter, as did the 'Stefaniani'.[101] This rearguard loyalty was after the end of the stable Tuscolano regime, an end which occurred with the revolt of 1044, so it is unlikely that these families had felt, or become, marginalized or oppositional in the decades of real Tuscolano power. But their links to the ruling family had not prevented them from drifting out of the city. And, once Tuscolano power had gone, they could not easily get back. In the upheavals of the 1040s and onwards, the *comites* were by now seen as external to Rome. The 'old aristocracy', which had dominated urban politics since at least 750, had turned into an outside force, in the most tranquil period for fifty years into the past and well over a century into the future. They left the field to much smaller families. The 'new aristocracy' would end up as dominant as their predecessors, but it would take another hundred years and more for this transformation to work itself through.

THE 'NEW ARISTOCRACY'

Rome's new leading stratum, as we have seen, begins to take form after the year 1000. Their members appear in public acts in the 1010s; and, increasingly from then on, in a variety of leases, usually *libelli*, both from newly documented churches and

---

[100] Alberico is last documented in *SCD*, n. 32 verso (a. 1030); he is dead by 1045 (Borgia, *Istoria*, pp. 167–8); but 'Vie et miracles du pape S. Léon IX', I.1, claims that he organized his son's simoniac election, which would mean he would have had to be alive in 1032; see also Beolchini, *Tusculum II*, p. 68, for a citation of him acting during Benedict's pontificate (and also p. 69 for Gregorio di Alberico, acting for his papal brother in 1036–43).

[101] *LP*, II, pp. 331, 334–5; 'Vie et miracles du pape S. Léon IX', I.3.

monasteries such as S. Maria Nova and S. Maria in Campo Marzio, and also from a smaller number of monasteries (S. Gregorio sul Celio and S. Ciriaco in Via Lata) whose documentation started earlier and carried on throughout our period. Only one family from this stratum can be traced earlier than the 990s, the Frangipane: they were descended from the Pietro *qui et* Imperiola who is, as we saw, the only person listed as a participant in the 963 Rome synod who is referred to as *de plebe*.[102] In the next half-century, a dozen similar families crystallized out of the top levels of the urban commercial and *rentier* elite, and emerged as politically active and, increasingly, surnamed families: early surnames are indeed associated with this stratum, and not the 'old aristocracy'. We do not know exactly why the Romans revolted against Benedict IX in 1044, but it cannot be easily doubted that it was the 'new aristocracy' that led the revolt; we will come back to this point (p. 245). They adapted themselves quickly to the new German-led regime. Indeed, the first document that gives us a full list of them is the best parallel in the post-1046 period to the 963 Rome synod or the 1014 Tribuco *placitum* as a roll-call of the city's elite: Nicholas II's Arci court case from April 1060. This is where we shall start, then, before working through in greater detail what we know of them.

The Arci case was similar to that at Tribuco in more than one way; for, in it, Pope Nicholas II and his archdeacon Hildebrand moved formally to remove the Ottaviani from the castle of Arci in the Sabina, in favour of the monastery of Farfa, much as Benedict VIII had removed the 'Stefaniani' from Bocchignano in 1014. The difference was that this time the pope simply did this through a court case in Rome, rather than after military action. (The Ottaviani did not turn up, and waited before they came to terms; but they did so exactly a year later, ceding not only Arci but Tribuco as well, which they had leased from Farfa subsequent to the 1014 *placitum*, for the massive pay-off of £126.) The case was the most formal documented gathering of the city's political community for a generation. Its witnesses began with five cardinals, plus two external bishops and Hildebrand as archdeacon; then followed Giovanni the urban prefect (this was Giovanni Tignoso from Trastevere, who had been appointed in January 1059 as one of Nicholas' first acts), five palatine judges, and two *dativi iudices*; then thirty-five lay witnesses, almost all of them clearly Roman—the only exception being two of the Guidi counts from north-east Tuscany, presumably present because Nicholas was also bishop of Florence. As usual, we cannot trace all of them; but those whom we can trace are significant.[103]

The list of the laity begins with Cencio *de Praefecto*, son either of the current prefect or of a predecessor. There were two Cencios who were the sons of prefects in this period, in fact: Cencio di Giovanni, who succeeded his father in the 1060s; and his rival Cencio di Stefano, who supported Honorius II/Cadalo of Parma in 1062 and imprisoned Gregory VII briefly in 1075, and whose brother killed Cencio di Giovanni in 1077—these being the most prominent Roman causes célèbres of the early Gregorian papacy. Since he was later so opposed to Hildebrand, historians

---

[102] Liutprando of Cremona, *Historia Ottonis*, ch. 9.
[103] *RF*, n. 906. For context, see also nn. 903–5 (905 is the pay-off).

tend to assume that Cencio di Stefano was absent from the great gathering of April 1060, but we cannot be sure of that, and Cencio di Giovanni was perhaps too junior (his father had only been prefect for a year) to head such a list as yet. Then follow Leone di Benedetto Cristiano, a close associate of Hildebrand and ancestor of the Pierleoni; Alberto di Ottone Curso, the first known named member of the Corsi family; Giovanni Bracciuto, from a prominent Trastevere family; Conte and Bertramo di Giovanni di Guido, Giovanni probably being the Giovanni *de Arci-praesbitero* who witnessed a court case in 1017;[104] Benedetto de *Aepiscopo*, clearly also from a high-status clerical family; and Cencio Fraiapane, the commonest early spelling of the Frangipane. The next two names belong to men who do witness elsewhere, but not in such a way as to tell us more about them; Giovanni di Balduino follows, who we know from a private document to have been an *opifex* or artisan;[105] then the first totally untraceable name; then two of the Tuscolani, Benedict IX's brothers, quite far down the list, and the only prominent 'old aristocrats' mentioned in the document, apart from the contumacious Ottaviani. Almost none of the rest of the list can be traced elsewhere, except for the Guidi counts from Tuscany near the end, and, with them, two members of the Sant' Eustachio family; but two more artisans, a goldsmith and a weaver, appear along the way, and one identifiable member of the 'medium elite' of Pigna, Durante di Giovanni di Atria (below, p. 283). It is reasonable to assume that after the Frangipane the witnesses become for the most part less prominent, with some notable exceptions. But up to then, the Arci text is a nearly complete list of Rome's new leadership in this early generation. Only one family that is prominent anywhere else in these decades is certainly absent, the *filii Baruncii*. The political aggregation around Nicholas and Hildebrand, a year after the fall of Benedict X, was the most extensive there would be for the next half-century.

So let us use the text as a guide, and look at its members more closely. We shall start with the families of those whom we know to have been at Nicholas' assembly: first, three heavily Hildebrandine families, the Pierleoni, the family of Giovanni Tignoso, and the Bracciuti; then two families prominent enough to take an independent line on occasion, the Corsi and the Frangipane. We shall next look at three oppositional families, the Sant' Eustachio, that of Cencio di Stefano, and the *filii Baruncii*, the third certainly absent in 1060, the first and perhaps the second present. We will then discuss a number of families (the Ceci, the *filii Astaldi*, the Normanni) who were not prominent in the political aggregations of the 1060s, but appear more clearly later in the century; then, finally, two families new in the twelfth century, the Boboni and the Papareschi. This will again involve a bit of exposition, but at least brief accounts are needed, as most of these families are poorly studied—the Pierleoni, at least, are reasonably well known, but only the Frangipane have a good recent published analysis.[106] That exposition will also give

---

[104] For this link, see *RF,* n. 504 and *SMVL,* n. 63.
[105] *S. Prassede,* n. 8.
[106] Thumser, 'Die Frangipane'. For general analyses of these families as a group, see Hüls, *Kardinäle, Klerus,* pp. 260–8; Moscati, *Alle origini,* pp. 124–38; Thumser, *Rom,* pp. 24–204;

us the data needed in order to analyse the 'new aristocracy' as a whole with greater confidence. At the end, we will look at one key issue, which was raised at the start of this chapter: how we can tell that these families were a distinct aristocratic stratum at all.

The Pierleoni first, then. Leone di Benedetto Cristiano is the first member of the family to be attested, as a *vir magnificus* and *negotiator*, leasing olive groves outside Porta S. Paolo from SS. Cosma e Damiano in Trastevere in 1051; his sons also held a mill on the Isola Tiberina, probably from the same monastery, by 1072. The story that the family had Jewish origins, which was already current by the late eleventh century, is confirmed by the epithet *Christianus* (i.e. 'convert') for Leone's father; but their conversion was probably not recent in 1051, for Leone's father has that epithet, not the merchant himself. Leone was very close to Archdeacon Hildebrand, and near-contemporary sources say that Leone was the dealer who paid off the Roman people with *pecunia*, on behalf of Hildebrand, to weaken the urban support of Benedict X in 1058–9 and Honorius II/Cadalo in 1062–4. Leone was probably dead by 1072 and his heirs were maybe young, for Pietro di Leone, his only named son, is visibly active rather later—he was prominent from the late 1090s to the 1120s, dying between 1124 and 1130. In that context, he is reported to have taken control over Castel S. Angelo for Urban II in 1098, to have put up Urban in his house beside S. Nicola in Carcere, where the pope died in 1099, to have facilitated the election of Paschal II immediately afterwards by paying off the Tuscolani, and then to have acted as the firmest supporter for Paschal and his two successors, including when Paschal fell out with the Corsi (see below). Pietro di Leone had eight sons and at least two daughters, who are the first people who can properly be called 'Pierleoni', after their father (and the surname is contemporary); this generation was active into the mid-twelfth century, and one of their number, Pietro Pierleoni, became a cardinal, at SS. Cosma e Damiano in Foro in 1112 (as a deacon) and at S. Maria in Trastevere in 1120 (as a priest), before becoming Pope Anacletus II in 1130.[107]

Petersohn, *Kaisertum und Rom*, pp. 162–71 (drawing on Petersohn, 'Der Brief', which is more restricted but more detailed). The family reconstructions in most of these need to be viewed with caution; Thumser, *Rom*, the most detailed by far, is much more careful, but focuses for the most part on the period after 1150. Moscati and Thumser both discuss more families than are analysed here. Note that the family histories in the collection entitled *Le grandi famiglie romane* seem to me mostly valueless, and I do not cite them.

[107] The best account of the early Pierleoni is Whitton, 'Papal policy', pp. 185–202; Fedele, 'Le famiglie', is the only fully published study, but is often problematic (not least in his attempt to link Gregory VI and VII to the family). Note that the frequent claim that Benedetto's original name was Baruch is an invention (accepted by Fedele, 'Le famiglie', p. 402), and has no justification at all. For the data cited here, in order, see: *SCD*, nn. 56 (a. 1051), 73 (a. 1072); *LP*, II, pp. 334, 336; cf. Benzone of Alba, *Ad Heinricum IV*, II.4, 9 (who is the first to stress the family's Jewish origins). For Pietro di Leone, esp. *LP*, II, p. 294; *LC*, I, p. 329; Sigebert of Gembloux, *Chronica*, p. 369; *CF*, II, pp. 232–3; *Liber Pontificalis*, ed. Přerovský, pp. 712, 720, 728, 734, 753–4; *Bullaire Cal. II*, n. 176. Most of his children are listed in Roger II's 1134 diploma, ed. Kehr, 'Diploma purpureo', pp. 258–9. For Pietro Pierleoni, Hüls, *Kardinäle, Klerus*, pp. 225, 189–91; and, in general, Palumbo, *Lo schisma*, and Stroll, *The Jewish Pope*. For Pierleoni financial support, see the overeager account in Zema, 'The houses of Tuscany and of Pierleone', pp. 169–75.

The Pierleoni were evidently financial dealers on a large scale, and Leone was a *vir magnificus*—as many merchants were, but signifying rank and respect—already in 1051.[108] We do not have to believe every story of their monetary pay-outs for popes (all of them popes in the Hildebrandine 'reform' tradition) to recognize that they had plenty of liquid cash, in coins or ingots (cf. above, p. 172). They had at least one mill, and we have seen how profitable these were (p. 151). They were based in the Isola Tiberina and immediately over the bridge to the left bank of the Tiber near S. Nicola in Carcere (probably the family church), and are not documented elsewhere in the city (including not ever in Trastevere, notwithstanding many claims to that effect in the literature). They may have disbursed money for the popes—not always their own money, we should remember—but they also gained handsomely from their support, as Caffaro di Caschifellone noted in his accounts of pay-offs to Roman clerics and laymen in return for cessions to the Genoese in 1120 (see further below, pp. 401–2): the Pierleoni got 155 silver marks (just over £100) from that set of transactions, plus jewellery for Pietro Leone and his wife. Similarly, the family got 240 *unciae* of gold annually (about 20 per cent more than Caffaro's one-off payment) from Roger II of Sicily in 1134, in return for their *fidelitas* to the rulers of the South, and perhaps had done so since the beginning of the century.[109] This is, significantly, an account of treasure, not land; and, indeed, if our Roman documents give us an accurate picture, the Pierleoni were slow to get land on a large scale. By 1107, it is true, they were leasing the castle of Isola Farnese from SS. Cosma e Damiano in Trastevere, and they kept it into the 1160s at least; in 1124 their opposition to Honorius II, a Frangipane-supported pope, was bought off by the cession of the important centre of Terracina (though they did not keep it for long); but they are never attested as major rural lords. They kept their hands on ecclesiastical and (after 1196) senatorial office, but their lack of commitment to land, whether owned or leased, is striking. They fell into eclipse after the 1220s.[110]

Giovanni Tignoso is in many respects an emblematic figure from the Hildebrandine party. As already noted, he was put into the urban prefecture by Hildebrand and Nicholas, at the start of 1059, even before Nicholas' papal coronation; he was from Trastevere, and (according to the *Annales Romani*) the Trasteverini had tipped the political balance in favour of Nicholas and against Benedict X. He is very likely to have been directly succeeded as prefect in the 1060s by his son Cencio, who was similarly close to Hildebrand/Gregory VII, right up to his assassination in office in 1077. Cencio di Giovanni was one of Pier Damiani's heroes, and in 1067–8 is

---

[108] Other merchants who were *viri magnifici* are listed above, Chapter 3, n. 115.

[109] *Codice diplomatico della Repubblica di Genova*, I, n. 31; Kehr, 'Diploma purpureo', pp. 258–9. Note that the latter text also refers to the family's military help to Roger in their *castellis et municionibus*. This might seem to make the Pierleoni figures in the landed military politics of the South; but they do not appear in the *Catalogus baronum* of the 1150s–60s (nor does any other Roman family), and the text in fact implies that this help is outside, not inside, Roger's kingdom. It seems to refer to military support, if/when needed, inside Lazio, and not to the family's direct possession of any such castles.

[110] ASR, SCD, cassetta 16, nn. 109, 118, 137; *Liber Pontificalis*, ed. Přerovský, pp. 753–4; for later offices and history, Thumser, *Rom*, p. 182.

praised by the latter as a wonderful preacher as well as a just judge, although prone to neglect his judicial duties because he prays too much (see further below, p. 390). Here, then, we have a family not just politically but also ideologically committed to the 'reform' programme; and Pier Damiani died in 1072, so his views were not affected by the martyr narratives that grew up around Cencio later.[111]

Giovanni Tignoso did not, however, die in office. In 1079, after his son's death, he and his two brothers Tebaldo and Cencio divided their collective property with the sons of a deceased fourth brother, Inghizzo, and listed the quarter share their nephews would receive: lands and signorial rights (*omni suo districto*) at Valerano along the Aurelia, a smaller set of lands at Marcelli and Campo di Merlo along the Portuense, a mill shared with Gregorio di Bracciuto, presumably on the Tiber, and lands around Albano and Ariccia. This was a substantial and wide-stretched possession if multiplied by four, although it may not have amounted to more than a few tenant-holdings in each place: it would be enough to make such a family prosperous as *rentiers*, but not enough to confer direct political power on its own. In this text, Giovanni *Tiniosus* and his brothers are called sons of Tebaldo *de Transti-berim*, and Tebaldo (son of Franco and brother of Inghizzo and Giovanni) appears several times in the period 1015–36 as a witness and lessee for SS. Cosma e Damiano in Trastevere; he held in *casale* S. Andrea on the Aurelia and in Traste-vere, and again in both Marcelli and Campo di Merlo.[112] It thus looks as if it was Tebaldo whose patronage by SS. Cosma e Damiano allowed the build-up of a solid set of *libelli* and emphyteuses in the Aurelia–Portuense sector, leading out of Trastevere, which then allowed Giovanni and his son to achieve the prominence of the urban prefecture during the period of rule of their close associate Hildebrand. After 1079, however, the family drop back out of view. In 1098, two witnesses to a Bracciuti land deal in Marcelli were Tebaldo di Cencio and Tebaldo di Cencio di Tebaldo, plausibly cousins from the next generation. In 1132, Tebaldo di Tebaldo, with a typical family name and Trastevere connections, made his will, an early Roman-law will (cf. below, p. 273); he held land by now in Criptule on the Portuense and in Marcelli, though he controlled only a few tenant-holdings by now; his son is called Giovanni Bracciuto. The latter Giovanni reappears as a witness to an 1145 court case, in a largely Trastevere context, among the region's

---

[111] Overall citations in Halphen, *Études*, pp. 149–51. For Giovanni, *LP*, II, p. 335 (p. 334 for Trastevere support for Nicholas); for Cencio's succession and death, Bonizone of Sutri, *Liber ad amicum*, VII–VIII (pp. 603, 611; he could have succeeded at any date between 1061 and 1067–8, the date of Pier Damiani's letters, *Epistolae*, nn. 145, 155, and cf. n. 135, and strictly there could have been another urban prefect between him and his father, but none is documented). For Cencio, Pier Damiani and the martyr narratives, see esp. D'Acunto, 'Il prefetto Cencio'.

[112] For 1079, SMT, n. 7. Note that the belief that Giovanni was dead by 1065—e.g. D'Acunto, 'Il prefetto Cencio', p. 2—is based only on a Tivoli charter of the kin of the late *Iohannes Tiniosus* but with no Roman context at all, *RF*, n. 942, and Tiniosus was a common nickname in the period; a better date might be 1067, for a similar set of heirs is attested in Rome, in the *regio* of Campo Marzio, SMCM, nn. 13–14; but neither stand up against as clear a text as SMT, n. 7, which is firmly located in Trastevere. That text just refers to *terrae* and the like, not to *casalia* or other 'estaty' words, which hints that the lands concerned are not huge. For Tebaldo, see SCD, nn. 24, 25, 35, 41, cf. *S. Gregorio*, n. 14 and SMVL, n. 63.

'medium elite'.[113] The prominence of the 1050s–70s for the family had evidently gone, and they had probably dropped back into the next social stratum.

The family of Giovanni Tignoso was clearly closely associated with the Bracciuti or Brachiuti, who were also from Trastevere, but less can be said about the latter family. The Giovanni Bracciuto of the Arci list was another prominent supporter of Hildebrand, although a persistent story claimed that he poisoned Pope Stephen IX in 1058. He was dead by 1073, when his heirs held a *turre* in Trastevere near a ruined Tiber bridge, the Ponte Antonini; it was his daughter Stefania who bought land in Marcelli in 1098 (two *pedicae* of grain-land, leased from SS. Cosma e Damiano, bought for the substantial price of £11), and it was presumably his son Gregorio who shared the mill with Giovanni Tignoso and his brothers in 1079. If a descendant of the family of Giovanni Tignoso was called Giovanni Bracciuto again, marriage must have linked the two at the end of the eleventh century. The family's early tower-house marks their status, at least in Trastevere, which fits their prominent appearance in the narratives of the 1050s–60s, and their high placing in the Arci list; but they did not retain any more status into later generations than did that of Giovanni Tignoso.[114]

The Corsi were much more important as a family, but have an uncertain and complex trajectory, which has not been properly explored; we need to set it out as clearly as possible. The Alberto di Ottone Curso of 1060 must be the Alberto di Oddone di Alberto 'Cors' [*sic*] who witnessed a castle lease made by SS. Cosma e Damiano in 1072, but he and his ancestors are not otherwise known. The family must have been notably rich and prominent supporters of Gregory VII if Henry IV took over the *domos omnes Corsorum* on the Capitolio in 1084, and made them his own political centre; but they fell out with Paschal II, who in 1106 destroyed the *Corsorum domūs omnes* (according to Cardinal Pandolfo), that is to say the houses of Stefano di Alberto, his brothers, and sons. Stefano, after a brief defence in S. Paolo fuori le Mura, moved his base to Montalto di Castro on the Aurelia in north-west Lazio, which he held for some time against Paschal. He vanishes from our sources thereafter, but Alberto di Stefano who, with his nephews, leased Castel di Guido, much closer to the city on the Aurelia, from S. Gregorio sul Celio before and after 1128, could well have been his son (the name Alberto is not so very common in Rome)—if so, the family still held it into the 1170s.[115]

[113] Respectively, *SCD*, n. 96; ACR, SCD, cassetta 16, n. 120; CVL 8044, ff. 4–16 for Giovanni *Brachiuti* in 1145; his son Scotto appears as a witness in 1190 in ASR, SCD, cassetta 16 bis, n. 158, another Trastevere document.

[114] For the poisoning, *LP*, II, p. 334, and Benone, *Gesta*, II. 9 (p. 379, who extends the claim to five or six popes). This odd story presumably means that people recognized the shift from Stephen, the last German pope, to the Tuscan Nicholas, the first pope for whom Hildebrand was archdeacon, as being a significant change. See also Benzone of Alba, *Ad Heinricum IV*, II.4. Later texts: SMT, nn. 5, 7; *SCD*, n. 96; ASR, SCD, n. 120. For a parallel but less prominent Trastevere family, the Maccii, see Chapter 5, n. 19.

[115] No focused analysis of the Corsi exists. For these references, in turn, *SCD*, n. 72 (a.1072); *LP*, II, p. 290; *Liber Pontificalis*, ed. Přerovský, pp. 710–14. Sigebert of Gembloux says that in 1099 'Alberto di Stefano' acted for Paschal II (*Chronica*, p. 369); did he invert the two names in error? For Castel di Guido see *S. Gregorio*, nn. 21–2 and 23 (a. 1177). Another possible relative is Alberto di Giovanni di Stefano, who was one of the prominent Romans who wrote formally to Lothar III on behalf of

The Corsi had a separate branch, however, who included Pietro Latrone *Corsorum*, a notable whose urban residence was a little to the south-west of the Capitolio, on the Ripa Graeca; he was a supporter of Gelasius II in 1118 and of Innocent II in 1130. Pietro Latrone's heirs took over Civitavecchia from Innocent in return for a large loan of £200, a pledge only repaid fifty years later, in 1193; the family meanwhile unsuccessfully defended it for Alexander III, of whom they were also major supporters, against Frederick Barbarossa in 1167. Civitavecchia is up the coast (and the Aurelia) from Rome, only some 35 km from Montalto, so these two branches of the Corsi were increasingly involved with this angle of Lazio. Pietro Latrone was also brother of the urban prefect Pietro 'II', who succeeded his father Pietro 'I' in 1116. These urban prefects are never, unlike Pietro Latrone, called 'Corsi', but Pandolfo is explicit about the fraternal relationship.[116] This adds a whole extra dimension to an already prominent family.

The urban prefecture of Rome in the twelfth century has generally been recognized as being dominated by a single family for long periods. Four prefects across the century were called Pietro; here I shall number them 'I' to 'IV' to avoid confusion. The first two were father and son, as just observed, and it was Paschal II's attempt to stop Pietro 'II' (in office 1116–24/30) succeeding his father that sparked off the most serious crisis in the city in his reign (below, pp. 344, 426). Pietro 'III' (in office 1141/3–60/70) and his son Pietro 'IV' (in office 1185–1223/30) are generally reckoned to be related to the first two, but the nature of the link has not been seen as clear (as a result, for most historians the numbering of the prefects begins with Pietro 'III'). One document, however, indicates directly that Pietro 'III' was the son of Pietro 'II', which allows us to see a father–son succession across all four, although there were breaks between the second and third, and probably between the third and fourth; from 1200 onwards, the prefecture was effectively hereditary. This branch of the family was one of the most influential players in the city in the century, eventual opponents of Paschal II, supporters of Gelasius II, opponents of Honorius II, and supporters of Innocent II, who gave the prefecture back to the family. In 1160, however, Pietro 'III' was a supporter of Victor IV and Barbarossa against Alexander III, breaking with the political position of his Latrone cousins, and Barbarossa indeed claimed the *possessio* of the prefecture between *c.*1159 and 1176, and later on in the 1180s–90s as well. Pietro 'IV' was very close to a succession of emperors; the prefects were, conversely, less often

---

Anacletus II in 1130 (see below, p. 430, and Petersohn, 'Der Brief', p. 506). Petersohn ('Der Brief', pp. 490–1) cautiously hypothesizes that this man was a Normanni, because the name Alberto appears later in the Normanni genealogy (see esp. Carocci, *Baroni*, pp. 381–6). I doubt that; the name is not attested until 1193 in that family; but it is interesting that that text (*S. Gregorio*, n. 24) is a lease of Castel di Guido to the Normanni, and it is possible that they had inherited both the castle and the name through the female line.

[116] Pietro Latrone: *Liber Pontificalis*, ed. Přerovský, pp. 738–9 (house in Ripa and *Corsorum*), 741 (brother of Pietro 'II' the urban prefect, for whose succession in 1116 see esp. *Liber Pontificalis*, ed. Přerovský, pp. 717–21); for 1130, *LP*, II, pp. 380, 382 and Kehr, II, pp. 348–50; *Landulphi Iunioris Historia Mediolanensis*, ch. 63; cf. *S. Agnese*, n. 7. For Alexander III, Maragone, *Annales Pisani*, s.a. 1168 (p. 42, cf. 43), with *LC*, I, n. 166, for the return of Civitavecchia. For other descendants of Pietro Latrone: *SMVL*, n. 156; *LC*, I, n. 114; *SMN*, n. 87; *S. Alessio*, n. 21; *Senato*, n. 42 (a senator in 1188).

close to the popes thereafter, and in the thirteenth century are best seen as a rural family.[117]

The 'Prefetti di Vico', as they were called by the 1240s, built up a rural lordship around Vetralla and the Lago di Vico, inland from Civitavecchia, in the later twelfth century, which they kept into the later Middle Ages. Pietro 'III' with his brothers in 1158 also received Civita Castellana, and Stefano di Alberto's old centre of Montalto, from Hadrian IV, in a pledge for 1000 marks which was once again only paid off in the 1190s. This consistent interest in the far north-west of Lazio helps again to make the links between the Corsi of the late eleventh century and the Prefetti of the late twelfth and onwards more solid. The Corsi were evidently laying the foundations for that rural power-base already before 1106. Earlier, it is much harder to tell. There had been Pietros acting as urban prefects before 1100; one in the 1050s, for Leo IX and then, later, Benedict X (he was dismissed in 1059 in favour of Giovanni Tignoso); and one in 1088 (if the latter was not the same as Pietro 'I'). The former of these (called *Petrus quondam prefectus Iohannis Michini*, a version of Benedict X's nickname) is said, in an 1144 agreement between the men of Corneto and the papacy, to have had control over the town in the past. Corneto is midway between Montalto and Civitavecchia; if this Pietro was an ancestor of Pietro 'I', this too would show some geographical continuity. But the link is too speculative for us to trust (it also makes the genealogical links between the family's various branches even harder to construct), and it is better to start this prefectural account around 1100. Indeed, in the late eleventh century it is easier just to say that the political focus of the Corsi family was, rather, in the neuralgic centre of Rome, the Capitolio, and not out in the countryside. The various branches of the Corsi, to sum up, given their prefectural association, can be argued to have been the most politically prominent family out of the 'new aristocracy' by 1100. They were also probably the first to get interested in rural lordship. But even for them the twelfth century was the clearest moment for that, not the eleventh.[118]

The Frangipane had a career trajectory that matched the Corsi, more closely than the other families mentioned hitherto. Pietro Imperiola or Imperio, who appeared in the 963 synod, held Farfa land in the Sabina, and was also an unruly tenant of

---

[117] For this sequence of Pietros, see Halphen, *Études*, pp. 151–6, and (with great caution) Calisse, 'I Prefetti di Vico', pp. 3–21; for 1160, Rahewin, *Gesta Frederici*, IV.77, 80; see also Hirschfeld, 'Zur Chronologie der Stadtpraefekten' (with some caution); and, more recently, Petersohn, 'Kaiser, Papst', who disposes of the supposed rivals to Pietro 'IV' as prefect at the end of the century. The very recent Berardozzi, *I Prefetti*, is now the basic analysis of this part of the family, and completely replaces, in particular, Calisse. Pietro 'III' had a brother called Giovanni *Prefecti* in 1158 (*LC*, I, nn. 167–8), whose father is most probably Pietro 'II', prefect between 1116 and 1124/30, rather than Ugo or Tebaldo (1130, 1133–41)—cf. also *S. Gregorio*, n. 7 for Pietro *Petri prefecti* in 1140, which shows that Pietro 'II' did indeed have a son named Pietro. The same Giovanni may perhaps have been Barbarossa's prefect Giovanni *Maledictus* in 1170: *LP*, II, p. 422, which may mean that the family held without a break in that period too. I am grateful here to discussion with Antonio Berardozzi, who emphasized for me, among other things, the Giovanni *Maledictus* connection.

[118] For the eleventh century see Halphen, *Études*, pp. 149–51 (a tenth-century Prefect Pietro, Halphen, *Études*, p. 147, is too far back to be relevant). For Civita Castellana, see *LC*, I, nn. 167–8; it was regained by the popes in 1195 (*LC*, I, nn. 178–83). Corneto: *LC*, I, n. 123 (for Benedict X as Giovanni *Mincius*, see *Chronica Casinensis*, II.99). Pietro 'II' also gained some rights over Formello near the Cassia in 1124: *Liber Pontificalis*, ed. Přerovský, p. 753, which the family kept: see Berardozzi, *I Prefetti*, p. 208 (a. 1180).

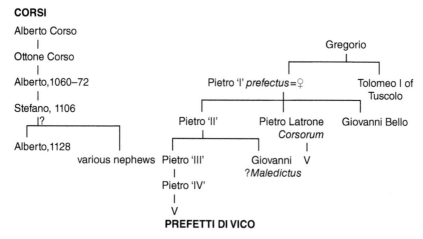

Genealogy 3

Subiaco and S. Erasmo sul Celio for land at Porta Maggiore in 966; he had the energy to force Subiaco to a substantial pay-off in a court case assembly full of major aristocrats. If all the people referred to as *de Imperio* and *de Imperator* in the next generations were his descendants, which is likely enough in view of the rarity of the name, the family included a *sutor* among his children and then a *negotiator* and a *scriniarius* among his grandchildren, situating them at the top end of the artisanate and lower end of the official strata; and, significantly for our genealogical reconstruction, they also included Pietro Fraiapane *de Imperator*, whose children gave a S. Maria Nova lease back to the church in 1039. One of these latter children was Leone, whom we have already seen attested (as Leone Fragapane) in the 1014 Tribuco witness list; with him, we move smartly out of the artisanal/professional level and into visible social prominence. Imperator may perhaps have been becoming a surname at the end of the tenth century; but Fragapane/Fraiapane, 'bread-breaker' (later spelt Frangentispanem in 1116 and 1125, and Frangipane in 1127) was even more certainly already one by the 1010s, if Leone inherited it from his father: the first known surname in Rome.[119]

The Frangipane are well documented, largely thanks to the closeness of their power-base, consisting of several tower-houses, to S. Maria Nova. The complex and incomplete detail of their family history has been well discussed by Matthias Thumser, and does not need to be reprised here. In brief: the Cencio Frangipane of the 1060 court case was probably Leone's grandson; by the start of the twelfth

[119] For the Frangipane, Thumser, 'Die Frangipane', is close to definitive. For the documents cited in this paragraph, in turn, *RS*, nn. 118–19 (a. 966) with *LL*, nn. 284, 334; *RS*, n. 106; *SMN*, nn. 13 and 11 (a.1039: the latter filled out from an eighteenth-century edition of a fuller text, Nerini, *De templo*, p. 390, plus BAV, CVL 11980, f. 5r, an authoritative Galletti MS edition; see Fedele, 'Sull'origine dei Frangipane', p. 501, the best work on the family before Thumser, and Thumser, 'Die Frangipane', p. 110n); and, for Leone, *RF*, n. 492 (a.1014). Later forms of the name: *SMN*, n. 36; *S. Gregorio*, n. 135; *CDC*, n. 312.

century there were probably two major branches of the family, and their genealogical relationships are unclear, but they consistently acted together. They were
also by now far more important in the city than their tenth-century predecessors.
Cencio was another close supporter of Hildebrand, and also of Desiderio of
Montecassino (briefly Pope Victor III, 1086–7). His son Leone was less of an
unambiguous member of the Hildebrandine party, as we shall see (p. 424), but
Giovanni Frangipane, perhaps his brother, was the host of Urban II in 1094 in his
firmissima munitio near S. Maria Nova, in one of the latter's attempts to take Rome.
In the unstable reign of Paschal II, the same Giovanni and another Leone Frangipane were leading papal supporters; Leone was later, however, as we saw at the start
of the chapter, a violent opponent of Gelasius II, together with his brother Cencio.
Calixtus II pulled down three Frangipane towers, but Cencio was reconciled to him
and headed his city militia (*masnada*). Leone, Cencio, and their cousin Roberto
imposed Honorius II on the cardinals against their will; and the Frangipane were also
the principal supporters of Innocent II in 1130 against the Pierleoni Anacletus II,
although the two latter families made peace later in the century.[120]

In the fifty years after 1100, the Frangipane were the most influential family in
Rome, along with the Pierleoni and the Corsi/Prefetti. They are also much more
visible as land dealers than either of the other two families, especially in S. Maria
Nova documents, of course: they dominated the zone between the Palatino and the
Colosseo, a monument which they partially controlled, and in 1177 the leaders
of the *regio Colossei* needed the *auctoritas dominorum de Frangenspanibus* to make
a pious gift to S. Giovanni in Laterano (see below, pp. 294–303). But they are also
found in late Subiaco documents (land outside Porta S. Giovanni), S. Gregorio
documents (in the Circo Massimo and the Settizonio), and S. Pietro in Vaticano
documents (land in Scorteclari); they seem to have had a base near S. Prassede on
the Esquilino, too.[121] This extended network of urban and suburban properties,
recorded in several different archives, puts into perspective the absence of equivalent Corsi and Pierleoni dealings; the Frangipane were more active and probably
larger-scale landowners than either. And it was not long before they moved outside
the Agro romano, too. Cencio Frangipane was briefly count of Ceccano in *Campania* under Honorius II; Adilascia, daughter of a different Cencio, had married
Rainerio count of Cornazzano before she made her will in 1137 (Cornazzano is very
close to Galeria, so this otherwise unknown count was probably from the comital
family of Galeria); Aldruda Frangipane married the count of Bertinoro in the
Romagna in 1142; and from the 1140s onwards the family developed a strong
power-base in *Marittima*: in Cisterna, Tivera, Ninfa, Monte Circeo, and in

---

[120] For all this, Thumser, 'Die Frangipane', pp. 112–27. For better terms with the Pierleoni later
on, see below, pp. 433–4.

[121] *SMN*, nn. 11, 13, 33, 36, 40, 45, 46, 49, 51, 65, 66, 72, 77, 87, 91, 92, 94, 95, 109, 116, 117,
118, 120, 124, 135, 152, 154, 159, 164 (by Roman standards, a giant set); Augenti, *Il Palatino*, p. 188
(a. 1177); *RS*, nn. 108, 107; *S. Gregorio*, n. 152; *SPV*, n. 23; also Kehr, II, pp. 348–50; and for
S. Prassede as *in fortiis Fraiapanum*, *Liber Pontificalis*, ed. Přerovský, p. 739. For the Frangipane in the
Colosseo in 1203, *Gesta Innocentii III*, ch. 139; cf. also the transactions from 1228 to 1232 recorded in
Fedele, 'Il leopardo e l'agnello', p. 214.

Terracina, where they were grasping and arbitrary lords across the second half of the century.[122] This strong political base in south-eastern Lazio matched—and overmatched—the Corsi/Prefetti base in the north-west, and it lasted into the thirteenth century of the *baroni*. But it, too, did not begin before the 1120s, and not really before the 1140s; before that, the Frangipane were very much an urban family.

The Sant' Eustachio, who appear at the bottom of the Arci list, are tricky to identify, because it is not clear when, and how far, *de S. Eustachio* and similar turns of phrase ceased to be simple geographical appellations and turned into surnames. But the two Sant' Eustachio *adstantes* in the Arci case were Sarraceno and Gregorio di Franco, and they link both backwards and forwards. Gregorio was presumably the son of the Franco *nobili viro a S. Eustati* of documents from 1000 and 1011; Sarraceno appears half a dozen more times after 1060, up to 1088; and in several of these latter documents he also appears with an Enrico *a S. Eustatio*. Enrico (fl. 1084–1105) was the father of another Enrico and Ottaviano, who were political players into the 1140s; the *filii Heinrici* of the later twelfth century were then the ancestors of the baronial family of Sant' Eustachio of the thirteenth.[123] The family thus seems to have been a real genealogical grouping, which allows us to trace the thirteenth-century family back to 1060 at least, and conceivably 1000, even if the exact links are sometimes unknown. In our period, they are overwhelmingly attested as witnesses, and not as landholders. But they were certainly prominent; in 1088 Sarraceno and Enrico were *consules comunitatis boum* (see below, pp. 393–7); in 1127 the later Enrico was one of six leaders of Rome in a Gaeta court case; in 1141 Enrico di Enrico called himself *Romanorum consul*; in 1178 his descendants were termed by Alexander III 'de nobilitatis in Urbe' and papal *fideles*. If the reference in the 1143 *Mirabilia* to the *turris* of Cencio *de Orrigo* (i.e. Enrico) on the Ripa Graeca is to this family—which is quite possible given that the name Enrico is not so common, even though the area is some 800 metres from S. Eustachio—then they were significant enough to provide almost the only reference to a living or recently dead person in the first version of that text. (This Cencio must be a recent figure, for Cencio di Enrico's two children are referred to in documents between 1148 and 1161.)[124] Their political allegiance was mostly

---

[122] *Liber Pontificalis*, ed. Přerovský, p. 755; *SMN*, n. 46; for *Marittima*, Thumser, 'Die Frangipane', pp. 131–42, with, for the Terracina plea against them from 1203–4, Contatore, *De historia Terracinensi*, pp. 52–7; Carocci, 'La signoria rurale', pp. 191–8. For Aldruda, see below, n. 173.

[123] *SMVL*, n. 24A and *RF*, n. 616 (Franco); *RF*, nn. 1076, 1085, 1095, 1097, 1115, 1278 (Sarraceno); *LP*, II, p. 345 (a. 1105); Petersohn, 'Der Brief', p. 506 (with pp. 492–3), with *PL*, CLXXIX, col. 707, n. 18 (a. 1130); *SMVL*, n. 165 (a. 1141); for the late twelfth century, Thumser, *Rom*, pp. 190–3; for the thirteenth, Carocci, *Baroni*, pp. 405–10. The Odalrico *de Sancto Eustachio* recorded at Clement III's 1098 synod (Benone, *Gesta*, V, p. 405) is in the right political faction, but his genealogical link to the family, if any, is unknowable. Carocci is cautious about the descent of the later family from Sarraceno or Enrico, but the Sabina connection (see below, n. 125) clinches it for me.

[124] *RF*, n. 1115; *CDC*, n. 312; *SMVL*, n. 165; *Epistolae*, ed. Loewenfeld, n. 282 (a. 1178); for Anacletus in 1130 see previous note. For Cencio di Enrico, *Mirabilia*, p. 62 (see Chapter 6, n. 177 for other references in the text to recent people, of whom the only one still living was Cencio Frangipane); for Cencio's children, see *Liberiano*, n. 17 (Imillia); *S. Prassede*, n. 26; *SMN*, n. 71; *SMCM*, n. 51 (Pietro; the first of these includes Pietro in a very high-status witness list—see below, n. 160); the stress

imperial; they consistently supported Henry IV and Clement III, then Silvester IV against Paschal II, though they swung around behind Anacletus II in 1130.

The Clementine allegiance of the Sant' Eustachio may be because the family were closely associated with Farfa, which, as an imperial abbey, kept close to both Henry IV and Henry V. S. Eustachio was the next-door church to Farfa's Roman base, S. Maria in the Terme Alessandrine. Farfa had bad relations with that church (above, p. 133), but evidently not with the leading local family. Sarraceno *illustrissimus vir* is once described as a monastic *fidelis*, and he also appears in purely rural documents for Farfa, up in the Sabina, as both a witness and as a monastic tenant, clearly marked as a *Romanus nobilissimus* in most of the texts. This Sabina connection is presumably also the background for the fact that the baronial family of Sant' Eustachio of the later thirteenth century is overwhelmingly attested in the central Sabina, between Catino and Vescovio; the family's link with the area was evidently long-lasting.[125]

Farfa's tenants and clients in the Terme Alessandrine area tended to be of relatively high status. They were often also families from the Sabina. Most prominent among them were the three sons of Pietro di Spampino, who appear as tenants and witnesses both in Rome and in the Sabina (mostly at Montelibretti) from the 1010s to the 1050s (by then, a new generation is simply called the *de Spampinis*); they accumulated quite a lot of monastic property, and acted as witnesses for Farfa, typically calling themselves *vir magnificus*, in a variety of places in the Sabina. Among other families, the brothers Gregorio and Urso di Bona (or di Urso di Malepassia), who leased the castle of Montelibretti from Farfa in 1000, were also tenants of houses in the Terme Alessandrine; and the family of Stefano *presbiter* di Giovanni Muto, who ceded back their Farfa leases in Rome in 1011 (land in the same city region, plus salt pans), were intermarried with the Sabina family of Azo and Teuzo di Benedetto, active *boni homines* for the monastery.[126] Stefano *presbiter* was probably, like the Sant' Eustachio, Roman, the others almost certainly Sabine, but the common Farfa connection brought all of them long-term leases in both. A structural link between the two areas seems to have lasted beyond the end of the Farfa documents for Rome.

The Sant' Eustachio take us away from the families who were securely in the Hildebrandine camp in the later eleventh century. Two other urban families were particularly opposed to Hildebrand/Gregory VII, and they can usefully be taken next. Cencio di Stefano is the most prominent figure here, and he receives a lot of

---

on Enrico in this group seems to rule out the possibility that the tower reference is to the Casa dei Crescenzi.

[125] As tenant, *LL*, nn. 1187, 1221 (a. 1085; in the latter, he is just called 'Sarraceno', and the name is not so rare, but the document has Astaldo di Astaldo, an associate of the Sant' Eustachio—below, p. 239—as a witness, and the document is Roman); as witness, *RF*, nn. 1278, 1085, 1095; for the thirteenth century, Carocci, *Baroni*, map facing p. 410.

[126] Spampini: in the city, *RF*, nn. 657, 658, 638, 668, 524, 710, 761, 775, 880; in Montelibretti, *LL*, nn. 1987, 631, 627, 628, 637, 664, 752; elsewhere in the Sabina, *RF*, nn. 687, 778, 835, 880, 893, 903. *Filii* of Bona/Urso: see Chapter 7, n. 12. Stefano *presbiter* and family: *RF*, nn. 652, 653, 654, 488, with, for Azo and Teuzo in the Sabina, Toubert, *Structures*, p. 1298n.

attention in the narratives for his hostility to Gregory, so we can trace him reasonably well. He was the son of an urban prefect, but Stefano does not appear as such in any document; the years 1037–50, when we know the name of no prefect, is the most likely period for his office. Cencio may or may not have been present during the Arci court case, as we have seen; if he was there, he was the first of the non-office-holding laity. He was certainly a supporter of Honorius II/Cadalo of Parma in 1062–4, and held Castel S. Angelo for the pope in the latter year. He also had a political link to the counts of Galeria. All this in itself makes it highly unlikely that Hildebrand and Alexander II would ever have made him urban prefect in the 1060s, but their choice not to do so exacerbated matters. So did Prefect Cencio di Giovanni's move against Cencio di Stefano's tower on the Ponte S. Pietro, an unpopular building because it was reputedly (so pro-Hildebrandine writers tell us) used as a base to extract tolls from people crossing to and from the Civitas Leoniana. Cencio di Stefano kidnapped the newly elected Gregory VII at Christmas 1075, in a prefiguring of the Frangipane kidnapping of Gelasius II in 1118; he took him to another tower in Parione (near the Ponte S. Pietro), but the pope was released by the Roman citizens, and his other towers were pulled down. Some sources claim that Henry IV was already involved in the kidnap plot; this seems unlikely. But after 1075 Cencio fled to northern Italy, to pro-imperial Pavia, where he soon died. His brother Stefano killed Cencio di Giovanni in 1077 and was himself killed as a result.[127]

The family was now both dispossessed and exiled, but Tebaldo di Cencio, who must have been relatively young at his father's expulsion, reappears in Rome as an active supporter of Clement III in 1089–98. This seems to have re-established the family in the city sufficiently well for them to have remained as major players under Paschal II. In 1103, Tebaldo was prominent enough for Paschal to appoint him, together with Pietro di Leone of the Pierleoni, as an arbiter of a major dispute between Farfa and the Ottaviani, in an initial (failed) hearing in S. Nicola in Carcere—here, Tebaldo supported Farfa, the imperial abbey, whereas Pietro favoured the Ottaviani (see below, p. 398). By now (by Paschal's reign at the latest), the family had begun to accumulate castles in Tuscia Romana, Fiano, Vacchereccia, Leprignano, and Civitella, a tight group about 35 km north of the city, on leases from S. Paolo fuori le Mura: S. Paolo several times claimed them in court (for example against Stefano di Tebaldo di Cencio in 1139), but also leased them back to the same family, into the 1180s, by when Stefano's son Cencio was the principal family member.[128] This did not take them out of urban politics, all the same. Stefano di Tebaldo was a supporter of Gelasius II in 1118 and of

[127] For Cencio di Stefano and his family, see Borino, 'Cencio del prefetto Stefano', and Whitton, 'Papal policy', pp. 223–6, 233–6, 244–52 (a better study, extending into the twelfth century too, although Whitton's theory of Cencio's Aretine origins does not convince). Basic texts: *LP*, II, pp. 336–7; Benone, *Gesta*, I.8 (p. 372); Bonizone of Sutri, *Liber ad amicum*, VI–VIII (pp. 595, 603–6, 610–11), followed by Paul of Bernried, *Vita Gregorii VII*, chs 45–51, 92.

[128] Tebaldo: Kehr, II, pp. 599–600; Benone, *Gesta*, V (p. 405); *CF*, II, pp. 232–3 (a.1103); and, for the castles, *S. Paolo*, nn. 4, 5, 7–11, with *Friderici I. diplomata*, n. 1195. For a genealogical table, di Carpegna Falconieri, 'Le trasformazioni onomastiche', p. 612.

Anacletus II in 1130. He was also in the entourage of Eugenius III, together with several Frangipane and Pierleoni, in 1153; he was present at the imperial council of Pavia in 1160; and he had an urban *turris* where Barbarossa's pope Paschal III stayed in 1168, so the pro-imperial alignment of the family evidently still persisted. Conversely, a Stefano di Cencio di Stefano di 'Tedaldo' was a *consiliator* for the Senate in 1150; his names are so much a family speciality that he could well be related, even if it is not easy to say how (cf. below, p. 450).[129] But, either way, the family had certainly made a comeback in the twelfth century, and they followed the Corsi-Prefetti and Frangipane route of urban political activism and rural castle-holding.

The other major anti-Hildebrandine family was the *filii Baruncii*, less clearly characterized but equally interesting. Cencio and Romano di Baruncio were also Honorius II/Cadalo supporters in the 1060s; Cencio's son Cencio *causidicus* (later, *iudex*) was in Henry IV's entourage in 1084, together with Sarraceno and Enrico *a S. Eustatio*. Cencio di Baruncio had at least four, and possibly six, sons, who crop up as witnesses for the next two decades, and a further generation can be tracked into the 1140s. One of the sons, Nicola di Cencio, was a *consul communitatis boum* in 1088, and in 1105 a supporter of Silvester IV along with his cousin Romano, Enrico *a S. Eustachio*, the Normanni, and some others. The *consules communitatis boum* are only attested in one document, in which, led by the urban prefect Pietro, they heard a formal plea of Farfa against the lord of Corese.[130] Not all nine *consules* can be traced elsewhere, but Sarraceno and Enrico are two of them again, and so is Leone di Cencio Frangipane. Gerardo di Crescenzio di Melioso may be the last known representative of the older 'Meliosi' family (above, p. 193). Astaldo di Giovanni di Astaldo was certainly a member of a prominent family from the Colosseo area, the *filii Astaldi*, whom we will look at in a moment. I will argue later (pp. 393–7) that these *consules* are among the earliest signs of the sort of collective aggregation by urban elites that would soon mark the *primo comune* in most central-northern Italian cities. Given that, Nicola di Cencio can be regarded as a city leader in the 1080s; but his *communitas* was also, as far as we can see, of a Clementine political complexion, with no Pierleoni, or any of the Trastevere families, listed as members (among families loyal to Gregory VII, only the Frangipane are listed, who thus had a foot in both camps).

The *filii Baruncii* mostly appear as witnesses; they had one judicial expert in the family, as we have seen; they were creditors of S. Ciriaco in Via Lata once, in 1098.

---

[129] See respectively *Liber Pontificalis*, ed. Přerovský, p. 734; Petersohn, 'Der Brief', p. 506 (with pp. 488–90, who sees the Stefano of the 1150s and onwards as a different person); *LC*, I, n. 91; Rahewin, *Gesta Frederici*, IV.77, 80; John of Salisbury, *The Letters*, n. 280, for Paschal III; *Senato*, n. 12. It is true that Stefano di Tebaldo would have to have been politically active late into his sixties to be the same man on all the above-mentioned occasions, and in the 1153 citation he has an 'infant' child with him, so might be a younger man; but *S. Paolo*, n. 11, at least makes it clear that the original Stefano was alive under Frederick Barbarossa, i.e. in or after 1155. I am more uncertain, on the other hand, as to whether there was a structural link between the family and the Tebaldeschi of the mid-thirteenth century; for the latter, Thumser, *Rom*, pp. 203–4.

[130] Hüls, *Kardinäle, Klerus*, pp. 261–2, is an initial guide. For references, *LP*, II, pp. 336, 345; *RF*, n. 1097 (a.1084); *SMVL*, nn. 121, 122, 123; ASR, SCD, cassetta 16, n. 109; *S. Gregorio*, nn. 34, 137 (a. 1131); *RF*, n. 1115 (*consules communitatis boum*).

In 1131, in one of the latest references to the family, Grisotto and Stefania di Stefano di Cencio di Baruntio, grandchildren of the 1060s' activist, appear as co-holders of a rural tower at Arciones on the Via Appia, arguably the first known example of a late medieval *casale* (that text also shows that they were married into the *filii Astaldi* family). Grisotto, with one ancestor elided, could have been the Grisotto di Cencio who was a senator in 1148 (below, p. 450). By 1144, their link to their ancestor, which is shown clearly hitherto in their patronymics, had stabilized as a surname, when Giovanni di Stefano *Baronchinorum*, presumably the brother of the last-named two, witnessed a papal cession. But the family is not visibly attested again; it would in my view be too speculative to add as a possible family member Nicola di Cencio, senator in 1163, for the names are too common.[131] They were probably less powerful examples of the 'new aristocracy' than many, even though they had moments of prominence. They are interesting for their Clementine sympathies. But they are also interesting because the Nicola di Cencio (di Baruncio) of 1088–1105 and his homonym of 1163 are both possible candidates for being the Nicolaus son of Crescens who was the builder of the well-known Casa dei Crescenzi on the Ripa Graeca beside the bridge over to Trastevere. That requires an excursus, for that house is the only surviving building which was certainly an aristocratic residence in our period, and it is a remarkable construction in itself.

The Casa dei Crescenzi as it now survives is the bottom half of a former tower-house, of considerable architectural complexity and ambition (see Figures 4.1 and 4.2). It has a set of rounded brick pilasters on its left-hand side, encased in flat walling, medieval in construction but made of reused classical brick, doubtless to echo the columns of the still-standing Tempio di Portuno immediately opposite. These are topped by capitals in newly cut brick, and then a reused classical marble pediment and an array of reused decorative elements mixed with brick decoration above, under an arcaded loggia, now mostly rebuilt. On its front, under a further classical pediment, it has a very elaborate doorway with a long inscription; and a window, partially decorated with a classical marble plaque (quite possibly taken from the nearby Tempio di Bellona), with another inscription indicating that a bust (*effigies*) of the builder (*auctor*) was once there. Inside, it has more classical and some new stone decoration, although less elaborate than outside. It is easily, for all its oddness, the most ambitious secular building surviving from our period, and its doorway inscription reveals that its builder was a Nicolaus, son of Crescens (i.e. Crescenzio or Cencio) and Theodora; Nicola's son was called Davide.[132]

---

[131] Respectively, *SMVL*, n. 122; *S. Gregorio*, n. 137 (for which see Carocci and Vendittelli, *L'origine della Campagna Romana*, p. 95); *Senato*, n. 12; *LC*, I, n. 123; *SMVL*, n. 200. Another conceivable family member is Romanus *Baroncinus*, a supporter of S. Gregorio sul Celio in the early 1140s (*S. Gregorio*, n. 7), who may also be the Romano di Barontio who witnessed *LC*, I, n. 123, along with Giovanni di Stefano *Baronchinorum*.

[132] For descriptions and analyses, see above all (excluding other, numerous, inferior accounts) Barbanera and Pergola, 'Elementi architettonici'; Pensabene, 'La Casa dei Crescenzi'; Montelli, 'Impiego dei mattoni'; Montelli, *Tecniche costruttive*. For the inscriptions, Forcella, XIII, nn. 1339–41. For the Tempio di Bellona, De Nuccio, 'La decorazione architettonica', p. 48, a reference I owe to Emanuela Montelli; I am grateful to her for discussion of this section, and also for a copy of her article, which is hard to find.

Figure 4.1. The Casa dei Crescenzi, side.

Figure 4.2. The Casa dei Crescenzi, front.

The date of this building and the identity of its builder have been under debate for decades, often unconstructively, even leaving aside the predictable claims that Nicola's family was the original 'Crescenzi'. Pietro Fedele, in one of his last and weakest articles, gratuitously attached Nicola di Cencio to a 'Nicola' (no father's name mentioned) active in 1062 among the supporters of Cadalo. Others have preferred the senator Nicola di Cencio of 1163, simply on the grounds of the paired (but, as just noted, common) names—although the other documented pairings of the names, in 1081, 1116, and in the citations of Nicola di Cencio di Baruncio (fl. 1088–1105), have not attracted discussion. (No other examples of a Davide di Nicola are attested.) The building is also generically dated to the early to mid-twelfth century by many people simply because the main inscription has many echoes of classical 'renewal', which are thought to mark that period. I shall argue later (pp. 348–50) that the idea of *renovatio* was present throughout our period, and that it does not attach itself specifically to the classicizing imagery associated (often rather romantically) with the early Senate; this dating argument is flawed, that is to say, and often circular. Richard Krautheimer had the good sense to ask the famous palaeographer Bernhard Bischoff to date the inscription, which he did, saying that it dated between the late eleventh century and the mid-twelfth, but probably closer to 1100. Most recently, however, Emanuela Montelli has proposed the mid-twelfth century on the basis of a detailed and comparative study of the layout of the reused brickwork of the house, which is well selected, very regular, and carefully carried out, evidently by experienced construction workers; this in itself argues for a period later than the introduction of the techniques used, around the end of the eleventh century. This fits the views of the other best recent analysts of the architecture, although they are more influenced by the supposed date of the sentiments of the inscription. Until a new study of the epigraphy of the latter is carried out (Bischoff was the touchstone of his generation, but this was somewhat out of his main field), the mid-twelfth century seems to me the best date for the building.[133]

The inscription is undeniably a grandiose text. Nicola di Cencio was proud of the contribution of his *domus sublimis* to renewing (*renovare*) the *decor* of 'old Rome' and of the 'great honour to the Roman *populi*' shown by his bust, and pensively conscious of the passing of earthly life. He was uninterested in Christian rhetorical elements, but certainly happy to use classical rhetorical tropes; whatever the problems of dating *renovatio* imagery, Nicola's inscription shows that such imagery was fully available to a rich architectural patron in the middle decades of the twelfth century.[134] That Nicola was from the highest elite, that is the 'new aristocracy', is shown not only by the scale and ambition of the house itself, but also by the remarkably boastful phrase 'primus de primis magnus Nicholaus', 'the first of the first, great Nicola', in his doorway inscription. (This, one could add, is also

---

[133] Fedele, 'Il culto di Roma', pp. 21–2 (citing Benzone, *Ad Heinricum IV*, II.3–4, pp. 202–4); Claussen, '*Renovatio Romae*', p. 121, and Maire Vigueur, *L'autre Rome*, p. 409 (two cautious supporters of the 1163 Nicola); Krautheimer, *Rome*, pp. 197, 354 (citing Bischoff); Montelli, 'Impiego dei mattoni'; Montelli, *Tecniche costruttive*, pp. 43, 138–9. Other people called Nicola di Cencio: *SMN*, n. 26 (a. 1081); ASR, SCD, cassetta 16, n. 111 (a. 1116)—very casual references.

[134] Forcella, XIII, nn. 1339–41.

less likely to indicate that he was part of a senatorial collectivity.) We are probably never going to be able to say with certainty who he was; Montelli's dating puts Nicola di Cencio di Baruncio, the most prominent man of this name in the documents, out of the running. But it is important to stress the geographical context of the building, already alluded to in Chapter 3. It is right beside the approach to one of the two main bridges to Trastevere, the Ponte S. Maria (now the Ponte Rotto), and would have been the most prominent building on the approach to the bridge, along with the Tempio di Portuno, by now the church of S. Maria Secundicerii, just on the other side of the bridge road. Furthermore, the houses of the Normanni (whom we will come to shortly) and of Pietro Latrone of the Corsi were on each side of S. Maria; and the main focus of the Pierleoni was only 200 metres to the north.[135] Nicola di Cencio had these major families as his most immediate audience; his innovative architecture, the grandiloquent sentences on his doorway, and the bust of himself, spoke directly to them. This seems to me more important than any reading of the detailed content of his message; he was being competitive inside a very narrow social group, and thought it possible to claim to be the equal of or superior to many of Rome's known political leaders. Given that, I am indeed inclined to ascribe the Casa dei Crescenzi to the *filii Baruncii*, who are the only family out of the thirteen discussed in this section whose geographical location is not clear in our sources, and who did at least have Nicola and Cencio in their naming repertoire; if so, they built it close to the end of their documented trajectory. But if it was a different family, it does not much matter; the building was built by a member of a family equivalent to those discussed here. It shows how bold, and how self-confident, their self-presentation could be. It is only a pity that the houses of their (probably richer) rivals do not survive, to show us how they responded.

It is not my aim here to set out a complete prosopography of Rome's 'new aristocratic' families in our period. There are too many unknowns, and words like 'probably' begin to make up too high a percentage of the genealogical links. I shall finish this exposition with only five more families, therefore, chosen to fill out some of the family types we have already seen.

First, the Ceci, whom we have met before (above, p. 165). Alberico di Pietro di Leone Cece was not in the 1060 lists, but he was all the same a long-standing associate of Gregory VII, whom the pope recommended to the North African ruler al-Nāṣir in 1076, presumably as a merchant. Alberico had been in the Tuscolano entourage in 1068, and had leased a mill near the Laterano in 1072; his father was from Trastevere, as a 1034 document tells us; his grandfather Leone Cece was one of Benedict VIII's *fideles* in 1015. In the next generation, Pietro di Alberico held land east of the city, which his widow Porpora sold off in 1140.[136] We cannot trace the family any later, but it is worth signalling it briefly here for all that, simply

135 *Liber Pontificalis*, ed. Přerovský, pp. 738–9.
136 *RF*, n. 502 (a. 1015); *SMVL*, n. 63 (a. 1034); *SMN*, n. 50 (a. 1140); for the other texts, see Chapter 3, n. 170.

because it shows that the social break between the now-rural 'old aristocracy' and the new urban families was not a complete one.

The *filii Astaldi a Coloseo* we have just met too; they figure as one of the *consules comunitatis boum* in 1088, but were otherwise very much a local family in the S. Maria Nova area: Astaldo di Crescenzio di Tedaldo, the earliest known family member, appears in 1055–60 as a dealer and witness there, holding no less than the Arco di Costantino, and the family was marked as *a Coloseo* into the 1140s. But they slowly gained wider prominence; already in 1084 Astaldo di Astaldo was in the entourage of Henry IV, alongside the Sant' Eustachio. The family started to witness more widely in the city and to own more widely too—at Orta Prefecti in 1118 and 1140; outside the Porta S. Giovanni, where they had a rural tower, in 1140 and 1156; and, thanks to a marriage with the *filii Baruncii*, on the Appia in 1131. In 1115, Paschal II used Astoldo *de Coloseo*, probably the 1088 consul, as one of the *prudentes viri de optimatibus suis* who resolved a dispute between S. Gregorio sul Celio and the *scola piscatorum* of the Porto lagoon. Later, they were significant enough a family to produce (in all probability) a *navalis prefectus*, Astaldo, in 1156 (he was paternal uncle of the wife of one of the Papareschi), and a cardinal in 1145–58, another Astaldo, of S. Eustachio and then S. Prisca. We can say that they were probably from this family, because other families used the name much more rarely until after the middle of the century; the naval prefect also seems to have been holding land from S. Maria Nova. Cardinal Astaldo must have been appointed by Celestine II or Lucius II in 1143–4, for Innocent II appointed no Roman cardinals and dismissed all those of Anacletus II; the date of his appointment lies firmly in the politically charged years of the early Senate. He must surely have been promoted at least in part to keep an influential family, presumably one close to their neighbours the Frangipane, on the papal side in a divisive period. But the family is not recorded later; this cardinal was not one who developed his family's fortunes, unlike some of his contemporaries and many of his successors.[137]

The Normanni used that name as a nickname right from their first citation in our sources, as supporters of Silvester IV against Paschal II in 1105. Stefano Normanno di Stefano di Oddone and his brothers were active there, and Stefano Normanno, a *fidelis* of Henry V, remained on bad terms with Paschal, at least until Henry interceded for him in 1111. They must have intermarried with the Frangipane before 1100, but are seldom found on the same political side. By 1118, as we saw at the start of this chapter, Stefano was a firm supporter of Gelasius II against Leone and Cencio Frangipane, his nephews, and he was left in charge of the city when the pope fled Rome. In 1120, he was close enough to Calixtus II to get some of the pay-offs that Caffaro of Genoa handed over to the Roman nobility. A Stefano Normanno of the next generation (by which time *Normannus* was evidently a surname) supported Victor IV in 1159–60; the family do not appear in urban

---

[137] In chronological order, *SMN*, nn. 16, 17; *RF*, nn. 1097 (a. 1084), 1115; *SCD*, n. 96; *S. Gregorio*, n. 34 (a. 1115); *SMCM*, n. 30; *S. Gregorio*, n. 137 (a. 1131); *SMN*, n. 50; *SMCM*, n. 42; *SMN*, n. 73 (a. 1156). For the cardinal, Pflugk, III, n. 63 (a. 1145) to *SPV*, n. 47 (a. 1158); see Doran, 'The legacy of schism', p. 94, who dates the appointment to December 1143.

documents at all in the middle third of the century, and next appear as lessees of the castle of Castel di Guido on the Aurelia from S. Gregorio in 1193, before spreading further along the Aurelia as a baronial family in the thirteenth century. Where this family came from cannot be said, unless they descended from the Stefano di Oddone who was, like Alberico Cece, in the Tuscolano entourage in 1068 (it would be too romantic to take seriously the idea, still popular, that the family came from Normandy via southern Italy). But it is clear that as soon as we hear of them they were a militarized elite family (they too had a house on the Ripa Graeca), and it is likely that they moved quickly into rural castle politics, perhaps well before 1193.[138]

We are by now firmly in the twelfth century, and new families henceforth more often have surnames from the start. One of the witnesses to the 1115 Porto *piscatores* case was a Pietro Bobonio *de Bobonis*, and it is pretty certain that Giacinto di Bobone, the first of the *optimates* who resolved the same case, was his relative too; for the man who made the later fortune of the Boboni had a similar name, Giacinto di Pietro di Bobone (he must indeed have been the 1115 Pietro's son: see p. 242 for a genealogy). The second Giacinto was a cardinal in 1143–4, another key Roman appointment in the early senatorial period, and remained so for nearly fifty years, until he became Pope Celestine III (1191–8). By the time he died, and certainly as a result of direct patronage from the cardinal/pope, his nephew Orso di Bobone di Pietro was in a strong enough position to dominate the early Roman baronage, and to rename part of the family, who were henceforth called, after him, the *filii Ursi* or Orsini. But the Boboni, like the *filii Astaldi*, must already have been significant enough for the pope (probably Celestine II, given Giacinto's later choice of papal name) to wish to keep them on side in 1143–4.[139]

Exactly who was a member of the Boboni family in our period is not clear—historians here have often underestimated how frequently the name is used after 1040 or so. It would be nice to propose that Bello di Bobone, a merchant who was powerful enough to make a personal trading treaty with the commune of Gaeta in 1124, was one, as historians frequently do, but there is no evidence for it. But Bobone di Bobone, who took in a hostage in 1134 on behalf of the Ottaviani to seal a political agreement over Silva Maior, and was a courtier of Innocent II in 1140 and Celestine II in 1143, is a much more definite family member. He witnessed for Celestine II in 1143 with his nephews Bobone and Graziano di Pietro; the former was the ancestor of the Orsini, so another nephew was their brother Cardinal

---

[138] *LP*, II, pp. 345–6; *Chronica Casinensis*, IV.38; *Liber Pontificalis*, ed. Přerovský, pp. 734–41; *Codice diplomatico della Repubblica di Genova*, I, n. 31; Rahewin, *Gesta Frederici*, IV.77, 80; *S. Gregorio*, n. 24 (a.1193; cf. *LC*, I, n. 166 for Cerveteri in the same year; the only other citation of the family as land dealers is as sellers, before 1166, of unspecified land to S. Croce in Gerusalemme, in Kehr, IV, pp. 226–8). For the thirteenth-century family, see Carocci, *Baroni*, pp. 381–6; Thumser, *Rom*, pp. 135–8. Stefano di Oddone: Gattola, *Historia*, I, pp. 233–4; house in Ripa: *Liber Pontificalis*, ed. Přerovský, pp. 738–9.

[139] *S. Gregorio*, n. 34; for cardinal Giacinto, see esp. Duggan, 'Hyacinth Bobone' and Doran, 'A lifetime of service', p. 39, for the strong likelihood that he was appointed by his papal homonym Celestine II. For the Boboni/Orsini, Thumser, *Rom*, pp. 47–51; Carocci, *Baroni*, pp. 387–400; Allegrezza, *Organizzazione di potere*, pp. 3–12.

Giacinto di Pietro. The elder Bobone also appears as tenant of part of a *trullo* in the city in 1149, in, significantly, the first document surviving in the Orsini archive, the oldest lay archive in Rome. It is generally reckoned that this *trullo* was part of the Teatro di Pompeio, because that theatre was later the focus of a major Orsini fortification (part of it survives above the Cinema Farnese on the Campo de' Fiori); the document in no way says so, but it is far from impossible. Giacinto/Celestine III, who was born around 1105, was also later said to be from the *regio* of Arenula, where the theatre is situated; so this was certainly a family base, in the heart of the developing quarters in the Tiber bend. Later figures who are more likely than not to be family members include Giovanni di Bobone di Giacinto, who had formerly held a lease of two houses in the trading area of the Civitas Leoniana, referred to in a text of 1151 (his brother Leone witnessed the 1149 *trullo* lease); and, as Jean Coste showed, the *Bovieri Romani* who took over the former castle of Empiglione behind Tivoli in pledge in 1159 when its owner, Subiaco, was short of money—for the Orsini held Empiglione on lease by 1247. If so, the Bovieri/Boboni concerned may have been the Bobone di Pietro of the 1143 document and his son Orso (he who gave his name to the Orsini), because they were politically active in this period; they appear as witnesses of a papal document of 1159, a pledge to Hadrian IV.[140] The Boboni thus take shape as a second-level family in papal entourages from the 1110s to the 1150s (but vastly more prominent later); as holders of city property in two commercially significant areas; and as rich enough in money to loan to Subiaco and get a large tract of land back (not a castle, though)—as well as being prosperous enough already in the 1130s to pay for a French (doubtless Parisian) theological education for the future Cardinal Giacinto, which trained the latter sufficiently for him to be among Peter Abelard's supporters at the time of the council of Sens in 1141.[141] They were second-level dealers in land and money as well as second-level courtiers, but were politically active, and well placed to be pushed upward to the baronial level by their cardinal.

We cannot look here at every one of the newer 'aristocratic' families of the twelfth century, such as the Scotti, the Malabranca, the *de Monumento*, the Annibaldi, the Parenzi, or the Capocci (see below, however, pp. 270–1, 299, for the last two).[142] None of these, however important later—the Annibaldi and the Capocci made it through to become *baroni* in the thirteenth century—leaves any significant trace in our documentation before 1150. One family may serve to close this list, however, the Papareschi or *de Papa*. This was the family of Innocent II, who came from Trastevere, and it certainly owed its later social position to that

---

[140] *CDC*, n. 302 (a. 1124); *SMVL*, n. 157 (a. 1134); *S. Gregorio*, n. 7 (a. 1140); *Codex diplomaticus*, ed. Theiner, I, n. 15 (a. 1143); *Regesto degli Orsini*, I, pp. 29–30 (a. 1149); for Celestine's origin, *LC*, II, p. 330; ASV, A. A. Arm. I–XVIII, n. 117 (a. 1151); *Chronicon Sublacense*, p. 22 (a. 1159)—see Coste, *Scritti*, pp. 455–6; *LC*, I, n. 112 (a. 1159). If the Boboni could be called Bovieri, then the *Bovisci* of *Liber Pontificalis*, ed. Přerovský, p. 734, who were supporters of Gelasius II, are doubtless the same family too; that version of the surname is known later.

[141] Bernard of Clairvaux, *Epistolae*, n. 189; John of Salisbury, *Historia pontificalis*, ch. 31.

[142] There are discussions of each in Thumser, *Rom*, pp. 28–42, 52–64, 126–30, 132–5, 175–80, 196–7.

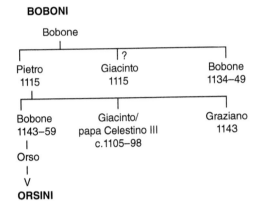

Genealogy 4

pope. Innocent (formerly Gregorio di Giovanni Gregorio, cardinal of S. Angelo in Pescheria) had several nephews, notably Guido *de Papa*, Giovanni Sarraceno, and Romano *de Papa*, as well as a niece, Purpura, who married Pietro 'III', the urban prefect of the 1140s–50s. Giovanni Sarraceno obtained much of Campo di Merlo on the Portuense in lease from S. Ciriaco in Via Lata in the late 1130s as a result of Innocent's direct intervention (above, p. 83); Romano was a *consul* in the court case of 1148 which showed how Innocent had intervened (cf. below, p. 404); Guido's son Giovanni was a senator in 1188; a cousin was a cardinal of S. Maria in Trastevere in the same year and onwards. Many of the family were also co-holders of the small city of Civita Castellana into the 1190s as a papal pledge, in inheritance from Purpura and Pietro.[143] None of this group are attested before Innocent's return to Rome in 1137–8 (the first reference is to Romano *de Papa*, who was an *amicus et fidelis* of S. Gregorio sul Celio in 1140, along with Cencio Frangipane and several other notables); there are a handful of eleventh-century references to people called *de Papa* and the like, but they cannot be connected to the later Papareschi, and there were plenty of other popes who left children and nephews. It would be difficult to doubt that it was Innocent who elevated the family from quite ordinary Trastevere origins to being lessees of estates, holders of Lazial cities, married into the Corsi, and consuls/senators—and, into the thirteenth century, *podestà* across central Italy, and baronial castle-holders in north-west Lazio under the new name *de Cardinale*. They remained a Trastevere family, all the same; Innocent's own prestige church was S. Maria in Trastevere, which he rebuilt from its foundations and decorated richly with mosaics (it was not his own cardinal's church, but it was that of his enemy Anacletus II: below, pp. 358–61); and the family continued as one

---

[143] Thumser, *Rom*, pp. 161–71; key documents include *SMVL*, nn. 162, 172 (a. 1148), 176, 182; *S. Gregorio*, n. 7 (a. 1140); CVL 8044, ff. 4–16; *SMN*, n. 73; *Senato*, n. 42 (a. 1188), with Hirschfeld, 'Zur Chronologie', pp. 106–7; ASV, fondo S. Trifone, n. 6; *LC*, I, nn. 180–2 (a. 1195), for the whole family and Civita Castellana.

of the lessees of the fishing lagoon beside the Porto salt flats into the 1290s (above, p. 104), along with other leading Trasteverini.[144]

The Papareschi, even more than the Boboni, were thus created by papal patronage. What is interesting here is how fast it happened. Innocent doubtless knew in 1138 that he would not have much time to position his family properly (he had five years, in fact); but he managed it. And his nephews were using the name *de Papa* even in his lifetime; it looks as if Innocent had created the family name Papareschi/*de Papa* as soon as he became pope, naming it after himself. This is a marker of Innocent's chutzpah, which we have ample evidence of elsewhere (below, pp. 432–4). But the family survived and prospered after his death as well. The trajectory the Papareschi followed was, apart from its speed, not wholly different from many of those we have seen in this section.

Now that we have seen a dozen families of the 'new aristocracy' sketched out, we need to consider what this quite heterogeneous group tells us about Rome's political society. I shall look at specifically political issues in Chapter 7, but their underpinnings belong here. We need to gain a sense of what sorts of resources and economic activities marked out this social stratum; what its various political alignments were; what sorts of roles gave its members social status; how its activities changed across the century and more up to 1150; and what marked, over all, the specific 'aristocratic' status of the group. One thing that should already be clear is that exactly what made these families *nobiles* or *optimates*, and distinguished them from the more local mercantile, money-lending, and *rentier* elite of each urban region, could sometimes be both labile and temporary; families regularly rose to become part of this 'new aristocracy'—and would continue to do so after 1150, with the arrival of new families such as the Malabranca and the *de Monumento*— but they could fall out of the aristocratic stratum as well, and return to being members of the 'medium elite' again, as has been proposed here for the families of Giovanni Tignoso and his associates the Bracciuti. We shall look at this point again at the end. All the same, they do fall into two distinct economic categories, and the trajectories of the various families related quite closely to this division.

Essentially, there seems to have been a basic difference inside the 'new aristocracy' of later eleventh-century Rome between a small group of prominent urban landowners and a rather larger group of less prominent ones. The leading group included the Corsi, the Frangipane (the dominant two), the family of Cencio di Stefano, and perhaps the Sant' Eustachio; by the early twelfth century we could probably add to them the Normanni. We cannot be exact about the early economic dealings of the first and third, but they certainly held houses and towers which were politically central, and they were serious political players. The Frangipane included artisans in the tenth century, but not in the eleventh, by when they were active land dealers—as we have seen, by far the most visible 'new aristocratic' dealers in eleventh-century documents—and had prominent fortified towers in the

---

[144] For the *de Cardinale* branch, Carocci, *Baroni*, pp. 343–8. For the lagoon in the 1290s, esp. *S. Gregorio*, n. 43.

S. Maria Nova–Colosseo area. (To be exact, the word *domus* is quite as frequent as *turris* in our documentation for these families; but the Frangipane *domūs* included a *firmissima munitio* by the 1090s, and it seems quite unlikely, in the ever more unstable situation of the period, that the others were not fortified too.[145]) The Normanni were a newer family, but married into the Frangipane, and were active in papal politics in the same way by the 1100s. The Sant' Eustachio are the least known, but, with the family of Cencio di Stefano, had the same sort of role in Clementine politics as the others had in the Hildebrandine tradition.

In the eleventh century, all these families were essentially based in the city or the Agro romano; this changed in the twelfth. By 1106 the Corsi had castles in north-west Lazio, and the Corsi/Prefetti kept that geographical power-base into the thirteenth century and later. The family of Cencio di Stefano was similarly focused on castles in Tuscia Romana by the 1110s; the Frangipane extended their interests outside the city later, but from the 1140s onwards were increasingly solidly based in *Marittima*. The Sant' Eustachio had a Sabina base already in the eleventh century, even if it is only in the thirteenth that we can pin it down properly. The Normanni are not documented holding castles until 1193, but they are not documented in the previous generation and may well have had them earlier. Three of these families thus had castles and signorial rights by the 1140s, with the others following soon after. These power-bases took all five families into the age of the *baroni*, even if none of them achieved the wealth and extent of castle-holding of the most successful baronial families.[146]

The other families we have looked at were different. They held urban and suburban land leases too, but, it seems, often on a smaller scale; and that land-holding did not usually build up subsequently, as far as we can see. They did not become major Lazio castle-holders in our period. The Pierleoni held Isola Farnese early, before 1107, but that was the only castle they held for long, just on the edge of the Agro romano; the family of Giovanni Tignoso already in 1079 held land on the Aurelia, similarly on the edge of the Agro romano, *cum omni suo districto*—with signorial rights, which were very rare indeed in the Agro (above, p. 50)—but no castle. Two of the families, the *filii Baruncii* and the *filii Astaldi*, are instead associated with an early *casale* and thus with a very urban form of economic management in the Agro romano in the mid-twelfth century; the Papareschi perhaps were beginning to be too, in the same period.[147] The two families out of this set to get involved in land deals outside the Agro, the Boboni and the Papareschi, did so only in the late 1150s and later, and in both cases, without doubt, because of the major political influence of ecclesiastical family members, a cardinal and a pope, after 1143 and 1138 respectively. And these were also the only two families out of the second group to make it as *baroni*; all the other families

---

[145] *Domus/munitio*: compare Bernold, *Chronicon*, p. 509, with Geoffroy de Vendôme, *Œuvres*, pp. 288–90.

[146] See above, n. 70, for the scale of wealth of major *baroni*.

[147] See Carocci and Vendittelli, *L'origine della Campagna Romana*, pp. 95, 128–9, and above, pp. 86–8.

disappeared, even the Pierleoni—although the three last known Pierleoni, a cardinal (Guido, cardinal deacon of the family church of S. Nicola in Carcere and then bishop of Palestrina, d.1228), a senator (Giovanni, single senator 1196–7, and a senior dealer under Innocent III), and a *podestà* of Florence (Uguccio di Giovanni, 1213) were of sufficient status that the family may simply have died out, as families do.[148] In the city, too, although nearly every family at this second level is known to have had a tower-house, only the Pierleoni seem to have organized a real political power-base, around S. Nicola and on the Isola Tiberina close by. We can trace the political alignments of most of the families, but, similarly, only the Pierleoni appear as real protagonists on the level of the Frangipane and Corsi, and of Cencio di Stefano—the others were followers rather than leaders, except when Giovanni Tignoso and his son were urban prefects, until the Boboni/Orsini moved onto the scene. So: this larger group had less ambitious territorial policies in the twelfth century, survived less long in most cases, and were less prominent politically; this goes with the likelihood that they were mostly also less wealthy.

It is well known that the Pierleoni dominated late eleventh- and early twelfth-century politics, along with (or against) the Frangipane and—the least famous, but not the least important, family of the three—the Corsi/Prefetti. For all that, it seems to me that the Pierleoni were the most prominent and richest of the second group, and not part of the first group. Their lack of commitment to landed power is one reason. They are also clearly documented as merchants and dealers, as also are the Ceci, possibly the Boboni, but seldom anyone in the first group (the Frangipane seem already to have left small-scale commerce behind soon after 1000)—until popes began to borrow massively from the Corsi and Frangipane, and the newer Malabranca, from the 1140s onwards.[149] Of course, our documents tell us mostly about land, and commercial references only occur by chance. It would not be possible to deny the proposition that the Frangipane had long been major financial operators, and it is indeed entirely plausible. But, if so, they were most probably commercially active as a spin-off of their wealth from dealings in land; for the Pierleoni, by contrast, the opposite was true, and it seems to have remained true. The Pierleoni must have been wealthy throughout, to remain central for so long, but there was a structural difference between the Frangipane and the Pierleoni which also marked a cleavage right across the 'new aristocracy'. It was not unbridgeable, as the Boboni and Papareschi found, but one needed a deliberate territorial politics to do so, preferably supported by powerful political office. We will come back to the issue of office in a moment.

One respect in which the two levels of the 'new aristocracy' were united was in their initial politics. It is highly likely that they were both generally involved in the uprising of the end of 1044 which temporarily expelled Benedict IX from the city, and which marked the beginning of the end of Tuscolano power. We have seen that the 'old aristocracy' mostly supported Benedict, and the near-contemporary *Annales Romani* insists on the unity of Roman action here—although left-bank

---

[148] Thumser, *Rom*, p. 182.   [149] See above, Chapter 3, n. 170.

Rome and Trastevere had fallen out by January 1045, which probably allowed the Ottaviani to nominate their own pope, Silvester III, and then allowed the counts of Galeria to reinstate Benedict for a short period. The reasons for the Roman uprising are not clear, but it closely matches the uprising in Milan in the same year against Archbishop Ariberto II and his *milites*, in which urban elites claimed, and gained, more formal standing in that city.[150] It would seem most probable that the 'new aristocracy' of Rome, too, wanted more of a role in the Tuscolano political system. There is, as a result, no reason to see 1044 as part of any ecclesiastical 'reform' movement. But there is equally no reason to think that any of the 'new aristocracy' were hostile to the German takeover of Rome in 1046. The close association of all of the early families with either Hildebrand or his German opponents by the 1060s can allow us to assume that they all saw advantages in the post-Sutri political, and possibly even ideological, settlement. But we cannot be more precise than that, because documents from the decade after 1046 are so scarce.

That initial unity had clearly broken down by 1062, when Bishop Cadalo of Parma was made Pope Honorius II by the regents of Henry IV against Bishop Anselmo I of Lucca, Pope Alexander II. By now, there was a breach between supporters of the German tradition of the 'reform' papacy and that represented by Archdeacon Hildebrand and his Tuscan popes. In Rome, the Hildebrandine alliance clearly covered the majority of the 'new aristocracy', in each stratum: the Corsi and Frangipane, and also the Pierleoni, the family of Giovanni Tignoso, the Bracciuti, and the Ceci were with Hildebrand; whereas the Sant' Eustachio, the family of Cencio di Stefano, and also the *filii Baruncii* were with Cadalo. Political opposition thus divided the 'new aristocracy' vertically, not along socio-economic lines. This division continued into the period of Clement III in the last two decades of the century, in which the *filii Astaldi* appear with Clement as well (and at least one Frangipane, although the family as a whole supported his opponents). But after 1099, when Paschal II and his successors for the most part ruled without rivals until 1130, these fairly clear divisions were replaced by a carousel of much less perman-ent rivalries, with the Corsi and Normanni opposed to Paschal but supporters of Gelasius II, the Pierleoni supporters of Paschal and Gelasius but opponents of Honorius II, the Frangipane opposed to Gelasius but supporters of Paschal and Honorius, and so on (see below, Chapter 7).

It may be for this reason that it seems to have mattered so little where in the city its leading figures had their power-bases. As already observed, we know the major locations of nearly every one of the families discussed in this section: in the Colosseo area, the Frangipane and the *filii Astaldi*; on the Capitolio, the Corsi; along the Ripa Graeca, the Pierleoni, the Normanni, another branch of the Corsi, and plausibly the *filii Baruncii*; in the *regio* Arenula, the Boboni; near the Pantheon, the Sant' Eustachio; in Parione and Ponte, the family of Cencio di Stefano; in Trastevere, the family of Giovanni Tignoso, the Bracciuti, the Ceci, and the Papareschi. The Trastevere families perhaps stuck together, and the Colosseo

---

[150] *LP*, II, p. 331, for Rome. For Milan, Arnolfo, *Liber gestorum recentium*, II.18–19; see further below, Chapter 7, n. 166.

families likewise, but in the Ripa area alliances and enmities were highly mobile. In 1116 the Pierleoni houses were bombarded from the Capitolio,[151] but apart from that this vicinity did not seem to present problems. Perhaps it was more important that the political heart of the city was shared.

One problem for the 'new aristocracy', which their predecessors had not had, was that the major ecclesiastical positions in the city were controlled by foreigners, who also did not, ever, use their office to establish family power-bases in Rome for themselves. This presumably was not predictable in 1046—even by the Germans; after all, Gregory VI, the major Roman victim at Sutri, was again proposed by Bishop Wazo of Liège as pope as early as 1047, on Clement II's death.[152] After that, however, the only fully Roman pope until 1130 was, briefly, Benedict X in 1058–9. We could add Hildebrand/Gregory VII himself, who was, though from Tuscany, very well rooted in the city, and its effective ruler from 1059 to 1083–4. But what we cannot add is all that many cardinals. On the basis of Rudolf Hüls' prosopography of cardinals from 1046 to 1130, only nine cardinals appointed in that period were certainly Roman (the origin of some two-thirds of the documented cardinals cannot be located, but nearly eighty were certainly non-Roman); nor did the percentage of Roman cardinals increase substantially before the return of the popes to Rome in 1188. Of the cardinals up to 1130, one was a Pierleoni, one an Ottaviani (hardly Roman by now), one a Papareschi, one a Boccapecora (Tebaldo of S. Maria Nova then S. Anastasia, who nearly became pope in 1124; his family are little known, but almost certainly belonged to the second 'new aristocratic' level). Thereafter, until 1188, we find two more Pierleoni, another Ottaviani, a Boboni, one of the *filii Astaldi*, and a Paparoni (not the same family as the Papareschi).[153] Not many of the 'new aristocratic' families looked to or gained high ecclesiastical office, that is to say; and only the Boboni and Papareschi really owed their standing to it (for the Pierleoni it was simply one element out of several, although it is probably significant that they provided cardinals and the Corsi and Frangipane did not). But the families also could not regularly base themselves on high ecclesiastical office, even if they wished to; the trend to non-Roman cardinals was too strong, and some popes (in the twelfth century Innocent II, and most popes between Eugenius III and the 1180s) were actively opposed to Roman appointments.[154]

Secular office-holding was, however, also less an accessible *cursus honorum* than it had been. The office of prefect of the city was becoming patrimonalized. Two families fought over it in the 1050s–70s, those of Giovanni Tignoso and Cencio di Stefano. By 1101 at the latest, however, a branch of the Corsi, later called

---

[151] *Liber Pontificalis*, ed. Přerovský, p. 721.

[152] Anselm of Liège, *Gesta episcoporum Leodiensis ecclesiae*, pp. 228–9; cf. Sennis, 'Gregorio VI'.

[153] Hüls, *Kardinale*, pp. 223–4, 225, 233–4, 235; for after 1130, Thumser, *Rom*, pp. 357–61, is an accessible survey. For the Boccapecora, *RF*, n. 492 (a. 1014, Benedetto *Boccapecu*), is the earliest reference, but then we have almost nothing until narrative accounts of the support of the *Buccapecorini* for Gelasius II in 1118 and Tebaldo's near-miss as pope in 1124 (*Liber Pontificalis*, ed. Přerovský, pp. 734, 751). The family appear casually in twelfth-century texts (*SPV*, n. 33, *SMCM*, nn. 43, 60, *SMVL*, nn. 143, 241, aa. 1113–92) as owners along the Cassia, Salaria, and Ostiense, but nothing more than that.

[154] Doran, 'The legacy of schism', pp. 76–81, 191.

the Prefetti, had got hold of the office, and held it for a minimum of 59 years in the twelfth century (and then on, without a break, long into the thirteenth)—only three other holders are known in the twelfth, restricted to the 1130s and then again, perhaps, to the 1170s. The Corsi/Prefetti do indeed seem to be the only 'new aristocratic' family who would happily have adapted to 'old aristocratic' practices if they had still been available. As to the territorial countships, these had either become hereditary (the Ottaviani in the Sabina, the Tuscolani in Tuscolo, the counts of Galeria), or had lost any real public authority by 1100 or so, or both. It is significant that the Frangipane, although they temporarily took the countship of Ceccano from its family holders in the 1120s, gave up that path, and are not attested with any particular office in their later *Marittima* power-base; unlike the Corsi, they never paid any long-term attention to offices of any kind in our period.

The core of the old aristocratic *cursus* had, of course, been the palatine offices, but here there was another change. These offices, after the mid-eleventh century, had less status, and were more often held by less rich families: families who had become *iudices* by profession, probably after a training either as *scriniarii* or, increasingly, as *causidici*, experts in Roman law. Only one of the 'new aristocratic' families we have looked at, the *filii Baruncii*, included a *iudex*, and he never became a palatine judge. Of the palatine judges themselves, even prominent ones have little traceable family or landholding context by now. Examples of this are Sassone di Elpiza, *secundicerius* in 1060–73 and active during the Cadalan schism; or Ferrucio, *secundicerius* for Clement III (1085–94; this is probably the Ferrucio who sold control of the Laterano palace to Urban II in 1094, for the name is rare) and then, having evidently changed sides, *primicerius* (1107–36) for a fifty-year career. A later *arcarius*, Gregorio (1139–66), called himself *de Primicerio*, which almost certainly means that he was Ferrucio's son, but this does not extend this essentially judicial family any further; all we know otherwise is that Ferrucio held a *feudum* from the monastery of S. Saba in 1126, which need not have been more than an upgrading of an ordinary agricultural lease. Later palatine judges, such as the *primicerius* Galgano, were clearly members of the 'medium elite' (below, p. 274), and so already, I would propose, were men like Sassone and Ferrucio.[155] The centrality of these judges to Rome's political system had faded with the rise of the cardinalate (which almost at once lost its Roman content too), and this was even more the case when the papal *camerarius* took over finance, presumably from the *arcarius*, in the early twelfth century.[156] Judicial office still had status, but by now no longer enough status for the greatest urban families to pursue.

Office-holding was, then, no longer the core marker of social prominence for Rome's leading families. A trend which had already partially begun in the late tenth

[155] Sassone: Halphen, *Études*, p. 111, with esp. Benzone of Alba, *Ad Heinricum IV*, II.3 (p. 202; it is not explicit here that Sasso was actually a supporter of Cadalo; Halphen thought he was an opponent, but the text does not say that either). Ferrucio and son: refs. in Halphen, *Études*, pp. 100, 112, 120–2; they miss out Geoffroy de Vendôme, *Œuvres*, pp. 288–90 and *SMN*, n. 42 (a.1126); see also below, p. 370. *Causidici* were certainly often from the 'medium elite': see below, pp. 268, 299.
[156] Jordan, 'Zur päpstlichen Finanzgeschichte', pp. 88–104; illuminating observations in Toubert, *Les structures*, pp. 1047–50.

century (above, p. 205) became precipitous by 1050. (If offices were what the 'new aristocracy' wanted out of the uprising of 1044, which we cannot know, then they were certainly doomed to disappointment.) The only external status indicators by now must have been simply closeness to the pope, or to the ever-changing sequence of popes. This is in itself a sufficient explanation for the violence with which the Frangipane, in particular (but not only them), dealt with papal elections in the first decades of the twelfth century: possession of papal favour was the only public role they could hold, so who was pope mattered inordinately. The Roman *nobiliores* are described by a Flemish abbot as attending the papal tribunal (*consistorium*) in 1141, *calamistati et sericis amicti*, 'with curled hair and cloaked in silks';[157] it becomes increasingly clear by the 1140s that, to maintain their social position, they had to. Papal patronage brought money or treasure as well, as we have seen and will see again (pp. 172–3, 417–19); that too was a necessary part of being an aristocrat, for it allowed for the financing, precisely, of this level of display, including, an increasingly important element, substantial entourages. Only when the 'new aristocracy' committed to the Senate, which was not until around 1190, was there a new political *cursus* to give them status and potentially money;[158] but soon after that the sharp increase in the number of Roman aristocratic cardinals gave them much more scope of all kinds.

Aristocratic status does not only depend on wealth, title and office, and closeness to rulers, the three markers we have looked at in most detail. It is true that one other typically important criterion for aristocracies, the imagery of noble ancestry, was absent in Rome in our period; no one made anything serious of long-ago family relationships, except the links to Alberico claimed by the Tuscolani. Legal definition was also not part of the habitus of aristocratic identity in this period in Rome, although it is at least the case that the word *nobilis*, which was a more restricted term by 1100, attached itself explicitly to nearly half the families discussed here (the Pierleoni, Corsi, Frangipane, Sant' Eustachio, and Orsini: below, p. 201), and generic words like *potentes* covered the political action of others as well. We can also presume that most of these families had peer recognition as political players, for each of the pre-1150 families we have looked at on the basis of their documentary appearances also appears as a protagonist in our scarce narrative sources, with the exception of the Ceci and the *filii Astaldi*. But status also typically depends on a network of other transactional elements: recognition by inferiors; display; and an exclusive education in whatever constitutes 'aristocratic' bearing in any given society. This must be why towers were an early marker of the 'new aristocracy', and it certainly must be why the Casa dei Crescenzi was so dramatically self-aggrandizing. The purple diploma from Roger II to the Pierleoni was also a remarkable sign of favour by an external figure, which was very potent for display purposes. So must have been the leopard (*lupardus*) which 'strangled' an unnamed woman in the *domus* of Cencio Frangipane in the time of Innocent II, according to notarized eyewitness testimony by a (necessarily very old) Tivoli priest in 1209; she

---

[157] See Müller, 'Der Bericht', p. 102.   [158] Thumser, *Rom*, pp. 231–56.

was buried in a marble sarcophagus in the doorway of S. Maria Nova, which was, indeed, quite as much of a piece of aristocratic display (a sarcophagus, i.e. a high-status burial, for an unnamed woman).[159] The major families also had entourages, who—as in other Italian cities—fought each other (such as the Normanni and Frangipane in 1118); the lay courtiers of Innocent II wore silk in 1141. These all cost money, so on one level they were simply markers of wealth, but they showed wealth that was used to establish their owners as socially distinct: as *nobiles* or *nobiliores*, indeed.

I have here rapidly tracked the elements of the aristocratic 'ideal type' set out at the start of the chapter (p. 184). But what is important to stress is that they marked out nearly all the families described here quite clearly—and few others. These families were the richest we can see documented in the century after 1050; only the Bracciuti do not appear explicitly as wealthy in that period, although our sense of the wealth of the Ceci is only really based on the commercial patronage of one of them by Gregory VII. They overwhelmingly dominate our accounts of who was closest to papal (or, occasionally, imperial) power in the city—even the Ceci and the *filii Astaldi*, absent from the narratives, figure here. They had at least some titles or offices: the urban prefecture (two rival families in the mid-eleventh century and then the Corsi), the naval prefecture (the *filii Astaldi*), the cardinalate (Pierleoni, *filii Astaldi*, Boboni, Papareschi), or various forms of consular title, or the title of *nobilis*—all except the Bracciuti, the Ceci, and the Normanni. They all visibly had towers or other fortifications by 1150, sometimes many, or else unusually impressive ones, except the family of Giovanni Tignoso, the Ceci, and the Papareschi. In the twelfth century, letters and documents emanating from a self-declared city leadership privilege most of these families (Pierleoni, Corsi, Frangipane, Sant' Eustachio, the family of Cencio di Stefano, Normanni) and few others.[160] The 'few others' who appear in such texts, and also in our narratives, such as the *Buccapecorini* and *Berizisi* in 1118, or, earlier, Cencio di Cencio di Roizone in 1088,[161] are in all identifiable cases families who otherwise appear in similar contexts, and were probably equally 'aristocratic' (certainly so in the case of the Boccapecora), but who for the most part escape the rest of our documentation.

This list of status markers makes it clear that many of our thirteen families were prominent according to all the criteria I have mentioned, and that most fulfilled the majority of them. The least prominent seem to have been the Bracciuti, whom we might see as thrust into the spotlight in the period of the German papacy and by Hildebrand, but unable to maintain that position—they were, that is to say, the most marginal of these families. The Ceci follow them, and then the family of Giovanni Tignoso, for all its dominance of the urban prefecture under Hildebrand/ Gregory and its holding of signorial rights. Interestingly, all three were Trasteverini,

---

[159] Ed. in Fedele, 'Il leopardo e l'agnello', p. 215; cf. the observations of Sandro Carocci in his 'Presentazione' to *La nobiltà romana*, at p. 1.

[160] For example *PL*, CLXIII, cols 1180–1, n. 98 (a. 1120); *CDC*, n. 312 (a. 1127); Petersohn, 'Der Brief', pp. 506–7 with *PL*, CLXXIX, col. 707, n. 18 (a. 1130); *S. Prassede*, n. 26 (a. 1153); *LC*, I, n. 91 (a. 1153).

[161] *Liber Pontificalis*, ed. Přerovský, p. 734; for Cencio see *RF*, n. 1115, and below, p. 283.

so slightly marginal to urban politics; and all three fade away in the twelfth century. They were, then, the closest documented 'aristocratic' families to the top edge of the 'medium elite', and they probably slipped back into it after their connection with Hildebrand ceased. But it is also important to emphasize that not one of the 'medium elite' families discussed in Chapter 5 is found in a similar political role before 1150, even to these three families, never mind the others. The only exception (below, p. 283) is one participant in the Arci assembly, participation in which, as we have seen, went well beyond the 'aristocracy'. As we shall see (pp. 271–7), we also cannot track wealth for members of that stratum that matches the wealth known for our 'aristocratic' families. If there were any other seriously rich families in corners of Rome (perhaps in expanding, but ill-documented, Parione) who are hidden from us because they did not participate either in the political self-affirmation of different types which I have just characterized, or in the landed transactions which our documents tell us about, they remained, precisely, hidden away. Instead, the 'medium elite' became senators, or legal experts, or else leaders of their *regiones*: very different markers of status.

The only arena where the 'medium elite' showed a similar commitment to these more prominent families was as military figures—as mounted horsemen, and as the builders of tower-houses—for a very wide 'medium elite' was militarized in Rome, as in every other twelfth-century city, as Jean-Claude Maire Vigueur has shown (see further below, pp. 262–6).[162] This certainly underpinned the permeability of Rome's social hierarchies. There must have been any number of 'medium elite' families who wanted to accumulate enough other status markers to be recognized, both by their neighbours and by established *nobiles*, as 'aristocratic'. This is precisely what Innocent II and Giacinto Boboni did for their families, pushing them through the barrier. Others (such as the Parenzi: below, pp. 270–1) followed later in the century. Indeed, all the 'new aristocracy' must have started like that originally, crystallizing up and out of a wider and less differentiated *plebs* (to use Liutprando of Cremona's word) in the first half of the eleventh century. But most did not manage it; either their wealth or their transactional status was not sufficient for them to make it as 'aristocratic'. And, except in such cases of social mobility, for all the permeability and fluidity of that divide between the two strata, it was evidently there; if we take the bundle of elements of the aristocratic ideal type, there was a clear separation between (most of) the Roman 'aristocratic' families and the rest. We thus see delineated a definable social group: that of the families who had the resources and social recognition necessary to be political players on the city level in their own right, and not just as part of a wider collectivity. This is the crucial mark of the 'new aristocracy'.

The 'new aristocracy' changed across the eleventh and twelfth centuries. It crystallized as a very urban group of families in the period 1010–80, and perhaps above all in the quarter-century of Hildebrand's dominance in the city. The families took sides when the 'reform' movement split, and some figures, like Leone di

---

[162] Maire Vigueur, *Cavaliers et citoyens*.

Benedetto Cristiano, or Cencio di Stefano, or, later, Cencio and Giovanni Frangipane, became active players for their respective popes, but they were seldom direct protagonists acting on their own account (perhaps only Cencio di Stefano, in his guerrilla action against Gregory VII in the 1070s). After 1100, however, several of the leading aristocratic families were very definitely independent players, as Paschal II and Gelasius II both found to their cost, and by 1124 and 1130 they were directly choosing popes. They were more ambitious by now, and their leaders were looking for the first time to landed power outside Rome's immediate hinterland. By the time the Senate was formed, in 1143–4, they were a papal-focused elite, against whom the early Senate defined itself: as the latter said to Conrad III in 1149, they were the *potentes urbis*, allied with the pope and the king of Sicily against Conrad and the Senate itself, who included not only the Pierleoni and the Frangipane but also the Tuscolani (no longer sharply distinguished), whose *fortitudines*, *turres*, and *domos* the Senate had seized.[163] By now, the social separation between 'aristocracy' and 'medium elite' had crystallized into direct political opposition. Who was representing 'the Romans' had dramatically changed: again. But the ambiguities of this process, which were many, need to be discussed in a focused way. That will be for the last chapter of this book.

ROME'S ARISTOCRACIES IN AN ITALIAN CONTEXT

We have already seen that the main families of the 'old aristocracy' of Rome had, as individual families, less landed wealth than did many tenth- and eleventh-century aristocrats in the *Regnum Italiae*: to use Tuscan parallels, they were roughly on a par with prominent city-level families in Florence (the city in the region with the biggest *contado*, so the best comparator) such as the 'Suavizi', who could at the top end hold 20 to 25 castles and estates, but did not match, any of them, the wealth of regional aristocracies like the Aldobrandeschi or the Guidi, who came to hold at least double that (pp. 207–8). To be more exact, the Fiorentino showed a clear hierarchy of wealth, with the Guidi firmly at the top (and extending well beyond the county), two or three other 'multizonal' families at the level of the 'Suavizi', holding castles and estates in several places in the diocese, as many again with about half that wealth, and then a larger set of 'zonal' families with one or two castles only.[164] If we exclude the Guidi, and also take into account the fact that castles hardly existed in the Agro romano, so that many relatively wealthy people never had them, Rome's 'old aristocratic' hierarchy was probably not dissimilar, although already in the eleventh century, a century earlier than in Florence, its leading families were developing geographical concentrations of signorial landholding. The collective wealth of the aristocracy around (say) 1000 was unusually great in Rome, but this is because of the combined resources of more families than most cities had, not the individual wealth of their leaders. Now that we have to consider

---

[163] *Senato*, n. 5.   [164] Cortese, *Signori, castelli, città*, esp. pp. 36–64.

the 'new aristocracy' as well, however, it is worth going a little further and later in these parallels, to get some sense of the variation there was in Italy north of Rome (I set aside the South, as less work has been done on this aspect of its history before the Norman conquest).

Lombardy and the Po plain in general are actually less easy to analyse from this standpoint than is central Italy—it is not entirely chance that Maria Elena Cortese's book on the Fiorentino is the most systematic county-level account of an eleventh-century aristocracy yet to appear. This is largely because, beside allodial property, so much aristocratic possession in the North was based on fiefs conceded by emperors and bishops, which were usually not recorded in documents, rather than on leases, as in Tuscany and Lazio, which were always conveyed through a written text; episcopal fiefs were also sometimes of ecclesiastical rights, largely to tithe, rather than land, so their economic content is harder to estimate; and the economic resources and local domination derived from signorial rights, which came to be heavier in the North, have to be added in as well. The historiography of the North has as a result tended to focus less on wealth, and more on genealogical reconstruction, on the reality of a division between an urban and a rural aristocracy, and on the nature and antiquity of the 'società cetuale' which north Italian (but not Tuscan or Lazial) documents demonstrate from time to time in their terminological separation between two aristocratic *ordines*, *capitanei* and *valvassores* (actually three, for the level of counts and marquises was regarded as distinct by Oberto dall'Orto in his famous formulation, dating probably to the 1140s).[165]

It is, all the same, possible to show roughly the same sort of hierarchical patterns of wealth as in Tuscany and Lazio, even if one bases oneself only on secondary literature focused on other issues, as I have done for the most part here. Families like the Canossa and the Obertenghi certainly matched the Guidi, and over-matched the Tuscolani; they were, however, as rare in the North as anywhere else in Italy. Comital families were the most likely to match the Tuscolani, *de Imiza*, and 'Suavizi', as with the counts of Padua and Vicenza, a single family, who had over fifteen estates, many with castles, or the Gisalbertingi counts of the Berga-masco, who had twenty to thirty castles under their family's control at different moments in the eleventh century, including a substantial set of lands around Crema which matched in size the territory of Tuscolo (although it was not under the sole control of the Gisalbertingi, for nothing matched the solidity of the blocks of land around Rome), or Bosone of Nibbianq, son of Count Gandolfo of Piacenza, who around 1000 had some eighteen estates, most with castles, on the western edge of that county. Some families of *capitanei*, however, came close to this level of wealth,

---

[165] See especially Keller, *Signori e vassalli*, and the reactions to it, of which recent ones (i.e. those subsequent to Keller's effective answer to earlier critics in his introduction to the Italian edition of his book, pp. xxiii–xxxiii—p. xxiii for 'società cetuale') include Grillo, 'Aristocrazia urbana, aristocrazia rurale', and *La vassallità maggiore*, especially the introduction by Andrea Castagnetti, pp. 7–23. Castagnetti stresses counts, in *La vassallità maggiore*, pp. 7–9; so do the collections of articles published as *Formazione e strutture*. Oberto dall'Orto on the various *ordines* is contained in *Consuetudines feudorum, recensio antiqua*, VIII.16 (pp. 127–8); for the date, see Classen, *Studium und Gesellschaft*, pp. 59–60.

as with the da Soresina of the Cremonese, who before their territorial eclipse in the 1030s (and their move to Milan) held a dozen castles and other estates as feudal dependants of the bishop of Cremona, which was not their whole wealth, as it did not include their evidently allodial centre of Soresina itself.[166]

These were mostly rural-based families, interestingly; that makes the North different from Tuscany and Lazio. Urban capitaneal families in the eleventh and twelfth centuries (and also lesser rural families, even *capitanei*, not to speak of *valvassores*) do not seem to have held so much. Very many capitaneal families only had a castle or two each.[167] Most civic leaders in the twelfth-century Po plain, whether *capitanei* or not, held little outside cities and their immediate surroundings—as could also be the case in Tuscany, where Enrico Faini calculates for Florence that two-thirds of the property held by elite urban families in the eleventh century was less than 10 km from the city (and this in a documentary context which, over all, illuminates the *contado* rather more than the city and its surroundings), a figure rising to a striking 92 per cent in the first half of the twelfth, at the height of the social separation there between city and countryside, though falling steadily thereafter, as the city expanded its authority. But there were always in the North some rich and urban-focused aristocratic families— families who were active both in episcopal followings in the eleventh century and in early communes in the twelfth—who had the equivalent of half a dozen castles or estates each (and at least some signorial rights), such as the Mozzi in Bergamo, the da Casalvolone in Vercelli, and the *de Porta Romana* in Milan.[168] These families contribute to make too sharp a separation between urban and rural aristocracies less crucial, although we need not doubt that this was very variable from city to city in the Po plain, as it certainly was in Tuscany—that, however, is a variability which still has to be worked out.[169]

Rome in the late eleventh and early twelfth centuries, the age of the 'new aristocracy', fits the range of these models too, but presents some clear originalities. As we have seen, even the most prominent of the newer families, the Corsi or the Frangipane or the family of Cencio di Stefano, did not control more than half a dozen castles each in the twelfth century, and the Frangipane, probably the richest

---

[166] Based on the data (often rough, as family possessions varied across time) in Rippe, *Padoue*, pp. 129–30; Menant, *Lombardia feudale*, pp. 80–7; Bougard, 'Entre Gandolfingi et Obertenghi', pp. 23–6, 42–8; Violante, 'Una famiglia feudale', pp. 673–83. For the Canossa, see e.g. Rinaldi, *Tra le carte di famiglia*, esp. pp. 53–97; for the Obertenghi see especially Ricci, *La marca della Liguria Orientale*, pp. 95–142.

[167] For example Rippe, *Padoue*, pp. 136–43; Menant, *Campagnes lombardes*, pp. 608–19; *La vassalità maggiore, passim*.

[168] Faini, *Firenze*, p. 359, with pp. 150–65; Menant, *Campagnes lombardes*, pp. 639–41 (Mozzi); Keller, *Signori e vassalli*, pp. 114–16, 169–70, with Panero, '*Capitanei, valvassores*', pp. 135–42 and Degrandi, 'Vassalli cittadini', pp. 22–5, 29 (da Casalvolone; the latter treats the family as very much the exception among the major capitaneal families of Vercelli in its urban orientation, however—doubtless it was determinant that the family's lands were quite dispersed, which made a city orientation more logical); Salvatori, 'I presunti "*capitanei* delle porte" di Milano', pp. 46–68.

[169] Note that the variability in the social (and military) base of the early commune is a different issue again, for that tends to melt urban aristocrats and richer *cives* together. For comparative overviews here, see Bordone, *La società cittadina*, pp. 160–82, and Maire Vigueur, *Cavaliers et citoyens*, pp. 220–46, 337–62; I am preparing a study on this topic.

of them inside Rome, did not enter castle/signorial politics until the very end of our period. They all held substantial landed estates in the ecclesiastically owned Agro romano as well, of course. We cannot quantify their number. But there is no evidence at all for large concentrations of leases held by individual families there in the documents that we possess for major landowners, S. Pietro in Vaticano, S. Ciriaco in Via Lata, S. Gregorio sul Celio, or SS. Cosma e Damiano in Trastevere; given that, it would be surprising if the Frangipane had as much as a dozen large estates in the Agro romano, and others doubtless had rather less. Again, the clear impression we receive is that the still-great lay landed wealth of the twelfth-century city was divided up among many families—and, in the Agro, not only the relatively substantial sets of holdings of the 'new aristocracy', which were already by 1150 beginning to crystallize in a few cases into *casali*, but the rather smaller-scale holdings of the 'medium elite' as well (see below, pp. 271–7, for orders of magnitude here). Even if we add in the Tuscolani, in the early twelfth century certainly no longer an urban family, and expanding their interests in that period into *Campania* (they were indeed the only surviving now-rural 'old aristocratic' family not to lose influence rapidly after 1100), we are still looking at only around ten castles newly in the family's hands at their high point around 1140, on top of the great block of land around Tuscolo itself. As for their sub-branch, the Colonna, who were by now separating their interests sufficiently from their Tuscolo cousins to survive the shipwreck of the latter's fortunes at the end of the twelfth century, which allowed them to become one of the greatest baronial families of all thereafter, they did not for their own part get beyond the control of a dozen castles, that is, perhaps twice the level of the family of Cencio di Stefano, until their great expansion in wealth following the patronage of a Colonna cardinal in the early thirteenth.[170]

Except of course for the Tuscolani/Colonna themselves, we are here looking at a far smaller landed base than the 'old aristocracy' of Rome had. Not one of the new urban families could in any way match the 'Suavizi' or the Gisalbertingi in landed resources in our period. But the best comparison with Tuscany and the North is not with the castle-holding families of the eleventh century, whether urban or rural, but, rather, the city-orientated families of the twelfth century. If we do this, we can see that the five leading Roman 'aristocratic' families were richer than all but a small number—usually no more than one or two per city—of the urban-focused families of the Centre-North, families like the Mozzi; and also that the holding of castles by this leading group, although a new development for the 'new' Roman families after 1100, did not at all make them less city-orientated, unlike in some other cities. From this standpoint, Rome was much more fully the centre of the socio-political life of its whole vast hinterland (far larger than that of any northern city, as we saw in Chapter 2) than were many northern and even Tuscan cities in the early twelfth century; and its leading group contained more relatively rich landed families than most cities seem to have had by now. The political protagonism of the individual

[170] Beolchini, *Tusculum II*, pp. 83–90; Carocci, *Baroni*, pp. 353–7.

families of the 'new aristocracy' after 1100, which is abundantly documented, and better so than that of the leading families in most other cities in our period, has some of its explanation here. More of these families could afford armed men to make up their *potentia*, to use the word for the Pierleoni following in 1111,[171] than in other cities; and they made the most of it, even without the help of ties of vassalage, which are little documented in Rome before 1150. And, by the same token, they had the resources, both individually and collectively, to make themselves more distinct from the rest of the Roman 'medium elite' than was possible or advantageous for the handful of equivalent families in other cities. (It is worth remembering that the much-discussed division between *capitanei*, *valvassores*, and *cives* inside Milan is not visible at the level of concrete political action after the earliest years of the commune.[172]) The 'new aristocracy' was not homogeneous; only its upper level, the five richest families, was or became really competitive with castle-owning families elsewhere in the peninsula. Rome was in that respect, as in many others, a more complex place than were most other Italian cities. But the protagonism of that aristocracy extended to both of its levels, and its relative wealth and relative social standing did as well, separating them from the 'medium elite' more clearly than in most cities, as we have just seen.

That is not the final point that needs to be made, however. For who, outside a few specialists, has heard of the 'Suavizi' or the Mozzi, for all their relative wealth and prominence? Let alone the names of most of the smaller-scale urban leaders of the early twelfth-century North. But every medievalist recognizes the names Frangipane and Pierleoni. This is for us because of the hold the papal grand narrative has had on the historiography, of course, and in the twelfth century it was the same; but not exclusively. Very few Italian urban leaders, however prominent, had much name recognition outside their own cities. But not only did Tolomeo II of the Tuscolani marry an illegitimate daughter of the emperor Henry V in 1116—this at least recognized the 'role of the absolutely highest level' which the family still held, in Valeria Beolchini's words—but Aldruda Frangipane in 1142 married the count of Bertinoro in the Romagna, whose possessions outmatched those of the Frangipane of that date by an order of magnitude (she later, in 1173, fought an imperial army to lift the siege of Ancona), and Oddone Frangipane in 1170, when the family were still in their first generation of castle-holding, married Eudoxia, niece of the Byzantine emperor Manuel I himself.[173] The Pierleoni for their part, although not part of the upper level of the 'new aristocracy' in wealth, were taken very seriously indeed by Roger II of Sicily (above, p. 224). So the 'new' families of Rome were operating on a national and international level, without visible difficulty, with landed resources that would have restricted them to the politics of single cities elsewhere

---

171 *MGH, Constitutiones*, I, n. 85.
172 Occhipinti, 'I *capitanei* a Milano'; Maire Vigueur, *Cavaliers et citoyens*, pp. 349–55.
173 'Ruolo di assoluto primo piano', Beolchini, *Tusculum II*, p. 88; Frison, 'Frangipane, Aldruda'. For 1170, Thumser, 'Die Frangipane', p. 136; Petersohn, *Kaisertum und Rom*, pp. 272–3; with the main source, *Annales Ceccanenses*, s.a. 1170 (p. 286). Maire Vigueur makes much the same point in *L'autre Rome*, pp. 191–4.

in communal Italy, and would have hardly got them an invitation to a royal Easter court anywhere else in Europe. They could do so because of the prestige of papal patronage (Alexander III is known to have brokered the second of the Frangipane marriages, and Innocent II doubtless played his part with Aldruda too)—and with the benefit of papal money too, which always added to their capacity for self-presentation (although it was Manuel who paid over *magna pecunia* in 1170 according to the *Annales Ceccanenses*, as indeed fits Roman dowry law). They could also do so because the city they were active in was no ordinary city; it dominated a whole region in a way no other north-central Italian city did, as well as being one of the largest in western Europe, even in the early twelfth century, when Milan had probably overtaken it in size and Venice and Paris were on the way to doing so as well. They could do so, that is to say, because Rome played by different rules; it conveyed far more symbolic capital. These rules were not entirely different; no one could completely escape the politics of land in our period, for example; and Roman aristocracies were not as distinct in their structure and values from those of the rest of Italy in most respects. But they were different enough for northern Italians to be as cold-eyed in their assessment of Roman political rivalries in our period as was Otto of Freising, or any 'reformer' from Lotharingia or France, that is to say men who did not understand the logic of urban politics at all.

This could be put the other way round as well. The Roman aristocracy, in every period, punched well beyond its weight; it was far more prominent than its resources ought to have allowed, particularly in the period of the 'new aristocracy', until the wealth of the *baroni* brought them more into alignment with European norms. But it needed help to do so. In the period after 1050, when titles and offices were less important, this meant that they needed a direct personal association with, and concrete resources from, popes, if they were to play on a wider stage than the city itself provided. This favoured any pope who himself had the protagonism to spread patronage and wealth around, as did the more able popes of the last century of our period, Gregory VII, Calixtus II, Innocent II. Popes did not always find it easy to do this, as we shall see later (pp. 417–20)—for example, for all their wealth, they actually had less disposable land than bishops in other cities, until after 1150—but they needed to do so if they were to stay on top of city politics. Each needed the other, then. That was not always possible, however, and, if not, there were alternative political possibilities as well. 'New aristocrats' did not only look to the popes; they were closely associated with the churches of their *regiones* too, as we shall see, as also with a more generic military identity, and both brought them politically closer to the 'medium elite'. The slow crystallization of the city commune took place in most cities in a vacuum of effective traditional political power, the hierarchies which looked to emperor and bishop. So too, to an extent, did they in Rome, where there are undoubted signs of a commune crystallizing along northern lines, linking together 'new aristocracy' and 'medium elite', during the relatively weak papacies of most of the first third of the twelfth century (below, pp. 436–41). Perhaps only the Corsi, more tied into traditional power structures as they were, would have resisted a communal choice under these circumstances. But the ambitions of the Roman 'aristocracy' went beyond that, or could go beyond that, if there was a pope who was prepared to be a protagonist, as Innocent II was in the years around 1140. When that happened, the 'aristocracy' stuck with the pope, and they and the non-aristocratic elite went different political ways. A discussion of how that actually happened will, however, have to be reserved for Chapter 7, after we have looked at the rest of the city.

5

Medium Elites and Church Clienteles
The Society of Rome's Regions in the Eleventh and Twelfth Centuries

We saw in Chapter 3 that Rome's small and bustling *regiones* were quite different from each other in their economic focus and in their overall prosperity.[1] How this worked at the level of social relationships is much harder to pin down. As usual, in the period before notarial archives begin, we only have restricted sets of data: a large number of urban leases and sales of leases; smaller sets of documents recording gifts to the church, and credit arrangements with pledges in land; and a few wills and dowry agreements, which sometimes have the advantage of listing all or most of the landed possessions of the author of the text. Rome also has rather less documentation than some more favoured cities, as we have seen. But we can use this material, all the same, and it is possible to say something about the different societies of at least some of the *regiones* of the city, those which are illuminated by the largest documentary sets we have. These are three in number: Trastevere (as seen through the eyes of the monastery of SS. Cosma e Damiano in Trastevere), Pigna (as seen from the monastery of SS. Ciriaco e Nicola—here, as before, S. Ciriaco—in Via Lata), and S. Maria Nova/Colosseo (as seen from the *diaconia* of S. Maria Nova). The local documentation for each hardly begins before 1000; in addition, it increases substantially in most areas after 1150. I shall therefore also use late twelfth-century material here to add to our understanding of how each *regio* changed; this chapter thus discusses the eleventh and twelfth centuries as a whole. Much of our reconstruction has to remain hypothetical, even in the best-documented case, S. Maria Nova, for the evidence has too many gaps. All the same, we shall find that the society of each of these three was indeed different, and this partly matches their economic contrasts. This chapter includes plenty of detailed workings-out of examples, because only by doing that can we get a sense of those differences. As in Chapter 4, that detail may fascinate some, but may alienate others. My defence, nonetheless, is that it seems to me necessary, if we want to get a sense of local societies with any accuracy at all.

The people who will stand in the foreground of this chapter are the broad stratum which I have already defined as the 'medium elite'. This is because the data we have, as just described, tell us far more about that stratum than they do

---

[1] See pp. 121–2 for definitions of *regiones*.

about any less prosperous and prominent social groups. A normal rural study (outside Rome's own hinterland, that is) can often say quite a lot about the rural poor, because they at least worked the land, and land is the basic focus of surviving documents for most of the Middle Ages. Inside cities, this is rather harder, because the urban poor do not appear in any detail in our sources, at least until sources that are less focused on the prosperous, such as criminal records or systematic registrations of witnessing (in civil cases, or, later, to establish the sanctity or heresy of local religious figures), begin to survive in usable numbers, which is very rarely before 1200; and archaeology, which will in the future be a basis for tracking them, has barely begun to provide us with the necessary data—even in Rome, which is well studied for our period, as we saw in Chapter 3. So the 'medium elite' will be our main focus in this chapter. I briefly characterized its difference from the 'aristocratic' strata at the start of Chapter 4, but we need to look at that in more detail to start with, so as to have a clear idea of the focus we need before we go into the detail of regional reconstructions. To begin with in this chapter, then, we shall look at the words used to define social groups in the eleventh and twelfth centuries in Rome, and at some of their implications. We shall then go on to look at five sample 'medium elite' families, some of the best-documented in Rome, in much the same way as we chased 'aristocratic' families in Chapter 4, so that we can get a sense of what sort of people they were, what sorts of resources they seem to have had, and how they dealt with the world around them. Finally, we shall look at the scale of wealth we seem to be dealing with when we characterize the 'medium elite' as a whole. I hope that all these, taken together, will give a useful framing for the three regional analyses to follow; and will allow us to develop hypotheses for how Rome's society hung together, at the end of this chapter and in the two following.

MEDIUM ELITES

Let us begin with hierarchies, as seen in the sources for Rome in the eleventh and twelfth centuries. Narratives, in particular, quite often see the Roman laity as a dyad, with *nobiles* counterposed to *populus* or *plebs*, *equites* to *pedites*, *maiores* to *minores*, and (once) *proceres* to *cives*.[2] It is easy to see these as characterizing, in a generic sense, elites and non-elites; it is much harder to be sure of where the boundary between them lay, if anywhere precise at all (*maiores* vs. *minores* is certainly in the terrain of the vague, but very few of these terms are really exact), especially as not all our narrative sources are written by Romans, and thus may be using different category systems. In fact, however, insofar as we can reach a degree of precision, the boundaries that each term tracked were different: sometimes between elites and non-elites, to be sure, but sometimes, equally, between 'medium' and 'upper' elites, reflecting the differences traceable between the 'new

---

[2] For example, in turn: *PL*, CXXIX, cols 699–700, n. 9; *LP*, II, pp. 345, 331, 389.

aristocracy' and the 'medium elite', as we saw at the end of Chapter 4. We therefore need to take them in turn.

Nobilis is the least problematic of these words, as it is the most consistent term of the set. It was fairly specific, and by 1100 did mean 'aristocrat' in most contexts. In the eleventh century and before, it had been used more vaguely to mean men and women of a variety of statuses, from the Tuscolani to rich artisans, as we have seen; the word steadily became much less common after 1060 or so, however. In twelfth-century Roman documents, it appears relatively seldom, but with more precision: it applied above all to well-known families such as the Frangipane, Pierleoni, Corsi, Sant' Eustachio (of whom Alexander III in 1178 said 'sunt nobilitatis in Urbe'), and, at the end of the century, *de Monumento* and Orsini. The few other documentary references to the word appear in a legal context, in which *nobilis* signified men of local public standing who had a judicial role (it applied, among others, to Cencio di Pietro of Pigna in 1156 and Gregorio di Berardo of S. Maria Nova in 1195, both from known 'medium elite' families, as we shall see). Outside that specific context, however, it was restricted to 'new aristocratic' families. *Proceres* and *potentes* are words with a roughly similar meaning, although they are rarer, and are always group words, not related to individuals; *senatus* before 1143 meant something similar too.[3] These are the words that represent the boundary between 'new aristocracy' and 'medium elite', then, and they are fairly consistent.

Populus, the opposite of *nobilis*, is a rather more ambiguous word. It meant the Roman people in general, as one would assume, but it had wider or narrower meanings according to context. In liturgical contexts the word *populus* had a very wide meaning indeed, covering all or most of the city, women as well as men, as we shall see in Chapter 6 (pp. 324–5). But normally it was used more narrowly, to mean smaller or larger groups of political players. In the 1044–73 section of the *Annales Romani*, for example, it seems to mean relatively influential Romans: as we saw in Chapter 3 (p. 172), their allegiance was often bought, and bought back, for *pecunia* at moments of political crisis. The author of that text elsewhere invokes the idea of a wide urban collectivity (the *omnes Romani in unum congregati*, collected together, who elect Silvester III in 1045), but when it comes to changing sides in return for financial pay-offs, it is much clearer that we are looking at a relatively small political leadership.[4] Of non-Roman sources, Falcone of Benevento was presumably referring to a similar group when he referred to the *populus* bought off by the supporters

---

[3] *Nobiles*: see in general *Codice diplomatico della Repubblica di Genova*, I, n. 32; *PL*, CXXIX, cols 699–700, n. 9, cols 706–7, n. 18; *S. Gregorio*, n. 7. For the Frangipane, *S. Prassede*, n. 26; Pflugk, III, n. 245; *PL*, CC, col. 178, n. 103; *LC*, I, n. 64. For the Pierleoni, Kehr, IV, p, 157. See further Kehr, II, pp. 348–50 (Corsi); *Epistolae*, ed. Loewenfeld, n. 282 (Sant' Eustachio); *Reg. Inn. III*, I. 325 (*de Monumento*); *Regesto degli Orsini*, pp. 31–2 (Orsini). In judicial contexts, *SMVL*, n. 187 and *SMN*, n. 145. *Proceres*: *LP*, II, p. 389 (note that this is Bosone, who was not Roman; but the word had a long history in the city). *Potentes*: see Petersohn, 'Der Brief', p. 506; *Senato*, n. 5; and note also the use of *potens persona* as a category of people to which tenants could not sell leases, a usage which is first attested in 1114 (SMT, n. 11), and is very common in documents by the end of the twelfth century. For *senatus* before 1143, see e.g. Beno, *Gesta Romanae aecclesiae*, I.7 (a. 1084); *MGH, Constitutiones*, I, n. 82 (a. 1111)—neither of them Roman sources.

[4] *LP*, II, pp. 331, 332, 334.

of Anacletus II in 1130; Bosone, in his slightly later account, referred to the same group as *maiores*.[5]

In other texts again, however, the political players referred to as the *populus* seem to have been more numerous. *Populus* or *plebs* is counterposed to *nobiles*, or to the *senatus* in its generic aristocratic sense, in several sources that describe political action in the late eleventh century or early twelfth, both Roman and external. Most specifically, Otto of Freising, in his description of the early Senate in 1145, says that the *populus Romanus* 'compelled all the *principes* and *nobiles ex civibus* to subjection to the *patricius* [the leader of the Senate]'; this clearly poses the *populus* as politically different from, as well as opposed to, the aristocracy of the city.[6] (I read *ex civibus* to mean that Otto, an outsider of course, saw these aristocrats as being urban, not rural. In Roman sources of our period, *civis* is not a common word, and is very seldom used before 1143, but it seems to denote a wide range of inhabitants of the city.) Similarly, the four men *de populo per unamquamquem contradam*, from each *contrada*, who agreed to swear on behalf of the Senate to Eugenius III in 1149, and the 800 *viri ex eodem populo* who swore to Alexander III a (very temporary) peace with Tuscolo in 1172, were clearly from a fairly wide group.[7] This latter *populus* would have included, at a minimum, what I describe as the 'medium elite', the leadership of the city's numerous *regiones*. It is very likely often to have extended beyond these local leaders, to a wider urban society. But it does not have to have included the whole of the (male) population of the city; not all urban inhabitants were characterized by any of the texts about political action, for there is no evidence that the urban poor were politically active in any significant or systematic sense.[8] Broadly, any of the people discussed in this chapter, whether prominent or not, could have been part of the *populus* of Rome as characterized in these twelfth-century sources. Conversely, they might well not, in many cases, have been in the *populus* who were important enough to be paid off by papal rivals in the 1040s and 1050s.

The word *equites* was certainly seen as meaning fighters on horseback as opposed to *pedites*, who fought on foot; but Rome's military engagement, too, had a relatively complex relation to hierarchy. A wide range of Romans were armed in every century, as shown in their involvement in wars with Tivoli and Tuscolo, and their defence of the city against German armies. Benzone of Alba described, in his

[5] Falcone of Benevento, *Chronicon*, col. 1203; *LP*, II, p. 380.

[6] Roman sources: *Codice diplomatico della Repubblica di Genova*, I, n. 32 (a papal bull from 1121); *PL*, CXXIX, cols 699–700, n. 9 (here *plebs*); Petersohn, 'Der Brief', p. 506 (here *plebs*). Non-Roman sources: Beno, *Gesta Romanae aecclesiae*, I.7; *Chronica Casinensis*, III.69, IV.37, 39, 40; *MGH, Constitutiones*, I, n. 82; Falcone of Benevento, *Chronicon*, col. 1167; Otto of Freising, *Chronica*, VII.31 (for 1145); cf. *Annales Casinenses*, p. 310, s.a. 1144 (here *populus minor*).

[7] 1149 and 1172: *Senato*, n. 8; *LP*, II, p. 424. *Cives* in Rome before 1143: Benzone of Alba, *Ad Heinricum IV*, I. 9 (not a Roman source); Petersohn, 'Der Brief', p. 506. People called *civis* later in the century are often aristocrats or at least privileged: e.g. *Senato*, n. 21; Kehr, II, pp. 358, 366–7; *Reg. Inn. III*, VI.214 (245). But *Senato*, n. 12, or *SPV*, n. 74, or *SMVL*, Baumgärtner, n. 14, are for much more ordinary people, and the contrast with *proceres* in Bosone in 1155 (*LP*, II, p. 389) indicates that he, at least, thought it meant non-aristocrats.

[8] See, among many, Frugoni, 'Sulla *Renovatio*', p. 162; Moscati, *Alle origini*, p. 25.

account of Rome in 1062, a 'Romanorum maxima multitudo, nullus eorum sine scuto', a great multitude of Romans, not one of them without a shield, and that was doubtless a feature of the city throughout our period. All the same, horsemen could be considered as part of an elite that excluded foot-soldiers. Jean-Claude Maire Vigueur, in an authoritative analysis, has argued that Italian cities in the twelfth and thirteenth centuries had above all a mounted army. Their *pedites*, ordinary foot-soldiers, certainly existed, but were less important militarily; conversely, *milites*, the standard word for horsemen in most cities, were an urban elite, even if not a tiny one—10–15 per cent of the population, on the basis of Piacenza figures from 1221, their families counted 'by hundreds rather than by tens' in sizable cities. *Milites* (or the *militia*) dominated urban politics, and by 1200 or so were in many cities coming to be called *nobiles* as well, in an extension of an earlier and more restricted aristocratic terminology.[9] In Rome in our period, the word *milites* is less common in this context. This is presumably because the Roman *militia*, or *scola militum*, was different, consisting of a long-standing and apparently large urban group, still prominent in ceremonials in our period, such as the *adventus* ceremony for emperors and popes (below, p. 333); a *scola militum* was active in land transactions as late as 1145.[10] In other documents and narratives, people called *milites* tend to appear in rural, rather than urban, contexts, as the armed entourages of counts and castral lords; in the city their rare appearances are normally in papal or aristocratic entourages. The use of the word *milites* as meaning a militarized social stratum in the city, or *militia* to mean an army (Gregory VII had one, for example), is mostly restricted to non-Roman accounts.[11] In Rome, the word *equites* was usually used instead. But even this word is not so very common, all the same; it does not by any means have the resonance that the word *milites* has in northern Italy.[12]

---

[9] Maire Vigueur, *Cavaliers et citoyens*, esp. pp. 217–19 (quote on 217), 275–83. See also Settia, *Comuni in guerra*, pp. 93–114, for the continuing importance of foot-soldiers in twelfth-century wars.

[10] *Scola/militia*: e.g. *LP*, II, p. 88 (a. 844); Beno, *Gesta Romanae aecclesiae*, I.1 and Benzone of Alba, *Ad Heinricum IV*, I.10 (a. 1084); Uodascalcus, *De Eginone et Herimanno*, p. 446 (a. 1120); *S. Alessio*, n. 14 (a. 1145); *LP*, II, p. 446 (a. 1179). So, too, Maire Vigueur, *L'autre Rome*, p. 187. Most of these are external accounts of *adventus*, but they still use a long-standing Roman terminology.

[11] For Gregory VII's *milites/militia*, see below, Chapter 7, n. 93. Elsewhere, Bonizone of Sutri, *Liber ad amicum*, VI (p. 595); Sigebert of Gembloux, *Chronica*, p. 389 (a. 1105); Maragone, *Annales Pisani*, p. 42 (a. 1168). The only Roman example I have seen of the word *miles* apparently being used as a social marker is *Liber Pontificalis*, ed. Přerovský, p. 739, in which Stefano Normanno is *miles Normannus*, in a very rhetorically heightened account however. Rural *milites* in Lazio are, however, quite common: e.g. *RF*, n. 1096; 'Documenti per la storia', n. 4; ASR, A. A. Arm. I–XVIII, n. 3655; *LC*, I, n. 179; *RS*, n. 191; *SMVL*, Baumgärtner, n. 14. *Milites* in papal/aristocratic entourages in the city: see *Liber Pontificalis*, ed. Přerovský, p. 739; Kehr, II, pp. 599–600; Falcone, *Chronicon*, col. 1167; *S. Gregorio*, n. 7; John of Salisbury, *Historia pontificalis*, ch. 27—here half Roman, half non-Roman sources.

[12] Kehr, II, pp. 599–600 (Urban II supported by *equites* and *pedites*); *LP*, II, p. 347 (Calixtus II buys the support of *equites* and *pedites*); and see the refs. in nn. 13 and 15 as well. In urban documents, however, *equites* only appear in *SMN*, nn. 13 and 15 (in both of these meaning any horse riders); they are slightly commoner in the countryside, e.g. *RF*, nn. 906, 1313; *Tivoli*, n. 16. Note finally the word *capitanei*; this word, imported from northern Italy and used for the most part by non-Romans, generally seems to mean a rural lord, as *comes* does in Rome as well. For non-Roman sources: *Chronica Casinensis*, III.19; Bonizone of Sutri, *Liber ad amicum*, VI (p. 595); *Conradi III diplomata*, n. 262 (apparently to urban Romans, but here copied from n. 261, to the Pisans); *LP*, II, 353, 357–9.

One reason for this may perhaps be because so much Roman warfare was actually intra-urban, between rival papal claimants or against imperial irruptions in the city, that the *pedites* were equally prominent inside fighting communities. The pitched battles in 1105, in front of the Laterano and in the Circo Massimo, between the supporters of Paschal II and those of his rival Silvester IV (the archpriest Maginulfo of S. Angelo in Pescheria), featured both *equites* and *pedites*, for example, with Roman *pedites* pursuing the supporters of Paschal throughout the *regio* of S. Maria Nova, and more than sixty horses supposedly killed. So did the Frangipane attack on Gelasius II in S. Prassede in 1118, which was carried out with *milites* and *pedites*, although here the force was a personal military entourage—what a papal accord with the Pierleoni in 1111 calls the latter's *potentia*. The Roman *minores* who (with the *maiores*) attacked Trastevere in 1044 according to the *Annales Romani* were perhaps not horsemen either.[13] We do not have detailed enough accounts of the wars with Tivoli or Tuscolo, or with imperial armies, to know whether *equites* were more to the fore there. It is quite likely, given Italian norms. But armed Romans were much more often called up for street-fighting, including when formally acting on behalf of the city—such as the twelve *regiones* (i.e. 'super-regions') of the city plus the Trasteverini and *Insulani* who joined the aristocracy to release Gelasius from the Frangipane earlier in 1118; these almost certainly were not simply *equites*. Regular military commitment was often, that is to say, not entirely an elite affair in Rome.[14]

Rome's male population was indeed, in one of our sources, simply made up of *equites* and *pedites*. Benedetto's *Liber politicus* from the early 1140s describes the games at Monte Testaccio on the first Sunday of Lent, the *ludus carnelevari*, to which it is the earliest reference. He envisages that the *pedites* go straight to the Testaccio, whereas the *equites* go first to the Laterano, and then ride with the pope and the urban prefect to meet the *pedites*.[15] We will look at this text again later, for its ceremonial aspects (p. 330), but it does at least show that Romans had a straightforward division between the two groups, and that each knew who they were. But that precision only works at the level of wide social groups. When it comes down to individuals, in Rome as in other major cities, we have little or no indication of who was an *eques* and who was not. At the most, we have chance and

For Roman sources, *PL*, CLXXIX, cols 706–7, n. 18 (*capitanei et comites*); *S. Gregorio*, n. 7 (*capitaneis et magno exercitu* who attack Oddone of Poli on Innocent II's orders); *Senato*, n. 42; *Gesta Innocentii III*, ch. 7 (here, at Innocent's election, the pope meets *cum magnatibus et nobilibus Urbis, multisque capitaneis et consulibus, ac rectoribus civitatum* at the Laterano, clearly a generic description). See in general Carocci, 'Una nobiltà bipartita', pp. 120–1n. Pietro di Paolo *capitaneus* was an early senator: *Senato*, nn. 12–13; *SMN*, n. 71; this characterization of an individual with the term is almost unique, however, and it is not possible to be sure of his social collocation.

[13] Respectively, *LP*, II, pp. 345–6 (a. 1105); *Liber Pontificalis*, ed. Přerovský, p. 739 (a. 1118); *MGH*, *Constitutiones*, I, n. 85 (a. 1111); *LP*, II, p. 331 (a. 1044).

[14] For external wars, see e.g. Maire Vigueur, *L'autre Rome*, pp. 196–9; in the fourteenth century, military commitment was relatively non-elite, however: Maire Vigueur, *L'autre Rome*, pp. 173–6. See this chapter, n. 81, for references to men who lost horses in the war of 1183 against Tuscolo and the imperial army. 1118: *Liber Pontificalis*, ed. Přerovský, p. 734.

[15] *LC*, II, p. 172.

implicit references. Romanucio di Romano di Frasia, who in 1157 divided his property with his brother, was a fairly modest member of the 'medium elite' living inside the Colosseo (below, p. 274); one of the items he ceded to his brother was his share of a *lorica*, a mail-shirt.[16] This was a marker of military commitment (and expense, and training) at the *eques* level, which probably also went with a home in the largest fortifiable classical monument in the city. Nor is this all that surprising; members of the 'medium elite', with (as we shall see) their two or three houses in the city and several plots of land in the vineyard belt, could certainly afford a horse and arms. It may well be that the *equites* mapped fairly well onto the membership of the 'medium elite', in fact—plus the 'new aristocracy'—which fits Maire Vigueur's general Italian picture. Rome had thirty-odd *regiones* and 30–40,000 inhabitants in the twelfth century (above, pp. 112, 121); this adds up to a thousand or so people per *regio*, some 200 families—although, of course, this is only an average, for regions will have varied greatly in size. If ten or twenty families of the 'medium elite' in each *regio* (plus one or two aristocratic families, where there were any aristocrats at all) made up the regional leadership, which, as we will see later in this chapter (e.g. p. 302), is a plausible order of magnitude, this would certainly fit the scale of 10–15 per cent of the population canvassed for the *militia* of Piacenza. Maire Vigueur likes to call all such people members of the 'noblesse urbaine';[17] I would resist this for the twelfth century, since Rome's *nobiles* were only the highest stratum of this wide group. But that its members could, and sometimes did, fight on horseback (at least ritually, at the start of Lent), thus distinguishing themselves from neighbours without horses, is very likely. And it is also true that the material–cultural projection of both elites had an increasingly military tone, as with the building of tower-houses by both *nobiles* and the richer members of the 'medium elite'; we shall see examples of the latter shortly.

This issue is historiographically important, for it links directly to the foundation of the Senate. Maire Vigueur links that process squarely to the *equites/militia*, seen as a wide but definable lay military elite, transporting his north Italian model to the city on the Tiber; with all the greater ease because Otto of Freising on two occasions actually links the events of 1143 and onwards with what he calls the *ordo equestris*. We shall see later that, as Arsenio Frugoni noted half a century ago, this marks Otto's classicizing terminology, not a specific knowledge of the social strata of Rome.[18] If that phraseology is left out, it is much more difficult to find evidence to link the early Senate with any particular form of military organization, such as would justify focusing on the equestrian element in its support. Not that we need doubt at all that the 'medium elite', in particular, was the core of the movement that took power on the Capitolio in 1143, or that it was militarized. But to call it a

---

[16] *SMN*, n. 75, and cf. e.g. Maire Vigueur, *Cavaliers et citoyens*, pp. 84–5, who stresses the expense of a *lorica* in this period.

[17] Maire Vigueur, *Cavaliers et citoyens*, p. 283; followed up in the Roman context in Marie Vigueur, *L'autre Rome*, pp. 185–7.

[18] See below, Chapter 6, n. 79 and Chapter 7, n. 151 for Otto, with (in particular) Frugoni, 'Sulla "Renovatio Senatus"', pp. 172–4. For Maire Vigueur, see *L'autre Rome*, pp. 309–10, and, in general, pp. 185–216; and also his 'Replica' in *Storica*, p. 141.

militia seems to me to obscure some vital differences. One is that the movement of 1143 and the decade following was, often, very hostile to *nobiles*. Otto of Freising tells us this quite explicitly in the citation from 1145 just mentioned, when he refers to the supporters of the Senate as the *populus* and their opponents as *nobiles* (and he is not our only source here: see below, pp. 442–5); we certainly cannot see, then, this political group as one which included all equestrians, from the Frangipane down to men like Romanucio di Romano di Frasia; and equally not as *only* including equestrians. Above all, the simple characterization of all of the city's leading groups as a *militia* obscures some quite clear social distinctions inside it, which were often—indeed, usually—of rather more importance than a common equestrian politics. If we want to understand Rome in the twelfth century, it is these distinctions that we need to get to grips with. We have already seen in Chapter 4 that the 'new aristocracy' can be divided into two socio-economic strata. The 'medium elite' were no more homogeneous either. It is the task of the rest of this chapter to see how socio-economic distinctions and regional solidarities worked inside the 'medium elite'; in Chapter 7 we will look at how that played out at the level of political action. I shall argue there that, whereas in most Italian cities the urban 'aristocracy' and 'medium elite' were political allies in the early commune—creating a common *militia* politics—in Rome, the divisions between the first and the second, and the regional loyalties visible in particular for the second, produced a different outcome.

To sum up, then: Rome did indeed have words to define social strata. *Nobilis* (or, less frequently, *potens*, etc.) marked the 'new aristocracy'; it is by now equally clear that *eques* could be used, if less often, to mark the 'medium elite' (plus, usually, the 'aristocracy' too). These were real and recognized distinctions. Their partial contradiction certainly helps to remind us that there was a continuum here, and that families could pass both up and down the social scale; as we have seen, on the margin status was doubtless negotiable; but the distinctions still existed. *Populus* was less consistent, and could refer to both very wide and relatively narrow groups, although it often, particularly in the twelfth century, seems to map fairly well onto the 'medium elite', this time in contrast to the 'aristocracy', with doubtless some non-elite elements too. But other markers can be described less easily through this terminology. These were relative levels of wealth, regional status, access to political power, which were all much more informally constructed, and have to be reconstructed through an analysis of practice. And formal hierarchical markers were also no more important than were either regional/communitarian identities and practices or the personalized clienteles of churches and aristocrats in creating solidarities in the city. So let us move on to these: sample families and then levels of elite wealth in this section, regional identities and clienteles in that following.

Five sample families

Most trackable 'medium elite' families are clearest in the twelfth century, as we shall see; but we can start our study of individual families with one early example, from the eleventh: the Maccii of Trastevere. They appear in a handful of documents, almost all for the monastery of SS. Cosma e Damiano, up to 1069. In that year, Gerardo *vir honestus* di Romano *de Maccii* leased from the monastery a quarter of a holding (*casale*) in Marcelli, SS. Cosma e Damiano's enormous estate just west of Trastevere, largely consisting of vineyards, *sicut detinuerunt Maccii*, 'as the Maccii held', plus a similar quarter of the *turricella* where Gerardo lived (with its own marble staircase) in Trastevere. This clearly shows a collective holding recognized as the family's, which was run from a tower-house in the city. Gerardo appears as a holder of vineyards on the boundary of another monastic lease slightly earlier in the same year. An earlier generation is documented in the 1020s, that of Gerardo's grandfather or uncles; in 1028 and 1033 the monastery made two emphyteutic leases, again in Marcelli, to Giovanni Maccius or Mazo and his brother Beno Pipa; the family name apparently began here, with a nickname (meaning 'mason'?). Beno Pipa was a *ferrarius*, a smith; with that ascription he witnessed a lease in Scorteclari across the river for the little-known monastery of S. Salvatore ad Duos Amantes in 1025. His son may be the Giovanni di Pipa who witnessed a SS. Cosma e Damiano lease in Porto in 1058. If Beno was also the Beno Macina who witnessed another monastic lease near Porto in 1041, then he had another brother, Romano, who did the same in 1046, and this Romano could well be Gerardo di Romano's father. After 1069, when Trastevere documents become rare for a century, they are harder to trace. Two brothers *de Maccio* witnessed in 1132 the will of Tebaldo di Tebaldo, one of the last known members of Giovanni Tignoso's family (see pp. 225–6); one of them, Teodoro, reappears as a witness to a court case of 1145, together with a Giovanni *Macii*. The name Maccio is known elsewhere, but is not very common, and both of these are Trastevere documents; I would be happy to assume that they show the family still active, and in significant contexts as well. But they do not reappear in later texts, and may have died out.[19]

The Maccii were, in fact, an entirely typical Trastevere family in their practice of leasing west of the city from SS. Cosma e Damiano. Tebaldo di Franco, Giovanni Tignoso's father, was just the same: a lessee in Marcelli, in *casale* S. Andrea to its north and (from S. Ciriaco) in Campo di Merlo to its south-west, together with being a witness for the monastery, again like the Maccii.[20] Beno was, unlike Tebaldo and Giovanni Tignoso, an artisan, and his brother Giovanni's nickname probably indicates that he was too. This is where the Maccii were socially at their origin, and indeed they may have remained so. But by the 1060s they had a tower, and an early surname, and a set of recognizable customary rights in Marcelli. Their horizon was restricted to that of their principal monastic landlord for the most part, and they died or faded out too soon to allow them to participate in senatorial politics. But they must have been prominent in Trastevere for all that; and their tower is not only documented earlier than that of the Bracciuti, but is actually, as

---

[19] For 1069, *SCD*, n. 70; for other Maccii, nn. 31, 39, 44, 49, 57, 69; ASR, SCD, cassetta 16, n. 120 (a. 1132); and *SMVL*, n. 49 (a. 1025); CVL 8044, ff. 4–16 (a. 1145). Di Carpegna Falconieri, 'Le trasformazioni onomastiche', p. 627, sees the family as 'nobile e ricco', which I think is an overstatement.

[20] *SCD*, nn. 24, 25, 35, 41; *SMVL*, n. 63. See above, pp. 224–6.

we have seen (p. 160), the earliest known in the whole of Rome. They were members of *an* elite, that from which Giovanni Tignoso, apparently the wealthiest of them, could be plucked by Hildebrand to become prefect of the city itself. The Maccii were not, however, and they stayed among the middling or 'medium' elite. *Rentiers*, artisans, public witnesses, but only in one or two regional contexts, or for one or two churches: that level is what marks them out.

The Carucini or Carucii appear slightly later, in the very early twelfth century, in the form of Benedetto di Leone Carucii *causidicus*, who witnesses a document of 1104. Benedetto was the uncle of Pietro *diaconus*, a native of Albano, who gave his house and lands in and around that city to S. Maria Nova when he joined the church at quite a high level in that year; Pietro said he was *de genealogia Dimidia Maza* on his father's side and a Carucini on his mother's: two family names. A member of the former, Giovanni Dimidia Mazza ('half mason'?), appears as a tenant on lay-owned land just beside S. Maria Nova (in the Basilica di Massenzio) as early as 1052, so Pietro's father's family had looked both to the city and to Albano for half a century. Much the same was true of Benedetto di Leone, for if he was a *causidicus* and the uncle of an adult in 1104, then he must have been training in the law in the city in the 1080s at the latest. The dual link with Rome and Albano continued here too, for in 1119 Benedetto *iudex* confirmed another Albano alienation to S. Maria, and his son Leone *causarum patronus* witnessed it, along with another Carucius—the name, although it is attested elsewhere, is again rare, so we must be dealing with the same family. Benedetto had evidently founded a family of judicial experts; and a second Benedetto di Leone, the well-known Romanist advocate and *causidicus* of the years 1137–62, was very probably his grandson. Here, then, we have Albano landowners (Pietro is one of the few laymen who seem to have owned their own land there), probably major figures in Albano given Pietro's proudly listed and unique double *genealogia*, who moved into Rome as senior clerics and judicial professionals. Unfortunately, we do not hear another word about their property dealings in the city. The second Benedetto, although he was very prominent in mid-century court cases (below, pp. 372, 404–7), never became a palatine judge; he does, however, appear giving *consilium* to the Senate in the very first documented lawsuit settled before it, in 1150. If he had heirs, they are not visible in our sources.[21]

The third family is that of Sassone *macellarius*, the butcher, a man who appears in S. Maria Nova documents from 1123 to 1140 and is invoked for some time after that. Sassone *macellarius*, son of Sinibaldo, was a witness to three church documents in the 1120s–30s; he was a tenant of the church in the same period, perhaps in the extramural vineyard area of Monte S. Ypoliti (above, p. 94), and certainly near S. Maria Nova itself in 1140. Sassone was probably dead by 1147, when his four sons took a S. Maria lease of two roofed *criptae* (here, as elsewhere, almost

---

[21] *SMN*, n. 33 for 1104; nn. 15, 38, for other citations. See above, p. 99, for the Albano context. For the second Benedetto di Leone, see Chapter 7, n. 47 (*Senato*, n. 12 for 1150); the best account is Chiodi, 'Roma e il diritto romano', pp. 1228–39. Moscati, *Alle origini*, p. 75, sees the two Benedettos as identical; this seems to me chronologically impossible.

certainly classical-period buildings) under the Palatino hill, but his sons and nephews appear as witnesses for the church up to 1164, and probably two further generations into the 1190s. The family appear on boundary clauses too, all close together in space: they held land in Caldararii (probably between S. Maria and the Colosseo) in 1152, on or under the Palatino again in 1160, and close to the Arco di Tito, on the via Sacra, in 1176. This last plot of land may be that referred to in the the *Liber Censuum*, dating to 1192, in which the *domus Saxsonis macellarii* is listed as one of those to whom annual payment is due for the erection of decorated arches along the via Sacra on Easter Monday (below, pp. 295–6, 328–9).[22]

Sassone was a butcher (an occupation which could lead to wealth and social position; by the fourteenth century it sometimes extended to the large-scale commercialization of animals); so was his father, and probably one of his nephews, Giovanni di Gregorio. It is interesting that none of his sons state that they themselves are *macellarii*, even though they are happy to mention their father's occupation. I am not sure how much weight to put on this, given the evident heredity in the family of this artisanal specialization in the first half of the twelfth century; we cannot see the *filii Sassonis* in any more status-filled activity, for example as legal experts or notaries, that might have persuaded them to abandon the butcher's profession, and a house and *criptae* along and close to the via Sacra will certainly have preserved their retail opportunities. What is clear, all the same, is that the family was prosperous and prominent in the *regio S. Mariae Novae*, with several separate but neighbouring houses and land-plots, for some fifty years, and that Sassone *macellarius* was remembered well after his death. They were closely associated with S. Maria, and were probably its tenants for all their lands. They were not, however, prominent in any other documented region of Rome, and did not make it through senatorial office, as far as we can tell.[23]

Finally, two families who appear above all in the *regio* of Campo Marzio and its immediate surroundings, in documents of S. Maria in Campo Marzio and S. Silvestro in Capite. One, the Cerratani, appears as early as 1076, when Bona di Romano Cerrotano ceded to her siblings a *cripta antiqua* and a *turris* built above it, situated near S. Lorenzo in Lucina, which, as we have seen, is early for tower-houses. Romano may have had a nickname, but it soon became a family name: in 1149, the heirs of Rogata *Cerratanorum*, 'of the Cerratani', appear on a boundary in the *regio* of S. Lorenzo in Lucina; her son Pietro di Rogata appears on a similar boundary, plausibly for the same property, in 1184, and witnesses the charter (a S. Silvestro lease) together with Giovanni Cerratanus. Pietro was the *procurator* of

---

[22] *SMN*, nn. 35, 41, 46, 47, 51, 61, 62, 64, 66, 79, 82, 87 (a forged text with a genuine model), 92, 109, and perhaps 159, with *S. Sisto*, n. 8; also *LC*, I, p. 300, and perhaps n. 98. This family has been studied several times: Moscati, 'Popolo e arti', pp. 486–7; Moscati, *Alle origini*, pp. 37–8; di Carpegna Falconieri, 'Le trasformazioni onomastiche', pp. 611–12, which again overstates the family's prominence; Ellis, 'Landscape and power', pp. 70–5, which is undermined by the belief that every Sassone in Rome must have been a member of the same family.

[23] Unless Giordano di Bulgamino (senator in 1191: *Senato*, n. 43) was a son of Bulgamino di Sassone; but the name is not uncommon. For the fourteenth century, see Lori Sanfilippo, *La Roma dei Romani*, pp. 262–89.

S. Maria in Campo Marzio in a major court case over parish bounds in 1188 (below, p. 308), so was clearly an influential local figure. His probable brother Ottaviano *Rogate* also held land in the *regio* of S. Lorenzo in 1194 (Rogata, though a common name in the eleventh century, is much rarer in the twelfth). A second Romano Cerratanus was certainly a relative too: he appears in three church archives as a creditor for pledges in land, in the city and outside it (on the Salaria and the Portuense), in the years 1158–82.[24] The Cerratani thus appear as surnamed landholders with a tower-house, based in the north of the city; as public figures in Campo Marzio; and also as rich enough to lend substantial even if not huge sums (£16 is the largest) to other Romans, extending themselves further geographically as they did so. But they, too, are not documented in the Senate, nor with any public roles that extended beyond the Campo Marzio-S. Lorenzo area.

Giovanni di Parenzo started in a similar way, but moved on much further. He appears as a witness for S. Maria di Campo Marzio in 1145–54, as does his son Giordano; the family was certainly local, for another son, Parenzo, is called *ab Campo Martis* when he witnesses for S. Maria in 1183; Azzone di Parenzo *a Campo Martio*, who lent money in return for a pledge in 1102, was probably an earlier member of the family too, since, although the name Parenzo is not uncommon, we are still in the same *regio*. Giovanni's sons Parenzo and Pietro leased half a *domus* in Campo Marzio from S. Maria in 1167, and it would not be surprising, given the earlier references to Giovanni in S. Maria's witnessing clientele, and the monastery's tenurial importance in the *regio*, if the family held all its Campo Marzio land from the monastery. The closeness of the family to S. Maria was cemented when Giovanni's daughter Sofia became a nun there, before 1161; she was one of the most senior nuns after the abbess in 1161–74, and had given to S. Maria a *pedica* of land out of the city, on the Salaria, when she joined the monastery, although the monastery leased the land back to the family.[25]

Thus far, the social profile of this family is parallel to that of the Cerratani (though without the latter's tower-house), and as localized. But Giovanni di Parenzo also had a successful legal career. He was an *advocatus*, witnessing court cases in 1155–62 which had no relation to Campo Marzio, along with the palatine judges; in 1179 he represented six papal creditors to whom Alexander III repaid £181, a large sum; in 1181 he was sent out to Velletri to hear a legal profession of adulthood by members of a rural aristocratic family; and in both 1157 and 1188 (by when he must have been at least in his late sixties, and probably older) he was a senator.[26]

This personal career turned out to be sufficiently solid to move Giovanni's family firmly up a social level: for the Parenzi, as sources by now intermittently call them,

---

[24] *SMCM*, n. 17 (a. 1076); *S. Sil.*, nn. 20, 35, 45; *PL*, CCIV, cols 1391–4 (a. 1188); for Romano Cerratanus as a creditor, *S. Sil.*, nn. 23, 27; *SMCM*, n. 54; *SMVL*, n. 216.

[25] *SMCM*, nn. 43, 44, 47–8, 52, 58, with *SMVL*, n. 126, for Azzone and *SMCM*, nn. 50, 52, 53, 55, 56, for Sofia.

[26] *S. Sisto*, n. 3; *LC*, I, n. 117 (with Benedetto di Leone); *SMVL*, n. 196; 'Documenti per la storia', nn. 10–11 (a. 1179); Borgia, *Istoria*, pp. 247–9 (a. 1181); Forcella, XIII.1 (a. 1157); *Senato*, n. 42 (a. 1188).

appear frequently in the early thirteenth century, as *podestà* of central Italian cities (generally in papal Umbria, at Orvieto, Perugia, and Foligno, but also at Lucca and Siena), and, three times between 1220 and 1245, as single senators of Rome.[27] This specialization in political leadership began in 1199, with Innocent III's nomination of Pietro di Parenzo as *dominus et rector* of Orvieto, even if this ended badly, with his murder by *heretici* a few months later—'heretics' here may, however, have included anyone in Orvieto incensed by Pietro's immediate banning of *ludus*, games in the *forum* at carnival time, and by his demolition of tower-houses in the city, as his thirteenth-century hagiography recounts.[28] This hyper-religious and pro-papal enthusiasm, and Innocent's patronage of it, was probably the reason why the Parenzi moved up in social prominence; conversely, it was not a political line pursued by at least some of his relatives—Parenzo di Parenzo, single senator in 1220 and 1225, was an active and sometimes excommunicated opponent of Honorius III.[29] It is not clear exactly how these, and other, Parenzi relate to Giovanni di Parenzo and his sons; these two may have been the children of Giovanni's son Parenzo, but *Parentii* may also simply have been a surname here. There is no doubt that they are related somehow, all the same; and that presents an interesting paradox. The family's prominent political role was clearly by the 1220s independent of any particular institutional patronage, if its members could be both pro- and anti-papal. Conversely, however, its members are not well attested in land deals outside Campo Marzio, whether in the city or beyond the walls—not even in Pigna, a well-documented *regio* immediately to the south. The most that can be said is that a Parenzo, conceivably related, was part of a consortium of *Romani cives* and Senesi who lent money to the bishop of Utrecht in the 1190s, money for which Innocent III had to threaten the bishop with excommunication to get repaid in 1204.[30] The family may thus have moved into papal and other finance, and this may have served as their economic base. By 1200 at the latest, they had clearly moved into the 'new aristocracy', presumably on the second, more mercantile, level (above, pp. 243–5). But they were not prominent members of it in economic terms, and, although their frequent hostility to popes may well have underpinned their city-wide status, it was unlikely to gain them more remunerative patronage. They did not become *baroni*, and after the 1260s they are hard to track.

The wealth of the medium elite

These five families were by no means unique; they are better documented than most others, but they show a set of characteristics that were widely shared across the city of Rome. They were all regionally prominent, as medium-level land dealers (twice with tower-houses) and creditors, lessees of land from the churches that kept

---

[27] See Thumser, *Rom*, pp. 175–80, 362–5, for a good survey of the whole family, with a focus on the thirteenth-century material. See also Fiorani Parenzi, *I Parenzi*, I, a better family history than many, which however still assumes that every Parenzo in Rome was a member of the family.

[28] Natalini, *S. Pietro Parenzo*, pp. 152–205, gives the text; ch. 5 for the *ludus*, and the *palatia et turres*. The best analysis is Lansing, *Power and Purity*, pp. 29–37.

[29] Thumser, *Rom*, pp. 178–9, 255–6.   [30] *Reg. Inn. III*, VI.214 (215).

our documents, and also witnesses for the same churches. They sometimes held, as with Pietro di Rogata of the Cerratani, more formal public positions for these churches, and they sometimes entered the churches/monasteries themselves as senior figures (Pietro of Albano, Sofia di Giovanni). We could see them as part of ecclesiastical clienteles, although these clienteles may have been seen by some of these families as being only stepping stones to wider social action. It is indeed quite likely that more successful families were in the economic/political spheres of influence of more than one such church; in the cases cited, only one church dominates our documentation in each *regio*, but there were several others, undocumented, close by—the Cerratani are a guide to this, for they appear in two archives, for monasteries 400 metres apart. Two of the five families, furthermore, were artisans at least by origin, something we saw less often in the 'new aristocracy'. (Merchants were, by contrast, often 'new aristocrats', but their social position was higher: see above, p. 145). The Cerratani may show us one way in which one could move from one status level to the other, on the back of the increasing intensity of urban credit as the economy developed after 1130 or so, which might well have also allowed a successful family to move to the far more elevated and remunerative level of offering credit to popes and non-Romans (above, pp. 164–6). We can see a political path for social ascent, as well: through legal specialization and/or the newly minted rank of the senatoriate, as with the Carucini and the Parenzi. The Parenzi perhaps show us both processes, economic and political, in parallel. It is probably not by chance that it is only that family that actually broke through, temporarily, to the 'aristocracy'.

The way the early Senate impinged on these 'medium elite' families will be looked at more closely in Chapter 7. Just as a matter of logic, however, early senators are likely to have come, above all, from the 'medium elite', even if the exact origins of rather few senators can be traced in detail: for very few of them were initially 'aristocratic', and the social category we are now looking at constituted the most influential non-aristocratic Romans there were around.[31] What we seem to see so far, however, is that these regional city leaders only sometimes made it into senatorial politics—maybe if they were particularly rich, or politically ambitious and agile, or if they had specific professional experience, for example in legal practice. In fact, as we shall investigate more closely later in this chapter, what is most likely is that there were regional-level political hierarchies inside the 'medium elite' as well, and that it was the top of those hierarchies that would most often have senatorial links. If there were a dozen or more leading families in the larger *regiones*, quite articulated local hierarchies were possible. This we shall look at in greater detail in a moment.

Before we do, however, we need to get a sense of the overall range of the property resources of regional-level elite members, so that we can set them against those of the 'aristocracies', discussed in Chapter 4. After 1050 and, in particular, after 1130, the growth of the use of classical Roman law procedures in the city (below,

---

[31] Moscati, *Alle origini*, pp. 24–7 and *passim*; and see below, pp. 447–52.

pp. 368–70) led to a greater use of wills which list all possessions, and, still more, marriage arrangements which can list or value the total property of the husband; a few systematic divisions of family properties between brothers, which survive across the same time frame, round out the set. A few of these are 'aristocratic'; some are clearly not elite members at all; but the 'medium elite' are a well-represented group here, and our texts do indeed give us a ball-park impression of the quantity and nature of their resources.

The completest lists of course come from wills, but there are actually only six that survive for the period before 1200, of which one is clearly 'aristocratic', Adilascia Frangipane in 1137; and both that text and three others are fairly vague as to scale.[32] But they are instructive as a group. The first known is the *testamentum* of Pietro di Sassone di Francone di Durante, who in 1087 gave two-thirds of his *domūs*, vineyards, and other lands to S. Maria in Via Lata and one third to the neighbouring S. Marcello, with life usufructs for his mother, sister, and nephews/nieces. This text is unhelpful as to the size of the landholding, but we also have a major court case from 1148–51 (the first surviving for a senatorial court: below, p. 407) in which S. Maria fought off the aggressive claims to Pietro's inheritance of Tedelgario and Giovanni di Rainaldo di Donadeo, otherwise unknown figures but plausibly the heirs of Pietro's sister Stefania, which states that the disputed land consisted of a water-meadow, three tracts of grain-land (*terra*), a vineyard near the Porta Pinciana, plus a *cripta cum cortinis*, that is, built land in the city. This was not a lot—enough to live off, but not much more; but Tedelgario and his brother temporarily defied the Senate to reject a compromise deal over it, so it evidently mattered to them. Given that one had to have a degree of political protagonism, however misguided, to be contumacious at a senatorial tribunal, to threaten it, and then to dig up the boundary stones fixed by the Senate, we could suppose the brothers to be at least 'medium elite' members: they will have had other land too, but this evidently would have added substantially to their resources had they got hold of it.[33]

Two other wills are more explicit. One is for Tebaldo di Tebaldo in 1132, whom I earlier proposed (p. 225) as being the heir of a Trastevere 'new aristocratic' family. I noted there that his holdings no longer seemed 'aristocratic' in scale, and that the family had returned to the 'medium elite', although doubtless to its upper stratum. Specifically, he disposed of his house (presumably in the city) to his wife and his unmarried daughters, plus two *pedicae* of land in Bravi (part of SS. Cosma e Damiano's Marcelli estate) valued at £24; his son Giovanni got *terre cum claustro* and a *pedica* in Criptule (like Marcelli, down the Portuense) valued at £50; Tebaldo also had other goods and loans valued at another £80, a few *solidi* which he gave for his soul (a rather small percentage), and furs, bedlinen, and grain, which went to his

---

[32] For Adilascia, *SMN*, n. 46, from which the only significant evidence is that half her dowry is valued at £50, which is a substantial figure (cf. below, p. 276; it was worth a quarter of the probably small castle of Cornazzano); other wills with little detail are *SMVL*, n. 182 (a. 1154), and *SPV*, n. 1188. The useful list in di Carpegna Falconieri, 'Sposarsi a Roma', p. 5n, includes some texts which are not wills.

[33] *SMVL*, n. 117, with *Senato*, nn. 12–13.

wife. An urban house, three or four tenant holdings, and enough movables to live in comfort, that is to say.[34] Later in the century, in 1185, Giovanni di Raineri left to his nephew Giovanni *Columpne* (who was almost certainly not from the Colonna family; these two are otherwise unknown) his share of rural property—a *turris*, stables and animal enclosures, grainlands, hemp-fields, and vineyards, mostly at Marana (the name of more than one small river east of Rome) and Albano (including a mill)—and also of some *domūs* in Rome (except for one house, disposed of separately). His wife Costanza, by contrast, got £100 in Provins money; of his other goods, his livestock, silver and gold objects, a £25 loan, and £5 more would be sold or given for his soul. This man clearly had the core of what would be called a rural *casale* in later centuries, with a strong pastoral orientation rather early, plus an Albano holding, houses in the city, and quite a lot of money and valuables. Childless, he was more mindful of his soul than Tebaldo had been. But the scale of wealth, although larger, is in the same order of magnitude.[35]

Three mid-century divisions between brothers give us an analogous picture. In 1155, the four sons of Oddone and Oresma divided a set of possessions with Sinibaldo di Sinibaldo, Oresma's son by a previous marriage—evidently this was all Oresma's inheritance or dowry (she, interestingly, was still alive). They amounted to two *domūs* and at least five *casarini* (here probably huts; one had a *cervinaria*, a wine shop, in it: see above, p. 131), including attached *orti*, on Montecitorio and just to its north and east, as well as a single vineyard outside the Porta Flaminia, and £14 in Lucchese money which Oresma kept. This property set included less extramural land this time, and certainly less money, but its core was a consistent and focused group of urban housing.[36] In 1157, the two sons of Romano di Frasia divided their father's inheritance, which was made up of a single house (a vane of the Colosseo), plus two or three pieces of arable land and vineyard outside the walls, plus a mail-shirt (see above, p. 265), and other unspecified movables; by 1170 they had increased their resources, for they were leasing at least two and possibly three vanes of the Colosseo from S. Maria Nova. One of the two, Pietro, in a marriage deal in 1173, listed the possessions he had by then, which consisted of a *domus* and a *cripta* (bordering his brother's) inside the Colosseo, and four or five vineyards or *orti* in the vineyard belt east of the city, mostly in the same places as in 1157 but by now at least twice as many.[37] In 1169, in a third example, the two sons of Galgano *iudex* divided their inherited land in Scorteclari, which consisted of four and a half *domūs* and two *casarini*, plus some salt pans on the coast and 40 *solidi* (£2) in Provins money. Most of these figures are otherwise unknown, but that is certainly not the case for Galgano *iudex*, who not only had evidently acquired judicial status, but must be the same man as the Galgano *primicerius et iudex* who held that office in 1138–51 (the name is rare). Galgano was active as a legal professional at the highest level in papal and then senatorial court hearings, but he had accumulated by

[34] ASR, SCD, cassetta 16, n. 120.

[35] ASV, A. A. Arm. I–XVIII, 5006, n. 3. Giovanni *Columpne* could be from the Colonna (Antonina) region, or (less likely) son of a woman called Columpna.

[36] *SMVL*, n. 185 (cf. *S. Sil.*, n. 22).   [37] *SMN*, nn. 75, 97, 100–1.

his death barely half a dozen houses plus salt pans, all doubtless held on lease. He shows, more clearly than any other, that palatine judges were no longer standard members of the 'aristocracy' by the twelfth century; but he also shows that even prominent members of the 'medium elite' did not have to be more than fairly modestly endowed with resources.[38]

Marriage agreements that followed classical Roman law are attested from 1056, but they only became standardized in their format and more frequent in number from the 1130s (below, p. 368).[39] Not all of them list the possessions of the husband, as Pietro di Romano di Frasia did, but they often allow a valuation of them. The typical marriage-gift pattern was by now for the wife or her family to give a dowry (*dos*) to her husband, which was returnable if either spouse died before children were born; and for the husband to give a *donatio propter nuptias* to the wife, worth half the *dos*, which she would inherit if he died first; this *donatio* was sometimes, however, described as 'half my possessions (*bona*)', which indicates that both gifts were calibrated according to the husband's resources, if possible—presumably, above all, in cases of relative economic equality between the families, which was of course not always the case. The husband kept control of both gifts during the lifetime of the couple, but characteristically, in order to guarantee the return of the *dos* to his wife's family if she died, he offered a pledge to his wife for it, usually valued in money, so we can calculate the values of those resources. In the marriage agreements that survive for the last two-thirds of the twelfth century, the scale of the dowry, and therefore, probably, the very rough value of the husband's resources, was—I simply list them—30 *solidi* in 1133 (pledged by a *copellarius*, perhaps a candlemaker), 40 *solidi* in 1155 (worth one house-plot in Pigna), 20 *solidi* in 1157 (worth roughly a house on the Palatino), £25 in 1160 (worth a *pedica* of land well out of the city at Colonna and a house in the Foro), 20 *solidi* in 1163 (probably worth two vineyards), £8 in 1173 (this is Pietro di Romano di Frasia, as we have seen worth two houses and several vineyards), £16 in 1173 (worth two vineyards), £10 plus a house on the Palatino in 1190, £35 in 1195 (worth a *pedica* of land, a meadow, and a mill in Silva Maior plus £13 in money), and £6 in 1198.[40]

This set certainly includes some non-elite members, for amounts between 20 and 40 *solidi* (£1–2) are not large. In another text of 1189 we have reference to a *dos* of 11 *solidi* (worth two-thirds of a vineyard), planned for by a family who had very

---

[38] *SMVL*, n. 205; Galgano's sister Bonella also owned, not on an enormous scale, in Arcioni east of the Trevi *regio*: nn. 217, 221. For his career as *primicerius*, see Halphen, *Études*, pp. 100–1, not a full list of his judicial activity, which I read as *SMVL*, nn. 162, 165; *S. Gregorio*, nn. 7, 82; *SPV*, n. 41; *Senato*, n. 12.

[39] *S. Prassede*, n. 7 (a. 1056); *SMCM*, n. 32 (a. 1133). See Toubert, *Les structures*, pp. 751–68, for the dowry system of Rome and Lazio, still the core analysis; di Carpegna Falconieri, 'Sposarsi a Roma'.

[40] *SMCM*, n. 32 (a. 1133); *SMVL*, n. 186 (a. 1155); *SMN*, n. 77 (a. 1157); *S. Sisto*, n. 5 (a. 1160); *SMVL*, n. 201 (a. 1163); *SMN*, n. 100 (a. 1173); ASR, SCD, cassetta 16, n. 143 (a. 1173); *SMN*, n. 133 (a. 1190); *SMVL*, n. 254 (a. 1195); *S. Sil.*, n. 48 (a. 1198). The currencies of these texts are all Lucchese or Provins coins, plus senatorial coins based on those of Provins; the former two had the same value in 1164 (ASR, SCD, cassetta 16, n. 146, eighth text on roll, a text which gives an exchange rate of 1 *denarius* of Pavia for 2 of Lucca or Provins).

few other resources indeed.[41] But Pietro in 1173 (from the family in the Colosseo with the mail-shirt), the 1160 husband (Gozo di Todero, whose brother was a *scriniarius*), the second 1173 husband (otherwise unknown), the 1190 husband (also unknown), and that of 1195 (the son of another *scriniarius*, who was marrying the daughter of the palatine *protoscriniarius*) apparently had rough total resources of between £8 and £35. These seem to have been sufficient for elite status, at least at the level of Rome's *regiones*, as the notarial/judicial qualifications in two of the cases further underline. As a comparison, the three marriage deals known for 'aristocratic' families in the same period, for the Prefetti and the Frangipane, were for much larger dowries of £130–200, in each case worth a portion of a castle.[42]

I do not wish to fetishize these figures, which can only be indicative. It is striking, apart from anything else, that the valuation of land fluctuates a lot in these documents, more than it normally does, which probably reflects the fact that marriage deals, however hard-headed, were not only for economic advantage—and the sums concerned could well sometimes have been inflated for effect. But the middle range of wealth seen here, that of Pietro di Romano di Frasia and the two *scriniarius* families, fits that of Galgano *primicerius*, and also the other wills and divisions already listed. It looks, in fact, as if only relatively high-status or prosperous people as yet made written wills, or documents recording land divisions; although, by contrast, poorer people could make written marriage contracts from the first. And a generic picture of medium-level elite resources can be created as a result: several houses in the city (but sometimes only two or three), several plots of land in the countryside (mostly in the vineyard belt), and, on occasion, quite a lot of money or treasure—often doubtless obtained from commerce, sometimes from war, sometimes from clerical relatives—and useful among other things for the credit market. From this standpoint, the tower-houses of the Maccii and Cerratani stand out as unusual, and it is interesting that the set of families with quasi-quantified resources, just discussed, also show us no surnames, unlike most of the five sample families I started with. Unusual also are the larger sums in money and movables of Tedaldo di Tedaldo and especially Giovanni di Raineri, who must have been very much on the richest edge of the 'medium elite'. We see clear signs of economic and social differentiation here. But the range of modest landed wealth (seldom, here as elsewhere, held in full property) seen in these land divisions and marriage agreements would doubtless have normally been enough to live on in rents, even excluding any artisanal, commercial, or financial operations that family members engaged in, or any dues from notarial/judicial activities, which are coming to be visible quite regularly among this group. This was what medium-level prosperity was like in Rome in our period. It was not necessarily enough to propel one to formal prominence, even in a *regio* of the city, still less to the Senate; but,

---

[41] *SMVL*, n. 234; the text makes it explicit that the vineyard, sold in the text to fund the dowry, was the most expendable of the bride's resources, a unique phrase; the *comminus* to S. Ciriaco in Via Lata was also unusually high, nearly a third of the value of the land, which hints at economic weakness.

[42] *SMN*, n. 46; 'Documenti per la storia', n. 25; *LC*, I, nn. 180–1. The first and the last are for £100 in Pavese money, which was worth £200 in Lucchese or Provins money (see above, n. 40, and also *SMN*, n. 99, a. 1171).

conversely, it was from this range of wealth that most of the city's leaders, at senatorial and regional levels alike, were recruited in the first fifty years of the Senate's existence.

This picture of the traceable activities and resources of 'medium elites', whether richer or less rich, more or less politically influential, is inevitably sketchy, even if it does allow at least tentative generalizations such as these just set out. But for more of a sense of how such families fitted into regional societies in Rome we must change focus, and follow the archival practices and political/economic interests of the churches and monasteries that kept our most substantial document collections. Secular families only emerge intermittently in any detail through that ecclesiastical gaze, but how churches dealt with their neighbours as a whole can give us more of a sense of how Roman regional societies functioned in the eleventh and twelfth centuries. The next section will be dedicated to this.

THREE ROMAN *REGIONES*

Trastevere

The monastery of SS. Cosma e Damiano in Trastevere (now called S. Cosimato) was founded, probably around 950, by Alberico's close associate Benedetto Campanino, a little south of the built-up sector of Trastevere; it may also have had a prior existence as a church or monastery. It was probably richer than the three titular churches of Trastevere, S. Maria, S. Cecilia, and S. Crisogono, and than the other main regional monastery, S. Pancrazio, just outside the walls on the Gianicolo. Almost all our Trastevere documents come from this monastery, with the addition of a few for S. Maria. Its urban land was overwhelmingly in Trastevere, both in the built-up streets of its north and east and the vineyards of its south and west, including up the slopes of the Gianicolo. It also owned almost all of the very large estate of Marcelli, immediately west of the city, other estates along the Aurelia and Portuense, notably Tertio and Palmi, and some holdings at Porto and in the Porto salt pans. In addition, up the Cassia to the north it held Isola Farnese, Campagnano, much of Cesano, and substantial lands in the diocese of Sutri, as well as vineyards in Albano, along with every other Roman church. This array of properties is visible from the considerable set of surviving original documents for the monastery (nearly two hundred up to 1200), but almost all are listed already in 1005 in the major papal confirmation to SS. Cosma e Damiano by John XVIII, and may largely go back to Benedetto himself.[43]

Trastevere was, as we have seen, a slightly separate region of the city, sometimes part of Rome, sometimes not entirely; but its inhabitants were not in any visible way unusual. They included potters, shoemakers, and ironsmiths, and they took

---

[43] For 1005, *Papsturkunden*, n. 419. For the history of the monastery, see esp. Barclay Lloyd and Bull-Simonsen Einaudi, *SS. Cosma e Damiano*. Note that Trastevere is not called a *regio* in texts between 1029 (*SCD*, nn. 34–5) and 1218 (ASR, SCD, cassetta 17, n. 213: see Hubert, *Espace urbain*, p. 94n), but it can readily be treated as one.

full part in the complex artisanal exchange of the city (above, p. 142). They also appear as witnesses to SS. Cosma e Damiano's documents for everywhere, and were also often tenants of its land: both in the city, and down the via Portuense to the sea. The Portuense, or more widely the whole agricultural sector between the Tiber and the Aurelia, was the basic zone of extension of Trastevere interest, in our period as also later. Trasteverini dominated the *scola piscatorum* who ran the fishing in the great lagoon behind the Porto salt pans, as a document of 1158 shows, notably the family of Pietro di Cencio di Guido and the recently aristocratic Papareschi, and, although salt tenants came from all over Rome, the *scola salinariorum*, the directive body for salt extraction, had strong Trastevere links too (for all this see above, pp. 103–5). The right-bank *regio*'s inhabitants were not by any means only interested in the lands of SS. Cosma e Damiano, too; any other church with land on the Portuense found itself with Trastevere tenants, the best-documented being the non-Trastevere monastery of S. Ciriaco in Via Lata, owner of most of Criptule and Campo di Merlo.[44] This consistent involvement of local inhabitants in the properties along the roads (and river) leading out of Trastevere helps to make up for a long gap in texts for the *regio* in the late eleventh century and early twelfth; for Trastevere itself our best documentation is restricted to the 1020s–70s, and then after 1160.

SS. Cosma e Damiano's local clientele in the early to mid-eleventh century consisted in part of families we have seen already, notably Tebaldo di Franco and his sons (including Giovanni Tignoso, prefect of the city in the 1060s), and the Maccii. They were in turn witnesses to monastic documents and monastic tenants, mostly in Marcelli, though in Tebaldo's case in S. Ciriaco's Campo di Merlo too. The family of Giovanni Tignoso, together with that of Giovanni Bracciuto, whose members were not monastic clients, were clearly among the leaders of Trastevere in the conflicts of the 1040s and 1050s, which pitched the *regio* against left-bank Rome, for and against rival popes; their support for Hildebrand and Nicholas II in 1058–9 was the direct reason for Giovanni Tignoso's promotion to the prefecture.[45] They mark a sharpness of Trastevere political action which is seldom as clear in later decades. Less prominent clients of the monastery were Donato di Crescenzio Cortese, who lived close to it (he is described as *a S. Cosmato* in 1078, the first appearance of the later name for the church), and who witnessed frequently for it for a decade; and Giovanni and Pietro *de Abbate* who witnessed from the 1050s to the 1070s, to be followed by the former's son Giovanni or Giannucio, who witnessed in 1098 and was a monastic tenant on the Isola Sacra at the Tiber mouth in 1091. Giovanni *de Abbate* also witnessed for S. Maria in Trastevere, so he had a more public role than the others: he was arguably a person of local status, an

---

[44] See Wickham, 'La struttura', pp. 194–205.

[45] See above, Chapter 4, nn. 111–114, for the family of Giovanni of Tignoso, and also the Bracciuti, who were not SS. Cosma e Damiano's clients (they appear instead, casually, in SMT, nn. 5, 7, and *SMVL*, n. 94), and who did not have any monastic land in any surviving document until Stefania di Giovanni Bracciuto bought two *pedicae* of land in Marcelli from another tenant in 1098: *SCD*, n. 96. For conflict narratives, see esp. *LP*, II, pp. 331, 334–5.

abbot's son no less, who was not simply a monastic client.[46] This is a distinction we shall see later too. We cannot say much more about the social environment of the eleventh century here, but it is at least clear that families could prosper through monastic links and gain a city-wide prominence, at least for a time; although I have argued that neither the family of Giovanni Tignoso nor the Bracciuti maintained 'aristocratic'-level status, we have also seen that Tebaldo di Tebaldo, probably descended from both, was on the richer end of the 'medium elite' in 1132.

The families of the later twelfth century associated with SS. Cosma e Damiano, after the break in Trastevere documents, seem to have been different ones. An important one was that of Giovanni di Astaldo, a monastic witness in 1164, whose sons Astaldo, Filippo, and Pietro were similarly witnesses in the 1170s–80s, and also tenants of SS. Cosma e Damiano for a house on the Gianicolo in 1178, together with agricultural land just inside the Trastevere walls in 1179. Giovanni's father was probably the Astaldo di Giovanni di Martignone who appears in 1139 as a witness for the monastery, and also in 1128 for S. Gregorio sul Celio for its Cancellata estate between the Aurelia and the salt pans. The family is certainly distinct from the *filii Astaldi* of the Colosseo, discussed earlier (p. 239), and was less prominent. All the same, Giovanni's sons Astaldo and Filippo both became senators in 1188–91, so they had a visible status. They had also moved into the world of local credit by 1182, when a loan of £20 owed by S. Ciriaco in Via Lata to Astaldo and his nephews, pledged against land in Campo di Merlo, was paid off by a new loan from the Cerratani of Campo Marzio. If Bonifacio di Nicola di Astaldo, a landholder in Palmi in 1192, was also a member of the family, then the Bonifacio *de Martinionibus*, a prior of the *scola salinariorum* in 1217, probably shows us that the family had an at least occasional surname, going back to the Martignone referred to in the 1130s. They were clearly, at least in part, clients of SS. Cosma e Damiano, but not necessarily easy ones: the 1179 lease refers to a prior dispute with the monastery, and the arbitration of two local figures. These included Ioattolo di Vitale *iudeo*, which is almost a unique citation in our texts, but is nonetheless a sign of the accepted participation of Jews in public life in the period, at least in Trastevere, where a synagogue is documented in the same year; Rabbi Yeḥiel, whom Benjamin of Tudela mentions as a scholar living in Trastevere in 1161, may well be the same man.[47]

---

[46] Donato: *SCD*, nn. 66, 69, 70, 78, 80, 84 (a. 1078). Giovanni, Pietro, Giannucio: nn. 55, 58, 72, 85, 90, 96; *SMT*, nn. 4, 5. Which abbot Giovanni and Pietro were sons of cannot be said; if he ruled SS. Cosma e Damiano (the most likely hypothesis), the best bet is Abbot Giovanni, documented 1026–36 (*SCD*, nn. 28–41).

[47] Giovanni di Astaldo and his sons: ASR, SCD, cassetta 16, n. 146 (eighth, twelfth, fifteenth, and sixteenth texts on roll, the last of these being the 1179 lease), cassetta 16 bis, n. 153; *SPV*, n. 56; *SMT*, n. 15; *Senato*, nn. 42, 43. Giovanni is actually first attested witnessing a Trastevere court case for S. Gregorio in 1145: CVL 8044, ff. 4–16. Astaldo di Giovanni di Martignone: S. Gregorio, n. 20; ASR, SCD, cassetta 16, n. 124 (the S. Gregorio text has his grandfather as *Marumoni*, which I take to be a misreading by the eighteenth-century compiler of the surviving text of the cartulary, or else of his source). Other texts: *SMVL*, n. 216 (a. 1182); ASR, SCD, cassetta 16 bis, n. 163 (eighth text on roll, a. 1192); Carbonetti Vendittelli, 'La curia dei *priores*', pp. 140–1 (a. 1217). See for the synagogue *SMVL*, Baumgärtner, n. 3; cf. Benjamin of Tudela, *The Itinerary*, pp. 5–6; he says there were 200 Jews in

The family of Giovanni di Astaldo was probably the most powerful the monastery had to deal with in the later twelfth century in the region, and the family dealt with more churches—and not only in Trastevere—than just this one. But it is worth stressing that SS. Cosma e Damiano at least kept an association with them; the two other clearly influential families in Trastevere in the late twelfth century that we know about, the 'aristocratic' Papareschi (above, pp. 241–3) and their opponents, the 'medium elite' *filii Grisotti*, who provided a senator in 1184, had almost no association with the monastery at all, and must have developed entirely different social networks in the *regio*.[48]

The other people who appear often in late twelfth-century SS. Cosma e Damiano documents were less prominent. Nicola di Alfedocia only appears in the monastery's archive. He was a monastic witness in the 1170s and 1180s too, and a tenant of monastic land in Trastevere twice in the 1170s–90s; he was also a monastic creditor for the small sum of 25 *solidi*, with a pledge of a vineyard inside the walls, before 1191.[49] The *de Pote* family, of whom six are known, were monastic witnesses for thirty years from 1168 onwards, and again are only known from documents of the monastery, except for one appearance as a witness in a S. Ciriaco lease for Criptule on the Portuense; they were clearly close to SS. Cosma e Damiano in these years, for Pietro *de Pote* is documented as a monk there between 1170 and 1191, for much of which period he was also the *yconomus* or financial administrator of the monastery.[50] The *filii Summeragi* were monastic witnesses and tenants across the same period, always, like Nicola di Alfedocia, for land inside the walls of Trastevere; they had some external interests as well, however, for Pietro di Gregorio Sumeragi was another *prior* of the *scola salinariorum* in 1217.[51] We are probably by now no longer at the level of the 'medium elite', however; notwithstanding Pietro *de Pote*'s career, there is no reason to think that any of these people were socially prominent. Nonetheless, here too, we find a mix of witnessing (i.e. being physically present while the monastery carried out transactions), tenancy, and credit, with the possibility of entry into the monastery itself for family members. These families were, above all, tenants in the city, as indeed

---

Rome, but does not say that any others lived in Trastevere. Other Jews taking part in public acts are attested in *RS*, n. 129 (a. 977) and *S. Alessio*, n. 21 (a. 1169).

[48] For the *filii Grisotti*, see above, p. 83, and Wickham, 'Getting justice', pp. 108–11. Pietro di Grisotto as senator: *Senato*, n. 39. The main references to the family focus on its substantial pledges and leases in Campo di Merlo and its troubled relation to its debtor and landlord, S. Ciriaco in Via Lata. Otherwise, CVL 8044, ff. 4–16; *S. Gregorio*, n. 55; and ASR, SCD, cassetta 16, n. 143, cassetta 16 bis, n. 163 (second and eighth texts on roll) are the likely citations. For SS. Cosma e Damiano, this consists of witnessing in 1173, 1191, and 1192. The other two senators who can be attached to Trastevere, Pietro di Stefano in 1188 and Sergio in 1191 (*Senato*, nn. 42–3), are also not identifiable in documents for the monastery.

[49] ASR, SCD, cassetta 16 bis, nn. 144, 145, 146 (sixth text on recto and fifth and sixth on verso), 154, 162 (a. 1191), 177.

[50] ASR, SCD, cassetta 16, nn. 138, 146 (seventh text on verso); cassetta 16 bis, nn. 162, 164, 171; *SMVL*, n. 259. Pietro is a monk from ASR, SCD, n. 140 to n. 162; he is first recorded as *yconomus* in n. 146 (ninth text on roll).

[51] ASR, SCD, cassetta 16, n. 146 (sixth and sixteenth texts on recto and fifth on verso); cassetta 16 bis, nn. 177, 180; Carbonetti Vendittelli, 'La curia dei *priores*', pp. 140–1.

was that of Giovanni di Astaldo; there seems by now to have been developing a separation between urban and rural tenants of the monastery, for rural tenants after 1150 or so hardly ever appear as monastic witnesses.[52] Urban tenants did, nonetheless, maintain systematic links to the salt pans of Porto as well.

There are other such families in the SS. Cosma e Damiano documents, which show a similar profile, but are more fragmentarily attested; they do not add anything to what has been said here. The monastic archive does, however, include two unpublished texts which are unique for the period and which flesh out our sense of the social environment around the church: they are each collections of documents on a parchment roll, twenty-four in the first case (from 1164 to 1180), eight in the second (from 1191 to 1192). The second, consisting of almost full texts, is all the work of a single *scriniarius*, Romano; the first is in note form, and not all in the same hand, and the *scriniarii*, when mentioned at all, are also not all the same, but it focuses on the affairs of SS. Cosma e Damiano, above all in 1177–9, and must have been created for the monastery. Romano's text is clearly an early version of a notarial register, and it is validated by his *siglum* at the end. The earlier text lacks that crucial validation, and must have been for the monastery's private use, but doubtless resembles the notes, *dicta*, referred to in many twelfth-century documents—for it is quite common for charters to say that a *scriniarius* later wrote it up as he found it *in dictis* of a deceased *scriniarius,* usually his father. (One of the texts in the first set here does this, in fact.) Both documents nonetheless give a detailed snapshot of monastic activities across a short space of time, inside the framework of a well-defined group of participants. The first mostly records monastic leases, with a few refutations, that is cessions back to the monastery, of existing leases (one held, atypically, *in feudo*), and a repayment of a pledge in land. The second mostly records the cessions of leases, bought back by the monastery, and two repaid pledges, plus a pious gift of land in Campagnano in Tuscia Romana, which is one of the few such gifts in the period. The land in both documents is mostly in Trastevere, less often down the Portuense, and only occasionally elsewhere.[53]

Both texts thus record essentially Trasteverino deals in monastic property. The transactions are often quite tightly spaced, a couple of days or a week apart, as in June 1177, February 1179, or October 1191, although then perhaps two months will elapse until the next. They represent a very local set of concerns. It is therefore interesting that very few of the participants, whether tenants, creditors, or witnesses, are recorded more than once. Some are: Gaudio *ferrarius*, Ruggero di Tancredi, Sasso di Rubeo and his son, and the small-scale client families already mentioned. But even these do not appear often, and the others come and go. It is clear that the immediate surroundings of SS. Cosma e Damiano were by now, given

---

[52] A rare instance is Guarnimento di Rainerio di Guido di Iaulino, who leased from the monastery in Marcelli in 1190 (ASR, SCD, cassetta 16 bis, n. 159, cf. cassetta 16, n. 138), and witnessed a monastic lease in Trastevere in 1179 (ASR, SCD, cassetta 16, n. 146, fifteenth text on roll).

[53] ASR, SCD, cassetta 16, n. 146 (eighth text on roll for *in dictis*), and cassetta 16 bis, n. 163. In general for *dicta*, see Pratesi, *Tra carte e notai*, pp. 481–501; the first mentioned in Roman documents is in *S. Gregorio*, n. 15 (a. 1067).

the expansion of Trastevere, rather more full of people, including artisans (half a dozen professions are mentioned), and the occasional immigrant from Tuscia Romana or Abruzzo. But it also seems that, apart from a small handful of slightly closer associates, the monastery relied for its daily business on bystanders rather than clients, and that it also had a substantial and diverse group of tenants. Between the eleventh and the twelfth centuries, the monastic gaze widened to include a considerable range of people, and it must be the case, given all these single appearances, that we are overwhelmingly looking at people without elevated status. That is significant; it marks a weakening in the political position of SS. Cosma e Damiano, as less connected to the relatively rich and powerful, but also a strengthening of its role as a local focus, in a region with a strong identity.[54] The monastery did pledge away some of its land in this period, but not on any substantial scale, and anyway redeemed its loans: if it had lost political standing, there are no signs that it was in financial trouble. It is easy, however, to see why it remained a regional focus; its ownership of such a high proportion of the south of Trastevere and of the lands down the Portuense, the natural hinterland of the Trasteverini, and its preparedness to lease it out, will have encouraged people to see it as such in every period. In these single references to tenants and witnesses, we thus see a cross-section of the inhabitants of the *regio*.

Pigna

SS. Ciriaco e Nicola in Via Lata lay just behind the *diaconia* of S. Maria in Via Lata, with S. Marcello, an early *titulus*, just opposite. This was the heart of the main demographic centre of medieval Rome, and the churches lay along one of the city's principal streets in every age. The *regio* of Pigna ran west from here to the Pantheon and south towards the Capitolio and its market; east across the road was SS. Apostoli, where Alberico's palace had been, inherited by the Tuscolani; and in fact S. Ciriaco was founded as a female monastery by Alberico's cousins, including Marozia 'II' ancestor of the Tuscolani, again around 950. It accumulated land in all directions: in the tenth century in Sutri and Ariccia, perhaps its earliest endowments; in the eleventh very extensively along the Portuense (Campo di Merlo, Criptule), along the Tiburtina, where its largest land block was (Silva Maior and Bolagai, probably Tuscolano gifts), and elsewhere too. In the city, Pigna was its main proprietorial focus, with some extensions east to Trevi and the Quirinale, and north to Campo Marzio, none of these being more than a quarter-hour's walk away.[55] S. Ciriaco's documents dominate our knowledge of

---

[54] Immigrants: ASR, SCD, cassetta 16, n. 146 (second text on verso: Cesano, Campagnano); cassetta 16 bis, n. 163 (third text on roll: Amiterno). ASR, SCD, cassetta 16 bis, n. 167 (a. 1194) has a witness named Transtiberinus, whose localized naming (unusual in Rome) underlines the identity of the *regio*.

[55] For the foundation, see Hamilton, 'The monastic revival', pp. 52–4; Wickham, 'La struttura', pp. 212–13n; for S. Ciriaco's lands in the Agro romano, see Wickham, 'La struttura', esp. pp. 203–5, 210–15. The first reference to the monastery is *S. Sil.*, n. 3 (a. 955); the monastic archive begins in 972 (*SMVL*, n. 6); its first urban document is *SMVL*, n. 26 (a. 1004).

Pigna, with the addition of a small handful of texts from each of S. Maria and S. Marcello, and the occasional surviving papal bull for other churches. Although this region was such a centre for everyone, S. Ciriaco's preoccupations thus govern our evidence, from 1004, when its urban documents start, up to 1187, when an unusual fifteen-year hiatus begins, with no more than a slight dip in the late eleventh and early twelfth, our normal low point for documents. Our evidence is again, as with SS. Cosma e Damiano but even more so, filled out by the involvement of locals in S. Ciriaco's extra-urban property-holding, particularly along the Tiburtina; this evidence does not show even those chronological dips, and indeed reaches a peak in the years around 1200.

Let us once again look at some of the people, and families, most closely associated with the monastery. Our information is relatively sketchy before the mid-twelfth century, and we can move here fairly quickly. An early family was that of Romano di Morino and his nephew Pietro di Crescenzio di Morino, who witnessed for S. Ciriaco on and off between 1029 and 1085 (the last reference is to Pietro's son Cencio, witnessing for another local church); they were also tenants in S. Ciriaco's vineyard area just outside the Porta Pinciana, that is to say roughly in the area of what is now the Villa Borghese (above, p. 95). Romano is referred to once, in 1034, as *vir magnificus*, showing at least local status, so he was presumably a member of the 'medium elite'; he was executor for deceased associates in that text, which indicates some public position. This was also probably the case for Giovanni di Atria, who is a witness for S. Ciriaco in 1057, as is his son Pietro in 1064 and 1073 (the last of these for land in Nepi, from where the family may have come); the social position of the family is shown by another son, Durante, who took part in the great papal court case concerning Arci in 1060, along with the city's entire secular leadership (above, p. 221–2).[56]

A slightly later figure, Giovanni di *domna* Bona di Berardo, was similar to the *filii Morini* as well. He first appears as a witness, in 1098–1106, and then in the first decade of the twelfth century he appears as a monastic tenant both in Pigna and in the Porta Pinciana vineyards. The use of the title *domnus/a* was widespread in Rome, well outside the 'aristocracy', but again indicates a claim to status, and Giovanni was assiduous in having it recorded for his mother in most of the texts concerning him; his own prosperity is indicated by one of his vineyard leases, in 1106, which uniquely includes a *palatium* in the vineyard. Giovanni di Bona is also recorded in the monastery's necrology (he died on 29 September), so he mattered to the nuns.[57] Finally, Cencio di Roizone, who witnesses between 1114 and 1158 (and his sons up to 1192), was almost certainly from the 'new aristocracy', for he appears in a S. Maria Nova document with the prestigious title of *Romanorum consul* in 1126, and must be—as Roizone is a fairly rare name—descended from the Cencio di Roizone *nobilis vir/vir magnificus* who

---

[56] Romano di Morino and family: *SMVL*, nn. 55, 62 (a. 1034), 70, 77, 79, 96; *SMCM*, n. 21 (a. 1085). Giovanni di Atria and family: *SMVL*, nn. 85, 92, 100 (a. 1073), 109; *RF*, n. 906 (Arci in 1060); *SPV*, n. 25; for Nepi origins, an indicator may be the rare name Atria in Nepi texts in *SMVL*, nn. 5, 28.
[57] See Chapter 2, n. 180, with Egidi, *Necrologi*, pp. 64–5.

was a monastic witness in the 1060s and whose son was a *consul communitatis boum* and thus a political player in 1088.[58] These men are among the monastery's best-attested witnesses up to the mid-twelfth century. They indicate that S. Ciriaco's clientele numbered rather more influential families than did that of SS. Cosma e Damiano, which the monastery's Tuscolano connections and central location probably explain. But the links between witnessing transactions around the monastery and renting land just outside the walls were strong in both cases.

In the years 1137–63, another monastic witness was Cencio di Pietro di Nicola. He held monastic land in Pigna, and also, like his predecessors, outside the walls: this time in Bolagai, part of the very large monastic estate on the via Tiburtina, which extended to Silva Maior and Reatina on the border with Tivoli (above, pp. 68–9). He did not witness so many charters, but he must have been a particularly important monastic client or associate, for many of the documents he witnessed were court cases or similar dispute-related texts. In 1148, he testified in a formal court for S. Ciriaco, to say that in 1140 he had witnessed a phony (*fenticio*) charter between the monastery and Grisotto di Ingizello of Trastevere, which was not intended by either party to be legally valid (cf. above, p. 83), so he was clearly trusted by the nuns; in 1156, similarly, Pope Hadrian IV sent him to Cave near Palestrina, one of S. Ciriaco's few castles, to act for the monastery against the aristocratic tenants of the castle—he went together with Oddone *scriniarius*, whom we will come back to.[59]

In the next generation we find a similarly named man, Pietro di Cencio di Nicola, who in two texts is called Pietro di Cencio di Pietro di Nicola, so he must be the son of the preceding—he evidently usually elided one of his ancestors. He was a witness for S. Ciriaco a few times in 1183–91, and a tenant of monastic land in Bolagai and, especially, Monte del Sorbo in Silva Maior, where, after his death in 1200, his sons also held land up to 1211 (they called themselves sons of 'Pietro di Cencio *de Pinea*', showing that the family was indeed based in the *regio*). Pietro di Cencio also collected rents for S. Ciriaco in Reatina, as the Silva Maior court case of 1201 relates. Already before 1179, he was rich enough and visible enough to be part of a consortium loaning money to Pope Alexander III, who repaid him £41 and 7 *solidi* in that year. And, in S. Ciriaco's temporary financial crisis in the late 1180s (above, p. 83), he also emerges as a moneylender to the monastery, against pledges of land once again in the Bolagai–Silva Maior–Reatina area, for the even larger sum of £127. Pietro di Cencio was certainly in the richest group of the 'medium elite' if he had that sort of disposable money, and he took over a measurable section of the monastery's estate until it was repaid. In 1200, his widow Gaita was herself

---

[58] *SMVL*, nn. 143, 149, 182, 189, 233, 241, with *SMN*, n. 42 (*consul*); for his eleventh-century homonym, *SMVL*, nn. 88, 91, and *RF*, n. 1115 (a. 1088), for Cencio Cencii Roizonis (cf. below, p. 396).

[59] *SMVL*, nn. 161, 172 (a. 1148), 178, 187 (a. 1156), 190, 195, 199 (land in Pigna), 208 (land in Bolagai). The other formal 1148 witness, Bonofiglio di Maridonna, had a similar standing: he witnessed documents for S. Ciriaco between 1125 and 1151 (*SMVL*, nn. 149, 177–8), and his heirs, who were also lessees of the monastery, carried on the tradition (*SMVL*, n. 244; *SMVL*, Baumgärtner, n. 5).

pledging land in Bolagai, after a dispute with Nicola di Tederico (otherwise unknown), for £120; it seems as if the dispute concerned an earlier loan from the latter. The family thus were not simply monastic creditors, but part of a wider and more complex credit market, connected to monastic land. They were certainly prospering as they did so, for the 1200 pledge by no means included all their extramural land. But they remained in this social and regional frame; they are never attested elsewhere in the city, and are not documented as senators.[60]

Cencio and his son Pietro are the clearest examples of quite a substantial group of monastic associates with similar trajectories in the second half of the twelfth century and beyond. They are sufficiently clearly delineated that it is worth looking at several of them. Oddone *scriniarius* wrote seventeen surviving monastic charters between 1135 and 1169. He was the son of the prominent *scriniarius* Falconio or Falcone, who worked for S. Ciriaco, but also for at least six other churches and monasteries, between 1100 and 1137, plus for the pope—he was also a palaeo-graphical expert, who transcribed tenth-century papyri for S. Gregorio sul Celio. Oddone was as prominent in the mid-century, and worked for even more churches, but over half of Oddone's surviving documents are for S. Ciriaco and, as we have seen, he was a legal representative for the monastery in 1156. Oddone's son Giovanni also wrote up some monastic documents, but he was less clearly a house *scriniarius* than his father or grandfather. Conversely, he was a monastic tenant in Bolagai in 1174, for land (held in *feudus*) which bordered on land held by the heirs of Cencio di Pietro. We cannot be sure that this was a Pigna family, but the long-lasting association that three generations of it had with S. Ciriaco documents produced tenancy and credit deals, just as it did for Cencio di Pietro and his son.[61]

Partial successors to this family were two judicial experts in the very late twelfth century and early thirteenth. One was Giovanni di Stefano, who was actually *protoscrinius*, a palatine judge, in 1195–1207 (he became *secundicerius* in 1210–17); he was engaged by S. Ciriaco in 1195 to serve the monastery *ex officio iudicis et avocati*, that is as its legal advocate, in return for a large lease at S. Onesto in Silva Maior, a block of land which would become the modern *casale* Marco Simone, and he does indeed appear as a judicial representative in many monastic documents of the next two decades.[62] Alicho di Romano Sordo was similarly an

---

[60] Witness: *SMVL*, Baumgärtner, n. 5: *SMVL*, nn. 235.II, 237. Tenant: *SMVL*, nn. 235.I, 257; *SMVL*, Baumgärtner, nn. 25, 30, 48a (*de Pinea*), 70, 78. Rent collector: *SMVL*, n. 280. Creditor: 'Documenti per la storia', nn. 10–11 (a. 1179); *SMVL*, nn. 227, 227A, 229, 261.I. Grandfather recorded as Pietro: *SMVL*, n. 237; 'Documenti per la storia', nn. 10–11. Gaita: *SMVL*, nn. 274–5.

[61] Oddone: *SMVL*, n. 187, as a representative; scribe from *SMVL*, Baumgartner, n. 2 (a. 1135) to *SMVL*, n. 204, plus *S. Agnese*, n. 8; *S. Prassede*, nn. 22, 23 (cf. 24), 29, 30, 33; *S. Alessio*, nn. 14, 18–21; *S. Sisto*, nn. 2, 4; *SMN*, n. 71; *S. Gregorio*, n. 55; *Liberiano*, n. 20. Falcone: *S. Gregorio*, nn. 34, 19, 20, and the transcriptions, nn. 1, 15, 68, 124 (cf. Carbonetti Vendittelli, '"Sicut inveni in thomo carticineo"'); *S. Prassede*, nn. 11, 12, 17, 19; ASR, SCD, cassetta 16, n. 102; Kehr, IV, pp. 450–1; *SMCM*, n. 30; *SMN*, nn. 42, 44, 45; plus *SMVL* from n. 125 to n. 160, over twenty times. Giovanni: *SMVL*, nn. 149, 208 (a. 1174).

[62] Giovanni's career: Halphen, *Études*, pp. 145–6, 113–14. For S. Ciriaco, *SMVL*, nn. 249–50 (a. 1195); as a monastic representative, nn. 253, 254, 258, 261, 265; *SMVL*, Baumgärtner, nn. 53, 64, 72, 76, 88, 90, 108. S. Onesto as Marco Simone: Coste, 'Il *castrum Sancti Honesti*'.

advocatus et scriniarius acting for S. Ciriaco in the years 1206–19 and tenant of land in Monte del Sorbo. The same mixture of monastic tenancy along the Tiburtina and professional expertise is visible in all three cases, stretching across half a century.[63]

Five other examples, not of professional experts, fill out this picture for the late twelfth century. Cencio Grosso was not from Pigna, but from Monti, as an 1188 document shows; he nonetheless appears with his brother Gregorio as a monastic witness in 1186–98 for lands all over the Agro romano, so must often have been at the monastery. He was a tenant in both Bolagai and Monte del Sorbo, as were his heirs, in documents between 1196 and 1225; he was also a monastic enforcer in Silva Maior in 1191–3, protecting S. Ciriaco's wood rights against the men of Tivoli by confiscating their tools, so he was evidently an active client. Once, in 1194, he appears as a monastic debtor, for £15, and he backed up a lay loan in 1201 as well. He was a rich dealer who had come into S. Ciriaco's orbit and prospered further there. But, like Giovanni di Stefano, he was already a public figure before he did so: he was a senator in 1185.[64]

Nicola Panico or di Panico was a more or less exact contemporary of Cencio Grosso; he was a monastic witness in 1189–95, and also a tenant in Monte del Sorbo from before 1189 to 1210. He was another monastic representative in Reatina in the 1190s, as the 1201 court case witnesses attest, but he gained more importance there later; by 1207 he was the monastery's *vicecomes*, bailiff, over the whole of Monte del Sorbo, a role he perhaps held from 1205, when he was leased a large *tenimentum* in Silva Maior, to 1210, when he became an oblate of the monastery (the closest he could get in spiritual terms to a monastery of nuns) and ceded the *tenimentum* back with a life usufruct. Nicola must have been from the city, for his early witnessing was for monastic properties well away from the Tiburtina, but here too his involvement in S. Ciriaco's affairs brought him substantial lands and an important supervisory role in Silva Maior.[65]

---

[63] Alicho: *SMVL*, Baumgärtner, nn. 44, 67, 90, 92, 108, 113. A further parallel for the mixture of professional, financial, and tenurial links in these cases, though certainly less close to the monastery, is Giovanni di Leone, *scriniarius* for seven churches, and important enough to have the *potestas dandi tutores et curatores* by 1192, a right apparently held only by one *scriniarius* at once (see below, n. 124), who appears as a creditor holding part of S. Ciriaco's large Lubbre estate in pledge for just under £12 in 1192, which is turned into a lease for his son in 1198. For the property deals, see *SMVL*, nn. 242, 260, cf. 263; for the documents he wrote, *SMVL*, n. 230, Baumgärtner, n. 3; ASR, SCD, cassetta 16, n. 146 (second text on verso), cassetta 16 bis, n. 163 (sixth text on roll); *S. Sisto*, nn. 10, 11, 13, 14; *S. Alessio*, n. 23; *LC*, I, nn. 165, 166, 178; *S. Gregorio*, n. 24; 'Documenti per la storia', n. 32. Nor was S. Ciriaco unique in making such deals with senior advocates; S. Alessio and S. Maria Tempuli did the same in the 1170s: *S. Alessio*, n. 22; *S. Sisto*, n. 8.

[64] Cencio Grosso: from Monti in 'Documenti per la storia', n. 14, a text which shows he was well-off; senator in *Senato*, n. 39 (= *SMVL*, n. 225b). Witness in *SMVL*, nn. 229, 237, 242, 244, 245, 246, 249, 251, 258, 260. Tenant in n. 255, with *SMVL*, Baumgärtner, nn. 17, 25, 117–18, 135. Enforcer in *SMVL*, n. 280. Debtor in n. 247 and creditor in *SMVL*, Baumgärtner, n. 18.

[65] Nicola di Panico: witness in *SMVL*, nn. 235.III, 242, 244, 252. Tenant in *SMVL*, n. 235.II, *SMVL*, Baumgärtner, nn. 39 (a. 1205), 87, 93. Monastic representative and *vicecomes* in *SMVL*, Baumgärtner, nn. 14, 52; as oblate, n. 70; cf. also n. 53, a court case against another tenant in Silva Maior. He is recorded in the monastic necrology as dying on 1 May: Egidi, *Necrologi*, pp. 30–1.

Leone or Leolo di Nicola di Leolo *de Camiliano* certainly came from close to
S. Ciriaco in Pigna, for the monastery was situated beside the Campus Camilianus.
He was a monastic witness from 1188. So was his son Pietro di Leolo by 1199, and
Pietro continued as such into the 1220s. Leolo and his brother were tenants in
Bolagai in particular, and also Monte del Sorbo, and they moved into Pilo Rotto in
Silva Maior before 1204 on a substantial scale, buying up monastic leases from a
locally based tenant, Viviano, who was facing financial and political difficulties.
Leolo had a wider public role: he was an agreed arbiter in the dispute faced by
Gaita, Pietro di Cencio's widow, in 1200, and a single agreed arbiter in a second
dispute in Bolagai in 1203; he also acted as a *procurator* for a deal by another tenant
there in 1204. Pietro di Leolo was an arbiter in 1221, too, in a text that calls him
iudex. He and his father never acted in a legal or paralegal capacity for S. Ciriaco
itself in any text we have, but the network of monastic tenants clearly regarded
them as serious and neutral figures, and they must have had local standing.[66]

Rufavelia and his probable nephew Stefano di Malagalia were tenants of
S. Ciriaco in Bolagai and Monte del Sorbo in the 1190s. Rufavelia was an
occasional monastic witness as early as 1169, and he had monastic tenures somewhere unspecified in 1177, when a senatorial court case established what rent their
cultivators should bring to his *domus* (above, p. 72)—the term *domus* implying that
Rufavelia was based in the city. So certainly was Stefano, who was a senator in
1186. Rufavelia's sons also took over some of Viviano's lands in Pilo Rotto in 1202;
they went to court against Leolo of Camiliano in 1204 over them, and bought him
out; they then continued to hold there in *beneficium* from S. Ciriaco for half a
century and more, along with their Malagalia cousins. It would be inappropriate
here to follow the details of their dealings further into the thirteenth century, but
these were complicated; this 'medium elite' city family must have derived a
substantial proportion of its resources from S. Ciriaco's land.[67]

A final example in this sequence is Bartolomeo *superista* or *vicecomes*, who in
some texts is called Bartolomeo di Giovanni *Tiburtini*—Tivoli being just beyond
Silva Maior. Notwithstanding his origin, he was *nutritus a parvulo* in S. Ciriaco,
brought up there as a child, as he said in a long testimonial in the 1201 Silva Maior
hearings; he then claimed to remember back to 1175, which is entirely possible, for
he appears as a monastic witness from 1183, and thereafter very frequently until
1201, when he seems to have died, perhaps in his forties. Bartolomeo, probably an
orphan brought into the city, was more clearly a monastic dependant than any of
the foregoing people, but he acted together with them; his titles show that he was a

---

[66] Campus Camilianus: *SMVL*, n. 115, a text of 1086. Leolo: as witness, nn. 233, 246, *SMVL*,
Baumgärtner, n. 35; as tenant with his brother, *SMVL*, nn. 270, 275, *SMVL*, Baumgärtner, nn. 33
(the 1204 Pilo Rotto text), 34, 131 (heirs of Leolo); as arbiter, *SMVL*, nn. 274–5 and *SMVL*,
Baumgärtner, n. 32a; as *procurator*, n. 35. Pietro di Leolo: as witness, *SMVL*, nn. 261, 274, 281,
SMVL, Baumgärtner, nn. 15, 35, 79, 81, 90, 92, 113, 135, 136; as arbiter/*iudex*, n. 115.
[67] Rufavelia: as witness, *SMVL*, nn. 204, 258; as tenant, *SMVL*, n. 210 (= *Senato*, n. 31), 255, 257.
Stefano: nn. 225 (= *Senato*, n. 37), 228 (*senator*; = *Senato*, n. 40), with *SMVL*, Baumgärtner, n. 25.
Heirs into the thirteenth century: *SMVL*, Baumgärtner, nn. 24 (a. 1202), 33 (a. 1204), 56, 81, 108,
155, 178, 262, 265, 277–8; see Carocci and Vendittelli, *L'origine della Campagna Romana*, pp. 44–5.

monastic bailiff, and publicly identified as such, and he collaborated with Cencio Grosso in his woodland guardianship, as well as being a monastic delegate to the local Ottaviani lords, and present at a variety of formal monastic acts in Reatina and Silva Maior. He is never recorded as leasing land from S. Ciriaco, but he had land from the nuns *iure feudi*, both down the Portuense in the Criptule area and in Bolagai, together with a horse and regular supplies of hay, as the monastery acknowledged in formal witnessing in 1199. Fiefs did not usually enter the documentary record, which would explain why he was never actor in any charter in his own right. He leased his Criptule land to the man who was by 1194 collecting up the entire monastic *tenimentum* of Criptule and Ciconiola, turning it into an early *casale*, Nicola di Giovanni di Riccio, who was far richer a figure than Bartolomeo, but who will have guaranteed the latter a steady rent. Bartolomeo marks the lowest social level of monastic property dealing, but it was in this case without doubt with a figure who can be associated, for almost the whole of his life, with the monastery itself in Pigna.[68]

We have quite a range of data here for the dealings between the monastery of S. Ciriaco and its clients or associates, enough to allow us to pin down both patterns and trends. The first is that there is a difference between the best-documented laity before and after the middle years of the twelfth century; before that, they leased monastic land in Pigna itself and in the monastic vineyards just beyond the northern walls of the city; thereafter, and particularly after *c.*1170, they leased overwhelmingly in Bolagai and Silva Maior. It is for this reason that I have extended my reconstructions into the early thirteenth century, to fill out the evidence for this new group. Why S. Ciriaco's associates suddenly pushed so firmly into the monastery's Tiburtina lands is not made explicit. Silva Maior was a land clearance zone, certainly, as its name shows, and as its surviving woodland, contested in the 1190s, also shows; indeed, Reatina to its south seems to have been cleared as late as 1160 or so (above, p. 85). But most of Silva Maior was also visibly settled by the 1120s, and Bolagai was probably a zone of old and continuous settlement; the majority of S. Ciriaco's land here was by no means a frontier area of new colonization. It is likely that a more immediate political reason allowed for a new attention to the territory: the military defeat of neighbouring Tivoli by the Romans in 1143, which left Silva Maior as much less of a frontier zone.[69] It is at least evident, however, that the monastic estates in this area had become newly available to be leased to intermediaries—none of these figures were cultivators—by the last few decades of the twelfth century. Some were locals, in fact, such as Viviano of Pilo Rotto and Giovanni Rubeus of Monte del Sorbo (above, pp. 75–7). But most

---

[68] Bartolomeo: as witness, *SMVL*, nn. 233, 235.III, 239, 244, 248, 250, 251, 258, 261–2, 267, 270, 276, 278, with *SMVL*, Baumgärtner, nn. 5 (a. 1183), 7, 15 (a. 1201), and ASR, SCD, cassetta 16 bis, n. 176 (a. 1193, a misplaced S. Ciriaco text). As feudal tenant in Criptule, *SMVL*, nn. 265, 268 (these two clinch the association between the *superistal vicecomes* and his Tivoli origin); cf. 246–7 for Nicola di Giovanni di Riccio in 1194. As witness in the 1201 hearings: n. 280.

[69] Thanks to Sandro Carocci for ideas about the political context of these developments. See in general Carocci and Vendittelli, *L'origine della Campagna Romana*, pp. 41–58; Wickham, 'La struttura', pp. 210–15.

were Romans, and were men who already had, or who at once developed, an association with the monastery. This contrasts notably with S. Ciriaco's other main group of estates, on the via Portuense, which were leased to Trasteverini, such as Grisotto di Ingizello, the Papareschi, and (probably) Nicola di Giovanni di Riccio, who had no other links to the monastery at all: there, the nuns recognized a certain geographical logic, and did not expect any personal links to their tenants.[70]

Bolagai and Silva Maior anyway became the preferred zone for lay Roman dealing in S. Ciriaco's land; and, once this happened, its huge size (some 40 km^2) allowed for a very substantial network of dealers. One could easily have obtained enough land to be a member of the city's 'medium elite' if one controlled only a small fraction of that territory, and it seems reasonable to conclude from the foregoing that many of the families we have just looked at indeed gained most of their wealth from there. This may even help to explain why there are no documents for Pigna itself in the 1190s: S. Ciriaco's entourage had become so much more interested in the Tiburtina. They held there by lease, *locatio*; by *feudum* or *beneficium*; and in pledge, set against credit agreements with the monastery. As we have seen (p. 82), leases and pledges had a parallel economic logic; we cannot be so sure about fiefs, which are less well documented, but they were regarded as similar to *locationes* in a number of texts, so probably were parallel too, while conveying some more immediate personal association (doubtless, given what we know of practice elsewhere in Italy, sealed with an oath) with the nuns of S. Ciriaco.[71] But all the men we have just looked at had some association with the monastery anyway, for they were witnesses, including also, in nearly every case, for documents unrelated to the Tiburtina, so they must have regularly frequented the monastic precinct. They were the people the monastery could turn to for support—for the witnessing of public acts, for legal and notarial expertise, for economic and legal representation on the ground in monastic properties, and increasingly for credit when the nuns needed it; and they gained handsomely for it.

S. Ciriaco's landed practices were, it is important to stress, not at all unique. We have seen how Trasteverini who were personally associated with SS. Cosma e Damiano ended up with monastic land down the Portuense, particularly in the eleventh century. In Chapter 4 (above, pp. 231–2), we also saw how Farfa in the early eleventh century leased to the same families both in its properties in Scorteclari west of the Pantheon and in the Sabina, close to Farfa itself, in particular at Montelibretti—sometimes to Romans, sometimes to *Sabinenses*, and sometimes to people who might be either. In the case of Silva Maior, we see S. Ciriaco building up tenants who were both Roman and local, and, although we cannot see any explicit introduction of families from Silva Maior into land in Pigna, the strong probability of moves to urban dwelling and leasing by originally rural inhabitants is

---

[70] See Wickham, 'La struttura', pp. 203–5, and above, n. 47. *SMVL*, n. 182 (a. 1154) is a single case of the Papareschi (at least two of them) witnessing for S. Ciriaco.

[71] *Beneficium*: *SMVL*, n. 153. *Feudum*: nn. 204, 208, 265, and *SMVL*, Baumgärtner, n. 14, for the Ottaviani in Silva Maior. Similar to *locatio*: a formulary linking them is visible in *SMVL*, nn. 161, 195, 212, 268.

at least represented by the (admittedly atypical) example of Bartolomeo *superista*. This politics of land is, needless to say, a classic medieval picture too; it is also one that is rather better documented than the artisanal and commercial world that also swirled through Pigna, with its merchants, ironworkers, and wheelwrights (above, p. 143), and also, as we have seen, judges and *scriniarii*, a world which was often, doubtless, more important in strictly economic terms. But Romans associated with S. Ciriaco did lease land, often large amounts, and sought to gain more of it; that they did so while being merchants or urban professionals as well did not lessen their interest in it. It is well known that Italian cities, with their prosperous urban landowners, were less separate from the rural world around them than were some of the more commercial centres of northern Europe. What our evidence shows, however, is the specific way Romans linked themselves to that rural world, and, sometimes, the way rural inhabitants linked themselves to the city: through the concrete landowning networks and clienteles of the richest churches and monasteries.

We cannot be sure that all the Roman clients or associates of S. Ciriaco came from Pigna. Giovanni di Bona probably did, out of the early group. After 1150, Cencio di Pietro and Pietro di Cencio certainly did, and so did Leolo of Camiliano; so, in effect, did Bartolomeo *superista*, and probably Nicola di Panico, given how much in the monastic entourage he was. Cencio Grosso did not; Monti is a kilometre away. We cannot say where the *scriniarius* families lived, nor Rufavelia and his heirs. The families we cannot associate firmly with Pigna were broadly those with the highest status, for Cencio Grosso and Stefano di Malagalia were senators, and the *scriniarii* included Giovanni di Stefano as a palatine judge. But one of the clearly Pigna families had considerable wealth, that of Pietro di Cencio, and others, Giovanni di Bona and Leolo of Camiliano, had visible public standing. What we can say is that, whether they came strictly from the area of the monastery or slightly further afield, all the above-named families wanted a monastic association. None of them are documented as tenants before they turned up as witnesses; but, even if above all they sought economic advantage, through leases and other cessions of land in the vast estates along the via Tiburtina, they were prepared to be connected to S. Ciriaco for long periods in order to do so. This was the monastery's effective entourage, particularly in the later twelfth century but also earlier. And all the people discussed in this section (with the exceptions of Bartolomeo *superista* and probably Nicola di Panico, who were monastic officials, and the 'aristocrat' Cencio di Roizone) were probably members of the 'medium elite': they were, as a whole, much richer and more prominent than the clientele of SS. Cosma e Damiano. The political support network of the nuns of S. Ciriaco was mostly not 'aristocratic', then; but, as a group, it was potentially fairly powerful in Roman dealing in the twelfth century. S. Ciriaco was certainly quite close to the Senate politically; several surviving senatorial documents in the first fifty years of its existence concern the monastery and were preserved in its archive.[72] One reason must be that some

---

[72] *Senato*, nn. 31, 34–40. Cf. also nn. 12, 13, 20, 45–52, surviving in the same archive, for neighbouring S. Maria in Via Lata, with *Reg. Inn. III*, II.230 (239).

senators were part of the monastic entourage. S. Ciriaco was effectively integrated into the dominant political structure of the late twelfth-century city.

How far can we extend these observations in the direction of an understanding of Pigna as a *regio*? That is not so easy. In Trastevere, SS. Cosma e Damiano was slightly outside the streets with the thickest settlement, where the old *tituli* were, and indeed did not have much link to some important regional families (the Bracciuti, the Papareschi, etc.), but it was a focus for all that, and Trastevere's identity was always clearly bounded and often strong, so one can say with certainty that the monastery was at least *one* regional focus. Pigna, for its part, was gaining in coherence. It existed as a territory of some kind by 955 (a citation of the church of S. Giovanni *in Pinea*); witnesses said they came from the area by 1027; by 1079 it is referred to as a *regio*, and it is often in later texts too; in 1151 and 1188 a senator is named as *de Pinea*, hinting that he may have been a local representative; Pope Clement III (1187–91) is called Paolo di Giovanni *Scolarii de regione Pinee* in the final segment of the *Annales Romani*, showing a recognition of local identity which had survived a long ecclesiastical career (a pity that the Scolari family, if his father's name was a real surname, is not documented elsewhere); by 1192 *Pinea* had a clear boundary, presumably of parish rights, with the *populus* of the churches of S. Maria domine Rose and S. Lorenzo, situated in the *Castellum Aureum* (the Crypta Balbi area just to the south).[73] But Pigna was always set closely between neighbouring *regiones* in all directions, Campo Marzio, Trevi, etc.; it would have been not only easy but normal to own land across regional boundaries here in the city's heartland, and Pigna cannot be said to show as strong a collectivity to identify with as did Trastevere. Occasional references to the *regio* of Via Lata may also have cut across its regional coherence.[74] It may well be that it would be its churches that would attract most loyalty, and they were numerous, thus fragmenting local identities further: not just S. Maria in Via Lata and S. Marcello, but S. Giovanni in Pigna, S. Maria sopra Minerva, S. Maria in Aquiro on its northern edge, and the powerful parishes of S. Marco to the south and SS. Apostoli to the east—and this is only to name the most important ones. We have few or no documents for most of these; without them, we cannot easily get the measure of Pigna as a community. S. Ciriaco, a monastery with no documented parish role, might indeed have simply been seen as the focus of a transregional entourage, who were brought into its orbit only because of its undoubted wealth.

We shall look at the role of parish communities shortly (pp. 306–11); it is indeed the case that they did not act in any obvious way to strengthen regional identities. But we can at least say that S. Ciriaco was an important focus of local attraction as well. It owned a substantial block, or blocks, of land in the area around or near the monastery. It was the means of the steady rise in prosperity of local families such as that of Giovanni di Bona, or Cencio di Pietro and his son. At a less clearly documented and more small-scale level, the monastery's Pigna land was a means of binding others to the community, as when the occasional monastic witness

---

[73] Respectively, *S. Sil.*, n. 3; *SMVL*, nn. 53, 105; *Senato*, nn. 13, 42; *LP*, II, p. 349; *SPV*, n. 79.
[74] *SMVL*, nn. 181, 232.

Cencio di Leone was given a lease in 1163 of a *casarinus* in Pigna, without an entry-fine, in return for the *servitium* 'which you have done to us and must do'. By now S. Ciriaco was leasing its Pigna land out in large part to relatively unknown people, who are most likely to have been locals.[75] Its witnessing entourage created a powerful political community, some of it local and all of it, increasingly, with leases on the Tiburtina; but it also had a string of lesser dependants in Pigna itself who were part of the network of (leased) land sales and urban building—and, of course, artisanal activity—discussed in Chapter 3. S. Ciriaco did, thus, have a defining role in Pigna, even if the *regio* was not fully cohesive as a collective unit.

S. Maria Nova/Colosseo

Of all the *regiones* that have an even partial documentation for Rome, the most coherent we know of was certainly S. Maria Nova, otherwise known as Colosseo. It was smaller in size than Pigna, and much smaller than Trastevere; it was also bounded by some less densely inhabited areas. Krautheimer saw it as cut off from the *abitato* of Rome; this, as we have seen, is untrue (pp. 115–17, 126), for there was always settlement in the Foro area to its west, and, for a long time, on the Celio to its east too. But the top of the Palatino to its south gives no sign in our evidence of any dense urban settlement, and, if there was more on the edge of Monti to its north, the Subura of classical times, it never appears in the generous documentation of the *regio*'s major church, S. Maria Nova, so a practical boundary clearly existed there.[76] The latter church (a *diaconia*), the Colosseo itself, now in part a huge housing block, and the Frangipane towers between them, were the real foci for this *regio*. In the case of S. Maria Nova's archive, we therefore do not have to face the problem of representativeness that the other two major document collections pose. The nearly 170 documents surviving for the church before 1200, overwhelmingly for the twelfth century, give us a good insight into the *regio*, especially as nearly half of them are for the *regio* itself (almost all the others being for the vineyard belt around the city to the north-east and south-east, especially S. Maria's estate at Monte S. Ypoliti outside Porta S. Lorenzo); we can effectively construct a picture of a local society here.

As with S. Ciriaco's Pigna, the eleventh century is less well attested, and can be looked at more briefly. The Frangipane are occasional tenants or subtenants of S. Maria Nova, and once donors to the church, in the latter's documents, starting in

---

[75] Cencio: *SMVL*, nn. 187, 195, 199 (a. 1163). The latest twelfth-century lease for Pigna, from 1187 (n. 232), is however to Leone *de Monumento*, a major urban aristocrat; he is not a lessee elsewhere, but is recorded in the monastic necrology: Egidi, *Necrologi*, pp. 36–7.

[76] S. Maria Nova the same *regio* as Colosseo: compare *SMN*, nn. 69 and 70. The Civitas Leoniana was as coherent a community (see above, pp. 137–40), but is not regarded as fully part of Rome in our sources. See Krautheimer, *Rome*, pp. 271, 314–17; Augenti, *Il Palatino*, pp. 102–10; and above, pp. 124–6, for settlement discussions. The term *Subura* survived in our period: see *Papsturkunden*, nn. 148, 564 (a flashy house in 1025 near S. Agata dei Goti); *SMVL*, n. 56; *S. Paolo*, n. 1, with *PL*, CLXXIX, cols 692–6, n. 4; *Senato*, n. 13; *SMN*, n. 93; *SMCM*, n. 58; *Liberiano*, n. 22; *RS*, n. 183. The absence of S. Maria Nova references in this group is striking in itself; the single citation is of a lay-to-lay sale of a church lease.

1039. We have seen (p. 230) that they had links to a variety of churches, and had lands in several different *regiones*, but their base was here—although not leased from S. Maria Nova (p. 125)—and it consisted by the end of the eleventh century of a network of towers, apparently interspersed with the dwellings of others. The *filii Astaldi*, also 'aristocratic' but less prominent (above, p. 239), transacted with S. Maria, including a large pious gift by Astaldo di Crescenzio in 1060 on behalf of his deceased wife Maria Bona, which referred to portions of houses, open land, and the Arco di Costantino itself; and they also witnessed church documents on occasion (as did, equally occasionally, the Frangipane).[77] Only one major, probably 'aristocratic', local family known from this period does not turn up in S. Maria's archive: that of Andrea di Pietro di Viola *de Coloseo*, who was a tenant both of S. Gregorio sul Celio (he leased the failed castle of Mandra Camellaria, formerly of the *de Imiza*, in 1024) and of S. Erasmo sul Celio (alongside the Frangipane). Andrea's grandson Rainerio di Guilia still held at Mandra Camellaria in 1128; another Rainerio di Guilia or Giulia is documented in the 1180s. The family's absence from S. Maria's charters throughout our period indicates that their base was probably the other side of the Colosseo, closer to the Celio.[78] They also show that not all the *regio* looked to S. Maria Nova. But it may be that the church was not yet a major elite focus in the eleventh century; even the Frangipane do not yet appear so very much. The families who appear most often are smaller ones. Gregorio di Michele *medico* and his son Gregorio *illustris vir* were active in 1018–63, and related to at least two *dativi iudices*; they leased S. Maria Nova vineyards on Monte S. Ypoliti north-east of the city and urban land by the church, and lent money to each other, as well as witnessing church documents; they also owned a house in the Basilica di Massenzio in full property in 1052, almost the first reference to lay landowning in the city. A substantial number of artisans also dealt with the church, *tessitores*, *erarii*, *calciolarii*, *sartores* (cf. above, pp. 141–3); they were its tenants and also witnessed on occasion, as with Giovanni Vecchio *rotarius* who (with his son Fazio and daughter Maria) appears half a dozen times between 1038 and 1103.[79] These were more obvious church dependants than were the 'aristocratic' families, and quite possibly all lived close to the church, in the densely inhabited tract between the steep slope up to the Palatino and the Basilica di Massenzio, almost all owned by S. Maria Nova, with the via Sacra running through the surviving monumental classical buildings in the middle.

[77] The first Frangipane document for *SMN* is n. 11, now an incomplete text, but recorded more fully by seventeenth- and eighteenth-century editors in BAV, CVL 11980, p. 5, and Nerini, *De templo*, p. 390n. See above, Chapter 4, n. 119. Later in the eleventh century, *SMN*, nn. 13, 15, 23, 25, are probable citations of the family. See in general Thumser, 'Die Frangipane'; Rodríguez López, 'La Torre Cartularia', pp. 321–6; Ellis, 'Landscape and power', pp. 61–70; Augenti, *Il Palatino*, pp. 89–102. For the *filii Astaldi*, *SMN* documents for the period are nn. 16, 17.

[78] Andrea and heirs: *S. Gregorio*, nn. 14, 131 (a. 1024), 169, 136 (a. 1128); *RS*, nn. 106, 102, 108, 107; 'Documenti per la storia', n. 19 (a. 1188). The younger Rainerio witnesses *SMN*, n. 114 (a. 1180), but it is a lay marriage charter, unconnected to the church.

[79] Gregorio and family: *SMN*, nn. 5, 12, 14, 15 (a. 1052), 16, 21. Giovanni Vecchio: nn. 10, 17, 27, 28, 32. Artisans appear in 18 of the 31 *SMN* charters up to 1100.

It is in the twelfth century, however, that our S. Maria Nova evidence really opens out, giving us usable information about a substantial number of local families, stretching from the Frangipane, through the 'medium elite', to people of less prosperous and status-filled origins. Unusually, also, we gain information about some of them from other sources too: in particular, three atypical texts, which do not have parallels in the other two *regiones* we have looked at in this section. As these three texts did not come from S. Maria Nova, they allow us some insights about people who were not the church's associates as well. Let us start by looking at how these three texts worked, so that we can come on to see how the information contained in them structures our more 'normal' information from S. Maria's own documents.

The first of these is a document only surviving in Onofrio Panvinio's sixteenth-century manuscript history of the Frangipane, recently republished by Andrea Augenti. Panvinio (d.1568) was a well-regarded antiquarian of the period and was close to the family; he does not have a good track record for reliability, but this text has many close connections with our original documents of the period, and I cannot see problems with it. It dates to March 1177, and in it twenty-five named men, acting for *aliis hominibus regionis Colossei, tam maioribus quam minoribus de Colosseo*, other men from Colosseo, both greater and lesser, and with the *auctoritate dominorum de Frangenspanibus*, the authority of the Frangipane, gave to S. Giovanni in Laterano all the rights they held over the Easter Thursday offerings to that basilica, as a pious gift for the benefit of their souls. It is clear that the *regio* here was operating as both a political and an economic collectivity, with an active local leadership, and many of the named men turn up in S. Maria Nova documents too. It is equally clear that they recognized the *auctoritas* of the Frangipane as they did so; in other words, that that family had some form of recognized supremacy over the activities of the *regio*. This document is unique in Rome in our period, in that no other text gives us any insight into the fact that *regiones* could form organized collectivities of this kind. It would be hard to claim that no other *regio* did so, at least as long as it had more structure than Pigna perhaps did; but the fact that this document is for Colosseo also fits with the other evidence we have for the unusual internal coherence of this part of Rome. Either way, however, we have a guide to who the leaders of Colosseo were in 1177.[80]

The second text is from 1188, and it is less unique to this region. One part of the complex dealing between Clement III and the Roman Senate in May of that year, which laid the basis for a stable political settlement after the pope's return to Rome

---

[80] Augenti, *Il Palatino*, p. 188, cf. pp. 106–7. Panvinio said the text survived in the Laterano archive; it does not now, for it is not recorded in the comprehensive recent register of the archive, Duval-Arnould, *Le pergamene*; in addition, BAV, CVL 8034, Galletti's MS cartulary for S. Giovanni in Laterano, does not have it, so it had probably vanished by the eighteenth century already—Galletti being the man who classified the archive in 1763. The text seems to me wholly authentic, given the names in it, but it is at least conceivable that Panvinio could have inserted the phrase *et auctoritate dominorum de Frangenspanibus*; however, *auctoritas* is used in this sort of context in the twelfth century (see e.g. *SMVL*, n. 196), so the phrase is not out of place. (I would not translate it 'signoria', as Augenti does: *Il Palatino*, p. 107.)

in March, was an agreement that the Roman church would reimburse a series of citizens of the city, some doubtless combatants, some clearly not, for the goods they lost during the *guerra pape Lucii*. This was the war of 1183 in which Lucius III, with the help of an imperial army, prevented the Romans from taking Tuscolo; during it, the imperial chancellor Christian of Mainz had also attacked the city.[81] We have a set of fourteen original documents from the winter of 1188–9 in which the pope (through his *procurator* Cencio) indeed reimbursed numerous Roman *deperdentes* of Monti, Biberatica, Colosseo, Arenula, Caccabarii, Trastevere, Ponte, Scorteclari, S. Maria in Aquiro, Colonna, Ripa, Marmorata, the Isola Tiberina, and Pigna, as well as a group of *senatores deperdentes*: that is to say, from around half of the *regiones* of the city, including some, such as Arenula and Caccabarii, which we know little else about. Eighty-three names can be made out in these documents, of which a quarter are attached to Monti, Biberatica, and Colosseo (which appear together as a 'super-region' in two of the texts, with different names listed in each); Colosseo is thus better represented than most *regiones* in the set, and in particular better than Trastevere (only three names) and Pigna (only three or four). The entire surviving series cost the papacy over £300, at the very least (not all the figures can be made out, and we certainly do not have the full set of texts); the war damage was evidently widespread and severe. The three *regiones* including Colosseo got some £88 of this; and that process furnishes us with another list of prominent local names, including several overlaps with the 1177 document.[82]

The third document is better known, but it is in some respects the most curious of all. In 1192, Cencio *camerarius* (the *procurator* of 1188 and the future Pope Honorius III) compiled the *Liber Censuum*, which is primarily a list of papal revenues (*census*), plus a cartulary of important documents; it also contains a miscellany of other useful texts, including detailed sets of instructions for the conduct of papal processions. We will look at the latter in Chapter 6; they are much studied, but are important for an understanding of how Rome functioned as a city. But one of them sheds light on S. Maria Nova/Colosseo in particular, and needs to be introduced here. It is a list of the payments (*presbyterium*) due each year from the papal treasury to *illis qui arcus faciunt*, those who made the elaborate but temporary arches over the papal processional route from S. Pietro to the Laterano every Easter Monday. These arches seem to have been structures decorated with

---

[81] See esp. *Annales Ceccanenses*, p. 287; *LP*, II, pp. 349–50. Note that the goods lost cannot have only been in the fighting itself, as assumed by Maire Vigueur, *L'autre Rome*, p. 198, as the 1188 texts contain several women ('Documenti per la storia', nn. 14, 16, 19, 20, with ASV, A. A. Arm. I–XVIII, n. 969, and Volpini, n. 10); he also attributes it to the 1167 war, whereas the 1188 texts always refer to Lucius III. Falco, 'Documenti guerreschi', pp. 1–6 (aa. 1186, 1188), also refers to the payment by the Senate of £25 to a man who lost horses and arms after being taken captive in the Lucius war (the Senate used money from the altar of S. Pietro!), and another 50 *solidi* to a man who just lost a horse; cf. *SMCM*, n. 54 (a. 1168), referring to ransoming (for £16) after that of 1167.

[82] The complete set is 'Documenti per la storia', nn. 12–20, plus five pieces left out by the editors, ASV, A. A. Arm. I–XVIII, nn. 966, 969 (for Pigna; there were more names originally, but only a few can now be made out, even using a UV lamp), 997 (the latter, for the *senatores*, is ed. in Hirschfeld, 'Zur Chronologie', pp. 106–7); and Volpini, nn. 10–11, documents from the Archivio Capitolare in Anagni. 'Documenti per la storia', nn. 14, 19 are for Monti, n. 16 for Trastevere.

precious metals and cloth; there may have been at least ninety of them, for that many payments are listed in the text, and the *regio* of Parione was paid a lump sum of £6 for its unspecified set of arches. The individual arches must, however, have been different in their scale, for the sums of money paid for them are quite diverse, from 4 *denarii* up to 30 *solidi* and sometimes more.[83]

The route used by the popes on Easter Monday can be fairly clearly tracked from the arch list, supplemented by Benedetto's *ordo* (see below, pp. 327–9, and Map 9). It ran along the Porticus S. Petri, past Castel S. Angelo and over the bridge, through an increasingly built-up Ponte and Parione, up what is now the via delle Botteghe Oscure to S. Marco, then around the Capitolio and into the Foro Romano; from there, it followed the via Sacra past S. Maria Nova and the Colosseo, and then up the hill to the Laterano, about 5 km in all. What is striking, however, is that over half the payments in the text cluster in a single 400-metre stretch from SS. Cosma e Damiano in Foro to the Colosseo, that is to say the *regio* of S. Maria Nova. Here, the payments are *domus* by *domus*, and are also unusually small, from 2 *solidi* downwards, and mostly less than a single *solidus*—only the Frangipane and a couple of other householders paid more. We cannot tell whether each house made its own small arch for the annual procession here, or whether they clubbed together to make bigger ones, but were rewarded separately; perhaps the latter. But we do have a detailed list of houses as a result, with their inhabitants named, situated presumably along the via Sacra itself or else very close by.[84] The householders of 1192 once again match up with many of the men of 1177 and 1188, as well as with plenty of people in S. Maria Nova documents; this text thus joins the other two as structuring elements for the sometimes chancier, but often more illuminating, appearances of local inhabitants in the archival record. Leaders of the *regio* in 1177, prominent victims of enemy attack in 1183, owners or tenants of houses along the via Sacra with ceremonial obligations in 1192: these are hardly a homogeneous group. But the overlaps between them are striking all the same, and they will recur often in this section.

In the light of these sources, let us now look at the clients and associates of S. Maria Nova that we can trace for the twelfth century. There are quite a number, and I shall track the best-documented of them family by family, once again to see how we can build up a picture of the lay social world, both around the church and less connected to it. We have already looked at one of these, the family of Sassone *macellarius*, who held church lands, a *domus* and *criptae* along the via Sacra, and appear in the 1192 list (they were paid the smallish sum of 8 *denarii* yearly); they were modest members of the regional 'medium elite', and frequent witnesses for the church (above, pp. 268–9). Only one other family, the Mancini, are as visible in our sources; but half a dozen others give us usable information too. Let us look at them in turn.

[83] *LC*, I, pp. 299–300. The best account is Twyman, *Papal Ceremonial*, pp. 210–14.
[84] *LC*, II, p. 154 for Benedetto (cf. Twyman, *Papal Ceremonial*, pp. 188–9); I, p. 300 for the S. Maria Nova houses.

The three sons of Pietro Mancinus were Girardo, Sassone, and Pietro, and are attested between 1123 and 1145 (their father appears only once, as a church witness in 1104). They and their heirs are the single best-attested family in the S. Maria Nova documents for the twelfth century, and can be tracked up to the 1192 arch list with security. Left-handed people are never uncommon, and there were quite a lot of people called *mancinus* in Rome in the twelfth century, most of whom cannot be related usefully to this family. But Pietro's sons and grandsons were a definable group with a local base, and his grandson Giovanni di Girardo (active 1158–92) used the name Mancinus again, by now presumably as a surname. The Mancini had no less than four houses along the via Sacra in 1192, those of Giovanni, Pietro di Gregorio Mancino, Sassone *de Manchino* (probably the house of the by-now deceased Sassone di Pietro), and an otherwise unknown Maria. Giovanni Mancino was third on the 1177 list of Colosseo leaders; Pietro di Gregorio was in the 1188 lists, with damaged goods worth the above-average sum of £7½. Throughout the century, the family appear as church witnesses for all kinds of transactions. They had land close to the church: beside the Arco di Tito and up the hill-slope of the Palatino, where Pietro di Pietro sold a church lease of a *casalinum* in 1139 for 4½ *solidi*, and Giovanni Mancino in 1160 pledged a *domus* (again clearly a S. Maria Nova tenure) for a loan of £5; and also some vineyards beyond the city walls to the south-east. We do not know what the Mancini did— the via Sacra houses hint at commerce, but what sort is never specified; we cannot be certain of the scale of their resources either (Giovanni's loan transactions are not huge in size). But several houses plus extramural vineyards are markers of the 'medium elite', and Giovanni's prominence in 1177 shows that he had a public role at the regional level.[85]

Berardo di Gregorio di Giorgio (active 1147–77) was certainly from the 'medium elite'; the lease he took of a *domus solarata* from S. Maria in 1161 (for an entry-fine of £3) says that it was on the via Sacra and bordered on his own *turris* (held, unusually for the area, from S. Paolo fuori le Mura). He was also sometimes a witness for S. Maria, as was, more often, his son Gregorio (active 1182–95). Gregorio and his brother Pietro di Berardo had public standing; they appeared together in 1195, as *nobiles viri*, overseeing a cession of land by a man to his brother's widow, a clearly tense intra-kin transaction. They had another house near the Colosseo in 1187; either this or the 1161 house would probably have been the *domus Berardi* mentioned by Cencio in 1192. So the family was prominent, with its own tower-house, and may appear as S. Maria's witnesses only because they lived close by and were locally important, not because they were the church's closest associates. It thus fits with our knowledge of Berardo that the first name on the list

---

[85] Mancini, witnessing and boundaries: *SMN*, nn. 30, 33, 35 verso, 41, 43, 44, 46, 51, 53, 54, 56, 79, 91, 109, 118, 119, 125, 133; as actors, nn. 47, 82, 99; plus Augenti, *Il Palatino*, p. 188; 'Documenti per la storia', n. 19; *LC*, I, p. 300. Pietro di Gregorio Mancino in 1188 must be part of the family, but his father is not otherwise attested. See for a brief discussion Moscati, *Alle origini*, p. 118. The account of this family in Ellis, 'Landscape and power', pp. 70–5, is too wide in its assumptions that other Mancini are related.

of Colosseo leaders in 1177 was *Bernardus Gregorii de Gregorio*, without any doubt
Panvinio's misreading for *Berardus Gregorii de Georgio*; in that year he was, perhaps,
the principal figure in the *regio*. And this also means that the *Berardus Gregorii Bone
Georgii* who was a senator in 1151 is quite likely to be the same man (*Bone* being
read as *bone memorie*, rather than as an extra generation); the Pietro di Berardo who
was a senator in 1188 could also be his son, although the name combination is less
rare. This is, anyway, the social stratum that produced many senators in the period,
so the identifications are at least plausible.[86]

Pietro di Roberto was second on the 1177 list; he has a less visible profile, but he
had a similar social prominence, for he was a senator in the same year. His brother
Giovanni leased a house from S. Maria Nova in 1184, and both brothers had
houses on the via Sacra in the 1192 lists, but they are relatively rare as witnesses for
the church. They did, however, keep the public status they had in 1177; Pietro di
Roberto's son Roberto was the third *nobilis vir* along with Berardo di Gregorio's
two sons in the intra-kin transaction of 1195.[87]

Romano and Rainucio di Bonella were a little less prominent. Romano was a
Colosseo leader in 1177, not very high on the list; he was one of the *deperdentes* in
1188, owed the substantial sum of £14; he is mentioned in the 1192 list. They were
probably somewhat older than Pietro di Roberto; Rainucio was a tenant of S. Maria
for a house near the church already in 1157, and witnessed in 1153. The family
were clearly reasonably prosperous, but they do not stand out; they also dealt with
S. Maria Nova only intermittently.[88]

Bobaciano di Romano di Rainucio (active 1153–77) may have been related to
them too, but is not linked to them in any text. He was also a Colosseo leader in
1177; by the date of the 1192 list he was doubtless dead, but he still gave his name
to the *domus Bobatiani*, which was remunerated with 12 *solidi* a year for its arch, by
far the highest figure in the S. Maria Nova section of the list. He held, and sold in
1153, a lease from the church of a *domus* on the Palatino slope, and his heirs held
vineyards on the Esquilino from S. Maria. Bobaciano only witnessed once for the
church in surviving documents, but he was locally respected; the marriage deal of
Pietro di Romano di Frasia in 1173 (see above, p. 274) put £2 of the pledge for
Pietro's dowry, an eighth of the total, into the hands of Bobaciano *de Coliseo* for safe
keeping and possible investment.[89]

A clearer client of S. Maria Nova was Giovanni di Benedetto. From 1176 until
the end of the century, he was a frequent witness for the church, as (once) was his
son Giovanni. He does not appear as a tenant of the church in any surviving lease,
but he appears as a landholder on the boundaries of leases for the Palatino slope in

[86] Berardo: Augenti, *Il Palatino*, p. 188; *SMN*, nn. 62, 83 (a. 1161), 87. Gregorio: nn. 118, 126
(a. 1187), 132, 133, 136, 145 (a. 1195); *LC*, I, p. 300. Senatori: *Senato*, nn. 13, 42, with Hirschfeld,
'Zur Chronologie', pp. 106–7. A Pietro di Berardo also held a *domus* in the Subura from S. Maria
Maggiore: *Liberiano*, n. 22.

[87] Augenti, *Il Palatino*, p. 188; *Senato*, n. 31; *SMN*, nn. 91, 99, 123, 145; *LC*, I, p. 300.

[88] Augenti, *Il Palatino*, p. 188; 'Documenti per la storia', n. 19; *LC*, I, p. 300; *SMN*, nn. 69, 76,
118, 120, 123.

[89] Augenti, *Il Palatino*, p. 188; *LC*, I, p. 300; *SMN*, nn. 69 (a. 1153), 81, 101 (a. 1173), 155, 161.

1188 and 1193, and must have held from S. Maria. His *domus* was listed in the 1192 arch list as well. Most of the figures we have just looked at were relatively seldom committed to church witnessing, even though they were all S. Maria's tenants; indeed, of all those I have so far analysed, only the Mancini, taken all together, were more frequent witnesses than Giovanni di Benedetto. Giovanni is never found in any other context, and he was doubtless much less important a figure than any of those so far cited, but he can stand as the sort of loyal and local member of the witnessing entourage that every church and monastery needed in Rome (and not only in Rome).[90]

Some other figures in S. Maria charters can be dealt with more rapidly. Peretto or Peretta witnessed several charters in the 1180s and 1190s; in one he is named as a *manisalcus*, a farrier. His son Giovanni leased a *domus terrinea* on the edge of the Palatino from S. Maria in 1187, so the family has a profile similar to Giovanni di Benedetto. Giovanni Suave and his two sons witnessed for S. Maria for fifty years, from 1153, without ever appearing as leaseholders, though they too doubtless also lived on church land.[91] Stanzone *sutor*, probably a shoemaker, witnessed sometimes in the 1180s and 1190s, and also leased two houses from S. Maria in 1183 and 1193, both on the via Sacra (oddly, he does not appear in the 1192 list); he was another artisan client of the church. So too must have been Romano *Comparapiper* or *Accattalpepere*, a pepper trader, who witnessed between 1185 and 1195; and also Ugolino *pelliparius*, a furrier, an occasional witness in the same period, and in the 1180s a tenant of S. Maria for a *domus solarata* for the large entry-fine of £10, and a vendor of another church lease for a house near the Colosseo for £9.[92]

This might make it seem that it was less influential people who were closer socially to S. Maria Nova, and the point is further made by some local men who have fewer church links or none at all, but who were prominent enough to be senators: Sassone di Oddone di Sassone, fifth on the 1177 Colosseo list, who was a senator in 1179, and never appears in charters for S. Maria Nova as a church; Giovanni di Cencio (attested 1171–88), probably based inside the Colosseo, who was sixth on the Colosseo list, was on the *deperdentes* lists in 1188, was possibly a senator in 1188, and is named as a *causidicus* in 1173, but only once witnessed for the church; Nicola *de S. Antonio* (which must be the church of that name re-established in a section of the ruined S. Maria Antiqua a little to the west), who held land near S. Maria Nova, witnessed only once, and was also a senator in 1188; and indeed Giovanni Capocci, a major senatorial leader at the end of the century, who makes an early appearance in the 1177 list, and held vineyards from S. Maria, but is never a witness for the church. We can add the Arcioni, based around the Arco di Costantino, who by the thirteenth century controlled the arch itself, but who only

[90] Witness: *SMN*, nn. 109, 121, 126, 134, 135, 136, 137, 140, 141 (Giovanni's son), 143, 168. On boundaries: nn. 132, 142, 143; and *LC*, I, p. 300.

[91] Perretta: *SMN*, nn. 120 (*maniscalcus*), 127, 129, 132, 142, 157; n. 127 features his son too. Giovanni Suave: nn. 74, 77, 91, 92, 95, 110, plus, for his sons, 141, 146, 167.

[92] Stanzone: *SMN*, nn. 119 (a. 1183), 120, 140, 141 (a. 1193); for *sutor*, see Chapter 3, n. 102. Romano: nn. 124, 126, 134, 146. Ugolino: nn. 121, 124, 126, perhaps 153.

witness a couple of times; and the sons of Romano di Frasia, 'medium elite' members also living in the Colosseo as we have seen, who never appear in S. Maria's own charters at all.[93]

Conversely, we must also remember that the most prominent church associates were the Frangipane themselves. They may not have leased their towers from S. Maria, but they leased other land, exchanged land with the church, and gave land in pious gift, including a large *curia* with two *domūs* in front of the church, apparently given by Adilascia Frangipane in 1137 and confirmed (perhaps after a dispute) by Leone Frangipane *Romanorum consul* in 1182. The Frangipane also introduced S. Maria to what was almost its only experience of landowning beyond the Agro romano, outside the family castle of Cisterna south of Velletri, in 1162. They witnessed for S. Maria, at least occasionally, and brokered the transactions of others; and they kept several of their own charters in S. Maria's archive.[94] No one in the twelfth century could have seriously doubted the interest the Frangipane had by now in S. Maria Nova. Indeed, they may well have been the patrons of the substantial rebuilding of the church which took place in this period, culminating in a formal rededication in 1161 by Alexander III; the immediately subsequent apse mosaic, unlike Innocent II's S. Maria in Trastevere two decades earlier, contains no reference to a pope, so the *committenza* could well have been local and lay.[95] So, given the formal *auctoritas* the family had in the *regio*, anyone opposed to the church would have risked alienating themselves from regional power structures altogether.

What is more likely, in fact, is that the closest clients and associates of S. Maria lived in the dense set of houses and *criptae* around the church and along the via

---

[93] Sassone di Oddone: Augenti, *Il Palatino*, p. 188; Piattoli, 'Miscellanea diplomatica (III)', pp. 166–7; this text, in which Sassone appears as a witness as *urbis senator*, is a canon law arbitration by the cardinal deacon of S. Maria Nova as papal delegate concerning a divorce in Pistoia, heard *in palatio S. Marie Nove*; this shows Sassone's connection with the region, and perhaps with the cardinal, but not with the church as landowner and patron. Giovanni di Cencio: Augenti, *Il Palatino*, p. 188; 'Documenti per la storia', n. 19; *Senato*, n. 42 (but *Senato*, n. 43, a. 1191, has a Giovanni di Cencio *de Porticu*, who is from the Civitas Leoniana and cannot be the Colosseo figure); *SMN*, nn. 99, 100–1 (a. 1173); the family link to Cencio/Honorius III, proposed by Thumser, *Rom*, pp. 59–60, 63, seems to me improbable. Nicola *de S. Antonio*: nn. 118, 127, 142, with *Senato*, n. 42 (cf. Hülsen, *Le chiese*, p. 199). Giovanni Capocci: see, for a survey of his later career and bibliography, Paravicini Bagliani, 'Capocci, Giovanni' (and see for his heirs, the baronial family, Carocci, *Baroni di Roma*, pp. 333–42; Thumser, *Rom*, pp. 53–64); he held vineyards from S. Maria Nova on the Esquilino and at Monte S. Ypoliti outside the walls (*SMN*, nn. 138, 156). Arcioni: *SMN*, nn. 81 (which says in a thirteenth-century dorsal note that the Arco is held by the family), 83, 121, 126, 136. (This Arcioni family is not the probably Trevi-based family of the same name, for which see Thumser, *Rom*, p. 42–5, plus, earlier, *Liberiano*, nn. 21–2, and perhaps *S. Gregorio*, n. 137.) Sons of Romano: *S. Gregorio*, nn. 75, 97, 100–1, none of them church documents. For housing in the Colosseo, see Rea, *Rota Colisei*.

[94] For the full Frangipane/*SMN* document set, see Chapter 4, n. 121. *Curia*: *SMN*, n. 118 (cf. 46). Cisterna: nn. 85–8, 105–6, 113, 115, 139, 144, 148–50, 163; although the key Frangipane gift, n. 87, is a forgery, it is near-contemporary, and transparently has an original base, for so many of the witnesses are traceable. (S. Maria Nova's only other estate outside the Agro was the *massa* Careia in Tuscia Romana, which it had trouble with: nn. 42, 68, 79, 92.) Frangipane witnessing: nn. 33, 45, 51, 77; brokering: n. 92; other transactions: nn. 95, 120, 135. Frangipane documents housed in S. Maria: nn. 49, 94, 116, 117, 152, 164.

[95] See now esp. Romano, *Riforma e tradizione*, pp. 335–43 (S. Romano and J. Enckell Julliard). For the rededication, *LP*, II, p. 403.

Sacra, and that people in the *regio* who had few or no links with it lived further away, in and around the *rota Colosei*, the classical monument itself, and the Arco di Costantino, or else on the far western edge of the *regio* beside the Foro Romano. That certainly fits the profile of the people mentioned in the previous paragraph, as also Bobaciano *de Coliseo*; by contrast, almost all the others discussed previously seem fairly clearly to be based close to S. Maria. This might seem a surprising pattern; we are dealing with distances of barely more than 200 metres from the church. But I think we can conclude that the *regio* of S. Maria Nova/Colosseo, although compact, politically organized, and on the edge of the built-up area of the city—which would have added to the coherence of its identity—was also micro-regionally divided, with S. Maria Nova operating only as a partial focus, even if a very important one for its immediate surroundings. Inside that micro-region, it was closely associated with some influential 'medium elite' families, such as that of Sassone *macellarius* and the Mancini, and was less close to others, such as that of Berardo di Gregorio (who was probably the most prominent non-aristocratic figure in the *regio* in the third quarter of the century). It was a real patron for a host of less influential families, many of them with artisanal specializations; and it was also durably close to the Frangipane. We could assume that the other regional figures had their own links to the Frangipane, who themselves, for example, held much of the *rota Colosei* by the start of the thirteenth century.[96] The latter family indeed provided the real axial power structure for the *regio*, with S. Maria only a subordinate patron.

S. Maria Nova thus had a more coherent local clientele than SS. Cosma e Damiano, but a smaller and less wide-ranging one than S. Ciriaco. This latter contrast is probably also because it had much less rural property than either; Berardo di Gregorio or the sons of Romano di Frasia might have wished to be distinctly closer to S. Maria if it had had a huge estate like Marcelli or Bolagai to lease. Its major property outside Rome, Monte S. Ypoliti, was a relatively small one in the vineyard belt, and, although its tenants there were probably not often cultivators (above, p. 94), they also did not always come from the *regio* around the church.[97] The economic base of the church was essentially the block of urban property closest to it. We have seen (p. 162) that by the end of the twelfth century S. Maria was exploiting this urban block reasonably effectively as an economic resource, but it was a socio-political resource too, the main element of its political attraction, and it attracted, above all, people who lived on the spot.

The *regio* of S. Maria Nova/Colosseo operated as a single political community, as we saw from the 1177 text, a community that, furthermore, had some form of economic identity, for otherwise it could never had held the rights to the S. Giovanni in Laterano offerings which it gave away in that year. (We can also

---

[96] *Gesta Innocenti III*, ch. 139; cf. *Codex diplomaticus*, ed. Theiner, I, n. 207, for the Frangipane cession of half the Colosseo, by then held *in feudum* from the papacy (*ecclesia Romana*), to the Annibaldi in 1244.

[97] Though the dorsal notes to *SMN*, n. 35, show a range of standard S. Maria Nova associates (including Sassone *macellarius* and Girardo Mancini) paying rents, probably for the vineyard area.

assume that the community had more collective resources than that; it is not likely that its members gave them all away for their souls in one go.) That community had at least one leader who was probably a senator very early, Berardo di Gregorio, and then several in the 1170s–80s; it must indeed have had others. The *regio* also had prominent professionals, such as Andrea *scriniarius*, fourth on the 1177 list and writer of nearly twenty S. Maria Nova documents, and also *iudices*/*causidici*, most of whom we have already encountered.[98] This means that, of the first six names on the 1177 list, four were known senators or probable senators, and the other two were Andrea *scriniarius* and one of the Mancini, either of whom could well have been a senator in other, undocumented, years: a clear set of regional leaders with senatorial connections. The well-known avoidance by the Frangipane of any direct senatorial involvement until the 1190s is partially nuanced[99]—at least after the first decade of the Senate, which had the Frangipane as a clear target, had passed—by the realization that some of its lay clients had an entirely normal relation to the Senate, with senatorial office available from the outset to leading members of the 'medium elite' of the *regio*. The 'medium elite' here numbered at least a dozen identifiable families, and, inside that group, regional-level leadership also extended to artisans, one of whom appears in the 1177 list.[100] We could, if we wanted, give part of this community a military interpretation, if we extended what we know about the fortification of the Colosseo through to the high degree of militarization and competitive tower-building described for 1203–4 in the *Gesta Innocentii III*, which resulted in a small war focused on the area between the Quirinale and the Colosseo, involving the Capocci and the Frangipane among others. But we can equally say that what the 1177 text shows us is a coherent regional community in which, even though a top senatorial-level leadership (and Frangipane dominance) is clearly visible, a much wider social network were political players, as with the *pelliparius* in 1177. I read this as a community in which regional identity and a regional clientelar network were more important than any division between an urban military stratum and a wider and more politically marginal urban collectivity. And it was the *regiones* that were at the base of the Senate, more than any separate stratum within them.[101]

This essentially lay socio-political community then overlapped with, and largely encompassed, the slightly smaller collectivity of the clients and associates of S. Maria Nova. Association with S. Maria was not essential in order to participate in the *regio*'s political community, certainly; but the church must have been by far the most important landowner there, and it thus had its own partially autonomous

---

[98] Andrea *scriniarius*: Augenti, *Il Palatino*, p. 188; *SMN*, nn. 61 to 114, for documents written by him. Giovanni *iudex* also appears in the 1177 text, and Giovanni di Cencio was a *causidicus*: above, n. 93.

[99] Thumser, *Rom*, pp. 231–2; *Senato*, n. 43 (a. 1191), mentions the first Frangipane senator.

[100] Stefano *pelliparius* appears in Augenti, *Il Palatino*, p. 188; Sassone *macellarius* can be seen as an earlier regional leader.

[101] Cf. the discussion between me and Jean-Claude Maire Vigueur in *Storica*, L (2011), pp. 129–34, 141–2; for the *regiones* and the Senate, see below, pp. 448–9. 1203–4: *Gesta Innocenti III*, chs 139–40.

patronage network, validated by Frangipane support. Berardo di Gregorio may not have needed S. Maria's backing to be locally prominent, but Sassone *macellarius* and the Mancini probably did. If we did not have the 1177 text, we would not see so clearly that the church was not squarely the political focus of its surroundings, but it cannot be decentred more than partially. Rather more than the two monasteries discussed in this section, its clientele was a major element in the construction of a coherent local society in the *regio*.

There were clear contrasts in the social structure of these three *regiones* in the eleventh and twelfth centuries. All three were artisanally active, as we saw in Chapter 3, with leather and ceramics prominent in Trastevere, iron and wood in Pigna, bronze and (after 1100) leather in S. Maria Nova; Trastevere also had half of the major river port of the city, and Pigna abutted onto the central market area north and west of the Capitolio. The port, plus Trastevere's rural hinterland, both inside the walls under the Gianicolo and right down the via Portuense to the sea, tied the right bank *regio* more closely to a specific rural sector than we see elsewhere, which added to a certain separation from the rest of the city which the Tiber had already created. S. Maria Nova had no such systematic rural links, but its location as a zone of relative population density on the edge of Rome's *abitato* made it, if not separate, at least internally coherent. Pigna, by contrast, lost some coherence because of its closeness to the market, and also to several other densely populated *regiones*. The church clienteles we have looked at mapped onto these contrasts in different ways again, with SS. Cosma e Damiano's associates looking to Portuense landowning at first but their successors becoming more and more a chance cross-section of the population of an expanding urban sector, whereas S. Maria Nova's were a much more representative sample of a more articulated community, dominated by what was probably Rome's richest twelfth-century 'aristocratic' family. By contrast, although those of S. Ciriaco in Via Lata were again a very coherent group, prosperous and very interested in the monastery's big extramural lands, the richer elements were less strictly connected to Pigna itself.

It is important to stress once again that these are only very partial pictures, built up out of land documents above all, which cannot tell us much about less formal social relationships, least of all in a city, where so much interaction did not even nominally relate to land. But they are enough to show us that there was great variation between Rome's *regiones*. We can only understand regional politics very sketchily in our period, but there must have been a major contrast between S. Maria Nova, where the Frangipane oversaw a clearly defined community, and Pigna, where 'medium elite' families from inside and outside the *regio* must have formed and reformed themselves around a variety of local churches. Even if, as is highly likely, the large and annually changing composition of the early Senate already had some representation from each *regio* (at least via the groups of *regiones* called here 'super-regions'), and even if this representation often (although doubtless not always) tended to privilege regional-level 'medium elites', the way the Senate would have impacted on each *regio* would nonetheless have been quite different, depending on how local social structures worked. Even the value of senatorial status will doubtless have been understood differently in each. This, too, must be remembered when we return to senatorial politics at the end of Chapter 7.

Conversely, we can generalize about Roman society as well. The pictures of the different clients and associates of these three churches, however diverse, do have certain elements in common. I have been trying in this and the previous two chapters of this book to separate out social strata in the city, the 'old' and 'new' aristocracies in Chapter 4, the 'medium elite' in this chapter, and less socially prominent groups both in this chapter and (as artisans) in Chapter 3. But, excepting the 'old aristocracy', which was leaving the city as urban documents begin (and which had seldom been clearly associated with specific urban regions), all these strata appear together in and around our documented churches and monasteries. SS. Cosma e Damiano dealt with the 'new' aristocracy only in the eleventh century; its 'aristocratic' clients/associates faltered thereafter, and successive Trasteverino 'aristocrats' (such as the Papareschi) looked to other local churches. S. Ciriaco dealt with relatively few 'aristocrats' (Cencio di Roizone is the most likely); S. Maria Nova dealt with the Frangipane all through, who became closer to the church as they became more influential. But in each case these 'aristocratic' families operated alongside 'medium elites' of a variety of different levels, and indeed others. We can usually only see through the church's own gaze the vertical relationships thus created, but the patronage relations each had with the church must have been at least partly mirrored in the secular world as well. Similarly to churches, both 'aristocratic' and 'medium elite' families needed urban and rural tenants (and *vicecomites* or *superistae*), to run their rural landholdings, witnesses for their transactions, as also—and not least—armed men to help them in their more direct interventions, that is, to sum up, clients; as well as political supporters and associates who might be their equals, and more powerful patrons for more difficult business too. We shall come to the similarities and differences between secular and ecclesiastical clienteles shortly, but both through the mediation of churches—the part we can see—and separately, these are the ways in which our social strata interpenetrated, in practice and on a daily basis, throughout Rome.

I argued earlier that the 'new aristocracy' can itself be divided fairly clearly into two strata, a smaller one more involved in a landed politics and a larger one, consisting of families usually less rich and less long-lasting, more focused on commercial activity (above, pp. 243–6). In this chapter, we have seen that there were also richer and less rich, more and less prominent, strata inside the 'medium elite' as well. It needs to be remembered again that these are also only rough categories, with no firm divisions in our period. That is to say: writers after 1100 could use words like *nobilis* for what I call the 'new aristocracy', and they were certainly calling attention to hierarchical differences when they did so; but exactly when it was that the family of Giovanni Tignoso, or the Parenzi, or indeed the Pierleoni, made it through from the 'medium elite' to the 'aristocracy', was probably as difficult to tell then as it is now, and probably also depended whom one was speaking to. This was even truer inside the 'medium elite', the ten to twenty leading families of each *regio*. Probably we can assume that its leaders were generally those who were most likely to become senators, as is implied by our S. Maria Nova evidence, but apart from that definable position, status was negotiable. Contemporaries of Sassone *macellarius*, or the Mancini, or the sons of Romano di Frasia (to use S. Maria Nova examples) will certainly have known better than we do how wealthy and influential they really were, how visible outside their *regio*, and so on; but how far they belonged to an elite, how high they were within its hierarchy, and how much authority attached to them rather than to their patrons, was likely to be up for continual negotiation, and, again, to be contested. It is fairly clear, too, that some richer artisans, and families of recent artisanal background, could be members of the 'medium elite'—Sassone *macellarius*, or the Maccii with their early surname and tower-house, can stand for the latter—but *how* influential they could be will remain unclear, and, once again, perhaps also was then.

These observations might seem to undermine any attempt to draw distinctions of wealth and status below the (itself negotiable) level of *nobilis*—let alone distinctions of class, save to say that only a small number of the people discussed in this chapter are likely to have worked with their hands most of the time: perhaps only some of the less-often attested artisans of S. Maria Nova, and some of the men who appear in the late twelfth-century quasi-notarial records of Trastevere. But the broad and fuzzy category of 'medium elite' at least allows us to recognize a specifically *regional* leadership, which visibly existed in S. Maria Nova, and must have existed in every other region as well, even if its dimensions and resources, and internal hierarchies, are likely to have been different across space and time. S. Ciriaco or S. Maria Nova transacted with all sections of the population, it is true, but they certainly greatly valued their links with members of the 'medium elite', Cencio di Pietro and his son Pietro or Stefano di Malagalia for S. Ciriaco, Sassone *macellarius* and the Mancini for S. Maria Nova. Although sometimes (often) we cannot be quite sure who was elite and who was not, we can recognize this aspect of social prominence and track it. Although we can never get as much detail about any of them as we would like, and although a total picture of the category is arduous to construct (and probably to read), we can get a sense of the rough resources of regional elites, and also some aspects of how they dealt. That they were situated in an ill-defined and constantly changing environment does not detract from that sense.

We have thus looked at regional difference inside Rome; but we have also been moving towards generalizations. These will be further developed in the final section of this chapter, in which we will return to the evidence for the whole of Rome. There, I want to look at the general problem of how social solidarity, factions, and geographically defined communities were constructed in the city. The evidence for this is rather more heterogeneous, for we will be looking at document sets of very different types, some of them small and obviously atypical, as well as a variety of narratives; but it will allow us to move out from our three best-documented *regiones* back to the city at large, as far as we can.

SOCIAL NETWORKS IN THE CITY OF ROME: PARISHES,
CLIENTELES, AND INFORMAL ASSOCIATIONS

We have now looked at the society of three of Rome's *regiones* in some detail. It is
clear from this that they had crystallized by the early twelfth century (at the latest) as
social bodies, although they varied considerably in their coherence; these regions
were indeed the basic building blocks of Roman political society, as can be seen in
the four oath-swearers to Eugenius III *per unamquamquem contradam* (i.e. each of
the *regiones* of the documents) in 1149, and again in similar oaths in 1188.[102] But
they were not the only local structures in Rome. In particular, they coexisted with
two other sets of collective groupings, *scolae* and parishes. How did these two relate
to Roman regional societies?

Scolae can be dealt with fairly fast, as we looked at them in Chapter 3
(pp. 152–4). They were professional and artisanal groups, with defined internal
hierarchies. They were probably also not geographically restricted, unless there were
so many people in any given profession or trade that there was more than one *scola*;
many artisanal groups were based in given regions, on the other hand, such as the
erarii of S. Maria Nova, which may have given some de facto geographical
localization. Some of them participated in Rome's extensive ceremonial activities,
which gave them public prominence; they also had judicial responsibilities for their
membership, at least for trade-related disputes, which we can see in particular for
rural *scolae* (above, pp. 103–5) in the early twelfth century. They were the oldest
associational groups that we can see in the city. Although they probably formed as
purely ceremonial groups, they can clearly be seen operating as what would
elsewhere be called guilds by the early twelfth century. They must have both
cut across *regiones* and acted as a model for the functioning of later and more
strictly geographical collectivities. So it is interesting that we cannot track any
structured relationship between them and the early Senate; there was none until
Brancaleone degli Andalò associated the *artes*, the name for guilds by then, with
his *popolo*-based regime in the 1250s. However they worked in practice by the
1140s, they were not used as political building-blocks then, although their
ceremonial role, as also (at least in the case of the *salinarii*) their judicial role,
continued for a long time. The equivalents of *scolae* were not, it must be
recognized, used as constitutive elements by any other Italian city commune
either; but there were also no others in which guilds have the same visibility in our
sources in this period.[103]

Parishes present different problems. In much of Italy, urban quarters as structured communities based themselves on parishes, as in, for example, Lucca or

---

[102] *Senato*, nn. 8, 42. See Chapter 3, nn. 32–3, for *contradae* and their relationship to *regiones*.

[103] For *scolae* in our period, see especially Moscati, *Alle origini*, pp. 51–65. For the judicial role of
the *salinarii*, see esp. Carbonetti Vendittelli, 'La curia dei *priores*'. In the regime of Brancaleone degli
Andalò, what are now called the *arti* were, as usual in Italy, fully represented (and re-formed into
thirteen corporations), but the 'super-regions' remained crucial elements as well: Duprè Theseider,
Roma dal comune di popolo, pp. 26–9; Lori Sanfilippo, *La Roma dei Romani*, pp. 67–8; Maire Vigueur,
'Arti o rioni?'.

Florence.[104] In Rome, where *regiones* were old, there was a clear alternative to parishes, and a stronger one; but parishes developed all the same. Tommaso di Carpegna Falconieri has recently and efficaciously sketched their complex history, and I follow him here. Rome, being so large, had always needed a geographically based *cura animarum*, which we could call parish structures, focused on rights to baptise; this was traditionally supplied by the late Roman and early medieval *tituli*, titular churches, of which there were twenty-five, plus the five great basilicas (S. Giovanni in Laterano, S. Maria Maggiore, and the extramural S. Pietro in Vaticano, S. Paolo, and S. Lorenzo), which also had baptismal rights. The eighteen *diaconiae* were later foundations, seventh- or eighth-century for the most part, and had an important role in the distribution of charity, but no initial parish function; they were, however, all founded in populated areas (many *tituli* were now, by contrast, isolated in zones of relative *disabitato*), and soon gained considerable local prestige. Around 900, the older parish geography of the city broke down, and the local role of the *diaconiae* becomes much more visible; it is very evident, for example, in the eleventh-century ceremony of the *laudes Cornomanniae*, which went back in some form at least to the late ninth century, in which the *populus* of each *diaconia* (called also a *parrochia*) processed with its archpriest to the Laterano on the Saturday after Easter (see below, p. 331). By the tenth century, indeed, many *diaconiae* had the basic elements of parish rights, that is to say local *cura animarum*, baptismal rights, and (increasingly lucrative) burial rights—and also archpriests, previously a right of *tituli* only. This process was partially reversed after 1050 or so, when 'reform' popes sought to re-establish a hierarchy between *tituli* (by now twenty-eight in number) and *diaconiae*. In terms of parish geography, the centrality of *tituli* was reaffirmed. But they were added to: the parish churches of the twelfth century (*matrices ecclesiae*) consisted of the *tituli*, the basilicas, several *diaconiae*, and some of the greater churches that had remained outside these structures, such as S. Croce in Gerusalemme and SS. Apostoli, which had long had effective parish rights, and both of whose heads became cardinal priests as well.[105]

By the twelfth century, effective parishes numbered over thirty. Some of them have surviving papal bulls which delineate the physical boundaries of the parish and its subject churches. Parishes, in turn, had a huge number of subject churches, usually called *capellae* in our sources; these steadily grew in number as Rome's

---

[104] Nanni, *La parrocchia*, pp. 145–54; Wickham, *Courts and Conflict*, pp. 252–6, 266–9; Davidsohn, *Storia di Firenze*, I, pp. 484–8, V, pp. 276–80. In Milan, the six *portae*, geographical quarters focused on the gates of the city, the basic political subdivisions in the twelfth century, were subdivided in their turn into *viciniae* based 'tendenzialmente' on parishes: Grillo, *Milano*, pp. 487–91 (p. 489 for quote); cf. Salvatori, 'I presunti "*capitanei* delle porte"', pp. 40–5, for their eleventh-century origins. Genoa also had non-parish neighbourhoods (called *compagne*, like the early commune itself): *Annali genovesi di Caffaro*, I, p. 25.

[105] See above all di Carpegna Falconieri, *Il clero di Roma*, pp. 195–234. For the *laudes Cornomannie*, *LC*, II, pp. 171–2. Twenty-eight *tituli*: see Alexander II's programmatic letter about *tituli* and *capellae*, Pflugk, II, n. 156. Burial rights are not referred to that often in Rome, but *SPV*, n. 16 and Pflugk, II, n. 284, show their importance. In *SMVL*, n. 80 (a. 1045), a layman gave a church and a cemetery to the monastery of S. Ciriaco.

population expanded geographically and demographically. In 1192, there is already evidence for 306 of them in the *Liber Censuum*, between parish churches and *capellae* (see Map 7 for a sample of them). *Capellae* themselves had subordinate parish rights over *cura animarum*, but they increasingly sought full rights, particularly over baptism.[106] All these churches were grouped together in the principal body of the non-papal Roman clergy, the *Romana fraternitas*, a forerunner of which is documented in an inscription in one of its main churches, the *diaconia* of SS. Cosma e Damiano in Foro, in 984, and which was running its own ecclesiastical tribunal by 1127 at the latest.[107] This was needed, for the complexity of the ecclesiastical structure of the city led to disputes at many levels: between parish churches of different types, over boundaries; between *matrices ecclesie* and *capellae* seeking independence; between *tituli* and *diaconiae* on the one side and monasteries, with their own claims to parish rights, on the other; and between everybody over that Roman speciality, complex ceremonial.

We know most about the structuring of parishes in our period through ecclesiastical disputes, which cluster in the twelfth century, for the twelfth century was in Italy the principal moment of the crystallization of the parish structure of the central Middle Ages.[108] Most of the surviving disputes concern the attempt by *capellae* to claim independence from their *matrix ecclesia*, which failed in every documented case; a series of popes, and the *Romana fraternitas*, all agreed on this, and insisted on the *iura parochialia* of the mother church: of which the key one, reappearing several times, is *obedientia*, although control over the *ordinationes* of chaplains was also important, and so were baptism, judicial powers, and 'reverences' or ritual rights. One particularly dogged *capella*, S. Salvatore de Curte, claimed autonomy from the *titulus* of S. Crisogono in Trastevere from Urban II, Calixtus II, Honorius II, Innocent II, Lucius II, Hadrian IV (twice), Alexander III, Lucius III, and Innocent III, always losing and never giving in.[109] One particularly interesting case from the 1180s set the female monastery of S. Maria in Campo Marzio against four neighbouring churches (three of them *capellae* of S. Lorenzo in Lucina) over the *parochiale iure populi* of a fairly small area, described in the documents by the houses and streets that delimited it. Lucius III (via a court case run by the *Romana fraternitas*) had recognized S. Maria's *populus*, in a charter then confirmed by both Urban III and Clement III, that is in texts dating from 1181 to 1188. The four churches, however, protested to Clement that the Lucius charter, although very recent, was a forgery, and that the *fraternitas* had never convened such a case; later in 1188, papal judges-delegate confirmed this, and the monastery lost. It is not as

---

[106] *LC*, I, pp. 300–4 (excluding seven monasteries in the list). For articulated lists, see di Carpegna Falconieri, *Il clero di Roma*, pp. 226–34; Passigli, 'Geografia parrocchiale', pp. 78–80; in both cases organized by parish with lists of subordinate *capellae*.

[107] For the *Romana fraternitas*, see Ferri, 'La *Romana fraternitas*', and especially di Carpegna Falconieri, *Il clero di Roma*, pp. 241–68: p. 242n gives a transcription of the 984 inscription. For 1127, Liverani, *Opere*, IV, pp. 258–64.

[108] See for bibliography Wickham, *Courts and Conflict*, pp. 266–9.

[109] S. Salvatore *de Curte*: see esp. *Reg. Inn. III*, II.144 (153), and cf. also *Bullaire Cal. II*, n. 227. Di Carpegna Falconieri, *Il clero di Roma*, p. 222n, gives a list of *capella* disputes; pp. 219–20n cite disputes over parish boundaries.

clear to me as to Clement's judges that the monastery was in the wrong, but either way it was clearly conceivable that monasteries, too, could have parish rights, at least on the level of *capellae*; that these subordinate parish communities were routinely called a *populus*; and that not only the main parishes but also *capellae* had detailed boundaries on the ground.[110]

Rome is not special in having cases of this type; indeed, it has fewer surviving parish disputes than some other cities. Throughout twelfth-century Italy—city and country alike—parishes, *capellae*, and nearby monasteries fought over election and ordination rights, obedience, and 'reverences'. Elsewhere in Italy, such cases could be exceptionally long and complex, and continually reopened, as parties made the expensive journey to (even more expensive) Rome, sometimes many times.[111] S. Salvatore de Curte, in its century-long campaign, was evidently prepared to take a similar financial risk. But the other point that comes from a comparison with the rest of Italy here is that, elsewhere in the peninsula, many of the participants in such cases were laymen: it was they who participated most keenly in local rituals, and, by watching them, could prove the right of one church against another.[112] The Roman parish cases feature few laity. It is true that we do not have surviving registrations of witness testimonies for Roman church cases, which would certainly have included more, but the one dispute that at least includes the names of witnesses—a 1127 dispute between SS. Apostoli and S. Marco over who should hold the cross in the procession of the Great Litany on 25 April—shows that they were overwhelmingly (four-fifths) clerical, although the laity did include a certain *laycus Gosbertus veteranus vir honestus probatus*, a respected layman of non-elite status, who could remember back to the 1070s. This was a more publicly visible case than many (it ended with SS. Apostoli's victory, proclaimed *clamantes per civitatem, ut mos est*, shouting throughout the city, as is customary), but it was still a largely clerical affair.[113]

This seems to me significant. Rome was of course full of clerics, thousands in number, who could do their own witnessing; but it is also the case that these parishes, whether at the level of *tituli/diaconiae* or *capellae*, never appear as the local bases of secular activity, as they do elsewhere. Even S. Maria Nova, a *diaconia* with an independent parish and also one of the major social and political foci of the *regio* named after it, does not appear as a basis for political protagonism (the men of the parish acting together, etc.) in the surviving documents for the church, which had,

---

[110] The records of this dispute survive, not in S. Maria in Campo Marzio's archive, but in that of one of the successful churches: ASV, Fondo S. Trifone, nn. 4–7, ed., rather scrappily, in *PL*, CII, cols 1469–70, n. 82, CIV, cols 1391–4, n. 92, and Kehr, IV, p. 239 n. 22. Note that *SMCM*, n. 62 (a. 1194), a papal confirmation of S. Maria's lands, sets out very carefully the relationship which the subordinate church of S. Andrea de Mortariis, a church not involved in the 1180s disputes, had with both the monastery and the *titulus* of S. Lorenzo in Lucina; the nuns had clearly learnt from their defeat.

[111] Emblematic for me is the Figline Valdarno case discussed in Wickham, *Dispute ecclesiastiche*, with its fourteen hearings; p. 78 for expenses.

[112] See the cases discussed in Wickham, *Dispute ecclesiastiche*, pp. 46–80; Wickham, *Courts and Conflict*, pp. 238–76.

[113] Liverani, *Opere*, IV, pp. 258–64; see di Carpegna Falconieri, *Il clero di Roma*, pp. 251–3.

after all, been selected for preservation by the clergy of S. Maria themselves. As for the area fought over by S. Maria in Campo Marzio in the 1180s, the *regio* of S. Lorenzo in Lucina was rather smaller than the parish of that *titulus*, which extended some way to the west and east, but it was more substantial than the tiny territories of the *capellae* that held off the monastery. The parish did not, at either level, act as the basis for regional identity, even though the *regio* of S. Lorenzo was named after its central church; the churches may well have been a social focus for their *regiones*, as S. Maria Nova was, and a ritual focus too of course, but they did not act to define them. And two-thirds of *regiones*, unlike these two, were not named after a church anyway. The secular districts of the city did not map well onto its parish structure. And it is the *regiones* that were the core of the political activity of Rome. The parishes, of course, were key to the city's ceremonial sector, which was huge, as we shall see in Chapter 6, and also to all activities inside the sphere of canon law. But there remained a certain separation of roles; clerics were focused on parishes, and on the churches as ritual centres, whereas the laity were focused on *regiones*, and on the churches as landlords and secular patrons. And Rome's parishes would not become more important as secular points of reference soon, either; into the late thirteenth century, parish locations were far rarer than regional ones in our documents.[114]

Rome's city clerics, in those hundreds of churches, were a large and important political community in themselves. After the 1040s they tended to be hostile to a 'reform' movement which increasingly marginalized them politically, in that popes added cardinals to *tituli* and *diaconiae*, who henceforth represented them in the papal Curia, but who were rarely themselves Roman or rooted in Roman traditions. Roman clergy were increasingly subject to control from above, as well, as the 'reforming' group around the pope directed their attention to traditional and beloved practices among the clergy (clerical marriage, for example; see below, p. 415). Small wonder that a sequence of popes opposed to the international hierarchy, from Benedict X in the 1050s to Victor IV in the 1160s, had strong support from the city clergy; so apparently did Arnaldo of Brescia, at least at the level of *capellani*.[115] These clerics were also closely linked to the laymen and laywomen who lived around them, who were their brothers and sisters, and who regularly attended services in their churches and processed in the major feasts of the ritual year. It is thus interesting that the Senate had no formal linkage with the city clergy at all; nor do the clergy appear in support of senatorial activities (except for moments of high religious ceremony such as papal *adventus*) in any text.[116] The Senate was almost certainly welcomed by Roman clerics, but, as with the *scolae*, it was not the product of any structured alliance with them. This in my view derives, above all, from the regional basis of secular political association, which was linked

---

[114] Hubert, *Espace urbain*, pp. 90–1.

[115] Di Carpegna Falconieri, *Il clero di Roma*, pp. 65–86. For Arnaldo, see a letter of Eugenius III to the Roman clergy from 1148, ed. *PL*, CLXXX, col. 1358, n. 311, condemning the fact that *capellani* have been persuaded by Arnaldo into disobeying their cardinals and *archipresbyteri*.

[116] *Adventus*: e.g. LP, II, pp. 387 (not explicitly mentioning the Senate), 446.

closely to local churches, but which did not depend on them. In this extremely ecclesiastical city, regional identity was the basis of an unusually autonomous secular solidarity. We will come back to the point later.

Lay clienteles mattered for churches and monasteries. They never needed secular political support more than when they were up against determined and powerful opponents whom they had to confront in court. In 1139, the abbot of S. Gregorio sul Celio raised a plea against Oddone of Poli in the most public space imaginable, Innocent II's Second Lateran Council, protesting at Oddone's usurpation of the monastery's rights over Poli itself and two subordinate castles, in the hills between Tivoli and Palestrina. We have the monks' account of the long and unsuccessful court case that followed, in which Oddone successfully requested delays in a dozen hearings between 1140 and 1143, when the pope died. Innocent probably had no intention of letting S. Gregorio win the case, in fact, and S. Gregorio never got Poli back. The case is fascinating for several reasons, and I will discuss it in more detail later (pp. 406–7); what is interesting for our purposes here, however, is that the monastery on each occasion turned up with its *amici et fideles*, who are often named. In May 1140 these are listed as Cencio Frangipane, Cencio and Massimo di Guido (the former was a monastic tenant on S. Gregorio's large Cancellata estate west of the city; his descendants were major figures in the fishing of the Porto marshes just to the south, which S. Gregorio had eminent rights over), Francone di Pietro di Francone (Pietro had been a judicial official in a major court case between S. Gregorio and the *scola piscatorum* over the same fishing rights already in 1115), Oddone di Francone (another Cancellata tenant), Romano *de Papa* (Innocent II's own nephew), Guidone and Gulferamo di Gulferamo (Guidone had been a witness to a church case over the rights of the bishop of Sutri in *c.*1120), and Rainerio di Benedetto *iudex*. Later lists of monastic *fideles* in the case include, among others, Galgano the *primicerius*.[117]

This galaxy of 'aristocrats', senior judicial officials, and prominent members of the 'medium elite', some of them with forensic experience, failed to win the case for S. Gregorio, even though the group included the pope's nephew. (Oddone, for his part, had the backing of the urban prefect, which must have been determinant on the other side.) But it is nevertheless important that the monastery could call on them, over and over, to come across to the Laterano to support its case—including Cencio Frangipane, an assiduous supporter, who certainly will have frequented the Laterano often enough on his own behalf, but who must have had other calls on his time too—and it is also important that the monastery felt it needed to have them there. In front of the pope, numerous and prominent supporters were clearly helpful. It is not so surprising that S. Gregorio's *fideles* were also its tenants, in

---

[117] *S. Gregorio*, n. 7, for the Poli text; for Cencio di Guido and Oddone di Francone, n. 20, and for Cencio's son Pietro and heirs, nn. 55, 43 (cf. above, p. 104), with SMT, n. 14 (a S. Gregorio charter, the only surviving original for the monastery); Pietro's brother Guido appears as a *consul* with Romano *de Papa* in SMVL, n. 172; for Pietro di Francone, *S. Gregorio*, n. 34; for Guidone di Gulferamo, 'Documenti per la storia', n. 22 (and *LC*, I, n. 123, for his son Romano). For Romano *de Papa*, above, p. 242; for Galgano, above, p. 274.

this case in its lands west towards the coast (where the Papareschi, heirs of Pope Innocent and Romano *de Papa*, would also hold from the monastery in the future, and perhaps did already). The Frangipane, whose power-base was close to S. Gregorio, were also logical allies, and indeed appear as witnesses to numerous monastic transactions from as early as 1014 and with a particular density in the second quarter of the twelfth century. In 1145 Cencio Frangipane, too, is found to be a long-standing leaseholder of S. Gregorio, of a *turris* in the Circo Massimo and of a section of the Settizonio, the large and fortified classical monument on the edge of the Palatino, just south of the Frangipane towers near the Colosseo and opposite S. Gregorio itself.[118] So, to return to generalizations: we have seen that the Agro romano and the city of Rome were overwhelmingly owned by the various churches and monasteries of the city. We have also seen that most of the Agro romano was leased out for quite low rents to urban 'aristocrats' and other *rentiers* (even though churches got profit from their lands too, at least by way of entry-fines). We are accustomed to conclude that what churches must have got in return was political support. This is exactly what S. Gregorio assumed it could count on in 1140, and it was right—that the support did not work in this case was unfortunate, but it was not because the monastery's supporters failed to present themselves.

S. Gregorio was a large landowner, with blocks of land of considerable size west of the city (Castel di Guido, Cancellata and the marshes) and east of the city (Mandra Camellaria, Moreni), plus castles further afield (at Calcata to the north and Poli to the east). It was already leasing to 'aristocrats' in the tenth century (its major clients then were the *de Imiza*, who had given the Settizonio to the monastery in the first place, in 975), and it continued to do so, although its clientele shifted to the 'new aristocracy'—the Frangipane from early on, and also the heirs of Andrea di Viola, another Colosseo family, who were either 'aristocratic' or at the top of the 'medium elite' (above, p. 293). It kept a much more 'aristocratic' clientele than any of the three churches/monasteries we looked at in the last section, too; Castel di Guido at the end of the twelfth century would be leased to the Normanni.[119] This illustrates the range that churches and monasteries had in constructing a network of *amici et fideles*, associates and clients. Both SS. Cosma e Damiano in Trastevere and S. Ciriaco in Via Lata also had very large estates in the Agro romano, but their clients were 'medium elites' rather than 'aristocratic', and (in the case of the Trastevere monastery) often less influential people still. They went, in effect, for a broad base of support, rather than a narrower and more powerful one, as with S. Gregorio. We cannot tell whether this was by choice or necessity. As it happened, to go with the 'medium elite' was probably the best strategy once the Senate came to rule Rome; conversely, 'aristocratic' backing might work better again by the thirteenth century, with the rise of the *baroni*. Which worked better could not be predicted in advance. But clienteles could evidently be constructed in a variety of different ways.

[118] Papareschi as monastic tenants: *S. Gregorio*, n. 43. Frangipane as tenants: n. 152; as witnesses: nn. 16, 135, 21–2, 82.
[119] *De Imiza: S. Gregorio*, nn. 151 (Settizonio gift), 4, 127, 12, 126. Castel di Guido: *S. Gregorio*, n. 24.

The solid basis for ecclesiastical clientele construction remained, however, the leasing of land. There were so many churches in Rome that lay political actors could be attached to several (as the Frangipane certainly were). Church clienteles could thus not be exclusive, and we do not get any particular stress on political loyalty in most ecclesiastical leases—the exceptions are clearly phrased as exceptions, and are also tenth-century rather than later.[120] But churches could, all the same, expect to build up networks of support when they leased, both in the city and in the countryside. This support was not just in crises, either; the Frangipane were regular witnesses for S. Gregorio, as well as its muscle in the papal court in 1140. And, as we saw in the previous section, it could run from the top of society to quite far down, creating networks at various social levels. Rome was a large and active city, but (within limits) the 'politics of land' worked as well there as it did in any part of Europe studied by Marc Bloch.

The preceding paragraph contains plenty of statements of the obvious. But it is worth setting them out again here because they seem to have applied, above all, to ecclesiastical clienteles. When we come to the construction of the clienteles and entourages of the secular 'aristocracy', can we assume that they were based on land in the same way? In the countryside, yes: we have clear evidence for the Sabina, and also for Tuscolo, as in the 1168 document in which Rainone of Tuscolo made the fiefs of his *milites* hereditary. But we cannot track this for the city. The tenants of 'aristocrats' will generally have been their clients, of course. The Frangipane secular land charters surviving in S. Maria Nova's archive are straightforward economic transactions, with no explicit political overtones, but, as with church leases, their beneficiaries could be expected to remain the family's supporters.[121] Conversely, the *auctoritas* the family had over the latter's *regio* (above, p. 294) cannot be shown to be on the basis of the distribution of land. And Roman 'aristocrats' probably for the most part did not actually have enough land under their direct control in the city, at least in the period of the 'new aristocracy' up to 1150, to build up large urban clienteles solely on the basis of it (unlike the tracts of baronial land in the city in existence by 1300, which could in principle be used for this);[122] nor, indeed, did they as yet hold so very much land in the countryside. So what means did the Frangipane have, to create the force of *milites et pedites* against whom Stefano Normanno fought in 1118, or did the Pierleoni have, to create the *potentia* which Paschal II recognized in 1111?

The answer is that we do not know for sure. But, as just implied, we have no reason to think that such entourages had to have been rewarded with land. Some of the more obvious non-land-based reward structures were furthermore not yet very developed. Some smaller families could associate themselves with more powerful ones to obtain papal castles in pledge, in return for loans, as Pietro di Atteia and

---

[120] Exceptions: *Statuti della provincia romana*, pp. 3–9 (a. 979); *Papsturkunden*, n. 393 (a. 1000).

[121] Sabina (and elsewhere in Lazio): Toubert, *Structures*, pp. 1157–79. Tuscolo: ASV, A. A. Arm. I–XVIII, n. 3655; a convenient edition is in Beolchini, *Tusculum II*, pp. 424–5. Frangipane charters: *SMN*, nn. 49, 94, 116, 117, 152, 164.

[122] Carocci, 'Baroni in citta', esp. p. 149; Maire Vigueur, *L'autre Rome*, pp. 222–8 relativises the force of urban baronial clientèles.

others did together with the Prefetti to take over Civita Castellana in 1158, but to participate in this way required a capital commitment that not every middling family had.[123] A century or so later, clienteles could be created through the assignment of ecclesiastical preferment, but the papal Curia was as yet relatively small, and also, across the period 1046–1188, only intermittently open to Romans; similarly, the secular city government was tiny in its permanent personnel throughout the twelfth century, so was not a major patronage resource even for the most Senate-orientated Roman 'aristocrats'.

I conclude that the major resource 'aristocrats' had to build up clienteles was movable wealth: *pecunia*, or, more specifically, silver, whether coined or not. Much of this came from the papacy, which dealt extensively in political gifts of silver. We have seen that support for popes in the schisms of the century after 1044 was typically created—and also undermined—by gifts of money/treasure to political players (see above, pp. 171–4 and below, pp. 417–19). The Pierleoni, Frangipane, Normanni, and Corsi/Prefetti also benefited directly from pay-offs such as the Genoese gifts to the Curia of 1120 (above, p. 164). And wider groups in society were accustomed to largesse in silver, as with the gifts of *denarii* in various contexts to lay participants in Easter ceremonies, and the payment of 'customary gifts' to the *populus* and to the senators in return for their swearing of fidelity to incoming popes (below, pp. 328, 347). The attraction of papal *pecunia* for people is obvious enough; but in the specific case of 'aristocratic' leaders such as the Frangipane and Pierleoni, it could be directly usable to construct support networks for them in their turn—networks of people who were already accustomed to expecting monetary largesse, as the ceremonial gifts just cited already show. This is hypothetical as a model for lay 'aristocratic' clientele-building, but it seems to me a reasonable hypothesis, and not a speculative one. Rome's political society was awash with *pecunia*, which came in from so many directions to make up the resources of the Roman church; so it would be entirely comprehensible for that *pecunia* to trickle down to the next level, the entourages of Rome's lay leaders.

This, however, means that, inside *regiones*, church clienteles and secular clienteles could have been differently constructed: land was the basis of the first, silver, at least in part, for the second. One cannot, of course, be categorical about the sharpness of that separation; nothing is as marked as that, and I am arguing anyway on the basis of logic, not direct evidence. Both will have been mediated, too, probably in particular the second, for military imagery and the prestige (and local political advantage) of 'aristocratic' connection were important in secular clienteles too, compensating in part for the potentially humiliating ambiguity involved with all gifts of money (not to speak of stable salaries) in our period. But it nonetheless seems to me likely that clients of, say, S. Maria Nova on the one side, and the Frangipane on the other, expected largely different things from their association with each. This is also likely to be a reason to think that individuals could consider

---

[123] Pietro di Atteia: *LC*, I, nn. 167–8.

themselves as clients of both, without ever having to worry about conflicts of interest: because attachment to each was constructed on different levels.

Romans of course dealt with each other in more informal ways as well: less geographically defined and less hierarchical. We cannot, unfortunately, track even one individual Roman in the full detail of his or her life (even to the extent to which such a life is illuminated from the outside by property transactions) until well after 1200; the sketchy paragraph-long accounts in the second section of this chapter are all we can glean. Even the Frangipane are hardly better documented than that as individuals; and the few Roman popes of the century after 1050 are seldom easier to track in detail in their family context—we know almost nothing of the family background of Innocent II, prominent though he was, and only Anacletus II has a set of known ancestors. So we cannot follow single people here in their social dealings. What follows, therefore, is a brief and fairly generic account of family strategies, structured through the life cycle of Romans with at least a minimum of landed property, across our period; because these strategies led directly outwards, from the family into the local community around them.

Brothers and sisters inherited equally in Rome at the start of our period, as any number of documents recording mixed-sex groups of landholding siblings testify. If they were fatherless and aged under twenty-five, their legal actions were subject to the confirmation of a *curator et tutor*, who was normally assigned by a palatine judge in the eleventh century, and by a range of judges and sometimes *scriniarii* by the later twelfth (one *scriniarius* at a time apparently had the *iurisdictio* of assigning *curatores* and *tutores* by the 1170s).[124] Such guardians were often kin, but did not have to be. After 1128 at the latest, the classical Roman distinction between the *tutor* and the *curator* re-emerged; the *tutor* was for children younger than twelve in classical law (an age is not specified in our period, but it seems quite plausible), and he or she acted directly for them; the *curator* was for twelve- to twenty-five-year-olds. In the later twelfth century, the commonest *tutrix* was the mother, if she had outlived her husband; mothers were much less often a *curatrix*, however (I have only found two examples). Late Roman law allowed mothers to be *tutrices* only if they did not marry again; there is no sign of this restriction in our period, although it appears in one of the documents in which a mother is appointed a *curatrix*.[125] *Curatores* were generally men, and we can assume that, if they were not kin, they were men of some local public standing—enough at least for them to be known to judges. Given the frequently low age of death and the high age of full adulthood,

[124] Earliest example of *curator et tutor*: *RF*, n. 667 (a. 1013). *Iurisdictio* of particular *scriniarii*, after 1171: *S. Sisto*, nn. 6, 7, 8; ASR, SCD, cassetta 16, n. 143; *Senato*, n. 29; *S. Pancrazio*, n. 9 (= 22); 'Documenti per la storia', n. 28, all for Cencio in 1171–9; *S. Sisto*, nn. 13, 14; *S. Alessio*, n. 23; *LC*, I, nn. 165, 166, 178–83; *S. Gregorio*, n. 24; 'Documenti per la storia', n. 32, all for Giovanni di Leone in 1192–1200.

[125] New pattern first in *S. Gregorio*, n. 21; the contrast in roles is clear in e.g. *LC*, I, nn. 180–2. Mother as *tutrix*: see for example *SMVL*, nn. 185, 218, 234; *SMN*, n. 93. As *curatrix*, SCD, n. 72 (a. 1072, citing Roman law); *S. Prassede*, n. 32 (a. 1164, citing the mother's promise not to remarry). See below, pp. 368–9, for the shifts in the direction of classical Roman law of pupillage, dowry, and the making of wills which characterized Rome around 1130.

there would have been a large number of tutorial and curatorial assignments in Rome; it must have been a standard task for judges, and curatorship, in particular, a standard role for men of local status.

The equal inheritance of women increasingly, however, simply represented a recognition of their right to a dowry, at least if they had brothers. In Rome, dowries were normal by the mid-eleventh century at the latest, matched, as we have seen, by a gift by the bridegroom of half the value of the dowry, in *donatio propter nuptias*, which is first documented in the city in 1056. This pattern was thus classical Roman already, even if the documents dealing with it became abruptly more common after 1130; it sharply distinguished Rome from Lombard Italy, where a *morgincap* from husband to wife of a quarter of his property was the only major marriage gift, although most of Lombard Italy picked up Romanist dowry-giving habits in the mid-twelfth century, and thus joined Rome's long-standing practice.[126] We have already seen (pp. 275–6) that the practice of giving marriage gifts, and guaranteeing their integrity in the event of the death of one or other spouse, led to very complicated pledging arrangements by the mid-twelfth century. The families who were joined in marriage took nothing for granted. So in 1197, at the death of Lorenzo di Maria di Giovanni, his son Pietro sold a vineyard outside Porta Flaminia for 8 *solidi* to pay for the return of the dowry of Lorenzo's widow Romana, Pietro's mother; this transaction was, however, directed by Romana herself, who had been given the *potestas* to do so in Lorenzo's will together with Pietro's *curator*, who was Romana's brother Angelo Bardello. There is every sign that this was a completely standard act. In 1192 Gerardo di Stulto sold a house in Campo Marzio for £12; because he was *pauper et senex*, from that sum he gave £7 to his wife Tropea *pro quitamento sue dotis et donationis*, to buy out her marriage portion: she had marital rights over his total property that were irreducible, no matter how 'poor' he was.[127]

So the pledging to preserve marriage deals seems to have worked. Conversely, however, daughters, in getting and keeping their *dos*, seem later in our period to have been more and more cut out of the sibling divisions of property which eventually followed parental death: the documents we have for land divisions from the 1060s onwards are in almost all cases between brothers (or brothers and nephews), not brothers and sisters.[128] But daughters/sisters kept hold of some land all the same, for a dowry was substantial in Rome, and, at least after their husbands died, they had full control over it. They sometimes gave it to their own daughters, whether for their dowries, or in inheritance, or in direct gift.[129] Women acting on their own are a minority of Roman document-makers, but a substantial

---

[126] *Donatio propter nuptias* first in *S. Prassede*, n. 7; *dos* first in *RF*, n. 990 (a. 1066). For the general history of marriage portions, see esp. Bellomo, *Ricerche sui rapporti patrimoniali*.

[127] *SMVL*, n. 256; *SMCM*, n. 60.

[128] *SMN*, n. 22 (a. 1065, the only division involving a woman); *SMT*, n. 7; *SMVL*, n. 185; *SMN*, n. 75; *SPV*, n. 53; *SMVL*, n. 205; *SMN*, n. 159. All but the first two postdate 1150. See in general here Toubert, *Les structures*, pp. 751–68; di Carpegna Falconieri, 'Sposarsi a Roma', esp. pp. 21–3; di Carpegna Falconieri, 'Sistemi familiari', pp. 209–12; Allegrezza, 'I legami di parentela'.

[129] Examples: *SPV*, n. 3 (a. 931); *RS*, n. 65 (a. 953); *SMN*, n. 31 (a. 1100); *SMVL*, nn. 217 and 221 (aa. 1182–3); *SMCM*, n. 64 (a. 1198).

minority, from start to finish; and husbands also routinely acted with wives in transactions, which very often explicitly involved the recognition of conjugal rights over property. This fits with the standard role of widows as *tutrices*, too: the space for female public action in Rome was not tiny, even if it was certainly restricted, and it was and remained rather greater than in Lombard-law cities in Italy.[130] All this also meant that marriage was and remained a serious commitment of property which involved both a male and a female player, and that their families could remain linked, as in the case of Lorenzo and Romana, thereafter.

At death, finally, Romans often made wills. They are referred to first in 994, though they are also implicit in our citations of executors (*fidei commissarii et testamentarii*), which begin in 978. The first surviving will dates to 1087; they too become more frequent after 1130, although, as we have seen (p. 273), they do not survive in large numbers even then. Executors, however, crop up in plenty of texts, particularly in the eleventh century, selling land of the deceased for their soul, or giving pious gifts directly to churches. They seem less often to be the kin of the deceased, or, if they were, they seldom say so. A few executors were judicial officials; quite a number were clerics. One only, in all the documents I have seen, was female (she was the dead man's widow, in a text of 1185).[131] The others were, as far as can be seen, laymen of no named office but with local public standing, who—presumably—knew the deceased well enough to be trusted to carry out their last wishes.

The point about this race through the life cycle is that, at all critical moments, families interacted with the society around them. *Curatores* did not have to be kin; executors frequently were not. Marriage pledges were essentially from husbands to wives, to safeguard legally the wife's rights over marriage portions, but they of course involved two families, not one, and furthermore often involved others as well: so in 1080, Barone di Guittone and three other men pledged land and movables in Pigna to S. Ciriaco in return for 100 *solidi* for Barone's marriage; in 1184, Carafiglia and her son Angelo sold a house in Campo Marzio for 100 *solidi*, which they invested with two associates 'at their risk', but which was nonetheless destined to be the *donatio propter nuptias* for Angelo's wife Costanza; in 1190, Nicola di Colobrino got from his wife Sergia £10 plus a house on the Palatino in dowry, and again invested some of the money, with Gerardo Tricatore.[132] The pattern of pledging was repeated in more unusual situations, too, as when in 1168 Pietro Sarraceno and his two brothers pledged two tracts of land north of the city to the professional moneylender Romano Cerratano for £16, which had been spent on

[130] Non-aristocratic women could appear in other public roles, such as, occasionally, as female witnesses (one example is *SMVL*, n. 105, a. 1079). In Albano there was even a female *iudex*, Rofreda, in the twelfth century, probably holding an honorific title, but a striking one for all that (*SMCM*, nn. 44, 45, 58).

[131] First will reference: *RS*, n. 167; first executors: *RS*, n. 114, and *S. Gregorio*, n. 4; first surviving will: *SMVL*, n. 117. Later wills: see above, nn. 32–35. Female executor: ASV, A. A. Arm. I–XVIII, n. 4999, n. 10; a husband is executor in *SMN*, n. 17. Judicial officials as executors: e.g. *S. Gregorio*, n. 4; *RF*, n. 1001; ASR, SCD, cassetta 16, n. 130. Clerics as executors: e.g. *RF*, n. 666; *RS*, n. 91; *SMVL*, n. 86; *SMN*, n. 30; *SMVL*, n. 135; *SMN*, n. 105.

[132] Pledges cited: *SMVL*, n. 106; *SPV*, n. 67; *SMN*, n. 133.

ransoming Pietro from the *Teutonici*, presumably in the war of the previous year.[133] The network of credit extended out from the family, or from two families tied in marriage, to include many other people, kin, neighbours, friends, moneylenders, or all four at once.

We should not overstate the ubiquity of credit deals; they were common of course, but they are only the best documented form of this sort of informal social interaction. The key point is, however, that men and women in Rome negotiated their way throughout their lives through relationships with a wide circle of people, and in public (all these acts of course included lists of witnesses to the relevant documents as well). The churches whose clienteles we explored in the last section were merely among the most influential of local social actors; there were very many others. Formal or informal links, links of friendship,[134] obligation, or of very specific credit/debit relationships, horizontal/communitarian or vertical/hierarchical links (to churches, 'aristocrats', regional leaders), all structured the societies of *regiones*. Indeed, it was the varying force of all these different sets of relationships, all put together, which created in their varying ways both the strong and focused community of the *regio* of S. Maria Nova/Colosseo, and also the weaker and more evanescent community of Pigna. All of them put together created, that is to say, the social fabric of the entire city.

This section has discussed social associations; and the 'associational urge' has long been canvassed as one of the bases for the communal movement in its widest sense.[135] This makes sense in Rome too; but we must not romanticize it. In a large and complex city, associations of this type had always existed; they were not a product of any new world after 1143, or 1084, or 1046. The reason why they may have had a different effect in the twelfth century is only because the basic and very long-standing structures of city government had failed at the end of the eleventh, leaving a power vacuum which had to be filled using as yet relatively informal, locally based, resources. Not only the Senate, but *regiones* themselves, took on a more prominent role to make up for that vacuum. We shall look at this in more detail in Chapter 7.

For now, however, we have to ask in this chapter what marks Rome out as different from any other Italian city in this period. This is not a straightforward question to answer, for not many cities have been analysed systematically from this standpoint in this period. Broadly, Rome's geographical spread meant that its *regiones* began to form early, by the eleventh century, and before the political crisis—unlike the *viciniae* and parishes of other cities, which are, above all, a twelfth-century development. They therefore mark a (necessarily) more geographically articulated city by 1000 at the latest, and indeed, given the long history of

---

[133] *SMCM*, n. 54.

[134] For friendship, see e.g. *SMN*, n. 14 (a. 1051), in which an ill woman gives a post-mortem gift to three laymen, 'pro magno amore et dilectione quam in vobis nunc habeo'.

[135] 'Moto associativo': the phrase is Romolo Caggese's, in *Classi e comuni rurali*, I, pp. 223, 225; cf., for the city of Pisa, Volpe, *Studi*, p. 401.

numbered regions in Rome, for centuries before. It may well have only been Rome for which such a regional identity was really strong in our period, much as it is only Siena, with its *contrade*, for which the same is true today. And it is certainly only Rome that allows us to construct and contrast regional societies in our period—whereas, in the late Middle Ages, this can be done (and has been) for plenty of other cities, with Florence at their head.[136] Rome has far fewer documents than, say, Lucca for the eleventh and twelfth centuries, but such a contrast would be impossible in the Tuscan city. In Lucca, the set of documents from any urban church archive reflect the society of the whole city; for us, however, SS. Cosma e Damiano's urban documents only tell us about Trastevere, S. Maria Nova's only about Colosseo. In Rome, regional analyses impose themselves. Those were real divisions, real separations, however much the city was also connected as a whole at other levels, as we shall see in Chapter 6.

As to social hierarchies, we saw in Chapter 4 how the 'aristocratic' strata of Rome compared with the parallel social groups of other cities. At the 'medium elite' level, too, Rome had plenty of close parallels elsewhere. Families who owned or leased a few houses in each of the city and the (near) countryside, maybe with judicial or notarial experience, sometimes with artisanal and mercantile involvement, and with a potential interest in communal office and in the status attached to such office: these represented an entirely normal stratum everywhere. They were the backbone of the *militia* politics studied by Maire Vigueur, across the whole of the peninsula. But, once again, elsewhere they were less tightly regionalized.[137] We would have to extend our field of study to the whole city of Lucca in order to get a sense of this social stratum. In Rome, inside whose walls ten Luccas could of course fit, we have to build up a picture of them, region by region, before we can generalize. And, at a different level of analysis, the more generous documentation of different artisanal professions in Rome allows us to see more easily here than elsewhere how some artisans could indeed be members of, or else socially close to, the 'medium elite', although here I would hesitate to draw a contrast with other cities; it is more likely in this case that Rome acts as a model for other cities, whose occupational specializations are more hidden from us. Where Rome differed, here again, was in the power of its regional politics, which meant that the society of each region, *rentiers* and artisans together, could be coherent enough to operate as a whole, rather than (or as well as) being divided between an equestrian military stratum of leaders and the others—even if it is important to stress that regional leaders operated politically at the level of the city as a whole as well, as we shall see in Chapter 7; they were not tied only to regional politics, or the Senate would never have been created. Rome had a larger, sometimes richer, and more proactive urban-

---

[136] e.g. Kent and Kent, *Neighbours and Neighbourhood*; Eckstein, *The District of the Green Dragon*.

[137] Maire Vigueur, *Cavaliers et citoyens*, pp. 254–62, for the economic base of early *militia* families; for one extra example, Lucca, see Wickham, *Courts and Conflict*, pp. 56–61, with other bibliographical citations. It must be added that an involvement of the different urban regions in the construction of the early commune has been hypothesized elsewhere, e.g. for Genoa and Milan, but the evidence for them is pretty fleeting: Bordone, 'Le origini del comune di Genova', p. 253, rejects the hypothesis, while Salvatori, 'I presunti "capitanei delle porte"', pp. 41–5, is cautiously positive for Milan.

focused 'aristocracy' than most cities did in the eleventh and twelfth centuries, which certainly conditioned the choices of the 'medium elite'; but, finally, it is equally important to stress that Rome also shows us a much more complex internal stratification inside all its elites, 'aristocratic' and non-aristocratic alike, which aided both alliance and opposition, according to circumstance.

The society of the city of Rome in the tenth to twelfth centuries will never be entirely clear. The city had many special features, which permit unusual angles of analysis—its range of artisans, and, as we are about to see, its complex processions—but, all the same, its restricted documentary base makes some wider analyses simply impossible. I have been trying in this chapter to get towards an understanding of Rome's non-aristocratic strata from a variety of angles: a collective portrait of some 'medium elite' families and of the global resources of members of that elite; an account of (parts of) the society of three *regiones*, seen in each case, above all, through the archives of only one church or monastery; an attempt to sketch some of the dominant social networks of the city at a fairly abstract level. If this works, it is only by following the rules of early Cubism, illuminating the angles rather than the whole. And, it is worth repeating, it also illuminates only the relatively prosperous non-aristocratic strata of the city; small vendors, carters, servants, beggars, and charity recipients—the vast swathe of what will in the future be called the *popolo minuto*—do not figure. They were not part of the world of ecclesiastical land transactions (though they certainly make up some of the more anonymous witnesses to church documents), so we cannot in this period reconstruct their social world at all. This is a great pity; but even the relatively prosperous only get the sideways angular views just characterized. Conversely, however, it was the 'medium elite' and the artisanal strata inside and just outside it, more than their poorest neighbours, which was at the core of the early Senate. This does not make our lack of information about their neighbours any better, but it at least means that we can confront the political analyses in Chapter 7 with less of a sense of dissonance.

6

The Geography of Ritual and Identity

In Chapter 5, I stressed the social division of Rome into its distinct *regiones*; Chapter 7 will also discuss how politically divided it was, above all in the crisis century of 1050–1150. But Rome as a city, however large and heterogeneous, was never in any danger of breaking up. No one who has looked at the narrative, topographical, or liturgical sources for the city in our period (which concentrate, in fact, in those same decades) could doubt the coherence of the city as a political, ideological, even geographical unit. Stefano Normanno's cry of 'we are Romans like you' to his Frangipane opponents—and relatives—in 1118 (above, p. 181), or the mental ordering of the city in the *Mirabilia* of 1140–3 by its largely classical monuments, gates, triumphal arches, baths, 'palaces', theatres, bridges, and cemeteries show a sense of its unity, which was taken for granted as much then as it is now.[1] That unity was explicitly expressed in topographical terms, even though it was precisely Rome's spacious regional topography and local loyalties that offered potential for fragmentation. What I would wish to argue here is that such unity should not be taken for granted. It was there, but it also had to be constructed, both consciously, through specific interventions, and—most often—unconsciously, through practice. That is the theme of this chapter. Here, I wish to argue that part of that construction was performative: through the regular practice, and also manipulation, of an unusually dense processional ritual, which will be the focus of the first section of the chapter, and through Roman uses of the city's past, both pre-Christian and Christian, that were unusually elaborate, which will be the focus of the second section. These are very far from understudied topics. But the extensive work on them deserves to be problematized more than it has been in most studies; it also needs to be set in a social and cultural context that was less exclusively papal than many historians assume. The *Romanitas* of the city (to use a word which does not appear in our sources) was a complex and inconsistent set of images, and needed to be worked on, and worked with, all the time, both by popes and secular Romans. It is that working which we will see developed in the pages that follow.

THE RITUAL CONSTRUCTION OF ROME

Rome's medieval religious liturgy is uniquely densely documented, above all in the dozens of *ordines* for church services, edited by Fabre, Andrieu, Schimmelpfennig,

---

[1] *Mirabilia*, esp. pp. 17–28.

and others. They allow historians to reconstruct the continual workings and reworkings of the ritual map of Rome across nearly every century of the Middle Ages, from the late empire onwards. All the same, it is the three twelfth-century *ordines* of Benedetto (1140–3), Albino (1189), and Cencio (1192), all edited in Fabre and Duchesne's *Liber Censuum*, that tell us most about processional ritual across the city in our period; these will be the central sources discussed here.[2] These texts focus on the major feasts only, but they were very numerous. Benedetto gives detailed accounts of around forty liturgical events, many involving masses at several churches in succession, as well as briefer references to less important ones; Albino fills out a smaller number with more details, especially of clothing; Cencio, too, focuses on a smaller number, but says much more about some of them (particularly about their financing) than do the other two. There has been discussion as to how much the liturgical world they describe was contemporary, as opposed to being a compilation of practices stretching a century or more into the past, much as people write about the main parallel to these texts, the mid-tenth-century *Book of Ceremonies* for Constantinople.[3] It is also clear, when Benedetto is compared to his two successors, that twelfth-century ritual was not static. But the main lines of a set of coherent ritual practices emerge with a fair degree of consistency in these sources, and to an extent they can be taken as a whole.

I will use Benedetto more than the others, for he certainly wrote during our period, in the papacy of his own *dominus*, Innocent II; he also dedicated his work to Cardinal Guido *de Castello*, who, as Celestine II (1143–4), became Innocent's successor as pope, which makes it clear that the work was completed before that succession. His work survives in a twelfth-century manuscript. Benedetto, a canon of S. Pietro in Vaticano and a *cantor* of the Roman church, can thus be placed quite exactly in the immediate milieu of Innocent's triumphal return to the city in 1138, and the restoration of what the latter saw as legitimate papal power (below, pp. 432–4). Benedetto's *Liber politicus* (i.e. probably, *polipticus*) can easily be seen as part of that restoration, both recording and seeking to re-establish papal rituals of all kinds. It is also clear that this work of compilation did not pause after the 1140s; there are signs of other texts being assembled and further developed between then and the 1190s, as also later.[4] Benedetto was certainly using earlier texts on occasion, as well; we cannot regard every detail of the *Liber politicus* as the work of an observer of the 1140s. Some of it is said explicitly to date back to

---

[2] For the twelfth century, see esp. *LC*, II, pp. 141–74 (Benedetto), 90–137 (Albino), I, pp. 290–316 (Cencio—with Schmidt, 'Die älteste Überlieferung'). See further Andrieu, *Les Ordines Romani*; Schimmelpfennig, *Die Zeremonienbücher*. For analysis, basic works are Schimmelpfennig, 'Die Bedeutung Roms'; Twyman, *Papal Ceremonial*; and, for an earlier period, Baldovin, *The Urban Character*, pp. 105–66; Latham, 'The ritual construction of Rome'.

[3] Schimmelpfennig, 'Die Bedeutung Roms', pp. 48–51, argues in particular that Benedetto looks back to before 1046 (see n. 5, however), as well as that his text was written by several authors (cf. n. 176 below). Compare, for the *Book of Ceremonies* (best but partial edition: Constantin VII, *Le Livre des cérémonies*, ed. Vogt), McCormick, *Eternal Victory*, e.g. pp. 160–1; Cameron, 'The construction of court ritual'.

[4] Schimmelpfennig, *Die Zeremonienbücher*, pp. 6–16, 141; a fragmentary *ordo* from the later twelfth century, the Basel *ordo*, is ed. Schimmelpfennig, 'Ein bisher unbekannter Text'.

Gregory VII's time, and some may well depict earlier practice still; but, conversely, there is enough material that links in with our other twelfth-century sources (including Albino and Cencio, but also casual references in narrative accounts) to allow us to be sure that it was not particularly idealized or anachronistic.[5] There was no real reason for it to be: papal ceremonial has been a stable part of Roman social and cultural practice for over a millennium and a half, and urban ceremonial for much longer. As does the *Book of Ceremonies*, Benedetto gives us a firm overall guide to a ritual world, even if some of his details relate more to the eleventh century (say) than the twelfth. And it is as an overall guide that I wish to use him here.

Benedetto was a *cantor*, and one of his principal concerns was to record the details of liturgical antiphons, mass by mass, demonstrating beyond doubt as he did so that membership of the *scola cantorum* in our period was a full-time (as also well-paid) job.[6] But he was also concerned to record all the participants in most of the feast days of the Roman church. The great majority of them involved the pope himself, normally with all the *curia*, or *ordines*, or *scolae* (here the cardinals, other Lateran clergy, and palatine dependents and servants of different kinds).[7] Benedetto in fact describes thirty-three ceremonies involving the pope directly, some of which lasted all day and a few of which included nocturnal vigils as well. As usual in the medieval church, these concentrated around Christmas and in the Easter period from the start of Lent to Pentecost, but they studded the rest of the year as well, with some ritual stress on the Purification of St Mary on 2 February, her Assumption on 15 August, her Birth on 8 September, and the Exaltation of the Cross on 14 September. This was, to put it simply, a lot of work for a pope. Large sections of his year were taken up with carefully choreographed ceremonial.[8] This ceremonial all took place with stand-ins if necessary (usually cardinals), whether the pope was in Rome or not, and there are certainly hints that he could, under some circumstances, not attend it all even if he was in Rome;[9] but our evidence converges to allow us to say that, in general, these were papal occasions.

[5] Gregory VII in Benedetto: *LC*, II, p. 171. I do not see how Schimmelpfennig, 'Die Bedeutung Roms', p. 51, manages to take the Christmas procession in Benedetto (*LC*, II, pp. 144–7) back to the pre-1046 period; his evidence here focuses on Gregory too (see below, n. 32). I agree with Herklotz, *Gli eredi di Costantino*, pp. 212–13, who argues that Benedetto does mostly have a contemporary context. For contemporary narratives, see e.g. below, nn. 67–70.

[6] For pay, see e.g. *LC*, II, pp. 143, 151, 156, 158 (Benedetto) and, in general, p. 90 (Albino).

[7] The *scolae* in the *ordines* are mostly sets of papal employees; the secular ones are listed in Cencio (*LC*, I, pp. 304–6), and include groups of, for example, *hostiarii*, doorkeepers (cf. also *LC*, nn. 158–9, a. 1188, for their oath), and *mapularii*, wardrobe-men; to these we must, of course, add the *scola cantorum*. See e.g. Twyman, *Papal Ceremonial*, pp. 189–93, for the secular group. They are thus distinct both from the artisanal and agricultural *scolae* (above, pp. 89–91, 103–5, 152–4) and the *scola militum* (above, p. 263).

[8] As was the ritual year of the emperor in Constantinople: see e.g. Liutprando, *Relatio*, chs 8–10, for a procession interrupting an embassy.

[9] Cencio, *LC*, I, p. 308 makes this clear for the *Letania Maior*. Innocent III in January 1199 sent presents to S. Pietro to make up for being too busy to come to services there: *Reg. Inn. III*, I. 534 (536). Di Carpegna Falconieri, *Il clero di Roma*, pp. 239–40, proposes that popes rarely processed by the twelfth century; this seems to me an exaggeration, except insofar as popes for the century before 1188 were very often away from the city, whether willingly or not.

Most of the ceremonies we are dealing with were stational liturgies: that is to say, the pope travelled from the Laterano palace to the church where the *statio* or *stacio* was, and then back to the palace afterwards: sometimes to S. Giovanni in Laterano itself, very often to S. Pietro in Vaticano or S. Maria Maggiore, but also to a variety of other churches, S. Croce in Gerusalemme, S. Stefano Rotondo, S. Lorenzo fuori le Mura, S. Adriano in Foro (the classical Senate house), S. Sabina, and others. Having a *statio* mattered; it was a big deal for S. Maria in Trastevere that Calixtus II transferred the 1 January *statio* to it in 1123. Benedetto does not mention this *statio*—proof that even his long list is not complete—but S. Maria in Trastevere sources certainly do: on 1 January 1124 the pope formally celebrated mass there, with cardinals, the clergy, all the *Lateranenses scolae*, and 'surrounded by a great crowd (*maxima turba*) of the Roman *populus*'.[10]

Let us follow four of these routes, four of the most elaborately discussed in our sources, to see what we are dealing with here: the liturgies for the Purification, Easter Monday, the Great Litany on St Mark's day (25 April), and the Assumption. (See Map 9 for the routes.) For the Purification, as for all Marian feast days, the *statio* was at S. Maria Maggiore; but, first, all eighteen of the city's *diaconiae* sent images of the Virgin *cum clericis et populo* to S. Adriano, creating, we must assume, a large gathering in the Foro Romano just outside it. The pope and cardinals went to S. Martina, a smaller church beside S. Adriano, where the pope sat outside and gave consecrated candles to clergy and people, then he sang mass in S. Adriano; then he walked barefoot past the arch of (the Foro di) Nerva, through the *forum Traiani* (which must be the Tempio della Pace, somewhat east of the Foro di Traiano), through the *arcus Auree* just north of S. Maria Nova, then up the hill past S. Pietro in Vincoli and S. Prassede to S. Maria Maggiore, where he sang mass again. Cencio adds that the diaconial images preceded him in this walk, *processionaliter cantando*, and that papal servants washed his feet once he got to S. Maria, where he put on shoes again.[11]

We need to pause here on the word *populus*. I argued earlier (pp. 261–2) that it was an ambiguous word in our period, which sometimes meant a restricted set of political players, and sometimes a wider array of Romans, including anyone—or anyone with a local status—who was not a *nobilis*. In these liturgical texts, it is certainly closer to the second of these, but is still wider, in that it denotes members of the laity in general; or else, even more clearly, members of the laity attached to particular churches, which in theory excluded nobody, however low status. We cannot, of course, say whether absolutely every able-bodied parishioner of a *diaconia* turned out for the Purification procession, or the *Laudes Cornomanniae* after Easter (below, p. 331)—rich and poor, male and female, adult and child;

---

[10] *Bull. Cal. II*, n. 408; see, for Calixtus's first celebration, *Necrologi*, ed. Egidi, I, pp. 88–9, and, for S. Maria's *statio*, esp. Kinney, 'S. Maria in Trastevere', pp. 199–204. For *stationes* in general, see e.g. Baldovin, *The Urban Character*, pp. 143–58; de Blaauw, *Cultus et decor*, pp. 28–40, 56–63; and, for the pre-900 period, Noble, 'Topography, celebration', pp. 83–91. The dates of *stationes* also needed popes to change them: an example is Alexander III moving the *statio* of SS. Apostoli from Thursday after Pentecost to 25 July: BAV, CVL 5560, ff. 7v–8r.

[11] *LC*, II, p. 148; I, p. 293.

prima facie, it does not seem likely that they did. The communities attached to *diaconiae* were anyway not necessarily the whole of Rome, in that other churches had parishes as well, and by the early twelfth century many *diaconiae* had also lost those parish rights they were beginning to accumulate a century earlier (above, p. 307). But other rituals involved more churches than *diaconiae*; and, overall, the impression created by these texts is that the *populus* included, in effect, anyone who wanted to participate and was allowed by their family to go. We can say nothing about female participation in our period, but women do appear in earlier sources for Roman and other Italian processions, and also had a visible role in later medieval processional practice, so it is unlikely that they were excluded in any systematic way; children, too, *pueri*, are mentioned explicitly in some instances, as we shall see.[12] We could equally say: the *populus* only included anyone who had the time to participate, in cases where the procession took place during working hours. It might therefore be that the liturgical *populus* sometimes in practice did not extend so very much past the 'medium elite' discussed in Chapter 5. But that was still a substantial slice of the population of the city, and could justify the use of phrases like *maxima turba*. And it also has to be said that there is no sense of exclusion in any of these citations; indeed, one gains the impression that some ceremonies, like Easter Monday as we shall see, involved as large a percentage of Romans as was practicable.

Next, the Great Litany. The *Letania maior* was a very old procession, dating back perhaps to the fifth century; in the eighth century, and probably earlier, it had run from S. Lorenzo in Lucina, north out of the city to the Ponte Milvio and back south to S. Pietro in Vaticano, following the rough route of a pre-Christian ceremony; it involved both clergy and laity from the first. By the late eleventh century, however, the procession had shifted completely and now began north of the Capitolio at S. Marco (whose saint's day 25 April was), whither 'all the crosses of the city of Rome, with clergy and *populus*, proceeded honourably *cum processione*', before going to S. Pietro, apparently directly: this was the ceremony indeed most closely linked with the Roman clergy as a separate body. Meanwhile, the pope said mass in S. Giovanni in Laterano, then proceeded, singing psalms with the *scola cantorum*, down past the Colosseo and S. Maria Nova, then to S. Marco, then west to the Ponte S. Pietro and over the bridge to the Civitas Leoniana and S. Pietro. In S. Pietro there was a distribution of money; the non-papal procession received a recompense (*presbiterium*) 'according to the custom of this day'; separately, the pope was given 20 *solidi* in Pavese money, the cardinals and cantors got 40 *solidi* in Lucchese money, the *scriniarii* got 10 *solidi*, and so on, presumably from the pilgrim offerings to S. Pietro, which are documented elsewhere as the source of these handouts. (The detail of the currency fixes this account in the mid-twelfth century; Lucchese money is barely documented earlier.)[13] Cencio filled out this

---

[12] For the *universae feminae* of Rome in 799 greeting Charlemagne, see *LP*, II, p. 6. For Ravenna in the early eighth, see the formal penitentials described by Agnello of Ravenna, *Liber pontificalis*, p. 304, in which the *populus* is segregated by gender. For later periods in Italy, see e.g. Trexler, *Public Life*, pp. 249, 252, 358–61, for Florence.

[13] For the early period, see Baldovin, *The Urban Character*, pp. 158–66, and esp. Dyer, 'Roman processions of the Major Litany'. For the route in 799, see *LP*, II, p. 4. In the twelfth century, see *LC*,

description with more details of the papal procession; the pope was again barefoot—he always was unless he was riding—but rested on a bed in several places, S. Clemente, S. Maria Nova, S. Marco, on the bridge, and once again outside S. Pietro. Cencio also tells us that all churches in the city which participated (some 80 are listed), got £25 in toto, a large sum, here explicitly from S. Pietro's altar, and he also gives us more details of the sums the pope and cardinals and other Lateran clerics and officials received, which are both much more complex than and slightly different from those in Benedetto. Cencio was interested in finance, as already noted, but his account of these handouts is much more elaborate than his description of the procession itself.[14]

The Assumption, in the heat of mid-August, began with a mass the previous evening at S. Maria Maggiore with the pope and his *curia*; then, at midnight, without the pope, the cardinals *cum omni populo* took the acheiropoietic icon of Christ (an icon believed not to be painted by human hands) from the Laterano basilica and carried it around the Campus Lateranensis, with the *curia* and the urban prefect with twelve men (presumably from Rome's 'super-regions'); then they took it down the hill to S. Maria Nova, where the feet of Christ on the icon were washed (small wonder the icon is in such a fragmentary state today), then to S. Adriano, where the same happened, then out north-eastwards and up to S. Maria Maggiore towards dawn, where the pope met them again. All this was instituted by Pope Sergius I (687–701), Benedetto said, to celebrate Mary's freeing of the *populus Romanus* from persecutions. (The *Liber Pontificalis* does indeed say that Sergius instituted a procession from S. Adriano to S. Maria Maggiore on that day; later on, the same text shows it in operation in 752 and 847.)[15] The *Ordo Romanus L*, a mid-tenth-century text from Mainz, fills this account out with a stress on light, for the whole event was lit by lanterns set on the houses along the route; so does a hymn to Mary *in nocte quando tabula portatur*, of *c*.1000, dedicated to Otto III, which also, like *Ordo L*, lays considerable stress on the participation of the *populus*.[16] This procession became ever more important, and by the fourteenth century was a focus of organized lay devotion, run through the confraternity of S. Salvatore, and featuring the leading guilds (*artes*) of the city.[17] We cannot document in our period more than an undifferentiated *populus*, but we can at least say that, as far as we

---

II, pp. 155–6. For the association with the Roman clergy, see di Carpegna Falconieri, *Il clero di Roma*, pp. 250–2.

[14] *LC*, I, pp. 307–10; p. 293 for the pope as *pedibus discalciatis* when he walked on foot.

[15] *LC*, II, pp. 158–9; for Sergius, 752 and 847, *LP*, I, pp. 376, 443; II, p. 110. This is perhaps the main ceremony which the popes came not to attend, above all once they began their thirteenth-century (and later) practice of summering in the hill towns east of the city (Paravicini Bagliani, *La vita quotidiana*, pp. 23 ff.); that practice is not systematically documented before Innocent III, however.

[16] *Ordo L*: Andrieu, *Les Ordines Romani*, V, p. 358 (this is the longest of the *ordines* edited by Andrieu, but it does not otherwise differ from the others in focusing almost exclusively on the liturgy inside churches, rather than on processions). Hymn: *MGH, Poetae*, V, pp. 466–8. The *populus grandis valde* is also stressed in Nicola Maniacutio's 1140s account, ed. in Wolf, *Salus populi romani*, pp. 321–5, at p. 324.

[17] See in general Wolf, *Salus populi romani*, pp. 37–78; Noreen, 'Sacred memory'; Maire Vigueur, *L'autre Rome*, pp. 237–40.

know, this is the only regular liturgical celebration in any of our twelfth-century sources which features the twelve Roman (super-)*regiones*, a metonym for whatever lay organization already existed before 1143.

It is worth adding that the symbolism surrounding this literal visit of Christ to his mother was complex. The *Song of Songs* was read in the evening Assumption mass, which in this period was taken as a love song to Mary, here representing the Church; indeed, Innocent II's apse mosaic in S. Maria in Trastevere, again dating to the early 1140s, also features an enthroned Christ with Mary, and quotes from the *Song of Songs*. Ernst Kitzinger argued in an influential article that the icon of Christ, when it arrived at S. Maria Nova, also formally met the icon of the Virgin housed in that church, and that they were enthroned together there (an argument backed up by the text of the Ottonian hymn); he further argued, very plausibly, that the S. Maria in Trastevere mosaic directly alludes to this.[18] The lay hierarchy of the city was here swept into a re-enactment of quite an elaborate theological argument, every year on a stifling August night.

I have skipped over the Easter Monday procession, which, of course, varies in date according to the year, but has to take place between 23 March and 26 April. It was, however, perhaps the most elaborate of all. For this, the *statio* was at S. Pietro, and the pope rode down there with his entourage, down the hill from the Laterano to the Colosseo, and then took a northern route, north-west through the Fori Imperiali and over the Quirinale, passing SS. Apostoli, crossing the via Lata (today's via del Corso), and reaching the Ponte S. Pietro via the *regio* of Campo Marzio. The return journey went from the bridge down through the Arco di Teodosio, Valentiniano e Graziano (now no longer existing, but near the southern end of the bridge), passing the *palatium Chromatii* (probably on what is now the via dei Banchi Vecchi), where the Jewish community gave *laudes* to the pope, then proceeding along roughly what is now via del Pellegrino, north of the Teatro di Pompeo through the *regio* of Pigna, past S. Marco, around the Capitolio and through the Foro Romano and Fori Imperiali, until it met the northern route again at the Colosseo. This southern route was the standard route from the Vaticano to the Laterano in our period, and was called the via Sacra in many narratives, and also documents. It ran through several heavily populated *regiones*, Scorteclari, Pigna, and S. Maria Nova/Colosseo, as well as the increasingly settled *regio* of Parione to the south-west of piazza Navona. It is interesting, though, that the northern route was developed as well, with its focus on the via Lata and the Campo Marzio. A high percentage of Rome's population was within a ten-minute walk of one route or the other.[19]

[18] Kitzinger, 'A virgin's face' (cf. *MGH, Poetae*, V, p. 467, lines 43–4), followed e.g. by Parlato, 'Le icone in processione'. The critique of this article by Tronzo, 'Apse decoration', pp. 174–84 does not convince. Kitzinger hung his argument in part on the 'un-Romanesque' head of Mary in S. Maria in Trastevere, which, he argued, was intended to resemble that of the S. Maria Nova icon ('A virgin's face', pp. 12–15); this is the least effective part of the argument, but is also unnecessary to it.
[19] *LC*, II, p. 154. For the location of the Arco di Teodosio, Valentiniano e Graziano, and the *palatium Chromatii*, see the *Lexicon topographicum urbis Romae*, I, pp. 95–6 (C. Lega), and fig. 120.

Benedetto essentially just gives us the routes here; Cencio fills this out with plenty of other details which do not seem to be later developments. For a start, Cencio makes it clear that the procession which returned from the Vaticano on Easter Monday was the model for the procession of the crowned pope after his election and consecration; and this allows us to be sure that the participants in and ordering of the Easter procession followed an elaborate pattern described in several sources from the twelfth century and indeed earlier: the pope rode close to the back, with only the urban prefect and the palatine judges a little behind him; then, in front of the pope, in order (the order varies very slightly in our texts): the *regionarius*, the archdeacon, the cardinal deacons, the *primicerius* of the *scola cantorum* with the *scola* and the subdeacons, the *advocati* and the *scriniarii*, the cardinal priests, the cardinal bishops and the abbots of Roman monasteries, any visiting bishops, two naval prefects, a subdeacon holding the papal cross, twelve *draconarii* (riders bearing banners, *vexilla* or *bandora*), a papal horse without a rider, and at the front the *maiorentini milites* or *maiorentes*, whose job was to get the *multitudo populi* out of the way.[20] The Roman *nobiles*, and, later, senators, were also involved, although where they fitted into the procession is less clear.[21]

It is evident from the role of the *maiorentini* that the organizers expected a crush. One reason was that at several points along the return route a papal official threw money (*denarii*, necessarily here coins) into the crowd: these *iacta*, 'throws', as they were called, took place in front of S. Pietro, at the *turris* of Stefano Serpetri in Parione (here, an official threw the money from the tower), at the *palatium* of Cencio 'Musca in Pugna' in the via de Papa (probably not much further along the road), at S. Marco, and at S. Adriano in the Foro Romano (here the official threw the money from nearby S. Martina). By Cencio's time, the Jews met the pope at the first tower, which was thus probably near the *palatium Chromatii*; they got 20 *solidi* for their *laudes* as well.[22]

The sense of occasion attached to Easter Monday was thus very considerable. It was, furthermore, greatly reinforced by the fact that, all along the southern route, the immediately local inhabitants erected ceremonial arches, every Easter Monday and also at papal coronations, for which as much as £35 was awarded annually, distributed among the arch-makers. These arches are documented from at least the

[20] *LC*, I, pp. 299–304 for Cencio on Easter Monday; for the equivalence to the coronation procession, p. 312. See in general Twyman, *Papal Ceremonial*, pp. 175–89. For the order of the procession, see *LC*, II, p. 146 (Benedetto, Christmas), 124 (Albino, coronation), I, p. 292 (Cencio, 26 December), 305 (*maiorentes* with the role of *multitudinem populi removendo* on coronation days); Schimmelpfennig, 'Ein bisher unbekannter Text', pp. 67–8 (Basel *ordo*, the coronation listing followed here). In the eighth century, a similar ordering already existed for Easter in *Ordo I* (Andrieu, *Les Ordines Romani*, II, pp. 69–71); note that in those days it was the *vestararius*, not the urban prefect, who rode at the back—compare above, p. 188.

[21] See the vaguer references in Schimmelpfennig, 'Ein bisher unbekannter Text', p. 63; Albino, *LC*, II, p. 124; and Cencio, *LC*, I, pp. 297, 298, 312.

[22] *Iacta* and Jews, *LC*, II, p. 124 (Albino), I, p. 299 (Cencio). Twyman, *Papal Ceremonial*, pp. 193–208, is the best commentary on the Jewish *laudes*, which included the formal presentation of the Torah. Krautheimer, *Rome*, p. 278 thought that the place for the Jewish *laudes* had changed: an unnecessary conclusion. On Jews in Rome, a basic guide is Champagne and Boustan, 'Walking in the shadows of the past'; see also Chapter 5, n. 47.

1110s. They were temporary constructions, and seem to have largely consisted of ropes across the street on which were hung (according to Albino) silver and gold pots, precious clothing, and jewels, as well as *turibuli*, incense-holders, provided by all the churches of Rome. The latter (according to Cencio) were remunerated in their turn with another £33, distributed among as many as 313 churches, most of which, except the larger ones, got 6 *denarii* each.[23] We looked at the arches before (pp. 295–6), in the specific context of S. Maria Nova, where arch-makers in particular clustered. But here the context is a wider one. It shows that Easter Monday was the focus of considerable work by Romans; and also, importantly, of large annual financial distributions by the pope from the altar offerings of S. Pietro: £68 for the arches, plus the *iacta*, plus the equally substantial sums which went to the clerics who participated in every *statio* at S. Pietro, and also to several *scolae* of palatine staff—enough, I would guess, to make the annual expense of the Easter Monday *statio* and its processions up to the round £100 mark, far more even than at the *Letania maior*. This was in a period when, to give an order of comparison, house prices in the city rarely exceeded £5, except for towers, which could go for £12. So, not only the bustle, the excitement, and the impressiveness of the procession, but also the simple cost of it, was very great; and it took place every year. It is not surprising that Cencio, the financial official par excellence, felt impelled to itemize it. But it must also have been worth it. The fact that the same Easter Monday procession was enacted at a papal coronation is a clear indicator that the annual event represented the affirmation of papal authority in the city. Indeed, the processional celebrations (not least the arches) allowed narratives of the coronation of a pope to say that 'the whole city was crowned with him' (*tota civitas coronatur cum eo*): the city recognized papal authority, but was also itself made special at the same moment.[24] This evidently justified such a giant cost. But the fact that the cost was quite so high has other implications too, to which we will return.

I have been discussing four liturgical high points of the year, when the involvement of the Roman *populus*, however defined, was particularly marked. But we certainly cannot assume that the other, numerous, Roman *stationes* and other feast days involving processions were met with lay indifference. Sometimes our texts explicitly invoke the lay population on other occasions too, as when the *populus* awaited the pope's processional return from S. Maria Maggiore, in the Campus Lateranensis, during the feast of the Exaltation of the Cross.[25] But even if purely clerical events were so routine that lay Romans sometimes hardly turned their

---

[23] For the arches, see *LC*, II, p. 124 (Albino), I, pp. 299–304 (Cencio); Schimmelpfennig, 'Ein bisher unbekannter Text', p. 70 (Basel *ordo*). Twyman, *Papal Ceremonial*, pp. 210–14, again gives the best analysis. As she notes (p. 212), the earliest direct reference to them is *LP*, II, p. 377 (a. 1120, in a text written over forty years later), with, already, *Chronica Casinensis*, IV.64 (a. 1118) for a papal visit to Capua, *ornatis plateis et arcubus Romano more*.

[24] *LP*, II, p. 152 (a. 858); *Liber Pontificalis*, ed. Přerovský, p. 734 (a. 1118); *Historia Compostellana*, III.23 (p. 457, a. 1130); *Gesta Innocentii III*, ch. 7 (a. 1198); see Twyman, *Papal Ceremonial*, pp. 212–13. Tower price: *SMCM*, n. 60 (a. 1192).

[25] *LC*, II, pp. 151, 152, 155, 158, 159 (Exaltation)—all from Benedetto.

heads, they had an effect all the same. Laterano clergy, including the pope, regularly rode or walked the streets of the city: once every ten days at the least (following a positivist and minimalist reading of Benedetto). The pope, even if he was not always there, was far more visible to his subjects than any other ruler in Europe; only the Byzantine emperor, wrapped in a similar, and without doubt genealogically related, network of processional ritual, was equally visible.[26] These moments of visibility were very physical, with light, noise, incense smells, and bustle. And the processions created a liturgical geography which tied the whole of the city together. Neither the Laterano nor the Vaticano was situated in the inhabited areas of Rome (the Civitas Leoniana was certainly inhabited, but was clearly seen as separate in many respects from the *urbs*), but the fourteen annual *stationes* in S. Pietro had to involve processions crossing the urban centre, mostly along the via Sacra; and there were regular papal visits to other churches in the centre as well. Only the processions from the Laterano straight to S. Maria Maggiore, S. Croce in Gerusalemme, and S. Lorenzo fuori le Mura were purely in the *disabitato*, the barely populated eastern half of Rome. Otherwise, the regular passage of large groups of clergy marked the experience of every Roman; and often there was active lay involvement; and sometimes there was money too.

The laity also had their own autonomous moments. Benedetto records four, presumably because they each included an element of papal participation, or *laudes* celebrating the pope, so there could have been more of them; but we can certainly say that at least these four were fairly elaborate. On 31 December, boys in groups danced in front of the houses of the city beating drums, one of them masked *cum maza in collo* (with a club around his neck, as Fabre thought? Or a barley loaf, as Boiteux has proposed? Or did he have a mask in the form of a *mazzancolla*, a prawn?); then, on 1 January, two boys blessed each house with an olive branch and by throwing salt into the fire, receiving sweetmeats in return. This ceremony was a far cry from the great pre-Christian Kalends of January celebrations, some elements of which continued into the eighth century, to Pope Zacharias' (mild) embarrassment, but it certainly had roots as deep as that, and its propitiatory role is clear in the good fortune the two boys offered, 'tot filii, tot porcelli, tot agni'. These boys reappeared in the middle of Lent, as well, this time with lances, banners, and bells, singing elaborate *laudes* to the pope in front of each house (in Latin and half-remembered Greek), this time receiving eggs in return.[27]

Adults for their part—this time, certainly a large proportion of the city's male population—assembled on the first Sunday in Lent, in effect at the final moment of Carnival, divided between *equites* and *pedites* (above, pp. 264–5). First they drank, then the *equites* went to the Laterano with the urban prefect to meet the pope, who rode with them to Monte Testaccio to meet the *pedites*. There they performed

[26] Links and parallels with Constantinople: see e.g. Baldovin, *The Urban Character*, pp. 167–234; see further n. 35 below, and n. 66 for Milan.

[27] *LC*, II, pp. 172–3; Fabre, *Le polyptyque*, p. 25 for the club; Boiteux, 'Cornomania e carnevale', p. 61 for the loaf. For Zacharias, *S. Bonifatii et Lulli epistolae*, ed. Tangl, nn. 50–1. Whether or not Benedetto wrote this part of the text (see this chapter, n. 3), the *laudes* the boys sang celebrated Innocent II, so the date is right.

games, *ludus*, explicitly to set aside internal conflict, and killed a bear, a bullock, and a cock, representing respectively the Devil, pride, and unchastity. This is the first surviving reference to the Testaccio games, which remained important throughout the Middle Ages, and became increasingly elaborate, with the development of a bull-fight Spanish style (clearly extending out from the killing of the bullock in the mid-twelfth), as well as jousts and horse races. These are regulated at some length in the 1360 communal statutes, and by then, at least, were seen as games of the city as an organized community; this seems indeed to be the case in our period too, with Romans acting perhaps as a commune, perhaps as an army, but certainly as a single body.[28]

The dialectic between secular and ecclesiastical collectivity was probably clearest in the *laudes Cornomanniae*, celebrated on the first Saturday after Easter. This was a ceremony organized by the eighteen *diaconiae* of the city, which were explicitly called *parrochiae*, 'parishes', in Benedetto's text; the *populus* of each collected at the diaconal church, where they met the archpriest and the *mansionarius* of the *diaconia*, the *mansionarius* wearing for the occasion a crown of flowers shaped into horns and carrying a bronze tambourine (*phinobolum*) with bells attached to it. Each *populus* went to the Campus Lateranensis, where the pope came out to meet them, and they each arranged themselves in a circle and sang *laudes* to him, with the *mansionarius* leaping about in the middle of the circle banging his tambourine. Each archpriest then sat backwards on a donkey brought out by the palace officials, on whose head was held a basin full of 20 *solidi* of money; the archpriest had three chances to lunge backwards and grab handfuls of the money, and could keep what he grabbed. The clerics of each *diaconia* then put crowns at the feet of the pope, and three of the archpriests set animals free: S. Maria in Via Lata set free a fox, S. Maria in Aquiro a cock, S. Eustachio a deer. Everyone then went home, but the *mansionarius* later, still dressed up, went around the houses of the parish playing his tambourine as before, throwing laurel on the fires of each, and giving sugar-cakes to the children, in return for a money gift from each *dominus domus*, each householder.[29]

This ceremony has had a certain amount of fairly speculative analysis, focused on the symbolism of each of the—let's face it, odd—details.[30] I will not add to that, save to say that the word 'carnivalesque', used in some of these analyses, does not seem to me appropriate for an event after Easter, that is to say after Lent and the Christian renewal of the Resurrection had put an end to the instabilities of the Carnival season. There were obviously comic elements, but they should not be seen as carnivalesque inversions, Bakhtin-style; they were part of a sequence which had clear links to Easter Monday, five days earlier, with the *populus* in both cases

---

[28] *LC*, II, p. 172; for the later development of the games, Sommerlechner, 'Die ludi Agonis et Testatie'; Maire Vigueur, *L'autre Rome*, pp. 178–84; *Statuti della città di Roma*, II.48, III.75–85. By then they were associated with similar events in the Campus Agonis (piazza Navona), see below, n. 48.

[29] *LC*, II, pp. 171–2.

[30] García Villoslada, 'El himno al papa Juan (IX?)' (with some unconvincing chronological hypotheses); Liver, 'Cornomannia'; Boiteux, 'Cornomania e carnevale'; di Carpegna Falconieri, 'Gioco e liturgia'.

collected to recognize papal authority, and getting money in return, even if distributed here in a burlesque manner—for sitting backwards on a donkey (or camel) was part of formal humiliation rituals for political losers in Rome, which went back to the late empire and still continued in the twelfth century.[31] The key point was the collective association between the different parishes of the city and the pope, this time in a less religious and more festive context, which was then also closed by a festive version of the same blessing ritual that the boys performed on 1 January.

The *laudes Cornomanniae* were no longer practised by 1140. Benedetto says Gregory VII ended it, one assumes in the 1080s, because of 'the cost of the war', perhaps because, although a total expense of (up to) £18 is much less than the £100-odd of Easter Monday, it was still not a small figure; but it has to be said that many other ceremonies cost more too, and it may well also be that the *laudes* did not suit the tone of the new ecclesiastical system Gregory was committed to. (This is one of only two ceremonies in the *Liber politicus* which are explicitly said to have been changed.)[32] The *mansionarii* locate the ceremony in an earlier period too, for Leo IX and then Gregory VII moved sharply to remove this 'semi-lay' category of sacristans from Rome in the mid-eleventh century; Alexander II, between them, also did much to reverse the trend towards regarding the *diaconiae* as Rome's basic parish network. So Benedetto must have been here working from a text dating to the third quarter of the eleventh century at the latest.[33] The only other citation of the ceremony is in a poem from the 870s–80s by Giovanni Immonide, biographer of Gregory I, which refers to it as a *sacerdotalis lusus*, a 'priestly game', in which the pope 'plays' and the *prior scholae* is crowned with horns—evidently in the ninth century the ceremony was slightly, even if not very, different.[34] But we should not see the *laudes* as simply being part of the 'pre-reform' past; they fitted closely with the Easter Monday and other ceremonies, and also the Testaccio games, in that they linked the whole city both together in itself and with the pope, whose ceremonial role included that of a distributor of money to the people.

*

Processions had been going on in Rome for centuries, and were not at all controversial in our period as a means of creating ritual aggregation. It is very likely that the big ritual battles were fought in the late empire or just after, when the public ritual of the newly triumphant church took to (took over) the streets, replacing its pre-Christian predecessors. Already in the eighth and ninth centuries, the *Liber*

---

[31] See McCormick, *Eternal Victory*, pp. 135, 144, 181, 186 for Byzantine parallels, and p. 50 for the late Roman use of camels; pp. 303–4, 314 for the Visigoths. For Rome (and Nepi) in our period, see Pier Damiani, *Epistolae*, n. 89 (pp. 539–40, John XVI in 998); *LP*, II, pp. 252 (a. 967), 345 (a. 1101), 347–8 (Gregory VIII in 1121: see Schreiner, 'Gregor VIII., nackt auf einem Esel'), and Penteriani, *Nepi*, p. 143.

[32] *LC*, II, p. 171; the other change is to the Christmas *statio*, from S. Pietro to S. Maria Maggiore (p. 145), which had already happened by 1075 (*LP*, II, p. 282; Bonizone of Sutri, *Liber ad amicum*, VII, p. 606).

[33] For the *diaconiae*, di Carpegna Falconieri, *Il clero di Roma*, pp. 208–9, 216, and above, p. 307; for *mansionarii*, below, pp. 414–15.

[34] *MGH, Poetae*, IV, p. 870.

Pontificalis shows a processional landscape closely parallel to that of the eleventh and twelfth, and the detailed differences between them will be of interest, above all, to expert liturgists. Such processions were, of course, primarily religious, but they did not only have a religious dimension, and the Easter Monday procession in particular—not to speak of the lay ceremonies just discussed—was important for the perennial reinforcement of the city as a single body, of course under the rule of the pope. The processional construction of the city will have already been import-ant when, before 1000 or 1050, more of the population lived scattered across the hills, the Quirinale, Esquilino, or Celio (above, pp. 116–18); but, as argued in Chapter 5, the newly crystallizing urban *regiones* came to matter more in the following century, and they, too, could be brought together in the processional tradition. Rome, like Constantinople—but like few other contemporary western cities, almost all of which were far smaller—was continually re-enacted by this sequence of open-air liturgical and/or festive moments.

In Constantinople, the tradition focused on imperial and patriarchal processions from and to the Great Church, Hagia Sophia, at its far eastern tip, overlooking the Bosporos. Some went from there to extramural or intramural religious sites and returned; some went around the walls; imperial *adventus*, which was common, began outside the city walls at the other end of town, either at their northern or (more usually) their southern end, entering the city from the west and linking all of it to the city's ecclesiastical and political heart in the east.[35] In Rome, the situation was similar, but slightly simpler; processions essentially began at the Laterano palace, just inside the walls, and returned to there. The built-up area of the city was traversed by routes, which rarely started from the centre; it was as if the central core of the city was held up in a spider's web of routes whose ends were the Laterano and Vaticano, part of Rome but separate from it at the same time (see Map 9).

The Vaticano was, however, also technically extramural. This mattered too. The formal *adventus* ceremony in Rome, for emperors, as also for popes who were consecrated elsewhere or else who had fled the city for political reasons and now returned, began way out of the city (sometimes as far north as Sutri), with elaborate welcomes from the *scolae* of the city's *militia*, the laity in ceremonial form, bearing banners, as is well attested from the eighth century to the twelfth and beyond. That procession traditionally came directly to S. Pietro, which was its focus; and by the ninth century the imperial palace was situated there too. Emperors stopped at S. Pietro, and did not normally undertake a ceremonial entry into the city proper, which, unlike their counterparts in Constantinople, they did not rule. (The principal exception was Henry IV in 1084, whose coronation was followed by processions to Rome's major churches, including, we are told, a meeting with the *scolae* of Rome's *regiones* at S. Giovanni in Laterano; this was certainly intended as the taking possession of the city by a victorious ruler, but Henry soon left, and did not return to Rome.) New or returning popes, however, typically stopped at

---

[35] See Baldovin, *The Urban Character*, pp. 178–202; Brubaker, 'Topography and public space', pp. 38–43; Brubaker, 'Processions and public spaces'; Berger, 'Imperial and ecclesiastical processions'; and, for *adventus*, McCormick, *Eternal Victory*, pp. 131–230.

S. Pietro but then moved into the city, over the Ponte di S. Pietro and along the via Sacra into the Laterano. Popes who were elected and consecrated at S. Pietro itself did the same.[36] The Easter Monday return replicated that post-consecration route, as we have seen, and thus could be seen, in formal terms, as representing an *adventus* from outside the walls. Hence, maybe, the decorated arches: they were in response to the pope entering and taking possession of his city.

All the same, so few popes actually were elected and consecrated at S. Pietro after 1046 that the commonest ritual, by the mid-twelfth century, seems to have become different. By 1100 it was the enthronement of the pope at the Laterano which, in effect, marked his formal taking of power in the city. And actual papal *adventus* from the 1130s onwards were as often directly to the Laterano, through the Porta S. Giovanni, as via the routes from S. Pietro. So, by Cencio's time, the wider taking-possession ceremony seems to have normally started from the Laterano, then gone to S. Pietro the Sunday after the enthronement, then returned: that is to say, it was less a matter of popes *entering* the city from an external S. Pietro, and more a matter of them moving *inside* the city, between its two poles, the Laterano and the Vaticano, both of them simultaneously part of Rome and not fully part of it, building up the spider's web already mentioned.[37]

One point is worth underlining here, however: the relative unimportance of Rome's walls themselves. Imperial *adventus* was elaborate, but stopped outside them. It is true that a papal *adventus*, after coronation elsewhere or after disputes with the city and exile, was often also a very elaborate event too, increasingly focused on a formal urban reception at the Porta S. Giovanni, with clergy, *populus* waving olive branches, all the papal *scolae*, judges and *scriniarii*, and the Jews carrying their laws: the Easter Monday community all gathered in one spot.[38] All the same, as we shall see in a moment, these were one-off events, representing very tense peace-making, which often failed. The regular processions of our period, discussed above, did not make anything of any of Rome's gates. Nor were there ever any processions around or along the walls: such as the classic protective measures seen for so many cities, in crisis or not, in earlier medieval centuries, the most famous of which was the parading of another acheiropoietic icon of Christ along the walls of Constantinople during the failed Avar siege of 626.[39] Rome was besieged,

---

[36] Classic narratives of imperial *adventus* to S. Pietro are *LP*, I, pp. 496–7, II, pp. 6, 88; *Annales Bertiniani*, s.a. 864 (pp. 67–8); *Annales Fuldenses*, s.a. 896 (p. 128); with, for later accounts, Tellenbach, 'La città di Roma', pp. 711–19. For *ordines*, see *Ordines coronationis*, ed. Elze, esp. pp. 34–5, 36–47, 62–9. The first of these (XIII. 5) is the only one to indicate an imperial entry into Rome itself. For Henry IV, Benzone of Alba, *Ad Heinricum IV*, I. 9–12. For papal *adventus*, Twyman, *Papal Ceremonial*, pp. 41–144 is currently definitive.

[37] Twyman, *Papal Ceremonial*, pp. 92–144 (this paragraph simplifies a very complex sequence).

[38] Falcone, *Chronicon*, col. 1221 (a. 1133, with little detail); *LP*, II, pp. 387 (a. 1145), 413 (a. 1165), 446 (a. 1178).

[39] For 626, see as a guide Pentcheva, 'The supernatural protector of Constantinople'. For other early processions around walls, see lists in Wickham, *Framing*, pp. 662n, 679. Contrast Pope Stephen II in 752, faced with the Lombard threat: he 'proceeded with the litany in the usual way' with the Laterano acheiropoietic icon, ending up as usual in S. Maria Maggiore, and simply adding *diversa sacra mysteria* (relics?) to the normal procession to emphasize its propitiatory importance (*LP*, I, p. 443; see further below, n. 63). In Rome, in fact, the exception that proves the rule is *LP*, II, p. 124, in which

often enough, by German emperors, in our period; but it never responded in this way. Its religious ceremonial did not encircle the city at all, and only relatively rarely even marked entry into the city. This marked Rome out from other cities, even from Constantinople, whose walls were as long. The *joyeuse entrée* bibliography, so generous for the early modern period, shows how important walls were in the cities of most of Europe, as markers of the start of major ceremonial moments. Even internally, the great St John's Day procession in late medieval Florence still processed around (most of) the old walls of the city—not the newer and longer late thirteenth-century walls, it is true, but encircling the old centre all the same.[40] But Rome was so big that its walls did not have to come into play in its normal ritual life. And, one is tempted to say, Rome was so self-absorbed that ritual protection may have seemed less relevant. Instead, the issue was internal structuration and unification, both religious (the joining together of relatively distant sacred spaces) and collective, involving both the ecclesiastical and the lay members of urban society; this is something that Roman ceremonial was amply concerned with.

The Campus Lateranensis, on the other hand, was an important space on its own account. It is here, a kilometre from the closest settled *regio* but inside the walls and just outside the papal palace, to the latter's north and west, that the pope could meet the Roman people, both literally and figuratively. The Roman aristocracy was, of course, familiar with the palace, internally as well as externally; by contrast, most of the *populus* did not get through its gate. But the *populus* did go to the Campus, to appeal to papal justice, to acclaim a new pope, to await the pope at the Exaltation of the Cross feast, or (until the 1080s) to perform the *laudes Cornomannie*. This is why the Campus was the location for some quite conscious pieces of papal self-presentation in material form. Perhaps the most important was the bronze statue of the Romulean she-wolf, a later version of which is now in the Musei Capitolini, which was considered by ninth- and tenth-century writers as *mater Romanorum*; this statue overlooked the place where popes did justice by the end of the ninth century, and Ingo Herklotz (whose important work I follow in this paragraph and the next two) has shown that it probably stood, throughout the medieval period, in or on the external portico of the papal palace, the same portico from which Hadrian I in the late eighth century, and perhaps his successors, had food distributed daily to Rome's *pauperes*. Charity, justice, and Roman origins were thus physically linked to the popes, and located at the entry to their palace in the Campus. By the thirteenth century at the latest, there was an inscription in bronze containing a law of Vespasian there too, which again attached the image of justice to the papacy. And there were other external statues located in the Campus as well: that of Marcus

Leo IV led the whole Roman clergy around the walls of the Civitas Leoniana in *c*.852, after its construction: for this was an extramural fortification. The imagery of the protective procession was thus evidently as well-known in Rome as elsewhere; but it was never used for Rome's own walls. Wolf, 'Icons and sites', p. 36 cites a Byzantine text of *c*.900 which refers to a procession around Rome's walls with an icon of Mary to ward off plague—presumably that of S. Maria Maggiore, and possibly referring to the plague of 590. This account has no resonance in Rome itself, and is most likely to reflect the assumptions of an inhabitant of Constantinople, where such processions had more of a history.

[40] Trexler, *Public Life*, pp. 250–1. See below, n. 59, for other bibliography.

Aurelius on a horse, the one now situated in the piazza del Campidoglio, which was believed to be a statue of Constantine; and the fragments of a huge stone imperial statue which are again now in the Musei Capitolini, a statue which this time really was of Constantine, but was then seen more generically as representing the city in its imperial role.[41]

Herklotz proposes that this sculpture gallery was essentially the work of Hadrian I.[42] His argument is attractive, although (as he stresses) hypothetical; but it is anyway certain that the wolf and Marcus Aurelius were there in the tenth century, by the start of our period, and likely enough that the others were too. What is important, however, is that whenever the *populus* or its individual members (including, as we have seen, the poor) came to the Laterano, it was this set of highly symbolic objects that they saw, essentially representing papal authority in the city. The Laterano was thus not only a somewhat distant palace, in the middle of vineyards and ruins, away from the daily activity of the city, but also a visible centre of political and ideological power. This was made clear every time Romans came to the Campus, in the heightened circumstances of religious ritual, which for many of them was twice a year at least—and for the most destitute, at least in the eighth century, could even be daily.

This was a long-standing situation; but the Campus Lateranensis was charged enough that it could allow more targeted interventions. The statue of Marcus Aurelius was particularly important here as a representation of right rule; the urban prefect Pietro, who had expelled John XIII from Rome in 965, was hung by his hair from it when the pope returned with Ottonian support a year later; when the controversial Pope Boniface VII died in 985, the *populus* dragged his body through the streets and left it under the same statue.[43] (It may be surprising that such an act did not occur more often, given the unpopularity of other popes too, but this, like the Synod of the Corpse in 897, may have seemed too extreme to repeat.) In the twelfth century, around 1140, Innocent II added to the sculpture gallery, by transporting the porphyry sarcophagus thought to be of the emperor Hadrian from Castel S. Angelo to the Campus, which added further to the imperial symbolism of the area. This addition was short-lived, for Innocent intended the sarcophagus to be his own tomb, and when he died it was moved again, to inside

[41] Herklotz, 'Der Campus lateranensis', revised and translated in *Gli eredi di Costantino*, pp. 41–94, is the most recent and best account of this. As usual, Richard Krautheimer got the main point earlier: *Rome*, pp. 192–7. For the she-wolf and the sculpture gallery, see also Erler, *Lupa, Lex und Reiterstandbild*. The surviving statue has now been shown on scientific grounds to be medieval, not Etruscan or Roman: see Carruba, *La Lupa Capitolina* (who shows that it is not antique, but hypothesizes a Carolingian date); and the technical articles in Bartoloni (ed.), *La lupa capitolina*, which, although discordant, lean towards a thirteenth-century date. (The counter-arguments in the same book do not convince. Alföldi et al., *Die römische Wölfin*, does not carry the debate usefully on.) But the wolf, if later than our period, must, of course, have had predecessors, given our written sources. I am very grateful to Giuliano Milani for advice and bibliography here. For the *lupa* as *mater Romanorum*, see *Libellus de imperatoria potestate*, p. 199; Benedetto of Monte Soratte, *Chronicon*, p. 145. For Hadrian I and the poor, *LP*, I, p. 502.

[42] Herklotz, *Gli eredi di Costantino*, pp. 75–87, and (explicit about the speculative nature of the argument) 214.

[43] *LP*, II, pp. 252, 259.

the basilica of S. Giovanni at the back of the Campus; all the same, the temporary display was significant. Innocent was not the only post-1046 pope to choose a classical sarcophagus for his tomb, but he chose the most symbolically significant one we know about, and his choice to display it first of all in the Campus marks a personalization of the imperial claims of the popes, a specific attachment of them to himself, which was remarkably overt.[44]

This fits Innocent II's personal tendency to very particular acts of power, as we shall see (pp. 432–4). He was not the only pope of the period to claim an authority that could be represented as imperial, both in the sense that he ruled in Rome as the heir of the classical emperors, and in the sense that he could deal with the German emperors as an equal and perhaps as a superior.[45] But Innocent, himself a Roman, here had Romans very specifically in his sights. It was them whom he was seeking to overawe and subjugate. This did not entirely work, as the establishment of the Senate on the Capitolio in 1143, when he was dying, shows; but that was a revolt against the pope who had tried harder to dominate the city, in highly authoritarian ways, than had any of his predecessors for a century. His Hadrianic addition to the Campus Lateranensis was part of that, and again it shows the importance of the area to the popes for the establishment of power.

The Campus Lateranensis was not Rome's only charged space. The Platea S. Petri was another, one where papal dominance was never contested by the Romans, for it was located in the pope's own Civitas Leoniana; but this square, bordered by palaces of both pope and emperor as it was, was the classic locus of opposition between the latter two, the literal field of battle on numerous occasions, as imperial visits went wrong, in 864, or 1014, or 1027, or 1111.[46] A third was the Foro Romano, on the via Sacra between the Laterano and the Vaticano. At its eastern end, S. Maria Nova, with its important icon of Mary, was a frequent stopping point for papal processions; but it was S. Adriano in Foro that appeared particularly often as a focus (as at the Assumption), or a starting point (as at the Purification), or as a site of popular assembly to receive money (as on Easter Monday). Why S. Adriano? It was a church since *c.*630, a *diaconia* since *c.*780, but does not appear as a major centre for political events in other respects; it was chosen as a meeting point for the rival factions of cardinals as Honorius II was dying in 1130, but only after a long discussion. But S. Adriano had been, in the classical period, the Senate House. I doubt that the Romans still knew that, for it is not so identified in the *Mirabilia* of *c.*1140, where its classical name is claimed to be the

---

[44] Herklotz, *Gli eredi di Costantino*, pp. 19–28 (with reference to other papal sarcophagi), 41. The main early source for Innocent here is the *Mirabilia* of 1140–3, p. 47, cf. pp. 14–15 (Innocent is not explicitly mentioned in the earliest manuscripts, but is in two from the 1190s). The sarcophagus was destroyed in the great fire at S. Giovanni of 1308, and Innocent was moved to S. Maria in Trastevere.

[45] Herklotz, *Gli eredi di Costantino*, pp. 95–158, and Stroll, *Symbols as Power*, pp. 180–93, stress this in particular.

[46] *Annales Bertiniani*, s.a. 864 (pp. 67–8, with the critical analysis of Buc, *The Dangers of Ritual*, pp. 70–9, an analysis valid for other such events too); Thietmar, *Chronicon*, VII.1; Wipo, *Gesta Chuonradi*, ch. 16; MGH, *Constitutiones*, I, n. 99 (for 1111, mostly from *LP*, II, pp. 338–43) with *Liber Pontificalis*, ed. Přerovský, pp. 714–16.

templum Refugii.[47] But they are much more likely to have known it in the eighth and ninth centuries, when many details of these ceremonies developed. For whichever reason, the Foro did still have quite a marked ritual centrality, even if not one that was visibly manipulated in our period for political purposes.

The other charged space was, of course, Rome's streets: the via Sacra above all, and secondly the streets from S. Adriano to S. Maria Maggiore, and the via Merulana from there back to the Laterano; but others too. These were interactive, particularly the via Sacra, as shown by the Easter Monday arches: they were foci for popular commitment, not just ecclesiastical self-presentation. Here it is simply worth noting that not all streets had this role; in particular, the via Lata, probably always Rome's biggest and most important thoroughfare, saw no known processions after the *Letania maior* was moved from S. Lorenzo in Lucina. The popes did not seek to appropriate every public space in the city; just those which were symbolically important to them.

The spaces in the city which were symbolically loaded in non-papal ways were, as far as we can see, fewer. (I say 'non-papal' rather than 'secular', for there was also religious symbolism attached to most of the following.) Monte Testaccio was one, but only for one day a year. The Campus Agonis (piazza Navona) may already have been the military training ground it would become in later centuries, although we have no clear notice of that yet.[48] The Senate's respect for the Colonna di Traiano (it was the object of senatorial protection in 1162[49]) may argue that this monument had a longer-term significance too. Our sources are so ecclesiastical that we cannot be certain of others, but the *Mirabilia*, not an especially papal text, gives little special prominence to most other public locations in its lists of monuments and its tour around the city. Castel S. Angelo mattered to Romans, for sure; its origin as Hadrian's mausoleum was perfectly well-known to them (to the author of the *Mirabilia*, for example), and its common appellation, the *castellum Crescentii*, after Crescenzio di Crescenzio's defence of it against Otto III in 998, shows that that traumatic event marked urban memory for centuries.[50] Castel S. Angelo, apparently exposed on the wrong side of the river, was in reality impregnable as a fortification; Crescenzio was the only defender to give in, vanquished by famine, and both Honorius II/Cadalo of Parma in 1064 and Gregory VII in 1084 held out in it, in the latter case for over two months. Its role as a fortification was, however,

---

[47] For S. Adriano, see *LP*, I, pp. 324, 509–10; *Historia Compostellana*, III.23 (p. 456; letter of the *universus Romanae urbis clerus et populus* to Diego of Compostela, a. 1130); *Mirabilia*, pp. 54–5. Paschal II restored it in 1100–01: see, in general, Claussen, *Die Kirchen der Stadt Rom*, I, pp. 21–38.

[48] The Campus Agonis was known as such from 958 (*LL*, n. 279), and is attested in numerous eleventh-century Farfa charters, but not in twelfth-century documents. The later jousting in the Campus Agonis (see refs. in n. 28) is not recorded in our period, but Vendittelli, 'Il *Campus Agonis*', plausibly proposes that its maintenance as an open and public space in earlier centuries, plus its name, argue for an earlier use of it by the city as a military training ground of some type.

[49] *SMVL*, n. 196; see below, n. 159.

[50] *Mirabilia*, pp. 46–7. The *castellum Crescentii* is referred to in the same source, p. 23, and in *Senato*, n. 41 (a. 1188); and by a host of narratives, largely external to the city, such as Arnolfo of Milan, *Liber gestorum*, III.17; Benzone of Alba, *Ad Heinricum IV*, VI. Praef; Ekkehard of Aura, *Chronicon*, p. 205; Gaufredo Malaterra, *De rebus gestis*, III.33, 37; *Tractatus Garsiae*, p. 22; Widone of Ferrara, *De scismate*, I.20; Otto of Freising, *Chronica*, VII.6, 14; Bosone, *LP*, II, p. 392.

as much papal as Roman, and it was a location one needed to control militarily, quite as much as a symbolic centre.[51]

Really, the only major non-papal—indeed, this time, fully secular—focus was the Capitolio. It was the location of the city's great market (above, p. 127), and it was seen as having once been (to quote the *Mirabilia*) the 'head of the earth (*caput mundi*), where consuls and senators used to live to govern the world': it, not S. Adriano, was thus recognized in those years as the ancient Republican centre of the city. It was a genuine centre of lay power. The Corsi, one of the most prominent families of the 'new aristocracy' (above, pp. 226–8), put their houses there; the *maxima multitudo* of Romans, including high aristocrats, who met Benzone of Alba in 1062 in his imperial mission on behalf of Cadalo, met him in the *palatium Octaviani* there; Henry IV in 1084 set up his own *domus* there— and not on Otto III's Palatino—once he had taken the city; the *Tractatus Garsiae* saw Urban II's occupation of the Capitolio as a metonym for his takeover of Rome at the end of 1098; Henry V met the *ordines* of the city there in 1117; and, of course, it was there that the Senate was located when it was (re-)established in 1143.[52] The senators built their own *palatium* there very fast, by 1151 at the latest, on the Tabularium at the back of the modern piazza del Campidoglio (far earlier than any other purpose-built communal *palazzo* in Italy); it may well be that it was also then or soon after that they set up the great Egyptian obelisk, with four lions at the base, that represented the commune for the rest of the Middle Ages (it survives today in the Villa Celimontana). The obelisk, set beside the Tabularium, over-looked the Foro Romano and the via Sacra up to the Laterano, and can easily be seen as a monumental reply to the Campus Lateranensis.[53] The foundation of the senatorial *palatium* also re-centred the city. Up to 1150, Rome had been suspended between the Laterano and the Vaticano, but now it had a formalized political focus, which has remained (outlasting the medieval commune itself) ever since. The processional routes—which tended to avoid hills where they could, for understand-able reasons—did not move, but they wound around and were overlooked by the senatorial power centre from now on.

The rhetoric of building and of monumentality in Rome in our period was very frequently expressed in terms of classical objects. The wolf (in an earlier version), Marcus Aurelius, the Capitoline obelisk, the Colonna di Traiano, and, of course, Castel S. Angelo, were just some of the many classical survivals that were employed here. Indeed, every one of the major classical buildings still existing inside Rome has at least some citation in our period, and most have numerous references. One would have to go well into the *disabitato*, to the Terme di Caracalla south of the

---

[51] For Cadalo, *LP*, II, p. 337; for Gregory, see Cowdrey, *Pope Gregory VII*, pp. 229–30. See, in general, D'Onofrio, *Castel S. Angelo*, pp. 113–42, with caution.

[52] *Mirabilia*, p. 51; *LP*, II, p. 290 with *RF*, n. 1097 for the Corsi and Henry IV; *Chronica Casinensis*, III.67; Benzone of Alba, *Ad Heinricum IV*, II.1; *Tractatus Garsiae*, p. 22; *Udalrici codex*, n. 178.

[53] Gramaccini, 'La prima riedificazione', pp. 34–9 (his link between the obelisk and rights over justice seems to me to go too far, though); Maire Vigueur, *L'autre Rome*, p. 311.

Aventino, to find a really neglected monument.[54] They were simply an ever-present part of the landscape. It is sometimes commented on in Britain that there is a wide cultural gap between a passer-by, perhaps an older one by now, who will give you directions in terms of churches ('go left at St Peter's, and right at the Methodist chapel'), and one who will do it in terms of pubs ('go along past the Red Lion, and right at the King's Arms'). It is thus interesting that Benedetto, when tracking papal processions, was so prone to give directions in terms of classical buildings, not churches. Here he is going from S. Anastasia on the Circo Massimo to the Ponte S. Pietro during the former Christmas procession: go by the *porticus Gallatorum*, and the *templum Sibille*, between the *templum Ciceronis* and the *templum Crinorum*, between the *basilica Iovis* and the *circus Flamineus*, by the *porticus Severinus*, the *templum Craticule* and the *insula Militena*, down to the *via Arenule*, past the *theatrum Antonini* and the *palatium Chromatii*, and under the *arcus Gratiani, Theodosii et Valentiniani*, to the bridge. Or again, going through the Foro Romano on Easter Monday: past the *privata Mamertini*, through the triumphal arch between the *templum Fatale* and the *templum Concordia*, between the *forum Traiani* and the *forum Cesaris*, through the *arcus Nerve*, between the temple of 'the same goddess' (Nerva??) and the *templum Iani*, up past the *asilum* by the path where Simon Magus fell, by the *templum Romuli*, to the *arcus Titi et Vespasiani* and the triumphal arch of Constantine.[55]

These are recognizable routes (particularly the second, traversing the archaeological zone of the Foro's ancient monuments as it does), but there is one significant absentee: anything medieval. Only Simon Magus is even a Christian image. The first route began in Ripa, full of important tower-houses, then went past S. Nicola in Carcere, S. Angelo in Pescheria, and probably S. Lorenzo in Damaso. The second went past S. Adriano, SS. Cosma e Damiano in Foro, and S. Maria Nova. All of these were important churches (and there were many others too), and S. Adriano and S. Maria Nova had considerable processional significance. They disappear from this mental geography nonetheless. Benedetto's text is not simply classicizing; where his processional accounts included ceremonial stops—that is, when he was not simply giving directions—he immediately switched to churches.[56] But, when he gave directions, he overwhelmingly thought in classical terms.

We will look again at the way the imagery of the classical world was used in our period in a moment. But it is important to recognize, before we do so, that, notwithstanding the rhetoric of *renovatio* of the Roman past of some twelfth-century writers and very many twentieth-century writers, there was interestingly little to renew. Romans had forgotten the real identity of the statue of Marcus Aurelius, and also, probably, that S. Adriano had once been the Senate House (they did not change their minds in our period, either), but it is quite striking how many

---

[54] The Terme di Caracalla are, nonetheless, cited by the *Mirabilia*, p. 20. Innocent II used their columns, perhaps the last complete set surviving in Rome's classical buildings, to rebuild S. Maria in Trastevere: Kinney, 'S. Maria in Trastevere', p. 319.

[55] *LC*, II, pp. 145, 154. See Kinney, 'Fact and fiction', who compares the first of these with the *Mirabilia*, shows that the identifications are not ridiculous, and defends Benedetto from the charge of antiquarian copying.

[56] e.g. *LC*, II, p. 156 for the *Letania maior*.

names Benedetto got roughly right. The *Mirabilia* attach many fantastic stories to monuments, but they are not, taking everything together, all that inaccurate either.[57] To manipulate the she-wolf, or the sarcophagus of Hadrian, was to use images which were permanently available, and did not have to be rediscovered: they were part not of the past, but of the present. They were like the ever-relevant symbolism of Michelangelo's 500-year-old Campidoglio today. So were all the temples that the clerics of Benedetto's processions walked by, for all that they were in ruins and had been, for centuries by now, used above all as quarries. In a way, this makes one issue I raised at the start of this chapter—why Rome did not fragment conceptually or politically—easier to deal with: because the city's settlement areas were not separated by fields of generic ruins, but by real classical buildings, with their own identities, even if in a highly dilapidated state.

All the same, the processional landscape that has been discussed in these last pages was of crucial importance. Romans were very attached to their *regiones*, and probably did not often move house from one to another. It is far from impossible that one might have found Romans who claimed never to have been outside them,[58] just as modern sociologists find twenty-first-century inhabitants of south London who claim they have never been north of the river, or inhabitants of the *sassi* of Matera who never went through the threatening archways into the *borghese* main street at the top of town until the cave dwellings were cleared in the 1950s. But Romans in our period did travel, processionally, and on a regular basis, and even more frequently they watched others doing the same. (The relative centralization of the city's economy, argued for in Chapter 3, also makes it likely that more Romans went to the Campidoglio market than that regional loyalty might imply.) There were moments in the year in which very many Romans would have found themselves in the Campus Lateranensis, and around several stational churches. The city was constructed performatively, under their feet, as they did so.

The bibliography on *adventus* and the *joyeuse entrée* largely focuses on major and dramatic single events—Constantius II's Roman triumphal entry in 357, so critically written up by Ammianus Marcellinus; Charles V or Henri II ceremonially entering Ghent in 1540 or Rouen in 1550; the contestation of the ceremonial traditions of Florence by new social groups (and the rising Medici, and Savonarola) in the fifteenth century; or the contestation of the processional landscape of Lyon between Catholics and Protestants in the mid-sixteenth. There is no doubt that these single events were dramatic in their effect—or at least in the narrativization of their effect, as Philippe Buc stresses, for each of our accounts of them is seeking to make points to its readers/hearers, rather than to give us unmediated reportage.[59]

[57] Kinney, 'Fact and fiction'.

[58] For the continuing (until very recently) social tightness of some Roman *rioni* see Herzfeld, *Evicted from Eternity*.

[59] MacCormack, *Art and Ceremony*, pp. 40–5; Waite, *Reformers on Stage*, pp. 158–9; Russell and Visentin, *French Ceremonial Entries*, e.g. pp. 29–54, 73–110; Trexler, *Public Life*, pp. 365–547; Davis, 'The sacred and the body social'—only a small percentage of the huge bibliography here. One exception, on the tradition of episcopal *adventus*, is Miller, 'The Florentine bishop's ritual entry'

But their effect (either in life, or in narrative) always depended on expectations of norms. It was precisely because everyone knew what the normal patterns of procedure were in the triumphal *adventus* processions in Constantinople that it mattered that the emperor John I in 971 was met by the patriarch outside the city gate, not at the Forum of Constantine, for example.[60] Minor changes in a processional geography could be read for their meaning, just as Kremlinologists worked out the changing political balance in the pre-1990 Politburo from the ordering of politicians on the balcony overlooking Red Square parades. But there needed to be that geography first for the meaning to be visible.

There are several issues that need to be untangled here. The first is that single, one-off, events were important, and had to be orchestrated effectively. The reception of Eugenius III in December 1145 at the Porta S. Giovanni by a crowd of people, *signiferi* with banners, *scriniarii*, judges, Jews, and the Roman clergy was not just the formal *adventus* of a newly consecrated pope; it followed his flight from Rome before his consecration in the spring of the same year because he would not recognize the Roman Senate, and the subsequent compromise agreement over the terms of papal recognition. Even then, the compromise did not hold, and Eugenius left Rome early in 1146, not to return until the end of 1149, when a new agreement was reached. A very similar *adventus* marked Alexander III's return to Rome in 1165 after the schism at his election in 1159 and the death of his rival Victor IV in 1164; Alexander had had little support in the city, so the reception had to be particularly elaborate, and Bosone's (pro-papal) narration of the event puts a lot of stress on the participation of *senatores cum nobilibus et magna cleri ac populi multitudo*, as well as *signiferi, scriniarii*, judges, and Jews again. This time he stayed nearly five years, weathering the German assaults on the city in 1166–7 with at least intermittent Roman support; the ceremonial worked, that is to say. But we can assume that it was nonetheless tense.[61] The narrativization of both events stresses their success, but this is part of the purpose of narratives. That for Eugenius could have been written up in a very different way, had we a senatorial account written after Eugenius had left Rome again. This was certainly the case for the failed, or, one could say, 'bad', *adventus* of Henry V to the Civitas Leoniana for his coronation as emperor in S. Pietro in 1111, which ended up with a pitched battle and the imprisonment of Pope Paschal II, a story told in a very different way by each side.[62] But the elements in play in the two papal *adventus* narratives, the particular groups of people and their banners, and so on, were those we are familiar with from all our

(which in fact argues for a direct effect of twelfth-century Roman rituals on those of northern Italy). On narrativization, see Buc, *The Dangers of Ritual*, pp. 15–157.

[60] McCormick, *Eternal Victory*, pp. 171–3. John I had temporarily been banned from the Great Church by the previous patriarch for his murder of his predecessor Nikephoros II, and this meeting at the gate showed clearly the end of patriarchal hostility.

[61] *LP*, II, pp. 387, 413; see Twyman, *Papal Ceremonial*, pp. 97–101.

[62] For the pope's side, see this chapter, n. 46; for Henry's side, e.g. Ekkehard of Aura, *Chronicon*, pp. 244–5; Otto of Freising, *Chronica*, VII.14 (more neutral). Compare once again Buc, *The Dangers of Ritual*, pp. 70–9, for 864.

other processional accounts. These were the dramatis personae of papal ceremony of all kinds.[63]

And that is the key point. These politically important, and dramatic, moments needed to draw on all of the regular ceremony of the ritual year to have any real purchase at all. But it was that regularity which marked real, permanent, acceptance of the political system of the city. When the pope was in Rome and accepted as ruler by its inhabitants, the Easter Monday procession, with his participation, was far more important for his stable political position than any one-off event. It was regularity, not a simple ad hoc ceremonial moment, that established rights. We see this sort of distinction made explicitly over and over in twelfth-century Italian legal disputes: repetition—of rent-taking, or of local church election procedures— established rights. Direct action, the unusual single event, did, it is true, set up a claim to a right. The violent invasion of land was a claim to possess it; the seizure of the keys to a church could be a claim to control the election of its priest. But for direct action to work in law, it had to be accepted, however unwillingly, by the other side—it had to start turning into a regularity. If the other side resisted, or went straight to court, then direct action was not probative.[64] So it was with papal *adventus* in Rome: if it failed to stick, as with Eugenius in 1145, although not with Alexander in 1165 (for a few years at least), then the ceremonial commitment was wasted, effectively valueless. The Romans meeting Eugenius III in December 1145 expected to see him processing on the next Easter Monday, which would have been much more significant for his authority. But he had abandoned the Laterano for Trastevere already in January 1146, and by Easter he had left the city altogether.[65] The negotiations therefore all had to begin again.

The regularity of procession, conversely, could itself be a stage for direct action: for the disruption of procession and other ceremonies was a particularly potent performative act, highly public, highly charged, and indeed upsetting to participants. In Milan, for example, when Archbishop Guido was excommunicated in 1066 by Alexander II for simony through the intervention of the leaders of the Pataria, Erlembaldo and Arialdo, Guido chose Pentecost to denounce the events from the cathedral pulpit; when Erlembaldo and Arialdo denounced him back in

---

[63] Note also the absence of relics in these accounts of one-off ceremonials. The use of relics by Stephen II in an earlier propitiatory act in 752 (above, n. 39) was atypical, and not repeated. It is true that popes between 750 and 850 moved many relics from suburban churches and catacombs to intramural churches with papal associations, in a clear centralization of spiritual power (see, most recently, Goodson, *The Rome of Paschal I*, pp. 197–256, 273–8); but they were not used transactionally in other respects, either then or later. That is to say, despite the huge collections of relics inside Rome as a result, above all in the Laterano but also in several other churches, and their standard use in many liturgical contexts (as with the icon of Christ for the Assumption), they were strikingly rarely used to make political points in the city, in strong contrast to the situation in Francia (cf., for example, Costambeys and Leyser, 'To be the neighbour of St Stephen', set against Smith, 'Old saints, new cults', for Frankish uses of Roman relics). The only relics in our period which produced politically controversial miracles were those of Clement III after 1100 (see p. 425). See also Chapter 4, n. 58, for miracles at SS. Bonifacio e Alessio being used, in a standard European way, to establish a cult; but that was of a new saint, a rarity in the city. I benefited here greatly from discussion with Julia Smith.

[64] Wickham, *Courts and Conflict*, pp. 83–8 and *passim*.

[65] Jaffé and Wattenbach, *Regesta pontificum*, II, pp. 29–32.

the church, there was an uprising against them and Arialdo was murdered shortly after. (We have the accounts of both sides here, and they roughly match, though they differ as to how much support the laity gave to the Pataria at the time.) It is evident that the Patarini deliberately chose to disrupt an episcopally dominated ceremony here, although it is probable that on this occasion they miscalculated and lost support.[66] In Rome, too, it was at the S. Maria Maggiore *statio* on Christmas night in 1075 that Cencio di Stefano kidnapped Gregory VII, although a popular uprising released him the following day. This was a remarkably overt act during one of the major ceremonies of the year, which must have been intended to make a major public point—even if the hostile voices which dominate our accounts of the event entirely hide what point it was.[67] A more successful example was the disruption in 1203 by the lords of Poli, who were being cheated out of their lands by Riccardo, brother of Innocent III, of the Easter Monday procession itself: they interrupted mass in S. Pietro, and abused the pope on his return walk. This very public assertion of rights gained substantial popular support, and Innocent had considerable trouble countering it.[68] A later instance was during the Assumption procession of (probably) 1239, when, at the moment when the icon of Christ was placed in the atrium of S. Maria Nova, some *blasphemi* called out a slogan in support of Frederick II: not a very significant act, one might think, but the fact that it got into the biography of Gregory IX shows, once again, how charged the moment was.[69]

Probably the best example of the disruption of the Roman ceremonial world to make a point in our period was Easter 1116. Pietro 'I' the urban prefect had just died; his supporters wanted his son Pietro 'II' to replace him; Paschal II wanted another candidate, apparently a son of Pietro di Leone, the first of the Pierleoni. There had already been some public trouble in S. Giovanni in Laterano on Easter Thursday, where the breaking of a vase of consecrated oil caused a certain upset; Pietro the younger then came into the church with torn clothing (*scissis vestibus*) to make his case during mass, to the indignation of the pope. His supporters gathered over the next days, and on Easter Monday blocked *cum tumultu* the outgoing procession at the *pons Traiani* (presumably Ponte S. Pietro), with Pietro again seeking confirmation in office, and they stoned the return procession from the Capitolio as well. By the end of the same week, Paschal had abruptly left for Albano; and Pietro 'II' remained in office. Our only detailed source for this focuses on the appalling behaviour of Pietro and his supporters—that is, the narrativization is one of improper, and by implication, non-probative behaviour—but the latter

---

[66] Arnolfo, *Liber gestorum*, III.18; Landolfo Seniore, *Historia Mediolanensis*, III.18 (the vaguest); Andrea of Strumi, *Vita Arialdi*, ch. 19 (and p. 1064n). Note that Milan also had a significant processional tradition, as is shown in the early twelfth-century *ordo* of Beroldo, a contemporary of Benedetto in Rome (*Beroldus*, esp. pp. 57–62, 83, 96–100, 113, 117–18, 122–6); but the twenty-odd processions described there were nearly all of clergy alone, and only the Palm Sunday procession across the city (pp. 96–7) had a substantial popular participation.

[67] Bonizone of Sutri, *Liber ad amicum*, VII (p. 606) is the core text; see Borino, 'Cencio del prefetto Stefano', pp. 431–6 for all the accounts; see further above, Chapter 4, n. 127.

[68] *Gesta Innocentii III*, chs 137–8.

[69] *Vita Gregorii IX*, ch. 42 (*LC*, II, p. 34). Cf. Ehrle, 'Die Frangipani', pp. 460–1.

had clearly played on the exceptional public sacrality of the Easter period with considerable effect, building up popular support across the days as they did so. It is also significant that (together with the 'bad' *adventus* of Henry V in 1111) this is virtually the only Roman event in Paschal's pontificate to reach the ears of non-Roman chroniclers; it had a resonance that echoed far beyond the Aurelian Walls.[70]

The force of the events of 1116, or 1203, lay in part in their rarity; if every Easter Monday had seen trouble of this kind, the force of each contestation—and of the processional event itself—would have been diminished. It was precisely the *uncontested* regularity of most such Easter celebrations which meant that the occasional big disruption was so serious a matter. The players were gambling for big stakes. But the possibility of disruption, however rare, also helped to keep the meaning of the celebrations in people's minds. Essentially, the fact that such events occurred in this way shows how important Easter Monday, or Christmas, or the Assumption, really were for Romans. Of course, these days were religiously important for any Christian, that is to say, for all of the city's non-Jewish inhabitants. But it was the great elaboration of the ceremonies on such days, a specifically Roman development, which created such an important public space for occasional one-off dramas. These were charged moments, and they had big audiences. Political points could be made all the more effectively. Conversely, when they were not, which was most of the time, the 'normal' political meanings of the ceremonies were regularly reinforced. The special nature of Rome; its unification through the regularity of processional routes; and papal authority over this special city—all these were constantly re-emphasized. This did not by any means signify that papal rule was actually accepted in the city, least of all in the crisis century which began in the 1040s, and then in the first decades of the Senate that followed. But it did mean that a version of a 'normal' papal authority never vanished; it also meant that the Senate was set quite a ceremonial challenge when it sought to establish its own autonomy after 1143. It tried to meet the challenge, but arguably it was too great a task, and the Senate in the end failed.

These observations can, however, also be reversed. Events like the Easter Monday procession were also moments for the affirmation of the coherence of the Roman *populus*, whose participation is constantly referred to in our sources. Papal authority was systematically reinforced in these rituals, and their evident penitential and propitiatory elements anyway implied the importance of the church (headed by the pope) which directed such penitential activity. All the same, popular participation had its own reinforcing role. This was not just a processional world for the clergy. There was a formal role for the armed laity in several ceremonies (particularly *adventus*), still described in this period with the early medieval terminology of the *scola militum* (cf. above, p. 263).[71] The *populus* was also integrally involved in a large number of different ceremonial days. *Nobiles* may have routinely ridden or

---

[70] *Liber pontificalis*, ed. Přerovský, pp. 717–21; cf., in less detail, *LP*, II, p. 344; Falcone, *Chronicon*, col. 1167; *Chronica Casinensis*, IV.60.

[71] Sigebert of Gembloux, *Chronica*, p. 369 (a. 1105); *LP*, II, p. 446 (a. 1179); cf. *S. Alessio*, n. 14. The 1179 reference relates to an *adventus*.

walked with the pope, as the urban prefect and (later) the senators certainly did; but a much wider portion of the city was often there as well, both as spectators and participants, and this portion could sometimes (Easter Monday; the *laudes Cornomanniae*; the Testaccio games) extend to nearly everyone. As we have also seen, Jews were also on occasion swept into this ceremonial space; when that happened, we can be fairly sure that the ceremony was intended to involve Romans as a whole, not just the community of the faithful. It was this popular involvement which did most to ensure that Rome itself was being created as a community by the ceremonial sphere. After 1143 the Senate may have had an uphill battle if it was ever to gain control of ceremonial space; but the Senate was made possible in the first place by a popular sense of community which ceremonies served strongly to reinforce. It was not only because popes like Innocent II were so powerful, domineering, and ambitious at a European level, that the emergence of the Senate was such a sharp break; it was also because popular identity in Rome was so focused and confident. The patterns described in this chapter went a long way to establish that identity. The pope was crowned; and, as we have seen, 'the whole city was crowned with him'.

Finally: this heightened world, and the scale of the resultant reinforcement of both the authority of the pope and the coherence of the *populus*, gives some perspective to the very large sums of money the church expended on many of these occasions. I have stressed Easter Monday (maybe £100), the *Letania maior* (in toto, at least £30), and the *laudes Cornomanniae* (up to £18); but such gifts, on a smaller scale, were standard in many other big feasts. Benedetto says that at Christmas and Easter the urban prefect received a 'double *presbiterium*' of 20 *solidi* (£1), judges and bishops got 4 *solidi* each, cardinals and deacons got 3 *solidi*, *cantores* and subdeacons and *regionarii* got 2 *solidi*, the naval prefects got 8 *solidi*, *scriniarii* got 10 *solidi*, *maiorentes* got 5 *solidi* (by Cencius' time in 1192 these figures had slightly changed, but by now also included senators); the different *ordines* of clerics, including the pope himself, got parallel gifts on many other feast days. How much this amounted to on each occasion is uncountable, for we do not know how many people were in each category, but £20 per occasion is a bare minimum here too, and it could have been much more.[72]

These sums came from the altars of S. Pietro, in most cases at least; that is to say, from the pilgrim traffic. They were in part simply salaries, parallel to the *beneficium* of £100 per annum which Innocent II established for judges and advocates as a collectivity in return for an oath of loyalty and of honest conduct. They were in part a repayment of expenses, as with the Easter Monday floral arches, or the payment to the pope at Advent of 20 *solidi* 'for the expense of the *curia* and his horses'.[73] But these gifts were also sacralized by being such a standard part of processional ritual. This was further reinforced by the *iacta* of money to the Roman crowds, which were in Albino's papal election *ordo* accompanied by public statements, 'I take no

---

[72] *LC*, II, pp. 146–7 (Benedetto), I, pp. 291–2, cf. 295–6, 306 (Cencio).
[73] Altars of S. Pietro: *LC*, II, pp. 90 (Albino), 143 (Benedetto). *Beneficium* to judges: *LP*, II, pp. 383–4. Advent payment: *LC*, II, p. 143 (Benedetto).

delight in silver and gold; what I have, I give to you', and 'He dispenses to the poor; his justice remains, for ever and ever.'[74] Such money was thus sacralized by its origins in pious gift, by the timing of its disbursement, and by explicit, if clichéd, statements. There must have been quite a lot more of such disbursements, too, unrecorded in our *ordines*, given the chance reference we have in 1177 to the rights of the *regio* of S. Maria Nova to receive all the oblations given on Easter Thursday, day and night, to the high altar of S. Giovanni in Laterano (see above, p. 294); and given the careful apportionings, recorded in some of our documents, of S. Pietro's offerings to a variety of other ecclesiastical uses—10 per cent of all of them for church rebuilding in 1053, all those from Easter Thursday to Easter Saturday to the bishop of Silva Candida in 1057, 25 per cent of all of them to the canons of S. Pietro in 1151.[75] If the S. Maria Nova rights had parallels elsewhere in the city, in particular, then the Roman populace as a whole regularly gained from pilgrim offerings of this kind: the whole city was structurally involved, that is to say, in such sacralized handovers of cash.

Money is still money, of course. It represented greed, metaphorically, and taking money (as opposed to land) was associated tightly with venality. Benedetto's and, especially, Cencio's careful accounting of how much should be paid on each occasion was in part intended to sidestep the venality issue, by standardizing payments. But they still could, at times, be refigured negatively. In the later twelfth century, 'customary fidelity' was sworn to newly elected popes and papal representatives by the Roman senators and *populus* in return for a *beneficium* of (in 1149) £500; this fitted easily into the ritualized disbursements listed above, but Innocent III could denounce it as corrupt in 1198, and he refused to pay it.[76] Over all, too, any outside observer could be relied on to see such gifts, in all circumstances, as part of the culture of corruption which was seen to characterize the whole city (see further pp. 171–4, 417–19).[77] All the same, the other point is that money (or gold and silver in other forms) was swirling around Rome, at least among its churchmen and its lay political class, which extended very widely. The papacy and the major Roman churches received money in a large variety of different ways, mostly from outside the territory of Rome.[78] The pope and the church had expenses too, of course, large and small. But one of these was keeping sweet the political actors in the city of Rome; and those actors anyway were fully aware of the large sums coming into the Laterano and Vaticano.

The sacral and the venal overtones of money gifts were not in contradiction. Rather, the ritualization of money transfers, their seamless weaving into Rome's processional cycles, was reinforced by the desire of Romans to get a share of the sums of money—unique for any city in the West—coming into Rome. And, on another level, the huge weight of that papal processional tradition, balanced against

[74] *LC*, II, pp. 123–4 (Albino).
[75] *SPV*, nn. 19, 43–4, 46, 60 (see further n. 77, a. 1191, when the bishop of Silva Candida claimed a larger share); *PL*, CXLIII, cols 828–9, n. 16 (a. 1057). See also Chapter 3, n. 86.
[76] *Senato*, n. 8; *LP*, II, n. 412; *Gesta Innocenti III*, ch. 8.
[77] See in general Wickham, 'The financing'.   [78] See Chapter 3, n. 198.

the confidence of Romans, partly created by their regular participation in those same processions, helped to ensure that the scale of money gifts was and remained very large. It is worth remembering that, in most medieval polities, rulers received from the ruled far more than they handed out in largesse. But in Rome, papal income was, to such a great extent, not derived from direct papal subjects that it became possible to reverse the rules of contemporary politics; in periods of the contestation of papal power, which dominated the 150 years after 1044, what was possible became necessary; so popes gave to the city rather more than they received from it. This added to Rome's Europe-wide reputation for venality, of course. It also further added to the cohesion of Rome and its *populus*, however defined, along the lines pursued in this chapter. But all of this was a result of the particular economic structure of the city and of its political system, as well as of the intensity, unique outside Constantinople, of the city's processional rituals and of popular participation in them.

*

PAST AND PRESENT IN ROME'S SELF-IMAGE

A good deal has been written about the classicizing imagery of *renovatio* which surrounded the creation of the Senate in 1143. It is certainly the case that early senatorial letters to German king-emperors make some play with Roman Republican imagery, either inviting Conrad III and/or Frederick Barbarossa to come and be Roman emperor together with the renewed Senate (and, more or less explicitly, against the pope), or else, even more boldly, setting out claims for the Senate's classical Roman legitimacy that challenged some of the rights of the emperor himself.[79] These letters have been added to the inscription over the door of the Casa dei Crescenzi, and to the various versions of the *Mirabilia urbis Romae*, and have come to be seen as part of a trend towards classical renewal, a new interest in Rome's pre-Christian past, which is regarded by many to have peaked in the early 1140s, the period of the earliest full *Mirabilia* text and the foundation of the Senate alike.[80] As the secular counterpart to a renewed interest in early Christian art, argued to be a specific feature of the papal 'reform' movement, this wide-ranging rediscovery of the past has come to be seen as no less than Rome's special contribution to the 'twelfth-century Renaissance'. The impact of that classic work of early twentieth-century *Geistesgeschichte*, Percy Ernst Schramm's *Kaiser, Rom und*

---

[79] Some of the most elaborate elements of this imagery come from the great stand-off between envoys of the Senate and Frederick Barbarossa in 1155, recorded by Otto of Freising, *Gesta Friderici*, II.29 (with Frederick's reply, II.30). These speeches cannot be regarded as representative of anything except Otto's own mental imagery (a point also picked up by Ingrid Baumgärtner in her review of Strothmann, *Kaiser und Senat*, in *Historisches Jahrbuch*, CXX, 2000, pp. 456–8, at p. 457), contra, e.g. Benson, 'Political *renovatio*', pp. 350–1; Strothmann, *Kaiser und Senat*, pp. 76, 150–7 (both of the latter know that the words are Otto's, but wish to accept their essential elements all the same). But the senatorial letters surviving in Wibald of Stablo, *Epistolae*, nn. 214–16, 347 (these four = *Senato*, nn. 5–8), 404 seem less reworked. See also Chapter 7, n. 151.

[80] This overall interpretation is summed up in Strothmann, *Kaiser und Senat*, pp. 78–216.

Renovatio of 1929, has here melded with US/UK-style Renaissance studies to produce a sense of a real cultural break in the mid-twelfth century, nothing less than 'the new rebirth of Rome', in Richard Krautheimer's phrase.[81]

The texts just referred to do undoubtedly show an interest in and a commitment to the classical past. They were not strikingly new, all the same, as indeed Schramm knew perfectly well, in that his hero was Otto III, over a century earlier; and indeed earlier texts still, notably the *Libellus de imperatoria potestate in urbe Roma*, from c.900, muse on the way that imperial rule was originally Roman alone, was lost to Constantinople, but was renewed and brought back to Rome in and after 800: the near-seamlessness of the past is here clear, with an imperial continuity which was always properly linked to the city (see below, p. 377). The word *renovatio* was also Otto III's, and of the Carolingians before him; even Sergius III (904–11) 'renews the empire', *imperium renovat*, according to a contemporary praise poem by Eugenio Vulgario. Although here, as in the *Libellus*, this 'renewal' referred to imperial or papal, not urban, authority, there is a conceptual continuity with Nicola di Cencio's desire to *renovare decorem* of 'old Rome' on the Casa dei Crescenzi (above, pp. 235–8), and, of course, with the *renovatio sacri Senatus*.[82] But what all this represents is not some great physical or constitutional rebuilding in the name of a vanished past, but, rather, a *constant* process of renovation. The word *renovatio* is in fact most frequently used in our sources simply to mean the renewal of a lease contract when it lapsed: a day-to-day, quasi-automatic process, far removed from the dreaming and fervency assumed by Schramm.[83] Rome was, of course, full of a classical and imperial past (both pagan and, with the great late antique basilicas, Christian). This past had not vanished, and no one in the city believed that it had lapsed. They disagreed as to who best embodied it (emperor, pope, or citizens), but it was always there to be used. And to be 'renewed', over and over in different contexts, just as modern governments constantly 'reform' functioning structures without often changing very much.

This broad-based continuity is recognized by much recent scholarship.[84] It still does not stop scholars from being excitable about all the different signs of twelfth-century 'Romerneuerung' which they think they see, but at least it means that the solidity of the pre-twelfth-century fabric of the city (and, until the late eleventh, of city government) is better recognized. The buildings were all around, as noted earlier on in this chapter. They were widely recognized as a special Roman feature. The *Liber Guidonis*, for example, a Pisan's-eye view of the history and geography of Italy and the Mediterranean dating to 1119, in the early years of Pisa's own

---

[81] Classics, apart from Schramm, include Benson, 'Political *renovatio*'; Krautheimer, *Rome*, pp. 161–202; and now Petersohn, *Kaisertum und Rom*, pp. 80–109, who stresses the imperial imagery of the Senate.

[82] *Libellus de imperatoria potestate*, pp. 191–9 (see below, n. 168 for the date); Schramm, *Kaiser, Rom*, pp. 42–3, 116 ff.; Eugenio Vulgario, *Sylloga*, n. 38, see Schramm, *Kaiser, Rom*, pp. 52–3; *Senato*, n. 12 and onwards.

[83] Examples of *renovatio* (the earliest is from 1019): *SMVL*, nn. 41–6, 61A; *RS*, n. 106; *SMCM*, nn. 16, 19; *SMN*, n. 51; *SPV*, n. 40; *S. Sil.*, n. 20.

[84] e.g. Claussen, '*Renovatio Romae*', p. 90 (a text otherwise focused on renewal, in this case in architecture); and Baumgärtner, 'Rombeherrschung'.

precocious commune, is a compilation of quite a number of classical and post-classical sources, including Dares Phrygius on the Trojan war and Paul the Deacon's *Historia romana*, as well as one of the Pisan victory poems of the late eleventh century; in this text, it is Rome's ancient buildings—and not Pisa's—which are listed and enumerated in a nine-page proto-*Mirabilia*, Augustan region by Augustan region.[85] And Rome's institutional history was long too. Papal government looked back to the late empire (or at least the Byzantine exarchate); the Roman aristocracy was so consistently called a *senatus* throughout the early Middle Ages that Arrigo Solmi could propose in 1944 in a book-length argument that the institution had remained intact the whole time—the argument is wholly unconvincing, but not ridiculous.[86] Ingrid Baumgärtner in 1989 argued strongly that an 'Antikenrezeption' has been overvalued in our analyses of the twelfth-century Roman commune, and that 'Rome's renewal on the part of the commune meant an activisation of already available elements'.[87] *Of course* the early Senate used classical imagery; it was so strong a part of their ideological toolkit, as it was for everyone in Rome, because it was all there already. This is the standpoint I wish to adopt as well. That ever-present past could always be 'renewed', in every century, but it was not any the less present for all that.

This does not mean, all the same, that nothing changed in the city at all. We will look in more detail in Chapter 7 at what I have already argued to be the major crisis in Rome's medieval history: the political and institutional breakdown of the century after 1046, which reached its nadir after 1084 and especially after 1100. It was that specific breakdown which ambitious popes from Innocent II onwards, and also the founders of the Senate, were reacting to, separately and in competition. This was a break at so many different levels—including in Rome's economic dynamism (above, pp. 156–7)—that it could not avoid having an effect on Rome's cultural production and representations, which I want to focus on here. But it cannot be mapped directly onto cultural changes, all the same; the latter visibly had a different periodization, and explanations for them do not all fit easily within any of the standard narratives for Rome, whether political/economic crisis, ecclesiastical 'reform', or the 'reception' of Antiquity. I will here concentrate on three aspects of cultural analysis: changes in the patronage of church building and church decoration; the deeper rooting, in the early twelfth century, of a dense set of legal practices deriving directly from Justinianic law; and—the one which shows the most stability—the way the past was remembered and used by Roman authors across our period. Our evidence for all these becomes more substantial after 1100 or so, as does that for processions, but, unlike in the case of processions, we can argue here for some genuine shifts in behaviour and attitudes. Not simple shifts, all the same: all three of these had different pacings from each other, never mind from the political environment inside which they operated.

---

[85] *Liber Guidonis*, ed. Campopiano, pp. 12–20. The Pisans identified unusually strongly with Rome, and sometimes called their city *Roma altera*: see e.g. Scalia, '"Romanitas" pisana' (p. 805 for the quote).
[86] Solmi, *Il Senato*.   [87] Baumgärtner, 'Rombeherrschung', p. 70.

Church building and decoration

By far the largest amount of surviving evidence for the building and decoration of churches in Rome in our period concentrates on the century after 1050, and especially from the 1080s onwards. Hardly surprisingly, it has therefore been seen through the interpretative grille of church 'reform'.[88] Nor would I want to contest that, at any rate not wholly. Indeed, surviving fresco cycles (including those, a substantial number, which are now only really legible through early modern watercolours and engravings), and the much rarer mosaic apses (there are only two surviving from the period 900–1150 in more than fragmentary form, the upper church of S. Clemente from around 1120, and S. Maria in Trastevere from around 1140), not only often have narratives and iconography that push known theological agendas, but were also, for ordinary Romans—that is, those who did not read theology—by far the most prominent guides to those agendas. But it seems to me that the process was more complicated than that, and that it had a variety of different roots, not all of them emanating from the papal court. Let us look at some aspects of this.

The first point is simply a warning: it is unwise to base too firm an argument on the pattern of surviving buildings. The tenth century is often seen as a void, 'the obscurest period of the history of Roman painting' (Matthiae), one in which, as early as 850 indeed, 'church building in Rome seems to have nearly stopped' (Krautheimer).[89] In fact, however, after the crisis of the decades around 900, there was a good deal of prominent monastic and church foundation, particularly by Alberico, his family, and his entourage, with SS. Cosma e Damiano in Trastevere (Benedetto Campanino) and S. Ciriaco in Via Lata (Marozia 'II' and her sisters) only being the most important; this continued into the late tenth and early eleventh century, with S. Maria in Pallara (Pietro *medicus*, 970s–90s), S. Trifone (Crescenzio the urban prefect, *c.*1005), and others. These churches, or at least their early medieval structures, mostly do not survive—the only exception with surviving decoration is S. Maria in Pallara, now called S. Sebastiano al Palatino—but they provided what would have been a normal continuity in building and artistic patronage from the 940s at the latest onwards.[90] A common narrative sees Roman fresco-work, in particular, as virtually restarting in the 1090s, under the influence of Desiderio's new (1060s) monastic church at Montecassino;[91] this

---

[88] See in general, for example, Toubert, *Un art dirigé*; Pace, *Arte a Roma*, e.g. pp. 69–85. I am very grateful in this section for detailed critiques by Leslie Brubaker and Lila Yawn.

[89] Matthiae, *Pittura romana*, 2nd edn, I, p. 196; Krautheimer, *Rome*, p. 166.

[90] See Hamilton, 'The monastic revival' for the tenth century; *Papsturkunden*, n. 424 (a. 1006) for S. Trifone. For church-building before 1050, see the complete survey in Coates-Stephens, 'Dark age architecture in Rome', pp. 204–22. For S. Maria in Pallara as a building, see above all Marchiori, *Art and Reform*; S. Sebastiano was a co-dedicatee of the church from the start (Marchiori, *Art and Reform*, pp. 178–9).

[91] The list is long here, but includes Toubert, *Un art dirigé*, pp. 193–238; Krautheimer, *Rome*, pp. 178–80; Kitzinger, 'The arts', pp. 638–42; Claussen, *Magistri doctissimi*, pp. 36, 239 (for decorated stone floors); Claussen, 'Renovatio Romae', pp. 87–94. Romano, *Riforma e tradizione*—now the fundamental text for the period after 1050—is much more cautious, pp. 166–8.

seems to me both unnecessary (in that there is no reason to suppose that a single rural church, however elaborate, would transform the decorative programmes of a whole city with its own long artistic tradition), and also unlikely, for reasons we shall come to.

That said, however, there is a strong probability that there was *more* building and decoration in churches from the late eleventh century onwards. This was in part simply because more entirely new churches were indeed being built, as Rome expanded; it is also, nonetheless, because older churches were being rebuilt, often on a larger scale—one of the reasons, indeed, why tenth-century (as also seventh-century) churches are so rare in the city. Innocent II's S. Maria in Trastevere was one of the first Roman churches to match the fifth-century S. Sabina in size, nearly seven centuries earlier; and inscriptions, commemorating the building or rebuilding of churches and the rededication of altars (which generally indicate substantial refurbishment), begin to survive from the period between 1046 and 1073, and then, after a gap for a generation, see a peak in the 1110s and 1120s: half of the inscriptions of this type from our whole period survive from those two decades, in fact.[92] What this actually means is an issue we will come on to, but at least it means that we have, in some cases, material to play with.

Hélène Toubert in 1970 published a highly influential article about the 'renou-veau paléochrétien' in Rome in the early twelfth century, which has set the tone for a generation. She argued that this was a period in which antique-style—both pagan and Christian—motifs were used, much more generally than they had been in the Carolingian period, such as square frames with swags of curtain, medallions, garlands, and masks; they are visible in churches like S. Maria in Cosmedin, S. Nicola in Carcere (both of which have rededication inscriptions from the 1120s), and in the exuberant populated vine/acanthus scroll of the mosaic apse of upper S. Clemente, from the same period. She ascribed this to a desire to return to the ideals of the apostolic period, which contributed to the valorization of the aesthetic of the first Christian centuries.[93] This fits, too, with a feature of the period which has been generally noticed, a considerable popularity in Rome of fresco cycles of the lives and deaths of early saints: St Benedict in S. Crisogono in, probably, the late 1050s (this saint, at least, certainly had a Cassinese ring, for he founded the latter monastery; furthermore, the cardinal priest of S. Crisogono was Federico abbot of Montecassino, before he became Pope Stephen IX in 1057), St Urban and St Cecilia in S. Urbano alla Caffarella a little way down the via Appia, and St Clement in S. Clemente in the 1090s, both Urban and Clement being early popes.[94] The 'reform' period was one in which early pontifical names were

---

[92] In chronological order, Forcella, IX.806, X.540–1, VIII.4, XIII.785–6, XI.262 (1047–73, plus Settele, 'Illustrazione', pp. 242–3, a. 1060); XI.766 (a. 1090, the only one between 1073 and 1110); X.727, VIII.717, V.341–3, IV.1311, XI.704, XI.767, XI.321, IX.1007, IV.743–4, XII.539, II.486–7, IV.260–1, IV.124 (1110s–20s), with the S. Clemente inscriptions ed. in Barclay Lloyd, *The Medieval Church*, pp. 60–2.

[93] Toubert, *Un art dirigé*, pp. 239–310.

[94] Brenk, 'Die Benediktszenen', Brenk, 'Roma e Montecassino' (with, more recently, Romano, *Riforma e tradizione*, pp. 79–87); Noreen, 'Lay patronage'; for S. Clemente, below, nn. 100–103.

commonly taken by popes—Clement II, Damasus II, Victor II, Alexander II, Urban II, Calixtus II, Anacletus II, Innocent II—and here were at least two of these, celebrated in fresco form. The models for these cycles, the visual lives of Peter and Paul in the fourth-century basilicas, were themselves late antique, and their use could thus be seen as part of this palaeo-Christian artistic interest too, as well as conceptual points of reference for ecclesiastical innovators keen to return to supposedly purer Christian periods.[95]

Broadly, this picture makes sense to me. It is true that (as Serena Romano has remarked) palaeo-Christian elements were often used in isolation, often simply for decorative effect, without any visible ideological charge, or else independently of any narrative cycle, as in lower S. Clemente, where the Clement scenes are separated from each other physically. It is also true that narrative cycles of saints do not by any means start neatly in 1046; there are Carolingian examples, such as S. Prassede; and, in our period, S. Maria in Pallara had late tenth-century cycles of both St Sebastian and St Zoticus (now lost, but recorded in early modern drawings), and S. Maria Antiqua preserves one for St Antony from roughly the same decades.[96] But they do become more common after the mid-eleventh century, and are part of a growing concern to make the sanctity, and saintly action, of relatively ordinary people (i.e. those from a later period than the apostolic age of Christ, Peter, and Paul) visible to a secular audience, as models to follow.[97] This was certainly part of a 'reforming' visual rhetoric, in a very wide sense, even if it is important to recognize that it was already beginning before 1000. And one sign of its wide acceptability in Rome is that we can see, from donor portraits and inscriptions, that several of the patrons of such visual sequences were not papal or even clerical, but lay figures: Pietro *medicus* in S. Maria in Pallara, Bonizzo in S. Urbano, Beno di Rapiza and his wife Maria *macellaria* in lower S. Clemente. Only Pietro is known elsewhere (he was a substantial landowner, and S. Maria's actual founder), but two of these were evidently from artisanal backgrounds, even if doubtless rich artisans. We could easily see all of them as members of the 'medium elite', and they were, in particular, almost certainly not from any of the aristocratic strata described in Chapter 4.[98]

---

[95] Kessler, *Old St. Peter's*, pp. 75–95; cf. Tronzo, 'The prestige of St Peter's'.

[96] Romano, 'I pittori romani', pp. 107–19; for S. Prassede, see Goodson, *The Rome of Pope Paschal I*, pp. 235–41; for S. Maria in Pallara, Marchiori, *Art and Reform*, pp. 188–200, 222–78; for S. Maria Antiqua, Osborne, 'The atrium of S. Maria Antiqua', pp. 204–5.

[97] See esp. Pace, *Arte a Roma*, pp. 69–85; Osborne, 'Framing sacred space'.

[98] This has not been presumed by other scholars. Guidobaldi, *San Clemente*, pp. 228–9, leans over backwards to try to make Beno and Maria aristocratic; Pace, 'Santità, aristocrazia', p. 317, sees 'espliciti segni di "esposizione" nobiliare' in their donor portraits, although he recognizes the fact that Beno by no means wears as decorative a costume as the 'real' aristocrats Sisinnio and Eufimiano (for whom see below); Carmassi, 'Die hochmittelalterlichen Fresken', pp. 38–63 offers a set of proposals about Beno and Maria's family connections with the family of Sassone *macellarius* (above, pp. 268–9), which at least aim at a more appropriate social stratum but still do not convince—there were plenty of *macellarii* in Rome; Romano, *Riforma e tradizione*, pp. 27, 130 develops Carmassi's hypotheses towards the aristocracy again. Note that lay patrons also appear in this period on frescoes which are not cycles of saints' lives, Beno in S. Gabriele sull'Appia, Romano *nipote de Mica* in S. Crisogono, Leone and his wife in S. Balbina, all of them again unknown elsewhere (Romano, *Riforma e tradizione*, pp. 21–2, 56–9, 76–7, 89–92, texts by S. Romano, J. Enckell Julliard, G. Bordi).

This middling social stratum thus contained men and women who bought into the ideals of post-apostolic sanctity, and were prepared to spend money to make these ideals visible to others. Such patronage also, of course, served to put their own name on that visual commitment, which could—would—further their own prestige; two of Beno and Maria's S. Clemente panels, showing in one a healing miracle by St Clement with a particularly large and prominent donor portrait of Beno and Maria and their children, adjoin the main internal entry to the lower church, and hit you as you go in (see Figure 6.2).[99] When we analyse the strength of the Pataria movement in Milan in the 1050s–70s, we know that it represented a substantially lay piety, for it was a popular movement directed against the marriages and simoniac elections of the Milanese clergy, including archbishops. In Rome, it is easy to see the parallel movement as only papal, for it was so often opposed by ordinary Romans (the clergy of Rome in the forefront); but Beno and Maria, like the tirelessly pro-Hildebrandine Pierleoni family (themselves probably fresco patrons by the 1120s, in S. Nicola in Carcere), show that many of the laity were very happy with the imagery of a more purist religious revival too.[100] It was an important feature of the spiritual world of the eleventh-century urban laity in Italy. This too, however, shows tenth-century roots, for it is present in Pietro *medicus'* S. Maria in Pallara. Like lay pious gifts to churches, which went back without any break to the late empire, lay patronage of church decoration was by no means new, and it could further the visualization of sanctity many decades before this became controversial or seen as part of 'reform', as it did from the mid-eleventh century onwards.

The test case study for this argument is S. Clemente, whose preserved lower church has four fresco panels of linked content, three of which have Beno and Maria's names on them, depicting the life of St Clement; the fourth, which features St Alexis (Figure 6.1), is identical in format and style, and is, I am sure rightly, always associated with the same high-quality pictorial programme.[101] They are dated by most scholars to the 1090s. The *terminus ante quem* for this is safe enough, for the lower church was mostly torn down by its cardinal priest Anastasio (fl. 1102–25), who built upper S. Clemente on top of it—it was almost certainly finished in his lifetime, so the building may have started early. Art historians have often assumed that the frescoes must also post-date 1084, the date of the Norman sack of Rome, which destroyed the nearby SS. Quattro Coronati, but that does not follow, for no fire damage is detectable in the lower church of S. Clemente (which has several earlier frescoes); all the same, the parallels to them are late eleventh century, the brickwork under the panels is late too, and I see no reason to doubt a late eleventh-century date. John Osborne argues that the appearance of St Nicholas in one of the

[99] Osborne, 'Proclamations of power', p. 169.

[100] Violante, *La Pataria milanese*, I, pp. 175–93; Violante, 'I laici nel movimento patarino'; Moore, 'Family, community', pp. 61–9. For S. Nicola in Carcere, see Romano, *Riforma e tradizione*, pp. 272–80 (F. Dos Santos); the association with the Pierleoni is likely but not proven.

[101] Basic analyses: Toubert, *Un art dirigé*, pp. 195–238; Guidobaldi, *San Clemente*, pp. 217–35; Pace, *Arte a Roma*, pp. 72–6; Osborne, 'Proclamations of power'; Carmassi, 'Die hochmittelalterlichen Fresken'; Filippini, 'The eleventh-century frescoes' (the fullest analysis); Filippini, 'La leggenda di sant'Alessio'; Romano, *Riforma e tradizione*, pp. 26–31, 129–50; Romano, 'Commedia antica'.

Figure 6.1. S. Clemente, lower church: S. Alexis fresco.

Figure 6.2. S. Clemente, lower church: donor portrait of Beno di Rapiza, Maria *macellaria* and their family.

frescoes suggests a date after the saint's translation to Bari in 1087, which seems most likely to me.[102]

Where analysts of the church have almost universally gone wrong is in attributing the guiding hand of Beno and Maria's patronage to the previous cardinal priest, Rainerio (1078–99), who became Pope Paschal II (elected in S. Clemente, indeed) in the latter year.[103] Rainerio was in reality out of Rome in Urban II's entourage or as a papal legate for the whole period 1084–98, except for a few contested moments in which the pope made irruptions into the city; Urban's allies may have controlled the S. Clemente area after 1094 (below, p. 424), but the situation was still one of war, and Urban and his cardinals anyway spent most of the next few years in France preaching the First Crusade. As Lila Yawn has recently and convincingly pointed out, pursuing suggestions by Valentino Pace and Tommaso di Carpegna Falconieri, frescoes of the life of Pope Clement I in S. Clemente, dating almost certainly to the reign of Pope Clement III (1084–1100), hardly have to be attributed to those of

---

[102] Osborne, 'Proclamations of power', has a sensible analysis of dating; pp. 163–4 for the absence of evidence for fire (see also Osborne, *Early Medieval Wall-Paintings*, p. 13), p. 165n for St Nicholas. Romano, *Riforma e tradizione*, pp. 26, 129, proposes 1078–84 as an alternative date to the 1090s, as had earlier, more sketchily, Bertelli, 'La pittura medievale', p. 229, but this is, above all, on the basis of a presumption of a pro-Hildebrandine reading of the programme, which seems to me unnecessary, as we shall see. The upper church was consecrated in 1118: see e.g. Riccioni, *Il mosaico absidale*, p. 3.

[103] See e.g. Toubert, Filippini, Romano, as n. 101, and a host of more casual references. Election in S. Clemente: *Liber Pontificalis*, ed. Přerovský, p. 705.

Clement's opponents who were not even in the city.[104] I conclude, again following Yawn, that the Beno and Maria frescoes probably date to before 1094, that is, to before the period when the church became contested territory again, making the plausible overall date range 1087–94. This Clementine association may very well, indeed, explain the partial demolition of the lower church during Paschal's pontificate. Like the later demolition and rebuilding of S. Maria in Trastevere—the titular church of Anacletus II before he became pope—by Anacletus' rival and enemy Innocent II, the transformation of S. Clemente can easily be seen as the physical annihilation of a church too closely associated with a defeated opponent. Evidently, this also means that Beno and Maria's lay piety can more easily be associated with Clement III than with his enemies. This does not have to be surprising at all, given that the papal 'reform' programme began with imperial popes, from Clement II onwards, but it is often forgotten by academic commentators. That piety could indeed be enthusiastic, but it did not commit patrons to any predetermined loyalty in the various papal schisms between 1044 and 1180. Nor did its visual forms have to be guided or organized by a clerical hand, for that matter, except insofar as any externally paid-for church decoration had presumably to be accepted by church incumbents. Which is to say: lay piety and church politics operate on wholly different levels, and we must avoid linking them at all tightly.

One aspect of the 'reform' agenda of lower S. Clemente is most visible in the St Alexis fresco: personal lay asceticism. Alexis was supposedly the son of the Roman senator Eufimiano, who became a wandering ascetic and returned to his father's house as a beggar to die, unrecognized, under the stairs; his cult probably spread to Rome from Syria in the 970s. The monastery of S. Bonifacio sull'Aventino had S. Alessio added to its titulature in the 980s, as we have seen (p. 203), and was collecting gifts from major Roman aristocrats by 987. By 1002, the whole Eufimiano story was known and accepted in the city, for that year shows the formal ratification by a large group of city leaders of a totally phony late Roman document recording the gift of Eufimiano's property to SS. Bonifacio e Alessio in memory of his son.[105] All of which once again shows that the veneration of an amateur (i.e. non-monastic) lay asceticism by no means began in 1046, and nor was it restricted to the 'medium elite'; it had high-aristocratic input from the start. All the same, in late eleventh-century S. Clemente the visual account of Alexis in rags, choosing not to be recognized by his grandly dressed parents until it is too late, makes sanctity precisely concrete. And in the S. Clemente frescoes, over all, it is the aristocracy that come off worst: the senatorial Eufimiano on his horse fails to recognize his son; and in another fresco the equally richly dressed Sisinnio (a courtier of Nerva in the

---

[104] Yawn, 'Clement's new clothes'; see, earlier, Pace, 'La Riforma e i suoi programmi figurativi', pp. 56–7; di Carpegna Falconieri, 'Storia medievale', pp. 153–4. Hüls, *Kardinale*, p. 160 and Servatius, *Paschalis II.*, pp. 15–32 track Rainerio's movements as cardinal.

[105] See Chapter 4, n. 58 for references, and Figure 6.1. *S. Alessio*, n. 1 is the 1002 ratification. The original Syriac life is *La légende syriaque*, ed. Amiaud; pp. 1–17 for a translation. For the fresco, see most recently Filippini, 'La leggenda di sant'Alessio'.

Figure 6.3. S. Clemente, apse mosaic.

earliest Clement I legend[106]), who disrupts Clement's mass, is blinded and com-
ically humiliated by miracles. The carefully labelled *dramatis personae* in these
complex scenes must have been explicated and commented on by clerics in
sermons—they are too dense for instant comprehension. But there is an edge of
a class-based critique to them which we also find in the activities of the Roman
populus after 1143; it is interesting to find it in non-aristocratic lay commissioning
half a century earlier.

Upper S. Clemente, like the slightly later S. Maria in Trastevere, has a much
clearer high ecclesiastical patronage, respectively a cardinal close to Pope Paschal II
and Pope Innocent II himself; their figurative decoration is also in mosaic, in the
apse, and this marks an expense and ambition that was most easily found in the
Curia (see Figures 6.3 and 6.4).[107] They are very different in style, of course, in that
they are not narrative in format, as apses never were. But they were also themselves
innovative. S. Clemente's huge inhabited vine-scroll is unique (the parallel fifth-
century scroll in the baptistery of S. Giovanni in Laterano, its closest model, does
not have people in it). S. Maria's array of saints, including Innocent himself as
founder, more conventionally flank a central divine figure, but on this occasion the

---

[106] For the Clement legend, see *Martyrium S. Clementis*, chs 5–14, a fourth-century text, clearly
followed by the fresco.

[107] Though major aristocratic families might take on such expense too, as—arguably—the
Frangipane did in S. Maria Nova in the 1160s: above, p. 300.

Figure 6.4. S. Clemente, apse mosaic: figures of lay workers.

figure is double, Christ in the centre enthroned with Mary, which is also not previously paralleled.[108] As noted earlier (p. 327), this latter image clearly represents the symbolic marriage between Christ and Mary-representing-the-Church, as quotes from the *Song of Songs* also present in the mosaic underline. This must have been a very important message for Innocent II, a man with his own programme for renewal, if he displaced the traditional centrality of Mary, in a Marian church, in order to do so. (See Figures 6.5 and 6.6. This displacement also had no successors; Christ and Mary reappear together in, for example, the late thirteenth-century Torriti apse of S. Maria Maggiore, but that is a slightly different image, the Crowning of the Virgin, and Christ is not at the centre.)[109] But in fact the S. Clemente mosaic represents the Church too, for the vine-scroll features the

---

[108] For good general introductions to both apses, Andaloro and Romano, 'L'immagine nell'abside'; Romano, *Riforma e tradizione*, pp. 209–18, 305–11 (J. Croisier), both with earlier references.

[109] Matthiae, *Mosaici medievali*, tavola 293; see Wolf, *Salus populi romani*, pp. 183–95.

Figure 6.5. S. Maria in Trastevere, apse mosaic.

Figure 6.6. S. Maria in Trastevere, apse mosaic: Pope Innocent II (left).

life-giving Cross at its heart, and then unrolls around small images of church fathers, and men and women performing domestic and agricultural tasks, which thus involve and privilege the whole Christian community; this association is made explicit by the mosaic inscription, which begins 'we have likened the Church of Christ to this vine'.[110] The Church as a concept is thus powerfully presented, in two very different ways, by builders who had, probably in both cases, destroyed churches associated with condemned papal predecessors. We can associate with this the papal fresco programmes in the Laterano Palace which Calixtus II, Anacletus II, and Innocent II each commissioned (they are now destroyed, but they were recorded by twelfth-century writers and sixteenth-century artists); these featured 'reform' popes trampling their papal opponents, the emperor Lothar III subjected to Innocent, and recent popes in the apse mosaic of a chapel, standing as if they were saints, representing what Ingo Herklotz has called 'Amtsheiligkeit'—the inherent sanctity of papal office.[111] It is important to stress that this very militant, theory-laden, version of 'reform' has little in common with the narratives of sanctity of the lay fresco patrons; it makes it less necessary still to see the latter frescoes as 'directed' by the Church.

S. Clemente and S. Maria in Trastevere were considerably less innovative in their architecture, however. Here they fit squarely into a tradition of basilica churches in reused brick, looking back to Carolingian foundations such as S. Prassede, and to great late Roman basilicas such as S. Sabina, with the pre-Michelangelo S. Pietro in Vaticano behind them all. S. Maria in Trastevere is one of the few contemporary constructions to have a transept like S. Pietro; its nave is also colonnaded, with a near complete set of matching columns, taken from the Terme di Caracalla, a highly ambitious architectural move which matches large fifth-century churches like S. Maria Maggiore, and again, not later ones.[112] As several commentators have observed, Innocent did not need to make this choice. He had spent the 1130s exiled in Pisa, so he knew what an ambitious and innovative stone cathedral could look like; he had visited France, so he could have seen buildings which were already moving away from Romanesque. He took the external blind arcading of the apse of S. Maria from Pisa's cathedral, so he was indeed looking around when he was there, but that was all.[113] Upper S. Clemente was equally traditional, and so was every other surviving church from the period. Perhaps the one that leaves the most striking architectural impression is Paschal II's rebuilt SS. Quattro Coronati from the 1110s, which has a high and solid apse (see Figure 6.7), dominating the slope of

[110] See esp. Toubert, *Un art dirigé*, pp. 268–305; Barclay Lloyd, 'A new look'; and the detailed survey of Riccioni, *Il mosaico absidale*, esp. pp. 37–64, who shows the considerable theological complexity of the iconography of the mosaic.

[111] Herklotz, *Gli eredi di Costantino*, pp. 95–158, translating and abbreviating 'Die Beratungsräume'—in which see p. 214 for 'Amtsheiligkeit'—with, for Innocent, Rahewin, *Gesta Friderici*, III.10 (for the displeasure of Barbarossa at seeing it in 1155). See also Stroll, *Symbols as Power*, pp. 106–214, the most detailed analysis of this interplay between papal political strategies and visual representation.

[112] Kinney, 'S. Maria in Trastevere', pp. 307–25. For the Carolingian background, see esp. Goodson, *Pope Paschal I*.

[113] Kinney, 'S. Maria in Trastevere', pp. 291–2, cf. 307.

Figure 6.7. SS. Quattro Coronati, external apse.

the Celio—that was certainly a deliberate projection of papal defensive power, on the edge of the Laterano quarter, in a difficult period—but the actual church at the top of the hill was relatively conventional (although unusually proportioned) and also quite small, made smaller by Paschal in fact.[114] The point is here that Rome's traditions of church architecture were so strong, so immanent, that innovation would have served no purpose. The purpose was to continue in that unbroken tradition. 'Being Roman' was enough for church builders; and Rome was Roman already.

There are many early twelfth-century churches surviving in Rome, seldom as entirely rebuilt as were the fore-mentioned, but all at least substantially repaired or enlarged; others include S. Lorenzo in Lucina, SS. Giovanni e Paolo sul Celio, S. Nicola in Carcere, S. Bartolomeo on the Isola Tiberina, S. Crisogono in Trastevere, S. Maria in Cosmedin, and S. Croce in Gerusalemme. S. Maria Nova followed, shortly after 1150 (see above, p. 300).[115] These were all large, if not quite as large as S. Maria in Trastevere. As just discussed, they were architecturally traditional, although they do begin to show two new developments, a portico and a campanile (the latter were new in Rome in the 1100s and expanded rapidly in the city, especially after 1140).[116] As inscriptions show, there were many other new churches in the 1110s and 1120s too—smaller in many cases, hence the fact that later rebuildings have again effaced most of the construction of this period. Indeed, some new churches in the Tiber bend must have been tiny, as well as lay-built, for the 1186 bull to S. Lorenzo in Damaso, the first attestation of most of the churches of Parione and Ponte which were subject to S. Lorenzo, includes S. Angelo *a domo Egidi de Poco*, S. Bartolomeo *a domo Iohannis Cagetani*, S. Nicola *de domo Cincii de Gregorio*, S. Andrea *a domo Fortisboliae*, and others of a similar type: chapels attached to private houses in effect, most of them unattested later.[117] It is the papal and richer clerical (or 'aristocratic') foundations and rebuildings, that is to say, that tend to survive, not those of the 'medium elite', which may give a misleading impression of the trends of the period. But these, at least, give one clear sign: there was money around.

This money is visible in several ways. First, the sheer size of S. Maria in Trastevere, or of SS. Quattro Coronati's apse, or plenty of other churches. S. Maria was mostly built between 1139 and 1143; it is unlikely to have been quite finished at Innocent's death in the latter year, but in his lifetime there is already reference to the *aureis metallis*, the gold background tesserae of the mosaic apse, which must have been one of the last things to be done.[118] The church's

---

[114] For S. Clemente, Barclay Lloyd, 'The building history'; Barclay Lloyd, *The Medieval Church*; Claussen, *Die Kirchen der Stadt Rom* I, pp. 299–347. See above, Chapter 3, n. 21, for SS. Quattro Coronati.

[115] See lists in Krautheimer, *Rome*, pp. 167–77; Romano, *Riforma e tradizione*, pp. 183–345; and Claussen, *Die Kirchen der Stadt Rom*, s.vv.

[116] Campanili: Priester, 'The belltowers', pp. 55–76.

[117] Ed. in Fonseca, *De basilica S. Laurentii*, pp. 250–5.

[118] 'Innocentius II dominus meus... ecclesiam sancte Marie trans Tiberim novis muris funditus restauravit et absidem eius aureis metallis decoravit': *LC*, II, p. 169 (Benedetto, who wrote before the pope's death in September 1143). Innocent's fourteenth-century epitaph in S. Maria in Trastevere says

construction had got that far in four years, in other words; this shows the capacity to command and pay a very large number of construction workers—to demolish the old church, to accumulate the extensive extra *spolia* for the new church, to rebuild, and to decorate richly—for it to be done in so short a time. Secondly, the splendour, that is, cost, of internal decoration itself. Fresco, the commonest wall decoration (far more common than mosaic) was not so expensive—not too expensive for lay patrons—but marble fitments were much pricier, and they could be very extensive, as the almost complete array in upper S. Clemente shows.[119] Thirdly, the early twelfth century also shows the rapid expansion of richly decorated floors, made out of many different types of stone, with swirls of 'cosmatesque' colour. These floors were by no means classicizing in their aesthetic. They are standard in all those churches and on through the thirteenth century, and their ambition is demonstrated by the fact that they are in many cases actually signed by their *marmorarius* creators: Paolo and his four sons in the early twelfth century, and his active grandson, Nicola di Angelo, later in the century; Rainerio and his descendants in the same time period; and many other families after them (note that the eponymous Cosmato worked much later, after 1260). These *marmorarii* are the first artists/artisans who consistently sign objects in medieval Roman history, and their commissions must have brought them unusual status, which normally implies wealth; their patrons must have been prepared to spend that money accordingly.[120]

The major period of the expenditure of this money seems to have begun under Pascal II (1099–1118), and continued under his successors, particularly Calixtus II (1119–24) and Innocent II (1138–43).[121] This concentration is interesting, particularly when it is contrasted with (less costly) lay patronage, which is documented on a small scale throughout the crisis century. First of all, it points out that the German and then Hildebrandine papacy of the period 1046–84 was not a particularly prominent patron of new buildings, even though that was a period when city government was still in good shape, and war had not really begun. (Inscriptions show some rebuilding in this period, as already discussed, but all patronized by the abbots and priests of their respective churches, except for some work by Alexander II in S. Giovanni in Laterano.)[122] It was rather more embattled popes and senior clerics who put money into large, ambitious, and expensive church architecture

the church was begun in 1140 and finished in 1148, which is not a strong basis for dating the completion of the church so late, but it would have to have been built very fast indeed to be entirely done by 1143, and the fact that Innocent's own figure on the mosaic apse has no square halo hints that it was finally finished after he died. See, for full argument, Kinney, 'S. Maria in Trastevere', pp. 206–18, with Gandolfo, 'Il ritratto', pp. 140–3.

[119] Claussen, 'Marmo e splendore', pp. 159–60; Claussen, 'Renovatio Romae', pp. 89–99; Claussen, *Die Kirchen der Stadt Rom*, I, pp. 325–43.

[120] Claussen, *Magistri doctissimi* is the basic survey; a nice synthesis is Maire Vigueur, *L'autre Rome*, pp. 386–93. Fresco painters did sometimes sign frescoes too; the earliest known is Crescenzio in the mid-eleventh century in S. Lorenzo fuori le Mura (Romano, *Riforma e tradizione*, p. 44, G. Bordi).

[121] See esp. Stroll, *Symbols as Power* (who, however, overstates the contribution of Anacletus II; in particular, her attribution of the upper S. Clemente mosaic to him, pp. 127–31, does not convince).

[122] See above, n. 92; Alexander II is in Forcella, VIII.4.

after 1100. They did so not just in a period of internal and external contestation, but in a period when Rome's political system was in crisis, and when all indicators of the economic prosperity of the city were negative (above, pp. 156–7), except the indicator of the building of these churches themselves. Such expense must, then, have been a partially defensive measure: sometimes literally so (SS. Quattro Coronati's impregnability), but, in general, a defensive show of strength and wealth in an otherwise difficult and uncontrollable time. It does not show that popes were re-establishing 'normality'; they were trying to convince. The solidity and expense of S. Clemente's imagery of the Church-as-vine was part of that rhetorical presentation, here attached to one of Paschal's close associates as a cardinal priest. So, doubtless, were the frescoes of the popes as 'saints' in the Laterano palace, in chapels and reception rooms not open to the wider public, but certainly visible to Roman aristocrats, and visitors from the rest of Europe. But we can at least see—as contemporaries also could, and were intended to, see—that popes in trouble were still rich, and capable of ambitious projects.

Innocent II is perhaps the exception to this defensiveness. The scale and speed of the destruction and rebuilding of S. Maria in Trastevere matches his forcefulness in other respects, after his triumphal return to Rome in 1138. It matches, in material terms, the much less expensive but still very overt appropriation of Hadrian's tomb for himself (above, p. 336), as well as his sharp-edged political acts (below, pp. 432–4). Innocent, for the first time in over fifty years, completely cowed the Roman church; he could afford to be offensive, not just defensive, in his expenditure. He roughly coincided with the beginning of the revival in Rome's economy, too. As we know, opposition to him did develop, and from an unexpected quarter, the city's non-aristocratic laity. But S. Maria and its dramatic apse, featuring Innocent himself in large format on the left (see Figure 6.6), is a monument to real papal aspiration and confidence. It would not last, but it could be built on by Innocent's namesake at the end of the century, and onwards from there.

This is a very quick run through a figurative art history and an architectural history which has attached to it hundreds of pages of recent prose. I have wanted to stress the cost of church building in Rome, and its lack of fit with the rest of the indicators of economic activity. I have also wanted to stress the variety of both patrons and imagery in the 'reform' period, which certainly (after 1100 at least) was associated with papal patronage, but which also had active lay interest from early on, and, indeed, roots well before 1046; this variety and heterogeneity are themselves reasons to see the generic label of 'reform' as inadequate—lay interest in personal asceticism and perhaps the criticism of aristocrats has little in common with the papal programmes of the 1110s and onwards. I have wanted to stress the dense intermixing of tradition and innovation in the city, which indeed can serve as an extended demonstration of how continuous *renovatio* worked when radical reconstruction was neither wanted nor needed. Above all, however, I think this brief account illustrates the complexity of the possibilities of material intervention in the church fabric of Rome: the huge range of the sort of messages that could be sent, and the sophistication of possible audiences. *Renovare decorum*, as Nicola di

Cencio put it in the Casa dei Crescenzi inscription,[123] was only a small part of it. Statements about lay asceticism, the solidity of the Church, papal 'sanctity' and imperial-style legitimacy, or the blindness of the aristocracy, could all be made, separately and together, along with improvisations on the classical past of several different kinds. The complexity of this developing semiological paradigm extended across to the more stable meanings conveyed by processions, too, as in the nod made by the S. Maria in Trastevere mosaic to the procession of 15 August (above, p. 327). And it extended to other aspects of Rome's cultural reproduction too, as we shall shortly see.

The paradoxes of Roman law

The second arena of change which needs discussion here is the use of Roman law in the city, and here the shift is simpler, although at least twofold: first, a marked increase in the detailed provisions of Justinianic law in documents, particularly family law, beginning in the mid-eleventh century and extending very considerably after about 1130; and secondly, the appearance of arguments in surviving documents based on citations and use of the *Corpus iuris civilis*, which begin (perhaps) in 1107, and which reach a peak in the 1140s–50s. It is important to stress that these changes are largely unrelated to the institutional history of Rome's law courts; as we shall see in Chapter 7, these went into crisis in the 1080s, and remained informal, often incoherent, until Innocent II's time. The increased use of Justinianic law was a cultural change, almost unconnected to political intervention, which is why it belongs in this chapter. But it is an important one, all the same.

Rome was, of course, a Roman-law city.[124] This was widely recognized throughout our period. It was underlined by the famous 998 case in which Abbot Ugo of Farfa successfully claimed to be heard by Lombard law in the city; there was no *iudex* there who knew Lombard law except his own advocate Uberto, who thus had to act as a judge in the case, and who wrecked it for the plaintiffs, the priests of S. Eustachio. In 1027, presumably by local request, Conrad II enacted that this would henceforth not be possible, and only Roman law could be used in the city by either plaintiffs or defendants.[125] But which Roman law? A series of legal historians, of whom the latest and most systematic is Giovanni Chiodi, have shown that the law cited in texts from the 990s onwards—not many texts, but half a dozen in the next two decades in particular—was the *Summa Perusina*, an early medieval epitome of the *Codex Iustinianus* (*CJ*); even the explicit citation of 'Justinian', in

---

[123] Forcella, XIII.1339 (see above, pp. 235–8).

[124] See classically Leicht, 'Lineamenti del diritto', and most fully Chiodi, 'Roma e il diritto romano'. Other important texts include Toubert, *Les structures*, pp. 1229–36, part of the general analysis at pp. 1191–348, by far the best account of Rome's legal system as a whole (see below, Chapter 7), and, for a context, Conte, 'Res publica'. Wickham, 'Getting justice', makes parallel arguments to those set out here, but is focused on the period after 1143. I am very grateful in this section for a critique by Emanuele Conte.

[125] Manaresi, n. 236 (see most recently Chiodi, 'Roma e il diritto romano', pp. 1162–85); MGH, *Constitutiones*, I, n. 37 (the date is presumably 1027, as this was when Conrad came to Rome).

this case *CJ* 7.43.8–9, in a court case of 999 (another case in which Ugo claimed the protection of Lombard law, this time unsuccessfully) in fact came from the *Summa Perusina*, as is clear from the phrasing.[126] Similarly, the direct quote from Justinian's '*Novella* 188', which appears in the proem of three texts from 1029–60, in which churches made emphyteuses to each other, is found in the *Epitome Iuliani*, another handbook, and this is by far its most likely source.[127] Romans up to 1050 or so evidently saw Justinian as their emblematic legislator, but in fact lived by a version of Roman law that was most probably customary in its essentials, and was simply backed up by relatively brief handbooks such as these two. That practical law recognized—I give the date of the first documentary example in each case, but I do not doubt that all were normal earlier as well—eminently Roman norms such as the legal autonomy of adult women (913), the difference between property-holding, most commonly called *ius*, and possession (919), *fidei commissarii* or executors (978) for *testamenta* or wills (994), the right to alienate freely (1012), a *tutor et curator* for minors (1013)—who remained minors until the age of 25, 'sicuti lex docet' (1057), a *donatio propter nuptias* contributed by a husband to a wife (1056, though the actual phrase does not predate 1093), and a *dos* contributed by the wife's family (1080, again without the actual phrase).[128] These all effectively conform to standard classical Roman practice, or a simplification if it. They are exactly what one would expect to find, indeed, in a city where no other sources of secular law had ever had any real force, but where law books and legal training had become relatively rare.

Charles Radding and Antonio Ciaralli have shown that no complete manuscripts of any parts of the *Corpus iuris*, except the *Novellae* as summarized in the *Epitome Iuliani*, circulated in the West before the eleventh century: the *Institutiones* was the first to be copied, in Rome in the early eleventh; the full *CJ* and the *Digest* followed later in the eleventh.[129] Clear citations of *CJ* which do not come from epitomes begin in 1047 (a law of Henry III) and 1058 (a Tuscan court case). The *Digest* is cited in another Tuscan case in 1076.[130] Rome fits this later eleventh-century date, too; *CJ* (7.65.1) is first cited directly in the great Arci case of 1060, which involved Pope Nicholas II and all of Rome's elite (above, pp. 221–2), although the *Digest* not until 1107 at the earliest, as we shall see. *CJ* must have come steadily into wider availability in the city from then on, for it is cited again (2.44.2) in 1072 to

---

[126] Manaresi, n. 254; *Summa Perusina*, ed. Patetta, p. 240. So did the same *CJ* quote in Manaresi, n. 285 (a. 1014). See Chiodi, 'Roma e il diritto romano', pp. 1144–50.

[127] *SMVL*, n. 54; *S. Alessio*, n. 6; *S. Prassede*, n. 8; *Iuliani Epitome*, ed. Hänel, p. 77 (actually n. 190 in the established text; note that the original *Novellae* only went up to n. 168); cf. Chiodi, 'Roma e il diritto romano', p. 1148. See also the phrase which appears with minor variants in *SMCM*, n. 2, *RF*, nn. 428, 628 (aa. 998–1012), 'omnem pactum quodcumque fecerit homo placitum vocatur, et ideo dictum est placitum, eo quod ex ambobus partibus placeat', which the first of these ascribes to a *liber iudicum*; I have not identified the (fairly banal) citation, but it may come from another summary text.

[128] Respectively, *RS*, nn. 115, 112, 114, 167; *RF*, nn. 656, 667; *SMVL*, n. 85; *S. Prassede*, n. 7; *SMN*, n. 30; *SMVL*, n. 106. (The reference to a dowry in *SMN*, n. 169, dated by the editor to the 980s, is in reality a text from about a century later, contemporary to the last-named.) See in general Toubert, *Les structures*, pp. 1229–36.

[129] Radding and Ciaralli, *The Corpus Iuris Civilis*, *passim*.

[130] MGH, *Constitutiones*, I, n. 50 (citing the *Novellae* as well); Manaresi, nn. 405, 437.

justify a special-case age of majority of 20, and also in the same year (7.52.6), in a more formulaic way, to emphasize the permanence of documents.[131] And one can see why, in a city already ruled by Roman law, a larger and more authoritative version of such law would easily slip into usage, once copies became easier to access, as long as trained legal experts were available to interpret it. How *dativi iudices* (the standard term for judges assisting court cases since the tenth century) were trained, and how this may have changed, is not clear (I will come back to this point), but *causidici*, legal experts, are at least occasionally documented in court cases and other major texts from 1084 onwards, and we can be fairly sure that *CJ*, at least, was part of their expertise from the start.[132]

What is striking, however, is that this knowledge soon spread out beyond simple citation. The content of daily legal practice, in particular, moved closer to that of classical law, often quite quickly. One example is pupillage. A man acting as *tutor et curator*, for fatherless minors below 25, is a common sight in eleventh-century documents. But classical Roman law actually kept the two roles separate; *tutores* acted for children under 12, whereas *curatores* acted together with older minors.[133] Between 1127 and 1128, city practice suddenly changed, and from then on the roles were always separate there too (women—generally mothers—were often *tutores*; *curatores* were almost all male: above, p. 315).[134] This must have been a deliberate choice by Rome's judicial establishment, for guardians were always assigned by *iudices*, indeed usually palatine judges; there had come a moment in which the latter decided to have a more legally exact system, and they stuck to it from then on. In any pre-industrial society it was common for fathers to die before children reached 25, so this was by no means a marginal shift.

An indicator of a different type is the generalization of Romanist dowries. The first documents are from the late eleventh century, and by 1093 we find the explicit structural linkage of *dos*, provided by the wife's family, and *donatio propter nuptias*, provided by the husband, for the first time. But it is from 1133 onwards that these gifts become standard, with regular rules coming in by the 1150s according to which husbands pledged property to ensure the repayment of dowry at the death of the wife.[135] Wills, too, although they are documented from the tenth century, move in a Romanist direction only from 1087, and the first full Roman-law will is in 1132.[136] The *Lex falcidia*, which established a minimum (a quarter) which direct heirs could expect from dying relatives, is less common in our documents, but is

---

[131] *RF*, n. 906; *SCD*, n. 72; *RF*, n. 1006.

[132] Early *causidici*: *RF*, n. 1097; *SMVL*, n. 121; *SMN*, n. 33; Ficker, *Forschungen*, IV, n. 92 (ASR, SCD, cassetta 16, n. 109).

[133] Buckland, *A Text-Book*, pp. 142–73.

[134] The last *tutor et curator* is in *SMN*, n. 45 (a. 1127), the first separate *tutor* and *curator* are in *S. Gregorio*, nn. 21–2 (a. 1128).

[135] *SMN*, n. 30 (a. 1093); *SMVL*, n. 155 (a. 1133); *SMCM*, nn. 32, 36 (aa. 1133, 1136); *SMN*, n. 46 (a. 1137), etc. See above, pp. 275, 316–17, for more on dowry; pledging by husbands begins with *SMVL*, n. 186 (a. 1155); *SMN*, n. 77 (a. 1157). See further Toubert, *Les structures*, pp. 751–68, who also uses material from southern Lazio; di Carpegna Falconieri, 'Sposarsi a Roma'.

[136] *SMVL*, n. 117 (a. 1087); ASR, SCD, cassetta 16, n. 120 (a. 1132).

first attested, used apparently accurately, in 1131.[137] In all these cases—all, it is worth stressing, concerning family law and succession—the signs are of quite a generalized shift, in or around 1130. This fits well with a date of 1128 for the introduction of a Romanist version of pupillage. But the shift in dowry and succession practices must have been as much bottom up as top down. We would not expect such worked-out documents for wills and dowries as we find in the 1130s if *scriniarii* and, indeed, ordinary lay actors had not absorbed the newly sharpened Romanist legal paradigm as well. I would presume that this was a longer process, which crystallized around 1130, but had earlier roots. On its back came later, more technical changes, doubtless generalized in documents through notarial training, such as the formal renunciation by women of the *ius et senatus consultum Velleianum* after 1160, which protected their rights over the property of husbands and children (e.g. *Novellae* 118.5, *Digest* 16.1.32), and the *exceptio non numerate pecunie*, increasingly standard after 1173, which renounced the right to raise legal cavils over sales and pledges in money (*CJ* 4.30).[138] It is hard to be sure whether these latter innovations were actually useful to people, rather than legalistic solutions to problems no one had posed, but they certainly added to the Romanist feel of our documentary corpus. Under Innocent II in 1138–43, *iudices* and advocates began to swear to uphold the '*constitutiones et leges*', in return for an annual salary; it is fairly clear that by then these laws were potentially the whole of the *Corpus iuris*.[139]

These changes were not the result of a single legislative enactment. In Pisa, the establishment of Roman law was indeed a well-defined legislative process, accurately datable to 1155–60, and visible in a variety of sources.[140] We have no sign whatsoever of an equivalent moment in Rome itself, presumably in 1127–33. However feeble our source base, we would have heard something of this; and Rome anyway did not need the sort of formal 'reception' of Roman law that formerly-Lombardist Pisa engaged in. But the changes were also not simply the casual result of a slowly expanding familiarity with long Romanist legal texts after the beginning of their availability in the late eleventh century. Something was going on around 1130, which extended technical versions of Roman law relatively suddenly into the lay community of the *urbs*. It is quite possible that this was, in each case, set off by choices on the part of Rome's palatine judges, as we saw for the changes in pupillage. All the same, it could only have happened if an increasingly Romanist legal training for *scriniarii* and presumably also *iudices* (as certainly for *causidici*) had already developed, making such a rapid shift practicable.

This process was early. It predated by thirty years the otherwise most precocious Romanist city in Italy, Pisa. Bologna, despite its *studium*, in existence by the 1120s at the latest, does not show such a density of lay legal practice until even later. Marie

---

[137] *S. Gregorio*, n. 137. Later examples are *SPV*, nn. 51, 74.

[138] *Senatus consultum Velleianum*: *S. Sisto*, n. 5 (a. 1160); *SMVL*, nn. 193, 198, 201 (aa. 1161–3), etc. *Exceptio non numerate pecunie*: *SMN*, n. 100 (a. 1173); *S. Sil.*, n. 36 (a. 1184), ASV, A. A. Arm. I–XVIII, 4999, n. 10 (a. 1185), etc.: by the later 1180s, it is standard in a high percentage of documents.

[139] *LP*, II, pp. 383–4.   [140] See for a survey Wickham, *Courts and Conflict*, pp. 114–28.

Louise Carlin, who traced similar processes of Romanization in Provence, dated them to the 1190s to 1210s in that region, and argued that Genoa—always a Roman-law city, as was Bologna—did not start them more than slightly earlier than that date either.[141] In Rome, people committed to the details of the *Corpus iuris*, at least insofar as they dealt with family and property law, in decades in which no other part of Europe was even thinking about them, outside rarefied training grounds such as the Bolognese *studium*.

This is important, for it gives a background to the other striking feature of early twelfth-century legal practice in Rome: the use, even if only in half a dozen legal disputes, of some very elaborate Romanist legal arguments. These cases have (mostly) been heavily studied, but they need to be set out again here, to show just how technical such arguments could be.[142] The first, and the most problematic, is a text of 1107 recording a dispute between SS. Cosma e Damiano in Trastevere and the Pierleoni family. The Pierleoni had leased all the monastery's land in Isola Farnese north of Rome, but after that lease a certain Bella died and left her land in Isola to SS. Cosma e Damiano; this land had once been the monastery's, but Bella's family had not paid any rent on it for fifty years, so monastic property rights were by now legally void. Should this be part of the lease to the Pierleoni or not? The monastery argued not, as it was by now a new acquisition; the Pierleoni disagreed. Both sides argued strictly by Roman law, and Cinzio, *rector* of SS. Cosma e Damiano, who is given the longest speeches and the best arguments in the text (the whole document is in *oratio recta*), cited several sections of both *CJ* and the *Digest* to back his position up, apparently successfully. The document is an odd one, however, for it has no reference to a *scriniarius*, so has no legal validity, and is also apparently a copy from later in the century; nor does it contain any formal decision on the dispute. The debate was heard before two *causidici*, with two palatine judges presiding, Ferrucio *primicerius* and Leone *secundicerius*, the first of whom is independently attested, as is at least one of the witnesses. It would be hard, given that, to dismiss the document as a total forgery. But, given that it is a one-sided monastic text, explicitly written 'lest later anyone, envious of justice, tries to deprive by evil will that which I [Cinzio] did', it is entirely possible that the sophisticated Romanist argument was added later, for extra effect. Either way, the arguments are presented as being set out before an informally constituted, even if expert, audience; there is no sign that the two palatine judges were acting on anyone's authority, and the atmosphere is one of an arbitration, not of a tribunal—which does fit the period, for Paschal II's reign actually shows us very few papally run court cases for the city of Rome at all.[143]

[141] Wickham, *Courts and Conflict*, pp. 157–9 for Genoa and Bologna; Carlin, *La penetration du droit romain*, pp. 89–116, 135–9, 145, 261–85.

[142] Esp. Padoa Schioppa, 'Il ruolo della cultura giuridica'; Besta, 'Il diritto romano'; Chiodi, 'Roma e il diritto romano', pp. 1206–39; Theisen, *Studien zur Emphyteuse*, pp. 230–49.

[143] Ficker, *Forschungen*, IV. n. 92 (the most recent of several editions); but the text has to be looked at directly in ASR, SCD, cassetta 16, n. 109. For Ferrucio, see Chapter 5, p. 248. Ilperino Cencii di Cencio Barontio, a witness, probably appears in *SMVL*, nn. 121–3 (a. 1094–99). The verso has the phrase *G(re)g(orius) scriniale* [sic] *complevi et absolvi*, a standard scribal clause, but the

We are on firmer ground with the next two cases. In 1124 and 1125, the bishops of Siena and Arezzo fought two of their five-centuries-long series of battles, over who should control the ecclesiastical rights of 21 *pievi* in central Tuscany, in the Laterano in front of Calixtus II and then Honorius II. In the second of these, and also in a contemporary *libellus* written for the Aretini, Roman law (both from *CJ* and the *Digest*) was extensively employed and critiqued to justify the *possessio* of ecclesiastical rights by each side, which the Aretini eventually obtained (leaving the issue of *proprietas* aside—it was, indeed, never returned to). It can be argued that this legal expertise was Tuscan, not Roman, and it was certainly ecclesiastical rather than lay; it marks a new level of legal sophistication in this early period of international appeals by churches to the Roman Curia. But the debate shows that the papal court was prepared to accept and able to adjudicate complex Romanist arguments by the 1120s.[144] Nor was this expertise restricted to canon-law cases in Rome. In the same period, in 1126, the monastery of S. Saba, in a case held before Pope Honorius, claimed an estate north of the city from S. Maria Nova using what would soon be called a *condictio*, an initial action invoking a specific Justinianic law (*CJ* 7.39.8.3); if this procedure was unsuccessful, as it turned out to be, it was only because S. Maria could show (quoting, among other things, *Digest* 44.4), that the action was an inappropriate one. It may be noted that Ferrucio, who had been *primicerius* in 1107, was the senior judge in this case too.[145]

Disputes from Anacletus II's reign (1130–8) have not survived his *damnatio memoriae* after his death, but these examples begin again in 1140, when the monks of Grottaferrata set out a long plea to Innocent II against the illegal acts of their neighbour Tolomeo II of Tuscolo. Such 'polittici delle malefatte' are not uncommon in Italy in the eleventh and twelfth centuries, but not many of them have a preface full of quotes from *CJ* (1.9.14, 2.1.13, 8.4.10, and 7.39.2) and the *Digest* (4.2.13); here again, this rhetorical recourse was not only available to the monks (or their legal advisors), but also presumed to be convincing to the pope and his judges.[146] In 1145, the most detailed of these cases sees Seniorile, *urbane prefecture causidicus*, acting both as a judge delegate for Celestine II and as elected arbiter by the parties, deciding a dispute over land on the Gianicolo between S. Gregorio sul Celio and S. Maria in Trastevere. Many things happened in this case, but it was structured at the start by Roman-law *condictiones* and exceptions (one was certainly based on *CJ* 4.9); it distinguished clearly between *dominium/proprietas* and *possessio* (as very many Roman cases did in this century, although this distinction at least had

---

hand is different. I am grateful to the Medieval History Seminar at the University of Birmingham for useful comments here. For citations of Roman law in the text, see Chiodi, 'Roma e il diritto romano', pp. 1208–13. For papal court cases from Paschal II's reign, see below, pp. 398–9.

[144] Pflugk, II, n. 295 (cf. Pasqui, *Documenti*, n. 9): see Besta, 'Il diritto romano'; Chiodi, 'Roma e il diritto romano', pp. 1217–23; Pennington, 'Roman law at the papal curia'.

[145] *SMN*, n. 42; Chiodi, 'Roma e il diritto romano', pp. 1213–17.

[146] 'Documenti per la storia', n. 4; Alibrandi, 'Osservazioni giuridiche'; Chiodi, 'Roma e il diritto romano', pp. 1223–7.

been well known in the city throughout our period); and other legal references, cited appropriately, include *Digest* 42.2.8 and *CJ* 7.39.2.[147]

A further pair of cases from the 1150s are linked by the presence in each of them, as an advocate for one of the parties, of Benedetto di Leone, an active member of a family of legal experts from Albano (above, p. 268); he was indeed present in the 1145 case among the judges as well. In 1151 he argued for S. Prassede against S. Croce in Gerusalemme before Eugenius III and his judges-delegate over a property east of the city, which S. Croce had in lease and was not paying the rent for, using *condictiones* based on *CJ* 4.65.33, 4.9, and the *condictio triticaria*. S. Croce replied with *Digest* 50.17.116.2 (misquoted); Benedetto cited *Digest* 41.2 in reply (calling it the *Nova Digesta*) and won, mostly because S. Croce admitted that it had previously paid the rent—so these legal subtleties were not really vital to the case. (S. Croce appealed this case to the Senate in 1160, but the Senate, on the advice of the *primicerius* and other senior judges, refused to hear the case after S. Prassede claimed the well-known Romanist *exceptio rei iudicate*, i.e. that the case was already decided, by the pope.) In 1155 Benedetto was acting for S. Agnese against S. Maria in Monasterio in another lease case, and both sides used standard Roman actions to set off the case, an *actio in rem*, a *condictio triticaria*, and the *interdictum 'uti possidetis'*, before Benedetto threw in a quote from *CJ* 4.6.23 and the case was then decided by witnessing, a charter, and swearing oaths.[148]

I have not been sparing here in technical citations, essentially so as to show that Romans, or at least the legal experts among them—*causidici*, advocates, and judges of different kinds—were well aware of the details of a considerable range of Roman law, not only initial actions but substantive law as well. They also knew how to argue on the basis of it. If not every case by any means actually hung on juristic arguments, they were all at least framed by such arguments. Nor was this restricted to lay legal experts; the ecclesiastics in the papal court had also become highly open to Roman law, by the 1120s at the latest.[149] It needs to be stressed that most cases in the city from the period up to the 1150s do not show such explicit use of Roman law; Rome was not like Pisa, where, once Justinian was formally adopted in 1160, his legal system was cited thereafter in every kind of dispute. All the same, the law was available in the city; and it was used not just in land cases, the great majority here, but also in entirely canon-law conflicts. It is not surprising that Bernard of Clairvaux could complain to Eugenius III around 1150 that 'laws resound daily in the palace, but those of Justinian, not of God'.[150] Papal judges, both ecclesiastical and lay, were often expert in the former.

---

[147] CVL, n. 8044, ff. 4–16. See further below, p. 404. This text, preserved in the well-known Galletti manuscripts, has been neglected by scholars. For *proprietas* and *possessio*, see Conte, 'Posesión y proceso'; Wickham, '*Iuris cui existens*', pp. 5–11.

[148] *S. Prassede*, n. 25 (cf. n. 28 = *Senato*, n. 17); *S. Agnese*, n. 10 = *S. Maria in Monasterio*, n. 1. See Chiodi, 'Roma e il diritto romano', pp. 1227–39.

[149] See Fried, 'Die römische Kurie', who indeed puts the start of the process earlier still. As early as the 1080s, Deusdedit's *Collectio canonum*, very much a curial product, had cited *CJ* and the *Novellae*: e.g. *CJ* I.311, 315–17, III.163–78. But there is a notable increase in casual references to Roman law in curial responses to strictly canon-law issues from the 1120s: see the debate between Mazzanti and Chiodi at the end of Chiodi, 'Roma e il diritto romano', pp. 1247–54.

[150] Bernard, *De consideratione*, I.4.5: 'quotidie perstrepunt in palatio leges, sed Iustiniani, non Domini'.

Aimerico (d.1141), *cancellarius* to Calixtus II, Honorius II, and Innocent II (he had the 1125 Siena–Arezzo judgement written), went further than this, for he asked the great Bolognese jurist Bulgaro to send him the first surviving synthesis of Romanist legal procedure, now usually called the *Excerpta legum*, probably already—though the date is not closely established—in the late 1120s. Whatever the date, Aimerico must have been disappointed; Bulgaro's short text is the most elementary guide possible, explaining in turn, very simply, what arbiter, judge, advocate, plaintiff, defendant each do, what accusation, witnesses, appeal, and so on are, and only towards the end getting into slightly finer procedural detail (mostly from *Digest* 50). Bulgaro must have thought the Roman Curia really backward; and that was the opposite of the truth.[151] As we saw earlier in the context of family law, no surviving Bolognese case is as tightly tied into legal argument as these Roman ones for decades; and even Pisa, the standard-bearer of Romanist legal practice in the later twelfth century, had got nowhere towards it before the 1150s.[152] Rome was unique in this early period in its commitment to the actual use of the *Corpus iuris* (the above-described examples are more than half of those known for the whole of Italy in the early twelfth century),[153] and was so from the 1120s at the latest—the period which saw the start of the shift to sharper Romanist distinctions in family law too.

So the shift in family law and in the substantive law on land ownership and possession (the subject matter of most surviving court cases) around 1130, plus a sophisticated understanding of Romanist legal procedure, go together to show that by the mid- to late 1120s a knowledge of Roman law was becoming generalized among, and was now consciously appropriated by, the professional strata of the city. Aimerico was not Roman, but Ferrucio, Benedetto di Leone, and a host of *causidici* and *scriniarii* certainly were; this knowledge did not need to come from anywhere other than a local training in (and experience in) using long and complex legal texts which evidently by now were available in the city. This, in particular, is too early for it to derive from Bologna; and the method of citation of legal sources, which Rome later probably transferred to Pisa, is a different one from that used in the Emilian city. In the early decades of the century, the professional strata were becoming systematically acquainted with *CJ* at least, and sometimes the *Digest* as well. This is most likely to have been a training emanating from the Laterano, for judges and *scriniarii*—whose normal full title was *scriniarius sanctae Romanae ecclesiae*—were linked closely to the papal administrative structure (even though by the early twelfth century a separate papal chancery was also forming); but it was a

---

[151] Bulgaro, *Excerpta legum*, ed. Wahrmund (with flaws; see further Fowler-Magerl, *Ordo Iudiciorum*, pp. 35–40). Conte, '*Res publica*', p. 199n also sees the text as not up to normal Bolognese quality standards, although Conte, 'Il Digesto fuori dal Digesto', shows that it does have an underlying theoretical argument. Pennington, 'The "big bang"', argues that Bulgaro is cited by Innocent II in Pisa in 1133–6, so this text probably predates that. It seems to me best located to periods in which Aimerico was in Rome, when his popes were running a broader legal system than the purely canon-law one Innocent controlled in his Pisan exile, which thus means it would date to before 1130. Fried, 'Die römische Kurie', p. 169 thinks the text is early too.

[152] See above, nn. 140–1.

[153] See Padoa Schioppa, 'Il ruolo della cultura giuridica', for others.

training, which was directed to the daily concerns of the lay majority of society, and was not focused on ecclesiastical matters.[154] Such a training, however it worked (we have no good evidence of a law school), may have begun under Paschal II, or even Clement III, but it was certainly fully in place by the time Aimerico became chancellor in 1123. Its crystallization then will also have been helped by the fact that the numbers of legal professionals were already, by 1000, higher in this unusually large city and in its unusually elaborate administration than they were elsewhere, and doubtless became more numerous still as the city expanded in the eleventh century; this meant that when Justinianic texts became more available in the second half of the eleventh they could find a better-informed community to receive them than anywhere else in Italy apart from the capital of the *Regnum Italiae* at Pavia (where a parallel development indeed took place).[155] This undoubtedly added to the cultural vitality of Rome after 1100—despite the institutional crisis which faced the city in the same period.

The converse of this is a paradox. The one major body in the city which did not use Roman legal texts at all in its procedures was the Senate. Apart from the brief 1160 case already cited, there are not even initial Roman actions in any senatorial court case surviving from the whole period 1150–1250, and no Romanist arguments at all. I have discussed this paradox elsewhere, and it does not need to be developed in detail in a book which, for the most part, stops in 1150, but the fact nonetheless needs to be stressed. Rome's daily legal practice had become, and remained, heavily influenced by the *Corpus iuris*, and palatine judges by 1150 probably all knew the Justinianic texts reasonably well; these judges worked for the Senate as much as for the papal palace. But senatorial cases remained resolutely pragmatic, focused on establishing facts, and eschewing legal distinctions. Even the *consilia* of legal experts, a standard part of senatorial forensic practice, remained firmly based on facts.[156]

This is very striking, given the rhetoric of both Republic and empire (and once, Justinian's *Institutiones*), employed in early senatorial letters to German rulers;[157] and it marks a clear limit to the commitment of the Senate to the classical past. It may be that the Senate did not feel it had to adopt such a legal rhetoric, for Rome (unlike Pisa) did not need the *Digest* to prove it was Roman. It may be that legal distinctions were somehow seen as too papal by now, and that the Senate reacted against the forensic intensity very visible in papal cases such as Seniorile's in 1145 (a case that had begun in 1143–4, a significant year), choosing to be more pragmatic in its judging instead. Whichever the reason—and I would hypothesize that both played their part—the rise of the Senate by no means furthered the

---

[154] See classically Kehr, 'Scrinium und Palatium'. For Rome and Pisa, Classen, *Studium und Gesellschaft*, pp. 73–4; see further for citation practices Conte, *Diritto comune*, pp. 75–7.

[155] Radding, *The Origins*.

[156] Wickham, 'Getting justice', pp. 121–4.

[157] See above, nn. 79, 81. Wezel's 1152 letter to Frederick Barbarossa (Wibald of Stablo, *Epistulae*, n. 404), is the only one of those texts which cites a (fairly simple) extract of Roman law, *Institutiones*, Preface and I.2.6; cf. most recently Thumser, 'Die frühe römische Kommune', pp. 135–45, at pp. 141–2; Petersohn, *Kaisertum und Rom*, pp. 135–7.

changes just described. Quite the opposite, in fact. After 1159, the popes were, for the most part, absent from the city until 1188; urban disputes no longer went to the papal court; and Romanist legal arguments abruptly stopped. Only one more such case survives for the whole period until Innocent III: a case heard by Alexander III in 1166, in his brief period in Rome in the late 1160s, between S. Cesario de Palatio and S. Marcello in Via Lata, which is again structured by possessory actions, and uses a clearly Romanist legal language in the judgement by the (eminently legally trained) pope.[158] Otherwise, Rome's precocity in Romanist argument was not just undermined by the rapid development of Bologna and Pisa, it was deliberately let slip by a Senate whose conception of itself and its roots was differently located. The Roman-ness of the Senate was clearly linked to buildings. In 1162 it famously put a preservation order on the Colonna di Traiano so that 'it should remain, whole and uncorrupted, to the honour of the whole Roman people, while the world lasts'.[159] We saw in the first section of the chapter the complex way it was linked to the Capitolio itself. But it was not linked to law, even though that law was all around it.

The sense of the past

The complexity of Rome's sense of the past is equally clear. Our accounts of that past are not numerous, but they do not by any means attach themselves to a single master narrative. How they are structured, however, is an interesting guide to the various strands of social memory available to Romans.

The succession of the popes beyond doubt determines the majority of our Roman narratives, for papal biographies are most of the substantial texts we have. The early medieval *Liber Pontificalis* had stopped in 886, and was not added to again in the systematic way that had been Roman palatine practice between the 640s and the 870s. Lists of popes continued nonetheless, in the tenth and eleventh centuries, with the origins of each pope and the exact length of his reign registered, and sometimes a longer text attached (for John XII and John XIII most notably), which is clearly more or less contemporary.[160] This was a model for later texts as well. The two main sequences of the so-called *Annales Romani*, for 1044–73 and 1116–21, both divide the text up at the accession of each pope with the same sort of initial rubric as in previous papal lists. And Cardinal Pandolfo, writing probably in the 1130s, sought to recreate the old *Liber Pontificalis* with a detailed set of papal biographies from Gregory VII to Honorius II; so also did Cardinal Bosone in the 1160s–70s, who began with a general papal narrative from the 880s to 1085, pretty

---

[158] *S. Marcello*, n. 7.

[159] *SMVL*, n. 196: 'ad honorem . . . totius populi Romani integra et incorrupta permaneat, dum mundus durat'. This famous text is most recently discussed in Conte, 'Archeologia giuridica', pp. 120–2; Peppe, 'Un "*investimentum*"'. See once more Baumgärtner, 'Rombeherrschung', esp. pp. 37–9, for contextualization.

[160] *LP*, I and II (pp. 1–198) for the text to 886; II, pp. 221–81 for 872–1073, with pp. ix–xx for the manuscripts (xiv–xv for John XII and XIII). On the end of the writing of the detailed *LP* in the 870s, see Bougard, 'Composition, diffusion et réception', pp. 131–4.

confused at the start, taken from Bonizone of Sutri, but then set out another biographical sequence beginning with Paschal II.[161] We see here a basic conceptual ordering of the past that had staying power: that the history of Rome was the history of the sequence of popes, and essentially nothing else. Other powers appear in that storyline, such as Roman, then Byzantine, then Frankish, then German emperors; but only insofar as they affected a history which was defined as papal. Alberico himself only appears in the papal works as the father of John XII, and in Boso's initial account he is hardly referred to at all.[162]

This was not the only way of seeing Roman history, all the same. An alternative view is clearly set out in the *Chronicon* of Benedetto of Monte Soratte, written shortly after 970. This history is justly famous for its confusions and inaccuracies, but what is more important here is its structure. It begins with the emperor Julian, and then runs through a collection of late Roman emperors and Ostrogothic kings, until Justinian, *peritissimus in mentem*, was elected *ab omni populo Romano*. Then followed Narses' invitation to the Lombards, and a uniquely imagined series of Lombard kings, interlaced with Byzantine emperors, leading to the Frankish conquest of Italy, and the century of Carolingian rule up to Guy of Spoleto and the period of Arab attacks ('the Hagarenes ruled in the Roman *regnum* for thirty years'). The next rulers to figure are Sergius III, Formosus (out of place), and John X; and then the *senatrix* (Marozia, execrated and unnamed), Alberico (a clear hero), his son John XII (a clear villain), and finally Otto I. The chronicle ends with a lament for the violence of Otto in Rome in 967, which is depicted as a sack of the city; it breaks off abruptly in the middle of a sentence, but its elegiac tone at the close indicates that the full text was not significantly longer.[163]

Benedetto was partially led by his sources, which included the very king-centred Paul the Deacon (second-hand), Einhard and the *Annales regni Francorum*, but not the papal *Liber Pontificalis*.[164] All the same, his very particular—indeed, very often weird—understanding of his sources evidently allowed him to shape them any way he chose; and it is clear that this choice was by no means structured by the papal narrative. He did mention popes in his narrative, and he had a papal catalogue, for he quoted it a couple of times (including a sentence on Lando, 913–14, one of Rome's obscurest pontiffs),[165] but popes in general only appear in chance references, apart from the Sergius III–John X period, and the rule of John XII. Otto I's reign is treated in more detail, and with this comes a fairly clear account of the misfortunes of his popes, but the overall picture is one in which the main legitimating element in Rome is external and secular rulership, with local Roman rulership, some papal but here again mostly secular, filling in in the early tenth century. Benedetto wrote from a totally Roman perspective, and saw the 'Saxon

[161] Respectively, *LP*, II, pp. 331–48, with the critical analysis of Whitton, 'The *Annales Romani*'; *LP*, II, pp. 282–328, but cited here from Paschal II onwards from the better text in *Liber Pontificalis*, ed. Přerovský, pp. 705–56 (Pandolfo); *LP*, II, pp. 353–446 (Bosone).
[162] *LP*, II, pp. 246, 353.
[163] Benedetto of Monte Soratte, *Chronicon*, ed. Zucchetti; pp. 28 for Justinian, 153 for the Hagarenes.
[164] Benedetto of Monte Soratte, *Chronicon*, ed. Zucchetti, pp. xxii–xxiii, xxvi–xxviii.
[165] Benedetto of Monte Soratte, *Chronicon*, ed. Zucchetti, p. 156.

king', Otto, as a foreigner, but the past was royal and imperial, not papal, for all that, except when secular rulers absented themselves.[166]

This imperial-Roman and Lombard–Frankish legitimism was not restricted to Benedetto of Monte Soratte. We need not be surprised to see it in Ugo of Farfa and the *Chronicon Farfense* of Gregorio of Catino, for Farfa was an imperial monastery and fiercely defended its autonomy from popes in all periods. (Both, however, give favourable attention to Alberico, who overthrew one of Farfa's emblematic Bad Abbots, Campone.)[167] But we do have to recognize the force of another early text, the *Libellus de imperatoria potestate in urbe Roma*. This dates to between 877 and 962; in the array of scholarship that has treated it, arguments have been put forward for a dating either to *c*.900 or *c*.950. Although I am unpersuaded by those who see it as a pro-Spoletan text, and therefore to be tightly located in the later 890s, its heavy focus on the 860s and '70s, and the absence of information thereafter, seem to argue for a date not too long after that period, so in or around 900 seems about right.[168] This text is the most pro-imperial manifesto, which is known to have come out of Rome or its immediate environs. It sees Rome as imperial Roman, then Lombard, then Carolingian: the latter 'holds the Roman *dominium* up to today'. It takes Lothar I's *Constitutio Romana* of 824, which had laid claim to an overarching sovereignty over Rome's legal system, and massively exaggerates its effect and range, ascribing it to Charlemagne: the judges of the emperor could 'compel the inhabitants [of Rome and its territory] to come to the *placitum*'; 'all the *maiores* of Rome were imperial men (*imperiales homines*)', and all the *vulgus* swore fidelity to the emperor; the imperial legate also controlled the city's finances. This lasted until Louis II's death (Louis faced down even Nicholas I, who apologized to him), after which Charles the Bald weakly ceded to the Romans 'the laws and customs of the kingdom (*iura regni et consuetudines illius*)', and kings/emperors lost control thereafter, with lamentable (but unspecified) results. But even then (unlike in Benedetto) we do not revert to a period of papal rule; it is the 'Romans', undefined, who benefited from Charles' privileges.[169] Even the violence of the Formosan crisis itself, with all its poisonous acts and equally poisonous texts (all of them, one should recognize, focused exclusively on canon law and papal or episcopal

---

[166] Benedetto of Monte Soratte, *Chronicon*, ed. Zucchetti, pp. 174–86. Monte Soratte had been a Carolingian-controlled monastery (as Benedetto knew: Benedetto of Monte Soratte, *Chronicon*, ed. Zucchetti, pp. 85, 96, 106, 146), but was not by now, and anyway the whole text, however critical of Romans, sees the world from their standpoint (cf. Benedetto of Monte Soratte, *Chronicon*, ed. Zucchetti, pp. xix–xx).

[167] *CF*, I, pp. 33–50 (Ugo), 301–66 (Gregorio)—the tenth-century sequences of each. For Gregorio's imperial perspective, see e.g. Toubert, *Les structures*, p. 81; Stroll, *The Medieval Abbey*, p. 7 and *passim*.

[168] *Libellus de imperatoria potestate*, ed. Zucchetti. For dating, see for an earlier dating, e.g. Lapôtre, *L'Europe et le Saint-Siège*, I, pp. 171–202; Arnaldi, *Natale 875*, pp. 38–40 (both favour a Spoleto connection); Brühl, 'Die Kaiserpfalz', p. 6; Buc, *The Dangers of Ritual*, p. 73; West, 'Communities and pacta', pp. 383–4. For a later dating, e.g. *Libellus de imperatoria potestate*, ed. Zucchetti, pp. lxx–lxxxiv; Schramm, *Kaiser, Rom*, pp. 64–6; Houben, 'La componente romana', p. 30.

[169] Quotes: *Libellus de imperatoria potestate*, ed. Zucchetti, pp. 194–5, 196, 197, 208. For the link to the *Constitutio Romana*, the most useful analysis is West, 'Communities and pacta', pp. 379–84.

precedent),[170] passed by the author of the *Libellus*, for whom the issue is simply Carolingian legitimacy.

The *Libellus* shows that there were people at the start of the tenth century who could see the popes as simply bishops inside the Carolingian state; Benedetto (who used the *Libellus*) shows that Rome's history could still be seen as a mostly secular narrative into the 970s. This indicates that there ought to have been a secularist political strand in the city that could make sense of both Otto III's domination in 998–1001 and Henry III's papal depositions of 1046. This is less easy to argue, however. Otto III left almost no trace in Roman narratives, if we except the *Vita S. Adalberti episcopi*, a life of Adalbert of Prague written for Otto himself by a monk of SS. Bonifacio e Alessio in Rome, Giovanni Canapario, which stresses Rome's welcome to the new emperor and his chosen new pope, Gregory V in 996.[171] Only the shadow of his memory was preserved, in that Castel S. Angelo was so widely— across Europe, indeed—called the *castellum Crescentii* in eleventh- and twelfth-century texts (including the Roman *Mirabilia*), thus attesting to the long-lasting memory of Crescenzio 'II''s unsuccessful defence of it against Otto in 998. This may simply be a marker of the weakness of Roman narratives during the century after Benedetto's text breaks off; but Henry III, too, is only remembered as a *papal reformer* in surviving Roman sources: as, that is to say, the catalyst for the appearance in the city of Clement II and his successors, and that in a fairly low-key way, too. Roman sources indeed, significantly, never engaged in any systematic condemnation of the *ancien régime* of the Tuscolani popes.[172] In the eleventh century, in other words, the traditional secular narrative seems to have become rather weaker. Emperors appear as supporters or opponents of popes, but imperial rule was not by now visibly part of the usable past for Romans, as far as we can tell.

It is nonetheless legitimate to wonder whether the possibility of imperial narratives had altogether vanished from the city. Otto III's rule was locally controversial and, by the end, universally rejected; it could be forgotten relatively easily, perhaps. Henry IV's rule from the Capitolio in 1084 may not have been so unpopular, however (below, pp. 423–4), and Henry V used the Capitolio again in a ceremony in 1117. It is true that Roman leaders sent a very cold letter to Lothar III in 1130, which suggests that Lothar should 'adapt yourself to Roman *leges*', and be civil to

---

[170] See *Auxilius und Vulgarius*, ed. Dümmler, pp. 59–94, 107–39; *Invectiva, passim*.

[171] Giovanni Canapario, *Vita S. Adalberti episcopi*, ch. 21 (*MGH, SS*, IV, p. 591).

[172] See above, n. 50, for the *castellum*. Bosone (not a Roman, but sometimes showing Roman sensibilities) recalls Crescenzio's defence in *LP*, II, p. 353. On the same page, he is also critical of John XIX's promotion from layman to pope, a rare negative comment on the first two Tuscolani popes; he also refers to the 1044–6 papal crisis as one of popes who *non regebant set vastabant pontificatum*, and were, as *tales pestes*, removed by Henry III, a more typical phraseology—cf., for example, the *Annales Romani*, in *LP*, II, pp. 331–2. But what this means is that the synod of Sutri was portrayed in Rome as a response to the immediate papal crisis, not as a sweeping away of the whole Tuscolano (and Teofilatto) political system. Note that, if Percy Schramm were right to date the *Libellus de ceremoniis aule imperatoris*, aka the *Graphia-Libellus*, an antiquarian and often fantastic account of the Roman imperial bureaucracy and ceremonial system, to *c*.1030, then an imperial interest would indeed be documented in the high Tuscolano period (*Kaiser, Rom*, pp. 192–217, but the whole book argues for an unbroken continuity here); but Herbert Bloch is convincing in his argument that it was compiled by Pietro Diacono of Montecassino, a century later ('Der Autor der "Graphia"', pp. 90–105).

Anacletus II, before he could be loved by Romans and became their *princeps*. But there are clear continuities, as Jürgen Petersohn has shown, between Henry V's dealings with the Romans on the one hand, and the altogether more enthusiastic letters of the Roman Senate to Conrad III in 1149, which invoke the *regnum et imperium* of Constantine and Justinian, and Gregory the Great's (supposed) subordination to Maurice, as a preferable alternative to papal power and the dominance of Roger of Sicily; throughout the early twelfth century (and later too), there were Romans who saw the empire as a major interlocutor for the Roman secular leadership.[173]

In 1149, the Senate was, to be sure, talking about Justinian, not Alberico, or even Charlemagne. But the point that emerges from the secular narratives is that the Romans did not make much distinction between them. The Carolingian period looked back to the classical Roman empire, to Constantine at least; and Benedetto's storyline did not envisage any real structural breaks until then—and, if the Arabs and Sergius III saw a break thereafter, Alberico and Otto I re-established secular power again. Even popes employed the imagery of Constantine, as the sculpture of the Campus Lateranensis shows (above, pp. 335–7), and they were by the 1120s also using the imagery of contemporary imperial power as well (above, p. 361). In that light, the senatorial use of Justinian simply seems like an updating of imperial imagery, in a city whose exposure to the *Codex Iustinianus* had recently become very considerable.

It cannot be said that a narrative of Roman history focused on secular rulers was as *strong* as that which was focused on popes. It is, as can be seen, necessary to explain away a gap of over a century in Roman secular storylines if one wants to explore continuities. But there was nonetheless, at least intermittently, a usable secular tradition which looked to Roman emperors and their successors, and not just to the papal storyline. Rome in practice tended to resist external interference, in every century, but it never lost its pride in its imperial past as *caput mundi*, and emperors were potentially part of that in every period.[174] Even Alberico arguably had become simply subsumed into the imperial narrative, as a fill-in between the Carolingians and Otto I; indeed Alberico showed himself to be fully conscious of this when he named his son *Octavianus*, Octavian, not a name used hitherto, implying that he himself could be seen as Julius Caesar, progenitor of a new imperial line.[175] (Crescenzio 'II' was only remembered as Otto III's brave opponent, however, and Giovanni di Crescenzio was not remembered at all.) But Charlemagne, Otto I, and Henry IV and his successors could potentially fit into the narrative without distortion; and Frederick Barbarossa in the decades after 1150 would do so with some force.

---

[173] For 1117, *Udalrici codex*, n. 178. For the text of 1130 and an exhaustive commentary, see Petersohn, 'Der Brief'; for the whole period from Henry V to Frederick I, see Petersohn, *Kaisertum und Rom*, pp. 7–194. For the 1149 letters, see above, n. 79.

[174] Schramm, *Kaiser, Rom*, p. 37 gives a full list of references to the use of *caput mundi* up to 1000. Twelfth-century examples include *Mirabilia*, p. 51; Wibald of Stablo, *Epistolae*, n. 214.

[175] For Ottaviano, e.g. Benedetto of Monte Soratte, *Chronicon*, pp. 171–2; Flodoard, *Annales*, s.a. 954.

This all gives a context to the *Mirabilia* tradition. If the *Mirabilia* text of 1140–3 is looked at on its own, it can easily be read as such a complete evocation of a classical past, with its obsessive lists of pre-Constantinian buildings, and its incredible stories about them attached to the late Republic and to Augustus, that the minds of scholars wander very easily into the well-worn paths of 'Renaissance' imagery.[176] And it is true that it focuses on an earlier period than any text we have just been looking at; of the twenty-odd emperors it mentions, only three post-date Constantine, plus three of the five popes; the latest of each come in a short narrative in which Boniface IV requests permission from the emperor Phocas to convert the Pantheon into a church around 608. Only four later people are referred to at all, casual references to mostly contemporary lay leaders. The *Mirabilia* text says that it is a description of the *tempus paganorum*, and this is broadly entirely correct.[177] It is deliberately not an evocation of the Christian past of the great basilicas, which were more dramatic in size and appearance than any but the grandest classical secular monuments, although Christian elements, of course, appear throughout the work. I do not see that the text is particularly an invocation of a Republican rather than an imperial Rome; the *tempus consulum et senatorum* is indeed referred to, but not nearly as often as emperors are. And the text lent itself easily to imperial readings, as shown most clearly in its reworking in 1155, presumably in the context of Frederick I's coronation, when it was inserted in a longer work called the *Graphia aureae urbis Romae* by the Cassinese monk, historian, and forger Pietro Diacono, alongside the *Libellus de ceremoniis aule imperatoris*, which (as noted above) Herbert Bloch shows to have been the work of Pietro himself. As a whole, then, the *Graphia* sets the *Mirabilia* into an essentially imperial framework, and it does so without any need to rewrite the latter except in some marginal details. Conversely, however, the papal tradition was not alarmed by the *Mirabilia* either, as shown by the fact that one of its early MS appearances is in Cencio's *Liber Censuum* of 1192.[178]

---

[176] *Mirabilia*, ed. Valentini and Zucchetti. The historiography on the text is endless; recent examples include Miedema, *Die 'Mirabilia Romae'* (focused on later manuscripts); Accame Lanzilotta, *Contributi sui Mirabilia* (focused on textual variants); Strothmann, *Kaiser und Senat*, pp. 93–127, 182–7; Kinney, 'Fact and fiction' (the best of this set); Hamilton, 'The rituals of Renaissance'; Riccioni, 'Rewriting Antiquity'. I accept the separation between the author of the text and Benedetto *cantor*, author of the processional *ordo*, argued for by Schimmelpfennig, *Die Zeremonienbücher*, pp. 14–15, developed in Schimmelpfennig, 'Die Bedeutung', pp. 50–1 (although he goes further than I would in dividing up the authorship of the *ordo*); the two texts are contemporary and have some interests in common, but are too far apart in their foci for them to be posited as having the same author without a much better demonstration than has been offered.

[177] Post-Constantinan popes: *Mirabilia*, pp. 44 (Symmachus), 41 (Pelagius), 35 (Boniface IV and Phocas); late emperors, apart from Phocas: p. 41 (Eudoxia, Arcadius, Theodosius II). Innocent II is referred to only in later twelfth-century MSS: see above, n. 44. Near-contemporary laymen: *Mirabilia*, pp. 23 (Crescenzio di Crescenzio, d. 998), 47 (Cencio the urban prefect, d.1077), 56 (Cencio Frangipane), 62 (Cencio *de Orrigo*: see above, p. 231). *Tempus paganorum*: *Mirabilia*, p. 65.

[178] *Tempus consulum et senatorum*: *Mirabilia*, pp. 32, 34, 51. Contra, e.g. the Republican readings of Krautheimer, *Rome*, p. 199; Herklotz, *Gli eredi di Costantino*, pp. 65–6, nuanced at pp. 215–17, a bibliographical survey. For the *Graphia*, see the exhaustive study of Bloch, 'Der Autor der "Graphia"'; see also Petersohn, *Kaisertum und Rom*, pp. 46–79 for the degree to which the *Graphia* is almost entirely un-papal; for the text of the *Mirabilia* in the *Graphia*, see Schramm, *Kaiser, Könige*, III, pp. 322–38. In the *Graphia*, it is true that some phrases in the *Mirabilia* are altered in an 'imperialist' direction; Herklotz, *Gli eredi di Costantino*, pp. 66–8, gives a list. But one cornerstone of the pro-Republican theory, the denial in

The *Mirabilia* is thus not a programmatic text, dedicated to a particular version of the Roman past. But it is, all the same, a clear evocation of the surviving glories of the pre-Christian period. This does not seem to me either as surprising or as new as some commentators believe. The text focuses on buildings, and the Romans, as we have amply seen, were always proud of their classical monuments; there had long been lists of them, as the *Itinerarium Einsidlense* of *c.*800 (which also includes churches) and the Pisan *Liber Guidonis* of 1119 (which does not) both show.[179] Benedetto's *Liber Politicus* even tracked papal processions by the classical buildings they passed (above, p. 340). The *Mirabilia* is simply a further exemplification of that interest. Its author, of course, knew that Rome was also full of grand churches, and was doubtless proud of that too, but these had parallels across Europe; the city's classical landscape had no parallel. And the other point that needs to be underlined is that Roman writers did not see that classical past as having gone away. They did not just have one genealogy connecting them to the ancient world, but two, the papal succession—which went back to the age of Nero (so the earliest *Liber Pontificalis* explicitly said about St Peter)[180]—and the classical/Carolingian/German imperial succession. And the intervening interventions in the city in themselves constituted a continuing process of renewal, with no breaks. (It was only external commentators who saw Rome as a wreck of its former self, and not all of them.) The *Mirabilia* from this standpoint was not so innovative, although it was certainly an enthusiastic and occasionally eccentric evocation of a past-in-the-present.

But it does, finally, need to be said that twelfth-century Romans did use the classical past more than most of their predecessors. The extension of Justinianic law in urban legal practice is the clearest sign of this. Another is naming. After Alberico's choice of name for his son, Ottaviano became a common name in the city. Of other classical names with little or no post-classical usage, *Nero* appears in documents in 1051, *Ptolomeus* in 1068 (the future count of Tuscolo), *Antoninus* and *Cycero* in 1110; and then, after 1150, *Iugurtha*, a Sutri notary, from 1161 (Sallust was clearly read in Sutri), *Achilles* from 1170, maybe *Anibal* from 1183, *Catilina* (the most surprising) from 1184.[181] In Milan (and many other cities), the naming changes of the twelfth century produced a large number of people named

---

the *Mirabilia* (p. 32) that the horseman in the Campus Lateranensis was Constantine, was not altered in the *Graphia*, which evidently did not see that it had anti-imperial implications (Schramm, *Kaiser, Könige*, III, p. 335). It is anyway less clear to me than to other commentators that a Republican programme could usefully be served by the re-identification of a single statue, without any other editorializing on the part of the text (see also, here, Herklotz, *Gli eredi di Costantino*, p. 216). I am with Miedema, *Die 'Mirabilia Romae'*, p. 9, that the author's position was 'ein literarischer, kein politischer'.

179 *Itinerarium*: most recent edition, Del Lungo, *Roma in età carolingia*, pp. 66–76. 1119 text: *Liber Guidonis*, ed. Campopiano, pp. 12–20.

180 *LP*, I, p. 118.

181 Respectively, *RF*, n. 824; *Chronica Casinensis*, III.60; *SMN*, n. 35; ASR, SCD, cassetta 16, n. 134; ASV, A. A. Arm. I–XVIII, n. 3654 = *LP*, II, pp. 422–3; *SMVL*, n. 222 (*Anibal* is the most problematic name of the set, though, for it may simply be an alternate spelling for the *Anibaldus senator* of 1171, *SMN*, n. 99, plausibly the ancestor of the Annibaldi: Carocci, *Baroni*, p. 311; Thumser, *Rom*, p. 28); *SPV*, n. 68.

or surnamed Caca- or Caga-, Cacainarca or Cagapisto ('shit-in-the-box' or 'shit-pesto'), showing a goliardic bounciness which was indeed one of the clearest northern Italian contributions to civic innovation and idealism. There were some of these in Rome too, but rather fewer.[182] Instead, the sedate figures of the classical world were invoked, together also with a steadily increasing number of new names formed from Deus, Deoteguardi, or Deusvossalvet, again particularly after 1150s as a consciousness of inhabiting the spiritual capital of the West presumably encouraged.[183] God and the classical past here went hand in hand, in developments that were beginning at the very end of our period. These legal and naming practices reached rather more people than any of the texts we have been looking at, too. As did the antique influences on both figurative and non-figurative decoration in churches, discussed earlier, although here most lay observers will doubtless not have picked up the specifically classical allusions.

The argument I am carefully stepping around here is that the foundation of the Senate was more than marginally influenced—still less determined—by the so-called *renovatio* of the classical past. Robert Benson in 1982 saw the early Senate as deviated by an illusion, 'the Romans' intoxication with Antiquity'; to Jürgen Strothmann in 1998, 'the *Mirabilia* are a component of the communication which led to the renewal of the Senate, whether Benedetto [i.e. the anonymous author] intended it or not'; and this is to cite only two studies out of many.[184] It is, of course, true that early senatorial letters to emperors did sometimes use a classicizing rhetoric (if less often than these two scholars believed), but this seems to me simply the consequence of an urban cultural environment, a set of available Roman storylines, that was long-standing and had many roots. People in Rome did indeed greatly value many aspects of the classical past—its buildings and monuments, pagan and Christian, the purist early Christian tradition of the martyrs, the unbroken continuity of papal power from the time of the Roman empire, the scarcely broken continuity of imperial valorization of the city, the Roman-ness of a largely imperial Roman law, and the always-immanent status of Rome as *caput mundi*. These manifold versions of the past-in-the-present (none of them needing any real *renovatio*, except Roman law) were available for a very wide array of political initiatives, and had long been. The popes used some of them, emperors used others, the early Senate a third set. This explains the relative intensity of the evocations of the past in the Roman Senate, as opposed to the different traditions available in other Italian communes, but it was not in itself a causal element of the events of 1143.

For, conversely, it has to be recognized that none of these storylines gave much autonomous role to the Roman *populus*, however that word was to be understood.

---

[182] For Milan, Menant, 'Une forme de distinction inattendue'. For Rome, *RS*, nn. 65, 76; *Papsturkunden*, n. 134 (these first three all for the same man); *SMVL*, nn. 76, 263; *SMCM*, nn. 44, 58, 62; *SPV*, nn. 51, 58; 'Documenti per la storia', n. 18. They begin in the 950s, but are only common after 1150.

[183] *S. Prassede*, n. 11 (the earliest, a. 1100); *SMVL*, n. 162; *SMCM*, nn. 35, 44, 55, 63; *SPV*, nn. 55, 56, 57, 65; *SMN*, nn. 53, 167; *S. Alessio*, n. 22; ASR, SCD, cassetta 16 bis, n. 154; *S. Gregorio*, n. 95; 'Documenti per la storia', n. 12 and ff.; *S. Sisto*, n. 13; *LC*, I, n. 183.

[184] Benson, 'Political *renovatio*', p. 359; Strothmann, *Kaiser und Senat*, p. 185. Contra: Baumgärtner, 'Rombeherrschung'; Miedema, *Die 'Mirabilia Romae'*, pp. 7–9.

The Romans are stressed plenty of times in them as players in the city's politics, sometimes positively (the *populus* electing popes in the pre-1046 period, and occasionally also later), sometimes negatively (Benedetto of Monte Soratte's repetitious invocation of their *consuetudo maligna* of rejecting their rulers),[185] but always in a subordinate role. This did indeed limit the early Senate's autonomous use of the past, and helps to explain its interest in imperial authority. It is not surprising that the Senate also began to name-check the traditions of the Roman Republic as a result as well, as did plenty of other Italian cities, but these were no more prominent in the available imagery of the past in Rome than they were anywhere else. The past gave the Senate its name, but did not particularly help its authority, that is to say. It did form a cultural environment in which the Senate inevitably had to operate, and it was a relatively unchanging one: for the twelfth century, even if it saw more writing, did not see radically different attitudes to the past. If, however, we want to understand how the Senate actually did develop, we will need to look elsewhere, at the social and political challenges faced by the city in the late eleventh and early twelfth centuries; these are the subject of Chapter 7.

*

What to me is most clear about the various cultural practices discussed in this chapter is their complexity, which is indeed dizzying at times. Rome's monumental landscape was a stage for a remarkable variety of cultural initiatives, and the multifaceted nature of its remembered past allowed as many more. This chapter has avoided more than occasional comparative analyses as a result, for nowhere (even Constantinople) could compete with this complexity. This resolves itself, however, into a network of practices and representations which remained fairly stable (although also acting as bases for disruption and contestation), and a second set which showed some innovation, particularly in the decades after 1100.

The most stable pattern discussed here was certainly the processional geography of Rome. Indeed, I have argued that this underpinned the identity of the city itself, and helped to maintain its unity. It foregrounded papal authority in the city, but at the same time involved and gave coherence to the Roman *populus* in its widest version. Processions took up a lot of time and energy, and were also an important means by which papal resources were distributed to Romans. They could be the outlet for tensions, but were also a favoured arena for expressing tension. This is all best documented after 1100, but its roots extended back for centuries, and similar patterns are certainly visible in the eighth and ninth. Rome through the processional system also saw the most important ecclesiastical foci of its symbolic geography constantly reaffirmed, and challenged the future Senate to come up with secular versions as well, which it rapidly did, with the new valorization of the Capitolio, Monte Testaccio, and (maybe already) piazza Navona. Almost as stable, I would argue, were Rome's uses of the remembered past, structured around the succession of popes, the city's imperial traditions, and, once again, the city's

---

[185] Benedetto of Monte Soratte, *Chronicon*, pp. 171, 179, 184.

landscape. These gave a variety of versions of the linkage between the past and the present, which could also connect to the ceremonial world, full of evocations of past events as that latter world was.

On that basis, nonetheless, we also see shifts. The greatly increased use of Roman law texts from the late eleventh century and especially after 1130 is one, certainly. It offered a density of cultural allusion that was largely new, or, at least, newly dense. And Romans began to do new things with visual culture, particularly in an ecclesiastical framework (although if we had more surviving secular buildings we would doubtless find more of the visual complexity of the Casa dei Crescenzi here too). This ecclesiastical innovation began before 1046, but was certainly spurred on by 'reforming' practices; conversely, it was itself manifold, some of it showing papal claims to imperial-style authority or supremacy in the city, some of it showing a renewed lay interest in a more purist and critical spirituality, which did not automatically underpin papal hegemony.

These shifts did not themselves have to lead in any direction. They are complex enough that they have been able to be used as supports for every one of the grand narratives that recent historians have employed, whether subtly or simplistically, to frame the period—papal 'reform', the twelfth-century 'Renaissance', the 'Roman revolution'. I have cast doubt on all these easy affiliations. But the point is that Rome's cultural world, whether changing or unchanging, was also complex enough to be a set of resources, a toy-box, for the use of every initiative and trend in our period too. Fervent opponents, like Crescenzio 'II' and Otto III, or Gregory VII and Clement III, or Anacletus II and Innocent II, or Innocent II and the early Senate, could each and all employ versions of the same sets of practices and images in competition with each other, creatively and continually. They could, and they did. How that competition actually worked in practice is the focus of what follows.

7

The Crisis, 1050–1150

The traditional system of Roman government, which dated back to the eighth century, lasted until the 1040s. Its crisis began with the synod of Sutri in 1046. It is not that the new regime of (initially) German popes automatically led to the collapse of the old system; Hildebrand/Gregory VII, at least, can be seen as a coordinator of innovative variants on it, which might have lasted had it not been for the civil war of the 1080s–90s. That civil war was indeed the catalyst for a series of sharp and irreversible political, institutional, and ideological changes throughout not only Rome and its territory, but the whole *Regnum Italiae* of central and northern Italy. Rome's particular history here has close parallels in the history of the northern half of the peninsula, parallels which will be explored further below; it could be said, then, that the Roman crisis began with Henry IV in 1084, not with Henry III in 1046. All the same, in Rome the later 1080s simply exposed the flaws in the political system which the first generation of 'reform' popes had sought to create; so we need to start in the 1040s in order to understand it. At the other end, it was not until the 1140s–50s that new types of political structure, the papal Curia and the Senate, finally crystallized. This did not in itself bring political stability— any more than Rome's pre-1046 *ancien régime* had been universally peaceful—but from then on conflict had a more stable set of tracks along which to run, and, by and large, it did so. This reconstruction process again has close parallels with those of the early communes in northern Italian and Tuscan cities, as we shall see.

The storyline of Rome's crisis is an Italian one, that is to say. This has long been known. It has not led to Rome being more than intermittently included among the exemplars of the historiography of the 'origins of the commune', as I complained in Chapter 1; mostly because a full understanding of Rome's moves in a communal direction has been, and still is, undermined by the moralism inherent in the 'reform' narrative. But many features of Rome's social and political structures did lead to Rome's experience being different, in a number of crucial respects. This chapter will thus, like several others, focus on both similarity and difference. I shall not, however, offer a full political history of the crisis here. A brief narrative was sketched out earlier (pp. 29–34), which can at least serve as a guide to readers; the 'political expedients' section below reprises some of that at greater length; but a detailed account, year by year, would do little more than repeat the reconstructions of dozens of (mostly) papal historians.[1] And it would not help the underlying problem, which is

---

[1] Such as Cowdrey, *Pope Gregory VII*; Ziese, *Wibert*; Servatius, *Paschalis II.*; Stroll, *Calixtus II*; Palumbo, *Lo scisma*; Stroll, *The Jewish Pope*.

to understand the changing structural constraints faced by Rome's rulers, and, more widely, Rome's elites—all the city's political players, indeed—when they made political choices.

This chapter therefore divides into four parts. In the first, I trace the history of Rome's judicial institutions, which can serve as a metonym for the changing governmental structure of the city as a whole. Then we shall look at the basic ground rules for Rome's politics and political economy, which acted as constraints on all those who sought to gain and exercise power in the city. Thirdly, I shall offer a brief chronological account of the attempts by certain major papal players— Hildebrand/Gregory, Clement III, Paschal II and his successors (including the responses of the Corsi, Frangipane, and Pierleoni), and Innocent II, to deal with the evolving political system as they found it. The events they engaged in are well known, but the changing structural constraints they faced have not been developed so much by historians. Finally, we shall look at the social basis of the commune, both before and after the foundation of the Senate in 1143, so that we can use the structural analyses both in this chapter and in preceding ones to see what changed in the social strata of the city as a whole. I am opposed to teleologies, so I am by no means dedicated to the view that the development of the commune was the only possible outcome of the crisis in Rome, but a book which finishes in 1150 cannot avoid the major shift that marks its end point. I hope, by exploring the relationship between structure and process, to push forward an understanding of development: doubtless not completely, but at least some way along.

FALL AND RISE OF A JUDICIAL SYSTEM

The basic structures of government in Latin Europe until well after 1150 revolved around war and justice. We tend to know less about the organization of the former than about the latter, for war is, above all, attested in narratives, mostly written by men who were not actually there, whereas justice is largely documented in court records which were supposed to be contemporary and to have legal validity in themselves as accurate accounts. Not all court records do this in any way perfectly; the standard template for recording north Italian public court (*placitum*) proceedings in the eleventh century, for example, gave very little space to the arguments of the parties, and only characterized in any detail the closing rituals of each dispute.[2] Roman records of disputes are slightly more circumstantial than that, however, in some cases at least; we get a certain sense of what went on in courts in every period as a result—as also of who was present to legitimize court proceedings, which was essential if the document was to have subsequent legal force. We can thus build up a sense of what, and who, was necessary in order to resolve a dispute in public. I have defended elsewhere the argument that the changing patterns of public legitimation in the widest sense, can, in the Middle Ages, best be studied through

---

[2] See in general Bougard, *La justice*, pp. 307–29; Wickham, 'Justice', pp. 185–9.

the history of *placita* and other forms of dispute settlement. (This needs to take into consideration, of course, all the ambiguities of the word 'public', but that was a standard word in the sources throughout our period, with roughly its modern meaning, as in the phrase *publica functio*.)[3] In Rome, indeed, this is in effect the only way to study political institutions as they worked in practice, for we know very little about the organization of the city's armies. What happened to justice is, anyway, illuminating and interesting in itself.

Pierre Toubert definitively analysed the structure of the Roman *placitum* up to 1080, taking the story on in less detail up to 1200, in a hundred pages of *Les structures du Latium médiéval*.[4] There is no need to repeat his insights at length. But we do need to start the story in the 1010s, because after that there is rather less evidence for a generation. I shall set the system up in the form it took in the 1010s, in the dozen surviving cases from the time of Giovanni di Crescenzio and Benedict VIII, before taking it forward into the later period.[5]

The classic *placitum romanum* (a convenient modern phrase; our sources just say *placitum*) consisted of a court president, who was the ruler of Rome or his delegate; some or all of the palatine judges, assisted by *dativi iudices* who were chosen case by case; a variable number of named Roman *nobiles*, who could make up a high percentage of the city's 'old aristocracy' in major cases; and numerous other unnamed *adstantes*, who might sometimes have been non-aristocratic.[6] They were thus large-scale operations, and are important for the prosopography of the Roman aristocracy, as we saw in Chapter 4. We only, of course, have cases involving the church as at least one party, and only cases concerning land, as is almost always the case in the documentary record we have in these centuries. We do not need to doubt that some lay-versus-lay cases were heard in the same way, but we cannot be sure how important a dispute needed to be—either in its scale or in the importance of the parties—in order to reach the attention of such an assemblage of notables. In the *Regnum Italiae*, *placita* were usually county assemblies which met (again, usually) three times a year, and seem to have heard whatever business came up on that occasion, although judicial hearings were not restricted to particular seasons. In Rome, we have examples of tenth- and eleventh-century *placita* in ten of the twelve months of the year; they may possibly sometimes have met at the request of the parties, and they also reassembled fairly readily to rehear cases.[7] Conversely,

---

[3] For *publica functio* see *Papsturkunden*, nn. 205, 345, 393, 420, 585 for the phrase, in use up to the 1020s. Other similar phrases followed later, such as the *ostis publicus* whose war damage justified the non-payment of vineyard rent in e.g. *SMVL*, nn. 133, 136, *S. Prassede*, n. 12 (aa. 1106–12). Rome, of course, followed Roman law, which made extensive use of the word *publicus*, but also Carolingian and post-Carolingian practice, which did likewise: see, for example, Sassier, 'L'utilisation d'un concept romain'. For *placita* as foci for legitimation and power, see e.g. Wickham, 'Justice', pp. 192–5 and *passim*. For a criticism, White, 'Tenth-century courts at Mâcon', pp. 58–61, focused on an earlier version of these arguments.

[4] Toubert, *Les structures*, esp. pp. 1191–257, 1314–48, effectively replacing the only previous survey, Hirschfeld, 'Das Gerichtswesen'.

[5] *RF*, nn. 616, 488, 657, 658, 637, 492, 502, 504, 506; *S. Gregorio*, nn. 126, 16, 14.

[6] Toubert, *Les structures*, pp. 1202–29.

[7] Toubert, *Les structures*, p. 1237, listing cases in nine of the months, with the addition of *S. Gregorio*, n. 14 (November 1019). *S. Gregorio*, n. 126, with two hearings in the monastery itself

the phrase *dum resideret* and similar near the start of several texts, 'while [the court president] was residing', a phrase probably borrowed from north Italian formularies, implies that there were also days set aside in advance for hearings, to which parties came to raise pleas.[8] Most of the city cases we have were heard in the *domus* of the court president, or else in the Laterano or in S. Pietro in Vaticano (where, in 983, a case was held 'intro ospitale in co usualis est nominati pape dormiendum', so, in effect, there too in the house of the president, Pope Benedict VII). The Laterano was not the dominant location that one might have expected, however, although the pope did indeed often preside over justice there—perhaps, as other sources say, in some cases under the statue of the *lupa*, overlooking the Campus Lateranensis, although sometimes visibly in the papal *camera* there too.[9]

The point about these *placita* was thus that they were standardized occasions, run by high-status legal experts, the palatine judges, and legitimated more widely by Rome's aristocracy. The whole of the city's political society came together regularly and frequently to run justice, that is to say, and the choreography of each case, while it was on one level unique every time because every case was different, on another level had considerable regularities as well. The 1010s *placita* show a stable political system, which continued to reproduce itself without visible change when, in 1012, the Tuscolano Benedict VIII replaced Giovanni di Crescenzio. This is more important for our purposes now than is the actual outcome of these cases. Some did not actually end, because of the contumacy of a party; some ended in a brokered agreement, an *amicalis pactuacio*; some ended in a *sententia*, and the *refutatio* of the loser. But all of them affirmed, and reproduced, the judicial authority of the political society of Rome, united in a structured assembly. The success of that authority, at least on the level of the churches and lay opponents who were parties in our cases, is shown by the rarity of private arbitrations surviving from the period to 1050; the accords and compromises we have are nearly all during or subsequent to formal hearings and ratified by palatine judges.[10] All this was normal in the 1010s, as it had been normal in the tenth century, by Alberico's time at the latest; more occasional texts show it already in the ninth. This sort of assembly politics was typical of early medieval Europe, and was regularized by the Carolingians; it was doubtless indeed the Carolingians who extended it to Rome,

---

in 1013, may be an instance of a case held at the request of a party; several hearings are also attested in e.g. *RF*, nn. 657–8. Bougard, *La justice*, pp. 207–9, shows that every month had *placita* in northern Italy, at least in an earlier period.

[8] Examples: Manaresi, nn. 236, 254; *RF*, n. 616. Compare almost any north Italian case in Manaresi, where '*dum*' or '*cum*' is formulaic.

[9] *Domus* of president: e.g. *RF*, n. 616, 637. Vaticano: *RS*, n. 185 (a. 983). Laterano: e.g. Manaresi, n. 254; *RF*, nn. 502 (papal *camera*), 1006. *RF*, n. 502 may be atypical, because Benedict VIII is here, uniquely, surrounded by his *fideles*, not by the *placitum* assembly, doubtless because Farfa's opponent was here his own brother Romano. See in general Toubert, *Les structures*, pp. 1237–41, who argues that the *placitum* was normally held 'de plein air', i.e. in a location accessible to a wide public. For the wolf, see Chapter 6, n. 41.

[10] Toubert, *Les structures*, pp. 1254–7.

for Roman practices are so close to those of Carolingian northern Italy.[11] By the eleventh century, such *placita* were rare in the Frankish world, but south of the Alps they were regular in most regions until the second half of the century. Rome fits this Italian pattern, then, although, as already noted, there are indications that *placita* were held even more often in Rome than they were in each county further north. It was clearly easy for Roman judges and aristocrats to come together frequently, and the more often they did so the more solid their political aggregation.

One narrative of a dispute may be enough to give a flavour of the Roman *placitum* process. In March 1012, Farfa laid a plea against Gregorio di Urso di Malepassia over a house in Rome *ubi dicitur Agones* (piazza Navona) and land in the southern Sabina, in what is now Montelibretti; Gregorio replied that his father and mother had held them from Farfa with a standard three-generation lease from Abbot Giovanni III (d.997). Farfa had already sought justice against Gregorio four months earlier, in December 1011, apparently for the same house (then said to be beside the Terme Alessandrine, just east of piazza Navona), from the *patricius* Giovanni di Crescenzio, who ordered the urban prefect Crescenzio to take care of it; Gregorio then refused to appear, and the monks went back to Giovanni to protest. He gave Gregorio three chances to delay (*indutia*), one of them brokered by Crescenzio di Benedetto count of the Sabina; then, in a final hearing the prefect, in his *domus*, with *iudices et nobiles Romanorum* including the *primicerius defensorum* and the *arcarius*, two *dativi iudices*, and fourteen named men (some from the Sabina), invested Farfa with the house in contumacy. This evidently worked to bring Gregorio to court, because it was soon after that the March document begins. This time it was heard directly by Crescenzio, the urban prefect, 'where were residing' the *primicerius*, the *prior* or *primicerius defensorum*, the *arcarius* (three palatine judges, this time), four *dativi iudices*, twelve named Roman aristocrats including Marino, the prefect's brother, and Crescenzio *comes* (presumably again the count of the Sabina), and 'all the illustrious men', plus eight *nobiles Sabinenses*. Gregorio showed his charters to the court, but 'it appeared to the most prudent lord prefect and all the *iudices* that the charters were forged (*falsidicae*)'. The prefect ordered other charters of Abbot John to be brought, to compare the hands, but they were in a different handwriting. Gregorio gave in—he seems to have been surprised more than anything—saying 'lords (*seniores*), I say truly that they are false; tell me what I should do'. The *iudices* said he should cede the disputed land at once, and the charters, which he did, and the *primicerius defensorum* cut a cross in the documents to invalidate them. Gregorio may have been right to be surprised, for he and his brother Urso *presbiter* certainly did have leases from Farfa; one survives from 1000 (a *libellus* for 29 years, renewable) for half the castle of Montelibretti itself, and Urso was probably also the tenant for three generations of a *cripta* in the Terme Alessandrine, a different building that is to say, in 991. The 1012 case has

---

[11] The earliest known Roman *placitum* is from 813 (*RF*, n. 199), in a period when Carolingian influence in Rome had begun. Presided over by Leo III, it already resembles contemporary Italian *placita* (e.g. Manaresi, nn. 14, 24) fairly closely.

the feel of a fit-up, in fact. But there was no doubt that such a defeat, in front of such an audience, was total.[12]

By far the commonest delegated president of court cases was the urban prefect, as in the case just cited, whose attested central role in 'civil' justice goes back to 993. As we saw earlier, the office of prefect was probably re-established, after a break of a century and more, under Alberico (p. 188), and it had become the second office in Rome after that of the ruler by 1000 or so, replacing the *vestararius*. The prefect remained in that role until well after 1200.[13] His judicial remit was indeed rather wider than simply deputizing for popes and other Roman rulers, or was by the 1060s. Cencio di Giovanni (prefect *c.*1065–77) is attested as in charge of what we would call 'criminal' justice, when he imprisoned his rival Cencio di Stefano for fraud, possibly in 1075 (the latter's brother Stefano in return killed Prefect Cencio in 1077). That 'criminal' responsibility continued, well after this initial period, into the twelfth century; it was Prefect Pietro 'III' who ran the execution of Arnaldo of Brescia in 1155, for example, and in the *ordo* of Albino of *c.*1190 we discover that the offerings on the altars of S. Pietro paid not only for the clergy and laity who took part in processions (above, p. 346), but also for the prefect's executioners—5 *solidi* for a hanging or beheading, 12 *denarii* per eye for a blinding, or per limb for a mutilation. It is quite likely that this responsibility attached to prefects from the start; it certainly had done to their early medieval predecessors. Such a judicial role is likely to have been much more summary and rapid than the civil disputes heard in the *placitum*, judging by Lombard and Tuscan parallels.[14] And the prefect's judicial responsibilities could extend even more widely, as it seems from a letter of Pier Damiani to the same Cencio di Giovanni in *c.*1068. Pier here criticized Cencio for not giving enough judgements because he spent too much time in prayer, saying that Pier had heard from 'those who have cases, that they do not manage to get from you the sanction of a legal judgement', and urging Cencio lest 'you neglect the discipline over such an innumerable *populus* as has been committed to you, and [lest], because of your own convenience, you disregard the common welfare of the *plebs*, which expects justice from you'. This unique text seems to indicate that the prefect also heard 'civil' disputes between less influential people than those who might appeal to the pope. It may also fit with other, wider, judicial roles which prefects certainly exercised in the mid- to later twelfth century, such as the care of (travellers on) roads, although these roles had not necessarily yet developed in the eleventh. One, the receiving of death duties from the inhabitants

---

[12] *RF*, nn. 657–8. In 657, Gregorio is *filius cuiusdam Bonae*, his mother. Other documents for the family are *LL*, nn, 441, 404; *RF*, n. 638 (Gregorio's father Urso is here son of Benepassia, evidently an alternative to Malepassia)—in this last text, from 1013, i.e. a year after the court cases, Gregorio gives two tenant-houses in Monterotondo, near Montelibretti, to Farfa: we cannot tell if in a context of coercion or of peacemaking or of piety.

[13] See Chapter 4, n. 16 for references.

[14] Bonizone of Sutri, *Liber ad amicum*, VII (p. 605); cf. Pier Damiani, *Epistulae*, nn. 145, 155; *Annales Palidenses*, s.a. 1155, p. 89; *LC*, II, p. 108 (Albino). See in general Halphen, *Études*, pp. 19–20, with more references. For summary criminal justice in early communal Italy, see e.g. Menant, *Campagnes lombardes*, pp. 429–33; Wickham, *Courts and Conflict*, pp. 130–1.

of the Civitas Leoniana, attested (and abolished) in 1123, certainly did not exist in the mid-eleventh—here, the prefect's role was clearly expanding.[15]

We could in principle conclude from this more fragmentary material that, for most Romans, the daily experience of justice in the city might have been focused, not on the *placitum* assembly, but on the person of the urban prefect; and the tone of our evidence also indicates that the prefect was running this sort of justice on his own. This in turn might indicate that Rome was, in this respect, more similar to the southern principalities. In Capua-Benevento and especially Salerno after 930 or so, court records show an expert *gastaldus et iudex*, increasingly just called *iudex*, as a sole judge, with aristocratic *adstantes* who are at most acting as witnesses, and who in Salerno only appear in a minority of cases. The idea that justice belonged to an assembly, whether of notables or of wider sections of the free (male) population, was, after all, a northern European practice, extending southwards with the 'barbarian' invasions of the Roman empire; although Capua-Benevento and Salerno lived by Lombard law, this aspect of Lombard political practice seems not to have rooted itself there as completely as it did in the *Regnum Italiae*.[16] Rome could, in this respect, be seen as a halfway house. It was not ever part of the Lombard or Frankish state, and it kept its Roman law, including the assumption, hard-wired into that law, that judicial experts were the most appropriate and legitimate judges; but it was also substantially influenced by Carolingian practices (more than the South was), and these practices, among other things, focused on judicial assemblies as the locations par excellence for the resolution of disputes. Maybe, then, in Rome these assemblies were only the top layer of a judicial system run by and intended for lay and ecclesiastical elites, with the rest of the population looking to the urban prefect, who would at most be flanked by a couple of judicial advisors and some very menacing armed men?

I raise this suggestion only to reject it, however. Such an image marginalizes the *placitum* too much. The fact is that not a single surviving document in the whole of our period attests to a formal civil dispute run by the urban prefect without an assembly, or refers to a preceding judgement of that kind, even casually.[17] Even if one might say, in the 1010s, that this was the result of the bias of our ecclesiastical sources, we could not do so as easily by the end of the eleventh century, by which time *placita* had disappeared. In that period, we find a variety of ad hoc procedures, as we shall see, but Salerno-style judicial magistrates are not one of them. Nor do they appear in the late twelfth century, when disputes of relatively ordinary people are sometimes recorded. We have to conclude that, whatever the judicial role of the prefect acting alone—and it clearly was and remained wide and important, from

---

[15] Pier Damiani, *Epistulae*, n. 155; for roads, *Reg. Inn. III*, II.275; see also n. 20 below. For 1123, see *Bullaire Cal. II*, n. 410, contrasted with *SPV*, n. 16, for 1053. Later, the urban prefect issued the first surviving judicial writ in 1148: see below, n. 49.

[16] Delogu, 'La giustizia', esp. pp. 263–8.

[17] Although palatine judges are referred to, apparently acting alone, in some documents recording a private accord or cession following a dispute; see below, nn. 18, 20, for examples. But there they were probably brokering a settlement, in a context which resembles (but is not identical to) a formal arbitration.

1000 to 1200 without a break, except in 1144–5 (below, pp. 433–4)—it was too summary to get preserved in writing. The world of judgements which needed to be, and could legally be, referred to in future written texts was the world of the *placitum*, as long as it lasted.

As already noted, the density of *placitum* texts in the 1010s is not repeated in the next few decades. In part, this is because Farfa, whose cartularies provide us with most of the texts of the 1010s, kept many fewer formal court case records after that, even in the Sabina; but it is not clear why other archives did not preserve them. We do have a handful of agreements after prior disputes, however; one, in 1034, was an accord made in the presence of a palatine judge, the *nomenculator*; another, in 1043, was a compromise agreement made after a dispute in front of Gregorio *consul*, brother of Pope Benedict IX, two senior ecclesiastics, the papal *cancellarius*, the *primus scriniarius* (i.e. the *protoscriniarius*, a palatine judge), and a *dativus iudex*. This could easily be seen as a cut-down *placitum*, with, by now, a slightly more ecclesiastical personnel, convened to ratify an agreement which was already being made.[18] The Tuscolani popes, anyway, maintained judicial assemblies; John XIX in 1026 heard a canon-law case in a chapel in the Laterano palace concerning ecclesiastical rights over a church in the castle of Galeria, brought to him by the bishop of Silva Candida, in the presence of six bishops, four deacons, and three cardinal priests, as was logical in a canon-law case, but also five of the seven palatine judges, a *dativus iudex*, the pope's brother Alberico *comes palatii*, and the *comes* of Galeria. (The case was an odd one, for in the middle of it the pope reacted to a suggestion of the Holy Spirit which 'came into my mind', and took the opportunity to ask why it was that the bishop of Silva Candida got so little in church dues (*redditum*) from Galeria as a whole, thus deviating the case entirely—over the protests of the bishop, who, quite reasonably, wanted the church dispute settled first.) There is no reason to think, overall, that anything much changed in the 1030s and early 1040s in the judicial practices of Rome, except that clerics and laity were more often acting together than they had before.[19]

This conclusion is reinforced by the court cases of the Hildebrandine period. We have a further handful of private agreements after disputes in the late 1050s, again, as in the Tuscolano period, brokered by one or more palatine judges (as many as four judges in a S. Ciriaco in Via Lata case of 1060). But the 1060 Arci case, in which Pope Nicholas II took on the Ottaviani counts of the Sabina over their occupation of a castle given to Farfa, shows the *placitum* assembly in good shape. As we have seen (pp. 221–2), the full array of Rome's secular elite were there, mostly

---

[18] Respectively, *SMVL*, n. 63 (the *nomenculator* is apparently chosen here because the case involves minors, and he had assigned the *curator*); *S. Alessio*, n. 6. For the 1020–60 'lacuna' see Toubert, *Les structures*, pp. 1211, 1316. For Farfa's decreasing number of court records for the Sabina, see Toubert, *Les structures*, pp. 1278–87, 1307–13; Wickham, 'Justice', pp. 229–31.

[19] *Papsturkunden*, n. 568 (the court is here called a *concilium*). A later assembly-based church court case is from 1049, in which the bishops of Porto and Silva Candida squared off over the control of S. Adalberto on the Isola Tiberina, but the location there is a formal synod of Leo IX, which is slightly different: *PL*, CXLIII, n. 7, cols 597–604. The closer association between clergy and laity went hand in hand with a greater conceptual separation between the two, which had begun well before 1046: see e.g. di Carpegna Falconieri, *Il clero di Roma*, pp. 91–3.

by now its 'new aristocracy', headed by Giovanni Tignoso the urban prefect, five of the seven palatine judges, and two *dativi iudices*; after them, as many as thirty-six men were named, most of them prominent enough to be identifiable elsewhere.[20] If the institutional structure of Rome had been harmed by Sutri and a non-Roman papacy, as would seem likely enough, given the halving of the volume of surviving documents for a decade after 1046 (above, p. 29), it had evidently recovered by now. The only change, though a significant one, was that this list was now headed by clerics: five bishops (three of them cardinals), Hildebrand as archdeacon of the Roman church, two cardinal priests, and a deacon. This looks back to the 1026 Silva Candida case, with its similar mix of ecclesiastical and lay; but in a formal land dispute it was new. It was followed up in 1072 when Hildebrand, still archdeacon, was the president in a case between Farfa and SS. Cosma e Damiano in Trastevere over possession of the monastery of S. Maria in Mignone in northern Lazio (one of a long-running sequence), together with bishops, cardinal priests, the urban prefect, and *iudicibus ac Romanorum maioribus*, unfortunately unnamed; and in 1073, when a minor part of the same case was reopened before Hildebrand, now Pope Gregory VII, and decided by the pope, bishops, prefect, *iudices* (including two palatine judges), and *nobilibus Romanis et Transtyberinis*. The presence of ecclesiastics, mostly cardinals, was thus by now normal in these big cases.[21] They were part of a stable practice of justice going on into Gregory's reign, which is also attested by the clearly routine duties of his prefect Cencio di Giovanni, already cited.

Ten years later, Rome was engulfed in civil war, more violently than at any time since 998, with Henry IV ensconced on the Capitolio, Gregory besieged in Castel S. Angelo, and the imperially backed Pope Clement III in the Laterano. Clement certainly intended to run at least ecclesiastical justice, and at the end of 1084, with Gregory by now exiled, he decided a dispute over a church between S. Marcello in Via Lata and the northern Lazio monastery of Acquapendente, with a full complement of bishops and cardinal priests, and Gregory's former archdeacon Teodino— Clement remarked rather smugly that it was a dispute which none of Leo IX, Victor II, Stephen IX, Nicholas II, or Alexander II had managed to end. Henry IV was running his own tribunal on the Capitolio too, as a Farfa case in April of the same year shows; this was called a *placitum* but was not in an assembly format—perhaps because it was an imperial case, perhaps because it was wartime, perhaps because it was called off and the parties came to terms *in amicabili compositione*—but it still featured four *iudices*, two *causidici* (one from the urban prefect's office), and at least

---

[20] Agreements: *SMVL*, nn. 85–8; clearly in 1057–60 S. Ciriaco was feeling the need to claim lost lands, presumably as a result of the end of the troubles of the previous decade. Arci: *RF*, n. 906. Note also de Rossi, 'Atto di donazione', a 1051 text in which a gift by a Roman *dativus iudex* to the cathedral of Arezzo (a very atypical grant to a church outside Lazio) is confirmed by no less than the urban prefect.

[21] *RF*, nn. 1006, 1013. *RS*, n. 48 may be a parallel example. See in general Toubert, *Les structures*, pp. 1316–19. Farfa tried to get back S. Maria in Mignone in courts of the *regnum Italiae* and imperial hearings, too: see Manaresi, n. 254 (*RF*, n. 437), *RF*, nn. 438, 439, 813, 1076–8.

two aristocrats from the Sant' Eustachio family in its witness list.[22] From here on until Clement's own exile from the city in 1099 we have only two cases, but they do seem to show the survival of the *placitum* tradition in some form. A *pactum* after a dispute (*lis*) in 1094 between S. Ciriaco in Via Lata and a lay family over a city tower-house was made in the presence of two palatine judges and four or five *placitorum causidici* as well as twelve named *nobiliores homines*, one of them a *iudex*, which is a large collectivity for any normal private deal. In 1088, still more clearly, Farfa raised a case in Rome over the castle of Corese in the Sabina in front of Pietro the urban prefect and nine city aristocrats, here called *consules communitatis boum*; there were no palatine judges or *dativi* here, or clerics for that matter, but the political community of the city was still being invoked as a judicial assembly.[23]

Here, however, for the first time, we can see difficulties in an argument that stresses continuity. The gap between 1020 and 1060 might not seem too worrying, given the scale of the Arci case and the apparent scale of the 1072–3 S. Maria in Mignone cases. But these are the only three large-scale formal *placita* of the old style that are clearly attested after 1020 in the whole century. The rest of Gregory's reign sees no such cases; and after the 1094 *pactum* there is another ten-year gap with no documented disputes at all, after which they are very heterogeneous. Given this, the less organized and structured 1088 and 1094 disputes may be showing a slow internal unravelling of the *placitum* tradition, in a way which we do not find in contemporary northern Italy, where judges and *adstantes* remained numerous for as long as *placita* lasted. (*Placita* reduced in number rapidly after 1085, however, in the regions of the *Regnum Italiae* where they are still attested, which were by now, above all, Lombardy, the western Veneto, and northern Tuscany.)[24] One interesting innovation in Rome is the term *bonus homo*. This was a standard synonym for *adstans* in the northern *placitum* tradition (extending south as far as the Sabina). But it was also a term used in the North for any prominent free man acting in a public role, potentially independently of wider hierarchies, as a witness to particularly important transactions, as an arbiter, and, increasingly in the growing vacuum of power in the *Regnum* from the 1080s onwards, as a political leader, including, in the twelfth century, the leaders of both urban and rural communities—and, again as far south as the Sabina, the leading stratum of castle society.[25] In Rome, the term had been unknown; but it suddenly appears in the 1090s, when in 1093 S. Maria in Via Lata faced off its neighbour S. Ciriaco in Via Lata over the boundary between the two churches with *maxima litigio*, until they came to terms by 'the intervention of *boni homines*'; in the 1094 *pactum* already mentioned,

---

[22] *S. Marcello*, n. 1; *RF*, n. 1097. A similar imperial case was heard before Henry came into the city, *RF*, nn. 1076–8 (see above, n. 21).

[23] *SMVL*, n. 121, *RF*, n. 1115.

[24] See Manaresi, nn. 465–84 and Wickham, 'Justice', pp. 203n, 216n, 220n, 239n, for the last *placita*.

[25] *Boni homines*: see e.g. Bougard, *La justice*, p. 119 and *passim*; a recent survey of their wider activity with earlier bibliography is Szabó, 'Zur Geschichte der *boni homines*'; for the Sabina, see esp. Toubert, *Les structures*, pp. 1292–303, 1332–6—*RF* has very many documents referring to *boni homines*, throughout our period.

the same phrase occurs.[26] In 1094, we know that such men were palatine judges and urban aristocrats; in 1093 we do not know who they were. But the term is clearly, in both cases, being used in its second north Italian meaning, not the first: that is to say, to denote prominent people who were simply there, acting in a public role which they may have started to define for themselves. Which means that we cannot be sure after all that the *primicerius, secundicerius, causidici*, and *nobiliores homines* of 1094 were acting as part of a surviving *placitum* tradition; there were a lot of them, so they were assembling in some way, but they may well have been filling a gap in the power structures of the city, informally, not demonstrating a continuity in old traditions.

This also forces us to ask questions about the *consules communitatis boum*, 'of the community of the oxen'. This collectivity, when it has been analysed (the only more than casual reference is the commentary by Laura Moscati), has been seen as a 'union of major entrepreneurs linked together by common interests', a cattle-men's cartel, possibly along the lines of the powerful *bovattieri* of the late thirteenth and fourteenth centuries, although that has recently been convincingly doubted.[27] And the fact that the 1088 group met to hear Farfa's case at the rarely attested monastery of S. Basilio might be significant here, for S. Basilio was situated at the northern end of the Foro di Augusto, not 100 metres from the location of what was was, by the fourteenth century, an important meat market, in the Arcanoe area (*Arcus Nervae*) at the northern end of the Foro di Nerva.[28] But, conversely, there is absolutely no sign of such a 'union' in any other text, and corporations of this kind are otherwise unknown before the mid-thirteenth century. Furthermore, as we have seen, cattle were relatively uncommon in the city until after 1200 (above, p. 144), so the political weight of a proto-guild of *bovattieri*, even if that guild had in reality concentrated on cattle imports, is anachronistic. I do not think we can see this as a *communitas* with common economic interests at all, that is to say; but, even if it was an economic association, it could not *only* be economic, for a monastic court case is the last thing we would expect a 'union of entrepreneurs' to be engaging in. As a socio-political association, however, which is the only alternative, the *communitas* is very interesting indeed.

The 1080s was a significant time. It is the period when informal leaders called *consules* were appearing in Pisa, the first north-central city to attest them; in the next

---

[26] *SMVL*, nn. 120–1. The only previous attestation of the phrase *boni homines* in Rome is in Farfa documents made in the entourage of Henry IV during his attack on the city in 1083, *RF*, nn. 1076, 1078.

[27] Moscati, *Alle origini*, pp. 52–4 (p. 53 for the quote: 'unione di grossi imprenditori legati tra loro da interessi comuni'); see also e.g. Halphen, *Études*, p. 29n; Carocci and Vendittelli, 'Società ed economia', p. 76; Maire Vigueur, 'Il comune', p. 120; Lori Sanfilippo, *La Roma dei Romani*, p. 60. For the fourteenth century, Gennaro, 'Mercanti e bovattieri'; Lori Sanfilippo, *La Roma dei Romani*, pp. 95–122; Carocci and Vendittelli, *L'origine della Campagna Romana*, pp. 198–200, the last two of which show that the later *bovattieri* were an association of agricultural entrepreneurs (including stock-raisers, but not exclusively), not cattle importers.

[28] Lori Sanfilippo, *La Roma dei Romani*, p. 263. Some support for the argument that this market already existed in the eleventh century is provided by the deposit of butchered cattle and horses found in the neighbouring Tempio della Pace: Meneghini and Santangeli Valenzani, *Roma nell'alto medioevo*, p. 178.

few decades there would be plenty more. They were by then ad hoc responses to the power vacuum which existed in most of the *Regnum Italiae*, and only slowly, across a generation or more, did their leadership crystallize into real political structures which aimed at the rulership of cities, in what we call the *primo comune*. I have argued elsewhere in the context of Tuscany for a version of what Gioacchino Volpe called the original private charter of the commune, because it seems to me that the beginnings of city communes were highly informal, and hardly institutionalized at all. One of the problems of Volpe's theory was the absence of much evidence for what he saw as private associations, held together by voluntary oaths, actually developing; when we see consuls acting in the Centre-North, it is in the name of the whole *civitas*, not of a restricted sworn grouping of urban leaders, right from the start.[29] But the 'community of the oxen' could be one such: a (doubtless sworn) association of Roman aristocrats, who needed to stick together, in a world where public structures were abruptly far weaker than they had been. There may well, indeed, have been more than one such association, given that its members—*filii Astaldi*, 'Meliosi', Sant' Eustachio, and *filii Baruncii* among others—were in large part demonstrably Clementine in affiliation, and contained no members of classic Hildebrandine families such as the heirs of Giovanni Tignoso and the future Pierleoni (cf. above, pp. 231–4; and see p. 424 below). So the *communitas boum* could be seen as a clear marker of the beginnings of a new type of political structure, one created by horizontal aggregation rather than called into being by court presidents and *iudices*, as the *placitum* was. This does have parallels with the sort of association which underpinned the *primo comune* in cities such as Pisa, Genoa, or Milan. And it is striking in that context that it actually appears running a court case, only four years after Henry IV and Clement III took Rome and Gregory VII fled; it was moving into 'public' activity pretty quickly, faster even than did the consuls in Pisa.

All the same, to propose communal origins in Rome as early as 1088, without qualification, is going far too fast. The Corese case looks both ways. First, it was actually presided over by the urban prefect, who thus maintained his traditional centrality and provided a clear element of continuity—which also means that the image of the *placitum* assembly does indeed, as already argued, attach itself to the case, at least in part. Second, the word *consul*, which was a new word in Pisa or Milan and thus leads us easily to look forwards to the developed *consulatus* of the early city commune, was not new at all in Rome, and was indeed one of the commonest words for 'aristocrat' in the tenth century, even if more recently it had come to attach itself to members of the Tuscolani family almost exclusively (see above, p. 197; below, pp. 436–7). In 1088, when the neologism had hardly developed at all in the Centre-North (its adoption in Pisa by 1080–5 was probably

[29] Wickham, *Courts and Conflict*, pp. 16–19, with previous bibliography, of which the key texts are Volpe, *Medio evo italiano*, pp. 87–118 (p. 104 for quote), and Cassandro, 'Un bilancio storiografico', esp. pp. 164–7 (consuls always acting in the name of the city—not in itself a controversial statement). I intend to develop the point elsewhere too. The most innovative recent study of the period does not discuss this issue: Maire Vigueur, *Cavaliers et citoyens*, pp. 337–62.

as much in imitation of contemporary Rome as a classicizing allusion), it is hard to see that in Rome it could have had any other meaning than just 'aristocrat', one in fact of a fairly traditional type in the city. Third, communes appeared in the Centre-North, and slowly at that, in a period of political crisis for Henry IV and his successors. Henry IV remained on top for most of the 1080s–90s, even if in a civil war situation, but Henry V was rather less present, and his successors still less, until Frederick Barbarossa sought (with temporary success) to turn back the clock in the 1150s; that intervening period was when communes crystallized.[30] It was different in Rome, where the pope, not the king/emperor, was sovereign, for he was much more regularly active in the city. Clement III was not always in Rome, but he largely was; the same is true for Paschal II and his successors.[31] Clement faced rivals, who imposed themselves in parts of the city several times (see below, p. 424), and who had some local support, but he had his own support too, indeed precisely from the families who made up the *communitas boum*. It would be hard to propose that, of all people, the *filii Baruncii* and the Sant' Eustachio were acting to fill a vacuum of legitimacy left by the very pope they were backing.

The *communitas boum* was new in structure, therefore, with likely parallels in the new informal measures being taken in equally troubled cities in the *Regnum Italiae*; but it did not intend to substitute itself for papal authority, and evidently not for the continuing centrality of the urban prefect. It was, all the same, likely to have come into existence, and, not least, come to public and juridical prominence, because city government was beginning to disintegrate internally; so were the *boni homines* of the 1093–4 agreements. The pope still ruled, but the institutions he had long ruled through were ceasing to operate. The traditional *placitum* never appears again. If that, the major organ of Rome's judicial system, is the marker of the city's *ancien régime* par excellence, then that regime was indeed, by the late 1080s and 1090s, finally ending. Toubert saw as the reason for this the introduction of cardinals as the leaders of the *placitum*, and the resultant downgrading and lesser consistency of the group of professional judges, plus the instability caused by the increasingly itinerant practice of the papal court.[32] The latter process had not yet really begun in the eleventh century, but it is at least true, without doubt, that popes and cardinals (of both parties) were by now overwhelmingly not Roman, and that the new institutional centrality of the latter thus privileged a non-Roman social group for the first time in the city's history. The idea that the (professional and secular) *placitum romanum* was, in some sense, the governing body of the city was seriously undermined by this. The only Roman left in a directive role was the urban

---

[30] See, for recent syntheses, with bibliography, Jones, *The Italian City-State*, pp. 130–51; Milani, *I comuni italiani*, pp. 16–29; a basic *Denkschrift* remains Keller, 'Gli inizi del comune'. For Pisa in 1080–5 and the first citation of consuls, see esp. Ronzani, *Chiesa e 'civitas' di Pisa*, pp. 190–9, who argues that the document in question dates to 1080–1.

[31] Clement III: judging by his few surviving letters and other chronicle references, in Jaffé and Wattenbach, *Regesta pontificum*, I, pp. 649–55, he was in the city perhaps half the time from 1084 to 1094, after which his position started to weaken (below, n. 96). Jaffé and Wattenbach, *Regesta pontificum*, I, pp. 702–839, implies 50–60 per cent for Paschal II, around 40 per cent for Calixtus II, and 75 per cent for Honorius II.

[32] Toubert, *Les structures*, pp. 1319–22.

prefect, and that was not enough. So the underlying logic which had kept the old institutions of government in operation had gone, and alternatives for political aggregation had to be found. This is where there was a place for associations like the *communitas boum*, even among the pope's supporters. It becomes unsurprising that it was attached to the urban prefect, and that it looked to the past as much as to the future. But it equally marked the fact that Rome's governmental structures would need to be re-established on different bases in the future.

The low point for all forms of documented dispute settlement in the *Regnum Italiae* tends to be the 1110s or 1120s, after which we find various new ways of dealing with 'civil' justice: an increasing number of formal arbitrations; episcopal courts, which were the bodies most likely to look back to *placitum*-assembly traditions (for the *placitum* had gone, except in the relatively conservative Veneto); and, by the 1130s, in several early adopter cities at once (in order of first reference, Genoa, Pisa, Milan, Piacenza, Lucca, Padua, Cremona, Verona), consular tribunals.[33] In Rome, the low point is the decade centred on 1100, but the subsequent picture is more heterogeneous still. I will take the dispute texts for Paschal II's reign as a whole so as to make the point. In 1103 a dispute between Farfa and the Ottaviani counts of the Sabina was entrusted, apparently by mutual agreement, to two Roman 'new aristocrats', Pietro di Leone and Tebaldo di Cencio, so that they could 'judge' it in their *curia*. This met in the Pierleoni church of S. Nicola in Carcere, and was by now called a *placitum*, with *causidici* acting for each party, and began with the Roman-law *sacramentum calumniae*. All of these are markers of a formally constituted court (though without any hint of an assembly); but Pietro di Leone is then referred to in Gregorio of Catino's (non-technical, but at least probably eyewitness) narrative as *arbiter constitutus*. He and his *socius* disagreed over the arbitration (*diffinitio*), however, and the case was removed from Rome back to the Sabina by the parties—another sign that it was an agreed arbitration, whatever else it was.[34]

A second case giving us mixed signals is the famous Roman-law debate between SS. Cosma e Damiano in Trastevere and the Pierleoni, dating to 1107. In Chapter 6, I cast doubt on this text for formal reasons, and wondered if the Romanist citations were added later, but the part of the text most likely to be authentic is the statement at the end that the case was *diffinitum* by two *causidici*, presided over (*presidentes*) by the *primicerius* and the *secundicerius*. This looks like another arbitration, but *diffinire* can be used for judgements too, and the presiding presence of palatine judges gives the whole dispute a substantial weight for an arbitration. If it was a formal tribunal, however, the text gives us no hint as to who set it up.[35] It could well be that it was simply an updated version of the 1050s cases in which agreements to end disputes were ordered and ratified by palatine

[33] Wickham, 'Justice', pp. 239–50; for Piacenza, Fugazza, *Diritto, istituzioni*, p. 20n; for Cremona, Menant, 'La prima età comunale', p. 236. In Genoa, such tribunals began around 1105, and in Pisa around 1110, as I shall discuss elsewhere.

[34] *CF*, II, pp. 232–3; see Stroll, *The Medieval Abbey of Farfa*, pp. 11, 101–32 for Gregory's direct participation, which is very likely but not certain.

[35] ASR, SCD, cassetta 16, n. 109; cf. above, Chapter 6, n. 143.

judges—we have another one of these in 1110, a S. Maria in Via Lata dispute with a layman, brokered by a later *secundicerius*. If this is the best reading of the case, then perhaps all the legal experts in 1107 might have been called *boni homines*, as in 1094. We have a further similar case from 1116, in which three *iudices* (one a *protoscriniarius*) from the Laterano made a *diffinitio* between Subiaco and the lords of Trevi over the castle of Ienne in the mountains between them.[36]

So far, then, Paschal's reign shows us palatine judges and (more rarely) major 'aristocrats' working more or less on their own, whether as judges, arbiters, or brokers, or a mixture of all three. Disputes did reach the pope as well, however, as we can see for both Paschal and his immediate successors. In 1115, S. Gregorio sul Celio was in dispute with the *scola piscatorum stagni*, the *scola* of the fishermen of the lagoon beside the Porto salt-pans (above, p. 103), over the boundary of the monastery's fishing rights in the marsh, as set out in the document of gift by Silvia, mother of Gregory the Great, dating to 604. (This text is a total forgery, probably confected for S. Gregorio in precisely these years, but it was accepted by both parties, and also by the pope.) The case was put to the bishop of Porto, but he hastened to put it before Paschal, as soon as the latter had got back from Benevento. Paschal was himself a party to the case, as the *scola* held their part of the lagoon in lease *per curiam*, that is, from the papacy, but the pope accepted S. Gregorio's reading of the document, and judged for the monastery, sending out eight men, many of them visibly from the Roman 'aristocracy', to *perscrutare* the boundary of the two halves of the lagoon. The text has numerous witnesses, but there is no sign that the pope was doing other than acting as a sole judge.[37] This also seems to be the case with a dispute between S. Paolo fuori le Mura and some inhabitants of Sutri, which Paschal in 1113 delegated to a Sutri *iudex* and Cardinal Divizone to resolve on the spot; and with a dispute over the castle of Cave in *Campania* between S. Ciriaco in Via Lata and the castle's lords, which went to Paschal (who judged for S. Ciriaco) and then in 1125 to Honorius II. Honorius, at least, was certainly a sole judge, in the Laterano, where he is seen granting the lords of Cave a delay *secundum ius legum* (we do not know with what result), even though here he had around him a whole *curia* of cardinals and *boni homines*. Papal judgements over secular matters, then, no matter how many people heard them, seem to have been decisions by the pope himself.[38]

We see similar but slightly more complex patterns in a later case, heard by Calixtus II in 1124 and again Honorius in 1126, a three-cornered dispute over the *massa* Careia in Tuscia Romana between the counts of Galeria, the *diaconia* of S. Maria Nova, and the monastery of S. Saba. Honorius' hearing is described in detail in the document for the case, which hung on a Romanist *condictio* and some other fairly simple Roman-law arguments (see above, p. 371). Here it is clear that Calixtus' hearing had involved Pietro 'II' the urban prefect as his deputy, and

---

[36] *SMVL*, n. 139; *RS*, n. 212 (this, if an arbitration, seems to have given everything to Subiaco; but the brief text may hide a more generous deal).

[37] *S. Gregorio*, n. 34, citing the forged n. 11.

[38] Andenna, 'Documenti di S. Paolo', pp. 35–8; *SMVL*, n. 149.

Honorius likewise used a cardinal and a lay 'aristocrat', Cencio di Roizone *Romanus consul*, but both popes made *sententiae* on their own. The parties queried Honorius' *sententia*, however, and so he entrusted six *iudices* (including one palatine judge, one *dativus iudex*, and three *iudices Beneventani*) to reach a final *consilium*. Five of the six agreed (S. Maria Nova said the sixth was bought by S. Saba), and the pope went with their *concordia*. Why Honorius backtracked is not quite clear (Cardinal Pandolfo later called him *rigidus in iustitia*, but he clearly was not in this case), but *consilia* of this type were common later in the century. If the pope sought to ensure final agreement, however, he failed, for S. Saba did not turn up the following day to the court, and S. Maria Nova did not get the *massa* Careia back for nearly thirty years. The pope clearly had expert advice here, but once again he was acting on his own as a judge.[39]

This is partially true even in our few canon-law cases for Rome and its environs. A dispute between the bishops of Tuscania and Sutri over ecclesiastical rights in Civitavecchia went to 'bishops and cardinals' in the Laterano, apparently during a synod; when they judged for Sutri, the bishop of Tuscania appealed to Pope Paschal, who heard it on his own and supported Tuscania. (The urban prefect signed this document, along with numerous clerics and an *iudex*.) Church synods were parallels to secular assemblies, of course (and would be for centuries into the future), but it was still up to the pope to decide here. Honorius, too, in a 1127 case between SS. Apostoli and S. Marco over precedence in a procession, heard the case, an increasingly complex one with several hearings, in the presence of bishops and cardinals, although he then asked the *Romana fraternitas* to arbitrate, and simply confirmed their decision; this was, in effect, the ecclesiastical equivalent of the secular *consilium* already mentioned, but bringing in the *Romana fraternitas* was once again a papal decision, which Honorius subsequently stuck to with some firmness, talking down the losing party, S. Marco.[40]

By far the most structured legal text surviving from the first quarter of the twelfth century was, however, none of these, but, rather, a document recording three hearings of the salt court, which survives in S. Maria Nova's archive, dating to 1118–19. In it, Duce *prior (scolae) salinariorum* with five *rectores* of the same *scola* heard a case between three members of it over three carts of salt, a case in which one party swore the formal *sacramentum calumniae* and the other refused, twice. This particular case was not going anywhere in these hearings, and why it ended up in S. Maria Nova's archive is even less clear. Nonetheless, its degree of formality and regularity—and collectivity, for six judges is a lot for a single *scola*—is striking. We saw in Chapter 2 that *scolae* could be highly organized, and that some had their own by-laws; here we can see them in operation. The salt court is documented again in

---

[39] *SMN*, n. 142; cf. Wickham, 'Getting justice', pp. 111–12. In the same period, Honorius and the urban prefect decided a S. Maria in Via Lata case: see *Senato*, n. 12 (a. 1151), and below, n. 54. For Pandolfo, *Liber pontificalis*, ed. Přerovský, p. 750.

[40] 'Documenti per la storia', n. 22; Liverani, *Opere*, IV, pp. 258–64 (see above, p. 309). A probable parallel, for Calixtus II, is referred to summarily in *Reg. Inn. III*, II.144 (153)—cf. *Bull. Cal. II*, n. 227, not a court case.

the early thirteenth century, when it still had a similar structure, to which was now added judicial *consilia*—and also strikingly high court fees.[41]

So: one sector of Roman society could organize regular justice in this period, for its own members. Perhaps we would know of others too, if similar lay documents had survived by chance in other church archives, but this is all we have. Land disputes, all the same, demonstrably did not have any form of regular framework. As far as we can see, they were sometimes appealed to the pope, who had full powers to decide them as he chose, either in a personal judgement or through the mediation of legal experts chosen by himself; or else they went to arbiters or judges chosen by the parties, who were usually trained legal experts—the most highly trained that parties could have found, indeed—but men who were, as far as we can see, acting informally and on their own. This was the period in which a systematic training in Roman law must have been developing in the city, for *iudices, causidici,* and *scriniarii* (above, pp. 367–74), but it did not extend at all to the reorganization of the structures of justice or dispute settlement. We can say that post-*placitum* justice was focusing firmly on the legal authority of the pope and his judges, which tells us something, at least, about the standing of papal power in the city. But the pope was not turning that authority into any institutional structure to replace the *placitum*, which tells us something else about that standing and that power. Even the urban prefect, whose institutional continuity and importance is undoubted (as the trouble over the succession to the office in 1116 showed: above, pp. 344–5; below, p. 426), is relatively little in evidence in our disputing texts in this period. Paschal and Honorius presided over a very makeshift urban government, as far as any of our sources tell us.

We should, however, pause on the word *curia*, for it has been the focus of serious discussion by historians, and its meaning is ambiguous. The word came, in eleventh-century Europe, to mean a court, in the sense of an entourage of a king, and soon of aristocrats too; in Rome the first clear example of this is a 1020 lease by the *comes* of Anguillara on the Lago di Bracciano, for a rent to be paid in *curia nostra*, and we have seen an urban example in the 1103 dispute heard in S. Nicola in Carcere; by 1089 the papal court was called a *curia* in a bull of Urban II to the city of Velletri, and this usage is often attested thereafter, as Karl Jordan showed in a classic article. The *curia* in the sense of entourage steadily became a more and more solid body, including both cardinals and leading Roman 'aristocrats' on occasion; by 1123 at the latest it was beginning to have officials attached to it (the first known is the *camerarius*), and in 1120 it was regarded by the Genoese as a formal body which had to be paid off in return for a favourable papal bull. We know that it included aristocrats then, for, as we have seen earlier (esp. p. 164), Caffaro of Caschifellone, one of the Genoese envoys, itemized the payments: 1700 marks to Pope Calixtus II, 300 to 'cardinals and bishops and *quibusdam laicis*' (this is the group also called the *curia* in the text), and 50 ounces of gold to the Roman clergy—as well as specific gifts to named people who were particularly important

[41] *SMN*, n. 37; see Carbonetti Vendittelli, 'La curia dei *priores*', for the thirteenth century, and above, pp. 103–4.

intermediaries: 303 ounces of gold to Bishop Pietro of Porto, £100 to the bishop of Acqui, 155 marks and some jewels to the Pierleoni, 100 to the urban prefect, 40 to Leone Frangipane, and 25 to Stefano Normanno. The *curia* was not always seen as both ecclesiastical and lay; the *Liber Politicus* of Benedetto *cantor* around 1140 seems to see it as an exclusively clerical body, for example. But very commonly it did include both, as one would indeed expect the entourage of any medieval ruler to do.[42]

From 1101 onwards, however, the *curia* was also being evoked in a specifically legal context, as a body which, together with the pope, judged canon-law cases from all over Europe. As is well known, such cases had been appealed to the pope for centuries, but much more frequently from the 1090s onwards, and they grew steadily thereafter, exploding in scale under and after Innocent II in the 1130s. From the 1110s, the papal law court which heard them was more and more often called a *curia*, and this too was systematized under Innocent.[43] This usage brought the word *curia* close to the word *consistorium*, the assembly of pope and cardinals, often to make legal decisions, which is a concept that developed across the same period, most clearly under Calixtus II. We have a good description of the *consistorium* in an eyewitness account of a canon-law hearing in the Laterano in 1141 by Abbot Hariulf of Oudenburg, who described it as being a place where Pope Innocent *in tribunal residebat* with his cardinals, with *Romanum nobiliores* standing and sitting at his feet: a mixture between court-as-entourage and law court, that is to say.[44]

Both of these usages converged in practice, then; both of them can be subsumed under the umbrella term 'the Curia', in the generic way that the word was increasingly used in the twelfth century, and is by historians now. But there soon came to be a difference in direction. When the pope was judging church cases, particularly in the increasing flood from the rest of Europe, the collectivity around the pope soon became more professionalized. This is shown already in the sequel to Hariulf's first audience, a few days later, when he met with just the pope and a handful of cardinals and was interrogated by the pope, before (in a third and fourth audience) the abbot and pope haggled over which judges-delegate in northern France would actually hear the case. The assignment of local judges-delegate (normally, not to actual litigants, but to their representatives who had come to Rome) indeed rapidly became the major task of the Curia in its legal role, and, when this happened, under Innocent II and his successors, one aspect of papal justice did begin to be institutionally firm again—although also always hugely expensive in 'gifts' such as those Caffaro paid. (Hariulf's account claims that the

[42] See in general Jordan, 'Die Entstehung', esp. pp. 125–52 (also developed by Sydow, 'Untersuchungen'), with CVL 8044, ff. 1–3 (a. 1020); Pflugk, II.178 (a. 1089—see Jordan, 'Die Entstehung', p. 127n for its authenticity); Jordan, 'Die Entstehung', pp. 139–41 for the *camerarius*; for Caffaro, see above, Chapter 3, n. 168; for Benedetto, see above, Chapter 6, n. 7.

[43] Jordan, 'Die Entstehung', pp. 130–2, 148–50; Pásztor, 'La curia romana' (for the long-term origins of the *curia*); Maleczek, 'Das Kardinalskollegium', pp. 59–73.

[44] See in general Sydow, 'Untersuchungen', pp. 52–5, 64–73; Sydow, 'Il "concistorium"'; Laudage, 'Rom und das Papsttum', pp. 27–30. For Hariulf, Müller, 'Der Bericht', p. 102.

papal *cancellarius* Aimerico warned him 'lest in the Roman *palacium* you give or promise anything to anyone; for if I find out you have done so, you will lose the help both of our advice and of the lord pope'. This is so heavily flagged in Hariulf's account—a clearly worked-up text—that one might well anyway be tempted to believe that the opposite had occurred, even if one did not have the wealth of counter-instances that are documented from the 1120s onwards.)[45] But when the pope was hearing non-ecclesiastical cases from Romans, whether clerics or laity, his *curia* was simply his entourage, and papal decision-making remained much more personalized and informal, as in the examples we have already seen.

No Roman court cases survive from Anacletus II's reign; they doubtless existed, but there was no point in keeping them when his régime was wiped away by Innocent II in 1138 (below, pp. 431–3). Under Innocent, in his Roman cases as in his canon-law cases for the rest of Europe, the patterns of justice became visibly more structured. If under Paschal we see a divergence between Romans who sought informally constituted legal expertise from palatine judges and *causidici* and Romans who sought papal decisions, under Innocent they begin to come together. Innocent put advocates and *iudices* onto his formal payroll, in return for their oath to deal with the *placita vel negotia Romanorum* according to the law. And we now see a flurry of appeals to the pope by local monastic plaintiffs, who were (or pretended they were) waiting for Innocent in order to right long-term wrongs done by lay tenants and neighbours. S. Paolo fuori le Mura made a formal plea in public in the Second Lateran Council in April 1139 against a number of laymen who (it said) held its castles unjustly, a claim repeated soon after in front of the urban prefect, cardinals, two palatine judges, a *dativus*, and four *causidici*. S. Gregorio sul Celio did exactly the same in the Lateran Council, pleading against Oddone of Poli, who held three of that monastery's castles, renewing its claim in 1140 in the presence of bishops, cardinals, the urban prefect, and several Roman aristocrats, as we shall see in a moment. In 1140 we have the text of a formal plea to the pope by the monks of Grottaferrata alleging violent acts by Tolomeo II of Tuscolo, using a developed Roman-law vocabulary; in the same period we also have an undated plea by SS. Cosma e Damiano in Trastevere against a smaller-scale set of misdeeds by the Pierleoni in the monastic castle of Isola Farnese. S. Alessio sull'Aventino, again in 1140, did the same against Tolomeo of Tuscolo, pleading over the promontory of Astura on the coast and its fishing rights. That time, at least, the pope acted promptly, sending a judicial messenger or *treuguarius* to call Tolomeo to the *curia*, and demanding that he came to terms, which he did.[46]

Innocent's reign thus marked a clear shift back to a more structured papal-orientated judicial system, which gets steadily better-documented in the years

---

[45] Müller, 'Der Bericht', p. 102; pp. 104 ff. for later audiences. For some counter-instances, see Chapter 3, n. 196; another, again from Calixtus' pontificate, is *Landulphi Iunioris Historia Mediolanensis*, ch. 48 *bis*.

[46] Payroll: see Chapter 6, n. 139. Cases: *S. Paolo*, nn. 7–8; *S. Gregorio*, n. 7; 'Documenti per la storia', n. 4; ASR, SCD, cassetta 16, n. 118 (for the family link to the Pierleoni, see Kehr, 'Diploma purpureo', pp. 258–9); *S. Alessio*, n. 13. Compare also the regular court held at Sutri by Innocent's delegates in 1142, *S. Gregorio*, n. 89.

immediately following, despite the political difficulties for the popes in the city after 1143—which in itself further indicates that the impetus for the system must have begun in the period of stability under Innocent. From now on, in fact, we have increasing evidence of a papal justice for property disputes from Rome, which is more organized and more professional, as well as more practised in the use of Roman law (see also above, pp. 366–75, for much of the following). The reign of Eugenius III (1145–53) shows it in particular. In 1145, we have the conclusion of an elaborate court case that had already begun under Celestine II in 1143, over the possession of an estate on the Gianicolo, between S. Maria in Trastevere and S. Gregorio sul Celio. This case was delegated by Celestine to Seniorile, *urbane prefecture causidicus*, an experienced judge who turns up in several major cases in the period, who acted with utmost care in his own *curia*, hearing Roman-law arguments, looking at the documents, going out to inspect the bounds of the estate, hearing and interrogating witnesses, listening to more Roman law, looking at more documents, going back to the estate, and finally giving sentence—both as *delegatus iudex* of the pope and as *electus arbiter* by the parties—in front of an authoritative group, three palatine judges plus a *iudex dativus* and another legal expert (all of whom gave him formal *consilium*), nine other *iudices*, advocates, and *scriniarii*, and an usually large and influential group of witnesses.[47] Some of the same legal experts turn up in a case of 1148 in which S. Ciriaco in Via Lata laid a plea against a lay tenant before the papal *vicarius* (Eugenius had not yet made peace with the Senate and was out of Rome), acting with two cardinals, a palatine judge, three *causidici*, and four *consules*, and also in the same year in a case between three churches over a large rural estate, heard before the same *vicarius*. In 1151, Filippo *sacellarius* gave sentence in a Subiaco case, again with a formal *consilium* from two *advocati* (including, as did the previous cases, one of the most active legal experts of the period, Benedetto di Leone). Again in 1151, Pope Eugenius himself decided a highly Romanist case between S. Prassede and S. Croce in Gerusalemme, though mandating four *iudices* actually to hear the case before him, *in curia* (Benedetto was here an advocate for S. Prassede), with the pope delivering his *sententia* in front of eight cardinals, several *iudices*, and 'many men'. In 1153, it was the turn of two other palatine judges, again with the help of advocates, to decide the *massa* Careia case again between S. Saba and S. Maria Nova.[48]

---

[47] CVL 8044, ff. 4–16; cf. above, p. 372. Seniorile reappears in *SMVL*, n. 162; *S. Paolo*, n. 7; *S. Gregorio*, n. 7; *S. Prassede*, n. 24; *SMVL*, n. 178, mostly court cases and arbitrations. Among other *advocati* featured in the case, Filippo reappears in *S. Paolo*, n. 7; *SMVL*, n. 161; *S. Gregorio*, n. 7; *S. Alessio*, n. 14; *S. Prassede*, n. 24; *Senato*, n. 12; and then as *sacellarius* in nine texts, three of them court cases, listed in Halphen, *Études*, pp. 138–9. Pietro di Ammattaguerra reappears in *SMVL*, n. 172; *Senato*, n. 12; *SMVL*, n. 196; and Pagano, 'La chiesa di S. Biagio', pp. 48–9. Benedetto di Leone reappears in *SMVL*, nn. 161, 172, 178, 195; *S. Prassede*, nn. 24, 25; *Senato*, n. 12; *S. Maria in Monasterio*, n. 1 = *S. Agnese*, n. 10; *LC*, I, nn. 91, 117; see Chiodi, 'Roma e il diritto romano', pp. 1228–9, for his involvement in Roman law, and above, p. 000. Note how many of these citations overlap. This influential group of *iudices* were nonetheless by now attached to the 'medium elite', not the aristocracy: see above, p. 248.

[48] *SMVL*, n. 172, one of the Campo di Merlo cases (see above, p. 83, and Wickham, 'Getting justice', pp. 108–11; Wickham, 'La struttura', pp. 203–5); *S. Prassede*, n. 24; *RS*, n. 169; *S. Prassede*,

Here, in the middle of the century, we see two things. The first is a by-now fairly predictable judicial framework (the phrase *ut moris est* or *more solito* is repeated for certain judicial procedures in both the 1143–5 Gianicolo case and the 1151 S. Prassede case), in which parties appealed to the pope and got skilled people to hear their cases. The second is a tight-knit set of those judicial experts, still headed by the urban prefect (who sent a judicial writ to a city aristocrat in 1148, one of the earliest that survives)[49] and the palatine judges, but extending to a dense group of *causidici*, who recur over and over, now giving judicial *consilia*, now acting as advocates. When we have our first example, in 1151, of a case that simply went to arbiters chosen by each side, between two tenants of S. Ciriaco, we discover without surprise that the arbiters were Seniorile and Benedetto di Leone: they must have known each other well, they were certainly experienced, and—evidently—not just popes and churches, but lay parties as well, were prepared to trust them.[50] This, at the end of our chronological period, could be seen as the end of the sequence of the fall and rise of a judicial system, for the community of legal experts associated with the papal Curia by the 1140s–50s was evidently capable of careful and trusted legal decisions, at a level of organization that we have not seen for nearly a hundred years. As has already been observed, it is also this period which sees the greatest concentration of detailed Roman-law arguments, even if only in a minority of cases; both Seniorile and Benedetto di Leone could handle them effectively.

The newly stabilized judicial system was, all the same, not a regularized process in the way that the *placitum romanum* had been. It was certainly not based on a judicial assembly, for a start. Instead, plaintiffs made their case directly to the pope or his *vicarius*, usually but not always in the Laterano, and then the pope, accompanied as he always was by a *curia* of cardinals and other notables, decided how to proceed. Sometimes he asked the urban prefect, or one or more palatine judges, or experienced *causidici* (Seniorile, as we have seen, was one for the prefect's office), to hear the case; sometimes a set of cardinals backed up by *iudices*; sometimes he pronounced sentence himself, with or without a *consilium* of legal experts. Parties would have increasingly known that they would benefit from the legal expertise of at least someone; but who, and how, were far from predictable, and the choice depended on the pope's will, not any set procedure. This shift, from assembly-based justice to what texts now sometimes call a *tribunal*, marked an important move from a world of collective legitimation, such as was important in Carolingian Europe, to a world in which the person of the ruler was the key element, no matter how large an entourage he had around him. It is particularly visible in France, where the main focus of the debate over the shift from Carolingian political

n. 25; *SMN*, n. 68. For the whole period, see Chiodi, 'Roma e il diritto romano', pp. 1227–39 for Romanist culture, and, earlier and summarily, Genuardi, 'Il papa Eugenio III'.

[49] *SMVL*, n. 171. Near-contemporary is an undated writ from Eugenius III, *PL*, CLXXX, col. 1564, n. 542.

[50] *SMVL*, n. 178 (another Campo di Merlo case, cf. above, n. 48); for a list of formal arbitrations and informal agreements, see Wickham 'Getting justice', p. 129 and n, with p. 120 for compromises. Toubert, *Les structures*, pp. 1324–30, seems to me to overstate their dominance.

structures to those of the twelfth century has been located.[51] But for it to work well, the ruler had to act appropriately as a judge. John of Salisbury remarked of Eugenius III, whom he knew, that his judicial sentences were 'so easily retracted', presumably by his successors, because he himself revoked too many earlier sentences, he relied too much on personal opinion (*spiritum proprium*), he was too suspicious, and he did not trust his advisors. John was probably talking about Eugenius' ecclesiastical judgements, and he had an axe to grind about Eugenius' cardinals, but the question of whether the pope—who, whatever his abilities, was a very busy man, and seldom from Rome itself—really was the most appropriate judicial authority for Romans undoubtedly poses itself.[52]

An instance of how things could go wrong comes from one of the Innocent II cases already mentioned. The monks of S. Gregorio sul Celio had leased their castle of Poli, near Palestrina, to a local aristocratic family, and found by the 1130s that they had lost control of it. As already noted, they made the very public step of standing up in the Second Lateran Council in 1139 and demanding justice against Oddone of Poli from Innocent II. This plea was renewed in more normal surroundings in February 1140 in the papal court, in the presence of cardinals, the urban prefect, and numerous *nobiles viri*; we have S. Gregorio's account of what followed. Oddone responded to every step in the plea by requesting a delay. The pope gave him a delay until 2 March, another until Palm Sunday, one for a further day, three more for two weeks each, one for another day, one for a week (we are now in June), one until July, one until September, another for a fortnight, then he stopped coming. In Lent 1141 S. Gregorio tried again, and Oddone again gained nine days' delay; only then did the pope lose patience and confiscate one of the lesser castles in dispute, but Oddone got more delays for Poli until the pope died in 1143 and S. Gregorio had to start again. The monastery never even got a proper hearing in the case, and certainly never got Poli back; Oddone gave it to Hadrian IV in 1157 and received it back as a papal fief, which ensured that S. Gregorio would have no chance in future, as it found out in an appeal to Innocent III in 1204. How did Oddone manage to spin it out for so long? The reasons he gave varied. He did not have sufficiently skilled advisers to hand; his ancestors had not been forced to appear, so why should he; his kin and supporters were not available, for they were busy fighting King Roger of Sicily—this appeal to high politics was certainly important, and the gap in the case in 1142 was likewise because the pope was involved in the war with Tivoli. He also clearly managed to win over the pope, notwithstanding Innocent's cross words, as reported by the monks at least: presumably because he had supporters in the papal entourage, particularly the urban prefect, as the text says. But on each of the dozen times Oddone sought delays, as

---

[51] Toubert, *Les structures*, p. 1322, for '*tribunal*'. For the shift in legitimation, see e.g. Wickham, 'Public court practice'; Bisson, *The Crisis*, stresses a similar shift in his wide-ranging study of power and violence. More continuist are Reuter, 'Assembly politics'; White, 'Tenth-century courts at Mâcon'; these two are among the few authors in the 'feudal revolution' debate to take the issue of judicial assemblies seriously.

[52] John of Salisbury, *Historia pontificalis*, ch. 21; for his views on cardinals, see ch. 38, and John of Salisbury, *Policraticus*, VI.24.

also on the other times he simply turned up a couple of days late, the abbot and monks of S. Gregorio had to appear in front of the pope, in different places in the city, with their own advocates, *fideles*, and aristocratic supporters such as the Frangipane (see above, p. 311, for that support). Oddone, with the de facto complicity of the pope, wore them down, and they lost.[53]

This was Innocent II, who was controversial in other ways; but the risks of a papal tribunal are rather more evident in this case than in, say, Seniorile's well-run Gianicolo case a couple of years later, in 1143–5. Knowing that a judicial hearing would bring you legal expertise might not be enough if you were not sure you would get a hearing at all. It is thus significant that the Senate, when it emerged from 1143 onwards, adopted quite a different judicial model, one visible from the first senatorial cases. In 1148, in the earliest case of all that survives, Tedelgario di Rainaldo di Donadeo raised a plea against S. Maria in Via Lata in front of twenty-five senators, whose stated task it was 'malitiosas lites, pravas contentiones omnino dirimere et resecare' (a phrase which recalls *placitum* texts), with a remit covering clergy, laity, the poor, the rich, and churches. The case revolved around a gift which a kinsman of Tedelgario had left to the church in 1087, but Tedelgario's side, whom the senators called *improbi litigatores*, 'dishonest litigators', turned out not to have any charters, whereas S. Maria had many, including a prior judgement against Tedelgario's father by Honorius II and the urban prefect. The senators sought a formal *consilium* from six *sapientes iudices* (including two palatine judges and Benedetto di Leone) and assigned two thirds of the disputed land to S. Maria in 1151, two and a half years later; twelve other *consiliarii* (with some overlap with the *sapientes iudices*) had confirmed the case in 1150, and a further set of nine at the end of the case. Tedelgario did not give in easily, and he and his brother dug up the bounds fixed on the land by the senators, but the Senate, moving more quickly this time, re-established the bounds and the judgement in the same month, with twelve senators signing. Over forty senators, across three years, were involved with this, plus nine non-senatorial legal experts, most of whom were appearing in the same years in papal cases.[54]

This pattern set the tone for the next four decades of senatorial judgements. One made one's plea to the whole Senate, and a substantial group of senators formed a judicial committee, which heard evidence and arguments, with the *consilium* of a group of legal experts (palatine judges, *causidici*, or advocates), which acted as the formal basis of the eventual senatorial judgement. Everything was then recorded by the *scriba* or *cancellarius senatus* or by other public officials, in a standardized format (this was unlike papal cases, which were usually written by the winning party).[55] As I stressed in Chapter 6 (pp. 374–5), the Senate did not use Roman-law arguments in its cases, including its *consilia*, some of which survive independently. This must

[53] *S. Gregorio*, n. 7. See Wickham, 'Getting justice', pp. 112–13, of which this paragraph is a revised version, and *LC*, I, nn. 101–2 (a. 1157), *Reg. Inn. III*, VII. 133 (a. 1204).

[54] *Senato*, nn. 12, 13; cf. *SMVL*, n. 117 (a. 1087). See above, p. 273, for Tedelgario.

[55] Wickham, 'Getting justice', pp. 113–14 and *passim*; for the senatorial chancery, see Bartoloni, 'Per la storia', pp. 2–13.

have been a conscious choice, given that the Senate had at its disposal exactly the same legal experts that the papal court had.[56] But what was even more conscious, it can scarcely be doubted, was the standardized regularity of senatorial justice. It is important to stress that the sorts of cases the Senate heard were identical to those that the newly organized papal court was hearing in the same years; so were the parties (mostly churches in our surviving documents, which is as usual because our archives are all ecclesiastical). Eugenius III was the first pope to recognize the Senate, and it may well be, as John Doran has argued, that it suited him that another body ran Rome instead of him,[57] but this was the area in which there was a direct and structural rivalry, between the papal and the senatorial legal systems. Each, however, offered what the other did not: juristic subtlety against procedural regularity, social status against being tried by one's peers. So the real end of the sequence of the fall and rise of a judicial system was that two systems crystallized around 1150, not one. That certainly marked Rome out from other north-central Italian cities, where by then, or soon after, an exclusively communal justice was hegemonic.

The other respect in which Roman senatorial justice was unusual in Italy by now was its collective nature. The tribunals of other Italian city communes were soon cut-down affairs: three consular judges were common, flanked by a couple of *nuntii*, and by few other people at all. Other communes did not, that is to say, seek to imitate the *placitum* assembly; initially, they may have felt that they did not have the legitimacy to do so, and by the 1150s the imagery of that legal assembly had faded. Communes were, of course, collective bodies, given authority by their belonging to the whole *populus* or *civitas*, and they did maintain popular deliberative assemblies, often called *contiones*; it may well be that this was seen as a sufficient collective legitimation for a justice which was rather simpler in style.[58] But in Rome, it is transparent in the 1148–51 Tedelgario case, and in its successors into the 1180s, that a collective imagery was being carefully respected; only after that did the city begin to adopt more streamlined, northern-style, practices.[59] The early Senate felt no insecurity about its legitimate inheritance of the world of the *placitum*, clearly. It is equally evident that Romans continued to value that world. But it is also likely that Rome was, above all, the city in which the imagery of public collectivity was particularly powerful. In Rome, unlike in any other commune, the Senate had a hugely powerful rival who could command large numbers of people— including Romans—in his court; the number of senators had to be unusually large so as to match that, and the Senate met in full sessions regularly, as its court cases

[56] Filippo *sacellarius*, just to take one example, acted for the pope in 1159 (*LC*, I, n. 117) and for the Senate in 1160 (*Senato*, n. 17).

[57] Doran, 'The legacy of schism', pp. 135–6.

[58] See e.g. Wickham, 'Justice', pp. 240–50; Wickham, *Courts and Conflict*, pp. 31–48. For *contiones*, see Coleman, 'Representative assemblies'; Grillo, 'La frattura inesistente', pp. 692–4; and below, p. 449; in the North, early consuls did sometimes judge in such assemblies.

[59] With one or two senators judging, and two experts giving *consilia*: see *Senato*, nn. 65–7, 77, 93, 96, etc. This practice doubtless came in when the college of senators was replaced by a single senator, from the 1190s (off and on) onwards.

show. Rome was also, more than any other, as we saw in Chapter 6, the city of processions, regular, large-scale, highly visible, collective gatherings, which were both tendentially papal and also stressed the participation of large numbers of lay Romans, year on year without a break; this too created a normative framework for a renewed space for public assemblies. Finally, the 1118–19 salt court text shows us that collective judgements did indeed continue in Rome during the period of crisis; at a popular level, there were surviving and active traditions which the Senate could draw on. The Senate had had to recreate the city-wide assembly format; it had gone, in the meantime, along with most of the city's traditional hierarchies. But its memory had survived, reinforced by these continuing practices, and its imagery was evidently still effective. Rome was thus the last city in Italy in which a version of the *placitum* could still be drawn on, and, with the exception of England and Scandinavia, perhaps also the last place in Europe.[60] This, too, marked the end of the fall and rise of a judicial system.

I have discussed elsewhere what happened to senatorial justice in the later twelfth century, and the ways in which it began both to work less well and to lose ground to the reviving papacy in the 1190s.[61] That takes us beyond my subject matter here, which is pre-communal, not communal, Rome. And it is also not needed for my argument. What should be clear from the preceding pages is the way that the re-crystallization of a functioning government in Rome, after the initial crisis, ended up with a bifurcation, and structural rivalry, of two separate political systems, papal and senatorial, both of which came to maturity in the same decade: the 1140s. What we have not so far confronted, however, is what the political roots of either that crisis or that bifurcation were. That is the task of the next three sections, the first of them focused on structures, the others on practices or processes—that is to say, on events.

THE RULES OF POLITICS IN ROME, 1050–1150

This section in large part reprises arguments made earlier in the book, summarizing them in a form of proto-conclusion, so that we can see where we have reached. So: how did Rome work politically, after the end of its *ancien régime*? If we want to investigate the threads which make up the network of political relationships today, then—as screenwriters and journalists alike advise us—we follow the money. Money did matter in Rome, as we have discovered, and as we shall see again; but we have to start off with a more fundamental piece of advice in any essentially agrarian society: follow the land. Who owned land in and around the city of Rome, and who took it in lease?

We have amply seen the answer to this question earlier, in Chapters 2 and 3. Roman churches and monasteries owned an overwhelming proportion of the land of the city and its surroundings, the Agro romano, up to 25 km out from the

---

[60] For England, see citations in Wickham, 'Public court practice', p. 27n.
[61] Wickham, 'Getting justice', pp. 114–16, 118–20.

Aurelian Walls. Even though its full control over that land started to slip after 1050—in the context, as usual, of political crisis—the situation only changed very slowly, and had not altered much by 1150, or by 1250 for that matter. This ecclesiastical predominance meant that there were very few lay landowners indeed, and also, as far as we can see, no peasant owners either. The Agro romano was, furthermore, not only controlled by church institutions, but also by bodies almost exclusively based inside, or just outside, the city's walls. Except for Grottaferrata, whose lands were focused around Tuscolo, there were also no autonomous land-owning monasteries in the Agro romano (see further above, p. 53).[62]

Rome's agrarian economy was thus totally controlled by the city, and by the churches in the city, in a pattern which had no parallels elsewhere in Italy. Anyone who wanted access to the fundamental source of wealth in our period had to deal with the city's churches and monasteries. And, even though it must be added that Rome's artisanal economy was intense and flourishing, that economy was based on urban land plots which were also owned by churches, and were sometimes exploit-ed quite intensively (above, pp. 139, 150–2). We have seen that what churches did with most of that land was lease it out to lay middlemen, on long-term or renewable leases of different kinds. Agrarian rents to churches were low, except in the vineyard belt immediately around the city and stretching down the hill below Albano, and except in the salt flats inland from Porto. It was also only in vineyard areas that churches leased, more than occasionally, directly to peasants. I have hypothesized that churches always made up for those low rents by high entry fines, which are first documented when *emphyteuses* are replaced by *locationes* in the late eleventh century (above, p. 79), but it must nonetheless be recognized that a high proportion of agricultural profit always went to lay middlemen, not to the churches and monas-teries who ultimately owned the land.

These lay middlemen were largely from the aristocracy of the city, first the 'old aristocracy', up to the mid-eleventh century, and then the 'new aristocracy', who begin to be documented from the early eleventh. It is not only not at all surprising that this should be the case, but indeed was inevitable, for the aristocracy would have to consist of the lay families who controlled the most land, and leasing was the only way that, for the first 25 km around the city, any members of the laity could get such control. For full ownership, one had to go further out, to the land of castles that made up the rest of Lazio. The 'old aristocracy' in the early eleventh century did that more and more; but the 'new aristocracy' did not even begin to follow them until the early twelfth, and, probably, did not in any case gain the bulk of their wealth from the rest of Lazio until a minority of them (plus one surviving 'old' aristocratic family, the Colonna) became the baronial families of the thirteenth. As we saw in Chapter 4, when the century of crisis opened around 1050, the 'old aristocracy' had already virtually all left the city. The city's remaining aristocratic players, the Frangipane, Corsi, Sant' Eustachio, Pierleoni, and so on, were based for

---

[62] See in general Wickham, '*Iuris cui existens*', and Wickham, 'La struttura', with Chapter 2, above, *passim*. For Grottaferrata's lands, 'Documenti di storia', n. 2. Farfa's few rural properties in the Agro romano, mostly on or near the via Salaria, are attested in *RF*, nn. 656, 637–8, 509, 587, 1026, 1134.

the most part on lands in the city and the Agro romano until 1150 at least: that is to say, on leases. So, still more, were members of the 'medium elite' in the city, who mostly had either urban leases or land in the vineyard belt and the salt-pans, as we saw in Chapter 5, though they too were increasingly active in the Agro romano in the twelfth century, again with ecclesiastical leases.

These leases were stable; churches never felt the need to extend the short-term leases that they did have (notably for vineyards and salt) to the rest of their property portfolio. But their stability did not mean that leaseholders could rely on them so completely that they could ignore the rights of the ultimate proprietors of the land, the churches. If they did, they might not get renewals of leases when they did come up; and they certainly would not get more land. Trouble between churches and lay leaseholders was endemic when it involved the lease of castles, beyond the limits of the Agro romano.[63] To aristocrats, castles were always worth the risk of such trouble; but they were also only a small part of the landowning of all Roman churches, which was often exclusively based on the city and the Agro romano, and sometimes only on the city and its vineyard belt. In these areas, leaseholders needed continued links with their landlords that were not only economic, but also social and political. We saw in Chapter 5 examples of churches and monasteries which had documented networks of links of precisely this type: S. Gregorio sul Celio with 'aristocratic' families, S. Ciriaco in Via Lata with members of the 'medium elite', SS. Cosma e Damiano in Trastevere with less prominent citizens, S. Maria Nova with several social strata from the Frangipane downwards in what was a particularly tightly knit *regio*. In each case, the laity were not only leaseholders from the church, but made up a social network focused on the church, and sometimes visibly acted to give political and judicial support to the church too—and to individual clerics, who would often (though it is hard to pin down the details in this period) be their brothers and uncles, and whose institutional prosperity doubtless spread out to their relatives too. There is good reason to suppose that these patterns were normal in Rome.

Roman elites thus, rather more than in other cities, depended for their wealth and status above all on relations with churches. (In other cities, it was certainly common for urban leaders to be bishop's vassals, and to hold land or parish rights from him, but they all also had allodial land as well.[64]) And the fact that Roman sociability was, for all but a few 'aristocratic' families, focused on single *regiones* meant that these churches were also an important element of the society of each *regio*. Churches were *in* such *regiones*, rather than acting to define them; Rome when it was built up territorially was a network of *regiones*, not parishes (above, pp. 308–11). These *regiones* were very coherent, and sometimes geographically far apart; Rome risked at least a degree of social fragmentation. We have seen in Chapter 6 that one of the tasks its processional geography had was to hold the city together, performatively. Few formal institutions could do as much here: perhaps

---

[63] e.g. *S. Paolo*, nn. 7–11, for castles in Tuscia Romana; *S. Gregorio*, n. 7, for Poli; ASR, SCD, cassetta 16, nn. 109, 118, for Isola Farnese; *SMVL*, n. 149, for Cave.

[64] For Lombardy, see, for example, Keller, *Signori e vassalli*, esp. pp. 102–18.

the *placitum* before the late eleventh century, as we have just seen, for, although undoubtedly dominated by the 'aristocracy', the assembly was open to all; certainly the Senate after 1143, as we shall see later; but little else in the intervening period in any systematic way. Rome remained a strong and coherent whole, above all in its political action; but in the decades of crisis above all, and also, pretty much, in every other period, the sociability of Romans was focused on their *regiones* themselves, and on the landowning churches in them.[65]

Another way of putting this is to say that Romans were focused on *churches*, but not on '*the church*'. One aspect of the fragmentation latent in Rome's society in the crisis century was that one person was not tightly involved in these ecclesiastical networks: the pope. In the *ancien régime* of the Carolingian papacy, the Teofilatto hegemony, and the Tuscolano period, there was indeed a political structure focused on the pope: it was the labyrinthine network of military, judicial, and clerical hierarchies, linked together (in the case of the first two) by the *placitum* assembly, which, although privileging the ('old') aristocracy, extended a long way down into urban society. This was beginning to break down in the early eleventh century with the decreasing tendency of aristocrats, either 'old' or 'new', to look to office-holding as a career, except for the still-central office of the urban prefect. This was further accentuated when, under the German and then Hildebrandine papacy, cardinals began systematically to be foreign, and also became politically central; the *placitum* faded, some time after the 1070s; the urban prefect was still a Roman office, but by 1100 it was virtually monopolized by a single family, the Corsi (later called the Prefetti), so was no longer an office other elite members could easily aspire to.

The resultant situation is often—and also in this book—expressed in terms of the alienation of secular Romans from the 'reform' papacy,[66] which was not only occupied by non-Romans but which also, increasingly, saw the city as an Other, a problem or an embarrassment, rather than the natural locus of papal rule, as popes had regularly seen it from the 550s to 1046, and would do so again later, in every century between 1188 and 1870 except the Avignon period. But the stripping out of the old political structures which united the city—and united it in a papal-dominated political system—revealed a more deep-seated issue as well: that day-to-day Roman loyalties were otherwise more focused on the individual churches of the *urbs* than on the papal church which symbolized it. This was even partially true of 'aristocrats'; the Frangipane were loyal as much to S. Gregorio and S. Maria Nova (and probably to other undocumented churches too) as to the papal court. Popes had their own lands too, and could deploy them for political purposes just as other churches did. The Frangipane expansion into *Marittima* after *c.*1140, for example, was as a result of papal cessions, which would ultimately, in this case at least, shift the balance of long-term Frangipane loyalty firmly to the pope, although that was

---

[65] Compare, for the strong and coherently organized *regiones/rioni* of the fourteenth century, Maire Vigueur, *L'autre Rome*, pp. 163–76; but these covered much larger territories, and therefore included many more people, than did those of the twelfth (cf. above, p. 122).

[66] e.g. Brezzi, *Roma*, pp. 234–6; di Carpegna Falconieri, *Il clero di Roma*, pp. 65–74, for the clergy too.

the result of mid-century changes, as we shall see in a moment. But the pope did not have limitless amounts of land in the Agro romano, and also controlled less of the rest of Lazio in the crisis century than either before or after.[67] And the landed policies of the other churches of the city were certainly not under papal control. The pope had, in fact, after the end of the old system of government, less of an aristocratic entourage based specifically on land cessions than did most north Italian bishops; that element of partial political centralization in Milan and other cities was not so easily available in Rome.

So what could an external pope, or any external political leader, do to have an impact on Rome at all? Otto III in his brief period of rule introduced two foreign popes, Gregory V and Silvester II, the first non-Italian popes for 250 years, but apart from that just relied on the 'old' aristocratic hierarchies that still existed. Why exactly this regime failed so quickly is not entirely clear, except for the simple reason that it followed forty years in which Romans had regularly revolted against every pope the Ottonians chose for them, whether Roman or external in origin. It may also be, though, as suggested earlier (p. 26), that Otto had his eye on the landed wealth of the city's churches, which, had he managed to appropriate it, would have been as rich a source of royal resources as was Lombardy or Saxony. When we see him confirming the possessions of SS. Bonifacio e Alessio in 996, or the rights of S. Gregorio sul Celio to Poli in 999, acts which were in no way in his remit had he remained just a patron of sovereign popes as his father and grandfather had been, we certainly see him in action as a direct ruler, the first layman to claim this role in full since the seventh century at the latest, and making the first step to claiming the right to dispose of land, not just to confirm it.[68] If that is what Otto was doing, however, he certainly failed, and no subsequent lay ruler until the nineteenth century even tried. Land remained in the hands of Rome's churches, and so, therefore, did local politics.

Another solution was to gain more control over Rome's churches themselves. This, it seems to me, is a major reason why the German popes chose foreign cardinals so fast, beside the obvious one, that is to say to create a critical mass for a directive community committed to 'reform'; for cardinals each had a church, whether a bishopric, a *titulus*, or a *diaconia*, under their direct control, so could potentially act as the focus of the local aggregation which was so important to Romans. This did not happen either, however. Cardinals were enmeshed in international politics; they were often sent as papal emissaries, they accompanied

[67] Thumser, 'Die Frangipane', pp. 128–42. The archive of the papal church is, sadly, mostly lost—only scattered texts from our period survive in the Archivio Segreto Vaticano and the *Liber Censuum*—so this is not possible to check in detail. The lands directly controlled by the pope in the Agro romano seem to have been to the east of the city, the sector with least evidence from other churches. The pope presumably also controlled the lands of S. Giovanni in Laterano, which were, however, fairly restricted in size in this period; and also of S. Pietro in Vaticano, which were huge, although also for the most part, as it appears from *SPV*, not leased out on any scale to aristocrats. For all this see Wickham, 'La struttura', pp. 206–7, 208; and above, p. 61.

[68] *Ottonis III diplomata*, nn. 209, 336 (= *S. Alessio*, n. 5; *S. Gregorio*, n. 3; note that Poli was already S. Gregorio's, *S. Gregorio*, n. 4). In 1000, however, *Papsturkunden*, n. 387, a letter from Silvester to Otto, sees the pope claiming his own *dominium* in the Sabina.

the pope outside the city, and, from the 1140s ever more insistently, they acted as judges-delegate for ecclesiastical disputes from across Europe. Their duties to their actual Roman church were increasingly restricted—probably for the most part to presiding over major feast days and stational processions (which, as members of the papal entourage, they had to be there for anyway), with the actual running of the church left to its *archipresbiter*, who was normally Roman. S. Maria Nova is the best test of this, for it is the only church with a cardinal to leave us a decent documentation. In the over 150 documents surviving from its archive between 1046 and 1200, the great majority of which involved the church directly, the cardinal deacon appears only ten times: four for the papal *cancellarius* Pietro in 1070–81, three for Tebaldo in 1110–19, two for the papal *cancellarius* Aimerico in 1140, and one for Bernardo in 1191; in most of these the *archipresbiter* of the church is present as well. Tebaldo, from the Boccapecora family, was one of a small handful of 'reform' cardinals who we know to have been Roman; but even he was only present in half of the documents from his cardinalate (1103–23). Aimerico (1123–41), from France, was a hugely influential *cancellarius*, but had still less of a role in S. Maria Nova's daily dealings. The other documents for the church up to 1140 were all headed by the *archipresbiter* or his subordinate priests, who were again all almost certainly of Roman origin.[69]

The papacy had one other hold over a church like S. Maria Nova: the possibility of internal reform. In 1060–3, Gregorio was not just *archipresbiter* of S. Maria Nova, but also *canonicus*: the *diaconia* had been transformed into a *canonica* with a college of regular canons. But already when Cardinal Pietro ran the church (which in the 1070s he did on his own, calling himself *rector et aucmentator*) it was called a *diaconia* again, and stayed so thereafter. In 1141–2, under Aimerico, the reform was tried again, and this time it held; S. Maria Nova was headed by a *prior* from 1142 on, assisted by canons, who are only occasionally called priests or deacons, and the church was often called a *canonica*. But it has to be said that one cannot detect the slightest change thereafter in its social networks or its landed practices. Although we do not know what the social origins of any of its priors were, the church remained a focus of its *regio*, and the betting would be that most or all of its canons remained as Roman as were the priests who preceded them—or as were their lay neighbours, who could well have been their relatives. And S. Maria Nova was one of the few regular *canonicae* in Rome to remain one across the century; the others were mostly as short-lived as was S. Maria's first experience.[70]

We can see popes having an effect on many practices of Rome's churches. S. Pietro in Vaticano, unusually rich as it was, and crucially important as a local political focus, saw its sixty *mansionarii*, the 'semi-lay' sacristans who ran the church and took a high percentage of its incomings from pilgrims (50 per cent in 1058),

---

[69] *SMN*, nn. 23–6, 35–6, 38, 50–1, 135 for cardinals; for *archipresbyteri* replacing cardinals as, in effect, parish priests throughout Rome, see di Carpegna Falconieri, *Il clero di Roma*, pp. 165–72.
[70] *SMN*, nn. 17–20 (a. 1060–3), 54 (a. 1142) onwards. See di Carpegna Falconieri, *Il clero di Roma*, pp. 183, 185–7, 188n (here he plausibly ascribes the 1141–2 *canonica* to Aimerico); in general, pp. 176–93 for canonical reform in general, which had started by 1043, before Sutri that is to say.

removed by Gregory VI and Leo IX, restored by Benedict X, and finally removed again by Gregory VII; that is to say, this link to the city—important in that *mansionarii* (for S. Pietro and many other churches) had been very active in the city as dealers and witnesses, in effect members of the steadily crystallizing 'medium elite'—was deliberately and permanently cut.[71] Furthermore, married clergy disappear from our sources. They had been normal everywhere in our ninth- and early tenth-century documentation; although in the early eleventh century formal marriage drops out of the texts, and instead we find priests acting with women who are not said to be their wives, up to here this was a change without much effect on family life. But after that, not only did the official rhetoric concerning clerical celibacy considerably increase, but such priests were, after 1070, replaced in the documents by priests without any visible families at all, which was a very different life experience.[72] These were real and rapid changes; and the Roman clergy, like that of most Italian cities, remained unhappy about 'reform' (maybe more unhappy than many laity) for two generations or more as a result.[73] Ecclesiastical culture slowly changed from then on and into the twelfth century, in Rome as elsewhere, with a growing separation between clerical and lay. But this was the limit of the impact the papacy had on Rome's churches; and on Rome's monasteries, as long as they did not seem to need internal reform (as with S. Anastasio ad Aquas Salvias, transferred by Innocent II to the Cistercians[74]), they had even less structural effect. Both churches and monasteries maintained their local roles as foci for Rome's lay social networks; the work of undermining that, or of refocusing the networks onto an ecclesiastical system the popes could control, had to be permanently in operation to be effective and was Sisyphean in nature. One look away, and churches returned to being responsive principally to the lay community which took its livelihood from church leases and in return supported their daily political needs. So, although most of Rome's resources were in the hands of its churches and monasteries, the process of controlling them was never a completely successful operation. Indeed, urban ecclesiastical institutions were, in the century after 1050 (and later), more often a barrier between the papacy and the laity than they were a conduit.

Another solution was one which had long existed and which continued: the processional tradition. We saw in Chapter 6 how that operated, to bring the pope and the Curia onto the streets, in public, regularly, and in return to attract the Roman *populus* into a ritual world which stressed papal dominance in the city. As we have seen, indeed, this did work. The public ceremonial world reinforced Roman identity, which helped the coherence of the city and its *populus*, but it

---

[71] Di Carpegna Falconieri, *Il clero di Roma*, pp. 136–48 for *mansionarii*; for changes in S. Pietro, see esp. *SPV*, n. 22 and Bonizone of Sutri, *Liber ad amicum*, VII (p. 603). For *mansionarii* of S. Pietro active in Rome, see e.g. *RS*, nn. 42, 134; *Papsturkunden*, n. 424; *SMVL*, n. 56; *S. Agnese*, n. 4.

[72] See di Carpegna Falconieri, 'Il matrimonio e il concubinato'.

[73] See di Carpegna Falconieri, *Il clero di Roma*, pp. 65–74. An emblematic text for the clergy of Milan defending clerical marriage is Landolfo Seniore, *Historia Mediolanensis*, e.g. III.5; see also the complexities related in the *Historia custodum Aretinorum*.

[74] *Vita prima sancti Bernardi*, II.48; cf. Loewenfeld, 'Documenta', n. 1, for Eugenius III's later confirmation.

also, and probably above all, stressed the centrality of papal sovereignty and ritual hegemony in a processionally united city. The Romans could, and did, oppose individual popes, but they did not usually oppose the concept of papal power in the city. The dice here were very much loaded in favour of support for papal rule. Alberico, earlier, had on his deathbed given up on his creation of a lay principate when he pushed for his heir to become pope (above, p. 24), and this remained the norm: the early Senate wished very much to get recognition (even though certainly not at all costs) from Eugenius III; if we go later into the Middle Ages, at the height of the Avignonese papacy, Cola di Rienzo's ideal of a not fully papal city only lasted a handful of months.[75] But, although this cultural and performative environment undoubtedly privileged papal hegemony (in a Gramscian sense), it did not privilege any particular version of papal government. Although individual popes, such as Innocent II or, later, Innocent III, could manipulate it in order to stress their own supremacy, the processional world did not substitute for absences in political infrastructures. It certainly did not favour any particular version of a 'reform' agenda; and the Senate, once in operation, had no trouble in fitting in with it as well.

We do, it is true, have clear hints that lay Romans were at ease with many aspects of the 'reform' agenda. The consistent support of the ancestors of the Pierleoni for the 'reform' papacy must have been a deliberate choice, and the piety of the prefect Cencio di Giovanni, evoked by Pier Damiani as we saw earlier in this chapter, can easily be seen as authentic. The donors of the late eleventh-century murals of S. Clemente seem to have favoured lay asceticism (above, pp. 357–8). Romans after 1050 could perfectly easily have developed their own lay 'reform' movement along the lines of the Milanese Pataria, had they not had a papal leadership devoted to doing just that. But this did not translate in Milan into a greater acceptance of 'reformed' archiepiscopal rule—indeed, in the end (even if for different reasons), Milan's commune crystallized very early.[76] And there is no sign in Rome that these indicators of a critical lay Christianity led in any particular political direction. The Pierleoni and Cencio were close associates of Hildebrand/Gregory VII, and they mark the success of the latter as an intermediary between the papal entourage and the 'new aristocracy', as we shall see in a moment; but the S. Clemente murals are best seen as reflecting the cultural world of Gregory's fierce opponent Clement III. Later, around 1150, both the Senate and Eugenius III had associations with rival leaders of 'reform' Christianity, respectively Arnaldo of Brescia and Bernard of Clairvaux; neither of these latter had much impact on Rome's politics, and their interventions only really mark the continued centrality to outsiders of Rome as an important political venue, but they certainly show again that uncompromising religious purism was not the patrimony of any particular political structure in the city.[77]

[75] e.g. Maire Vigueur, 'Cola di Rienzo'; di Carpegna Falconieri, *Cola di Rienzo*, pp. 66–138.

[76] For Cencio, D'Acunto, 'Il prefetto Cencio'; for the Pataria and the commune in Milan, the classic is Keller, 'Pataria und Stadtverfassung'.

[77] See in general Frugoni, *Arnaldo da Brescia*, and below, pp. 444–5.

The popes and their entourage after 1050 were perfectly well aware that they had to overcome the weak links they had with Rome as a city. For all their complaints about Romans, they also (mostly) recognized that they did have to rule Rome, and that they needed to find some way of getting over the dual problem of the alienation of Romans from a papal entourage which was increasingly foreign, and the slow dissolution of the governing structures of the city, particularly in the civil war period after 1084—both of which were likely to reinforce the local church-focused loyalties and regional commitment that have just been characterized. If they could not control the local churches, what they had to do, and indeed sought to do, was to bring Rome's 'aristocracy' on side. This was the standard medieval choice, reflecting, indeed, standard medieval realities; even in Italy, where communes would soon—to an extent—involve wider social groups, these new institutional forms were not politically coherent alternatives to traditional aristocratic hierarchies until after 1100 in a very few cities (only Genoa and Pisa) and after 1130—indeed often after 1150—in the others. Even the Pisans did not react against their own most visible aristocratic family, the Visconti, until 1153.[78] The main lay political players until the 1140s in Rome were the 'aristocracy' too. The task of the popes of the crisis period was to seek to involve the 'aristocracy' in the political community around individual popes, and, if possible, in the political direction favoured by each pope, even though the traditional structures which achieved this were failing.

What would bring Rome's 'aristocrats' stably into the papal court? A generic sense of status, certainly, of closeness to the ruler, as with the Roman *nobiliores* in Innocent II's *consistorium* in 1141 (above, pp. 249, 402). It is interesting that popes never in this period established a set of papal titles that might have conveyed that status, unlike emperors in the same period, who were happy to give titles like *comes sacri palatii* or *missus imperatoris* to urban aristocrats in other Italian cities.[79] 'Aristocrats' in Rome were by now just called by notably generic words such as *nobilis* (above, p. 261), or else, more rarely, *Romanorum consul*, which was the opposite of a papal term (below, pp. 436–7). It may be that, since popes did not in this period have so very much accessible land, they could not plausibly invent an aristocratic hierarchy which would only, so to speak, exist on paper. But the status certainly mattered, and indeed it put the most successful of these families on the European map in a way that they could never have achieved on their own (above, pp. 256–7).

The other attraction of closeness to the pope was gifts of money, or, more generally, treasure (including the patronage of some trading activities, as with Alberico Cece and Cencio Frangipane under Gregory VII: above, p. 165). This was available to popes thanks to incomings of all kinds, as we have seen at several

---

[78] For the Visconti, see Volpe, *Studi sulle istituzioni comunali a Pisa*, pp. 3–5, with *Statuti inediti della città di Pisa*, I, pp. 18–19 (a. 1153).

[79] See e.g. Wickham, *Courts and Conflict*, pp. 24–8, for Lucca; in Milan, by contrast, where most early twelfth-century *iudices* were *iudices et missi* of named kings/emperors, it only marked a professional qualification: see Andenna, 'Dall'Orto, Oberto', for an example, and, in general, *Gli atti del comune di Milano*, nn. 4–23.

points in this book: in rents from the city and the Agro romano, customs dues, renders from European monasteries, constant gifts from foreign powers—some stable (from England or, later, Sicily), some one-off but still substantial—as well as money for papal privileges, money for justice, and the ever-renewing supply of money from pilgrims.[80] I have invoked the handouts of gold and silver to rival groups of supporters in Rome in the century after 1050 several times in this book (esp. Chapter 3, pp. 171–4), and they were both well documented and, apparently, of great importance.[81] They were particularly frequent when there were two popes, and they were an absolutely standard way of building up and of undermining factional support under such circumstances.[82] We know that, in less tense moments, money flowed to aristocrats as a result of participation in the papal court too, as with the large rewards coming to the Pierleoni and the prefect Pietro 'II', and the slightly smaller ones received by the Frangipane and Normanni, when the Genoese came to Rome in 1120 (above, p. 402). It is entirely possible that aristocrats who were sufficiently close to the pope received the sort of 'money fief' which we know the Pierleoni got from Roger of Sicily in 1134: 240 *unciae* of gold (or the equivalent in kind) per year in return for sworn *fidelitas*, *servitium*, and *ligium hominium*, liege homage.[83]

The pope was short of available land, then, but he had plenty of gold and silver and other movables. It would be only sensible to use this to keep the support of the major lay political players in Rome, the city's 'aristocracy', even in times of peace, not to speak of times of schism, when rivals would certainly be doing the same. Conversely, it has to be stressed that no aristocrat could have relied only on such money. It was land which was the inescapable basis for status in the medieval period, before the massive economic expansion in some Italian cities allowed the richest bankers and merchants to gain status other ways, and even papal favour and papal silver would not be enough on their own for lasting position; and land, whether in the city or outside, as we have seen, depended on associations with Rome's churches more than on the pope. The land 'new aristocrats' thus gained was substantial, but not, especially for second-tier aristocrats, enormous; it was not for the most part greater than their counterparts had elsewhere in Italy (see above, esp. pp. 252–6). The Pierleoni, the most likely leading family in the city in our period to have an origin in finance, and closely associated with a long sequence of popes, got their first castle and their only long-held one, Isola Farnese, not from a pope but from SS. Cosma e Damiano in Trastevere, shortly before 1107.[84] But what those landholdings did give one, in this period, was enough status to be able to be a player in the papal court, and thus to have access to money on top of that pre-existing landed base. The money, easily divisible as it was, could then, some of it,

---

[80] See Chapter 3, n. 198 for references; cf. above, pp. 137–8, 174–5, for pilgrims.
[81] See in general Wickham, 'The financing'.
[82] As for example Pier Damiani, *Epistulae*, n. 89; Berthold, *Chronicon*, p. 380; Bernold, *Chronicon*, pp. 431, 439; *Pontificum Romanorum vitae*, ed. Watterich, II, p. 110.
[83] Kehr, 'Diploma purpureo'.   [84] See Chapter 4, n. 110.

be redistributed down lay 'aristocratic' clienteles, and could get into the rest of the city.[85]

This situation could be put schematically as follows: the regional-level Roman political economy focused on land, and local churches and monasteries; the papal political economy, and, through that, secular 'aristocratic' clienteles, focused on gold and silver (cf. above, pp. 313–14 The latter was indeed highly interesting to aristocrats, and kept them in the papal court, particularly when the pope was sufficient of a protagonist, as with Calixtus II and Innocent II, to attract the 'aristocracy' away from regional-level alliances with the 'medium elite', which were always there as well. The wealth of the popes also helps to explain the growing factional involvement of the aristocracy in papal elections, which reached an extreme with the Frangipane-controlled elections of Honorius II in 1124 and Innocent II in 1130, and of that of the Pierleoni Anacletus II in rivalry to Innocent. Indeed, with the shift of the palatine judges from the high aristocracy to being legal professionals, and the monopolization of the office of prefect by a single family, the pope was, in this period, the only major office to fight over, which added to the potential for factional instability in the city—a potential amply realized in the early twelfth century. But the attraction of money was not enough. In part, as just observed, this was because money could not match land as a rich and status-filled resource. In part, it was because money was always double-edged: it was a rich and deserved reward for one's friends, but a corrupt bribe for one's enemies. It may be because of this, to an extent, that the Senate in its early years had a perceptible anti-aristocratic element: the 'aristocracy' could be seen as having been 'bought' by the pope. The penalty for being closer to the pope was a reduced link to the city even for the 'aristocracy' itself, not just the foreign cardinalate. This is why popes had to be effective protagonists, which not all were, for this form of patronage to work fully.

We will look at these suggestions again later in the chapter. They certainly cannot stand as flat generalizations, for this would mean that the papacy could never re-establish itself stably in Rome, which would make the considerable successes of Innocent II in the early 1140s (see below, pp. 432–4), and Hadrian IV in the late 1150s,[86] difficult to explain, not to speak of the revival of papal power under Celestine III and Innocent III. Those successes were, however, partly because the rules changed again; the steady revival of papal territorial power, first in *Marittima* and western *Campania*, and later in ever wider areas of eastern and northern Lazio, under precisely these popes, gave them landed territories that they could—and did, as the *Liber Censuum* shows us—use once again to reward support in the normal medieval way. Innocent II was on the cusp: a successful pope in the tradition of the popes of the crisis century, but also just beginning to be able to use Lazial landed resources to back this up as well, even if not to the extent which Hadrian IV and Innocent III could. But even before that the pope did always gain by being the recognized sovereign of the city. Documents were always dated by him

---

[85] Thanks to Marco Vendittelli for a useful discussion of this point.
[86] See, for Hadrian, e.g. Bolton, *'Nova familia beati Petri'*.

(except in brief years of real political uncertainty, when incarnation dates were used). Even with the feeblest popes, such as Gelasius II, there were always people ready to give him the benefit of the doubt. All the same, it was always difficult to turn this generalized hegemony into real action, in the crisis century. It was not impossible, but it was necessary to work hard for it, and few managed it successfully. It greatly helped if the pope was himself a Roman, as two of the three most successfully dominant popes in the crisis century were, Gregory VII (by adoption) and Innocent II. These two, plus Calixtus II, really did know how to deal with the city, as no other popes of the period did. But being Roman was not necessarily enough either; at the end of the reigns of both Gregory and Innocent, if for widely different reasons, the city rejected them. Ruling remained hard, that is to say, even for them.

This is as far as a purely structural analysis will take us. What I have hoped to make clear in this section is that the objective difficulties of the popes in having any real effect on the city of Rome between 1050 and 1150 had a variety of causes, and were certainly not willed by anyone. They were the result of a network of social changes, which were undoubtedly set in motion by the unaccustomed dominance of foreign popes and cardinals after 1046, and accentuated by the post-1081 civil war, but were also linked to internal processes as well, the slow separation of the 'old aristocracy' from traditional offices, the lack of involvement in them of the 'new aristocracy' (except the office of prefect for the Corsi/Prefetti), and the strong tendency of Romans of all social levels to look to the land-based clienteles of local churches rather than to the papal-sponsored lay hierarchy (such as it was). These elements of disintegration resolved themselves in the 1140s, as we have seen in the first section of this chapter, into two rival institutional foci, the Senate and what one can by now generically call the Curia. But it will be for the next two sections to show how, in practice, Curia and Senate each crystallized politically in the early twelfth century.

POLITICAL EXPEDIENTS IN THE CRISIS DECADES

As stated earlier, it is not my aim to write a political history here. In narrative-poor Italy, there is, anyway, less evidence for what follows than for much found elsewhere in this book. Rather, I want to set out briefly and fairly synthetically what were the problems, relating to Rome, faced by the successive popes, and how (and how successfully) they dealt with them, using here too material discussed earlier. I will start with Hildebrand/Gregory VII, and then in turn move to Clement III, Paschal II and his successors, Anacletus II, and finally Innocent II. I skip over popes whose reigns in Rome were too short for them to have any useful purchase in the city. After Innocent, papal expedients were swept into the history of the early Senate, and will be discussed in the final section of the chapter.

The German papacy of the first few years after 1046 had relatively little documented connection with Romans of any kind. How papal rule in the city was actually organized is not at all easy to tell; there are relatively few documents for the period, and narratives are generic. The *Annales Romani*, for example, tell us that the Roman *populus* was prepared (for gifts) to receive back the Tuscolano Benedict IX at Clement II's death in 1047, but also stress that the *plebs* sought new popes from the emperors at each vacancy.[87] What effect even Leo IX (1049–54), the only long-lasting German pope, and one with a personal reputation for ecclesiastical rigour and personal sanctity, really had on the city is hard to tell; he anyway spent much of his reign confronting the Normans, until they destroyed his army at Civitate in 1053. Some Roman opposition, which remained attached to Benedict IX until his death in 1055–6, was perhaps taken for granted in these early years, and the survival of the German popes relied on the availability, at least potentially, of German and later Tuscan armies in their support. The first major figure from the Roman clergy to be reabsorbed into the papal entourage was Hildebrand himself. He had followed Gregory VI into exile in 1046, but became a monk in Germany and was taken back to Rome by Leo IX at the start of his reign. He was a senior figure in the papal court by the mid-1050s. After Henry III's death in 1056, three popes followed who were close associates of Marquis Gottifredo of Tuscany: his brother Stephen IX (1057–8), Nicholas II who was also bishop of Florence (1059–61), and Alexander II who was also bishop of Lucca (1061–73). In these years Hildebrand—who was born in Tuscany—was still more important, and in 1058–9 he became archdeacon of the Roman church, head of the Roman clergy, and second only to the pope in the city. Under Alexander, in particular, he ruled Rome during the pope's frequent stays in Lucca. His own succession as Pope Gregory VII was one of the easiest in the century, and he had strong explicit support from the Roman *populus*. He ruled Rome with relatively little opposition from 1059 to 1083.[88]

Hildebrand did have opponents, all the same, changing across time. At Stephen IX's death, the Romans in fact elected Benedict X (1058–9), bishop of Velletri, who had strong support from the *comites qui circa urbem erant*, the 'old aristocracy' of the the Tuscolani, the Ottaviani, and the counts of Galeria. Hildebrand sent money via Leone di Benedetto Cristiano, ancestor of the Pierleoni, to gain support for Nicholas II from the Roman *populus* (Benedict X had done the same earlier). This worked, and Benedict was expelled from the city and then, eventually, forced to submit; he was enclosed in S. Agnese and lived there till his death in the mid-1070s, though still keeping some popular support—all this according to the *Annales Romani*, with some details (notably the money) supported by other sources.[89] Here Hildebrand can be seen as an effective link between the 'reform' papacy and at least some of Rome's 'new aristocracy', a group which also included Giovanni Tignoso, whom he made prefect in 1059, Giovanni Bracciuto—both of these from Trastevere (above, pp. 224–6)—and Cencio Frangipane, most of whom

[87] *LP*, II, pp. 332–4.

[88] For all this, see Cowdrey, *Pope Gregory VII*, pp. 37–58, 71–4, 314–29, 213–29. For Hildebrand's standing under Nicholas and Alexander, our best source is Pier Damiani, *Epistulae*, nn. 49, 57, 63, 65, 75, etc.

[89] *LP*, II, pp. 334–6, with Pier Damiani, *Epistulae*, n. 58 and Benzone of Alba, *Ad Heinricum*, VII.2.

were involved, among other things, in the election of Alexander II in 1061. But already in April 1060 Nicholas and Hildebrand had collected almost the whole Roman 'new aristocracy', and even the Tuscolani, together in the great Arci court-case, in the largest political aggregation since the 1010s.[90]

The events of 1058–9 marked the last attempt of the Tuscolani and other members of the 'old aristocracy' to choose a pope on their own in the traditional way. All candidates from the rest of the century, and thereafter as well, came from the 'reform' tradition, which thus lost any particular political or factional colouring in itself. But this divided after 1059, between those who saw the emperor as the major guarantor of papal legitimacy and those who did not. Bishop Cadalo of Parma was elected Pope Honorius II in the German court at Basel against Alexander in 1061, and twice, in 1062–3 and 1064, had a certain success in Rome. Hildebrand and Leone di Benedetto had to give many gifts to the Romans to regain support in the city, which was then backed up by Tuscan and Norman armies. The Roman aristocracy was by now clearly divided too, with the *filii Baruncii* and Cencio di Stefano, son of a former prefect, among those in support of Cadalo (as were also the Tuscolani and the counts of Galeria, who were clearly by now motivated above all by hostility to the Hildebrandine affinity).[91] It was this group who remained Hildebrand's opponents from now on. Cencio di Stefano, as we have seen, kidnapped Gregory at the Christmas mass in 1075, and his brother Stefano had Gregory's urban prefect Cencio di Giovanni Tignoso killed in 1077. This was a clearly unreconciled family. But all the signs are that Hildebrand/ Gregory remained hegemonic in the city, especially after Cadalo/Honorius failed in his attempts to become pope, and that Cencio di Stefano's affinity was in a restricted minority from then on. It was the Roman *populus*, in some form at least, which released Gregory the next day in 1075, lynched Stefano in 1077, and destroyed family towers on both occasions.[92]

Hildebrand/Gregory must have been an effective dealer. He was, it is true, lucky in his moment. We saw earlier that it is likely that the 'new aristocracy', or many of them, were the force behind the Roman revolt of 1044 against Benedict IX (p. 245), and they were also likely, even if with some slippage at times, to have been potentially favourable to the 'reform' papacy as long as Tuscolani popes were the alternatives, that is to say up to 1059 at least. Hence, too, the major collective aggregation against the Ottaviani, which is clearly documented at Arci in 1060. But that aggregation had needed some orchestration if it even included the Tuscolani as part of it; and Hildebrand, with his closest supporter Leone di Benedetto, had to re-establish it twice in periods of crisis, against Benedict X and then against Cadalo. Hildebrand was thus both close to the 'new aristocracy' as a whole in its initial decades of dominance in the city, and capable of manipulating its factions

---

[90] Election of Alexander: e.g. Benzone of Alba, *Ad Heinricum*, II.4. Arci: *RF*, n. 906; see above, pp. 221–2.

[91] *LP*, II, pp. 336–7, with Benzone of Alba, *Ad Heinricum*, II.3, 9, 10.

[92] Bonizone of Sutri, *Liber ad amicum*, VII–VIII is the most detailed account; for full lists of sources see Cowdrey, *Gregory VII*, pp. 327–8; D'Acunto, 'Il prefetto Cencio', pp. 5–9.

effectively once it began to divide into them. There were structural elements to this control as well. Hildebrand ran a version of the *placitum* assembly into the 1070s, as we have seen; it must have been he who asked Cardinal Deusdedit to compile the first survey of rights of the Roman church in the 1080s; and two very different sources say that he was active in establishing an armed *militia* of some kind in Rome and its environs, which only became controversial in 1082, when a *conventus* of cardinals refused to support the use of church property to pay for it.[93] He also had close relations with the urban prefect and with the latter's own judicial authority. So: Hildebrand/Gregory fully ruled Rome, and kept the support of the Romans. He could do this while also acting as the unchallenged leader of the 'reform' movement at a European level, and, particularly after he became pope, sending directives to the rulers of most of the continent. But, in contrast to his European-level activities, Hildebrand's rule in Rome was relatively traditional in its basic elements; we cannot easily track cultural initiatives, for example (his close ally Desiderio of Montecassino's spectacular new abbey church of the 1060s had no contemporary parallel in Rome).[94] Here, innovation was probably not needed, at least, not for the moment.

The Hildebrandine consensus lasted until 1083–4, but then fell apart. The edginess of the 1082 *conventus* is already a sign of it. Gregory VII and Henry IV's 1070s confrontations turned to war in 1080, and Henry attacked Rome, seeking the imperial coronation which Gregory refused him, in 1081, 1082, 1083, and 1083–4, every year getting slightly further into the city. By 1083, it must have been obvious to the Romans that Henry was not going to stop, and that their own military resistance might not be sufficient; they certainly will also have realized that this trouble had began with a pope condemning a German king, and not, as was more usual hitherto, the other way round. In 1084 it was the king's turn to distribute *pecunia* among the citizens; the slowly weakening consensus in support of Gregory rapidly tipped over, and at Easter the Roman *populus* acclaimed Henry as emperor and Clement III (1084–1100) as pope. The Norman attack on the city in May to release Gregory from Castel S. Angelo, which devastated at least the Celio in the south and the northern *regio* of Campo Marzio, did not help Gregory's wider support. The only Hildebrandine supporters we can still be sure of were the Frangipane and the Corsi, though we can probably also again include the future Pierleoni. It was these who were now the minority in a largely Clementine city.[95]

I have stressed the Clementine consensus before, but there is no doubt that Clement III faced more serious structural problems than Hildebrand/Gregory had.

---

[93] For the *militia*, see Landolfo Seniore, *Chronicon*, III.15; Widone of Ferrara, *De schismate*, I.2; Zaferana, 'Sul "conventus"'. Deusdedit, *Collectio canonum*, contains the survey; it is dedicated to Victor III, but could not have been compiled later than 1084, with the expulsion of the Hildebrandine party from Rome.

[94] For the abbey church, see e.g. Bloch, *Monte Cassino*, I, pp. 40–71. For Gregory's fairly traditional rule in Rome, see e.g. Cowdrey, *Gregory VII*, pp. 314–21.

[95] For Henry and Gregory, see Cowdrey, *Gregory VII*, pp. 213–31; for the Normans, Hamilton, 'Memory, symbol and arson'. For hostility to Gregory, see esp. Widone of Ferrara, *De schismate*, I.20, an eyewitness (he was in Clement III's entourage) but extremely *parti pris*. For the Corsi, *LP*, II, p. 290; for Cencio Frangipane see this chapter, n. 97. Only one Roman charter dates by Gregory after he left the city, *SMN*, n. 27, for a Frangipane-associated church.

He was pope during a civil war, and his own rivals Victor III and Urban II did frequently seek to get into the city, to the Settizonio in 1086, to Trastevere and the Civitas Leoniana in 1087, to the Isola Tiberina in 1088, throughout much of Rome briefly in 1089, to the Frangipane *munitio* beside S. Maria Nova in 1093 and to the Laterano in 1094 (which Urban may well have kept hold of), again in 1097, and then throughout Rome in 1099. But charters dated by Victor are unknown in the city, and there are only three for Urban, as against twenty-nine for Clement; such dating clauses indicate a hegemony for Clement that was near-total until 1094, after which the Romans mostly dated by the incarnation until Paschal II's first document in 1100. Clement, on this basis, was broadly accepted in the city for ten years, with more neutrality visible in the last five years of his reign, when he probably no longer controlled the Laterano, although 1098 saw a briefer revival of his hegemony.[96]

It was in the decade of Clement III's fullest hegemony that the judicial documents already discussed (pp. 393–8) belong. These may well show the beginnings of institutional breakdown in the city, as we saw, although they certainly also show Rome's urban prefect and palatine judges operating in a Clementine political framework. In the 1088 Corese case, too, the *consules comunitatis boum* certainly included known pro-imperial families like the Sant' Eustachio and the *filii Baruncii* (not that of Cencio di Stefano, but only because there was then a generation gap; his son, the now-adult Tebaldo di Cencio, was, however, active in Clement's last church council in 1098); but it is significant that it also included Leone di Cencio Frangipane. A Cencio Frangipane, presumably Leone's father, was so close to Gregory VII that he had accompanied him to Salerno and then joined Desiderio of Montecassino/Victor III in 1086–7. Another relative, Giovanni, hosted Urban II at S. Maria Nova in 1094, and went to France with him a year later. Such moments of exile show real commitment. So, in 1088, either the family had decided, as aristocrats often do, to support both sides at once, or else in that year Clement simply seemed, even to Romans of the Hildebrandine party, to have won. Either way, the 1088 text shows Clement to have gone beyond the restricted factional support available to Cadalo, and even beyond the support for him in 1084. Not all the 'new aristocratic' families were with Clement, but the Frangipane were among the two most powerful. If the Pietro who was urban prefect in 1088 was the same man as the one who died in 1116 or his relative—which is unprovable, but conceivable, given the frequency of the name Pietro among the later hereditary prefects—then

---

[96] For narratives of the attacks by Victor and Urban, see Cowdrey, *Abbot Desiderius*, pp. 194–7, 207–8, with *Chronica Casinensis*, III.66, 68–9; Becker, *Papst Urban II*, pp. 98–113. The takeover of the Laterano in 1094 is related in Geoffroy of Vendôme, *Œuvres*, pp. 288–90; I conclude it may have been permanent because Urban started to register letters from the Laterano for the first time in January 1097, and frequently thereafter (Jaffé and Wattenbach, *Regesta pontificum*, I, pp. 691–700). Documents dated by Urban in the city are *SMN*, n. 28; *SPV*, n. 29; *S. Gregorio*, n. 134 (aa. 1089, 1092, 1096); twenty-seven documents date by Clement up to 1094, but, after 1094, only two texts date by Clement, and nine by the incarnation. Cowdrey, *Gregory VII*, p. 231 says that no pope established himself in the city in 1084–94, but this is wrong. See, for 1098, Ziese, *Wibert*, pp. 241–59.

the other major family, the Corsi, whose houses Henry IV had burned in 1084, had swung behind Clement too.[97]

Clement thus had real support, at least from the aristocratic and palatine elite, up to 1094 at least, when it was probably Ferrucio *secundicerius* who handed the Laterano to Urban for a large pay-off. We also know, from the S. Clemente frescoes, that some of the 'medium elite' probably backed him too. What we cannot tell, however, is what he did with that support; his eventual failure led to a *damnatio memorie* that was too total. He certainly ran church councils, although every pope did that; he presided over a substantial polemical literature as well. His experience as imperial chancellor for Italy in the early years of Henry IV, and as archbishop of Ravenna from 1073, might have allowed him to develop a more personalized political pragmatism, but we cannot track it.[98] All we can say is that he held Rome together for a decade after the fall of Gregory VII, in a very difficult situation. His tomb in Civita Castellana was the site of miracles, reported from the local bishop to Henry IV: six from blindness, two from deafness, six from paralysis, three from fever, two from deformity, one from leprosy, one from dysentery, one from insanity, one (more novel than the others, but with a close parallel to a miracle of Leo IX) from an over-tight iron belt worn by a hermit, which miraculously broke—as well as supernatural punishments of people who doubted him. Paschal II, when he heard this, had his bones thrown in the Tiber.[99]

Paschal II presided over a situation both better and worse. After Clement's death in 1100, he faced down three rival popes in the city by 1105, and then ruled for thirteen years without papal opposition, the longest unopposed single reign in the whole crisis century. He took over some palatine judges who had been Clement's: Cencio, who had been *primicerius* for both Gregory and Clement, is recorded under Paschal as well in 1101 (although he may have switched sides in 1094 with Ferrucio, for a Paolo *primicerius* appears in two Clementine councils in 1095–8), after which Ferrucio himself became *primicerius* for thirty years (above, p. 248).[100] All the 'new aristocracy' were also now back in the city, but the factional division which we have already seen still continued. Paschal could count on the Pierleoni and the Frangipane; when he left Rome for Puglia in 1108, he handed the rule of the city to Pietro di Leone and Leone Frangipane (probably not the same as the 1088 figure; the twelfth-century Leone is attested until 1133). Pietro 'I' the urban prefect was also securely on Paschal's side in 1105, and so even was the strongly Clementine Tebaldo di Cencio, who ran the Farfa dispute together with Pietro di

[97] For references, see Thumser, 'Die Frangipane', pp. 113–16, plus *RF*, n. 1115 (a. 1088). For the urban prefects, see above, pp. 326–8.

[98] See in general Ziese, *Wibert*; Robinson, *Authority and Resistance*, pp. 44–6, 96–100, 160–3, 172–9 (for the polemical literature); Dolcini, 'Clemente III, antipapa'; and now esp. Longo and Yawn, *Framing Clement III*.

[99] *Udalrici codex*, n. 108, pp. 194–6; see Ziese, *Wibert*, pp. 270–3; Bertolini, 'Istituzioni, miracoli, promozione del culto dei santi'; Longo, 'A saint of damned memory' (p. 5 for Leo IX, referring to 'Vie et miracles du pape S. Léon IX', II.10).

[100] Halphen, *Études*, pp. 99–100, and above, Chapter 4, n. 155.

Leone in 1103 (above, p. 398).[101] Conversely, the pope's opponents were also numerous. Maginulfo/Silvester IV in 1105, in particular, had the support of the *filii Baruncii* and the Sant' Eustachio, as one might expect, but also Stefano Normanno and his brothers—Stefano, first cited here, was Leone Frangipane's uncle—as well as lesser-known figures such as Berizone *a S. Maria in Aquiro* and his brother Stefano. Silvester, with German support, achieved a papal consecration, and won two pitched battles against Paschal's forces, at the Laterano and at the Circo Massimo, until Silvester's resources ran out and he left with the German army.[102] This might have led to a wider consensus around Paschal, but he now, in 1106, fell out with the Corsi, relatives of his supporter the prefect Pietro; he had their *domūs* on the Capitolio destroyed, and pushed their faction out of the city, to their rural castles in north-west Lazio—a tough action, but one that had plenty of potential repercussions. In 1108 the Tuscolani, previously allied to Paschal, turned against him too. Cardinal Pandolfo, whose account this is, remarks that when Paschal came back from Puglia the same year, 'he could not fully tell who his enemies, and who his *fideles* and associates, were'.[103]

The sense that Paschal was not on top of events is further strengthened by the way he handled the two major crises of the rest of his reign. The debacle of the coronation of Henry V in 1111 does not need narration here; suffice to say that Paschal made bold and perhaps unwise proposals to Henry in order to resolve the Investiture Dispute, and then the coronation was interrupted by violence, the city rose in revolt against Henry, and Paschal was imprisoned by the Germans for two months, before a controversial treaty agreed near Tivoli ensured a successful coronation and Henry's departure. Notwithstanding Glauco Cantarella's nuanced defence of Paschal's political and theological line, especially given the difficult position he was put in, nobody came out of this well—not least in the eyes of the Romans, whose grain-lands Henry had ravaged.[104] In 1116, matters did not go any better. This was the moment in which, at the death of the urban prefect Pietro 'I', Paschal wished to replace him with his own choice (Falcone of Benevento, writing in the 1140s, says his choice was a son of Pietro di Leone, which, given the latter's closeness to Paschal, is likely enough); a popular movement, however, confirmed Pietro's son Pietro 'II' in the office instead, and Paschal had to face disruptions to the Easter Thursday mass in S. Giovanni in Laterano and then attacks on the Easter Monday procession, as we have already seen (p. 344). Not only did Paschal never get Pietro di Pietro out of the prefect's office, but he lost control of Rome and half of southern Lazio (Tolomeo I of Tuscolo, the younger Pietro's uncle, changed sides twice) in the last two years of his reign. Pietro di

---

[101] *Liber Pontificalis*, ed. Přerovský, p. 712 (cf. Thumser, 'Die Frangipane', pp. 117–18); *LP*, II, p. 345 for 1105; *CF*, II, p. 232 for 1103.

[102] *LP*, II, pp. 345–6; for Stefano Normanno as a Frangipane uncle, *Liber Pontificalis*, ed. Přerovský, p. 740.

[103] *Liber Pontificalis*, ed. Přerovský, pp. 711–14 (p. 713 for quote).

[104] Most of the relevant texts are in *LP*, II, pp. 338–43, *MGH*, *Libelli de lite*, II, pp. 658–75, and *MGH*, *Constitutiones*, I, nn. 82–101. For an articulated narrative, see Cantarella, *Pasquale II*, pp. 93–153.

Leone's tower-houses around S. Nicola in Carcere were bombarded by *machinae* on the overlooking cliff of the Capitolio, where Corsi power had been located. Henry V was back in Rome too, and had absorbed the prefect Pietro and Tolomeo of Tuscolo into his entourage. Paschal barely made it back to Rome before he died in 1118.[105]

I would not hesitate to call Paschal politically inept. But the situation he faced in Rome was not as easy to control as the absence of papal rivals between 1105 and 1118 might make it appear, even setting aside the disruptive potential of every imperial visit. We have seen that the judicial apparatus of the city was by now at the low point of its coherence (pp. 398–401), and that Rome's exposure to two decades of war had also led to an economic downturn which lasted well beyond Paschal's reign (pp. 156–7). The only institution that worked effectively was the papal chancery, under the capable control of Giovanni of Gaeta, who was *cancellarius* for Urban and then Paschal, without a break for thirty years, but that wholly ecclesiastical institution had little connection to the problems of controlling the city.[106] Paschal was a builder, on the other hand. Whether he named himself after Paschal I because the latter had gained the *Ludowicianum* from Louis the Pious in 817 (a short-lasting imperial recognition of papal immunity in the territory of Rome, which was prominent in the apparatus of papal canonists in the late eleventh century), or because the first Paschal built such impressive churches, he certainly emulated this last characteristic, and restored the war-damaged SS. Quattro Coronati and S. Lorenzo in Lucina, as well as, presumably, acting as a patron for Cardinal Anastasio's destruction and large-scale rebuilding of S. Clemente.[107]

Paschal was thus making prominent interventions in the city, but from a position of institutional weakness. His expulsion of a branch of the Corsi from the city in 1106, and his attempted weakening of another branch in 1116, could be seen as other such interventions. Perhaps so also was his courting of Gregorio and Tolomeo of Tuscolo and the latter's cousin Pietro Colonna, who were by now no longer automatic opponents of the 'reform' papacy, and who could thus be dealt with as political players, particularly outside the city. But, in an urban political environment in which there were by now no real institutions of government (except the prefect's office) or formal secular hierarchies, the only way of dealing with the city was to seek to associate leading aristocrats, one by one, with the papal court, probably, as we have seen above, with the help of gifts of gold and silver; or, if they were opponents, to marginalize them without comeback. This was an inherently unstable game to play, not unlike those children's games in which one has to set all the silver balls into holes in the box at once, without disturbing others. Paschal did not play the game well, but it was hard to.

---

[105] See esp. *LP*, II, p. 344; *Liber Pontificalis*, ed. Přerovský, pp. 717–21; Falcone, *Chronicon*, cols 1167–8.

[106] Kehr, 'Scrinium und Palatium', pp. 103–12; see further for the papal chapel Elze, 'Die päpstliche Kapelle', pp. 147–51.

[107] Church restorations and rebuildings: see above, pp. 363–5. For Paschal II's naming after Paschal I, see alternatively Cantarella, *Pasquale II*, pp. 26–7 (cf. Costambeys, *Power and Patronage*, pp. 315–22), or Osborne, 'Proclamations of power', p. 156n.

In principle, it was possible to unite the aristocracy of the city, or nearly all of it. We see this briefly in 1118, at the election of Gelasius II, the former *cancellarius* Giovanni of Gaeta, who would be much less effective as pope than he had been as an administrator. This was held in S. Maria in Pallara, 'between the *domos* of Leone and Cencio Frangipane', as the members of the electoral meeting, the cardinals, and *multi Romani de senatoribus ac consulibus*, 'thought the place very safe', to quote Cardinal Pandolfo. They evidently expected Frangipane support, and not what actually happened, which was a violent irruption into the church by Cencio Frangipane and the kidnapping of the new pope. In reaction to this, a *multitudo Romana* from the whole city assembled on the Capitolio, led by the urban prefect Pietro 'II', Pietro di Leone, Stefano Normanno, Stefano di Tebaldo (grandson of Cencio di Stefano), Stefano di Berizone (son of one of Silvester IV's 1105 supporters), the Boccapecora, the Boboni, and several others; they sent messengers to demand the pope back, which Leone Frangipane soon conceded. All the major players in the city since 1100 were here united, except for the *filii Baruncii* and the Sant' Eustachio: united against the Frangipane, but since the *coup de main* of that family was so unexpected, the latter could have as easily been there too, as *Romani similes vobis* in Stefano Normanno's words to the Frangipane, who were again attacking Gelasius, later in the same year.[108]

There clearly did exist, then, a sense of a collectivity of the aristocratic leadership of the city by now, of the *senatores ac consules*, as Pandolfo said. An able pope could make something of that collectivity. Calixtus II, when he returned to Rome in 1120 after Gelasius' ignominious exile and death, with the added push of a victory over Henry V's last imperial pope, Mauricio of Braga/Gregory VIII in 1121, could establish a balance of power in the city. He handed out '*pecunia* in the city, and many *equites* and *pedites* did *fidelitas* to him', as the *Annales Romani* said: a generalized generosity, paid for by Calixtus' equally generalized accumulation of gifts of all kinds from litigants and supplicants. A letter from Calixtus survives from 1120 which refers to oaths sworn to him after his arrival in Rome by Pietro di Leone, the prefect Pietro 'II', Leone Frangipane, Stefano Normanno, and Pietro Colonna, all there at once.[109] Calixtus favoured the Pierleoni above all, but used both the stick and the carrot on the Frangipane: he pulled down several of their tower-houses, but also encouraged Cencio Frangipane to build up an armed *masnada* for him. But it still took a great deal of skill (and money), such as only Calixtus had, to do so; and Calixtus was in Rome for only four years, so there was less time for things to go wrong.[110]

The other problem in this whole period was, essentially, that the 'new aristocracy' was now different. The moment of maximum aggregation—and aggregation around a pope—was in 1060, when the social stratum was newly defining itself as a political elite, and also, probably, when it was still relatively restricted in wealth and

---

[108] *Liber Pontificalis*, ed. Přerovský, pp. 727–41 (p. 731, 734, 740 for quotes).

[109] *LP*, II, p. 347 (quote); *Bull. Cal. II*, n. 176 (a. 1120).

[110] *Liber Pontificalis*, ed. Přerovský, pp. 748, 753 for the Frangipane. See in general Laudage, 'Rom und das Papsttum'; Stroll, *Calixtus II*, pp. 296–7.

political presence (even the first tower-houses are not yet attested). But in the years of civil war and political breakdown, any elite family was much more likely to seek to increase its own landholding and economic stability above all, that is to say in association with other city churches and monasteries, buttressed by more informal accords such as the *communitas boum*. And the families which were most successful at this, such as the Corsi/Prefetti, the Frangipane, and (despite political vicissitudes) the heirs of Cencio di Stefano, plus also the Pierleoni, who, although less rich in land, had made the decision to stick with the Hildebrandine tradition of 'reform' popes and gained handsomely from it, were—as any stabilized aristocracy would— by now looking for more. By 1100, these families were the most active lay players in the city, and it was they whom the popes most needed to keep on side, together, more intermittently, with the Tuscolani, who had maintained more of an interest in the city than did the other 'old aristocrats', and who by now had marriage links with the urban prefects. Paschal's reign is the first where we can see the leading urban families dealing in castles (above, p. 244). This was a marker of aristocratic status everywhere in the twelfth century, so such a move was only to be expected, but it brought more problems for popes: notably that most castles were not actually in papal gift, and papal patronage was thus weakened. Popes would need to control rather more of Lazio than they yet did to satisfy their aristocratic clients with castles themselves; that was not achieved until the 1140s–50s and later, above all, by Innocent III and his successors.

In this period, then, what the popes could give the 'new aristocracy' was different, and indeed less. *Pecunia* was one reward, as we have amply seen; titles and offices were not, as we have also seen; otherwise, all the pope really had to offer were more intangible and transactional signs of status, associated with being close to him: the right to counsel the pope, plus a reasonable chance that the pope would act on that counsel; the ability to control whom else might be rewarded. Pietro di Leone had that under Paschal (he was Paschal's negotiator with Henry V over investitures, and his son Pietro was made cardinal of SS. Cosma e Damiano in Foro, a rare promotion for a Roman, in the years 1111–13); it is likely that it was this accentuated prominence of one lay figure which caused the 1116 prefecture business to get out of hand.[111] The Prefetti branch of the Corsi normally had it too, simply by right of the office of prefect, the only lay office still to carry transactional weight, as long as they could hold onto it (hence again the intensity of 1116). The Frangipane were more on the edge, both under Paschal and under Calixtus: major figures, entrusted with some elements of political power, but not the most central ones. It must be for this reason that they eventually concluded that their best hope was with controlling the choice of pope. Presumably their extreme, and never explained, hostility to Gelasius II was because their own preferred candidate (we do not know whom) was not elected in 1118. They did not make the same mistake in 1124, when they, with the help of Cardinal Aimerico, the influential papal *cancellarius*, and cardinal deacon of S. Maria Nova, the Frangipane

[111] *MGH, Constitutiones*, I, nn. 85–6; Hüls, *Kardinale*, p. 225.

church par excellence, forced Honorius II on an unwilling cardinalate, according to Pandolfo's account—they paid off Pietro the prefect and Pietro di Leone with gifts of castles. This put the Frangipane firmly into the centre of the picture for the next few years; Cencio Frangipane even became count of Ceccano for a brief period: the family's first taste of power in rural Lazio. But it further upped the stakes of political rivalry in the city.[112]

The schism of 1130 is treated with embarrassment by historians, and with a good deal of *parti pris* (expressed at surprising length), whether for Anacletus II or Innocent II, both of whom had good claims to canonical election as the rightful pope. There has been considerable argument about which wings of the 'reform' movement each represented, and about the extent to which the double election was an ideological battle. I am more convinced by the arguments of historians such as Palumbo and Stroll, who play down ideological differences.[113] But, whatever the ideologies involved, the schism was also the logical consequence of the election of 1124, and that of 1130 was planned for on both sides. Pietro di Leone was by now dead, but his sons, the Pierleoni, would not be taken by surprise again; for their part, the Frangipane and Cardinal Aimerico were reluctant to lose the position they had gained. The election would be performed by cardinals, not by lay magnates, but the cardinals were clearly also divided, and therefore decided on an electoral college of eight to propose a candidate to the others, so as to achieve concord. In the end, at Honorius' death, a partially different group of cardinals (including Aimerico) secretly elected Gregorio cardinal deacon of S. Angelo in Pescheria as Innocent II, whereupon the other cardinals in Rome, a slightly larger number, elected Pietro Pierleoni, by now cardinal priest of S. Maria in Trastevere, as Anacletus II. (Both were prominent clerics, and may have been the candidates all along.) Of the Roman laity, Innocent only had the support of the Frangipane and the Corsi, and he took refuge in Leone Frangipane's house before moving to his home *regio* of Trastevere, and soon out of the city entirely, for he was faced with the hostility of most other Romans, including the clergy. The differing accounts of each party at least agree on these minimum facts, and they do indeed show both that trouble was expected, and that Innocent had little Roman support. Innocent's side did not deny that, but, of course, argued that lay Roman support for Anacletus was bought, 'corrupting the *maiores* and oppressing the *minores*', as Bosone later put it.[114]

Anacletus' wide following among what Bosone calls the *maiores* is best shown in a formal letter on his behalf to the German king Lothar III of three months later, from the citizens of Rome led by named *potentes*. These were Ugo the urban prefect and his brothers, Stefano di Tebaldo, Alberto di Giovanni di Stefano, Stefano di Berizone and his brother Berizone, Enrico and Ottaviano of the Sant' Eustachio, and, most significantly, Leone and Cencio Frangipane. The 1130s were one of the

---

[112] *Liber Pontificalis*, ed. Přerovský, pp. 750–5.

[113] See in general Klewitz, 'Das Ende'; Palumbo, *Lo scisma*; Palumbo, 'Nuovi studi'; Schmale, *Studien zum Schisma* (developed, among others, in Chodorow, *Christian Political Theory*, pp. 18–46); Stroll, *The Jewish Pope*; Doran, 'The legacy of schism', pp. 44–63.

[114] See n. 113 for accounts of the events of 1130; for Bosone, *LP*, II, p. 380 (who says the Corsi supported Innocent; some of them certainly did by 1133—see n. 116).

only two decades of the twelfth century (the other perhaps being the 1170s) in which the Corsi were not prefects, although we do not know which family Ugo belonged to. (We also do not know the reason for the loss of the prefecture by the Corsi, at some point during Honorius' reign, but it may well have been a result of Pietro 'II''s early opposition to Honorius' election; it anyway must have affected the family's political choices in this period.) But the Corsi may have been part of this group all the same; although this Alberto is not otherwise known, the names Alberto and Stefano are both *Leitnamen* of the Corsi. The presence of the Frangipane, and of the Corsi if they were there, can only be explained by their felt need to adapt to an overwhelming Roman consensus in favour of Anacletus.[115] This consensus recalls that of 1118 in favour of Gelasius; nor did it obviously break down later, although there were exceptions, notably the Frangipane, who changed sides again by 1132 and stuck to Innocent thereafter, as also by 1133 did one of the Corsi, Pietro Latrone, and the next urban prefect, the equally unknown Tebaldo. Anacletus held on to Rome until his death in January 1138. When Innocent appeared with an imperial army in 1133 for Lothar's imperial coronation, he and his troops were restricted to the Laterano and the Aventino in the *disabitato*.[116] Only one Roman charter dates by Innocent before 1136, when opinion in the city apparently began to divide; even then, though, documents date by Anacletus until two months before his death.[117]

Anacletus and Innocent were both Roman popes, the first to be fully Roman since Benedict X. But there is no doubt that only Anacletus initially committed to the city. In his propaganda, aimed at persuading the kings and bishops of Europe of his rightful papacy, he makes much of his Roman support, which clearly he saw as helping to give him legitimacy; he was elected 'at the request of the *populus*' (as Gregory VII had been); he had performed the coronation ritual and procession along the via Sacra as popes should do.[118] Unfortunately, as we have already seen, the destruction of Anacletan documents and the reversal of his acts by the eventually victorious Innocent deprives us, as with Clement III, of much of a sense of what Anacletus actually did in the city. The 1130s remain something of a blank as a result. The reorganization we can attribute to Innocent could well have partial Anacletan roots, but we cannot say more than that.

---

[115] The letter is ed. and commented on by Petersohn, 'Der Brief' (see above, Chapter 4, n. 115 for the Corsi). A similar list of notables is given in a letter of Anacletus to Lothar, *PL*, CLXXIX, col. 707, n. 18.

[116] *Udalrici codex*, n. 259 (a. 1132); *LP*, II, p. 382 (a. 1133); cf. Thumser, 'Die Frangipane', pp. 126–8. For Lothar in Rome, see esp. Doran, 'The legacy of schism', pp. 67–9. Note that Pietro Latrone was Innocent's *procurator* in Rome in 1135 (*Landulphi Iunioris Historia Mediolanensis*, ch. 63); he may have kept hold of some sector of the city.

[117] Roman documents before 1138 dating by Innocent: *S. Sil.*, n. 17 (a. 1134); *SMCM*, n. 37 (a. 1136); ASR, SCD, cassetta 16, n. 121 (a. 1136); *SMN*, n. 46 (a. 1137); *SMVL*, n. 161 (1137). In 1137, documents still dating by Anacletus are ASR, SCD, cassetta 16, n. 122; *SMCM*, n. 38; *S. Prassede*, n. 19.

[118] *Pontificorum Romanum vitae*, ed. Watterich, II, p. 186 (quote); for rituals, e.g. *PL*, CLXXIX, cols 699–700, 704–5, nn. 9, 15.

Innocent won the propaganda war. Lothar was persuaded quite early, and the rest of northern Europe soon followed, thanks to Bernard of Clairvaux's support, and not a little antisemitic hostility to Anacletus' Jewish forebears; of major players, only Roger of Sicily held out for Anacletus.[119] Innocent's court at Pisa in the 1130s was thus the international focus of the papacy, and not Rome. Rome was marginalized in Innocent's rhetoric, and all the hostility of northern Europeans to Roman political practices could be let loose. But Innocent was himself Roman, and this was relevant too. It is interesting that, when he was at Liège with Lothar in 1131, he performed the ceremonies for the fourth Sunday in Lent 'as if in Rome on the via Triumphalis', with St-Lambert in Liège referred to as the *Capitolium*.[120] His points of reference remained Roman, then, at least in part. It might sometimes seem that Innocent vs. Anacletus was a return to the popes of Henry III's time, cancelling out and reversing Gregory VII vs. Clement III, with imperial support once again necessary to overcome the irremediable Roman-ness of Rome, and with Anacletus' Roman support actually posed as a disadvantage; but Rome mattered more than that in Innocent's *imaginaire*. He was back in the city at the very end of Anacletus' reign, and for the last five years of his papacy he ruled from there more firmly than any pope had done since Gregory VII.

Innocent in Rome in 1138–43 was certainly vengeful. We have documents in which cessions of Anacletus or his associates are annulled, and even one in which a lease is voided only because it was made during Anacletus' reign.[121] (We have, however, enough Anacletan texts to be sure that this was not universally carried out.) All of Anacletus' cardinals (many of whom were Roman) were deposed at the Second Lateran Council in 1139, and Innocent appointed no Roman cardinals thereafter. Unlike with Paschal in 1099, no palatine judge under Anacletus is documented as keeping his office; the urban prefect Tebaldo did, but he, as we saw, came out for Innocent in 1133.[122] We have seen plenty of signs of Innocent's particular protagonism in Rome: his appropriation of the sarcophagus of Hadrian and his location of it in the Campus Lateranensis, together with the development of a wider imperial imagery (pp. 336–7); his demolition and expensive/ambitious reconstruction of Anacletus' former titular church, in Innocent's own heartland of Trastevere (pp. 358–65); the systematic recording of papal ceremonies by Benedetto *cantor* (p. 322); Innocent's energetic and sometimes unprincipled support for the developing landholdings and careers of his own family, the Papareschi, whose status he effectively created, in the first of a long line of medieval examples of papal nepotism (pp. 241–3). Innocent failed to stop Roger II from conquering south-central Italy (he was actually briefly imprisoned by the Normans after a battle

---

[119] For antisemitism, see esp. Stroll, *The Jewish Pope*, pp. 156–78.

[120] Anselm of Gembloux, *Continuatio*, p. 383: see Doran, 'The legacy of schism', p. 66.

[121] Kehr, V, pp. 14–15 (a. 1138 = S. Pancrazio, n. 14); *SMCM*, n. 42 (a. 1140, the lease); Kehr, II, pp. 348–50 (a. 1140).

[122] Doran, 'The legacy of schism', pp. 75–8; Maleczek, 'Das Kardinalskollegium', pp. 75–6; for Tebaldo, Halphen, *Études*, pp. 152–3, and esp. Hirschfeld, 'Zur Chronologie' (I would, however, date the final reference, *S. Gregorio*, n. 7, as extending into 1141, not 1140 as Hirschfeld thought; see above, p. 406).

in 1139), but he did succeed, after reverses, in imposing his will on Tivoli in 1141–3. Innocent was both forceful and cynical, as his smiling and faintly menacing treatment of Hariulf of Oudenburg in 1141 demonstrates with unusual immediacy.[123] But he certainly also knew that he had to keep control of Rome, and he did so structurally. As we have also seen earlier in this chapter, he put *iudices* and advocates on his payroll, and encouraged a wave of pleas from churches against the laity; Rome's papal judicial system, and also the collectivity of expert judges, in effect begin in his reign. (Innocent in Pisa had also extensively developed the system of judges-delegate in canon-law cases.) He put his stamp on the city in a variety of ways, systematically and very fast, with more of an interest in innovation than any predecessor since the great Carolingian popes.

And it is in this same way that Innocent systematically courted the Roman aristocracy, including even its Anacletan wing. This is one of the most striking of Innocent's many political acts, and one that contrasts in particular with his treatment of Roman cardinals. The Frangipane of course did well out of Innocent, and were prominent in his court; it is in these years that Aldruda Frangipane made her rich marriage to Rainerio count of Bertinoro (above, p. 256); and, since it was just after his death that they got Terracina in *Marittima* from Celestine II, in 1143–4, and Monte Circeo from Lucius II in 1145 (these two popes had been close associates of Innocent), it is entirely possible that Innocent was the donor to the family of the gateway to *Marittima*, the castle of Cisterna, which they certainly controlled later. We see here the beginnings of a new landed politics in action. Pietro Latrone, Innocent's other early supporter, for his part gained Civitavecchia, in return for a pledge of £200, which his heirs kept till 1193. Pietro Latrone's relatives also regained the office of urban prefect by 1143, the date of the first appearance of the prefect Pietro 'III'. Of the clearly Anacletan families, Enrico of Sant' Eustachio remained prominent, calling himself *Romanorum consul* in 1141.[124] But it is particularly important that we also find Anacletus' brother Leone Pierleoni in Innocent's entourage already in 1140, and Leone, with his son Pietro, were *delegati presidis* of Sutri for the pope in 1142. The Pierleoni had come to terms fast; they prostrated themselves at Innocent's feet at Pentecost 1138 and sworn him *ligia fidelitas*, in return for (so the *Chronica Casinensis* says) *immensa pecunia*. So the way was open to peace here; but it is still notable that Innocent kept to the implicit bargain.[125] This was his choice, and it paid off.

---

[123] Müller, 'Der Bericht', e.g. pp. 103–4, 113–14: here Innocent's joyful face (*hylari vultu*) and smiling (*subridens*) words hide some elegant but dangerous manipulation. When Innocent 'laid his eyes' (*oculos ingecerat*) on some of S. Ciriaco in Via Lata's land for his nephews, the nuns went to the extreme of a fake lease to show the pope that it was not in their possession (*SMVL*, n. 172).

[124] Thumser, 'Die Frangipane', pp. 131–2; *LC*, I, n. 166 for Civitavecchia; Halphen, *Études*, pp. 153–4 for Pietro 'III' the prefect (the first text for him is the undated text following *S. Paolo*, n. 7, which must date to 1141–3 given the argument in n. 122); *SMVL*, n. 165 for Enrico of Sant' Eustachio.

[125] *S. Gregorio*, nn. 7, 89 (aa. 1140–2); for 1138, Bernard of Clairvaux, *Epistolae*, n. 317; *Chronica Casinensis*, IV.130. Leone was also by now Tolomeo II of Tuscolo's father-in-law, and acted for him in a court case in 1140, *S. Alessio*, n. 13. See in general Fedele, 'Le famiglie', pp. 421–2.

The point here is that it was, of all people, Innocent II, the most uncompromising pope of the first half of the twelfth century, who ended the running battles of aristocratic factions that had marked the city since the 1060s, culminating in the Frangipane-Pierleoni stand-offs of 1124 and 1130. Open competition between these two families does not in fact resurface from this moment onwards; rather, they came to be seen as a pair, the object of the hostility of the Senate in 1149, or the beneficiaries of papal generosity during the siege of Rome in 1167, or, between them, the great majority of the Roman aristocrats entitled *Romanorum consules* in the half-century after 1150.[126] The Corsi, too, were on side, thanks to their renewed control over the office of prefect and an ever solider hegemony over the castles of north-west Lazio. Innocent managed to wrap these leading families into the papal entourage on a stable basis; and it must have been stable, for it continued across the travails and frequent papal elections that marked the decade after Innocent's death. These were evidently the *nobiliores* who attended the *consistorium* in 1141. What Innocent had to give them now was not just money but castles (at least the Corsi and Frangipane), and administrative roles, which, under Innocent, were actually beginning to exist. This held them in the papal court and on the papal side in the next political conflicts faced by the city, over the Senate.[127]

For, as is well known, Innocent's systematic hegemony did not convince everyone in Rome forever. The Roman aristocracy may have been persuaded, but we can assume that much of the Roman clergy were permanently alienated by the demotion of their cardinals. The Roman *populus*, too, were unimpressed by Innocent's terms to Tivoli, whether they were made before or after Roman victory over the rival city in July 1143: no destruction of the city walls, and the continuance of urban self-government, in return for a recognition of papal (not Roman) sovereignty. It was now that, as Innocent was dying in September, it revolted, and set up the Senate on the Capitolio.[128] This was, however, not just the result of summer events in 1143, but of a parallel narrative of Roman collective politics to set against the papal narrative of the last few pages. This is what we have to turn to in the final section of this chapter.

THE SOCIAL ORIGINS OF THE COMMUNE

A currently standard account of the first fifty or so years of an Italian city commune goes roughly like this. In the civil war period of the 1080s–90s, cities were ruled by fairly ad hoc groups of urban notables, following in some cities traditions which

[126] 1149: see below, p. 444. 1167: *LP*, II, p. 417; cf. Maragone, *Annales Pisani*, p. 43 (1168 by Pisan dating = 1167 *stile comune*; here these two families support Alexander together with the Corsi). *Consules*: see lists in Vendittelli, 'Romanorum consules', pp. 226–7, and below, p. 436.

[127] Celestine II in 1143–4 added to this group the Boboni and the *filii Astaldi* as well, for he made members of each family cardinals (above, pp. 239–40). Petersohn, *Kaisertum und Rom*, pp. 162–71 argues that in the second half of the twelfth century the Roman aristocracy was largely pro-imperial; this seems to me overstated, but it also relates to a period later than that covered in this book.

[128] See e.g. Fedele, 'L'èra del senato'; Rota, 'La costituzione originaria', pp. 41–53.

went back to urban revolts against bishops in the 1030s–60s, and in most cities the military leadership of armies. Increasingly, their leaders, leading members of the urban *militia*, came to be called *consules*, and they were sometimes explicitly connected together with the rest of the city by collective oaths of peace. Consuls, however, are not continuously documented in any city except Genoa and Pisa until around 1140; although they were annually elected in many cases earlier than that, it took some time for the 'consulate' to be seen as a formal office in most cities. Instead, consuls, the bishop, and leading aristocratic families are seen, in turn or together, as running cities and, where they controlled them, *contadi*, in the few documents we have that attest to urban government in the early twelfth century. That 'government' was in the first decades of the century still highly informal. Consuls do, nonetheless, become more and more prominent in our sources: in war, in justice, and in general, as operating with a city-wide authority that is often called *publicus*. As we have seen (p. 398), formal consular justice appears in leading cities in the 1130s, even though many other cities do not have evidence for it until the late twelfth century; when that justice appears, plus in some cases (Genoa and Pisa again) early *brevia* and *constituta*, something that we can call a 'commune' in institutional terms can be said to exist, even if the noun *commune* is as yet rare. It was that communal structure, newly institutionalized but still culturally rather frail (how much social status a consul, elected by a city *populus*, really had as opposed to a castle-holding *nobilis*, whether city- or country-dwelling, is uncertain), that Frederick Barbarossa sought to regain control over in the 1150s–70s; it was his eventual military failure which gave city communes the formal legitimation which they had previously lacked, as well as a self-assurance which they developed extensively in years to come.[129]

This account puts some stress on the initially informal nature of the commune, and on a process of institutional crystallization which took a generation to complete. If we have that model in mind, it is not so hard to construct a similar narrative for Rome, at least up to the 1130s. Before we do, however, we have to remember that the plural words *consules* and *senatores,* as also *senatus,* were systematically used in Rome to mean 'aristocrats' or 'leading men', throughout the eleventh century (and indeed earlier) and well into the twelfth, in narratives and documents: as with the *consules, senatores,* and *populus* of Rome who greeted Victor III in 1087 according to the *Chronica Casinensis,* the *senatores ac consules* who participated in the election of Gelasius II in 1118 according to Cardinal Pandolfo, or the *consules et maiores civitatis* who were part of Innocent II's 1141 entourage in the document recording the S. Gregorio vs. Oddone of Poli court case—and these are only some of a large number of examples. ('*Senatus*' was indeed a sufficiently neutral word that it was used, by writers such as Pier Damiani, to mean purely ecclesiastical leaders.)[130] All

---

[129] A good modern survey is Milani, *I comuni italiani*, pp. 21–60, with bibliography. I analyse early communes in this way in *Courts and Conflict*, pp. 16–40, and will return to this issue elsewhere. A recent case study is Faini, *Firenze*, pp. 262–320, for a decidedly unprecocious commune.

[130] *Chronica Casinensis*, III.69 (cf. also IV.61); *Liber Pontificalis*, ed. Přerovský, p. 731; *S. Gregorio*, n. 7. *Senatus* used ecclesiastically: see Jordan, 'Die Enstehung', pp. 123–5.

this marked Rome's particular links to the past, which included the knowledge that Rome had always been the location par excellence of both consuls and senators (their seat identified, the *Mirabilia* said around 1140, as being on the Capitolio). In the specific case of consuls, it also linked to the tenth-century use of *consul et dux* as an honorific title for individual Roman aristocrats, although later, as we have also seen (p. 197), both *consul* and *senator* were consistently used as specific titles by the Tuscolani, in formulations such as *omnium Romanorum consul* (1059), *consul et dux atque senator* (1065), or *Romanorum senator* (1068).[131] The detailed differences between such formulations were clearly of no importance; the important fact was that the titles were then seen as a Tuscolano monopoly. The use of these terms on their own do not, that is to say, mark any special political or social change in Rome, except presumably the fading of respect for Tuscolano authority—unlike in any other city, where *consul* was a neologism, and *senator* unheard of.

This Roman lexical tradition notwithstanding, we do all the same see the same sort of developments in the city as we can find elsewhere. The *consules comunitatis boum* of 1088 are one example, an apparently private association of Clementine aristocrats, called to judge a dispute together with the urban prefect. So is the growing tendency from the 1090s onwards for the palatine judges and other legal experts to deal with disputes in the city without recourse to higher authorities (above, pp. 393–7). Another instance is the use of the title *Romanorum consul* by 'new' urban aristocrats as well as by the Tuscolani, starting with Cencio Frangipane in 1084–6 in a narrative, the *Chronica Casinensis*, and then, a generation later, in documents: Cencio di Roizone in 1126, Leone—almost certainly Leone Pierleoni—in 1127, his father Pietro di Leone (d.1124/30) in a text of 1134, Cencio and Oddone Frangipane in 1139, Tedelgario in 1141, Enrico di Enrico of the Sant' Eustachio and Rogerio *scriniarius* in 1141. This seems by the 1120s to be a specific honorific title, in that only named individuals held it (more than one of these texts identify a single person as a *Romanorum consul* out of longer lists, including of 'aristocrats'), and a case might even be made for the claim that it was by then an annual office. I would not make such a claim, because after this period of a relatively wide availability of the title (which extended to 1148, when the consuls Guido di Cencio di Guido, Romano *de Papa*, Romano di Paolino and Giovanni *causidicus* are recorded), we enter nearly four decades in which the only *Romanorum consules* were either Pierleoni or Frangipane, many of whom held the title for years on end.[132] By then, the valency of the title had, however, evidently changed. What of the 1120s–40s, though?

In that earlier period, it is at least very likely that the title *Romanorum consul* was restricted to 'aristocrats', and also legal experts, two of whom are so recorded. The Pierleoni, Frangipane, Sant' Eustachio and Papareschi are all 'consuls of the

    [131] Borgia, *De cruce*, n. 4; Hoffmann, 'Petrus diaconus', n. 2; Gattola, *Historia*, I, pp. 233–4.
    [132] *Chronica Casinensis*, III.39, 66, 68 (and, still for Tolomeo I and II of Tuscolo, IV.25, 61, 125, and Hoffmann, 'Petrus diaconus', n. 4); *SMN*, n. 42 (a. 1126); *CDC*, n. 312; Kehr, 'Il diploma purpureo'; *SMN*, n. 49; *S. Gregorio*, n. 7; *SMVL*, nn. 165, 178. See Moscati, *Alle origini*, pp. 138–41; Vendittelli, '*Romanorum consules*', pp. 226–7. I read *S. Gregorio*, n. 7 differently to Vendittelli. The latter is the best guide to the continuing changes of meaning of the title.

Romans'. Cencio di Roizone, who was based in Pigna as we have seen, must be related to the Cencio di Cencio di Roizone who was a consul of the 'community of the oxen' in 1088 (see above, p. 284); Guido di Cencio di Guido was probably the son of the Cencio di Guido who figures among the high-status entourage of S. Gregorio sul Celio in 1140, and was, as we have also seen (p. 311), a Trastevere notable. Only Tedelgario and Romano di Paolino cannot be placed socially.[133] The title was particularly commonly used in papal court cases, to denote important lay figures in the judicial action, as was the case in 1126, 1140, and 1148. The 1141 citation also shows the two consuls working together with the *primicerius*, to give greater judicial weight to a transaction (though the transaction concerned is an apparently straight-forward lease). We could thus see the title as two-fold: as already assigned to at least some Pierleoni and Frangipane, perhaps as of right (plus sometimes, still, to counts of Tuscolo), and also as a quasi-judicial title used for a wider range of aristocrats who operated as adjuncts to the palatine judges. The title is still a significant one, all the same, for it very specifically attached such aristocrats to 'the Romans' as a collectivity—and not, in particular, to the papacy.

Such an attachment gains further force from the 1127 text, for this is an unusual document. It is a very short text preserved in the Montecassino cartulary, the *Registrum Petri Diaconi*, a cartulary full of forgeries; but this one seems sound, not least because it is barely more than a note—it has no witnesses or notary—so could not have been legally useful in this form. In it, Leone *Romanorum consul*, three Frangipane (Leone, Cencio and Pietro), the otherwise unknown Filippo di Alberico, and Enrico of Sant' Eustachio, *una cum sexaginta senatoribus et cuncto populo Romano urbis*, concede freedom of navigation to the ships of Montecassino. Clearly here Rome as a secular community is granting a right, a right which, it is important to add, had previously been granted by two popes, Victor II and Nicholas II, in 1055–9. That community has six aristocratic leaders, one of which is a *consul*, and is then made up of sixty senators and 'the whole *populus*'. Laura Moscati has stressed that the figure of sixty is not so far from the fifty-six senators of the formally constituted full Senate of the years around 1190.[134] This point might indeed be significant, especially as the exact number fifty-six was not canonical earlier (fifty is the number in 1150 and 1167), but I would note that a contemporary document from Lucca, dating to 1124, before the consular régime was fully established there, similarly refers casually and vaguely to 'sixty consuls' resolving a dispute collectively.[135] Since all other references to *senatores* in this period generically refer to the urban aristocracy, it would seem to me conceivable that the 'sixty' is a generic number here too, and simply means 'the whole

---

[133] Tedelgario might be the plaintiff in the first senatorial court case of 1148–51, *Senato*, n. 12 (see above, p. 407), but the name is not unparalleled. Romano di Paolino rents a house in Trastevere in ASR, SCD, cassetta 16, n. 126, which fits the fact that two of the other consuls of 1148 are clearly Trasteverini.

[134] *CDC*, n. 312; Moscati, '"Una cum sexaginta senatoribus"'. For previous papal cessions, see above, Chapter 3, n. 174.

[135] *Senato*, n. 11 = Maragone, *Annales Pisani*, p. 13; Maragone, *Annales Pisani*, p. 44 (these could be vague citations, too, of course; both dates are a year later in Maragone, who is calculating with the Pisan dating system). Compare *Il regesto del Codice Pelavicino*, n. 50, for Lucca.

aristocracy'. The text is not less important, for all that, for it still shows a large urban aggregation, led by lay 'aristocrats', making the sort of concession that popes had formerly made.

If we think of the 1127 text as simply a demonstration of a secular urban aggregation, we can find others too. One, not very clearly characterized by Cardinal Pandolfo, is the collectivity of 'wicked men' who elected Pietro 'II' as urban prefect in 1116, 'without consulting the *patres* and *primores*'; the collectivity is later called a popular tumult, *tumultus populi plebisque*, and it was, however much Pandolfo wished to delegitimize it, enough to face down the pope and force him to leave the city. But it must have been this same group whose leaders, the new prefect and *consules*, invited Henry V to Rome in the same year according to the *Annales Romani*; so we could easily see it once more as an urban collectivity with 'aristocratic' leaders. A second such collectivity is better described by Pandolfo, because this time he was in favour of it: the reaction against the Frangipane kidnapping of Gelasius II in 1118. Here, as we have just seen, the *multitudo Romana* was headed by ten 'aristocratic' families (the prefect Pietro was listed first); to these were added the twelve *regiones* of the city, plus *Transtiberini* and *Insulani*, all armed and assembled on the Capitolio. A third is the collective letter to Lothar III of 1130 to support Anacletus II, signed by members of six 'aristocratic' families (again headed by the prefect), *reliqui Romane urbis potentes*, the palace judges and *nostri consules* [here the *Romanorum consules* in judicial guise?] *et plebs omnis Romana*.[136] We have, that is to say, more and more examples of urban collectivities operating autonomously in this period. They are almost as common as an image as the factional rivalries of these and other sources; indeed, the evocation of such collectivities was intended in 1118 and 1130 precisely to claim that this group, unlike its opponents, represented the whole city, and was not a faction. They are collectivities with 'aristocratic' leaders, but these leaders in each case operate together with a wider grouping, and clearly gain legitimacy by so doing: usually, what is claimed to be the whole of the 'aristocratic' elite, and always a wider *plebs* and/or *populus*. This collectivity is entirely secular, and, although it often operates to support popes, it can also oppose them, or even (as in 1127) substitute for them. It may well be this collectivity which the *Romanorum consules* also represent in the same period. And it looks remarkably like the collectivities which are regularly attested in the first, informal, generation of city communes elsewhere in Italy.

These texts are perfectly well known, and have been used for well over a century. Gregorovius saw them as showing an 'aristocratic republic', 'the consular rule of the nobility', an oligarchy but not a commune; Halphen saw the *Romanorum consules* simply as papal officials, separate from any wider collectivity; Solmi saw all these aggregations as signs of the unbroken continuity of the Roman Senate from antiquity to the renewal of 1143. Rota argued them all away, even (with some difficulty) the 1127 document, denying that any 'real political self-representation'

---

[136] *Liber Pontificalis*, ed. Přerovský, pp. 717–20, 734 (a. 1118); *LP*, II, p. 344; and cf. *MGH, Constitutiones*, I, n. 82 for Henry V's letter to a similar Roman collectivity in 1111, and *Regestum Pisanum*, n. 302 (a. 1126). For 1130, Petersohn, 'Der Brief', pp. 505–7.

preceded the revolution of 1143. (This would presumably also be the case for those, like Brezzi, who do not discuss the issue at all, and limit themselves to criticizing the easily contested views of Solmi.) More recently, Moscati rather avoided committing herself as to what the 'sixty senators' actually meant for the proto-history of the Senate, but seemed to imply sympathy with those, like Frugoni and Arnaldi, who saw senatorial imagery as a strong ideological element in Rome which could be drawn on from time to time, but perhaps not yet for communal purposes: 'the consciousness of a past which modifies and reforms itself, and indeed contradicts itself, but is not ignored'. Petersohn, discussing the 1127 and 1130 texts, referred to the 'oligarchically defined structure of pre-communal Rome'.[137] All these writers, in their different ways, were engaging in institutional readings, both of the Senate of 1143 and of the political world that preceded it: either these texts show a structured institution, or else, if they show an informal collectivity—which, it should be fairly clear, they do—they cannot be used as part of a communal narrative. It is only quite recently that some historians, more conscious of the way interpretations of north Italian communes have changed in the last generation, have taken some of these texts more seriously: for Carocci and Vendittelli, the 1127 text 'seems to have had a more real and concrete role as a deliberative organism than has hitherto been attributed to it', and that the senators 'were acting in the name of the Roman people in the arena of public law, substituting for the popes'; for Maire Vigueur, the same text 'ought to persuade us to relativise seriously the revolutionary character of the *renovatio senatus* of 1143', and he adds that the Romans had their own army by now, and that it was 'del tutto inverosimile', entirely implausible, that this was only under the control of the pope. He went further: the Romans had a relative autonomy of action in justice, the economy and the army well before 1143, in a gradual process starting in the late eleventh century, and, overall, 'the famous revolution of 1143 perhaps does not deserve the fame of a founding event which is usually ascribed to it'.[138]

I would not go as far as that last citation, and in fact Maire Vigueur a few years later drew back from it himself, and now called the 1143 uprising 'one of the most decisive events in the history of Rome'.[139] But I fully associate myself with these latter authors in seeing that that event by no means came out of nowhere. The question is, however, what really was happening in the 1110s and 1120s, and how it linked with what came later. Early communes in northern Italy were led, almost

---

[137] Gregorovius, *History*, IV, pp. 459, 461; Halphen, *Études*, pp. 31–4; Rota, 'La costituzione', pp. 34–7 ('vera e propria rappresentanza politica'); for Brezzi on Solmi, *Roma*, p. 530; Moscati, '"Una cum sexaginta senatoribus"', p. 545 ('la coscienza di un passato che si modifica, si riforma, e al limite si contraddice ma non si ignora'; cf. Frugoni, 'Sulla "Renovatio Senatus"'; Arnaldi, 'Rinascita, fine'); Petersohn, 'Der Brief', p. 500.

[138] Carocci and Vendittelli, 'Società ed economia', pp. 79–80 ('sembra insomma avere un ruolo di organismo deliberante più reale e concreto di quanto gli sia stato finora attribuito'; 'agiva in nome del popolo romano in materia di diritto pubblico, sostituendosi ai pontefici'); Maire Vigueur, 'Il comune romano', pp. 120–1 ('dovrebbe indurre a ridimensionare seriamente il carattere rivoluzionario della *renovatio senatus* del 1143'; 'la famosa rivoluzione del 1143 non merita forse la fama di evento fondatore che generalmente riveste'), cf. Maire Vigueur, *L'autre Rome*, pp. 306–8.

[139] Maire Vigueur, *L'autre Rome*, p. 305.

universally, by a few castle-holding aristocrats, together with a leading stratum of landed urban notables from families which included *iudices, causidici*, notaries, canons of the cathedral, and probably (though we almost never have the documents to tell us this) merchants and rich artisans. This is also the stratum which, as Maire Vigueur has elsewhere shown, constituted an urban mounted *militia*.[140] Some highest-ranking aristocrats (the families in each city who were the equivalents to the Corsi, say) often avoided being consuls in the early period, but they remained closely associated with the political structures that were crystallizing around consuls. In Rome, it was much the same. We do not have any real signs of annual offices in Rome, but they are intermittent in our evidence in most cities; in Milan, for example, certainly a precocious commune, we have names of consuls in 1117, then 1130, and more regularly only from 1138. Indeed, it is almost certainly the case that there were not consuls every year in the initial phases of some communes (Vercelli, for instance), and that cities returned to being happy with more informally constituted groups of leaders, out of which generals or magistrates would emerge as necessary, as had already been the case everywhere in the 1090s. A durable informality is certainly what we appear to see in Rome, with the Frangipane, Pierleoni, Corsi/Prefetti (the prefecture was of course a genuine office, but not annual) and Sant' Eustachio by now clearly part of the leading group, but with a wider public participation that could be called on as necessary, extending to the other *proceres/potentes/senatores*, sometimes explicitly to a professional stratum, and also linking together with a less well-defined *populus* or *plebs*. The only real Roman originality is the importance of the *regiones* in 1118, which, although these were the more formal 'super-*regiones*' rather than the smaller *regiones* Romans in practice identified with (see above, p. 121), certainly mark the cellular nature of Roman political practice, which was much stronger here than elsewhere, a point we shall return to.[141] What we would expect to see next would be annual offices, perhaps in the 1130s, which might be initially taken up by slightly less important families, some aristocratic, some judicial, with the Frangipane, etc., sticking to the vaguer and perhaps more prestigious title *Romanorum consul* for a decade or so before coming into the annual cycle. That would have been the next stage if Rome continued to follow Italian trends; and it was that stage that Rome did not 'reach'. We do not know much about Rome in the 1130s; but the 1143 uprising had a different orientation.

What this hypothetical narrative of course leaves out is the popes. All the sequence of papal expedients referred to in the previous section of this chapter can get forgotten if one focuses too hard on a communal narrative, but they undoubtedly happened. In other cities, bishops were of course important; they sometimes held formal comital powers from emperors and therefore controlled

---

[140] Maire Vigueur, *Cavaliers et citoyens*, esp. pp. 254–75.

[141] For Milan, see lists in *Gli atti del comune di Milano*, pp. 537–40. For Vercelli, Grillo, 'Il comune di Vercelli', pp. 172–5; cf. Milani, *I comuni italiani*, pp. 24–5. For the internal subdivisions of other cities in the early commune, see Grillo, 'La frattura inesistente', pp. 695–6; they were much less prominent than in Rome.

cities in institutional or legal terms; and, even when they did not (as in Milan or Lucca or Pisa), they were rich and powerful players, with urban aristocrats as their vassals. But popes were far more powerful; and they were sovereigns in Rome. The 'early commune' that I have just been characterizing is exactly the body which would crystallize in a period of political uncertainty (there were two popes for a twenty-year period) and the breakdown of traditional institutions, which took place in Rome as everywhere else. But the emperors were hardly visible in the *Regnum Italiae* for a full half century after 1100, in the period of maximum institutional incoherence in the north and centre of the peninsula, whereas popes were present in Rome at least as often as not, as we have seen. It was easier, just because of that, for popes, and the rich papal court, to re-establish ideological and political hegemony in the city: if not over the *populus*, at least over the aristocracy. An unwise pope such as Paschal II in 1116 could alienate a substantial wing of the aristocracy sufficiently to get it to react with popular support; later, the alternative 'communal' version of political protagonism in 1127 seems to have been at least as strong as the papal court of a colourless pope such as Honorius II. But the leading aristocratic families did look to popes, throughout our period, *as well as* to Rome as a collectivity. If a pope appeared who could really involve them, either by force of character, by largesse, or by providing a revived set of papally focused institutions for aristocrats to be active in, then regional and communal leadership would potentially be much less attractive.

This is exactly what happened under Innocent II. The force of his political and institutional project was great and wide-ranging, and we have often seen its signs across this book. All the major aristocratic families were brought on board. And, in so doing, Innocent cut these families off from the *populus* (whomever this group actually consisted of—we will come back to this shortly), which they had been happy to represent for a generation; wealth, power, even by now land were now available from the papal court to a wide range of notables on a scale not seen since the 1070s, and simply representing and leading the *populus* could not compete. The standard communal narrative was here decisively deviated.

Communes were of course not inevitable developments in Italy. In the South, they seldom appear. Gaeta, Benevento (by now a papal city) and, more uncertainly, Naples are the only examples; large and important cities such as Bari or Salerno remained parts of stable hierarchies looking to single rulers, and, as far as we can see, were content to do so. The fact that Gaeta and Benevento moved in a communal direction (in each case short-lived; Benevento's commune only lasted from 1128 to 1130, and was ended as a formal body by Anacletus II) can best be explained by the fact that both experienced the sort of institutional breakdown that characterized most of northern and central Italy; conversely, this was absent in a city such as Salerno, long a capital, whose ruling family shifted from being Lombard to being Norman fairly rapidly in 1077.[142] Urban elites could happily continue to be part of

---

[142] For Benevento, the basic source is Falcone, *Chronicon*, cols 1202–6. See in general Oldfield, *City and Community*, pp. 45–81; and, for specific cities, Skinner, *Family Power*, pp. 197–202 (on Gaeta), and several articles in Delogu and Peduto, *Salerno nel XII secolo*.

princely hierarchies, which indeed did not offer the problems of status uncertainties that early consuls could experience, as long as those hierarchies remained strong. They could also, under these circumstances, also continue to be key figures in the clientelar hierarchies which extended, through them, down into the rest of the population. This is arguably the political structure which Innocent wished to created, or recreate, in Rome (and which Anacletus and Innocent also sought to do in Benevento, with at least intermittent success); and, given these southern examples, such a project was by no means unfeasible.

It did not, however, work in Rome. Innocent could bring the aristocracy on board, but not the rest of the city. This is amply shown by the revolt of 1143 itself, which we will come on to in a moment. Exactly why the rest of the city was less persuaded by Innocent's protagonism is, as we might expect, less clear. Probably in part it was because the wider *populus* was more used to some element of protagonism itself by now, as a result of the developments of the 1110s and 1120s, so, now abandoned by its aristocratic leaders, moved to claim it directly, perhaps also following the visible models of the Centre-North. Presumably the *populus* was, as already proposed, also unconvinced and/or alienated by Innocent's own political acts. But it also seems to me crucial, as was stressed in Chapter 5 and earlier in this chapter, that the political communities of Rome were focused on *regiones*, and on the local churches which provided everyone with land, rather than on hierarchies which led upwards to the papal court. The *regio* of S. Maria Nova/Colosseo was dominated by the Frangipane, and might therefore have looked to the papal court via the Frangipane connection, valuing, perhaps, the papal silver which that aristocratic family could distribute. Probably that was the idea. But the *regio* could also have reacted against the fear that the papal court would take the Frangipane away from them, into a different, and non-regional, political world. The regional community would then potentially be capable of acting independently of the Frangipane, associating itself with the local churches for preference, and choosing its own autonomous politics, particularly in the first decades of the Senate. This is a hypothetical reconstruction (one which we shall return to); but we do know that the *regio*'s most prominent local figure in 1177, Berardo di Gregorio di Giorgio, was a senator as early as 1151 (above, pp. 297–8), in a period in which tensions between the Senate on the one hand and the pope and his aristocratic allies on the other were still quite high. And we do, of course, also know that the foundation of the Senate was a violent and hostile act. There was a genuine break, that is to say, which cannot be argued away, so some version of these hypotheses has to have reflected the real situation. And the Senate that was founded was something new.

Given all the pages devoted to the early Roman Senate by twentieth-century historians, the actual evidence for it is surprisingly meagre. The first formal document for it is not until 1148. We are reliant on a handful of brief narratives, none of them by Romans, and some official letters. The narratives say that the *populus Romanus* rose up against Pope Innocent, who died in September 1143, and set up a Senate; Bosone calls the people *novitatis amator* and says the Senate was created 'under the pretense of the utility of the *respublica*'; Otto of Freising says it was created in hostile response to Innocent's relatively generous terms to Tivoli in the summer of 1143, 'seeking to renew (*renovare*) the ancient dignity of the *urbs*'; the word 'new' is used in similar but even more generic sentences by Romualdo of Salerno, Godfrey of Viterbo, and the *Carmen de gestis Frederici*. The Senate must thus have begun in August or September 1143.[143] A year later, Lucius II, Innocent's second successor (pope from March 1144 to February 1145), entered into renewed and more serious conflict with the Senate. According to Bosone, he forced the senators to 'descend from the Capitolio and abjure the Senate', but when he fell ill the *populus Romanus* refused to go along with this; Godfrey of Viterbo says that Lucius attempted unsuccessfully to storm the Capitolio with a powerful *militia* in order to remove the senators, but the pope was wounded by thrown stones and died later from his wounds.[144] We cannot assess the accuracy of either of these rival accounts, both of them written some time later; but we can say, from the dating clauses of later senatorial documents, which—uniquely among Italian communes—often date by the *renovatio sacri senatus*, that that era began in August or September 1144; the summer evidently marked a sufficiently important reorganization of the Senate that 1144, not 1143, was officially remembered as its starting-point thereafter.[145] This was also the approximate period in which, as numerous sources relate (always telegraphically), the Senate took Giordano Pierleoni as its leader, calling him a *patricius*, the title Crescenzio 'II' and his son Giovanni had used in the 990s–1000s, but also the title used in Rome by emperors such as Charlemagne and Henry III. The creation of the *patricius* and the formal *renovatio* of the Senate must be related; whether this preceded or succeeded Lucius II's attack on the Capitolio is less clear.[146]

Lucius' successor Eugenius III, elected in February 1145, was not consecrated in S. Pietro, as the senators, who controlled the church, refused to allow it unless he recognized the Senate; he spent the year in northern Lazio, fighting senatorial Rome with military support from Tivoli, Tuscolo, and the Normans. In this period the Senate took over the *regalia beati Petri*, the pope's rights in the city, and abolished the powers of the urban prefect; it is plausible that the *patricius* was intended to replace the prefect from the start. Two sources, John of Salisbury and Otto of Freising, also say that the senators destroyed the *palatium* of Cencio Frangipane to spite the pope (John), and/or destroyed 'not only the *turres* of certain illustrious laymen, but also the *domūs* of cardinals and clerics' (Otto). Eugenius and

---

[143] *LP*, II, p. 385; Otto of Freising, *Chronica*, VII.27; Romualdo of Salerno, *Chronicon*, p. 228; Godfrey of Viterbo, *Pantheon*, p. 261; *Carmen de gestis*, l. 808. See in general for the whole period 1143–54 Fedele, 'L'êra del senato'; Brezzi, *Roma*, pp. 317–39; Frugoni, 'Sulla "Renovatio Senatus"'; Rota, 'La costituzione' (the most detailed, up to 1145, but also too schematically positivist and legalist as an account); Strothmann, *Kaiser und Senat*, pp. 128–87; Schultz, '*Poiché tanto amano la libertà . . .*', pp. 136–62 (a convenient but traditional overview); Schmitz-Esser, '*In urbe, quae caput mundi est*'; Doran, 'The legacy of schism', pp. 85–178; Petersohn, *Kaisertum und Rom*, pp. 80–109.

[144] *LP*, II, p. 386; Godfrey of Viterbo, *Pantheon*, p. 261.

[145] For the date, the best guide is Bartoloni, 'Per la storia', pp. 24–7.

[146] Otto of Freising, *Chronica*, VII.31; Romualdo of Salerno, *Chronicon*, p. 228; John of Salisbury, *Historia pontificalis*, ch. 27; *Annales Casinenses*, p. 310 (saying Giordano was allied with *parte totius populi minoris*). See, on Giordano, Moscati, *Alle origini*, pp. 143–51, among others.

the Senate came to terms in December 1145. In their agreement, the pope recognized the Senate, and, in return, the Senate recognized papal authority, the office of *patricius* was abolished and the prefecture restored.[147] The agreement did not last long, and Eugenius left the city soon after; final peace was not made until 1149, when, in a text preserved in the letter collection of Wibald of Stablo, the senators agreed to swear fidelity to the pope, with four oath-swearers per *contrada*, and to restore the papal *regalia* and *pecunia* taken from churches, in return for a *beneficium* of £500, 'as the Romans have been accustomed to swear to the Roman popes'. It was shortly before that peace, earlier in 1149, that the *senatus populusque Romanus*, one of the first references in the crisis century to the ancient SPQR, wrote to the German king Conrad III in the classicizing terms recalled earlier (p. 379), inviting him to Rome to be crowned emperor and restore the Roman empire, invoking Constantine and Justinian as his forebears, and attacking the pope and his Sicilian alliance; more concretely, the Senate related how it had taken over the *fortitudines*, *turres*, and *domos* of the *potentes urbes* who supported the pope and the king of Sicily, notably the Frangipane, the Pierleoni and the Tuscolani—except Giordano Pierleoni, who was now described as the senatorial *vexillifer*, standard-bearer, presumably indicating that he had remained a senatorial leader, but with a less controversial title.[148] This thus confirms, a few years later, what John and Otto already claimed for 1145, that is to say the targeting of the houses of the aristocratic supporters of the pope. Presumably this ended with the 1149 papal peace, which was more lasting than that of 1145.

Tensions nonetheless remained high. They were not helped by the fact that the purist preacher Arnaldo of Brescia was now in Rome, influential *in publicis contionibus*, i.e. senatorial assemblies, as John of Salisbury said later; another 1149 letter to Conrad, from an unnamed senator (i.e. not from the Senate as a body), invites him to take the pope in hand, 'lest wars or homicides are done in the world by priests. For it is not permitted to them to hold the sword or the calix, but [only] to pray . . .', which are known to be Arnaldian views. It may also be from this wing of the popular movement in Rome that an otherwise unknown Wezel wrote a letter to the new German king, Frederick I, in 1152, which addresses him, insultingly, as *clarissimus* (an ancient senatorial title), not as *rex*, and argues at length that only the Senate can make him emperor. And it was certainly in this context that Eugenius

---

[147] For this period, basic are Otto of Freising, *Chronica*, VII.31 (quote), 34 (agreement); *LP*, II, pp. 386–7; John of Salisbury, *Historia pontificalis*, ch. 27 (quote).

[148] Wibald, *Epistolae*, nn. 347, 214, 215. Conrad replied in 1151, not to the Senate, but to an older collectivity, the urban prefect, the *consules*, *capitanei*, and *omni populo Romano tam minoribus quam maioribus*: Wibald, *Epistolae*, n. 345 (= *Conradi III diplomata*, n. 262; the argument by Petersohn, *Kaisertum und Rom*, pp. 116–17, that by *consules* Conrad meant the Senate, does not convince). For SPQR, see esp. Beneš, 'Whose SPQR?', pp. 876–81, and (for an earlier citation for the year 1117) Petersohn, *Kaisertum und Rom*, p. 24, cf. p. 70. For these letters as a whole, see among many Benson, 'Political *renovatio*', pp. 341–50; Thumser, 'Die frühe römische Kommune' (the best guide). Doran, 'The legacy of schism', pp. 124–76, is the fullest recent account of Eugenius and the Senate; it is more eirenic than I would be about their relationship (they were sometimes on civil terms, it is true, but a relatively relaxed relation between the pope and the Senate before 1188 is only really attested for Hadrian IV).

III wrote to Wibald himself, as an imperial advisor, in the same year, claiming that Arnaldo had stirred up a *rusticana quedam turba absque nobilium et maiorum*, 'some sort of rustic mob without aristocrats or elites', two thousand strong, who planned on 1 November 1152 to elect a hundred permanent senators (called *sectatores* in the text), two consuls, one for internal city affairs, the other for external affairs, and their own emperor. This sounds like a pope frightened by wild rumour; whatever the truth of it, Eugenius made peace with the city yet again at the end of the year.[149] Nor had relations between the pope and the city been universally bad even before; a treaty between the Roman Senate and the commune of Pisa in 1151 begins 'we fifty senators by the grace of God [and] by the lord Eugenius the Pisan pope...'. When Hadrian IV, a tougher pope than Eugenius, finally placed an interdict on Rome in 1155 unless the city expelled Arnaldo, the *clerus et populus Romanus* made the senators concede, just before the great Easter processions. Arnaldo fled Rome, but was caught by Frederick Barbarossa on his way to the city for his imperial coronation, and handed over to the urban prefect, who had him executed.[150] The anticlericalism of Arnaldo and his supporters will certainly have struck a chord with a city whose relations with Eugenius (not to speak of Lucius, and indeed Innocent) had so often been hostile, but I conclude that the senatorial conflict with the pope was most of all over secular matters, and Arnaldo was, however interesting, a sideshow.

Let us stop this narrative here, with Frederick's coronation—scene, in fact, of yet another violent skirmish between Germans and Romans, and plenty of signs of tension between emperor and pope; but an analysis of these would take us into the political world of the late twelfth century and of the developed commune, which is not the subject matter of this book. Instead, we need to take stock of the decade which began in 1143, to see what the socio-political situation actually was.

Historians have chewed over every last morsel of information that can be drawn from the scarce sources for the early commune. I am rather more cautious about the reliability of narratives than most of my predecessors; Otto of Freising, in particular, has done several generations of over-trusting historians some damage by couching his descriptions of the Roman Senate in a rhetorical frame containing too many classical allusions, even though Arsenio Frugoni remarked on this fact already in the 1950s.[151] Accordingly, I have given an account here based as far as

---

[149] John of Salisbury, *Historia Pontificalis*, ch. 31; Wibald, *Epistolae*, nn. 216, 404, 403; with commentary from Frugoni, *Arnaldo da Brescia*, pp. 69–76; Thumser, 'Die frühe römische Kommune', pp. 128–46; Schmitz-Esser, '*In urbe, quae caput mundi est*', pp. 33–42; Doran, 'The legacy of schism', pp. 143–53. There is controversy over how Arnaldian the first of these letters is, but I am convinced by Thumser, pp. 128–9, and by Schmitz-Esser. Frugoni remains the basic, and minimalist, guide to Arnaldo and his importance in Rome; he is still to be preferred to the cautious arguments for a greater role for Arnaldo in Schmitz-Esser, '*In urbe, quae caput mundi est*', esp. pp. 40–2.

[150] *Senato*, n. 11; *LP*, II, p. 389; Otto of Freising, *Gesta Friderici*, II.28.

[151] Frugoni, 'Sulla "Renovatio Senatus"', pp. 172–4, with Frugoni, *Arnaldo da Brescia*, pp. 65–7 ('L'*ordo equestris* è dunque qui invenzione culturale di Ottone', a citation found in both texts), commenting in this case on Otto of Freising, *Gesta Friderici*, I.28, II.28–30, on the *ordo equestris* (which Moscati, *Alle origini*, pp. 25–6 and Maire Vigueur, *L'autre Rome*, pp. 309–10 are happy to take to the letter). For Otto, *Gesta Friderici*.II, 29–30, a highly artificial and classicizing account of the stand-off between senatorial representatives and Frederick I in 1155, see above, Chapter 6, n. 79.

possible on letters and documents, which certainly helps to shorten my own narrative. But even this brief account makes clear the genuine novelty of the events of 1143–4 and their aftermath. The *populus Romanus* was no longer a minor player in an aristocrat-led, or papal-led, city community; it was constituting itself as a direct rival to the popes and their allies. Only Giordano Pierleoni, out of the 'aristocracy', is associated with the early Senate (and, once, the *populus minor*) in these texts; it is common enough for popular revolts to look for isolated aristocratic leaders or figureheads, and this was presumably the case here.

The systematic hostility of the Senate to the pope should not be overstated. It sought papal recognition, and after it received this in 1145, it recognized some form of papal superiority ever after, as far as we can see: the first senatorial document, from the end of 1148, certainly does. But an early hostility to the 'aristocracy' is very evident. The Frangipane, Pierleoni, and the urban prefect were explicitly targeted (Hadrian IV agreed in 1158 to help the prefect Pietro 'III' and his associates rebuild their *domūs* in Rome, as part of an agreement by which he paid them the enormous sum of 2000 silver marks for war damage).[152] This has relatively little parallel in other Italian communes, before the *magnati–popolo* conflicts of the thirteenth century. And unparalleled also is the institutional ambition of the new Senate; it not only had its own dating system, but also a *scriba* or *cancellarius* and a seal, as early as 1148; it very soon developed a distinctive round minuscule script; by 1151, again precociously, it had a *palatium* on the Capitolio, as we have seen (p. 339).[153] The early senators thus had a project, and it was a project that, whatever their occasional classicizing rhetoric, was above all to establish an unusually self-aware, and also unusually anti-aristocratic, version of a contemporary north Italian consulate. This would have been radical anywhere, and was all the more radical when it was set against the papal politics of the previous decades, culminating in the wide-ranging hegemony of Innocent II. The excitement of being part of the early senatorial experiment also led to ever bolder measures, especially in 1144–5, with the institution of the *patricius* and the attack on the prefect's office, in a way common in radical movements—and also interestingly parallel to the ever-greater ambition of the rhetoric and planning of the 'reform' papacy with Umberto of Silva Candida and Pier Damiani a hundred years before. Revolt soon institutionalized itself, and the 'aristocrats' mostly ceased to be enemies, even if they were not yet senators; but Hadrian IV and his successors henceforth faced an autonomous and self-confident urban government which no pope even tried to undermine again until Innocent III, and which for the thirty-year period 1159–88 was far better-rooted in the city than the popes were. This is why this book stops in 1150: not because the Senate is in any way the 'natural' culmination of the trends I have been tracing in this book, but because the whole political set-up of the city would henceforth be so different.

---

[152] *LC*, I, nn. 167–8.
[153] Bartoloni, 'Per la storia', pp. 2–6, 28–41 (see also for the seal Petersohn, *Kaisertum und Rom*, pp. 106–8); *Senato*, n. 11; cf. Maire Vigueur, *L'autre Rome*, p. 311.

What, however, we need to return to is the issue of who the *populus Romanus* who did all this actually was. We have seen a variety of possible meanings for the word *populus*: the probably fairly restricted elite group to whom *pecunia* was distributed by rival papal candidates; a wider group, often counterposed in our source to *nobiles* or *potentes*, which certainly included the 'medium elite' of richer artisans, legal experts and small-scale *rentiers* discussed in Chapter 5, and must have also extended more widely, though doubtless not to the urban poor; and the *populus* which took part in processions, which could in principle include almost the whole city (see pp. 324–5). I do not think there can be much doubt that the Senate was led above all by the 'medium elite', for the simple reason that the Senate was often opposed to *nobiles*, and the next most prominent social stratum was the 'medium elite'. We have seen in S. Maria Nova/Colosseo, the only *regio* which gives us adequate documentation for this (pp. 297–8), that several of its leaders in 1177, most of them visibly part of that elite, are identifiable as senators in our very intermittent senatorial lists. Participation in and commitment to the Senate seems to have extended more widely as well, however, as we shall see in a moment, fitting the citations earlier in the twelfth century of the *populus* as a larger political group. I earlier (pp. 262–6) defended the view that this characterization is a more helpful one for Rome than the image, common in the recent historiography of the Senate, of it being based on a mounted *militia*, although the difference between the two views is not huge, and it cannot be doubted that the Senate of the 1140s was very interested in fighting Tivoli, just as that of the 1170s–80s was very interested in fighting Tuscolo. It is, however, worthwhile coming back to the senatorial lists and looking at them as a whole, to see how many of the early senators can actually be located socially.

We have reasonably long lists of senators for 1148, 1150, 1151, 1157, 1162, 1166, and 1177, plus casual references to senators appearing in ones and twos for another seven years up to 1180. We know the Senate best in the first decade or so of its formal documentation; the only better-documented period is 1185–91, which shows a partial move towards a more aristocratic involvement immediately preceding the institution of rule by single senators from 1192 onwards, but the late 1180s takes us too far beyond the period of this book, and I will not consider them here.[154] Given that there were often fifty-plus senators at any one time, it is fairly likely that we do not have a full count in any year except, probably, 1188 and 1191. Before 1180 we know the names of eighty-six of them, however. Not one of them is a senator in more than one documented year up to 1180; however incomplete our lists, this shows an annual turn-over of senators which was probably substantial, and which contrasts with other cities, where early lists of consuls (even though normally made up of rather smaller numbers) often show the same names cropping

[154] Lists in Bartoloni, 'Per la storia', pp. 76–86, with the addition of Pagano, 'La chiesa di S. Biagio', pp. 48–9 (a. 1154) and ASR, SCD, cassetta 16, n. 138 (a. 1168). 'Aristocratic' families which begin to be referenced in the senatorial lists in 1188 and 1191 include the Malabranca, the Papareschi, the Corsi, the Frangipane and the Orsini; they are as yet a small minority, however. For the 1190s, with the single senator, see above all Thumser, *Rom*, pp. 239–46, with Moscati, 'Benedetto "Carushomo"'.

up again and again. Were we to assume that senators only ever served once, and once per family, twenty years would see a thousand and more men serving, which would represent over 10 per cent of the families in the city even if we accept, probably as an outside estimate, a population level of up to 40,000 for the end of the twelfth century (cf. p. 112). We cannot, of course, make these assumptions (there are, for example, some senators serving more than once by the 1180s), but it gives us an order of magnitude to start from. We might guess that at least 5 per cent of urban families had a member who was a senator up to 1180, as a rough ball-park figure. We clearly have no reason to suppose the restriction of senatorial office to a tiny leading group, but, all the same, if the 'medium elite' was 10–15 per cent of the population (see above, p. 263), not all its members could realistically have expected to reach senatorial status, especially as I doubt that all senators came only from that stratum: senatorial office was necessarily, somehow, representative.

The first point to be made about the early senatorial lists is that less than a third of them can be identified elsewhere, or socially located, with any degree of confidence at all; this too is in sharp opposition to the situation in other cities. Indeed, even taking into account the fact that some of them have very common names, which could in principle be that of numerous people in our sources (such as Giovanni di Berardo, the first senator of all listed in 1148), half of them never appear even hypothetically in any other text. This might simply show that the senators we cannot place came from ill-documented *regiones* like Ripa or Caccabarii or Ponte, which must be true in many cases, but it is, taken across the whole set, also likely that many of them were from less elevated backgrounds, from social strata which were less likely to get into our documentation—the fact that most identifiable senators were from the 'medium elite', as we shall see in a moment, does not have to be more than a consequence of the fact that most people who are identifiable in our texts were reasonably prosperous. This, as with the fact that early senators are only documented for single years, is indicative rather than probative, but both together point clearly in the direction of a relatively wide social inclusiveness for senatorial membership. It has often been proposed that the fifty-six senators, the apparently standard number by 1190 or so, were made up of four from each of the fourteen 'super-regions'; the mathematics does not add up well (twelve Roman *regiones* plus Trastevere makes thirteen), and there were anyway not always fifty-six in the earliest years,[155] but the idea that the Senate was constituted regionally certainly fits the emphasis on *regiones* in so many of our sources, both documents and narratives, and also, perhaps, the fact that the 1177 Colosseo regional leadership is so well represented in our lists. A small handful of senators were identified by their *regio*—in 1150 Lorenzo from the Subura; in 1151 Giorgio from Equo Marmoreo (the Quirinale) and Stefano *scriniarius* from Pigna. If *regiones* chose senators, however, they may not have restricted themselves to leading families; Bentevegna in 1148 was a *pictor* and Giorgio of Equo Marmoreo in

---

[155] See Halphen, *Études*, pp. 58–60, already critical; Doran, 'The legacy of schism', p. 137, sums up the issue; see above, n. 135 for fifty senators in some years.

1151 was a *sartor*, so some artisans clearly qualified, although such ascriptions are rare in the senatorial lists, and these may perhaps have been elite artisans.[156]

The force of *regiones* in the early Senate needs a little more comment. The best instance of a *regio* operating as a real community is Colosseo in 1177, and that cannot be invoked as a sign of a collectivity of action which helped the operative coherence of three decades earlier, in the 1140s. But the appearance of the twelve 'super-*regiones*' in 1118 (above, p. 121) shows that a regionalization of political practice pre-existed 1143; indeed, on the fringe of our vision we find early references to *decarcones* in 965 and 1062, who were certainly representatives *de vulgi populo* at the former date, when Otto I hanged twelve of them, which may conceivably imply a regional association.[157] If, then, as I have just proposed, the early Senate was constituted regionally, this might well have been not such a new development, even if it is also quite plausible that *regiones* became more coherent in the decades around 1100 as a result of the breakdown of traditional forms of political authority and government, just as signorial territories, parishes, and urban and rural communes did elsewhere in the peninsula.[158] In the twelfth century, as we saw in Chapter 5, *regiones* structured the social fabric of the city. Men and women may have been loyal as much to their *regio* as to the city, as can be seen in particular for Trastevere, and it is probable (although impossible to demonstrate) that the Senate, and the importance of senatorial office, was understood slightly differently in each, as local social structures differed. This also means, however, that loyalty to a *regio* is likely to have been at least as important as loyalty to any given social stratum. If senators were chosen regionally, there is no reason to presume from the start that elite status always mattered more than the ability to be an effective spokesman for a regional society. Membership of the 'medium elite' was probably normal for senators, but does not have to be assumed to be axiomatic; and, where artisanal groups were locally influential, their leaders with less social status could fulfil the task as well as could others. This fits the predominance in our early senatorial lists of men whose origins and social connections are unknown.

This point is, finally, reinforced by what little we know of the Senate as a 'public sphere', in Habermasian terms. I have argued that Arnaldo of Brescia was a marginal figure to the main political activity of the Senate, but he certainly had a following, sometimes a vocal one, and sometimes (to popes) a disturbing one. The fact that John of Salisbury says that he was vocal *in publicis contionibus* (above, p. 444) is simply a marker of the fact that, to John, his appeal was demagogic and not institutional. But it is still interesting that John—who knew Rome, even if a little later than this—assumed that it was in assemblies that Arnaldo gained his support. Other city communes had *contiones* from the start, gatherings of a wide range of people, as part of their projection into the city, but these had less of a role as locations for real public debate after consuls gained institutional standing in the second third of the twelfth century.[159] In Rome, we have a faint sign that assembly-

---

[156] *Senato*, nn. 12, 13.   [157] *LP*, II, pp. 252, 336.
[158] Cf., e.g. Wickham, *Community and Clientele*, pp. 234–41.
[159] Coleman, 'Representative assemblies', esp. pp. 203–7.

based debate was part of the structure of the Senate, even though it had formally constituted senators at the same time; and we have more than a faint sign that this was the context for the development of a radical religious wing for senatorial politics, which, however marginal here, was very rare elsewhere. This gives further force to the proposal that Rome's Senate was the focus of a relatively widely based popular political aggregation.

If we simply focus on the twenty-four senators we do know a little more about, we can get a better sense of the strata which made up its leadership. For a start, a maximum of two were perhaps aristocrats, Grisotto di Cencio in 1148, who might well be linked to the *filii Baruncii* (as Gregorovius already noticed), and Stefano di Cencio di Stefano di Tedaldo in 1150, whose ancestors' names are *Leitnamen* in the family of Cencio di Stefano. If these possible links hold good, it is interesting that the two families concerned had a heavily pro-imperial past.[160] Seven of the twenty-four, nearly a third, were *scriniarii*, *causidici*, or *advocati*, that is to say from the stratum of legal professionals who were so often consuls in northern cities. One of these, Giovanni di Parenzo (senator in 1157 and then again in 1188), we have seen rising from the 'medium elite' towards the aristocratic level his sons certainly reached, but, if he did so already himself, this is unlikely yet to have been the case in 1157 (above, pp. 270–1). The *advocatus* Pietro di Rubeo (senator in 1150) also appears as a *dativus* or with palatine judges in two senatorial court cases of the 1160s, and was part of the expert legal group around Benedetto di Leone and Seniorile (above, p. 404). Gregorio *de Primicerio* (senator in 1151) is in some ways the most interesting of the set, for he was actually a palatine judge, *arcarius*, while he was senator; he held that office from 1139 to 1166, and was, as we have seen, almost certainly son of the *primicerius* Ferrucio (above, p. 248).[161] The palatine judges moved seamlessly between the papal Curia and the Senate anyway, but this is the extreme example of it. They were by now, as we saw for the *primicerius* Galgano (p. 274), members of the 'medium elite'.

With the the other identifiable senators up to 1180, we are usually clearly in the same 'medium elite' category too. Some only appear as landholders on the boundaries of documented properties, so we cannot place them socially. Of the others, though, three of them (in 1151, 1177, 1179) were among the leaders of the *regio* of Colosseo in 1177 (above, pp. 297–8). Two appear elsewhere as creditors of churches, Sebastiano di Gualtrada (senator in 1148, creditor of S. Alessio for the sum of £9 in 1165) and Giovanni di Cencio di Pantaleone (senator in 1151, probably a creditor of Grottaferrata in 1160). Several reappear, sometimes more than once, as church witnesses, and one, Gregorio di Peregrino (senator in 1151),

---

[160] Grisotto: *Senato*, n. 12 with *S. Gregorio*, n. 137 (a. 1131)—see above, p. 235, including for Nicola di Cencio, senator in 1163 (*SMVL*, n. 200), a less likely aristocrat—and Gregorovius, *History*, IV, p. 497n. (Gregorovius' other identifications are, however, worthless. He has been followed in this by distressingly large numbers of subsequent scholars, who find the Berizoni, or Boboni, or even, amazingly, the Crescenzi behind any one of the common patronymics in the senatorial lists. It would be unfair to name names.) Stefano: see above, p. 234.

[161] Pietro di Rubeo: *Senato*, nn. 12, 17; *SMVL*, n. 196; possibly also *SMVL*, nn. 175, 176, 193. Gregorio *de Primicerio*: *Senato*, n. 13; see Chapter 4, n. 155.

was part of S. Ciriaco in Via Lata's witnessing community for significant court cases, so was certainly at the 'medium elite' level. So also, probably, was Anibaldo (senator in 1171), who, although very plausibly the ancestor of the baronial Annibaldi family in the next century, does not appear as more than a small-scale dealer in this period. One, finally, Rustico di Nicola di Rustico (senator 1151) was probably the son of the Nicola di Rustico who was a vineyard tenant on the Portuense in 1115 and a leader (third in a long list) of the *scola piscatorum* in the Porto marshes in 1155; this probably puts him among the 'medium elite' of Trastevere.[162]

These, then, were the known leaders of the Roman *populus* in the mid-twelfth century: a tiny handful of possible aristocrats, and then judges, *scriniarii*, leaders of *regiones*, financial dealers, members of church witnessing groups, and probably reasonably well-off artisans. Behind them, we can presume, stood the rest of the 'medium elite' of the city—and, as I have proposed, less prosperous groups too, those whose social context cannot be documented. The senatorial project from the start involved hostility to the pope and to *nobiles*, and it would have been important, therefore, to have generated as wide a social collectivity as possible. So the Senate would have consisted of a wide range of people, representing that wider commitment, the *populus minor* of one text; but it would all the same, we need not doubt, have been *most* representative of the 'medium elite', who make up the senators who are easiest to track. On one level, this is exactly what one would expect; already Gregorovius assumed, without doing the prosopography himself, that the 1148 senators were mostly 'people of the burgher class (*fast nur bürgerliche*), names hitherto unknown to history'.[163] Exactly these middling social groups filled the consular offices of other cities, too. But in other cities they had not taken on the city aristocracy frontally, let alone the pope. In most other cities, that is to say, the 'medium elite' joined with local aristocrats to form *militia*-led communal systems. In Rome, instead, for specific local reasons, the alliances swung a different way, and these ordinary, even if doubtless militarily trained, local leaders joined with less powerful members of their regional communities to seize control of a city from its 'aristocratic' leadership, fought the pope to a standstill, and then held onto power for fifty years. They lost full control of it, back to the 'aristocracy' and the pope, in the 1190s and onwards, but it was quite a run all the same, and the institutions they created remained.

Rather than simply sitting back to admire this at least partially popular success, as did Gregorovius, so conscious as he was of the Risorgimento parallels, or Brezzi, with his invocation of 'l'età eroica' of the commune, it is worth reprising what

---

[162] Sebastiano: *Senato*, n. 12 with *S. Alessio*, n. 20; Giovanni di Cencio: *Senato*, nn. 12–13, with *S. Sisto*, n. 5 (his own name is here lost in a lacuna, but his father's and rare grandfather's name are preserved; the creditor here might be his brother instead). Gregorio di Peregrino: *Senato*, n. 13, with *SMVL*, nn. 149, 172, 187. Another example is perhaps Giovanni di Sassone, witness in CVL 8044, ff. 4–16 (a. 1145), a major court case, and doubtless father of Nicola, senator in 1188 (*Senato*, n. 42). Anibaldo: *SMN*, n. 99, with (probably) *SMVL*, n. 222; cf. Carocci, *Baroni di Roma*, p. 311; Thumser, *Rom*, pp. 28–30. Nicola di Rustico: *SMVL*, n. 144; *S. Gregorio*, n. 55; cf. above, p. 104; Rustico is a very common name, but this is the only Nicola di Rustico in our documents.

[163] Gregorovius, *History*, IV, pp. 496–7 (*Geschichte*, IV, p. 469). See, more exactly, Moscati, *Alle origini*, pp. 24–6.

causal processes made it possible, in Rome in particular.[164] One is that Roman local associations were old, with *scolae* operating as coherent trade-based groups, and with *regiones* as increasingly visible and powerful points of reference, the latter of which can be argued, as I have just done, to be among the building blocks for the commune itself. A second and related explanation has also already been amply discussed earlier in this chapter, that regional loyalties were largely structured by the churches in them which owned and leased out all the land, and were very hard indeed for popes to maintain any influence in, which allowed the further development of autonomous forms of social action in the city. A third explanation was discussed in Chapter 6, the fact that the ceremonial and processional world of Rome was so unusually strong, and that, although it clearly buttressed papal power and hegemony in the city, it also acted to give the Roman *populus* its own ceremonial identity. The processional world also helped to keep alive the traditions of assembly which were otherwise lost when *placita* ceased in the last decades of the eleventh century—hence, in particular, the unusually collective, assembly-based, nature of senatorial justice in the 1140s to 1180s (above, p. 408), as well as debate in the *contio*, less well-attested. A fourth explanation lies in the wealth of the city and the scale of its artisanal economy, explored in Chapter 3, which sustained more people to make up the *populus*, and created a more broad-based prosperity for its leaders, the 'medium elite'. Rome had faced recession since the 1080s, and was by 1143 dropping behind Milan in economic and demographic terms (above, pp. 178–9), but it was also reviving economically in the 1140s, and was still rich and active by the standards of anywhere else. I set aside, however, a fifth explanation, the interest in antiquity and *renovatio* which supposedly animated the early Senate; as argued earlier, these were simply longstanding—very Roman—rhetorical trappings and images of the past which anyone could use, and Innocent II used them as much as did his senatorial opponents (above, pp. 336–7); anyway, the Senate carefully avoided one of their most obvious potential elements, the use of Roman law (above, p. 374). But four explanations do seem to me sufficient to give a proper context to the actions of the *populus*, once it broke with the pope and the 'aristocracy', and took off on its own. The *populus* had an unusual organizational coherence in mid-twelfth-century Rome, and a potentially autonomous one; it had more capacity for independent action than did its equivalents in other Italian cities, as yet. It was precocious, here as in so many other ways. And it needed to be; Innocent II was quite an opponent to take on, even on his deathbed.

Was Rome in the pre-communal period more of a northern, or more of a southern, city? This is a version of a question that has become, in its reworkings over the last two centuries, uselessly polemical and essentialist; 'the North' and 'the South' of course barely exist as real entities. But it is fair to ask where, in our period, the best parallels to Rome's endlessly complex social development really lie, and I will end this book by trying to engage with the question.

---

[164] Gregorovius, *History*, IV, pp. 510–11n; Brezzi, *Roma*, p. 317.

I have stressed most of all northern parallels in this book, so it is only fair to begin with them. Rome was not part of the *Regnum Italiae*, but it was of continual interest to Carolingian and then German kings, who needed to be crowned emperor in Rome to be able to rule legitimately in Italy. Such coronations were moments of great tension in Rome (street battles routinely resulted from them), and German king/emperors deposed and appointed more bishops of Rome than they did the prelates of any other Italian see. Rome was in some respects directly influenced by Carolingian political practices, most particularly in the development of the *placitum* assembly as the basic location for the collective self-assertion of the city's political players, in the ninth to eleventh centuries. It was also influenced by northern political crises. The relative power-vacuum in immediately post-Carolingian Europe in the early tenth century had less effect, except insofar as it allowed the Teofilatto family to develop its innovative dynastic politics; but the civil war in (Germany and) Italy in the 1080s and 1090s had a direct effect on Rome. Rome faced, along with all north Italian cities, an urban version of the 'feudal revolution' crisis, as the traditional sources of political legitimacy began to crumble in the civil war period. Rome, like other north Italian cities, then faced an early twelfth century dominated by ad hoc political and administrative expedients, as we have seen at length at the start of this chapter, until it, as other cities did, developed structures of communal government, even if these were in Rome also set against revived structures of episcopal (papal) power as well, which were not a feature of most of the North.

The narrative of Roman socio-political history thus follows northern lines, particularly in the final crisis century of the 250 years covered by this book, because the city was so closely tied into northern political structures, regardless of its formal autonomy. There were structural reasons why Rome had plenty of parallels in the northern cities, too. Rome was traditionally ruled by bishops. So were many cities in the *regnum Italiae* (and also, with temporary exceptions, very few cities in the South).[165] Episcopal rule was very difficult indeed to organize dynastically—in Rome, only the Tuscolani ever managed it—and thus there was potential for disturbance and rivalry at every episcopal election. The stakes were lower in northern Italian cities, because bishops were not actually sovereign, but the episcopacy was the most important office open to local inhabitants in most cities (counts were usually either royal appointments or dynasticized offices), so local politics revolved around such elections; as often in the Middle Ages, disturbance and rivalry on the one side and political aggregation and commitment on the other had a close structural relationship. The political aggregation associated with disputed elections was not different in papal Rome, but was even more important given Rome's sovereign autonomy. Aristocratic family politics in many periods (the 850s, the 980s, the 1120s) focused on this to the exclusion of almost everything else, and could be renewed at particularly short notice because popes were usually elected at a greater age than were other bishops, and so had shorter reigns. The only

---

[165] I develop this point in '"The Romans according to their malign custom"', focused on the late ninth and early tenth centuries.

difference between the tensions in Rome and those in, for example, Milan under Archbishop Landolfo II (979–98) is that those in Rome are slightly better documented. And, similarly, lesser-aristocratic uprisings against unpopular bishops happened in the same way; there is a clear parallel between the revolts against the bishops of Cremona and Milan in the 1030s–40s and that against Benedict IX in Rome in 1044.[166]

These structural parallels are reinforced when we consider different aristocratic strata. Every demographically expanding city sees constant replacements of leading families. In our period, particularly after 1000, this often showed itself through an earlier generation of rising families, with military or judicial roles or mercantile wealth, who gained sufficient comital or episcopal patronage that they could obtain, and attach themselves to, castles in the countryside; an autonomous, castle-based, signorial lordship then became more attractive and solid than the competitive bustle of urban hierarchies. Such families did not necessarily move out of cities or, indeed, of city politics, but urban offices and professions were taken over by newer families. We can see this in Milan, where *valvassores* of the eleventh and early twelfth centuries, military families holding fiefs (although not castles), are on occasion visibly the heirs of merchants, metal-workers and moneyers, and also in early twelfth-century Lucca, where one generation of *iudices* could become the next generation of castle-holding *milites*.[167] Every city was different in detail, but the patterns were the same. We can certainly see them in Rome, where the (here very long-lasting) 'old aristocracy' in the city until the 1010s became the rural *comites* of the 1050s, and was replaced by a 'new aristocracy'—which then in its turn obtained castles in the 1100s and onwards, and experienced at least one wave of replacements, before its then-current leaders struck gold under Innocent III and formed a more permanent stratum of *baroni* in the centuries to follow.

Which generation of urban leaders happened to be there when the crisis hit in the decades around 1100 and cities moved in a communal direction was almost chance. But how close the current generation of urban leaders in the 1110s or 1120s were to becoming castle lords and the like did, from city to city, affect the degree to which that leadership felt too grand to be associated with the earliest commune and the consent of less socially prominent strata: some early city communes were relatively aristocratic in leadership and style (and were often associated with episcopal vassalage), others were not.[168] Similarly, later in the twelfth century, it affected the pacing by which more, or less, ruralized castle lords came to be associated with communal structures which by then were more imposing, more powerful, and thus more status-filled (as all such lords did by 1200 except for a handful of families). These observations are not in conflict with Jean-Claude Maire Vigueur's recent insistence that the *primo comune* was the work of the

---

[166] For Landolfo, Arnolfo, *Gesta*, I.10; for the revolts, see classically Violante, *La società milanese*, pp. 186–213; Tabacco, *Egemonie sociali*, pp. 226–32, 401–10.

[167] Keller, *Signori e vassalli*, pp. 192–207; Wickham, *Courts and Conflict*, pp. 56–60.

[168] See e.g. Bordone, *La società cittadina*, pp. 160–82; Maire Vigueur, *Cavaliers et citoyens*, pp. 220–46.

urban mounted *militia,* for all urban leaders were indeed militarily trained, and had a certain group identity; but the way that the large and militarized leading group of each city was internally articulated, and how the constant replacement of elites impacted on the slowly crystallizing commune, was different from place to place, and that difference seems to me the crucial one to understand.[169] It was certainly different in Rome, as we have seen, where the early Senate was directly opposed to those 'new aristocrats' who were becoming castle lords and papal clients; but the difference was inside a recognized range of north Italian parameters.

Having said all this, it is necessary also to stress contrasts with the North, and southern parallels. Rome was an independent city, ruling most of the large area today covered by an Italian *regione.* It was in this respect most similar to Capua, Benevento, and Salerno (and the very much smaller Naples, Gaeta, and Amalfi) before the Normans conquered them all (except the city of Benevento) between 1058 and 1139. Under the Teofilatto family, Rome developed a dynastic leadership with close similarities to the southern principalities, and it is obviously not chance that Alberico adopted the southern title of *princeps.* Even after that family drew back from secular rule—that is to say when the new *princeps* Ottaviano di Alberico became Pope John XII in 956—the old principle that Rome had both its own independent political structure and a territory, much larger than a simple diocese, to rule, as did Capua-Benevento and Salerno, continued. A senior Teofilatto-Tuscolano figure like Stefania *senatrix* could be given a whole city territory, Palestrina, to rule in 970.[170] And in every period the issue of local territorial rule remained an important part of Roman patronage—Lazio could not, as a northern diocese could, all be run directly from the city.

This had permanent structural results. Who was *rector* of the Sabina continued to matter in the tenth and eleventh centuries, even though the internal structure of the Sabina fragmented into castle-based territories as the latter century wore on. So did who was *comes* of *Campania,* at least in the tenth; and ruling Terracina was an important role throughout our period, coveted by Crescenzi, Pierleoni, and Frangipane alike.[171] Roman control over the whole of Lazio steadily disintegrated in the eleventh century (it parallels Benevento before the Normans here, although not Salerno); but the principle that it was all by rights ruled from Rome remained, and popes from Nicholas II, through Honorius II, to Hadrian IV made often effective moves to regain various sections of the old *territorium S. Petri,* before the comprehensive reunification under Innocent III. Tivoli was one of the first to begin to break away, in 1001, and was (as Innocent II found) one of the hardest to subdue, but on the other hand Segni, Anagni, and Ferentino in the west of

---

[169] Maire Vigueur, *Cavaliers et citoyens, passim*; pp. 339–49, 355–62 for the dominance of the consulates of northern cities by the *militia*; 246–7, 342–6 for the variability of the relationship between castle lords and communes. For a Lucchese example of a city family apparently too grand to enter the consulate at the start, Wickham, *Courts and Conflict*, pp. 24–28. I shall discuss this issue at greater length in future work.

[170] *Papsturkunden*, n. 205. The document just conveys the *civitas* of Palestrina, but the bounds approximate to those of its diocese.

[171] Falco, *Studi*, II, pp. 401–15, nuanced in Toubert, *Les structures*, esp. pp. 988–98, 1024–31.

Campania were, after an extension of Roman control in the 1120s, safe bases for papal power, which popes took advantage of whenever they were exiled from Rome in the mid-1140s onwards, and especially in the 1160s–80s.[172]

The purpose of raising this is not to introduce, at the last moment, a territorial element into what is avowedly an urban history, but rather to stress the wide geographical scale of Roman dominance. None of the other Lazio cities were even distant rivals to Rome as socio-economic or political foci, a fact which itself had economic implications for Rome, as we saw in Chapter 3. Furthermore, the existence of this wider hinterland, however hard it was to control in practice for much of our period, also made possible the creation of the Agro romano, that enormous area around the city, as big as many whole dioceses elsewhere in the peninsula, in which Rome had total hegemony, and in which its churches had a near-total ownership of the land, as we saw in Chapter 2. This was a political and economic phenomenon, producing great wealth for the city, which had no parallels whatsoever in the north of Italy; a similar dominance over a smaller area, is, however, one of the reasons why Naples was one of the principal cities of the South.[173] Later, when Innocent III completed his reconquest, he created a geographical canvas on which a new and vastly rich stratum of *baroni* could base their castle-holding; that new stratum renewed the comparisons which can be made with the South, for in wealth and lifestyle they were most similar to the contemporary aristocracies of the southern *Regno* of the Staufer and Angevins.[174] But the links of at least parts of the whole of Lazio to Rome were older than that, and allowed for a relatively wide geographical scale in politics even in the period of maximum incoherence. When Paschal II expelled some of the Corsi from Rome in 1106, they went to Montalto di Castro, a full hundred kilometres from Rome.[175] No northern city *contado* stretched anything like so far.

Rome was thus closely linked to the wider history of the north of Italy; but not only. Being an independent state, southern-style, continued to matter. Rome's Byzantine past, another element that by now looked south, also brought a complexity of government practices which was far greater than any city-state, however large, might be thought to need. Rome's traditional structures of government were indeed uniquely complex in early medieval Latin Europe, as we have seen (pp. 189–90), with its aristocratic hierarchies of palatine and other offices, headed by the *vestararius* (later, the urban prefect) and the seven palatine judges, several of them with names inherited from the Byzantines (as medieval Romans well knew).[176] These hierarchies threaded through the assembly politics of the *placitum romanum*, and gave it a notable coherence. The *placitum* broke down in the late eleventh century,

---

[172] See in general, Toubert, *Les structures*, pp. 1073–8. For Tivoli in 1001, Pier Damiani, *Vita beati Romualdi*, ch. 23; Thangmar, *Vita Bernwardi*, chs 23–4.

[173] For the landowning concentration around Naples, see Martin, *Guerre, accords*, pp. 114–38; for the economic complexity of the city, see most recently Carrero, *Napoli*, pp. 359–419.

[174] See esp. Carocci, *Baroni di Roma*.

[175] *Liber Pontificalis*, ed. Přerovský, pp. 712–13.

[176] See e.g. the so-called 'ältere römische Richterliste', ed. *MGH, Leges*, IV, p. 663; cf. Schramm, *Kaiser, Rom*, pp. 27–8; Schramm, *Kaiser, Könige und Päpste*, I, pp. 130–44.

and the palatine judges lost their aristocratic status, but they continued to structure Rome's now de-institutionalized legal system, and (as did the prefect) provided an element of continuity. So did Rome's *scolae*, heirs of ceremonial trade associations which had some Byzantine roots, which were by the eleventh and twelfth centuries proto-guilds with, often, highly coherent collective structures. And Rome's processional and ceremonial practice, another Byzantine inheritance, but made possible and necessary by the city's geographical scale, maintained a public world of large groupings of people which, if they had no deliberative role, at least had a performative one; and this did not break down in the crisis century at all.

All these elements, listed in the previous paragraphs, in fact supported a greater level of structural continuity in the period 1050 (or 1080) to 1150 than any northern city experienced. The survival in the Laterano of the court of the city's long-term rulers, the popes, a court capable of operating on a larger scale than that of any contemporary ruler inside Italy until Roger II unified the South, also acted as a major element in political aggregation. These elements of continuity, which were all in turn supported by the city's wealth (even in the economic crisis of the decades around 1100), by no means attenuated the political crisis which hit city government in Rome after 1080, but they did allow its re-establishment thereafter. Even if the city's administrative coherence collapsed during the period of the crisis, its renewal was largely complete by the 1140s. And then the elements of continuity allowed the recreation of structures which were more similar to the past than those managed in most of Italy. It is striking how assembly-based, how 'Carolingian', Roman senatorial activities still were; they were much more large-scale and collective than most political activities were elsewhere, not just in Italy but in most of Europe. The Byzantine inheritance thus helped Rome to remain a Carolingian city. This is ironic; the Romans by no means valued much of the Carolingian political project. But they did take on Carolingian assembly practices; and these survived even the years of the great crisis. The Roman Senate was new, just as the papal Curia was new, in the 1140s, but each of them had deep roots in the past, both in ways they recognized and ways they did not.

Bibliography

A. PRIMARY SOURCES

1. Locations of unpublished material

Archivio di Stato di Firenze, fondo documentario: Fiesole, S. Bartolomeo della badia dei Rocchettini; S. Pier Maggiore

Archivio di Stato di Roma [ASR]

ASR, fondo Benedettini e Clarisse in SS. Cosma e Damiano, cassette 16-16 bis-17 (photographs of the documents are available online on the archive's website, at http://www.cflr.beniculturali.it/Pergamene/pergamene.php?lar=1024&alt=768)

ASR, fondo Clarisse in S. Silvestro in Capite, cassette 38-38 bis

Archivio Storico Capitolino, Archivio Orsini

Archivio Storico del Vicariato, Archivio del Capitolo di S. Maria in Trastevere, n. 532; unnumbered charters for S. Maria in Trastevere are from n. 35 in the same archive, a seventeenth-century cartulary, entitled *Copia simplex instrumentorum ac bullarum contentam in libro primo authentico venerlis ecclesie S. Marie Transtyberim, extracto mense Iulii, Anno Dni 1654*

Archivio Segreto Vaticano [ASV]

ASV, Archivum Arcis, Armari I–XVIII

ASV, fondo S. Trifone

Biblioteca Apostolica Vaticana, Codices Vaticani Latini [CVL; the fondo Galletti is CVL 7854-8066]

2. Published sources

Acta pontificum romanorum inedita, ed. J. von Pflugk-Harttung, 3 vols (Tübingen, 1881, Stuttgart, 1884–6).

Agnello of Ravenna, *Liber pontificalis ecclesiae Ravennatis*, ed. D. Mauskopf Deliyannis (Turnhout, 2006).

Albarelli, I. M., 'Septem bullae ineditae ad ecclesiam Sancti Marcelli Romae spectantes', in *Monumenta ordinis Servorum Sanctae Mariae*, ed. A Morini and P. Soulier, 16 vols (Brussels, 1897–1916), II, pp. 191–211.

Andenna, G., 'Documenti di San Paolo fuori le mura, fra cui un placito papale del 1113, nel codice XXXIV (71), ora trafugato, della Biblioteca Capitolare di Santa Maria di Novara', in A. Degrandi et al. (eds), *Scritti in onore di Girolamo Arnaldi* (Rome, 2001), pp. 25–39.

Andrea of Strumi, *Vita sancti Arialdi*, ed. F. Baethgen, *MGH, SS*, XXX.2 (Leipzig, 1934), pp. 1047–75.

Annales Beneventani, ed. G. H. Pertz, *MGH, SS*, III (Hannover, 1839), pp. 173–85.

Annales Bertiniani, ed. G. Waitz, *MGH, SRG*, V (Hannover, 1883).

Annales Casinenses, ed. G. H. Pertz, *MGH, SS*, XIX (Hannover, 1866), pp. 303–20.

Annales Ceccanenses, ed. G. H. Pertz, *MGH, SS*, XIX (Hannover, 1866), pp. 275–302.

Annales Fuldenses, ed. G. H. Pertz and F. Kurze, *MGH, SRG*, VII (Hannover, 1891).

Annales Palidenses, ed. G. H. Pertz, *MGH, SS*, XVI (Hannover, 1859), pp. 48–98.

Annales Romani, ed. L. Duchesne, in *LP*, II, pp. 331–50.

Annali genovesi di Caffaro e de' suoi continuatori dal MXCIX al MCCXCIII, ed. L. T. Belgrano, I (Rome, 1890).

Anselm of Gembloux, *Continuatio*, ed. L. C. Bethmann, in *MGH, SS*, VI (Hannover, 1844), pp. 375–85.

Anselm of Liège, *Gesta episcoporum Leodiensis ecclesiae*, ed. R. Koepke, *MGH, SS*, VII (Hannover, 1846), pp. 189–234.

Arnolfo of Milan, *Liber gestorum recentium*, ed. C. Zey, *MGH, SRG*, LXVII (Hannover, 1994).

Auxilius und Vulgarius, ed. E. Dümmler (Leipzig, 1866).

Baumgärtner, I., 'Regesten aus dem Kapitelarchiv von S. Maria in Via Lata (1200–1259)', *QFIAB*, LXXIV (1994), pp. 42–171, LXXV (1995), pp. 32–177.

Benedetto of Monte Soratte, *Chronicon*, ed. G. Zucchetti in *Il Chronicon di Benedetto monacho di S. Andrea del Soratte e il Libellus de imperatoria potestate in urbe Roma* (Rome, 1920), pp. 3–187.

Benjamin of Tudela, *The Itinerary of Benjamin of Tudela*, ed. and trans. M. N. Adler (London, 1907).

Beno, *Gesta Romanae aecclesiae contra Hildebrandum*, ed. K. Francke, *MGH, Libelli de lite*, II (Hannover, 1892), pp. 366–422.

Benzone of Alba, *Ad Heinricum IV. imperatorem libri VII*, ed. H. Seyffert, *MGH, SRG*, LXV (Hannover, 1996).

Bernard of Clairvaux, *De consideratione ad Eugenium papam*, in *Sancti Bernardi Opera*, III, ed. J. Leclercq and H. M. Rochais (Rome, 1963), pp. 393–493.

Bernard of Clairvaux, *Epistolae*, in *Sancti Bernardi Opera*, VI–VIII, ed. J. Leclercq and H. M. Rochais (Rome, 1974–7).

Bernold of Konstanz, *Chronicon*, ed. I. S. Robinson, *Die Chroniken Bertholds von Reichenau und Bernolds von Konstanz*, pp. 383–540.

Beroldus, Ecclesiae Ambrosianae Mediolanensis kalendarium et ordines, ed. M. Magistretti (Milan, 1894).

Berthold of Reichenau, *Chronicon*, ed. I. S. Robinson, *Die Chroniken Bertholds von Reichenau und Bernolds von Konstanz*, pp. 161–381.

Bonizone of Sutri, *Liber ad amicum*, ed. E. Dümmler, in *MGH, Libelli de lite*, I (Hannover, 1891), pp. 571–620.

[Bulgaro,] *Excerpta legum edita a Bulgarino causidico*, ed. L. Wahrmund, Quellen zur Geschichte des römisch-kanonischen Processes im Mittelalter, IV.1 (Innsbruck, 1925).

Bullaire du pape Calixte II 1119–1124. Essai de restitution, ed. U. Robert, 2 vols (Paris, 1891).

Bullarium Basilianum [in ASV, Basiliani], ed. in P. Battifol, 'Ungedruckte Papst- und Kaiserurkunden aus Basilianischen Archiven', *Römische Quartalschrift*, II (1888), pp. 36–63, at pp. 39–48.

Bullarum, privilegiorum ac diplomatum amplissima collectio, ed. C. Cocquelines, III (Rome, 1740).

Carmen de gestis Frederici I. imperatoris in Lombardia, ed. I. Schmale-Ott, *MGH, SRG*, LXII (Hannover, 1965).

Cartario di S. Maria in Campo Marzio (986–1199), ed. E. Carusi, Miscellanea della Società romana di storia patria, XVII (Rome, 1948).

Catalogus baronum, ed. E. Jamison (Rome, 1972).

Chartae latinae antiquiores, LV, ed. R. Cosma (Zürich, 1999).

Chronicon Sublacense (aa. 593–1369), ed. R. Morghen, *Rerum italicarum scriptores*, 2nd edn, XXIV.6 (Bologna, 1927).

Cronica pontificum et imperatorum S. Bartholomaei in Insula Romani, ed. O. Holder-Egger, *MGH, SS*, XXXI (Hannover, 1903), pp. 189–222.

Chronica monasterii Casinensis, ed. H. Hoffmann, *MGH, SS*, XXXIV (Hannover, 1980).

Codex diplomaticus Amiatinus, II, ed. W. Kurze (Tübingen, 1982).

Codex diplomaticus Cajetanus, I–II, = *Tabularium Casinense*, I–II (Montecassino, 1887–91).

Codex diplomaticus dominii temporalis S. Sedis, I, ed. A. Theiner (Roma, 1861).

Codice diplomatico del Senato romano dal MCXLIV al MCCCXLVII, I, ed. F. Bartoloni (Rome, 1948).

Codice diplomatico della Repubblica di Genova, ed. C. Imperiale di Sant'Angelo, 3 vols (Rome, 1936–42).

Colotto, C., 'Il "De monasterio Sancti Pancratii et Sancti Victoris de Urbe", unico testimonianza superstite di un archivio medievale romano perduto', *ASRSP*, CXXVII (2004), pp. 5–72.

Conciliorum oecumenicorum decreta, ed. G. Alberico et al., 2nd edn (Basel, 1962).

Conradi III. et filii eius Heinrici diplomata, ed. F. Hausmann, *MGH Diplomatum regum et imperatorum Germaniae*, IX (Vienna, 1969).

Consuetudines feudorum, recensio antiqua, ed. in K. Lehmann, *Das langobardische Lehnrecht* (Göttingen, 1896), pp. 84–148.

Constantin VII Porphyrogénète, *Le livre des cérémonies*, ed. and trans. A. Vogt, 2 vols (Paris, 1967).

de Rossi, G. B., 'Atto di donazione di fondi urbani alla chiesa di S. Donato in Arezzo, rogato in Roma l'anno 1051', *ASRSP*, XII (1889), pp. 199–213.

Deusdedit, *Collectio canonum*, ed. V. Wolf von Glanvell, *Die Kanonessammlung des Kardinals Deusdedit*, I (Paderborn, 1905).

Die Chroniken Bertholds von Reichenau und Bernolds von Konstanz, 1054–1100, ed. I. S. Robinson, in *MGH, SRG*, NS XIV (Hannover, 2003).

Die Urkunden und Briefe der Markgräfin Mathilde von Tuszien, ed. E. and W. Goez, *MGH, Diplomata*, 5 ser., II (Hannover, 1998).

'Documenti per la storia ecclesiastica e civile di Roma', ed. E. von Ottenthal, *Studi e documenti di storia e diritto*, VII (1886), pp. 101–22, 195–212, 317–36, and continuing.

Donizone, *Vita Matildis*, ed. L. Bethmann, *MGH, SS*, XII (Hannover, 1856), pp. 348–409.

Duval-Arnould, L., *Le pergamene dell'Archivio Capitolare Lateranense* (Rome, 2010).

Ecclesiae S. Maria in Via Lata tabularium, ed. L. M. Hartmann and (for vol. 3) M. Merores, 3 vols (Vienna, 1895–1913).

Ekkehard of Aura, *Chronicon universale*, ed. G. Waitz, *MGH, SS*, VI (Hannover, 1844), pp. 33–231.

Epistolae pontificum Romanorum ineditae, ed. S. Loewenfeld (Leipzig, 1885).

Eugenio Vulgario, *Sylloga*, in *MGH, Poetae*, IV.1, pp. 406–44.

Falco, G., 'Documenti guerreschi di Roma medievale', *BISIME*, XL (1921), pp. 1–6.

Falcone of Benevento, *Chronicon*, in *PL*, CLXXIII, cols 1151–1262.

Fedele, P., 'Carte del monastero dei SS. Cosma e Damiano in Mica Aurea, secoli X e XI', *ASRSP*, XXI (1898), pp. 459–534, XXII (1899), pp. 25–107, 383–447, republished as a book with the same title, ed. P. Pavan, Codice diplomatico di Roma e della regione romana, 1 (Romae, 1981).

Fedele, P., 'Tabularium S. Mariae Novae ab an. 982 ad an. 1200', *ASRSP*, XXIII (1900), pp. 171–237, XXIV (1901), pp. 159–96, XXV (1902), pp. 169–209, XXVI (1903), pp. 21–141.

Fedele, P., 'Tabularium S. Praxedis', *ASRSP*, XXVII (1904), pp. 27–78, XXVIII (1905), pp. 41–114.

Fedele, P., 'S. Maria in Monasterio. Note e documenti', *ASRSP*, XXIX (1906), pp. 183–227.

Fedele, P., 'Un codice autografo di Leone Ostiense con due documenti veliterni del sec. XII', *BISIME*, XXXI (1910), pp. 7–26.

Federici, V., 'Regesto del monastero di S. Silvestro de Capite', *ASRSP*, XXII (1899), pp. 214–300, 489–538, and continuing; the registers in the edition have been checked against ASR, fondo Clarisse in S. Silvestro in Capite, cassette 38–38 bis.

Ferri, G., 'Le carte dell'archivio Liberiano dal secolo X al XV', *ASRSP*, XXVII (1904), pp. 147–202, 441–9, and continuing.

Flodoard of Reims, *Annales*, ed. P. Lauer, *Les Annales de Flodoard* (Paris, 1905).

Friderici I. diplomata, ed. H. Appelt, *MGH, Diplomatum regum et imperatorum Germaniae*, X (Hannover, 1975–90).

Gaufredo Malaterra, *De rebus gestis Rogerii Calabriae et Siciliae Comitis et Roberti Guiscardi ducis fratris eius*, ed. E. Pontieri, *Rerum Italicarum Scriptores*, V, 1 (Bologna, 1928).

Geoffroy of Vendôme, *Œuvres*, ed. G. Giordanengo (Turnhout, 1996).

Géographie d'Édrisi, trans. P. A. Jaubert, II (Paris, 1840).

Gerbert of Aurillac, *Epistulae*, in *Die Briefsammlung Gerberts von Reims*, ed. F. Weigle, *MGH, Die Briefe der deutschen Kaiserzeit*, II (Weimar, 1966).

Gesta Innocentii III, ed. in *PL*, CCXIV, coll. xvii–ccxviii.

Giorgi, I., 'Il regesto del monastero di S. Anastasio ad Aquas Salvias', *ASRSP*, I (1878), pp. 49–77.

Giovanni Canapario, *Vita S. Adalberti episcopi*, ed. G. H. Pertz, *MGH, SS*, IV (Hannover, 1841), pp. 581–95.

Gli atti del comune di Milano fino all'anno MCCVI, ed. C. Manaresi (Milano, 1919).

Gli atti privati milanesi e comaschi, ed. C. Vittani, C. Manaresi, and C. Santoro, 4 vols (Milan, 1933–69).

Godfrey of Viterbo, *Pantheon*, ed. G. Waitz, *MGH, SS*, XXII (Hannover, 1872), pp. 107–307.

Gregorii VII Registrum, ed. E. Caspar, *MGH, Epistolae selectae*, II (Berlin, 1920–3).

Gullotta, G., 'Un antico ed unico documento sul monastero di S. Maria e S. Nicola in "Aqua Salvia"', *ASRSP*, LXVI (1943), pp. 185–95.

Herimanni Augiensis chronicon, ed. G. H. Pertz, *MGH, SS*, V (Hannover, 1844), pp. 67–133.

Hildebertus Cenomannensis episcopus, *Carmina minora*, ed. A. B. Scott (Leipzig, 1967).

Hincmar, *De ordine palatii*, ed. T. Gross and R. Schieffer, *MGH* (Hannover, 1980).

Historia abbatiae Cassinensis per saeculorum seriem distributa, ed. E. Gattula, I (Venice, 1733).

Historia Compostellana, ed. E. Falque Rey (Turnhout, 1988).

Historia custodum Aretinorum, ed. A. Hofmeister, *MGH, SS*, XXX.2 (Leipzig, 1934), pp. 1468–82.

I diplomi di Berengario I, ed. L. Schiaparelli (Rome, 1903).

I documenti di S. Andrea 'de Aquariciariis', 1115–1483, ed. I. Lori Sanfilippo, Codice diplomatico di Roma e della regione romana, 2 (Rome, 1981).

I papiri diplomatici, ed. G. Marini (Rome, 1805).

I placiti del 'Regnum Italiae', ed. C. Manaresi, 3 vols (Rome, 1955–60).

Ibn Hauqal, *Configuration de la terre*, 2 vols, trans. J.H. Kramers and G. Wiet (Beirut-Paris, 1964).

Il 'Liber Floriger' di Gregorio di Catino, ed. M. T. Maggi Bei, I (Rome, 1984).

Il Chronicon Farfense di Gregorio di Catino, ed. U. Balzani, 2 vols (Rome, 1903) [*CF*].

Il regesto del Codice Pelavicino, ed. M. Lupo Gentile = *Atti della società ligure di storia patria*, XLIV (1912).

Il regesto del monastero dei SS. Andrea e Gregorio ad Clivum Scauri, ed. A. Bartola, 2 vols, Codice diplomatico di Roma e della regione romana, 7 (Rome, 2003).

Il Regesto di Farfa, ed. I. Giorgi and U. Balzani, 5 vols (Rome, 1879–1914).

Il Regesto Sublacense del secolo XI, ed. L. Allodi and G. Levi (Rome, 1885).

Innocentii III regesta sive epistolae, ed. in *PL*, CCIV–CCVI; partial re-ed. in *Die Register Innocenz' III.*, ed. O. Hageneder et al., 10 vols continuing (Graz, 1964; Vienna, 1979–). [Where the numbering in each edition is different, I cite Hageneder's and add *PL*'s in brackets.]

Inscriptiones Christianae urbis Romae septimo saeculo antiquiores, ed. G. B. De Rossi, 2 vols (Rome, 1857–88).

Invectiva in Romam pro Formoso papa, ed. in E. Dümmler, *Gesta Berengarii imperatoris* (Halle, 1871), pp. 137–54.

Inventari altomedievali di terre, coloni e redditi, ed. A. Castagnetti et al. (Roma, 1979); XII, Vescovato di Tivoli, pp. 249–75, is ed. A. Vasina.

Iscrizioni delle chiese e d'altri edifici di Roma dal secolo XI fino ai giorni nostri, ed. V. Forcella, 14 vols (Rome, 1869–84).

Italia sacra, ed. F. Ughelli, I, 2nd edn (Rome, 1717).

Iuliani Epitome latina Novellarum Iustiniani, ed. G. Hänel (Leipzig, 1873).

Jaffé, P. and Wattenbach, W., *Regesta pontificum romanorum*, I, II (Leipzig, 1885–8).

John VIII, *Epistolae passim collectae* and *Registrum*, ed. E. Caspar and G. Laehr, *MGH, Epistolae*, VII (Berlin, 1928), pp. 313–29 and 1–272.

John of Salisbury, *Historia pontificalis*, ed. M. Chibnall (Edinburgh, 1956).

John of Salisbury, *Policraticus*, ed. C. C. I. Webb, 2 vols (Oxford, 1909).

John of Salisbury, *The Letters of John of Salisbury*, II, ed. W. J. Millor and C. N. L. Brooke (Oxford, 1979).

Justinian, *Codex Iustinianus, Digesta, Institutiones, Novellae*: all in *Corpus iuris civilis*, ed. T. Mommsen et al., 3 vols (Berlin, 1928–9).

Kehr, P., 'Diploma purpureo di re Roggero II per la casa Pierleoni', *ASRSP*, XXIV (1901), pp. 253–9.

La légende syriaque de saint Alexis, l'homme de Dieu, ed. A. Amiaud (Paris, 1889).

Landolfo Seniore, *Historia Mediolanensis*, ed. L. C. Bethmann and W. Wattenbach, *MGH, SS*, VIII (Hannover, 1848), pp. 32–100.

Landulphi Iunioris Historia Mediolanensis, ed. C. Castiglioni, *Rerum Italicarum scriptores*, V.2 (Bologna, 1934).

Lauer, P., 'Un inventaire inédit des revenus fonciers de la basilique du Latran au XIIe siècle', *Mélanges d'archéologie et d'histoire*, XLII (1925), pp. 117–24.

Le carte del decimo secolo nell'Archivio arcivescovile di Ravenna, ed. R. Benericetti, 3 vols (Ravenna-Faenza, 1999–2002).

Le carte ravennati dei secoli ottavo e nono, ed. R. Benericetti (Faenza, 2006).

Le carte ravennati del secolo undicesimo. Archivio arcivescovile, ed. R. Benericetti, 4 vols (Faenza, 2003–7).

Le Liber Censuum de l'église romaine, ed. P. Fabre and L. Duchesne, 3 vols (Paris, 1905–10).

Le Liber Pontificalis, ed. L. Duchesne, 2 vols (Paris, 1955).

Le più antiche carte del convento di San Sisto in Roma (905–1300), ed. C. Carbonetti Vendittelli, Codice diplomatico di Roma e della regione romana, 4 (Rome, 1987).

Libellus de imperatoria potestate in urbe Roma, ed. G. Zucchetti in *Il Chronicon di Benedetto monacho di S. Andrea del Soratte e il Libellus de imperatoria potestate in urbe Roma* (Rome, 1920), pp. 191–210.

Liber Guidonis compositus de variis historiis, ed. M. Campopiano (Florence, 2008).

Liber instrumentorum seu chronicorum monasterii Casauriensis, Bibliothèque nationale, Codex Parisinus Latinus 5411, published in facsimile by the Amministrazione provinciale dell'Aquila (L'Aquila, 1982).

Liber largitorius vel notarius monasterii Pharphensis, ed. G. Zucchetti, 2 vols (Rome, 1913–32).

Liber pontificalis nella recensione di Pietro Guglielmo OSB e del card. Pandolfo, ed. U. Přerovský, 3 vols, Studia gratiana, 21–23 (Rome, 1978).

Liber pontificalis prout exstat in codice manuscripto Dertusensi, ed. J.-M. March, (Barcelona 1925).

Liutprando of Cremona, *Antapodosis, Historia Ottonis* and *Relatio de legatione Constantinopolitana*, in *Liudprandi opera*, ed. J. Becker, *MGH, SRG* (Hannover, 1915), pp. 1–158, 159–75, 175–212.

Livy, *Ab urbe condita*, ed. M. Müller and W. Weissenborn, 4 vols (Leipzig, 1930–3).

Loevinson, E., 'Documenti del monastero di S. Cecilia in Trastevere', *ASRSP*, XLIX (1926), pp. 355–404.

Loewenfeld, S., 'Documenta quaedam historiam monasterii S. Anastasii ad Aquas salvias illustrantia', *ASRSP*, IV (1881), pp. 399–404.

Loewenfeld, S., 'Acht Briefe aus der Zeit König Berengars', *Neues Archiv*, IX (1884), pp. 515–39.

Lori Sanfilippo, I., 'Le più antiche carte del monastero di S. Agnese sulla Via Nomentana', *Bullettino dell' 'Archivio palaeografico italiano'*, NS, II–III (1956–7), II, pp. 65–97.

Ludovici II. Diplomata, ed. K. Wanner, *MGH, Diplomata Karolinorum*, IV (Munich, 1994).

Maragone, Bernardo, *Annales Pisani*, ed. M. Lupo Gentile, *Rerum italicarum scriptores*, 2nd edn, VI.2 (Bologna, 1930–6).

Martyrium S. Clementis, in F. X. Funk (ed.), *Opera patrum apostolicorum*, II (Tübingen, 1881), pp. 28–45.

MGH, Constitutiones et acta publica imperatorum et regum, I, ed. L. Weiland (Hannover, 1893).

MGH, Leges, IV, ed. F. Bluhme (Hannover, 1868).

MGH, Libelli de lite imperatorum et pontificum, II (Hannover, 1892).

MGH, Poetae latini aevi Carolini, III, IV, V, eds L. Traube, P. De Winterfeld. K. Strecker (Berlin, 1896–Leipzig, 1937).

Mirabilia, ed. Valentini and Zucchetti, *Codice topografico*, III, pp. 3–65.

Miracula [de S. Alexio confessore], in *AASS Jul.* IV, cols 258–61, accessed through http://acta.chadwyck.co.uk/.

Monaci, A., 'Regesto dell'abbazia di Sant'Alessio all'Aventino', *ASRSP*, XXVII (1904), pp. 351–98, and continuing.

Monumenta epigraphica christiana saeculo XIII antiquiora quae in Italiae finibus adhuc extant, I, ed. A. Silvagni (Rome, 1943).

Müller, E., 'Der Bericht des Abtes Hariulf von Oudenburg über seine Prozessverhandlungen an der römischen Kurie im Jahre 1141', *Neues Archiv*, XLVIII (1929), pp. 97–115.

Necrologi e libri affini della provincia romana, I, ed. P. Egidi (Rome, 1908).

Odo of Cluny, *Vita sancti Geraldi Auriliacensis*, ed. A.-M. Bultot-Verleysen (Brussels, 2009).

Ordines coronationis imperialis, ed. R. Elze, *MGH, Fontes iuris germanici antiqui*, IX (Hannover, 1960).

Otto of Freising, *Chronica*, ed. A. Hofmeister, *MGH, SRG*, XLV (Hannover, 1912).

Otto of Freising and Rahewin, *Gesta Friderici I. imperatoris*, ed. G. Waitz and B. De Simson, *MGH, SRG*, XLVI (Hannover, 1912).

Ottonis I diplomata, ed. T. Sickel, *MGH, Diplomatum regum et imperatorum Germaniae*, I (Hannover, 1884).

Ottonis III diplomata, ed. T. Sickel, *MGH, Diplomatum regum et imperatorum Germaniae*, II.2 (Hannover, 1893).

Papsturkunden 896–1046, ed. H. Zimmermann, 2 vols (Vienna, 1988–9).

Papsturkunden in Italien, ed. P. F. Kehr, 6 vols (Rome, 1977).

Pasqui, U., *Documenti per la storia della città di Arezzo nel medio evo*, 3 vols (Florence, 1899–1937).

Patrologiae cursus completus, series latina, ed. J.-P. Migne, 220 vols (Paris, 1844–55) [*PL*].

Paul of Bernried, *Vita Gregorii VII papae*, in *Pontificum Romanorum . . . vitae ab aequalibus conscriptae*, ed. J. B. M. Watterich, 2 vols (Leipzig, 1862), I, pp. 474–545.

Piattoli, R., 'Miscellanea diplomatica (III)', *BISIME*, LVII (1941), pp. 151–204.

Pier Damiani, *Epistulae*, in *Die Briefe des Petrus Damiani*, ed. K. Reindel, *MGH, Briefe der deutschen Kaiserzeit*, IV, 4 vols (Munich, 1983–93).

Pier Damiani, *Vita beati Romualdi*, ed. G. Tabacco (Rome, 1957).

Pontificorum Romanorum vitae, ed. I. M. Watterich, II (Leipzig, 1862).

Regesta Honorii papae III, I, ed. P. Pressutti (Rome, 1880), pp. li–cxxiv.

Regesti dei documenti dell'Italia meridionale, 570–899, ed. J.-M. Martin et al. (Rome, 2002).

Regesto degli Orsini e dei conti Anguillara, I, ed. C. de Cupis (Sulmona, 1903).

Regesto del capitolo di Lucca, ed. P. Guidi and O. Parenti, 4 vols (Rome, 1910–39).

Regestum Pisanum, ed. N. Caturegli (Rome, 1938).

Regesto della chiesa di Tivoli, ed. L. Bruzza (Rome, 1880).

Romualdo of Salerno, *Chronicon*, ed. C. A. Garufi, *Rerum italicarum scriptores*, 2nd edn, VII.1 (Bologna, 1919).

S. Bonifatii et Lulli epistolae, ed. M. Tangl, *MGH, Epistolae selectae*, I (Berlin, 1916).

Schiaparelli, L., 'Le carte antiche dell'Archivio Capitolare di S. Pietro in Vaticano', *ASRSP*, XXIV (1901), pp. 393–496, XXV (1902), pp. 273–354, and continuing.

Scriptorum veterum nova collectio et Vaticanis codicibus edita, V, ed. A. Mai (Rome, 1831).

Settele, G., 'Illustrazione di un'antica iscrizione esistente nella chiesa di S. Silvestro in Capite', *Dissertazioni dell'Accademia romana d'archeologia*, III (Rome, 1829), pp. 231–66.

Sigebert of Gembloux, *Chronica*, ed. L. C. Bethmann, in *MGH, SS*, VI (Hannover, 1844), pp. 300–74.

Statuti della città di Roma, ed. C. Re (Rome, 1880).

Statuti della provincia romana, ed. V. Federici et al. (Rome, 1930).

Statuti inediti della città di Pisa, I, ed. F. Bonaini (Florence, 1854).

Stevenson, E., 'Documenti dell'archivio della cattedrale di Velletri', *ASRSP*, XII (1889), pp. 63–113.

Summa Perusina, ed. in F. Patetta, *Adnotationes codicum domini Iustiniani (Summa Perusina)* (Roma, 1900) = *Bullettino dell'Istituto di diritto romano*, XII (1899).

Thangmar, *Vita Bernwardi*, ed. G. H. Pertz, *MGH, SS*, IV (Hannover, 1841), pp. 754–82.

Thietmar of Merseburg, *Chronicon*, ed. R. Holzmann, *MGH, SRG*, N.S. IX (Berlin, 1935).

To eparchikon biblion, the book of the eparch, le livre du préfet (London, 1970).

Tractatus Garsiae, ed. R. M. Thomson (Leiden, 1973).

Trifone, B., 'Le carte del monastero di S. Paolo di Roma dal secolo XI al XV', *ASRSP*, XXXI (1908), pp. 267–313, and continuing.

Udalrici Babenbergensis codex, ed. P. Jaffé, *Bibliotheca rerum germanicarum*, V, *Monumenta Bambergensia* (Berlin, 1869), pp. 1–469.

Ugo of Farfa, *Destructio monasterii farfensis*, in *CF*, I, pp. 27–50.

Ugo of Farfa, *Exceptio brevis relationum*, in *CF*, I, pp. 61–70.

Uodascalcus, *De Eginone et Herimanno*, ed. P. Jaffé, *MGH, SS*, XII (Hannover, 1856), pp. 429–47.

Valentini, R. and Zucchetti, G., *Codice topografico della città di Roma*, 4 vols (Rome, 1940–53).

'Vie et miracles du pape S. Léon IX', ed. A. Poncelet, *Analecta Bollandiana*, XXV (1906), pp. 258–97.

Vita Gregorii IX, in *Le Liber Censuum*, II, pp. 18–36.

Vita prima sancti Bernardi Claraevallis abbatis, ed. P. Verdeyen (Turnhout, 2011).

Volpini, R., 'Per l'archivio pontificio tra XII e XIII secolo: i resti dell'archivio dei papi ad Anagni', *Rivista di storia della chiesa in Italia*, XXXVII (1983), pp. 366–405.

Wibald of Stablo, *Epistolae*, ed. P. Jaffé, *Bibliotheca rerum germanicarum*, I, *Monumenta Corbeiensia* (Berlin, 1864), pp. 76–622.

Widone of Ferrara, *De scismate Hildebrandi*, ed. R. Wilmans and E. Dümmler, *MGH, Libelli de lite*, I (Hannover, 1891), pp. 529–67.

Wipo, *Gesta Chuonradi imperatoris*, in *Wiponis Opera*, ed. H. Bresslau, *MGH, SRG*, LXI (Hannover, 1915), pp. 1–62.

B. SECONDARY LITERATURE

Abulafia, D., *The Two Italies* (Cambridge, 1977).

Accame Lanzilotta, M., *Contributi sui Mirabilia urbis Romae* (Genoa, 1996).

Adams, I. C. M., 'A History of the Roman Monastery of S. Paolo fuori le mura in the Later Middle Ages', PhD thesis, University of St Andrews, 1973.

Ait, I., 'Per un profilo dell'aristocrazia romana nel XI secolo', *Studi storici*, XXXVIII (1997), pp. 323–38.

Alba Calzado, M., 'Apuntes sobre el urbanismo y la vivienda de la ciudad islámica de Mérida', in *Excavaciones arqueológicas en Mérida 2001. Memoria 7* (Mérida, 2004), pp. 417–38.

Alba Calzado, M., 'Diacronía de la vivienda señorial de *Emerita* (Lusitania, *Hispania*)', in G. P. Brogiolo and A. Chavarría Arnau (eds), *Archeologia e società tra tardo antico e alto medioevo* (Mantua, 2007), pp. 163–92.

Alföldi, M. R. et al., *Die römische Wölfin* (Stuttgart, 2011).

Alibrandi, I., 'Osservazioni giuridiche sopra un ricorso de' monaci di Grottaferrata al pontefice Innocenzo II', *Studi e documenti di storia e diritto*, VIII (1887), pp. 201–12.

Allegrezza, F., *Organizzazione di potere e dinamiche familiari* (Rome, 1998).

Allegrezza, F., 'I legami di parentela e la loro percezione presso l'aristocrazia romana (secoli XI-XV)', in *La nobiltà romana nel medioevo*, pp. 187–97.

Althoff, G., *Otto III*, Eng. trans. (State College, PA, 2003).

Andaloro, M. and Romano, S. (eds), *Arte e iconografia a Roma* (Milan, 2002).

Andaloro, M. and Romano, S., 'L'immagine nell'abside', in eaedem, *Arte e iconografia a Roma*, pp. 73–102.

Andenna, G., 'Dall'Orto, Oberto', *DBI*, XXXII (Rome, 1986), pp. 145–50.

Andrieu, M., *Les ordines romani du haut moyen âge*, 5 vols (Louvain, 1931–61).

Annis, M. B., 'Ceramica altomedievale a vetrina pesante e ceramica medievale a vetrina sparsa provenienti dallo scavo di San Sisto Vecchio in Roma', in Paroli, *La ceramica invetriata*, pp. 394–417.

Antonetti, S. and Rea, R., 'Inquadramento cronologico delle tracce di riuso', in Rea, *Rota Colisei*, pp. 283–333.

Apollonj Ghetti, B. M. et al., *Esplorazioni sotto la confessione di San Pietro in Vaticano*, I (Rome, 1951), pp. 225–44 (C. Serafini).

Arnaldi, G., 'Papa Formoso e gli imperatori della casa di Spoleto', *Annali della facoltà di lettere e filosofia*, I (1951), pp. 85–104.

Arnaldi, G., 'Alberico di Roma', *DBI*, I (Rome, 1960), pp. 646–56.

Arnaldi, G., 'Rinascita, fine, reincarnazione e successive metamorfosi del senato romano (secoli V-XII)', *ASRSP*, CV (1982), pp. 5–56.

Arnaldi, G., *Natale 875*, I (Rome, 1990).

Arnold, D., *Johannes VIII.* (Frankfurt, 2005).

Augenti, A., *Il Palatino nel medioevo* (Rome, 1996).

Augenti, A., 'Roma tra la tarda Antichità e l'alto Medioevo', *Reti medievali rivista*, XI.2 (2010), DOI: 10.6092/1593-2214/51.

Baldassarri, M. et al., 'Analisi archeologiche ed archeometriche su ceramiche invetriate da fuoco rinvenute a Pisa', *Atti, XXXIX convegno internazionale della ceramica* (Albisola, 2006), pp. 177–90.

Baldovin, J. F., *The urban character of Christian worship* (Rome, 1987).

Barbanera, M. and Pergola, S., 'Elementi architettonici antichi e post-antichi riutilizzati nella c.d. Casa dei Crescenzi', *Bullettino della Commissione archeologica comunale di Roma*, XCVIII (1997), pp. 301–28.

Barbini, P. M., 'Ceramica invetriata dallo scavo della catacomba di S. Senatore ad Albano', in de Minicis, *Le ceramiche di Roma*, II, pp. 66–71.

Barceló, M. and Toubert, P., *'L'incastellamento'* (Rome, 1998).

Barclay Lloyd, J., 'A new look at the mosaics of S. Clemente', in A. Duggan et al. (eds), *Omnia disce* (Aldershot, 2005), pp. 9–27.

Barclay Lloyd, J., 'Masonry techniques in medieval Rome, c.1080-c.1300', *Papers of the British School at Rome*, LIII (1985), pp. 225–77.

Barclay Lloyd, J., 'The building history of the medieval church of S. Clemente in Rome', *Journal of the Society of Architectural Historians*, XLV (1986), pp. 197–223.

Barclay Lloyd, J., *The Medieval Church and Canonry of S. Clemente in Rome* (Rome, 1989).

Barclay Lloyd, J. and Bull-Simonsen Einaudi, K., *SS. Cosma e Damiano in Mica Aurea* (Rome, 1998).

Barelli, L., 'Ecclesiam reparare', *Palladio*, XXXVIII (2006), pp. 5–28.

Barelli, L., *Il complesso monumentale dei SS. Quattro Coronati a Roma* (Rome, 2009).

Barrow, J., 'Ideas and applications of reform', in T. F. X. Noble and J. M. H. Smith (eds), *The Cambridge History of Christianity*, III (Cambridge, 2008), pp. 345–62.

Bartoloni, F., 'Per la storia del Senato Romano nei secoli XII e XIII', *BISIME*, LX (1946), pp. 1–108.

Bartoloni, G. (ed.), *La lupa capitolina. Nuove prospettive di studio* (Rome, 2010).

Bartoloni, V. and Ricci, M., 'Produzioni ceramiche da un contesto dei secolo XI–XII a Tarquinia', in de Minicis, *Le ceramiche di Roma*, II, pp. 100–6.

Baumgärtner, I., 'Rombeherrschung und Romerneuerung', *QFIAB*, LXIX (1989), pp. 27–79.

Becker, A., *Papst Urban II (1088–99)* (Stuttgart, 1964).

Bedini, E., 'I reperti faunistici', in Rea, *Rota Colisei*, pp. 405–35.

Bedini, E., 'I resti faunistici', in Saguì and Paroli, *Archeologia urbana*, pp. 623–38.

Belli Barsali, I., 'La topografia di Lucca nei secoli VIII-XI', in *Atti del V Congresso internazionale di studi sull'alto medioevo* (Spoleto, 1973), pp. 461–554.

Bellomo, M., *Ricerche sui rapporti patrimoniali tra coniugi* (Milano, 1961).

Beneš, C. E., 'Whose SPQR?', *Speculum*, LXXXIV (2009), pp. 874–904.

Benson, R. L., 'Political *renovatio*', in R. Benson et al. (eds) *Renaissance and Renewal in the Twelfth Century* (Cambridge, MA, 1982), pp. 339–86.

Beolchini, V., *Tusculum II* (Rome, 2006).

Berardozzi, A., *I Prefetti* (Rome, 2013).

Berger, A., 'Imperial and ecclesiastical processions in Constantinople', in N. Necipoğlu (ed.), *Byzantine Constantinople: Monuments, Topography and Everyday Life* (Leiden, 2001), pp. 73–87.

Bertelli, C., 'La pittura medievale a Roma e nel Lazio', in idem (ed.), *La pittura in Italia. L'Altomedioevo* (Milan, 1994), pp. 206–42.

Bertolini, M.G., 'Istituzioni, miracoli, e promozione del culto dei santi: il caso di Clemente III antipapa (1080–1100)', in S. Boesch Gajano and L. Sebastiani (eds), *Culto dei santi, istituzioni e classi sociali in età preindustriale* (L'Aquila, 1984), pp. 71–104.

Bertolini, O., 'Per la storia delle diaconie romane nell'alto medioevo sino alla fine del secolo VIII' in idem, *Scritti scelti*, I, pp. 311–460.

Bertolini, O., *Scritti scelti di storia medioevale*, 2 vols (Livorno, 1968).

Besta, E., 'Il diritto romano nella contesa tra i vescovi di Siena e d'Arezzo', *Archivio storico italiano*, 5 ser., XXXVII (1906), pp. 61–92.

Bianchi, L., *Case e torri medioevali a Roma*, I (Rome, 1998).

Bisson, T. N., *The Crisis of the Twelfth Century* (Princeton, 2009).

Bloch, H., 'Der Autor der "Graphia aureae urbis Romae"', *Deutsches Archiv*, XL (1984), pp. 55–175.

Bloch, H., *Monte Cassino in the Middle Ages*, 3 vols (Rome, 1986).

Blunt, C. E., 'Anglo-Saxon coins found in Italy', in M. A. S. Blackburn (ed.), *Anglo-Saxon Monetary History* (Leicester, 1986), pp. 159–69.

Boiteux, M., 'Cornomania e carnevale a Roma nel medioevo', *La ricerca folklorica*, VI (1982), pp. 57–64.

Bolton, B., '*Nova familia beati Petri*', in eadem and Duggan, A. J. (eds), *Adrian IV. The English pope (1154–1159)* (Aldershot, 2003), pp. 157–78.

Bonaccorsi, I., 'Marino I', *DBI*, LXX (2008), pp. 499–502.

Bordone, R., *La società cittadina del regno d'Italia* (Turin, 1987).

Borgia, A., *Istoria della chiesa, e città di Velletri* (Nocera, 1723).

Borgia, S., *De cruce veliterna commentarius* (Rome, 1780).

Borino, G., 'L'elezione e la deposizione di Gregorio VI', *ASRSP*, XXXIX (1916), pp. 141–252, 295–410.

Borino, G. B., 'Cencio del prefetto Stefano', in idem (ed.), *Studi gregoriani*, IV (Rome, 1952), pp. 373–440.

Bossi, G., 'I Crescenzi', *Dissertazioni della Pontificia accademia romana di archeologia*, 2 ser., XII (1915), pp. 49–126.

Bossi, G., 'I Crescenzi di Sabina Stefaniani ed Ottaviani (dal 1012 al 1106)', *ASRSP*, XLI (1918), pp. 111–70.

Bougard, F., 'Entre Gandolfingi et Obertenghi', *MEFRM*, CI (1989), pp. 11–66.

Bougard, F., *La justice dans le royaume d'Italie de la fin du VIIIe siècle au début du XIe siècle* (Rome, 1995).

Bougard, F., 'Composition, diffusion et réception des parties tardives du *Liber pontificalis* romain (VIIIe–IXe siècles)', in idem and M. Sot (eds), *Liber, gesta, histoire* (Turnhout, 2009), pp. 127–52.

Bougard, F. et al., 'Du village perché au *castrum*', in G. Noyé (ed.), *Structures de l'habitat et occupation du sol dans les pays méditerrannéens* (Rome, 1988), pp. 433–65.

Bougard, F. et al. (eds), *Théorie et pratiques des élites au Haut Moyen Âge* (Turnhout, 2011).

Bratchell, M., *Medieval Lucca and the Evolution of the Renaissance State* (Oxford, 2008).

Brenk, B., 'Die Benediktszenen in S. Crisogono und Montecassino', *Arte medievale*, II (1984), pp. 57–65.

Brenk, B., 'Roma e Montecassino', *Revue d'art canadienne/Canadian art review*, XII (1985), pp. 227–34.

Brentano, R., *Rome before Avignon* (London, 1974).

Bresslau, H., *Handbuch der Urkundenlehre für Deutschland und Italien*, I, 2nd edn (Leipzig, 1912).

Brezzi, P., *Roma e l'impero medioevale (774–1252)* (Bologna, 1947).

Brogiolo, G. P., and Gelichi, S., 'Ceramiche, tecnologia ed organizzazione della produzione dell'Italia settentrionale tra VI e X secolo', *La céramique médiévale en Méditerranée* (Aix-en-Provence, 1997), pp. 139–45.

Brubaker, L., 'Memories of Helena', in L. James (ed.), *Women, Men and Eunuchs* (London, 1997), pp. 52–75.

Brubaker, L., 'Topography and the creation of public space in early medieval Constantinople', in M. de Jong et al. (eds), *Topographies of Power in the Early Middle Ages* (Leiden, 2001), pp. 31–43.

Brubaker, L., 'Processions and public spaces in early and middle Byzantine Constantinople', in press.

Brühl, C. R., 'Die Kaiserpfalz bei St. Peter und die Pfalz Ottos III. auf dem Palatin' [1954], in idem, *Aus Mittelalter und Diplomatik*, 2 vols (Munich, 1989), I, pp. 3–31.

Buc, P., *The Dangers of Ritual* (Princeton, 2001).

Buckland, W. W., *A Text-book of Roman Law*, 3rd edn (Cambridge, 1963).

Caggese, R., *Classi e comuni rurali nel medio evo italiano*, 2 vols (Florence, 1907–8).

Calisse, C., 'I Prefetti di Vico', *ASRSP*, X (1887), pp. 1–136, 353–594.

Cameron, A., 'The construction of court ritual', in D. Cannadine and S. Price (eds), *Rituals of Royalty* (Cambridge, 1987), pp. 106–36.

Camilli, A. and Vitali Rosati, B., 'La ceramica a vetrina pesante da ricognizione di superficie nel territorio capenate', in de Minicis, *Le ceramiche di Roma*, I, pp. 48–51.

Cammarosano, P., *Italia medievale* (Rome, 1991).

Cammarosano, P., *Nobili e re* (Bari, 1998).

Camobreco, F., 'Il monastero di S. Erasmo sul Celio', *ASRSP*, XVIII (1905), pp. 265–300.

Campese Simone, A., 'Fra l'*Ara Coeli* e Piazza Bocca della Verità', *AM*, XXXI (2004), pp. 441–55.

Cantarella, G., *Pasquale II e il suo tempo* (Naples, 1997).

Cantini, F., 'Ritmi e forme della grande espansione economica dei secoli XI-XIII nei contesti ceramici della Toscana settentrionale', *AM*, XXXVII (2010), pp. 113–27.

Cantini, F., 'Dall'economia complessa al complesso di economie (Tuscia V-X secolo)', *Post-classical Archaeologies*, I (2011) pp. 159–94.

Carbonetti, C., 'Tabellioni e scriniari a Roma tra IX e XI secolo', *ASRSP*, CII (1979), pp. 77–156.

Carbonetti Vendittelli, C., 'Precisazioni sui primi documenti riguardanti il castello di Vaccareccia nel territorio Collinense', *ASRSP*, CV (1982), pp. 145–55.

Carbonetti Vendittelli, C., 'La curia dei *priores et consiliarii campi salini* a Roma agli inizi del Duecento', in A. Mazzon (ed.), *Scritti per Isa* (Rome, 2008), pp. 115–41.

Carbonetti Vendittelli, C., 'Scrivere e riscrivere', in L. Pani (ed.), *In uno volumine* (Udine, 2009), pp. 35–52.

Carbonetti Vendittelli, C., '"*Sicut inveni in thomo carticineo iam ex magna parte vetustate consumpto exemplavi et scripsi atque a tenebris ad lucem perduxi*"', in C. Braidotti at al. (eds), *Scritti in memoria di Roberto Pretagostini*, I (Rome, 2009), pp. 47–69.

Carbonetti Vendittelli, C., 'Il sistema documentario romano tra VII e XI secolo: prassi, forme, tipologie della documentazione privata', in J.-M. Martin et al. (eds), *L'héritage byzantin en Italie (VIIIe–XIIe siècle)*, I (Rome, 2011), pp. 87–115.

Carlin, M. L., *La pénétration du droit romain dans les actes de la pratique provençale (XIe–XIIIe siècle)* (Paris, 1967).

Carmassi, P., 'Die hochmittelalterlichen Fresken der Unterkirche von San Clemente in Rom als programmatische Selbstdarstellung des Reformspapsttums', *QFIAB*, LXXXI (2001), pp. 1–66.

Carocci, S., *Tivoli nel basso medioevo* (Rome, 1988).

Carocci, S., 'Una nobiltà bipartita', *BISIME*, XCV (1989), pp. 71–122.

Carocci, S., *Baroni di Roma* (Rome, 1993).

Carocci, S., *Il nepotismo nel medioevo* (Rome, 1999).

Carocci, S., 'Pontificia o comunale?', in A. Mazzon (ed.), *Scritti per Isa* (Roma, 2008) pp. 155–72.

Carocci, S., 'Baroni in città', in Hubert (ed.), *Roma nei secoli XIII e XIV*, pp. 139–73.

Carocci, S., 'La signoria rurale nel Lazio (secoli XII e XIII)', in Spicciani and Violante (eds), *La signoria rurale*, I, pp. 167–98.

Carocci, S., '"Metodo regressivo" e possessi collettivi', in D. Boisseuil et al. (eds), *Écritures de l'espace social* (Paris, 2010), pp. 541–55.

Carocci, S. and M. Vendittelli, 'Società ed economia (1050-1420)', in A. Vauchez (ed.), *Roma medievale* (Rome and Bari, 2001), pp. 71–116.

Carocci, S. and M. Vendittelli, *L'origine della Campagna Romana*, Miscellanea della Società romana di storia patria, XLVII (Rome, 2004).

Carriero, L., 'Napoli tra X e XII secolo', Tesi di perfezionamento, Scuola normale superiore, Pisa, a.a. 2010/2011.

Carruba, A. M., *La Lupa Capitolina* (Rome, 2006).

Casini, T., 'Signoria e società rurale nella Toscana nordorientale nei secoli XII–XIII', Dottorato di ricerca in Storia medievale, Università degli studi di Firenze, 2009.

Cassandro, G., 'Un bilancio storiografico', in G. Rossetti (ed.), *Forme di potere e struttura sociale in Italia nel Medioevo* (Bologna, 1977), pp. 153–73.

Castagnetti, A., *L'organizzazione del territorio rurale nel medioevo* (Turin, 1979).

Castagnetti, A. (ed.), *La vassallità maggiore del Regno Italico* (Rome, 2001).

Castagnoli, F., 'Il tempio di Roma nel medioevo', *ASRSP*, LXX (1947), pp. 163–9.

Cavazzi, L., *La diaconia di S. Maria in Via Lata e il Monastero di S. Ciriaco* (Rome, 1908).

Cecchelli, C., 'Roma medioevale', in F. Castagnoli et al., *Topografia e urbanistica di Roma* (Bologna, 1958), pp. 189–341.

Champagne, M. T. and Boustan, R. S., 'Walking in the shadows of the past', *Medieval Encounters*, XVII (2011), pp. 464–94.

Chavarría Arnau, A., 'Case solarate e *domus* incastellate', in eadem (ed.), *Padova: architetture medievali* (Mantua, 2011), pp. 21–33.

Chiodi, G., 'Roma e il diritto romano', *Settimane di studio* 49 (2002), pp. 1141–254.

Chodorow, S., *Christian Political Theory and Church Politics in the Mid-twelfth Century* (Berkeley, 1972).

Christie, N. (ed.), *Three South Etrurian Churches* (London, 1991).

Claridge, A., 'A date for the medieval settlement at the Vicus Augustanus Laurentium (Castelporziano)', in Paroli and Delogu, *La storia economica di Roma*, pp. 287–93.

Classen, P., *Studium und Gesellschaft im Mittelalter* (Stuttgart, 1983).

Claussen, P. C., *Magistri doctissimi Romani* (Stuttgart, 1987).

Claussen, P. C., 'Renovatio Romae', in B. Schimmelpfennig and L. Schmugge (eds), Rom in hohen Mittelalter (Sigmaringen, 1992), pp. 87–125.

Claussen, P. C., *Die Kirchen der Stadt Rom im Mittelalter, 1050–1300*, 3 vols continuing (Stuttgart, 2002–10).

Claussen, P. C., 'Marmo e splendore', in Andaloro and Romano, *Arte e iconografia a Roma*, pp. 151–74.

Coarelli, F., 'L'*urbs* e il suburbio', in A. Giardina (ed.), *Società romana e impero tardoantico*, II (Roma and Bari, 1986), pp. 1–58, 395–412.

Coates-Stephens, R., 'Housing in early medieval Rome, AD 500–1000', *Papers of the British School at Rome*, LXIV (1996), pp. 239–59.

Coates-Stephens, R., 'Dark age architecture in Rome', *Papers of the British School at Rome*, LXV (1997), pp. 177–232.

Coates-Stephens, R., 'The walls and aqueducts of Rome in the early middle ages, A.D. 500-1000', *Journal of Roman Studies*, LXXXVIII (1998), pp. 166–78.

Coates-Stephens, R., *Porta Maggiore. Monument and Landscape* (Rome, 2004).

Cohn, S. K., *Creating the Florentine State* (Cambridge, 1999).

Coleman, E., 'Representative assemblies in communal Italy', in P. S. Barnwell and M. Mostert (eds), *Political Assemblies in the Earlier Middle Ages* (Turnhout, 2003), pp. 193–210.

Collavini, S., *Honorabilis domus et spetiosissimus comitatus* (Pisa, 1998).

Collavini, S., 'Le basi materiali della contea dei conti Guidi tra prelievo signorile e obblighi militari (1150 c.-1230 c.)', *Società e storia*, CXV (2007), pp. 1–32.

Contatore, D. A., *De historia Terracinensi libri quinque* (Rome, 1706).

Conti, E., *La formazione della struttura agraria del contado fiorentino*, I (Rome, 1965).

Conte, E., 'Archeologia giuridica medievale', *Rechtsgeschichte*, IV (2004), pp. 118–36.

Conte, E., '*Res publica*', in V. Colli and E. Conte (eds), *Iuris historia* (Berkeley, 2008), pp. 193–212.

Conte, E., *Diritto comune* (Bologna, 2009).

Conte, E., 'Posesión y proceso en el siglo XII', in E. Conte, M. Madero (eds), *Procesos, inquisiciones, pruebas: Homenaje a Mario Sbriccoli* (Buenos Aires, 2009), pp. 97–121.

Conte, E., 'Il Digesto fuori dal Digesto', in D. Mantovani and A. Padoa Schioppa (eds), *Interpretare il Digesto. Storia e metodi* (Pavia, in press).

Corretti, A., *Metallurgia medievale all'isola d'Elba* (Florence, 1991).

Cortese, M. E., 'Castelli e città', in R. Francovich and M. Ginatempo (eds), *Castelli*, I, (Florence, 2000), pp. 205–37.

Cortese, M. E., *Signori, castelli, città* (Florence, 2007).

Cortese, M. E. and Francovich, R., 'La lavorazione del ferro in Toscana nel medioevo', *Ricerche storiche*, XXV (1995), pp. 435–57.

Cortonesi, A., *Terre e signori nel Lazio medioevale* (Naples, 1988).

Cortonesi, A., 'L'economia del casale romano', in M. Chiabò et al. (eds), *Alle origini della nuova Roma. Martino V (1417–1431)* (Rome, 1992), pp. 589–601.

Cortonesi, A., *Ruralia* (Rome, 1995).

Costambeys, M., *Power and Patronage in Early Medieval Italy* (Cambridge, 2007).

Coste, J., 'I casali della Campagna di Roma all'inizio del Seicento', *ASRSP*, XCII (1969), pp. 41–115.

Coste, J., 'I casali della Campagna di Roma nella seconda metà del Cinquecento', *ASRSP*, XCIV (1971), pp. 31–143.

Coste, J., *Scritti di topografia medievale* (Rome, 1996).

Coste, J., 'Il *castrum Sancti Honesti*', in Mari et al., *Il Lazio tra Antichità e Medioevo*, pp. 40–55.

Cowdrey, H. E. J., *Pope Gregory VII, 1073–1085* (Oxford, 1998).

Crescimbeni, G. M., *L'istoria della chiesa di S. Giovanni avanti Porta Latina, titolo cardinalizio* (Rome, 1716).

D'Acunto, N., 'Il prefetto Cencio di Giovanni Tignoso nelle fonti del suo secolo', *BISIME*, XCV (1989), pp. 1–44.

D'Onofrio, C., *Castel S. Angelo* (Rome, 1971).

Davidsohn, R., *Storia di Firenze*, 8 vols (Florence, 1956–78).

Davis, N. Z., 'The sacred and the body social in sixteenth-century Lyon', *Past and Present*, XC (1981), pp. 40–70.

Day, W. R., 'The population of Florence before the Black Death: survey and synthesis', *Journal of Medieval History*, XXVIII (2002), pp. 93–129.

Day, W. R., 'Antiquity, Rome and Florence; coinage transmissions across time and space', in C. Bolgia et al. (eds), *Rome across Time and Space* (Cambridge, 2011), pp. 237–61.

Day, W. R., *Florence before Dante: The Early Development of the Florentine Economy, c. 1115–1265* (Leiden, in press).

De Angelis, G., *Poteri cittadini e intellettuali di potere* (Milan, 2009).

de Blaauw, S., *Cultus et decor* (Rome, 1994).

De Francesco, D., 'S. Eufemia e il *lacus Turni* presso Albano dall'età tardoantica al basso medioevo', *MEFRM*, CIII (1991), pp. 83–108.

De Francesco, D., *La proprietà fondiaria nel Lazio* (Rome, 2004).

de Grossi Mazzorin, J., 'Il contributo dei reperti archeozoologici', in Spera, *Lo scavo . . . di San Paolo*, in press.

de Grossi Mazzorin, J. and Minniti, C., 'Lo studio dei resti animali', in N. Parmegiani and A. Pronti (eds), *S. Cecilia in Trastevere* (Rome, 2004), pp. 283–305.

de Luca, I., 'Ritrovamenti dei secoli IX-X dai Fori di Cesare e di Nerva', in R. Meneghini and R. Santangeli Valenzani (eds), *Roma. Lo scavo dei Fori Imperiali 1995–2000. I contesti ceramici* (Rome, 2006), pp. 93–108.

de Minicis, E. (ed.), *Le ceramiche di Roma e del Lazio in età medievale e moderna*, 6 vols (Rome, 1994–2009).

de Neeve, P. W., '*Fundus* as economic unit', *Tijdschrift voor Rechtsgeschiedenis*, LII (1984), pp. 3–19.

De Nuccio, M., 'La decorazione architettonica dei templi del Circo Flaminio', in S. F. Ramallo Asensio (ed.), *La decoración arquitectónica en las ciudades romanas de occidente* (Murcia, 2004), pp. 37–53.

De Simone, A. and Mandalà, G., *L'immagine araba di Roma* (Bologna, 2002).

Degrandi, A., 'Vassalli cittadini e vassalli rurali nel Vercellese del XII secolo', *Bollettino storico-bibliografico subalpino*, XCI (1993), pp. 5–45.

Del Lungo, S., *Roma in età carolingia e gli scritti dell'Anonimo augiense* (Rome, 2004).

Delfino, A., 'L'epigrafe di Pietro dalla Torre dei Conti', *Bullettino della Commissione archeologica comunale di Roma*, XCVIII (1997), pp. 301–28.

Delogu, P., 'Territorio e cultura fra Tivoli e Subiaco nell'alto medio evo', *Atti e memorie della società tiburtina di storia e d'arte*, LII (1979), pp. 25–54.

Delogu, P., 'The rebirth of Rome in the 8th and 9th centuries', in R. Hodges and B. Hobley (eds), *The Rebirth of Towns in the West AD 700–1050*, CBA research report, LXVII (London, 1988), pp. 32–42.

Delogu, P., 'La giustizia nell'Italia meridionale longobarda', *Settimane di studio*, XLIV (1997), pp. 257–312.

Delogu, P., 'L'importazione di tessuti preziosi e il sistema economico romano nel IX secolo', in idem (ed.), *Roma medievale. Aggiornamenti* (Florence, 1998), pp. 123–41.

Delogu, P., 'Rome in the ninth century: the economic system', in J. Henning (ed.), *Post-Roman Towns. Trade and Settlement in Europe and Byzantium*, I (Berlin, 2007), pp. 105–22.

Delogu, P. and Esposito, A. (eds), *Sulle orme di Jean Coste* (Rome, 2009).

Delogu, P. and Peduto, P. (eds), *Salerno nel XII secolo* (Salerno, 2004).

Delogu, P. and Travaini, L., 'Aspetti degli abitati medievali nella regione sublacense', *ASRSP*, CI (1978), pp. 17–34.

Delumeau, J.-P., *Arezzo. Espace et sociétés, 715–1230* (Rome, 1996).

Devroey, J.-P., *Économie rurale et société dans l'Europe franque (VIe–IXe siècles)* (Paris, 2003).

Di Branco, M., *Storie arabe di greci e di romani* (Pisa, 2009).

di Carpegna Falconieri, T., 'Le trasformazioni onomastiche e antroponimiche dei ceti dominanti a Roma nei secoli X–XII', *MEFRM*, CVI (1994), pp. 595–640.

di Carpegna Falconieri, T., 'Torri, complessi e consorterie', *Rivista storica del Lazio*, II (1994), pp. 3–15.

di Carpegna Falconieri, T., 'Sposarsi a Roma', *Ricerche storiche*, XXV (1995), pp. 3–33.

di Carpegna Falconieri, T., 'Gioco e liturgia nella Roma medievale', *Ludica*, III (1997), pp. 51–64.

di Carpegna Falconieri, T., 'Sistemi familiari a Roma in base ai cartari. Secoli X–XII', in E. Sonnino (ed.), *Popolazione e società a Roma dal medioevo all'età contemporanea* (Rome, 1998), pp. 199–219.

di Carpegna Falconieri, T., 'Storia medievale', *Studi romani*, XLVI (1998), pp. 145–58.

di Carpegna Falconieri, T., 'Il matrimonio e il concubinato presso il clero romano (secc. 8–12)', *Studi storici*, XLI (2000), pp. 943–71.

di Carpegna Falconieri, T., 'Giovanni di Crescenzio', *DBI*, LVI (2001), pp. 1–4.

di Carpegna Falconieri, T., *Cola di Rienzo* (Rome, 2002).

di Carpegna Falconieri, T., *Il clero di Roma nel medioevo* (Roma, 2002).

di Carpegna Falconieri, T., 'Marozia', *DBI*, LXX (2008), pp. 681–5.

di S. Quintino, G., 'Monete del X e dell'XI secolo scoperte nei dintorni di Roma nel 1843', *Atti e memorie della Reale Accademia di scienze di Torino, scienze morali storiche e filologiche*, 2 ser., IX–X (1849), pp. 1–116.

Di Santo, A., *Monumenti antichi, fortezze medievali* (Rome, 2010).

Dilcher, G., *Die Entstehung der lombardischen Stadtkommune* (Aalen, 1967).

Dilcher, G. and Violante, C. (eds), *Strutture e trasformazioni della signoria rurale nei secoli X–XIII* (Bologna, 1996).

Dolcini, C., 'Clemente III, antipapa', *DBI*, XXVI (Rome, 1982), pp. 181–8.

Doran, J., 'The legacy of schism', PhD thesis, Royal Holloway, University of London, 2008.

Doran, J., 'A lifetime of service in the Roman church', in Doran and Smith, *Pope Celestine III*, pp. 31–79.

Doran, J. and D. J. Smith (eds), *Pope Celestine III (1191–1198)* (Farnham, 2008).

Duby. G., *Hommes et structures du moyen âge* (Paris, 1973).

Duchesne, L., 'Notes sur la topographie de Rome au moyen-âge', *Mélanges d'archéologie et d'histoire*, X (1890), pp. 225–50.

Duggan, A. J., 'Hyacinth Bobone: diplomat and pope', in Doran and Smith, *Pope Celestine III*, pp. 1–30.

Duprè Theseider, E., *Roma dal comune di popolo alla signoria pontificia (1252–1377)* (Bologna, 1952).

Dyer, C., *Standards of Living in the Later Middle Ages* (Cambridge, 1989).

Dyer, J., 'Roman processions of the Major Litany (*litaniae maiores*) from the sixth to the twelfth century', in Ó Carragáin and Neuman de Vegvar, *Roma felix*, pp. 113–37.

Eckstein, N. A., *The District of the Green Dragon* (Florence, 1995).

Ehrle, F., 'Die Frangipani und der Untergang des Archivs und der Bibliothek der Päpste am Anfang des 13. Jahrhunderts', in *Mélanges offerts à M. Émile Chatelain* (Paris, 1910), pp. 448–85.

Ellis, M., 'Landscape and power', in J. Hill and M. Swan (eds), *The Community, Family and Saint* (Turnhout, 1998), pp. 61–76.

Elze, R., 'Die päpstliche Kapelle im 12. und 13. Jahrhundert', *Zeitschrift der Savigny-Stiftung für Rechtsgeschchte, kanonistische Abteilung*, XXXVI (1950), pp. 145–204.

Epstein, S. R., 'Cities, regions and the late medieval crisis', *Past and Present*, CXXX (1991), pp. 3–50.

Epstein, S. R., *Freedom and Growth* (London, 2000).

Erler, A., *Lupa, Lex und Reiterstandbild im mittelalterlichen Rom* (Wiesbaden, 1972).

Esch, A., *Lucca im 12. Jahrhundert*, Habilitationsschrift, Universität Göttingen, 1974.

Esch, A., 'Überlieferungs-Chance und Überlieferungs-Zufall als methodisches Problem des Historikers', *Historische Zeitschrift*, CCXL (1985), pp. 529–70.

Esposito, D., *Archittettura e costruzione dei casali della Campagna Romana fra XII e XIV secolo* (Rome, 2005).

Fabre, P., *Le polyptyque du chanoine Benoît* (Lille, 1889).

Faini, E., *Firenze nell'età romanica (1000–1211)* (Florence, 2010).

Falco, G., *La santa romana repubblica* (Milan, 1954).

Falco, G., *Studi sulla storia del Lazio nel medioevo*, Miscellanea della Società romana di storia patria, XXIV (Rome, 1988).

Fea, C., *Storia delle saline d'Ostia* (Rome, 1833).

Fedele, P., 'La battaglia del Garigliano dell'anno 915 ed i monumenti che la ricordano', *ASRSP*, XXII (1899), pp. 181–211.

Fedele, P., 'Una chiesa del Palatino', *ASRSP*, XXVI (1903), pp. 343–80.

Fedele, P., 'Le famiglie di Anacleto II e Gelasio II', *ASRSP*, XXVII (1904), pp. 399–440.

Fedele, P., 'Il leopardo e l'agnello di casa Frangipane', *ASRSP*, XXVIII (1905), pp. 207–17.

Fedele, P., 'Ricerche per la storia di Roma e del papato nel secolo X', *ASRSP*, XXXIII (1910), pp. 177–247, XXXIV (1911), pp. 75–115, 393–423.

Fedele, P., 'Sull'origine dei Frangipane', *ASRSP*, XXXIII (1910), pp. 493–506.

Fedele, P., 'Per la storia del Senato romano nel secolo XII', *ASRSP*, XXXIV (1911), pp. 351–62.

Fedele, P., 'L'êra del Senato', *ASRSP*, XXXV (1912), pp. 583–610.

Fedele, P., 'Il culto di Roma nel medio evo e la casa di Niccolò di Crescenzio', in *Il Centro di studi di storia dell'architettura* (Rome, 1940), pp. 17–26.

Federici, V., *I monasteri di Subiaco*, 2 vols (Rome, 1904).

Feniello, A., *Napoli. Società ed economia (902–1137)* (Rome, 2011).

Fennell Mazzaoui, M., *The Italian Cotton Industry in the Later Middle Ages, 1100–1600* (Cambridge, 1981).

Fentress. E. and Goodson, C., 'Villamagna (FR): l'eredità di una villa imperiale in epoca bizantina e medievale', *AM*, XXXIX (2012), pp. 57–86.

Fentress. E. and Goodson, C., 'Structures of power: from imperial villa to monastic estate at Villamagna (Italy)', in A. Reynolds (ed.), *Power and Place*, in press.

Ferri, G., 'La "Romana Fraternitas"', *ASRSP*, XXVI (1903), pp. 453–66.

Ficker, J., *Forschungen zur Reichs- und Rechtsgeschichte Italiens*, 4 vols (Innsbruck, 1868–74).

Filippini, C., 'The eleventh-century frescoes of Clement and other saints in the basilica of San Clemente in Rome', PhD thesis, The Johns Hopkins University, 1999.

Filippini, C., 'La leggenda di sant'Alessio nella chiesa di S. Clemente a Roma', in S. Romano and J. Enckell Julliard (eds), *Roma e la Riforma gregoriana* (Rome, 2007), pp. 289–303.

Fiorani Parenzi, M. A., *I Parenzi*, I (Rome, 1978).

Fiore Cavaliere, M. G., 'Le terme alessandrine nei secoli X e XI', *Rivista dell'Istituto nazionale d'archeologia e storia dell'arte*, ser. 3, I (1978), pp. 119–45.

Fletcher, R. A., *Saint James's Catapult* (Oxford, 1984).

Fliche, A., *La réforme grégorienne*, 3 vols (Louvain, 1924–37).

Fonseca, A., *De basilica S. Laurentii in Damaso libri tres* (Fano, 1745).

Formazione e strutture dei ceti dominanti nel Medioevo, ed. C. Violante and A. Spicciani, 3 vols (Rome, 1988–2003).

Fossier, R., *Enfance de l'Europe* (Paris, 1982).

Fowler-Magerl, L., *Ordo Iudiciorum vel ordo iudiciarius* (Frankfurt, 1984).

Franceschi, F. and Taddei, I., *Le città italiane nel Medioevo. XII–XIV secolo* (Bologna, 2012).

Francovich, R. and Valenti, M., 'La ceramica d'uso comune in Toscana tra V–X secolo', in *La céramique médiévale en Méditerranée* (Aix-en-Provence, 1997), pp. 129–37.

Fresi, E. and de Santis, C., 'Reperti ceramici', in Spera, *Lo scavo . . . di San Paolo*, in press.

Fried, J., 'Die römische Kurie und der Anfang der Prozessliteratur', *Zeitschrift der Savigny-Stiftung für Rechtsgeschichte, kanonistische Abteilung*, LIX (1973), pp. 151–74.

Frison, C., 'Frangipane. Aldruda', DBI, L (1998), pp. 221–2.

Frugoni, A., 'Sulla "Renovatio Senatus" del 1143 e l'"Ordo equestris"', *BISIME*, LXII (1950), pp. 159–74.

Frugoni, A., *Arnaldo da Brescia nelle fonti del secolo XII* (Rome, 1954).

Fugazza, E., *Diritto, istituzioni e giustizia in un comune dell'Italia padana* (Padua, 2009).

Fumagalli, V., *Coloni e signori nell'Italia settentrionale, secoli VI–XI* (Bologna, 1978).

Galletti, P. L., *Del vestarario della santa romana chiesa* (Rome, 1758).

Gandolfo, F., 'Il ritratto di committenza', in Andaloro and Romano, *Arte e iconografia a Roma*, pp. 139–49.

García Villoslada, R., 'El himno al papa Juan (IX?) de las Laudes Cornomanniae', *Miscelánea comillas*, XXXII (1974), pp. 185–205.

Gargiulo, M., 'La torre del Circo Massimo e alcune testimonianze sull'insediamento della famiglia Frangipane nel Palatino', *ASRSP*, CXXIV (2001), pp. 5–23.

Garzella, G., *Pisa com'era* (Naples, 1990).

Gennaro, C., 'Mercanti e bovattieri nella Roma della seconda metà del Trecento', *BISIME*, LXXVIII (1967), pp. 157–203.

Genuardi, L., 'Il papa Eugenio III e la cultura giuridica a Roma', *Mélanges Fitting* (Montpellier, 1908), II, pp. 387–90.

Gerstenberg, O., *Die politische Entwicklung des römischen Adels im 10. und 11. Jahrhundert* (Berlin, 1933).

Gerstenberg, O., 'Studien zur Geschichte des römischen Adels im Ausgang des 10. Jahrhunderts', *Historische Vierteljahrschrift*, XXXI (1937), pp. 1–26.

Gibson, S. and Ward-Perkins, B., 'The surviving remains of the Leonine wall', *Papers of the British School at Rome*, XLVII (1979), pp. 30–57, LI (1983), pp. 222–39.

Ginatempo, M. and Sandri, L., *L'Italia delle città* (Florence, 1990).

Goodson, C. J., *The Rome of Pope Paschal I* (Cambridge, 2010).

Görich, K., 'Die *de Imiza*', *QFIAB*, LXXIV (1994), pp. 1–41.

Görich, K., *Otto III.* (Sigmaringen, 1995).

Gramaccini, N., 'La prima riedificazione del Campidoglio e la rivoluzione senatoriale del 1144', in *Roma, centro ideale della cultura dell'Antico nei secoli XV e XVI*, ed. S. Danesi Squarzina (Milan, 1989), pp. 33–47.

Grassi, F., *La ceramica, l'alimentazione, l'artigianato e le vie di commercio tra VIII e XIV secolo*, BAR, I2125 (Oxford, 2010).

Gregorovius, F., *Geschichte der Stadt Rom im Mittelalter*, 4th edn, 8 vols (Stuttgart, 1886–96), trans. A. Hamilton, *History of the City of Rome in the Middle Ages*, 8 vols (London, 1894–1902).

Grillo, P., 'Aristocrazia urbana, aristocrazia rurale e origini del comune nell'Italia nord-occidentale', *Storica*, XIX (2001), pp. 75–96.

Grillo, P., *Milano in età comunale (1183–1276)* (Spoleto, 2001).

Grillo, P., 'Il comune di Vercelli nel secolo XII', in *Vercelli nel secolo XII* (Vercelli, 2005), pp. 161–88.

Grillo, P., 'La frattura inesistente', *Archivio storico italiano*, CLXVII (2009), pp. 673–700.

Guidi, I., 'La descrizione di Roma nei geografi arabi', *ASRSP*, I (1878), pp. 173–218.

Guidobaldi, F., *San Clemente* (Rome, 1992).

Güll, P., *L'industrie du quotidien* (Rome, 2003).

Haldon, J. F., *Byzantium in the Seventh Century*, 2nd edn (Cambridge, 1997).

Halphen, L., *Études sur l'administration de Rome au moyen âge* (Paris, 1907).

Hamilton, B., 'The monastic revival in tenth-century Rome', *Studia Monastica*, IV (1962), pp. 35–68.

Hamilton, B., 'The monastery of S. Alessio and the religious and intellectual Renaissance of tenth-century Rome', *Studies in Medieval and Renaissance History*, II (1965), pp. 265–310.

Hamilton, B., 'The house of Theophylact and the promotion of religious life among women in tenth-century Rome', *Studia monastica*, XII (1970), pp. 195–217.

Hamilton, L. I., 'Memory, symbol, and arson', *Speculum*, LXXVIII (2003), pp. 378–99.

Hamilton, L. I., 'The rituals of Renaissance', *Medieval Encounters*, XVII (2011), pp. 417–38.

Hartmann, L. M., *Urkunde einer römischen Gärtnergenossenschaft vom Jahre 1030* (Freiburg im Breisgau, 1892).

Hartmann, L. M., 'Grundherrschaft und Bureaukratie im Kirchenstaate vom 8. bis zum 10. Jahrhundert', *Vierteljahrschrift für Social- und Wirtschaftsgeschichte*, VII (1909), pp. 142–58.

Herklotz, I., 'Der Campus lateranensis im Mittelalter', *Römisches Jahrbuch für Kunstgeschichte*, XXII (1985), pp. 1–43.

Herklotz, I., 'Die Beratungsräume Calixtus II. im Lateranpalast und ihre Fresken', *Zeitschrift für Kunstgeschichte*, LII (1989), pp. 145–214.

Herklotz, I., *Gli eredi di Costantino* (Rome, 2000).

Herrmann, K. J., *Das Tuskulanerpapsttum (1012–1046)* (Stuttgart, 1973).

Herzfeld, M., *Evicted from Eternity* (Chicago, 2009).

Hirschfeld, T., 'Das Gerichtswesen der Stadt Rom vom 8. bis 12. Jahrhundert wesentlich nach stadtrömischen Urkunden', *Archiv für Urkundenforschung*, IV (1912), pp. 419–562.

Hirschfeld, T., 'Zur Chronologie der Stadtpraefekten in der Zeit der Erneuerung des Senates', *QFIAB*, XVI (1914), pp. 93–107.

Hocquet, J.-C., 'Le saline', in L. Cracco Ruggini et al. (eds), *Storia di Venezia*, I (Rome, 1992), pp. 515–48.

Hodges, R., et al., 'Excavations at Colle Castellano', in K. Bowes et al. (eds), *Between Text and Territory* (London, 2006), pp. 187–223.

Hoffmann, H., 'Petrus Diaconus, die Herren von Tusculum und der Sturz Oderisius' II. von Montecassino', *Deutsches Archiv*, XXVII (1971), pp. 1–109.

Houben, H., 'La componente romana nell'istituzione imperiale da Ottone I a Federico II', in *Roma antica nel medio evo* (Milan, 2001), pp. 27–47.

Hubert, É., 'Patrimoines immobiliers et habitat à Rome au moyen âge', *MEFRM*, CI (1989), pp. 133–75.

Hubert, É., *Espace urbain et habitat à Rome du Xe siècle à la fin du XIIIe siècle* (Rome, 1990).

Hubert, É. (ed.), *Roma nei secoli XIII e XIV, cinque saggi* (Rome, 1993).

Hubert, É., 'Évolution générale de l'anthroponymie masculine à Rome du Xe au XIIIe siècle', *MEFRM*, CVI (1994), pp. 573–94.

Hubert, É., 'Gestion immobilière, propriété dissociée et seigneuries foncières à Rome aux XIIIe et XIVe siècles', in O. Faron and É. Hubert (eds), *Le sol et l'immeuble* (Rome, 1995), pp. 185–205.

Hubert, É., 'L'*incastellamento* dans le Latium', *Annales. Histoire, sciences sociales*, LV (2000), pp. 583–99.

Hubert, É., 'L'organizzazione territoriale e l'urbanizzazione', in A. Vauchez (ed.), *Roma medievale* (Rome and Bari, 2001), pp. 159–86.

Hubert, É., 'Rome au XIVe siècle', *Médiévales*, XL (2001), pp. 43–52.

Hubert, É., *L'«incastellamento» en Italie centrale* (Rome, 2002).

Hubert, É., 'La construction de la ville', *Annales. Histoire, sciences sociales*, LIX (2004), pp. 109–39.

Hüls, R., *Kardinäle, Klerus und Kirchen Roms 1049–1130* (Tübingen, 1977).

Hülsen, C., 'I *saepta* e il *diribitorium*', *Bullettino della commissione archeologica comunale di Roma*, 1893, pp. 119–42.

Hülsen, C., *Le chiese di Roma nel medio evo* (Florence, 1927).

Insalaco, A., *La 'Città dell'Acqua', the archaeological area of the vicus Caprarius* (n.p., 2008).

Jones, P. J., 'Economia e società nell'Italia medievale: la leggenda della borghesia', in *Storia d'Italia, Annali*, I (Turin, 1978), pp. 187–372.

Jones, P. J., *The Italian city-state* (Oxford, 1997).

Jordan, K., 'Zur päpstlichen Finanzgeschichte im 11. und 12. Jahrhundert', *QFIAB*, XXV (1933–4), pp. 61–104.

Jordan, K., 'Die Entstehung der römischen Kurie', *Zeitschrift der Savigny-Stiftung für Rechtsgeschichte, kanonistische Abteilung*, XXVIII (1939), pp. 97–152.

Katermaa-Ottela, A., *Le casetorri medievali in Roma* (Helsinki, 1981).

Keary, C. F., 'A hoard of Anglo-Saxon coins found in Rome and described by sig. de Rossi', *The Numismatic Chronicle*, 3 ser., IV (1884), pp. 225–55.

Kehr, P. F., 'Scrinium und Palatium,' *Mittheilungen des Instituts für österreichische Geschichtsforschung, Ergänzungsband*, VI (1901), pp. 70–112.

Kehr, P. F., *Italia pontificia*, 10 vols (Berlin, 1906–75).

Keller, H., 'Pataria und Stadtverfassung', *Vorträge und Forschungen*, XVII (1973), pp. 321–50.

Keller, H., *Adelsherrschaft und städtische Gesellschaft in Oberitalien. 9. bis 12. Jahrhundert* (Tübingen, 1979), Ital. trans. as *Signori e vassalli nell'Italia delle città (secoli IX–XII)* (Turin, 1995).

Keller, H., 'Gli inizi del comune in Lombardia', in R. Bordone and J. Jarnut (eds), *L'evoluzione delle città italiane nell'XI secolo* (Bologna, 1998), pp. 45–70.

Kent, D. V. and Kent, F. W., *Neighbours and Neighbourhood in Renaissance Florence* (New York, 1982).

Kessler, H. L., *Old St. Peter's and Church Decoration in Medieval Italy* (Spoleto, 2002).

Kinney, D., 'S. Maria in Trastevere from its founding to 1215', PhD thesis, New York University, 1975.

Kinney, D., 'Fact and fiction in the *Mirabilia urbis Romae*', in Ó Carragáin and Neuman de Vegvar, *Roma felix*, pp. 235–52.

Kitzinger, E., 'A virgin's face', *Art Bulletin*, LXII (1980), pp. 6–19.

Kitzinger, E., 'The arts as aspects of a Renaissance: Rome and Italy', in R. L. Benson et al. (eds), *Renaissance and Renewal in the Twelfth Century* (Cambridge, MA, 1982), pp. 637–70.

Klewitz, H.-W., 'Das Ende des Reformpapsstums', *Deutsches Archiv*, III (1939), pp. 371–412.

Kölmel, W., 'Beiträge zur Verfassungsgeschichte Roms im 10. Jahrhundert', *Historisches Jahrbuch*, LV (1935), pp. 521–46.

Kölmel, W., *Rom und der Kirchenstaat im 10. und 11. Jahrhundert bis in die Anfänge der Reform* (Berlin, 1935).

Krautheimer, R., *Rome: Profile of a City, 312–1308* (Princeton, 1980).

Krautheimer, R. et al., *Corpus basilicarum Christianarum Romae*, 5 vols (Rome, 1937–77).

La signoria rurale in Italia nel medioevo (Pisa, 2006).

La nobiltà romana nel medioevo, ed. S. Carocci (Rome, 2006).

Lanciani, R., 'L'atrio di Vesta', *Notizie degli scavi di antichità*, 1883, pp. 434–97.

Lanciani, R., 'Il "Campus salinarum romanarum"', *Bullettino della Commissione archeologica comunale di Roma*, 1888, pp. 83–91.

Lansing, C., *Power and Purity* (Oxford, 1998).

Lapôtre, A., *L'Europe et le Saint-Siège à l'époque carolingienne*, I (Paris, 1895).

Latham, J. A., 'The ritual construction of Rome', PhD thesis, University of California, Santa Barbara, 2007.

Laudage, J., 'Rom und das Papsttum im frühen 12. Jahrhundert', in K. Herbers (ed.), *Europa an der Wende vom 11. zum 12. Jahrhundert* (Stuttgart, 2001), pp. 23–53.

Le Jan, R., *Famille et pouvoir dans le monde franc (VIIe–Xe siècle)* (Paris, 1995).

Lecuyer, N., 'De la ville à la campagne', in *La céramique médiévale en Méditerrannée* (Aix-en-Provence, 1997), pp. 419–27.

Leicht, P. S., 'Lineamenti del diritto a Roma dal IX al XII secolo', in Brezzi, *Roma*, pp. 561–92.

Lenzi, M., *La terra e il potere*, Miscellanea della Società romana di storia patria, XL (Rome, 2000).

Lenzi, M., 'Per la storia dei *casalia* del territorio romano nell'alto medioevo', in Carocci and Vendittelli, *L'origine della Campagna Romana*, pp. 307–24.

Lexicon topographicum urbis Romae, ed. E. M. Steinby, 6 vols (Rome, 1993–9).

Leyser, C., 'Episcopal office in the Italy of Liudprand of Cremona, c.890-c.970', *English Historical Review*, CXXV (2010), pp. 795–817.

Leyser, C. and Costambeys, M., 'To be the neighbour of St. Stephen', in K. Cooper and J. Hillner (eds), *Religion, Dynasty and Patronage* (Cambridge, 2007), pp. 262–87.

Leyser, K., *Medieval Germany and its Neighbours 900–1250* (London, 1982).

Liver, R., 'Cornomannia. Etymologisches und Religionsgeschichtliches zu einem stadtromischem Fest des Mittelalters', *Vox romanica*, XXX (1971), pp. 32–43.

Liverani, F., *Opere*, 4 vols (Macerata, 1858–9).

Lohrmann, D., 'Schiffsmühlen auf dem Tiber in Rom nach Papsturkunden des 10.-11. Jahrhunderts', in K. Herbers et al. (eds), *Ex ipsis rerum documentis* (Sigmaringen, 1991), pp. 277–86.

Longo, U., 'A saint of damned memory', in Longo and Yawn, *Framing Clement III*.

Longo, U. and Yawn, L. (eds), *Framing Clement III, (anti)pope, 1080–1100*, in *Reti medievali rivista*, XIII.1 (2012), http://rivista.retimedievali.it.

Lopez, R. S., 'À propos d'une virgule: le facteur économique dans la politique africaine des papes', *Revue historique*, CXCVIII (1947), pp. 178–88.

Lori Sanfilippo, I., 'I possessi romani di Farfa, Montecassino e Subiaco – secoli IX–XII', *ASRSP*, CIII (1980), pp. 13–39.

Lori Sanfilippo, I., *La Roma dei Romani* (Rome, 2001).

MacCormack, S. G., *Art and Ceremony in Late Antiquity* (Berkeley, 1981).

McCormick, M., *Eternal Victory* (Cambridge, 1986).

McCormick, M., *Origins of the European Economy* (Cambridge, 2001).

Maetzke, G., 'La struttura stratigrafica dell'area nord-occidentale del Foro Romano come appare dai recenti interventi di scavo', *AM*, XVIII (1991), pp. 43–200.

Maetzke, G., 'Produzioni ceramiche a Roma', in de Minicis, *Le ceramiche di Roma*, I, pp. 9–16.

Maggi Bei, M. T., 'Sulla produzione del sale nell'alto medio evo in zona romana', *ASRSP*, CI (1978), pp. 354–66.

Magna, L., 'Gli Ubaldini del Mugello', in *I ceti dirigenti dell'età comunale nel secoli XII e XIII* (Pisa, 1982).

Maire Vigueur, J.-C., 'Les «casali» des églises romaines à la fin du Moyen Âge (1348–1428)', *MEFRM*, LXXXVI (1974), pp. 63–136.

Maire Vigueur, J.-C., 'Cola di Rienzo', *DBI*, XXVI (Rome, 1982), pp. 662–75.

Maire Vigueur, J.-C., 'Il comune romano', in A. Vauchez (ed.), *Roma medievale* (Rome and Bari, 2001), pp. 117–57.

Maire Vigueur, J.-C., 'Arti o rioni?', in L. Gatto and P. Supino Martini (eds), *Studi sulla società e le culture del Medioevo per Girolamo Arnaldi* (Florence, 2002), pp. 327–40.

Maire Vigueur, J.-C., *Cavaliers et citoyens* (Paris, 2003).

Maire Vigueur, J.-C., *L'autre Rome* (Paris, 2010).

Maire Vigueur, J.-C., 'Replica', *Storica*, L (2011), pp. 137–42.

Maleczek, W., 'Das Kardinalskollegium unter Innozenz II. und Anaklet II.', *Archivum historiae pontificiae*, XIX (1981), pp. 27–78.

Manacorda, D., *Crypta Balbi* (Rome, 2001).

Manacorda, D., 'Castra e burgi a Roma nell'alto medioevo', in *La nobiltà romana*, pp. 97–135.

Manacorda, D. et al., 'La ceramica medioevale di Roma nella stratigrafia della Crypta Balbi', in *La ceramica medievale nel Mediterraneo occidentale* (Florence, 1986), pp. 511–44.

Mandarini, L. V. and Paganelli, M., 'Note preliminari sulla ceramica comune del saggio E* della basilica di San Clemente, Roma', in de Minicis, *Le ceramiche di Roma*, III, pp. 23–33.

Marazzi, F., *I 'patrimonia sanctae Romanae ecclesiae' nel Lazio (secoli IV–X)* (Rome, 1998).

Marchiori, M. L., 'Art and reform in tenth-century Rome: the paintings of S. Maria in Pallara', PhD thesis, Queen's University, Kingston, Ontario, 2007.

Mari, Z. et al. (eds), *Il Lazio tra Antichità e Medioevo* (Rome, 1999).

Martin, J.-M., *Guerre, accords et frontières en Italie méridionale pendant le haut moyen Âge* (Rome, 2005).

Martorelli, R., *Dalla 'civitas Albona' al 'castellum Albanense'* (Rome, 2000).

Matthiae, G., *Mosaici medievali delle chiese di Roma* (Rome, 1967).

Matthiae, G., *Pittura romana del medioevo*, 2nd edn, 2 vols (Rome, 1987–8).

Mayer, E., *Italienische Verfassungsgeschichte von der Gothenzeit bis zur Zunftherrschaft*, 2 vols (Leipzig, 1909).

Menant, F., *Campagnes lombardes au moyen âge* (Rome, 1993).

Menant, F., *Lombardia feudale* (Milan, 1994).

Menant, F., 'La prima età comunale (1097-1183)', in G. C. Andenna (ed.), *Storia di Cremona. Dall'alto medioevo all'età comunale* (Cremona, 2004), pp. 198–281.

Menant, F., *L'Italie des communes (1100–1350)* (Paris, 2005).

Menant, F., 'Une forme de distinction inattendue', in D. Boisseuil et al. (eds), *Écritures de l'espace social* (Paris, 2010), pp. 437–56.

Meneghini, R., 'L'attività delle officine ceramiche nell'area del Foro di Traiano, fra il XV e il XVI secolo, attraverso i dati archeologici più recenti', in R. Meneghini and R. Santangeli Valenzani (eds), *Roma. Lo scavo dei Fori Imperiali 1995–2000. I contesti ceramici* (Rome, 2006), pp. 127–43.

Meneghini, R. and Santangeli Valenzani, R., *Roma nell'altomedioevo* (Rome, 2004).

Meneghini, R. and Santangeli Valenzani, R., *I fori imperiali* (Rome, 2007).

Metcalf, D. M., 'The Rome (Forum) hoard of 1883', *The British Numismatic Journal*, LXII (1993), pp. 63–96.

Miedema, N. R., *Die 'Mirabilia Romae'* (Tübingen, 1996).

Milani, G., *I comuni italiani. Secoli XII–XIV* (Bari, 2005).

Milano e il suo territorio in età comunale. Atti del XI Congresso internazionale di studi sull'alto medioevo (Spoleto, 1989).

Miller, M. C., 'The Florentine bishop's ritual entry and the origins of the medieval episcopal *adventus*', *Revue d'histoire ecclésiastique*, XCVIII (2003), pp. 5–28.

Miller, M. C., 'The crisis in the Investiture Crisis narrative', *History Compass*, VII/6 (2009), pp. 1570–80.

Mini, A., 'Le torri urbani di Arezzo', in E. de Minicis and E. Guidoni (eds), *Case e torri medievali*, III (Rome, 2005), pp. 169–80.

Molinari, A., 'Le ceramiche rivestite bassomedievali', in Saguì and Paroli, *Archeologia urbana*, pp. 357–484.

Molinari, A., 'Dalle invetriate altomedievali alla maiolica arcaica a Roma e nel Lazio (secc. XII-XIV)', in S. Patitucci (ed.), *La ceramica invetriata tardomedievale dell'Italia centro-meridionale* (Florence, 2001), pp. 27–42.

Molinari, A., 'Siti rurali e poteri signorili nel Lazio (secoli X–XIII)', *AM*, XXXVII (2010), pp. 129–42.

Molinari, A., 'Gli scavi al n. 62 di Piazza Navona tra "microstorie" e "grandi narrazioni"', in press.

Montel, R., 'Un *casale* de la Campagne Romaine de la fin du XIVe siècle au début du XVIIe: le domaine de Porto', *MEFRM*, LXXXIII (1971), pp. 31–87.

Montel, R., 'Le "casale" de Boccea, d'après les archives du Chapitre de Saint-Pierre', *MEFRM*, XCI (1979), pp. 593–617, XCVII (1985), pp. 605–726.

Montelli, E., 'Impiego dei mattoni nella casa dei Crescenzi in Roma', in S. Huerta et al. (eds), *Actas del sexto Congreso nacional de historia de la construcción, Valencia, 21–24 octubre 2009* (Madrid, 2009), pp. 909–18.

Montelli, E., *Tecniche costruttive murarie medievali* (Rome, 2011).

Moore, R. I., 'Family, community and cult on the eve of the Gregorian reform', *Transactions of the Royal Historical Society*, 5 ser., XXX (1980), pp. 49–69.

Moreland, J., 'The Farfa survey', *AM*, XIV (1987), pp. 409–18.

Moreland, J. et al., 'Excavations at Casale San Donato, Castelnuovo di Farfa (RI), Lazio, 1992', *AM*, XX (1993), pp. 185–228.

Moreland, J., and Pluciennik, M., 'Excavations at Casale San Donato, Castelnuovo di Farfa (RI), 1990', *AM*, XVIII (1991), pp. 477–90.

Morelli, C. et al., 'Scoperte recenti nelle saline portuensi (*Campus salinarum romanarum*) e un progetto di ricerca sulla ceramica di area ostiense in età repubblicana', in A. Gallina Zevi and R. Turchetti (eds), *Méditerranée occidentale antique: les échanges* (Soveria Mannelli, 2004), pp. 43–55.

Moscati, L., 'Due documenti dei conti di Tuscolo sul traffico marittimo', *ASRSP*, CI (1978), pp. 367–74.

Moscati, L., 'Popolo e arti a Roma prima della "renovatio Senatus"', *Studi romani*, XXVI (1978), pp. 478–502.

Moscati, L., *Alle origini del comune romano* (Rome, 1980).

Moscati, L., '"Una cum sexaginta senatoribus"', *Clio*, XX (1984), pp. 531–45.

Moscati, L., 'Benedetto "Carushomo" *summus senator* a Roma', in *Miscellanea in onore di Ruggero Moscati* (Naples, 1985), pp. 73–87.

Muir, E., *Civic Ritual in Renaissance Venice* (Princeton, 1981).

Nallino, M., 'Un' inedita descrizione araba di Roma', *Annali dell'Istituto universitario orientale di Napoli*, n. ser., XIV (1964), pp. 295–309.

Nanni, L., *La Parrocchia studiata nei documenti lucchesi dei secoli VIII–XIII* (Rome, 1948).

Nardella, C., *Il fascino di Roma nel medioevo* (Rome, 1997).

Nardi Combescure, S., *Paesaggi d'Etruria meridionale* (Florence, 2002).

Natalini, V., *S. Pietro Parenzo* (Rome, 1936).

Nerini, F., *De templo et coenobio sanctorum Bonifacii et Alexii historica monumenta* (Rome, 1752).

Niermeyer, J. F., *Mediae latinitatis lexicon minus* (Leiden, 1976).

Noble, T. F. X., *The Republic of St. Peter* (Philadelphia, 1984).

Noble, T. F. X., 'Topography, celebration, and power', in M. de Jong et al. (eds), *Topographies of Power in the Early Middle Ages* (Leiden, 2001), pp. 45–91.

Noreen, K., 'Lay patronage and the creation of papal sanctity during the Gregorian reform', *Gesta*, XL (2001), pp. 39–59.

Noreen, K., 'Sacred memory and confraternal space', in Ó Carragáin and Neuman de Vegvar, *Roma felix*, pp. 159–87.

Notizie degli scavi di antichità, 1885, p. 428; 1886, pp. 25–6.

Ó Carragáin, É. and Neuman de Vegvar, C. (eds), *Roma felix: Formation and Reflections of Medieval Rome* (Aldershot, 2007).

O'Donovan, M. A., 'The Vatican hoard of Anglo-Saxon pennies', *The British Numismatic Journal*, XXXIII (1964), pp. 7–29.

Occhipinti, E., 'I *capitanei* a Milano', in Castagnetti, *La vassallità maggiore*, pp. 25–34.

Oldfield, P., *City and Community in Norman Italy* (Cambridge, 2009).

Osborne, J., *Early Medieval Wall-paintings in the Lower Church of San Clemente, Rome* (New York, 1984).

Osborne, J., 'The atrium of S. Maria Antiqua, Rome', *Papers of the British School at Rome*, LV (1987), pp. 186–223.

Osborne, J., 'Proclamations of power and presence; the setting and function of two eventh-century murals in the lower church of San Clemente, Rome', *Mediaeval Studies*, LIX (1997), pp. 155–72.

Osborne, J., 'Framing sacred space', *Analecta romana Instituti Danici*, XXX (2004), pp. 137–51.

Pace, V., *Arte a Roma nel Medioevo* (Naples, 2000).

Pace, V., 'Santità, aristocrazia e milizia nella percezione d'immagine del medioevo romano', in *La nobiltà romana*, pp. 313–21.

Pace, V., 'La Riforma e i suoi programmi figurativi', in S. Romano and J. Enckell Julliard (eds), *Roma e la Riforma gregoriana* (Rome, 2007), pp. 49–59.

Padoa Schioppa, A., 'Il ruolo della cultura giuridica in alcuni atti giudiziari italiani dei secoli XI e XII', *Nuova rivista storica*, LXIV (1980), pp. 265–89.

Paganelli, M., 'Area N-O del Foro Romano', in L. Paroli and L. Vendittelli (eds), *Roma dall'antichità al medioevo*, II (Rome, 2004), pp. 180–203.

Paganelli, M., 'Produzioni ceramiche a Roma del VI al XIII sec.', in de Minicis, *Le ceramiche di Roma*, I, pp. 17–29.

Pagano, S. M., 'La chiesa di S. Biagio "de Anulo" (già "de Oliva") e il suo archivio', *ASRSP*, CVII (1984), pp. 5–50.

Palermo, L., *Il porto di Roma nel XIV e XV secolo* (Rome, 1979).

Palermo, L., *Mercati del grano a Roma tra medioevo e Rinascimento*, I (Rome, 1990).

Palermo, L., *Sviluppo economico e società preindustriali* (Rome, 1997).

Palumbo, P. F., *Lo schisma del MCXXX*, Miscellanea della Società romana di storia patria, XIII (Rome, 1942).

Palumbo, P. F., 'Nuovi studi (1942–1962) sullo schisma di Anacleto II', *BISIME*, LXXV (1963), pp. 71–103.

Panero, F., '*Capitanei, valvassores, milites* nella diocesi di Vercelli durante i secoli X-XII', in Castagnetti, *La vassallità maggiore*, pp. 129–59.

Pani Ermini, L., '*Forma urbis*', *Settimane di studio*, XLVIII (2001), pp. 255–323.

Pani Ermini, L. and de Minicis, E., (eds), *Archeologia del medioevo a Roma* (Taranto, 1988).

Pannuzzi, S., 'Ceramica dipinta in rosso nel Lazio meridionale', in de Minicis, *Le ceramiche di Roma*, VI, pp. 31–41.

Paravicini, A., *Saggio storico sulla prefettura urbana dal secolo X al XIV* (Rome, 1900).

Paravicini Bagliani, A., 'Capocci, Giovanni', *DBI*, XVIII (1975), pp. 596–8.

Paravicini Bagliani, A., *Il trono di Pietro* (Rome, 1996).

Paravicini Bagliani, A., *La vita quotidiana alla corte dei papi nel Duecento* (Rome and Bari, 1996).

Parlato, E., 'Le icone in processione', in Andaloro and Romano, *Arte e iconografia a Roma*, pp. 55–72.

Paroli, L., 'Ceramica a vetrina pesante altomedievale (Forum Ware) e medievale (Sparse Glaze)', in Saguì and Paroli, *Archeologia urbana*, pp. 314–56.

Paroli, L., 'La ceramica invetriata tardo-antica e medievale nell'Italia centro-meridionale', in Paroli, *La ceramica invetriata*, pp. 33–61.

Paroli, L. (ed.), *La ceramica invetriata tardoantica e altomedievale in Italia* (Florence, 1992).

Paroli, L. and Delogu, P. (eds), *La storia economica di Roma nell'alto medioevo alla luce dei recenti scavi archeologici* (Florence, 1993).

Partner, P., *The Lands of St. Peter* (London, 1972).

Passigli, S., 'Geografia parrocchiale e circoscrizioni territoriali nei secoli XII-XIV', in Hubert (ed.), *Roma nei secoli XIII e XIV*, pp. 45–86.

Passigli, S., 'Per una storia dell'ambiente nel Medioevo', tesi di dottorato, VIII ciclo (1992–5).

Pásztor, E., 'La curia romana', in *Le istituzioni ecclesiastiche della "societas christiana" dei secoli XI–XII* (Milan, 1974), pp. 490–504.

Patterson, H., 'La ceramica a vetrina pesante (Forum Ware) e la ceramica a vetrina sparsa da alcuni siti della Campagna Romana', in Paroli, *La ceramica invetriata*, pp. 418–34.

Patzold, S., '"Adel" oder "Eliten"?', in Bougard et al., *Théorie et pratiques des élites*, pp. 127–46.

Pauler, R., 'Giovanni XIII', *DBI*, LV (2000), pp. 577–82.

Pavolini, C., 'Aspetti del Celio fra il V e l'VIII-IX secolo', in L. Paroli and L. Vendittelli, *Roma dall'antichità al medioevo*, II (Rome, 2004), pp. 418–34.

Peacock, D. P. S., *Pottery in the Roman World: An Ethnoarchaeological Approach* (London, 1982).

Pennington, K., 'The "big bang"', *Rivista internazionale di diritto comune*, XVIII (2007), pp. 43–70.

Pennington, K., 'Roman law at the papal curia', available at <http://faculty.cua.edu/pennington/PenningtonRomanLawLateranII.htm>.

Pensabene, P., 'La Casa dei Crescenzi e il reimpiego nelle case del XII e XIII secolo a Roma', in V. Franchetti Pardo (ed.), *Arnolfo di Cambio e la sua epoca* (Rome, 2006), pp. 65–76.

Pentcheva, B. V., 'The supernatural protector of Constantinople', *Byzantine and Modern Greek Studies*, XXVI (2002), pp. 2–41.

Penteriani Iacoangeli, M. P. and Penteriani, U., *Nepi e il suo territorio nell'alto medioevo (476–1131)* (Rome, 1986).

Pentiricci, M., 'Palazzo della Cancelleria', in de Minicis, *Le ceramiche di Roma*, I, pp. 30–9.

Peppe, L., 'Un "*investimentum*" del Senato romano del 1162 d.C.', in *Studi per Giovanni Nicosia*, VI (Milano, 2007), pp. 121–33.

Pergola, P., et al. (eds), *Suburbium* (Rome, 2003).

Petersohn, J., 'Kaiser, Papst und praefectura Urbis zwischen Alexander III. und Innocenz III.', *QFIAB*, LX (1980), pp. 157–88.

Petersohn, J., 'Der Brief der Römer an König Lothar III. vom Jahre 1130', *Deutsches Archiv*, L (1994), pp. 461–507.

Petersohn, J., *Kaisertum und Rom in spätsalischer und staufischer Zeit* (Hannover, 2010).

Peyer, H. C., *Zur Getreidepolitik oberitalienischer Städte im 13. Jahrhundert* (Vienna, 1950).

Pfaff, V., 'Aufgaben und Probleme der päpstlichen Finanzverwaltung am Ende des 12. Jahrhunderts', *Mitteilungen des Instituts für österreichische Geschichtsforschung*, LXIV (1956), pp. 1–24.

Pini, A. I., *Città, comuni e corporazioni nel medioevo italiano* (Bologna, 1986).

Pini, A. I., *Vite e vino nel medioevo* (Bologna, 1989).

Poláček, L., 'Ninth-century Mikulčice', in J. Henning (ed.), *Post-Roman Towns. Trade and Settlement in Europe and Byzantium*, I (Berlin, 2007), pp. 499–524.

Potter, T.W. and King, A. C., *Excavations at the Mola di Monte Gelato* (London, 1997).

Pratesi, A., *Tra carte e notai* (Rome, 1992).

Priester, A. E., 'The belltowers of medieval Rome and the architecture of renovatio', PhD thesis, Princeton University, 1990.

Prigent, V., 'Les empereurs isauriens et la confiscation des patrimoines pontificaux d'Italie du Sud', *MEFRM*, CXVI (2004), pp. 557–94.

Provero, L., *L'Italia dei poteri locali, secoli X–XII* (Rome, 1998).

Quilici, L., 'Roma, Via di S. Paolo alla Regola. Scavo e recupero di edifici antichi e medioevali', *Notizie degli scavi di antichità*, 8 ser., XL–XLI (1986-7), pp. 175–416.

Quirós Castillo, J. A., *El incastellamento en el territorio de la ciudad de Luca (Toscana)* (Oxford, 1999).

Racine, P., *Plaisance du Xème a la fin du XIIIème siecle* (Paris, 1980).

Radding, C. M., *The Origins of Medieval Jurisprudence* (New Haven, 1988).

Radding, C. M. and Cianelli, A., *The Corpus Iuris Civilis in the Middle Ages* (Leiden, 2007).

Rapetti, A. M., *Campagne milanesi* (Cavallermaggiore, 1994).

Ratti, N., *Storia di Genzano con note e documenti* (Rome, 1797).

Rea, R. (ed.), *Rota Colisei* (Venice, 2002).

Recchia, V., *Gregorio magno e la società agricola* (Rome, 1978).

Redi, F., *Pisa com'era* (Naples, 1991).

Reuter, T., 'Assembly politics in western Europe from the eighth century to the twelfth', in P. Linehan and J. L. Nelson (eds), *The Medieval World* (London, 2001), pp. 432–50.

Ricci, M., 'Appunti per una storia della produzione e del consumo della ceramica di cucina a Roma nel medioevo', in de Minicis, *Le ceramiche di Roma*, III, pp. 34–42.

Ricci, M., 'I reperti archeologici dal sottoscala XXXVI', in Rea, *Rota Colisei*, pp. 344–403.

Ricci, M., 'La bottega delle olle acquarie in età federiciana', in de Minicis, *Le ceramiche di Roma*, VI, pp. 42–6.

Ricci, M. and Vendittelli, L., *Museo nazionale romano—Crypta Balbi, ceramiche medievali e moderne*, I (Milan, 2010).

Ricci, R., *La marca della Liguria Orientale e gli Obertenghi (945–1056)* (Spoleto, 2007).

Riccioni, S., *Il mosaico absidale di S. Clemente a Roma* (Spoleto, 2006).

Riccioni, S., 'Rewriting Antiquity, renewing Rome', *Medieval Encounters*, XVII (2011), pp. 439–63.

Rinaldi, R., *Tra le carte di famiglia* (Bologna, 2003).

Rippe, G., *Padoue et son contado (Xe–XIIIe siècle)* (Rome, 2003).

Robinson, I. S., *Authority and Resistance* (Manchester, 1978).

Robinson, I. S., *The Papacy, 1073–1198* (Cambridge, 1990).

Rodríguez López, A., 'La Torre Cartularia', in R. Mar (ed.), *El Palatí* (Tarragona, 2005), pp. 313–28.

Romano, S., 'I pittori romani e la tradizione', in Andaloro and Romano, *Arte e iconografia a Roma*, pp. 103–38.

Romano, S., *Riforma e tradizione 1050–1198. Corpus*, IV (Milan, 2006).

Romano, S., 'Commedia antica e sacra rappresentazione', in G. Bucchi et al. (eds), *Figura e racconto, figure et récit* (Florence, 2009), pp. 53–88.

Romei, D., 'La ceramica a vetrina pesante altomedievale e medievale dal castello di Scorano (Capena, Roma)' in Paroli, *La ceramica invetriata*, pp. 438–54.

Romei, D., 'Produzione e circolazione dei manufatti ceramici a Roma nell'alto medioevo', in L. Paroli and L. Vendittelli (eds), *Roma dall'antichità al medioevo*, II (Rome, 2004), pp. 278–311.

Romei, D., 'La ceramica medievale proveniente dal castello di Scorano (Capena, Roma)', in de Minicis, *Le ceramiche di Roma*, III, pp. 124–38.

Romeo, C., 'Crescenzio de Theodora', *DBI*, XXX (Rome, 1984), pp. 657–9.

Romeo, C., 'Crescenzio, figlio di Benedetto', *DBI*, XXX (Rome, 1984), pp. 664–5.

Romeo, C., 'Crescenzio Nomentano', *DBI*, XXX (Rome, 1984), pp. 661–4.

Ronzani, M., *Chiesa e "civitas" di Pisa nella seconda metà del secolo XI* (Pisa, 1996).

Rossetti, G., 'Il lodo del vescovo Daiberto sull'altezza delle torri', in *Pisa e la Toscana occidentale nel medioevo*, II (Pisa, 1991), pp. 25–47.

Rostowzew, M., *Geschichte der Staatspacht in der römischen Kaiserzeit bis Diokletian* (Leipzig, 1902).

Rota, A., 'La costituzione originaria del comune di Roma', *BISIME*, LXIV (1953), pp. 19–131.

Rovelli, A., 'La *Crypta Balbi*. I reperti numismatici. Appunti sulla circolazione a Roma nel Medioevo', in *La moneta nei contesti archeologici. Esempi dagli scavi di Roma* (Rome, 1989), pp. 49–95.

Rovelli, A., 'Monete, tessere e gettoni', in Saguì and Paroli, *Archeologia urbana*, pp. 169–94.

Rovelli, A., 'Monetary circulation in Byzantine and Carolingian Rome', in J. M. H. Smith (ed.), *Early Medieval Rome and the Christian West* (Leiden, 2000), pp. 85–99.

Rovelli, A., 'Emissione e uso della moneta', *Settimane di studio*, XLVIII (2001), pp. 821–52.

Rovelli, A., 'Nuove zecche e circolazione monetaria tra X e XIII secolo', *AM*, XXXVII (2010), pp. 163–70.

Russell, N. and Visentin, H. (eds), *French Ceremonial Entries in the Sixteenth Century* (Toronto, 2007).

Saguì, L., 'Lo scavo', in Saguì and Paroli, *Archeologia urbana*, pp. 15–95.

Saguì, L., 'Area delle "Terme di Elagabalo"', in C. Panella (ed.), *Scavare nel centro di Roma* (Rome, 2013), pp. 13–51.

Saguì, L. and Paroli, L. (eds), *Archeologia urbana a Roma: il progetto della Cripta Balbi. V, L'esedra della Crypta Balbi nel medioevo (XI–XV secolo)* (Florence, 1990).

Salvadori, F., 'Campioni archeozoologici italiani di età tardoantica e medievale', tesi di dottorato, Università degli studi di Siena, 2009–10.

Salvatori, E., *La popolazione pisana nel Duecento* (Pisa, 1994).

Salvatori, E., 'I presunti "*capitanei* delle porte" di Milano e la vocazione cittadina di un ceto', in Castagnetti, *La vassallità maggiore*, pp. 35–94.

Sansterre, J.-M., 'Formoso', *DBI*, LXIX (Rome, 1997), pp. 55–61.

Santangeli Valenzani, R., 'Tra la *Porticus Minucia* e il Calcarario', *AM*, XXI (1994), pp. 57–98.

Santangeli Valenzani, R., 'Residential building in early medieval Rome', in J. M. H. Smith (ed.), *Early Medieval Rome and the Christian West* (Leiden, 2000), pp. 101–12.

Santangeli Valenzani, R., 'Vecchie e nuove forme di insediamento nel territorio', in Pergola, et al., *Suburbium*, pp. 607–18.

Santangeli Valenzani, R., 'Forme dell'insediamento nel suburbio di Roma tra X e XI secolo', in P. Gioia (ed.), *Torre Spaccata* (Rome, 2008), pp. 299–304.

Santangeli Valenzani, R., 'L'insediamento aristocratico a Roma nel IX-X secolo', in M. Royo et al. (eds), *Rome des quartiers: des vici aux rioni* (Paris, 2008), pp. 229–45.

Santangeli Valenzani, R., *Edilizia residenziale in Italia nell'altomedioevo* (Rome, 2011).

Sassier, Y., 'L'utilisation d'un concept romain aux temps carolingiens', *Médiévales*, XV (1988), pp. 17–29.

Savigni, R., *Episcopato e società cittadina a Lucca (1086–1225)* (Lucca, 1996).

Sayers, J., *Innocent III* (London, 1994).

Scalia, G., '"Romanitas" pisana tra XI e XII secolo', *Studi medievali*, XIII (1972), pp. 791–843.

Schaube, A., *Handelsgeschichte der romanischen Völker des Mittelmeergebietes bis zum Ende der Kreuzzüge* (Munich, 1906).

Schilling, B., *Guido von Vienne—Papst Calixt II.* (Hannover, 1998).

Schimmelpfennig, B., 'Ein bisher unbekannter Text zur Wahl, Konsekration und Krönung des Papstes im 12. Jahrhundert', *Archivum historiae pontificiae*, VI (1968), pp. 43–70.

Schimmelpfennig, B., *Die Zeremonienbücher der römischen Kurie im Mittelalter* (Tübingen, 1973).

Schimmelpfennig, B., 'Die Bedeutung Roms im päpstlichen Zeremoniell', in B. Schimmelpfennig and L. Schmugge (eds), *Rom in hohen Mittelalter* (Sigmaringen, 1992), pp. 47–61.

Schmale, F.-J., *Studien zur Schisma des Jahres 1130* (Köln, 1961).

Schmid, K., *Gebetsdenken und adliges Selbstverständnis im Mittelalter* (Sigmaringen, 1983).

Schmidt, T., 'Die älteste Überlieferung von Cencius' Ordo Romanus', *QFIAB*, LX (1980), pp. 511–22.

Schmitz-Esser, R., '*In urbe, quae caput mundi est*. Die Entstehung der römische Kommune (1143-1155)', *Innsbrucker historische Studien*, XXIII–IV (2004), pp. 1–42.

Schneider, F., 'Zur älteren päpstlichen Finanzgeschichte', *QFIAB*, IX (1906), pp. 1–37.

Schramm, P. E., *Kaiser, Rom und Renovatio* (Leipzig, 1929).

Schramm, P. E., *Kaiser, Könige und Päpste*, 5 vols (Stuttgart, 1968–70).

Schreiner, K., 'Gregor VIII., nackt auf einem Esel', in D. Berg and H.-W. Goetz (eds), *Ecclesia et regnum* (Bochum, 1989), pp. 155–202.

Schultz, K., '*Poiché tanto amano la libertà . . .*' (Genoa, 1995).

Schwarzmaier, H. M., 'Zur Familie Viktors IV. in der Sabina', *QFIAB*, XLVIII (1968), pp. 64–79.

Schwarzmaier, H. M., *Lucca und das Reich bis zum Ende des 11. Jahrhunderts* (Tübingen, 1972).

Sennis, A., 'Gregorio VI', in *Enciclopedia dei papi*, II (Rome, 2000), pp. 148–50.

Serlorenzi, M. and Saguì, L., 'Roma, Piazza Venezia', *AM*, XXXV (2008), pp. 175–98.

Servatius, C., *Paschalis II. (1099–1118)* (Stuttgart, 1979).

Settia, A. A., *Castelli e villaggi nell'Italia padana* (Naples, 1984).

Settia, A. A., 'Lo sviluppo di un modello', in *Paesaggi urbani dell'Italia padana nei secoli VIII–XIV* (Bologna, 1988), pp. 157–71.

Settia, A. A., *Comuni in guerra* (Bologna, 1993).

Sickel, W., 'Alberich II. und der Kirchenstaat', *Mittheilungen des Instituts für österreichische Geschichtsforschung*, XXIII (1902), pp. 50–126.

Skinner, P., *Family Power in Southern Italy* (Cambridge, 1995).

Smiraglia, E. and Zanotti, M. G., 'Ceramiche medievali dallo scavo della nuova basilica circiforme della via Ardeatina', in de Minicis, *Le ceramiche di Roma*, III, pp. 171–82.

Solmi, A., *Il Senato romano nell'alto medio evo (757–1143)* (Rome, 1944).

Sommerlechner, A., 'Die ludi Agonis et Testatie', *Römische historische Mitteilungen*, XLI (1999), pp. 339–70.

Sommerlechner, A. (ed.), *Innocenzo III, urbs et orbis* (Rome, 2003).

Spera, L., *Il paesaggio suburbano di Roma dall'Antichità al medioevo* (Rome, 1999).

Spera, L., 'Le forme della cristianizzazione nel quadro degli assetti topografico-funzionali di Roma tra V e IX secolo', *Post-classical archaeologies*, I (2011) pp. 309–48.

Spera, L. (ed.), *Lo scavo 2007–2009 nell'orto dell'abbazia di San Paolo*, in press.

Spicciani, A. and Violante, C. (eds), *La signoria rurale nel medioevo italiano*, 2 vols (Pisa, 1997–8).

Sprenger, K.-M., 'The tiara in the Tiber', in Longo and Yawn, *Framing Clement III*.

Spufford, P., *Money and Its Use in Medieval Europe* (Cambridge, 1988).

Squatriti, P., *Water and Society in Early Medieval Italy, AD 400–1000* (Cambridge, 1998).

Stafford, P., *Queens, Concubines and Dowagers* (London, 1983).

Stafford, P., 'Women and the Norman Conquest', *Transactions of the Royal Historical Society*, 6 ser., IV (1994), pp. 221–49.

Storia di Milano, III (Milan, 1954).

Storia economica e sociale di Bergamo. I primi millenni, II (Bergamo, 1999).

Stroll, M., *The Jewish Pope* (Leiden, 1987).

Stroll, M., *Symbols as Power* (Leiden, 1991).

Stroll, M., *The Medieval Abbey of Farfa* (Leiden, 1997).

Stroll, M., *Calixtus II (1119–1124)* (Leiden, 2004).

Stroll, M., *Popes and Antipopes* (Leiden, 2012).

Strothmann, J., *Kaiser und Senat* (Cologne, 1998).

Supino Martini, P., *Roma e l'area grafica romanesca (secoli X–XII)* (Alessandria, 1987).

Sydow, J., 'Untersuchungen zur kurialen Verwaltungsgeschichte im Zeitalter des Reform-papsttums', *Deutsches Archiv*, XI (1954–5), pp. 18–73.

Sydow, J., 'Il "concistorium" dopo lo schisma del 1130', *Rivista di storia della chiesa in Italia*, IX (1955), pp. 165–76.

Szabó, T., 'Zur Geschichte der *boni homines*', in D. Balestracci et al. (eds), *Uomini paesaggi storie* (Siena, 2012), pp. 301–22.

Tabacco, G., *Egemonie sociali e strutture del potere nel medioevo italiano* (Turin, 1979).

Tellenbach, G., 'La citta di Roma dal IX al XII secolo visto dai contemporanei d'oltre frontiera,' in *Studi storici in onore di Ottorino Bertolini*, 2 vols (Pisa, 1972), II, pp. 679–734.

Tellenbach, G., *The Church in Western Europe from the Tenth to the Early Twelfth Century*, Eng. trans. (Cambridge, 1993).

Theisen, F., *Studien zur Emphyteuse in ausgewählten italienischen Regionen des 12. Jahrhunderts* (Frankfurt, 2003).

Thumser, M., 'Die Frangipane', *QFIAB*, LXXI (1991), pp. 106–63.

Thumser, M., *Rom und der römische Adel in der späten Stauferzeit* (Tübingen, 1995).

Thumser, M., 'Die frühe römische Kommune und die staufischen Herrscher in der Briefsammlung Wibalds von Stablo', *Deutsches Archiv*, LVII (2001), pp. 111–47.

Tiberini, S., 'Origini e radicamento territoriale di un lignaggio umbro-toscano nei secoli X-XI', *Archivio storico italiano*, CLII (1994), pp. 481–559.

Tomassetti, G., *La Campagna romana, antica, medioevale e moderna*, new edn, ed. L. Chiumenti and F. Bilancia, 7 vols (Florence, 1979–80).

Torelli, P., *Un comune cittadino in territorio ad economia agricola* (Mantua, 1930).

Toubert, H., *Un art dirigé* (Paris, 1990).

Toubert, P., *Les structures du Latium médiéval* (Rome, 1973).

Toubert, P., '*Scrinium* et *palatium*', in idem, *L'Europe dans sa première croissance* (Paris, 2004), pp. 419–61.

Travaini, L., 'Rocche, castelli e viabilità fra Subiaco e Tivoli', *Atti e memorie della società tiburtina di storia e d'arte*, LII (1979), pp. 65–97.

Trexler, R. C., *Public Life in Renaissance Florence* (New York, 1980).

Tronzo, W., 'The prestige of St Peter's', in H. L. Kessler and M. Shreve Simpson (eds), *Pictorial Narrative in Antiquity and the Middle Ages* (Washington, DC, 1985), pp. 93–112.

Tronzo, W., 'Apse decoration, the liturgy and the perception of art in medieval Rome', in idem (ed.), *Italian Church Decoration of the Middle Ages and Early Renaissance* (Bologna, 1989), pp. 167–93.

Twyman, S., *Papal Ceremonial at Rome in the Twelfth Century* (London, 2002).

Valenti, M., *L'insediamento altomedievale delle campagne toscane* (Florence, 2004).

Vehse, O., 'Das Bündnis gegen die Sarazenen vom Jahre 915', *QFIAB*, XIX (1927), pp. 181–204.

Vehse. O., 'Die päpstliche Herrschaft in der Sabina bis zur Mitte des 12. Jahrhunderts', *QFIAB*, XXI (1929–30), pp. 120–75.

Vendittelli, M., 'Diritti e impianti di pesca degli enti ecclesiastici romani tra X e XIII secolo', *MEFRM*, CIV (1992), pp. 387–430.

Vendittelli, M., '*Romanorum consules*', in *La nobiltà romana nel medioevo*, pp. 211–36.

Vendittelli, M., 'Testimonianze sui rapporti tra romani e i vescovati di Metz e Verdun nel secolo XIII', *ASRSP*, CXVIII (1995), pp. 69–99.

Vendittelli, M., 'Élite citadine', in *Les élites urbaines au moyen âge* (Rome, 1997), pp. 183–91.

Vendittelli, M., *'In partibus Anglie'* (Rome, 2001).

Vendittelli, M., 'Mercanti romani del primo Duecento "in Urbe potentes"', in Hubert (ed.), *Roma nei secoli XIII e XIV*, pp. 89–135.

Vendittelli, M. (ed.), *Sutri nel medioevo* (Rome, 2008).

Vendittelli, M., 'Il *Campus Agonis* nei secoli centrali del medioevo', in press.

Vendittelli, M., *Mercanti del tempio* (Rome, in press).

Venni, T., 'Giovanni X', *ASRSP*, LIX (1936), pp. 1–136.

Vera, D., *'Massa fundorum'*, *MEFR. Antiquité*, CXI (1999), pp. 991–1025.

Violante, C., *La società milanese nell'età precomunale* (Bari, 1953).

Violante, C., *La Pataria milanese e la riforma ecclesiastica*, I (Rome, 1955).

Violante, C., 'I laici nel movimento patarino', in *I laici nella «societas christiana» dei secoli XI e XII* (Milan, 1968), pp. 597–697.

Violante, C., 'Quelques caractéristiques des structures familiales en Lombardie, Émilie et Toscane aux XIe et XIIe siècles', in *Famille et parenté dans l'Occident médiéval* (Rome, 1977), pp. 87–147.

Violante, C., 'Una famiglia feudale della "Langobardia" nel secolo XI', in *Studi filologici letterari e storici in memoria di Guido Favati*, II (Padua, 1977), pp. 653–710.

Volpe, G., *Medio evo italiano* (Florence, 1961).

Volpe, G., *Studi sulle istituzioni comunali a Pisa*, 2nd edn (Florence, 1970).

Waite, G. K., *Reformers on Stage* (Toronto, 2000).

West, G. V. B., 'Communities and *pacta* in early medieval Italy', *Early Medieval Europe*, XVIII (2010), pp. 367–93.

White, S. D., 'Tenth-century courts at Mâcon and the perils of structuralist history', in W. C. Brown and P. Górecki (eds), *Conflict in Medieval Europe* (Aldershot, 2003), pp. 37–68.

Whitton, D., 'The *Annales Romani* and Codex Vaticanus Latinus 1984', *BISIME*, LXXXIV (1972–3), pp. 125–43.

Whitton, D., 'Papal policy in Rome, 1012–1124', DPhil thesis, Oxford University, 1979.

Wickham, C., 'Historical and topographical notes on early medieval South Etruria', *Papers of the British School at Rome*, XLVI (1978), pp. 132–79; XLVII (1979), pp. 66–95.

Wickham, C., *The Mountains and the City* (Oxford, 1988).

Wickham, C., 'Economia e società rurale nel territorio lucchese durante la seconda metà del secolo XI', in C. Violante (ed.), *Sant'Anselmo vescovo di Lucca (1073–1086)* (Rome, 1992), pp. 391–422.

Wickham, C., 'La mutación feudal en Italia', in A. Malpica and T. Quesada (eds), *Los orígines del feudalismo en el mundo mediterráneo* (Granada, 1994), 31–55.

Wickham, C., 'La signoria rurale in Toscana', in Dilcher and Violante, *Strutture e trasformazioni*, pp. 343–409.

Wickham, C., 'Justice in the kingdom of Italy in the eleventh century', *Settimane di studio*, XLIV (1997), pp. 179–255.

Wickham, C., *Community and Clientele in Twelfth-century Tuscany* (Oxford, 1998).

Wickham, C., *Dispute ecclesiastiche e comunità laiche* (Florence, 1998).

Wickham, C., '"The Romans according to their malign custom": Rome in Italy in the late ninth and tenth centuries', in J. M. H. Smith (ed.), *Early Medieval Rome and the Christian West* (Leiden, 2000), 151–66.

Wickham, C., 'Paludi e miniere nella Maremma toscana, XI–XIII secoli', in J.-M. Martin (ed.), *Castrum 7* (Rome, 2001), pp. 451–66.

Wickham, C., *Courts and Conflict in Twelfth-century Tuscany* (Oxford, 2003).

Wickham, C., *Framing the Early Middle Ages* (Oxford, 2005).

Wickham, C., 'Public court practice; the eighth and twelfth centuries compared', in S. Esders (ed.), *Rechtsverständnis und Konfliktbewältigung* (Cologne, 2007), pp. 17–30.

Wickham, C., '*Iuris cui existens*', *ASRSP*, CXXXI (2008), pp. 5–38.

Wickham, C., *The Inheritance of Rome* (London, 2009).

Wickham, C., 'La struttura della proprietà fondiaria nell'agro romano, 900–1150', *ASRSP*, CXXXII (2009), pp. 181–238.

Wickham, C., 'The financing of Roman city politics, 1050–1150', in P. Guglielmotti et al. (eds), *Europa e Italia* (Florence, 2011), pp. 437–53.

Wickham, C., 'Getting justice in twelfth-century Rome', in C. Dartmann et al. (eds), *Zwischen Pragmatik und Performanz* (Turnhout, 2011), pp. 103–31.

Wickham, C., 'The origins of the signoria in central Lazio, 900–1100', in D. Balestracci et al. (eds), *Uomini paesaggi storie* (Siena, 2012), pp. 481–92.

Wickham, C., 'Albano in the central middle ages', in G. Barone et al. (ed.), *Ricerca come incontro* (Rome, 2013), pp. 209–26.

Wickham, C., 'The changing composition of early élites', in Bougard et al., *Théorie et pratiques des élites*, pp. 5–18.

Wolf, G., *Salus populi romani* (Weinheim, 1990).

Wolf, G., 'Icons and sites', in M. Vassilaki (ed.), *Images of the Mother of God* (Aldershot, 2005), pp. 23–49.

Wood, I., *The Missionary Life* (Harlow, 2001).

Yawn, L., 'Clement's new clothes', in Longo and Yawn, *Framing Clement III*.

Zaferana, Z., 'Sul "conventus" del clero romano nel maggio 1082', *Studi medievali*, VII (1966), pp. 399–403.

Zema, D., 'The houses of Tuscany and of Pierleone in the crisis of Rome in the eleventh century', *Traditio*, II (1944), pp. 155–75.

Ziese, J., *Wibert von Ravenna. Der Gegenpapst Clemens III. (1084–1100)* (Stuttgart, 1982).

Zimmermann, H., 'Parteiungen und Papstwahlen in Rom zur Zeit Kaiser Ottos des Grossen', *Römische historische Mitteilungen*, VIII–IX (1964–6), pp. 29–88.

Zimmermann, H., *Papstabsetzungen des Mittelalters* (Graz, 1968).

Index

Adalard of Corbie 190
Adalbert of Prague, saint 203, 204n., 378
Adammulo, *scandolaro* 146n.
Adilascia Frangipane 230, 273, 300
Ælfwynn, queen of Mercia 24n.
Æthelflæd, queen of Mercia 24n.
Agnello of Ravenna 325n.
agriculture 4, 35–8, 41, 66, 70, 76–7, 80,
    84–90, 94–5, 105, 107–10, 116–18, 136,
    142, 146, 168, 179, 248, 278–9, 361, 410;
    see also grain; vineyards, vineyard belt, wine
Agro romano 8, 27, 39–43, 46–7, 50, 52–88,
    96–110, 122, 136, 141n., 155, 157,
    168–70, 174, 176–7, 187, 193, 206–7,
    217–18, 230, 244, 252, 255, 282n., 286,
    300, 312, 409–13, 418, 456
Agusto 131n.
Aimerico, *cancellarius* and cardinal 373–4, 403,
    414, 429, 430
Albano 36, 37n., 42, 50, 52, 54, 56, 61–2, 64,
    67, 69–70, 74–6, 92, 97–102, 106–10,
    143, 145, 148, 152, 157, 168, 177, 179,
    193–4, 200, 204, 207, 213, 225, 268, 272,
    274, 277, 317n., 344, 372, 410
Alberico, prince 4, 15, 23–8, 34, 43, 47, 54, 58,
    114, 116, 126, 130, 154, 170, 182, 187–8,
    190–2, 194–8, 201n., 205, 209, 211, 249,
    277, 282, 351, 376–7, 379, 381, 388, 390,
    416, 455
Alberico 'III' 195–6, 220
Alberico of Spoleto 23
Alberico di Pietro di Leone Cece (Alberico
    Cece) 165, 166n., 167, 238, 240, 417
Alberto di Ottone Curso (or Corso) 203,
    222, 226
Albino, author 322–3, 328–9, 346, 347n., 390
Albino, *arcarius* 215–16
Aldobrandeschi, family 207, 208, 252
Aldruda Frangipane 230, 231n., 256–7, 433
Alexander II, pope 30, 129n., 165, 233, 246,
    307n., 332, 343, 353, 364, 393, 421–2
Alexander III, pope 59, 82, 100, 125, 164–5,
    227, 231, 257, 261, 262, 270, 284, 300,
    308, 324n., 342–3, 375
Alexis, saint 204, 286n., 357, 403
Alicho di Romano Sordo 285, 286n.
Amato, *prior* of *scola ortulanorum* 89
Ammianus Marcellinus 341
Anacletus II, pope 14, 32–4, 127, 223, 227n.,
    230, 231n., 232, 234, 239, 242, 262, 315,
    353, 357, 361, 364n., 371, 379, 384, 403,
    419, 420, 429–3, 438, 441–2
Anastasio, cardinal 354, 427

Anastasio, *bibliothecarius* 22, 188
ancien régime 28, 186–220, 378, 385, 397,
    409, 412
Andrea, *arcarius* 192
Andrea, *scriniarius* 302
Andrea, *secundicerius* 217
Andrea *de Coloseo* 114
Andrea di Pietro di Viola *de Coloseo* 293, 312
Andrea of Strumi 344n.
Andrieu, Michel 321
Anibaldo, senator 381n., 451
Anicia, gens 210
Annibaldi, family 208, 241, 301n., 381n., 451
Anselm of Liège 247n.
Anselmo I, bishop of Lucca, *see* Alexander II,
    pope
Anselmo of Gembloux 432n.
Ansone, husband of Urza 98
Aqua Tuzia 92–100
Arab invasions 22–3, 44, 58, 65, 133, 155, 376
Arcadius, Byzantine emperor 380n.
arcarius, *see* judges, palatine
Arcioni, family 299, 300n.
Arialdo, Patarene leader 343–4
Ariberto II, archbishop of Milan 246
aristocracy 5, 16, 21, 26–32 114–18, 123, 128,
    136, 140, 145–6, 149, 152, 154–5, 158,
    160, 164–70, 181–277, 311–14, 319–20,
    357, 363, 388–403, 410–12, 417–19, 422,
    424–9, 433–57
    hierarchy and status, social strata 4, 21,
    26–30, 34, 133, 146, 181–6, 194–8, 205,
    223, 243–5, 248–54, 256–7, 260–6, 272,
    276, 278–80, 282–3, 287, 290, 297–8,
    302–5, 314–16, 319–20, 353–4, 394–5,
    409, 412, 417, 419–20, 427–8, 440–2,
    449, 454–7
    'new aristocracy' 29–30, 34, 56, 115, 146,
    165, 167, 182–6, 213, 220–58, 260–1,
    265–6, 271–3, 304, 313, 393, 398, 410,
    412, 416, 418, 420–2, 428–9, 454–5
    'old aristocracy' 23, 29, 52, 56, 182–222,
    239, 245, 248, 252–58, 304, 410, 412–13,
    420, 422
    titles 24, 26, 58, 89–90, 145, 182, 184,
    186–99, 204–6, 212–13, 215–17, 249–50,
    257, 283, 287–8, 317n., 417, 429, 454
    wealth 206–8, 244–5, 249–57, 269, 271–77,
    305, 428–9
    women 24, 28, 53, 195, 204, 208–12, 261,
    275, 315–18, 367–9, 415
    see also offices, officials; social structure and
    change